Facing the Other Way
THE STORY OF 4·A·D

MARTIN ASTON

The Friday Project
An imprint of HarperCollins*Publishers*
77–85 Fulham Palace Road
Hammersmith, London W6 8JB
www.harpercollins.co.uk

First published by The Friday Project in 2013

1

A catalogue record for this book is
available from the British Library

ISBN 978-0-00-748961-9

Printed and bound in Great Britain by
Clays Ltd, St Ives plc

MIX
Paper from
responsible sources
FSC
www.fsc.org   **FSC˚ C007454**

FSC™ is a non-profit international organisation established to promote
the responsible management of the world's forests. Products carrying the
FSC label are independently certified to assure consumers that they come
from forests that are managed to meet the social, economic and
ecological needs of present and future generations,
and other controlled sources.

Find out more about HarperCollins and the environment at
www.harpercollins.co.uk/green

ACKNOWLEDGEMENTS

In the category of Indispensible, I have to start with Ivo Watts-Russell, for resisting his normal impulse to let the music alone do the talking, and for granting me so much time, commitment and unexpected copy-editing skills. And to Tate, Moke and Emmett, for their part in hosting me. To George, for his part too. Thanks also to Vaughan Oliver, for dedication and contributing extraordinary artwork. To Mat Clum, for his patience and endurance over the course. To the Mieren Neukers of Ladywell, for insight and encouragement. To my HarperCollins editor Scott Pack, for commissioning this book, and project editor Rachel Faulkner, editorial assistant Alice Tarbuck and copy editor Nicky Gyopari, for the finesse. To 4AD, especially Steve Webbon, Rich Walker, Annette Lee, Simon Halliday and Ed Horrox, for assistance/ archive. To Madeleine Sheahan, for advice and Spanish translation, and Craig Roseberry, the one and only 4AD Whore – I know what this means to you. And finally, to three 4AD fan websites, Lars Magne Ingebrigtsen's eyesore.no, Jeff Keibel's fedge.net and Maximillian Mark Medina's themysteryparade.com, for comprehensive listings.

Thanks to my two families – in London, Mum, David, Penny, Katie, Vicki and Christopher, Louis, Tess, and in Michigan, Mom Clum, Doug and family, Liz and family, Nate and Bruce, Mindy and Tom.

Many thanks to everyone I interviewed for the book, but especially Miki Berenyi, Mark Cox, Nigel Grierson, Robin Guthrie, Kristin Hersh, Robin Hurley, Matt Johnson, Brendan Perry, Simon Raymonde, Chris Staley and Anka Wolbert. Special thanks to John Grant and John-Mark Lapham, for sound and vision.

Thanks to my nearest-and-dearest: Brenda and Trish, Kurt, Mark, Pixie, Eloise and James, Sara, Will and Harriet, Merle and Gary, Joanna MLNOV, Laura, Yael, Meir and family, Duncan, Amanda, Madeleine, Mary Pat, Gordon, Catherine and Arvo, Nicole, Angela, Hop, Sarah and Foster, Cat my foxymoron, Dr John and Michael, Kat, Peter, Gabby and Trixie, Emma, Jessica and family, Clare and Antoine, Yas, Lauren and Sam, Jesper, Christine and Naomi, David, Yvette and family, Christina, Olivia and Bif, Patrick and Karl, Justin, Lisa and family, Cushla, Felicity, Dean and Britta, the Nervas, the Dutch, Jon and Patricia, Diana and Tim, cousin Jenny, Jim Fouratt, Steve, Mr Stroopy Mumblepants and Spencer, Bob and Jeff, Pat, John, Lynn, Siuin, Debbie, Jude, Sigrid, Amy, Laurence, Miriam and Viva, Jane, Richard, Huw and Dan, Edori and family, Susie and Mark, Lisa, and my Nunhead pals (Karolina, Lukasz, Hugo and Hannah, Claire, Andrew and Eva, John and Katrina, Carolyn, Jeremy and Max).

Thanks also to Tony Bacon, Ralf Henneking, James Nice, LightBrigade PR, José Enrique Plata Manjarrés and Andy Pearce, and to anyone I have inadvertently missed out, and also not credited for quotes, which I've done my upmost to do.

I finally want to thank Tim Carr, one of the insightful people I talked to for this book, and one of 4AD's greatest supporters, *in memoriam*.

This is dedicated to my father Basil, *in memoriam*, and to my mother Patricia. Thanks for not insisting I pursue a career in merchant banking.

To Moray, *in memoriam*. I hope you are grooving in your home disco, reading, writing and meditating, looking forward to tralaalaa o'clock.

Imagine a scene on a beach. A barbecue for friends and colleagues. Some of them like each other and some of them don't. The man in charge, responsible for inviting them all, and responsible for feeding them, suddenly self-combusts. In his confused, mad dash to reach the water, to put out the flames, he ricochets into those closest to him and knocks them down, even starting minor fires over their bodies. Before he reaches the ocean, he passes through a pile of fireworks lying on the beach for use in a display later that night. All hell breaks loose, with everyone on the beach scattering, trying to save themselves. The man has now reached the water and finds he has gone out too far and has forgotten how to swim. He is drowning but unable to call for help. He is totally aware of the chaos on the beach that he is responsible for and has left behind but, because he's drowning, can do nothing to prevent the destruction. He is puzzled as to why no one is coming to his rescue. Meanwhile, everyone to a man back on the beach is thinking, 'You stupid cunt. What did you do that for, you've ruined everything' and 'For fuck's sake, just swim'.

(George, 2013)

CONTENTS

INTRODUCTION

When a fan of 4AD, and of the British independent label scene of the Eighties in general, heard I was writing this book, he asked me, 'Is there much drama in the 4AD story?'

True, the story of 4AD doesn't feature a TV presenter-cum-entrepreneur who starts a record label whose most iconic frontman commits suicide and initiates a Che Guevara-style cult; nor does it involve the decision to invest heavily in a nightclub that goes on to become an epicentre of the biggest dance music boom in UK history, rejuvenating both youth and drug culture, the combined legacy of which soon enough bankrupts said label.

That would be the suspenseful saga of Manchester's Factory Records, 4AD's principal peer in the world of pioneering, inventive and maverick independent labels. For both labels, the visual aesthetic was as crucial as the music, yet, in many ways, south London's 4AD, formed in 1980, was the anti-Factory: its spearhead, Ivo Watts-Russell, was more of a recluse than a media-savvy self-promoter, and 4AD had no recognisable ties to the zeitgeist – nor to any cultural trend, in fact. All of *that*, Ivo felt, was irrelevant; only the artefact mattered – the music and its exquisite packaging. In the mid-Eighties there were constant references to 'the 4AD sound': a beautiful, dark, insular style.

If the 2002 fictionalised film about Factory Records was called *24 Hour Party People*, what might a film about 4AD be titled – *Eight Hours Chilling, and Then Bed*?

But whilst 4AD's story may be less sensational and populist than Factory's, it is equally gripping, the label's A&R vision being that much greater, and its subsequent cast of characters even more fascinating and beguiling. Under Ivo, 4AD's vision chimed with a rare era in British pop history when there was a sizeable market for innovation and experimentation. The artists he was drawn to were trailblazers, outsiders whose unique perspective invariably included a troubled, sometimes irreconcilable relationship with the mainstream (scoring the UK's first independently released number 1 single was as much the beginning of the end for 4AD as it was the start of a new era), and with each other, like a dysfunctional family – and that includes the staff at the record label.

Like the motion of the swan's legs beneath its ineffably elegant glide across water, below the surface of 4AD's dazzling and enigmatic artwork and music the human drama unfolded. 4AD's journey began as a shared discovery of a new world of sound and opportunity in the aftermath of the punk rock revolution. But its community was progressively fractured by splits, rivalries, writs, personal meltdowns, addiction, and depression – not least of the victims being 4AD's most iconic artists Cocteau Twins, Pixies and The Breeders, and the label boss as well.

Though 4AD became increasingly popular in the first half of the Nineties, the shifts in the cultural climate and music business practise, as the major labels and the mainstream sought to exploit 'alternative music', was enough to shatter Ivo's dream to the point that he sold up in 1999 and disappeared into the New Mexico desert, cutting all ties to the music industry.

Also unlike Factory, 4AD has survived – some even claim that in the twenty-first century, the label, under new stewardship, has reclaimed its former glory. However, it is the Eighties and Nineties, the years under Ivo's tutelage, that are the real story. This is the period that *Facing the Other Way* concentrates on: a time in which the word

'4AD' became an adjective, when 4AD was the most fanatically appreciated and collected of record labels, whose legacy casts a long shadow over contemporary music, from dream-pop, goth, post-rock and industrial to Americana, ambient, nu-gaze and chillwave. Not forgetting Pixies' indelible influence on Nirvana, whose impact pushed alternative rock into the mainstream, after which there was no return.

There was no return for Ivo either. His non-existent profile since the end of the twentieth century means that one of the great sagas of British-label history had not been told. That is, until I went looking for him in 2010.

I'd been a 4AD fan throughout the earlier years, from Bauhaus' early singles to The Birthday Party and Cocteau Twins, and as soon as I started writing about music, in 1983, I'd had a close working relationship with Ivo. Over the years, I've covered numerous 4AD artists, and been beguiled and exhilarated by the procession of sounds and names: Dif Juz, This Mortal Coil, Dead Can Dance, Throwing Muses, Pixies, The Wolfgang Press, His Name Is Alive, Lush, Red House Painters, Tarnation … But, in the wake of Ivo's retreat, our last correspondance was in 2002 (regarding some sleevenotes I was writing about one of Ivo's favourite 4AD signings). Arguably, a book on 4AD could have been written then, but it makes more sense now, with the label's reputation, and myth, increasing year on year. This is a testament to a label that existed purely on its own terms, out of time and place with the rest. Facing the other way. Sometimes it's the quiet ones you have to look out for …

1

DID I DREAM YOU DREAMED ABOUT ME?

Creativity is a product of a diseased mind.

(Dee Rutkowski, 2011)

I have the strangest dreams every night … been going on for months. Unlike my waking life, the dreams are full of strangers that I am forced to interact with. I'm not sure whether I experience greater feelings of alienation asleep or awake.

(Ivo, by email, 2012)

Yes: I am a dreamer. For a dreamer is one who can only find his way by moonlight, and his punishment is that he sees the dawn before the rest of the world.

(Oscar Wilde, sometime in the late nineteenth century)

May 1985. The phone rings at Ivo's home on a Saturday afternoon. 'It's David Lynch's assistant: are you free to talk to him?'

The American film director behind the startling, surreal *Eraserhead* and the dramatically different, but equally affecting, biopic *The Elephant Man* had a new film in pre-production, titled *Blue Velvet*, and he'd fallen for a song that he wanted to use for the opening sequence, set at a high-school prom.

The song was a cover of Tim Buckley's 'Song To The Siren', a mercurial, exquisite ballad that described, in aching and elaborate homage to the ancient Greek poet Homer's epic *The Odyssey*, the inevitable damage that love causes. Buckley's original, which the Californian singer-songwriter had written and first recorded in 1968, wasn't at all well known, even by 1985. Between 1966 and 1974, he'd recorded a startling array of music over the course of nine albums, from folk rock to jazz to avant-garde to funky soul and AOR. It all ended with a snort of heroin at an end-of-tour party. With rock and pop culture yet to turn nostalgic, Buckley's reputation had died with him, and punk rock's Stalinist purge of the past had ensured that Californian singer-songwriters of all pedigrees were discourteously dismissed.

But this new cover version of 'Song To The Siren', by a studio-based collective named This Mortal Coil, had sprung up in a very different climate. Punk had given way to its more experimental, artful offspring, post-punk, alongside the new electronic sound, and the synthesised pop called New Romantic. 'Song To The Siren' had spent more than a hundred weeks in the British independent music charts during 1983 and 1984, and its fame had reached America, as David Lynch's interest illustrated. He regards TMC's version as *his* all-time favourite piece of music: 'That song does something to me, for sure,' he told the *Guardian* newspaper in 2010.

In either version, 'Song To The Siren' was an easy track to be infatuated with, given its sorrowful, elegiac mood, and its lyrics haunted by images of the sea and of death. The singer of This Mortal Coil's version was Elizabeth Fraser, whose performance – supported in spirit by the guitar of her musical and romantic partner Robin Guthrie – suggested that she was the siren of *The Odyssey* personified, luring sailors/lovers to a watery grave.

In their daily lives, Fraser and Guthrie were known as Cocteau Twins, recording artists for the independent music label 4AD. It was 4AD's co-founder, and singular leader, Ivo Watts-Russell, that had taken Lynch's call that afternoon. 'As happens,' Ivo recalls, 'when the film went into production, my friend Patty worked as an assistant to the producer on *Blue Velvet*. She'd call me, whispering, "David and Isabella [Rossellini, the female lead] are in the corner *again*, listening to 'Song To The Siren'," before shooting a scene.'

The cover version, recorded in 1983, had been Ivo's idea. The late Tim Buckley is his all-time favourite singer, and 'Song To The Siren' is still his all-time favourite song. 'Not since Billie Holiday had recorded "Strange Fruit" was a song and lyric so suited to a voice as Tim Buckley's was to "Song To The Siren",' he reckons.

By 1985, the inimitable Elizabeth Fraser had become his favourite living singer. And here was Lynch, requesting not just the music for *Blue Velvet* but Fraser and Guthrie to mime on stage in the prom scene. However, the lawyers for Buckley's estate demanded $20,000 for the rights, scuppering Lynch's plans (the film's total budget was only $3 million). The director quickly turned to composer Angelo Badalamenti, who attempted to mirror the track's displaced, eerie mood with a new song, 'Mysteries Of Love', sung by the American singer Julee Cruise with her own take on haunting, ethereal projection. Starting with *Blue Velvet*, and most famously on his TV series *Twin Peaks*, Lynch fashioned a world that appeared seamless, unruffled and presentable on the surface, but scarred and disturbed underneath, foaming with a barely controllable darkness. As *Twin Peaks'* FBI Special Agent Cooper declared, 'I'm seeing something that was always hidden.'

In 2006, Ivo pointed to a similarity between label and director. 'I feel that 4AD is like David Lynch,' he told the *Santa Fe Reporter*. 'If you say to somebody, "It's kind of like a David Lynch movie", you kind of know what you're getting. It was like that in the same way for a certain period at 4AD: "It's kind of like a 4AD record". Actually, that probably meant it had loads of reverb.'

By this, Ivo wasn't referring to something hidden – more that it was a brand that could be identified, where the term 4AD had become an adjective of sound. Yet in the music that the label was producing, there was the same sense of beauty as a mask for the true emotions coursing beneath. By 1985, the so-called 'classic' 4AD sound was all about dark dreams and hidden depths, performed by supposed fragile characters on the verge of anguish and breakdown. Take Elizabeth Fraser. After the drooling reception for her performance in 'Song To The Siren', she didn't grow in confidence, but began to sing in what resembled a made-up language, or simply by enunciation, making it impossible to be understood. With a voice like hers, she didn't need words; it was all there in her delivery, a shiver of emotion from agony to ecstasy.

March 2012. It's been thirteen years since Ivo stood down from running 4AD and sold his 50 per cent share of the label back to his business partner Martin Mills, the head of the Beggars Banquet group of companies. But his legacy clearly lives on. The weekend edition of the *Guardian* has just published a feature on 4AD. 'What is it about a record label that makes it the sort of place you want to spend time in?' asks writer Richard Vine. 'When it first emerged in the 1980s, 4AD felt like one of the most enigmatic worlds, the sort of label that you wanted to collect, that brought a sense of "brand loyalty" way before it occurred to anyone to talk about music in such crass terms.'

Vine cites Ivo as the reason, adding, 'But arguably just as important to the label's cohesion was designer Vaughan Oliver and photographer Nigel Grierson whose covers gave 4AD its distinct, haunted, painterly quality. It felt like you were peeking into a carnival full of beautiful freaks who didn't want to be seen.'

So much of the music released on 4AD during Ivo's era had this same creative tension, beauty masking secrets, feelings buried, persisting in anxious dreams and suppressed fear, hope and anger; lyrics that don't explain emotion as much as cloud the issue, penned by a carnival full of beautiful freaks who didn't want to be seen. Isn't that what music does best, express feelings that words can't articulate? Emotion that can't be attached to a view or opinion, to a time or a place, is often the most timeless and precious.

People have long attached an obsessive importance to 4AD, and cited its enduring influence. On its own, This Mortal Coil's 'Song To The Siren' drew extravagant praise. At the time, vocalists Annie Lennox (Eurythmics) and Simon Le Bon (Duran Duran) voted it their favourite single of the year. Today, Antony Hegarty (Antony and the Johnsons) calls it, 'the best recording of the Eighties'. The song was to make an indelible impression. 'For years, I was spellbound by the Julee Cruise catalogue but I didn't know why,' says Hegarty. 'It was so beautiful and yet so horribly cryptic; there seemed to be something terrible lurking beneath the breathy sheen. Years later, I understood when I discovered that Lynch had originally wanted to license "Song To The Siren".'

Irish singer Sinead O'Connor was just seventeen when her mother was killed in a car crash. 'It was the record that got me through her death. In a country like Ireland where there was no such thing as therapy, self-expression or emotion, music was the only place you had to put anything. I played "Song To The Siren" nearly all day, every day, lying on the floor curled up in a ball, just *bawling*. I couldn't understand the words much, but [Fraser's] way of singing was the feeling I didn't how to make. I still can't move a muscle when I hear her sing it.'

July 2012, Ivo is driving from his New Mexico home in Lamy towards Santa Fe to an appointment with a new therapist, with Emmett sitting pillion; his black Newfoundland-Chow mix is the most eager of Ivo's three dogs to go along for the ride, and Ivo loves his company anyway. Clouded memories of former sessions, in the inevitably elusive pursuit of happiness and to understand the nature of depression, persist as he passes through the jagged, barren landscape, the sun playing shadow games on the mounds of burrograss, the rust-coloured earth framed 360 degrees by the mountains. So much beauty and light. But inside his head, sadness and darkness.

On arrival, Ivo is pleasantly surprised when the therapist agrees Emmett can stay. 'That's the way to do therapy,' Ivo reckons. 'And Emmett loves our time together.' But Ivo is not here to discuss Emmett, except in relation to how dogs have taught him to love unconditionally. 'Something I have struggled to do with people,' he says.

The black dog at his feet during the session has a special significance for Ivo. Depression is often known as 'the black dog', as British politician Winston Churchill famously labelled it. In 1974, towards the end of his young life, the British folk singer Nick Drake wrote 'Black-Eyed Dog' about the same subject. *'A black-eyed dog he called at my door/ A black-eyed dog he called for more/ A black-eyed dog he knew my name ...'*

Andrew Solomon's book *The Noonday Demon: An Atlas of Depression* summarised such depression: 'You lose the ability to trust anyone, to be touched, to grieve. Eventually, you are simply absent from yourself.'

'Try running a record company with two offices and over a dozen members of staff with countless artists looking to you for advice, guidance and financial support in that condition,' says Ivo.

Up in the high desert of New Mexico, 7,000 feet above sea level and 18 miles outside of the state capital Santa Fe, the community of Lamy is comfortably off the beaten track. It was once a vital railroad junction: the Burlington Northern Santa Fe (BNSF) line – colloquially known as the 'Santa Fe' – was to stop in Santa Fe but the surrounding hills meant that Lamy was a more practical destination. But few people disembark here now. The restaurant (in what was the plush El Ortiz hotel) and tiny museum are outnumbered by the rusting, abandoned rail carts, memories of a more prestigious past. Not many people live here either: the 2010 census gave a population count of 218.

By nightfall, a hush descends; it's the kind of place where you come to get away, or hide away, from it all. To give an idea of its isolation, America's first atomic bomb was tested just two hours away. It's a landscape on to which you can put your own impression, and also disappear into. 'I've moved to where I feel my most comfortable,' Ivo confesses. 'But people just think I'm eccentric.'

It's here, on a ridge outside of Lamy, that Ivo built his house. On the roof, you can see 360 degrees to the surrounding mountains. To the left, the Manzanos; straight ahead towards Albuquerque, the Sandias; to the right above Los Alamos, the Jemez and the Sangre de Cristo ranges that host ski season. Trails lead through the rock and scrub, but generally only dog walkers follow them; the remoteness is both impressive and comforting. In his decidedly modernist house, which stands out among New Mexico's predominantly pueblo architecture, Ivo lives with his three dogs, his art, his music and his privacy. It's an idyll, a hideaway, a fortress, possibly even a prison. Sometimes the only sounds are the sighs, whines and occasional barks of his dogs. The sun bakes down for much of the year. The skies are huge, the silence deafening.

Among the albums is a box set of This Mortal Coil recordings that Ivo recorded back in the day with a revolving cast of musicians, some close friends and others mere acquaintances. Some remain friends; others he hasn't seen, talked or corresponded with for many years. No expense was spared in the mastering of this music or the packaging of the collectors CD format known as 'Japanese paper sleeve', though the high-end quality is more like stiff card, like it's a book or a piece of art. These miniature reproductions of the original vinyl album artwork, only reproduced by specialist manufacturers in Japan, is the antithesis of the intangible digital MP3 that now defines music consumption. 'I'm fascinated by the quality of what the Japanese do, and the obscurity of some of the releases they archive and document,' Ivo says. 'Record companies say that no one buys finished product anymore. So why not give them something of beauty?'

Shelves and drawers in Ivo's rooms contain thousands of these limited edition box sets, which he trades as a hobby, to turn a profit if he can, ordering early and then selling on once they have sold out. After a period of not even being able to listen to music, it has again become an obsession. The music industry, or rather 4AD's place in it, used to be an obsession as well. Not anymore. Now it's a foggy, jumbled-up memory of highs and lows, a black dog growling at the foot of his mind.

Much contemporary music has a similar effect. Edgy, glitchy electronic music, the currency of the present technological age, 'is just wrong for my brain,' Ivo shrugs. He also admits he very rarely sees any live music anymore; too many people, too much fuss. The concept of the latest sound, the latest trend, the hyped-up sensation, leaves him cold. It has to be music that exists for its own sake. Music that can provide what he describes as 'solace and sense'. For the most part, Ivo explains, 'it doesn't involve the intellect, but evokes an emotional response. It draws one away from analysis, from the brain constantly questioning.'

This music often comes from his past, discovered in his youth or while he was building 4AD's catalogue, when he experienced epiphanies, love affairs, drug trips, through a cassette demo or a live show, before there was even the awareness of a black dog or what it meant to run a business. Music from the worlds of American folk and country appear to provide the most solace and sense these days. But the uncanny world of progressive rock rooted in the Sixties and Seventies, fusing the techniques of classical and avant-garde music to play havoc with tempo, texture and access, has become a recent fascination. 'Give me originality,' he says. 'Give me something challenging. I listen to music now and I'm always running an inventory in my head of what it reminds me of. I mean, if you're going to copy, to mimic, without putting an ounce of yourself into it …'

Ivo hasn't recorded any of his own music since 1997, when he assembled a series of cover versions under the name The Hope Blister. 'There have been a couple of times where I've talked about it,' he admits. 'I sent tapes out for people to consider, but I couldn't go through with it. In any case, I haven't had an original idea for years. In fact, I have no idea how I was ever that imaginative.'

Yet despite his disappearance into the desert and retirement, Ivo's opinion clearly still stands for something. Colleen Maloney, 4AD's head of press through the Nineties and currently at fellow south London independent Domino, heard that Ivo had fallen for *Diamond Mine*, a collaborative album between Scottish vocalist King Creosote and British electronic specialist Jon Hopkins that Domino had released in 2011. Ivo's name subsequently appeared on a press advertisement beside the quote: 'the best vocal record of the last twenty years'.

'It's so full of atmosphere, so sharp and so sad,' he says, nailing the very qualities that so often elevated the music released on 4AD to such sublime heights. But, as the cliché goes, the higher you climb, the harder you can fall. Beneath the beauty, lies a deeper ocean of emotion in which to drown.

2 1980(i)

PIPER AT THE GATES OF OUNDLE
(axis1-axis4)

Far from Lamy, the ancient market town of Oundle in the UK has a markedly different flora, fauna and geography – flatter, greener, though just as sedate. In a rural idyll 70 miles north of London In the county of Northamptonshire, Oundle is also isolated: 12 miles from the nearest main town of Peterborough, and almost surrounded on three sides by the River Nene.

The house where Ivo grew up was also isolated – the driveway to the main house was half a mile long. The Watts-Russells are inextricably linked to Oundle: records show that Ivo's ancestor Jesse Watts-Russell Junior built the town hall and the church, though it's the ancient church in the nearby village of Lower Benefield that can be seen through the avenue of trees from the estate's manor house.

Ivo's family came from aristocratic money, but while they still own much of the land in the area, the low-rent tithes set by his grandmother in the 1930s drastically reduced the income. The farmhouse property where Ivo was raised while his grandmother occupied the manor house had broken windows in every room. 'Sixty years earlier, the family name was a presence – my grandparents' marriage was society news,' he recalls. 'But the reality was five of us in one bedroom, and the farm itself was only a modest success.'

Ivo's father served in the British army in Egypt before and during the Second World War, and in Germany afterwards, before returning to Oundle in 1950 to run the estate farm. Ivo was born four years later, named after Ivo Grenfell, a cousin on his grandmother's side and brother of the First World War poet Julian Grenfell, whose famous war poem 'Into Battle' was published the same month he was killed in 1915. Ivo was the youngest of eight, with two brothers and five sisters. By the time his grandmother had died in 1969 and Ivo's family moved into the manor house, all his siblings had left home. His other brother Peregrine (known as Perry) remembers Ivo assisting with the move in a rare bonding exercise with an emotionally distant father.

'My older sister would joke, though not necessarily so, that the first time our dad talked to us was when we'd each turned fifteen, and he'd say, "OK, get on the tractor and drive". He was a very aloof man, who lost his own father when he was seven and was raised by a tyrannical Victorian English mother. We never related emotionally to either parent.'

Ivo's mother was diagnosed with tuberculosis when he was born in 1954, keeping her and the baby apart for three months for fear of passing on the potentially fatal disease. It was a harsh domestic regime of a father with a farm to run and a mother raising eight children without modern appliances ... 'I don't remember many visitors,' says Ivo. 'My uncles would come for the weekend, and then we'd have fun.'

In any environment of emotional deprivation, any form of art can become a vital lifeline, a source of comfort, inspiration and imagination. Ivo's pre-teen memories were of the rousing film soundtracks to *South Pacific* and *The Sound of Music*. Even earlier, *West Side Story*, the first 'teen' musical, was his introduction to the culture of attitude, fashion and sex (*'Got a rocket in your pocket, keep coolly cool, boy!'*). All three musicals emphasised the urge to escape, from 'Climb Every Mountain' and 'Over The Rainbow' to the lovers Tony and Maria from *West Side Story* believing, *'there is a place somewhere'* – a better place, beyond the control of authority and circumstances.

Eight children meant pop music was always in the Watts-Russell house. For Perry, it was The Beatles and The Rolling Stones. 'There was a three-year age gap between me and Ivo,' he says, 'so they couldn't be his soundtrack to adolescence.' Ivo has no memory of why the first single he bought at the age of six was 'I Can't Stop Loving You' by R&B legend Ray Charles. EPs by The Who and The Kinks followed, but his epiphany, the road from Oundle to Damascus, was The Jimi Hendrix Experience miming to the trio's debut single 'Hey Joe' on a 1967 edition of BBC TV's weekly flagship music show *Top of the Pops*. Their Afro hairstyles alone would have triggered intrigue in middle England, even consternation. But it was Hendrix's sound – liquid, sensual, aching, unsettling, alien – that had coloured the imagination of an impressionable twelve-year-old, thrilled at the subversive invasion of a drab farmhouse lounge.

'My sister Tessa and my parents were watching too and I remember a shared feeling of jaws dropping, of confusion,' Ivo recalls. 'I thought, this is having an impression, and being very interested by that. The next Saturday, I listened to [BBC radio DJ] John Peel's *Top Gear*, with sessions by Cream, Hendrix and Pink Floyd. I bought Hendrix's *Are You Experienced* and Pink Floyd's equally mind-altering *Piper At The Gates Of Dawn*. I'd finally found, to paraphrase John Lennon, the first thing that made any sense to me. My gang.'

These weren't the cool Sharks or Jets gangs of *West Side Story*, but the freaks, in all their animalistic glory. In this first flowering of psychedelia, the possibilities were endless. 'How mad was [Pink Floyd's] "Apples And Oranges" as a single?' says Ivo. 'What a brilliant reflection of the times. Aurally and visually, this was the counter-culture, the hope for the future.'

Despite his advanced tastes, Ivo – or George as he was affectionately known – wasn't allowed to join Perry and his friends at a concert with the epic bill of American R&B singer Geno Washington and the kaleidoscopic heaviness of Pink Floyd, Cream and The Jimi Hendrix Experience. His first ever show was more pop-centric but still staggering – The Who, Traffic, Marmalade and The Herd. 'Ivo was much more obsessive about music than I was,' Perry recalls. 'He wasn't yet distracted by girls, so music was the means by which you formed an identity. It spoke to him in ways that regular life didn't. He'd listen to Peel religiously, while I was so taken up with school.'

While his older brother studied intensely to pass his Oxbridge entrance exams, Ivo wasn't academic (or sporty), and music played an even more defining role. 'I felt like I didn't belong anywhere,' he says. 'I couldn't relate to anything I was being taught.'

His first chance to physically escape came that summer of 1968. Aged fourteen, Ivo and a school friend plotted to follow their friend Peter Thompson, one year older, to London. Thompson was squatting in a dilapidated house in the city centre near Marble Arch, helping to distribute Richard Branson's first venture, the free magazine *Student*. It was in this house, which doubled as *Student*'s HQ and Branson's living space, that Ivo smoked hash for the first time. But his education in this new illicit high was short-lived after an errant joint smoked by another schoolboy implicated Ivo.

His subsequent expulsion from school alongside two other boys made the news in Peterborough. 'Our family's position in society in that part of rural England stretched back two hundred years,' says Perry. 'It was a traumatic, life-affecting experience for Ivo and he was treated as a pariah. Maybe it drove him towards music being even more of a saviour.'

The cloud's silver lining turned out to be the offer of a place at a nearby technical college where the class system, peer pressure and school uniforms didn't apply, and girls were everywhere. Ivo persisted with buying records with odd-job cash, guided by John Peel's tastes; his next pivotal discovery was the Los Angeles quartet Spirit, led by prodigious teenager Randy California, a peer and friend of Jimi Hendrix who specialised in an 'infinite sustain' guitar technique, by aligning guitar feedback with the note that creates it. Ivo recommends the delicately searing solo in 'Uncle Jack' from 1968's debut album *Spirit*: 'I still get the same tingling feeling as when I first heard it.'

The doors of perception swung open to the sound of The Nice's keyboard-heavy *The Thoughts Of Emerlist Davjack* and Deep Purple's proto-heavy *Shades Of Deep Purple*, and especially The Mothers of

Invention's heavy satire *We're Only In It For The Money*, which Ivo found more intriguing and challenging than Hendrix. For starters, chief Mother Frank Zappa mocked not only the establishment's corporatisation of youth culture but the hippie dream too, hard to take for dreamers such as Ivo. Zappa claimed both sides were 'prisoners of the same narrow-minded, superficial phoniness'.

More crucially, the album was assembled like a collage, an anarchic and operatic meld of jazz, classical and rock that consistently changed tack. 'All these noises and whispers, the chop-ups and talking ... It proved to be incredibly influential on me, how something that cropped up in one song reappeared in another seven tracks later,' Ivo recalls. 'It made me think about how an album could be assembled. And if that kind of record can become normal, it suggests one is really open to pretty much anything in music. And that was me set. I had this ongoing relationship with whatever was contained within a twelve-inch-square sleeve. That's what I lived for.'

Ivo soon got to see The Mothers of Invention on stage. Other formative concert experiences were psychedelic seers King Crimson and Pink Floyd. To Ivo, Syd Barrett was the personification of cool, and even once Barrett's fragile eggshell mind had broken, like the acid Humpty Dumpty, he believed fully in Floyd's subsequent journey to the outer reaches of space rock. The realisation that music could be a journey sent Ivo on his own quest to unearth music of an equivalent mindset.

A recommendation to investigate the burgeoning acid rock scene over on America's west coast introduced Ivo to traditional folk/country roots, through Buffalo Springfield's newly liberated frontman Neil Young and the collective jamming of The Grateful Dead. 'I was exposed to more than the electric guitar individuality that English bands had,' he recalls. And it wasn't long till Ivo was exposed to acid itself, experiencing his first hallucination in Kettering's Wimpy hamburger bar in the company of his friend (and future heavy metal producer) Max Norman. Ivo's parents allowed Max's band to rehearse in a cottage on the family estate; Ivo acted like their roadie: 'I'd bash away at the drums, but I never dreamt of picking up a guitar or learning an instrument. I was the only one of the eight kids to not have piano lessons, though musically none of us were remotely gifted.'

In 1972, when they were eighteen, Max and Ivo hatched a plan to move to London, which failed after one day when the friend they hoped to stay with turned them away. A month later, Ivo returned alone. Drawn to High Street Kensington because of its popular hippie market, he spotted a shop on Kensington Church Street called Norman's with Floyd's *Piper At The Gates Of Dawn* (already five years old) in the window. It was run by a father and daughter partnership. 'The place was shabby and out of time but it still appealed to me, so I asked if they had a job going. By the time I'd got home, the father had called, saying I could help on the record side. I think his plan was to train me to run the shop with his daughter.'

Ivo and two college friends subsequently moved into a basement flat in nearby Earls Court, stricken by damp and frogs in the kitchen, but there's no place like home. 'Behind the counter, that was my territory,' Ivo says, 'just as behind my desk at 4AD later on. But I was still incredibly shy.'

Six months later, Ivo had had enough of Norman's. 'The stock was limited and we'd get asked for a Steely Dan album but we didn't have a clue because it was only on import. It was a road to nowhere.' In an early and risky show of self-determination, he left Norman's and moved in with his sister Tessa's boyfriend in the nondescript outer west London suburb of Hanwell. One day, exploring the busier streets of nearby Ealing, he found a branch of Musicland, a more clued-in record retailer. After boosting his credibility by asking for the album *Alone Together* by [Traffic's] Dave Mason, he asked the manager, Mike Smith, for a job. Smith happened to need an assistant, but he accurately predicted Ivo would be managing his own Musicland branch within two months.

Ivo ran Musicland in the deeply dull suburb of Hounslow – had the Sixties even reached Hounslow, let alone the Seventies? – but he managed to return to Ealing when Musicland – now called Cloud Seven after a takeover – transferred Mike Smith to another branch. It was now 1972, the time of glam rock, a revolution in dazzling sound and satin jackets, which helped British pop escape the cul-de-sac of denim and hard rock, a world of singles as well as albums. But Ealing, with its copious clubs, bars and students, had held on to its Sixties dream, as one of London's musical epicentres, the birthplace of British jazz and blues where The Rolling Stones had got their first break.

One regular at the Cloud Seven shop was Steve Webbon. A few years older than Ivo, Webbon had boosted his credibility by quizzing Ivo about country rock pioneer Gram Parsons – and then asking about a job. Ivo hadn't heard of Parsons, but he'd found his assistant.

Steve Webbon currently runs the back catalogue department of both 4AD and Beggars Banquet labels. In the late Sixties, he studied at Ealing Art School, moving on to unemployment benefit and spending most of it in Cloud Seven, in thrall to the sound of west coast American music. Manned by its two Yankophiles, Cloud Seven stocked up on what Gram Parsons had labelled 'cosmic American music', before he died, like Tim Buckley, of a heroin overdose. Nowadays, people call it Americana, a repository of roots music that pined for a simpler, humanistic society while rejecting the flash and excess of rock'n'roll. Only in the shape of Bob Dylan and The Band's return to American roots did British audiences pay attention; in America as well as the UK, Parsons' raw, Nashville-indebted sound was overshadowed by the softer, sweeter bedsitter folk of the era's million-selling singer-songwriters such as Carole King and James Taylor.

Next to this, Ivo felt glam rock and its more adult cousin art rock to be inauthentic. 'It was too "look at me", too frivolous. I later learnt that there was depth there, and obviously there was something different about David Bowie. But his Ziggy Stardust explosion had put me off, and Alice Cooper and Roxy Music weren't serious enough either.'

Ivo was happy in his domain behind the Cloud Seven counter: 'I was having a whale of a time. Until I got mugged, that is.' It was just before Christmas 1973; the victim of a second mugging that evening died from the attack. Carrying the night safe wallet after shutting up the shop, Ivo was knocked unconscious, landing face first and breaking his nose: 'I was freaked out, and left London, back home to Oundle, to the womb. But I immediately knew I'd made a stupid mistake.'

After two months, Ivo called Cloud Seven and got a desk job at the company head office. He graduated to conducting impromptu stock checks (to catch potential thieves among the staff) before managing the branch in Kingston, a relatively unexplored satellite town just south of London. Yet it was home to a thriving student campus, and the Three Fishes pub, an enclave of American west coast and southern rock: 'Everyone wore plaid shirts, drove VW vans and listened to The Grateful Dead,' Ivo recalls.

The Kingston shop was first on the import van's route from Heathrow airport, so Ivo was the first to lay his hands on albums such as Emmylou Harris' *Pieces Of The Sky*, Tim Buckley's *Sefronia*, and Bill Lamb and Gary Ogan's *Portland*, pieces of exquisite rootsy melancholia that he'd sticker with recommendations and sell a hundred copies of each. Ivo became especially infatuated with Buckley's five-octave range and equally audacious ability to master different genres. He began ordering album imports such as Spirit's *The Family That Plays Together* and Steve Miller's *Children Of The Future* because they had gatefold sleeves, made from thick board; the packaging was part of the appeal, tangible objects to have and to hold. Pearls Before Swine's use of medieval paintings that were rich in symbolism but gave no indication of the music inside was another alluring draw.

But again Ivo became restless. Once he'd received the Criminal Compensation Board's cheque for £500 to fix his broken nose, Ivo forwent the operation (it was later paid for by the National Health Service) and went travelling with his friend Steve Brown, hitchhiking through France, taking the train through Spain and then the boat to Morocco, in the footsteps of those who'd sought out premium-grade hashish. After two months of beach-bum life, a cash-depleted Ivo was back in London, seeking work again. Steve Webbon, now managing the Fulham branch of a new record shop, Beggars Banquet, said the owners were looking for more staff.

One of the owners was Webbon's old school friend Martin Mills. They'd stayed friends while Mills attended Oxford University;

Webbon remembers hedonistic nights in student dens, where casual use of heroin was part of the alternative lifestyle, though, he adds, 'Not Martin, he was more disciplined, not stupid like some others.' Mills' room would resonate to west coast classics: 'The Byrds, Moby Grape, Love, The Doors,' Webbon recalls. 'English groups weren't that inspiring – we were more interested in the next Elektra Records release. That was the kind of record label to follow, and ideally to be part of.'

Elektra had been founded in 1950 by Jac Holzman and Paul Rickolt; each invested $300. During the Fifties and early Sixties, the label had concentrated on folk music, but also classical, through its very successful budget Nonesuch imprint, sales of which helped to fund music of a more psychedelic nature, starting with the bluesy Paul Butterfield Band, Love, The Doors and a nascent Tim Buckley. The Nonesuch Explorer Series was a pioneer in releasing what became known in the Eighties as world music. Put simply, Holzman ran the hippest, coolest, trendiest and also the best record label around. But, like Ivo, he too got restless, and in 1970, Holzman sold his controlling share in Elektra, which became part of the Warner Brothers music group. Holzman stayed in charge until 1972, when it merged with Asylum Records, which specialised in west coast singer-songwriters, from Jackson Browne and Linda Ronstadt to Joni Mitchell and The Eagles. Politics and rivalries under the Warner umbrella made for a bumpy ride, but the quality of the music rarely wavered.

It's very unlikely the Warners corporation would ever have considered housing its record companies in the rabbit warren of rooms and corridors that made up 15–19 Alma Road in Wandsworth, south-west London, where Martin Mills' Beggars Banquet and associated labels have their offices. A suitably alternative, homespun space for the world's most successful independent label group, Mills' lawyer James Wylie once described the label's operation as, 'a Madagascar off the continent of Africa that is the music business, part of the same ecosystem but with its own microclimate'.

Not even the success of Adele, signed to Beggars imprint XL, whose 2011 album *21* is the biggest selling album in the UK since The Beatles'

Sergeant Pepper in 1967, has encouraged Mills to move – nor his half of a recent $27.3 million dividend based on his profit share. Mills also owns half of the Rough Trade and Matador labels, and all of 4AD. Mills – and Ivo – moved here in 1982, when more than 25 million sales would have been a ridiculous, stoned fantasy.

Born in 1949, Mills was raised in Oxford, and he stayed on to study philosophy, politics and economics at the prestigious Oriel College. Piano lessons had come to nothing when The Beatles and the Brit-beat boom arrived, though Mills says he favoured 'the rougher axis' of The Rolling Stones and The Animals, just as he enjoys live music much more than recordings, making him the opposite of concert-phobe Ivo. 'I cared about music above anything else,' he says, but when he failed to get a positive response to job requests sent to every UK record label he could find an address for, his upbringing demanded common sense. While taking a postgraduate degree in town planning, he shared a flat in west Ealing with Steve Webbon.

But he found he couldn't give up on music. Scaling back his ambitions, Mills then began a mobile disco with a friend from Oxford, Nick Austin, who was then working for his father's furnishing company. The pair named their enterprise Giant Elf (a riposte to J. R. R. Tolkien's already iconic *The Hobbit*) before Mills claims they needed a new name after receiving too many hoax calls alluding to Giant Elf's supposed gay connotation. A subsequent team-up with a friend's mobile disco, called Beggars Banquet, provided the means.

Mills also drove a van for Austin's father while signing on for unemployment benefit – 'a desirable scenario back then,' he smiles. But the benefit office forced him into a full-time job, and for two years, Mills worked for The Office of Population, Census and Surveys (managing the statistics for the Reform of Abortion act) but he landed a job at the Record & Tape Exchange, a well-known record shop trading in second-hand records in Shepherd's Bush, not far from Ealing.

Soon, Mills and Austin were discussing running their own second-hand record shop, which would sell new records too. Each borrowed £2,000 from their parents and, in 1974, opened Beggars Banquet in

Hogarth Road, Earls Court. 'It was a buzzing, backpacker type of place, with lots of record shops,' says Mills. 'But we'd stay open later than the others, until 9.30pm, selling left-field undergraduate stuff, west coast psychedelia, folk and country, but also soul, R&B and jazz-funk. We brought in Steve Webbon, who knew about record retail. By 1977, we had six shops.'

Beggars Banquet had given Ivo a job, and in a reversal of roles, he became Webbon's assistant after the latter had moved to the Ealing branch. But so much of music, culture, and record retail was fundamentally shifting. The first real wave of opposition to the stagnating scenes of progressive, hard and west coast rock was the neo-punk of Iggy and The Stooges and the New York Dolls, which soon triggered a new wave of stripped-back guitars, centred around the CBGB's club in the States (Patti Smith, Television) and the wilder exponents of so-called 'pub rock' in the UK (Doctor Feelgood, The 101ers). The first wave of London-based independent labels (Stiff, Chiswick, Small Wonder) sprang up to meet a growing demand, while Jamaican reggae imports were also rising. Not far behind was the new Rough Trade shop in west London's bohemian enclave of Notting Hill Gate, whose founder Geoff Travis was to bolt on a record label and a distribution arm.

Beggars Banquet's first expansion was as a short-lived concert promotions company. 'We saw the opportunity for artists that people didn't know there was demand for,' says Mills, beginning with German ambient space-rockers Tangerine Dream in 1975 at London's grand Royal Albert Hall. Only a year later, Mills says he saw a palpable shift in audience expectations while promoting the proto-new wave of Graham Parker, whose support band The Damned was the first punk band to release a single. 'Punk turned our world upside down. No one wanted the kind of shows in theatre venues that we'd been promoting. People wanted grotty little places, so we stopped.'

A Beggars Banquet record label came next. The Fulham branch turned its basement into a rehearsal space for punk bands, one being London-based The Lurkers. A shop named after a Rolling Stones album was now primed to put rock 'dinosaurs' such as the Stones to the sword. Fulham branch manager Mike Stone had doubled up as The Lurkers' manager. 'Every label had a punk band now, and no one was interested in the band,' says Mills. 'So we released the first Lurkers single ['Shadows'] ourselves. We had no clue how to, but we found a recording studio and a pressing plant in a music directory and we got distribution from President, who manufactured styluses.'

John Peel was an instant convert to punk, including The Lurkers, who sold a very healthy 15,000 copies of 'Shadows' on the new Beggars Banquet label. The profits funded *Streets*, the first compilation of independently released punk tracks. That sold 25,000, as did The Lurkers' debut album *Fulham Fallout*.

Nick Austin spearheaded the talent-spotting A&R process. 'He'd have ten ideas, and one was good, the rest embarrassing,' says Steve Webbon. Subsequent Beggars Banquet acts such as Duffo, The Doll and Ivor Biggun (the alias of Robert 'Doc' Cox, BBC TV journalist turned novelty songsmith) were fluff compared to what Rough Trade and Manchester's Factory Records were developing. 'We were a rag-bag in the early days,' Mills agrees. 'A lot was off-message for punk. But our fourth release was Tubeway Army, after their bassist walked into the shop with a tape.'

Tubeway Army, marshalled by its mercurial frontman – and Berlin-era Bowie clone – Gary Numan, would catapult Beggars Banquet into another league, with a number 1 single within a year. But Numan's demands for expensive equipment for the band's first album, and other label expenses, stretched the company's cash flow, and Mills says that only Ivor Biggun's rugby-song innuendos (1978's 'The Winker's Song' had reached number 22 on the UK national chart) staved off near bankruptcy. Mills and Austin were businessmen, not idealists, so when they had to find a new distributor (the current operators Island had had to withdraw due to a licensing deal with EMI), they got into bed with the major label Warners. The licence deal meant that Beggars Banquet wasn't eligible for the new independent label chart that would launch in 1980, but it did inject £100,000 of funds. 'It was an absolutely insane figure,' says Mills. 'How could Warners expect to be repaid?'

The answer to repaying Warners was Tubeway Army's bewitching, synthesised 'Are "Friends" Electric?' and its parent album *Replicas*, which both topped the UK national chart in 1979. So did Numan's solo album *The Pleasure Principle*, released just four months later. The Faustian deal effectively meant that Beggars Banquet became a satellite operation of Warners, even sharing some staff. 'We'd become something we hadn't intended to be,' says Mills. 'One reason we [later] started 4AD was that it could be what Beggars Banquet had wanted to be: an underground label, and not fragmented like we'd become.'

While working in the shop, Ivo had only been a part-convert to the punk revolution. 'I liked some of The Clash's singles but their debut album was so badly recorded, it didn't interest me at all. But I'd seen Blondie and Ramones live, and I quickly came to enjoy punk's energy and melody. But I didn't need punk to wipe away progressive rock. I'd been listening to what people saw as embarrassing and obscure country rock – no one was interested in Emmylou Harris or Gram Parsons back then. But I just loved voices, like Emmylou, Gram and Tim [Buckley].'

Of the new breed, Ivo preferred the darker, artier, and more progressive American bands such as Chrome, Pere Ubu and Television, who had very little in common with punk's political snarl and fashion accoutrements. Steve Webbon, however, appeared to more fully embrace the sound of punk and its attendant lifestyle. 'Those customers that were still into the minutiae of country rock were very dull,' he recalls. 'And that music had become more mainstream and bland. I spent the Seventies on speed: uppers, blues, black bombers. It must have been wearing for Ivo.'

Ivo had been forced to take charge on those days when Webbon disappeared to drug binge or during his periods of recovery. Ivo himself dipped into another torpid period of indecision. 'Being behind the shop counter, with these children coming in every night, their hair changed and wearing safety pins, was exciting, but it got pretty boring too. So I left again.'

This time, Ivo flew to find the Holy Grail – to California. His brother Perry was taking Latin American studies at the University College of

Los Angeles and could provide a place to stay. When Ivo's visa ran out after just a matter of months, he again went back to the devil he knew; Beggars Banquet rehired him to train managers across all its shops. But after just one hour in the job, he quit again: 'I felt like a caged animal.'

After claiming unemployment benefit for six months, the local job centre forced Ivo to apply for a job as a clerical worker at Ealing Town Hall. He once again turned to Beggars, and Nick Austin – clearly a patient man – re-employed him to do the same training job. In the summer of 1979, Ivo was even allowed an extended holiday, returning to California, where he and his friend Dave Bates first conceived the idea of a record label, and of opening a record shop with a café in Bournemouth on the south coast. Both operations were to be named Freebase (friends of Ivo's had claimed they invented the freebasing technique of purifying cocaine). Ivo even went as far as registering the name: 'Thankfully, it never happened. Imagine being behind a company called Freebase. In any case, the shop and café was pure fantasy.'

Ivo's first thought for the Freebase label was to license albums by the San Francisco duo Chrome, purveyors of scuzzy psychedelic rock/ electronic collage. Instead, the band's creative force Damon Edge suggested Ivo should buy finished product from him instead, which he was unable to afford.*

The next opportunity came after Alex Proctor, a friend from Ivo's Oundle days who was working at the Earls Court shop, passed on a demo. Brian Brain was the alter ego of Martin Atkins, the former drummer of Sex Pistol John Lydon's new band Public Image Limited (or PiL). Ivo had recommended his tape to Martin Mills, who didn't show any interest. 'But then I got talking to Peter Kent, who was managing Beggars' Earls Court branch,' Ivo recalls.

Ivo's cohort in forming a record label now lives in the Chicago suburb of Rogers Park, two blocks from Lake Michigan's urban beach.

---

* After starting 4AD, Ivo did import copies of Chrome's second album *Half Lip Machine Moves* before introducing the band to Beggars Banquet, which released the band's next three albums, starting in 1980 with *Red Exposure*.

It's his first ever interview. 'I've always considered myself as a bit player on the side,' says Peter Kent. 'I know people who are just full of themselves, but I'm more private. And being a Buddhist, I like to live in the present rather than regurgitate the past.' But he is willing to talk, after all. 'It's nice to leave something behind,' he concedes.

Kent didn't hang around for long in the music business, partly by choice but also due to illness (he has multiple sclerosis). Among other part-time endeavours, he works as a dog sitter, which would give him and Ivo plenty to chat about. But during the time that they worked together, Ivo says, he knew nothing about Kent's private life.

Born in Battersea, south-west London, his family's neighbour was the tour manager of the Sixties band Manfred Mann, which gave the teenage Kent convenient entry to London's exploding beat music boom. Kent says he DJed around Europe while based in Amsterdam, 'doing everything that you shouldn't'. He adds that, 'A friend was a doctor of medicine in Basle, who'd make mescaline and cocaine. Peter Kent isn't my real name; Interpol and the drug squad were looking for me at one point. It's a long story.'

Kent also says that British blues vocalist Long John Baldry was his first boyfriend before he dated Bowie protégé Mickey King who he first met, alongside Bowie, at the Earls Court gay club Yours or Mine. After returning from Amsterdam, Kent appeared to calm down when he started managing Town Records in Kings Road, Chelsea, next door to fetish clothing specialists Seditionaries, run by future fashion icon Vivienne Westwood and future Sex Pistols manager Malcolm McLaren. He also ran a market stall-cum-café in nearby Beaufort Market, next to future punk siren Poly Styrene of X-Ray Spex fame. By 1976, Kent had opened his own record shop, called Stuff, in nearby Fulham but it didn't make a profit and so he took the manager's post at Beggars Banquet's Earls Court branch. The label's office, and Ivo's desk, was upstairs.

The origins of 4AD are contested. Kent says an avalanche of demos had been sent in the wake of Tubeway Army's success: 'Part of my job was to listen to them with the idea of forwarding the good ones to

Beggars. I also said it was a great idea to start a little label on the side, and Martin said that's what Ivo also wanted to do.'

Martin Mills recalls Ivo and Peter Kent approaching Nick Austin and himself with a plan, while Ivo sticks to the story he told *Option* magazine in 1986. 'We'd regularly rush upstairs to convince Martin and Nick that they should get involved with something like Modern English, as opposed to what they were involved with. Eventually, Beggars got fed up with us pestering them and said, "Why don't you start your own label?"'

Whatever the story, Mills and Austin donated a start-up fund of £2,000. Kent got to christen the label, choosing Axis after Jimi Hendrix's *Axis: Bold As Love* album. 'Ivo and I clicked as people,' says Kent. 'It was like I was Roxy Music and he was Captain Beefheart, but we appreciated where each other was coming from. He was mellower; I was more outgoing. But I wouldn't say I ever knew him well.'

'Ivo and Peter were a good double act,' recalls Robbie Grey, lead singer for Modern English, one of 4AD's crucial early signings. 'They were similar in their background too, neither working class, so straight away you were dealing with art college types.'

Steve Webbon: 'Peter was great. Very tall, dry sense of humour. And he had all these connections. He wasn't as into music as Ivo, he was more into the scene. He'd go to gigs while Ivo would more listen to your tape.'

Ivo: 'Peter was so important to 4AD from the start. Most of the early stuff was his discovery. While I was running around servicing the other shops, he was the go-getter. He knew people. I liked everything enough to say yes, but I didn't know what I was doing.'

One part of the plan was for Axis to play a feeder role for the Beggars Banquet label, so that those artists with commercial ambition could make use of Beggars' distribution deal with Warners. Another idea was to launch Axis with four seven-inch singles on the same day: 'To make a statement, and to establish an imprint,' says Ivo. 'Other independent labels at that point, such as Factory, were imprints. It meant something.'

Factory's first release, *A Factory Sampler*, had featured four bands, including Joy Division and Sheffield's electronic pioneers Cabaret Voltaire. Axis' first quartet, simultaneously released on the first business day of 1980, wasn't quite as hefty. Nor did it include Brian Brain, which would have instantly given the label a newsworthy angle, or another mooted suggestion, Temporary Title, a south London band that used to rehearse in Beggars' Fulham basement, whose singer Lea Anderson was a 'floating' Saturday shop assistant across the various Beggars Banquet shops. Instead, out of the pile of demos emerged three unknown entities, The Fast Set, Shox and Bearz, and one band that had released a single on east London independent Small Wonder: Bauhaus, who was to save Axis from the most underwhelming beginning.

The single given the honour of catalogue number AXIS 1 was The Fast Set's 'Junction One'. London-based keyboardist David Knight was the proud owner of a VCS3 synth, popularised by Eno, whose demo was played in the Earls Court shop by his friend Brad Day who worked there on Saturdays. 'Peter Kent said if I wanted to record an electronic version of a glam rock track, he'd release it on this new label,' recalls Knight. 'The Human League had covered Gary Glitter's "Rock And Roll", and there were lots of other post-modern, semi-ironic interpretations around. I knew T. Rex's "Children Of The Revolution" had only two chords, which suited me. Peter put me in a studio to record it, but he needed another track, which I knocked out on the spot, which became the A-side. I don't know why.'

At very short notice, Knight and three cohorts played a show at Kent's request. Budding film director John Maybury (best known for his 1998 Francis Bacon biopic *Love Is the Devil*) projected super-8 images on to them and named them The Fast Set, because the quartet were so immobile on stage. Maybury also designed the cover of 'Junction One'. The Fast Set's synth-pop had a bit of early Human League's sketchy pop but not its vision or charm. 'For starters, I was no singer,' says Knight. 'My vocals were appalling!'

AXIS 2 and AXIS 4 were demos that had been posted to the Hogarth Road shop. 'She's My Girl' was by Bearz, a quartet from the south-west of England that wasn't even a band, says bassist Dave Gunstone. 'The singer John Goddard and I had an idea to make a record – we liked the new wave sound, but we didn't even have songs before we booked the studio. We found a drummer, Mark Willis, and David Lord produced us and played keyboards. I was a signwriter for shops and vans then – and you can hear I'm not a musician. But Ivo called to say he was interested in signing us. We went up to see him and Peter – to be in the office with Gary Numan gold discs on the walls, it was dream come true.'

They called themselves The Bears until Ivo (who says it would have been Peter Kent) pointed out other bands had already used the name, 'so he said "stick a z on the end"', says Gunstone. 'Neo-psychedelic vocals over an attractively lumpy melody' (*NME*) and 'nostalgia pop' (Peter Kent) are fair appraisals of the song, given the dinky Sixties beat-pop and Seventies bubblegum mix, while the B-side 'Girls Will Do' was tauter new wave.

Shox were also hopeful of a stab at success via the new wave conceit of a misspelt name – though the photo on the cover of vocalist Jacqui Brookes and instrumentalists John Pethers and Mike Atkinson in one bed was horribly old school. The most prominent British weekly music paper, *New Music Express* (*NME*) also approved of 'No Turning Back': 'Fresh and naturally home-made, like The Human League once upon a time'. Peter Kent's comment, 'I have no memory of it whatsoever', also hits the mark.

AXIS 3, 'Dark Entries', was an altogether different story. Peter Kent recalls being in the Rough Trade shop. 'I was buying singles for Beggars Banquet, and Geoff Travis was there, playing some demos. I heard him say he didn't like it, and I said, "Excuse me?" Geoff said I could take it. The energy was unbelievable, and the sound was so different from everything else around. Forty-eight hours later, I was in Northampton to meet Bauhaus.'

Ivo: 'If Peter did go to Northampton, that was another thing that he didn't tell me! I first met Bauhaus in the Earls Court shop where Peter had intercepted the tape they were intending to deliver to Beggars Banquet. Peter came to find me in the restaurant over the road and insisted I come back immediately to listen to it and meet the band.'

According to Bauhaus' singer Peter Murphy, 'Peter said, "I'm having you lot". Ivo didn't want us. That's what Peter said at the time. Ivo's a mardy bugger! And really sarcastic [laughs]. But when we walked into the Beggars office, Ivy [Murphy's affectionate nickname for Ivo] was working there, and he looked at us after hearing the music and said yes!'

Via a Skype connection to Turkey's capital Istanbul, where Murphy has lived since marrying his Turkish wife and following the Islamic belief of Sufism, the former Bauhaus singer still looks sleek and gaunt, his celebrated 'dark lord' persona intact. Traffic whirs away in the background, but it cuts out when Murphy puts on 'Re-Make Re-Model' from Roxy Music's epochal 1972 album debut, presumably to set the scene for our conversation, by showcasing Bauhaus' roots in both glam and art rock.

'I was fifteen,' Murphy begins, 'and I didn't know if it was male or female, but I saw this pair of testicles peaking out under a Kabuki outfit, and it was the most erotic moment. It felt angelic.' The photographic object of his affection was David Bowie, in his Ziggy Stardust leotard. Roxy Music's synthesiser magus Brian Eno, says Murphy, 'was maybe even more magical, awesome in that raw, lo-fi way, the drums on his solo records so flat and thick and stocky, with none of that fucking reverb bollocks that Ivo would swamp things in!'

The Bauhaus siblings, David and Kevin Haskins, both now live in California – David J, as the bassist calls himself, is in Encinitas, 95 miles from Kevin Haskins Dompe (he's since bolted on his wife's maiden name) in Los Angeles. Both willingly testify to a similarly shared epiphany – July 1972, when Bowie – in the guise of Ziggy – sang 'Starman' on *Top of the Pops*. 'I was hooked, and I knew I had to do this myself.'

There's one missing voice – guitarist Daniel Ash. Though he lives in California as well, he hasn't communicated with any of his former bandmates since the band's 2008 album *Go Away White*. Ash, the others say, prefers tinkering with his beloved motorbikes over any remembrance of the past.*

Playing guitar, David J had graduated from his first band, Grab a Shadow, and having encouraged Kevin – still just thirteen – to learn the drums, they'd joined Jam, a hard rock covers band. 'And then punk happened,' says Haskins Dompe. 'David took me to The 100 Club to see the Sex Pistols, The Clash and the Banshees. The next day I cut off my hair and wore my paint-splashed polyester pyjamas to art school.'

After the demise of the pair's short-lived punk band The Submerged Tenth, David J had bumped into fellow art school student Ash, who he'd known since kindergarten. 'We clearly had a connection,' says David. 'We both loved dub reggae, and Bowie.' Haskins and Ash subsequently formed The Craze, which, Haskins Dompe says, 'played new wave power-pop, which Daniel didn't like, so that ended'. Ash asked Haskins Dompe to join a new band fronted by Ash's old school friend Peter Murphy, but excluding David J. 'Daniel felt David's ideas were too strong, but he relented,' says Haskins Dompe. 'I could see the chemistry between them.'

David J had watched the others rehearse. 'They were so streamlined and stark, and Peter had such charisma, and looked amazing. They had a bassist, but his looks and personality didn't fit, so I joined.'

Peter Murphy: 'David was sensitive, smart, self-interested, a dark horse. Kevin could be narky and uppity, but he was our sweet angel. I was very overpowering but we were respectful of each other, though there was a lot of unspoken, repressed tension.'

---

* For all his protestations about ditching the past, in March 2013 Ash announced an event he called *Truth Be Told*, to be staged in Las Vegas over one weekend in May. Comprising music, Q&A sessions, parties, accommodation and food, with tickets starting at $2,000 to be sold by auction, the weekend included a private concert in a Las Vegas mansion, with material spanning Ash's career, from Bauhaus and his Tones on Tail and Love and Rockets bands to solo material. This followed a similar twice-the-price Miracula Sessions in 2012. Maybe those spare bike parts are very expensive, though Ash planned to donate an unspecified amount of his proceeds towards creating a music rehearsal space for children in the Los Angeles area.

The battle of wills that marked Bauhaus to the end produced the necessary sparks at the start. Written only weeks after David J joined, the band's debut single 'Bela Lugosi's Dead' was a cavernous, dub-enhanced nine-minute drama with the epic mantra, '*undead, undead, undead,*' in honour of Bela Lugosi, the Hungarian actor most famous for his 1931 portrait of Dracula. 'We surprised ourselves, because it was ambitious and didn't follow anyone else,' says David J. Every major label (and Stiff) declined to release it, before the fledgling London independent label Small Wonder stepped in. 'Theirs was the only response that didn't think the track was too long.'

Thirty-four years on, 'Bela Lugosi's Dead' remains Bauhaus' signature classic; it hung around the new UK independent singles chart (launched two weeks after Axis) for two years. It also helped spawn a genre that proved to be as contentious for the band as it was for the future 4AD. It's said that the term 'gothic' was used by Factory MD Tony Wilson to describe his own band Joy Division, but it was also applied to the ice queen drama of Siouxsie and the Banshees. Soon enough it would be shortened to 'goth', and wielded as a pejorative term, to describe an affected version of doom and angst.

The problem was, as Ash said, goth came to define bands with 'too much make-up and no talent'. Bauhaus were undeniably talented, but Murphy had a habit of shining a torch under his chin as he prowled across the stage. This was fine by Kent: 'I wanted more than people just standing there on stage, and Peter was already one of the best frontmen,' he says. Murphy relishes the memory of a Small Wonder label night at London's Camden Palace, 'me in a black knitted curtain and jockstrap,' he recalls. 'We scared the fuck out of everyone that night, all these alternative über-hippies moaning about everything. After punk, everybody ran out of things to moan about.'

Actually, the opposite was true. Post-punk had plenty of targets to kick against in 1980 and its bristling monochrome was a suitable soundtrack to the economic and social depression of an era presided over by the hate figure of Conservative prime minister Margaret Thatcher: tax increases, budget cuts, worker strikes, nuclear paranoia, Cold War scare-mongering and record post-war levels of inflation (22 per cent) and unemployment (two million). But goth bands didn't articulate social injustice or political turmoil. This version of disaffection and dread was more *Cabaret*, an escape from the gloom, with lots of black nail varnish. Bauhaus' 'Dark Entries', for example, was inspired by the decadent anti-hero of Oscar Wilde's novel *The Picture of Dorian Gray*. 'A story of great narcissism and esoteric interior,' says Murphy. 'A rock star's story.'

Axis' founders didn't appear driven by causes or campaigns either. Ivo didn't favour political agitators such as The Clash or Gang of Four, but more the open-ended oblique strategies of Wire or the acid psychodrama of Liverpool's Echo & The Bunnymen. In fact, Ivo felt that the name Axis had unwanted political connotations. 'Peter [Kent] may have been thinking of Hendrix but, for me, Axis related to [Nazi] Germany, like Factory and Joy Division. It was a stupid name.'

It was a stroke of fortune that the label was forced into changing its name before the imprint, or the association, stuck. An existing Axis in, of all countries, Germany, read about the launch of the UK version in the trade paper *Music Week*; the owners allowed all the remaining stock on the UK label to be sold before they had to find a new name. '4AD was grasped out of the air in desperation,' says Ivo.

A flyer that freelance designer Mark Robertson had laid out to promote the launch of Axis worked on the concept of a new decade and a new mission. In descending order down the page was written:

1980 FORWARD
1980 FWD
1984 AD
4AD

'What I loved about 4AD was that it meant nothing,' Ivo recalls. 'No ideology, no polemic, no attitude. In other words, just music.'

3 1980 (ii)

1980 FORWARD
(bad5-bad19)

The spirit of rebirth behind the change of name from Axis to 4AD was underlined by the need for fresh blood, given that The Fast Set, Bearz and Shox would never again record for 4AD. Sales of Bauhaus' 'Dark Entries' meant that 4AD would re-press the single another three times, while Shox's 'No Turning Back' was temporarily given a Beggars Banquet catalogue number (between the changeover from Axis to 4AD) for a second pressing before the band vanished. Dave Gunstone's dream was quickly over when Ivo informed Bearz that their new demos weren't good enough. The Fast Set would resurface, but only once, in 1981, with a second T. Rex cover, 'King Of The Rumbling Spires', on the first compilation of synth-pop, released by a new independent label, Some Bizzare, in 1981. But while the album's new inductees Depeche Mode and Soft Cell were to use *Some Bizzare Album* as a springboard to superstardom, David Knight retired The Fast Set.* Even the

---

* Of all Axis' lesser-known luminaries, Bearz producer and keyboard session player David Lord has done the best, as an engineer/producer for artists such as Peter Gabriel, Tears For Fears, Peter Hammill, Tori Amos and Goldfrapp. David 'Fast Set' Knight became a studio-based collaborator (and lover) of British singer-cum-performance artist Danielle Dax. However, Shox vocalist Jacqui Brookes fronted the synth-pop band Siam and released a solo album, *Sob Stories*, for major label MCA.

31

revolutionary Do It Yourself opportunities of the punk and post-punk movements bred more frustrated failures and dead ends than established breakthroughs.

Conditioned by the pre-punk era of beautiful artwork and hi-fi, Ivo also embarked on raising the quality of the packaging and sound after judging the production company that Peter Kent had employed for Axis: 'They were among the worst-sounding vinyl I'd ever heard, in really poor-quality sleeves.'

This spirit of rebirth was to be reinforced by 4AD's official debut release. Ivo had been doing his round of the Beggars Banquet shops and had returned to Hogarth Road: 'Peter was behind the counter with all of Rema-Rema. When I heard their music, I knew it was a sea change for 4AD.'

On the seventh floor of a council-block flat overlooking the hectic thoroughfare of Kilburn in north-west London, Mark Cox not only remembers the first time he met Ivo, but the last – the pair remain friends thirty-three years on, and he is the only former 4AD musician who visits Ivo in Lamy. But then Cox knows all about staying the long course. He's lived in this flat for three decades, and recently tackled the contents of a cupboard for the first time in two of them, where he discovered a Rema-Rema cassette that brought on a rush of nostalgia. 'We only ever released one EP, you see,' he sighs. One of the potentially great post-punk bands was over before it had even begun.

Cox grew up further out, in London's leafy and stiflingly conservative suburb of Ruislip, near the famous public school of Harrow. Cox himself ditched his educational opportunities at another public school in the area, snubbing the exam that could have led to university qualification. Two weeks into an apprenticeship in carpentry and joinery, he was on tour with Siouxsie and the Banshees, American punks The Heartbreakers, and Harrow's own punk ingénues The Models.

At school, Cox had found himself at odds with his schoolmates' preference for hard rock, preferring Seventies funk and Jamaican dub, and like most every proto-punk, Bowie and Roxy Music. While fending off the attention of bullies for his skinhead haircut, he had bravely ventured into the still-underground society of London's gay nightlife, whose liberated clubbers had thrown the nascent punk scene a vital lifeline. 'You could wear different clothes, dye your hair and wear make-up there,' Cox recalls. 'And everyone was having a good time.'

Cox first met Susan Ballion, the newly christened Siouxsie Sioux, at Bangs nightclub, and seen, up close, John Lydon/Johnny Rotten at Club Louise. But he'd actually befriended Marco Pirroni, who'd played guitar in the impromptu stage debut of the original Banshees and then started The Models with singer Cliff Fox, bassist Mick Allen and drummer Terry Day. Cox was employed as The Models' roadie – he owned a car while the rest of the gang couldn't even drive – and even occasionally become a fifth Model on stage, in his words, 'making noise on a synthesiser over their pretty songs'.

Released in 1977, the band's sole single 'Freeze' was poppy enough, but its bristling, scuffed energy was far from pretty. There was evidently more ambition than two-minute bites such as 'Freeze'. As Cox recalls, 'Marco showed me you didn't need to go to college for ten years to play music. I discovered Eno and his exploration of sound. I became interested in rhythm, frequency and vibration.'

When Mick Allen introduced his friend Gary Asquith to the gang, Cox recalls that The Models split into two camps, 'and one was Mick, Gary, Marco and me'. Though they didn't know it at the time, they'd become Rema-Rema.

The divisive problem was Cliff Fox: 'He just wanted to be David Bowie,' says Asquith, 'which had become a real problem.' As Fox pursued his own path, abruptly terminated by a fatal heroin overdose, the remaining four friends combined for a minimal, chugging and quintessentially post-punk tour de force titled 'Rema-Rema', named after the Rema machine manufacturers in Poland: 'It sounded industrial, like Throbbing Gristle,' Cox explains. Rema-Rema became the band's name too, signifying the shift from the simple punk dynamics of The Models.

'Marco wanted to go places, do things,' says Gary Asquith. 'It moved fast for everyone.' Another north London resident, living in Kentish Town, adjacent to the more famous swirl of Camden Town, Asquith still comes across as the same 'larger-than-life, livewire, I'm-tough Cockney' that Mick Harvey of The Birthday Party recalls. Asquith admits that he and Mick Allen were typical teen rebels. 'But no knife crime!' he claims. 'And no drugs either – though there were later. But at first, it was food! After rehearsals, we'd descend on Marco's parents' house, who being Italians, always stocked the fridge.'

Suitably fuelled, Rema-Rema quickly abandoned the drum machine that was being adopted by every synth-pop band and advertised for a human drummer. Dorothy Prior, known as Max, added Velvet Underground-style metronomic thump to Rema-Rema's coarse energy, as well as becoming Marco's girlfriend. With Mick Allen now singing, the band's demos had drawn interest from the major-affiliated progressive label Charisma, keen to update and rebrand, but the label baulked at Allen's lyric on the track 'Entry', *'and you fucked just like Jesus Christ'*.

Cox says that Rema-Rema – already a fragile coalition – even considered splitting up, but Peter Kent saw the band play and immediately suggested they release a record on 4AD. Four tracks, two studio and two live, were proposed for a twelve-inch EP, *Wheel In The Roses*. Ivo devised a catalogue system to differentiate between releases: the prefix AD was for a seven-inch single, BAD for a twelve-inch, CAD for an album, and the numbering would identify the year. As the label prepared for the EP, Rema-Rema supported Throbbing Gristle and Cabaret Voltaire at London's basement club underneath the YMCA, but their 'big moment', according to Asquith, had been supporting Siouxsie and the Banshees and The Human League at London's art deco palace The Rainbow Theatre; David Bowie was at the side of the stage to watch The Human League, but Asquith says it felt like the bar had been raised and Rema-Rema could garner the same kind of press appreciation as the others. The only problem was that Marco left the band before *Wheel In The Roses* was even released, and the remaining members were beginning to doubt whether they would continue without him.

Pirroni had been seduced by an offer from the equally ambitious Stuart Goddard who, as Adam Ant, had lost his original backing band to Malcolm McLaren's new project, Bow Wow Wow (former Models drummer Terry Day was also to join the new Ants). Pirroni remained supportive enough to attend a band meeting with Beggars Banquet, where Ivo recalls Nick Austin insisting anything 4AD signed had also to sign to Beggars' publishing wing, and for at least five years. 'This for a band that was no longer together! It was very surreal.'

No deal was struck, but 4AD still released *Wheel In The Roses*: 'It still stands out from that era,' Ivo reckons. 'Hearing Marco's rockist guitar, wailing and screeching, but with very controlled feedback, over something that was so post-punk, was very unusual. It carried forward the idea that this little thing Peter and I had started would really mean something.'

Wheel In The Roses sounded something like a gang out of *A Clockwork Orange* expressing itself through music. The opening 35 seconds of gleeful howls and screams prefaced the menacing crawl of 'Feedback Song', a combative mood that extended through a pounding 'Instrumental' and a live take of 'Rema Rema'. A second live song, 'Fond Affections', showed a startlingly tender and melodic streak, though the mood was undeniably eerie. The EP's sleeve image was equally layered: a 1949 photo of two imposing Nuban tribesmen in Sudan taken by British photographer George Rodger that Mick Allen had doctored by drawing a tiny red rose between one of the men's fingers.

Despite Rema-Rema's short-lived promise, Ivo felt he'd learnt a valuable lesson. 'I understood punk much more after meeting Rema-Rema. They were real individuals, not aggressive, but they'd get in your face and argue their point. They believed in themselves, so you supported that even more than their music. Those people deserved support.'

To that end, Ivo hired Chris Carr, a freelance PR who was promoting bands such as Siouxsie and the Banshees and The Cure, to work on the Rema-Rema EP. Carr says he doesn't recall any reviews in the music press, which was disappointing for a record of such steely adventure, but without a band, what were its chances? But Carr says he was keen to continue working with Ivo. 'He wasn't remotely interested in what the majors were doing, only in developing the punk ethos, where punk meets art, and not for commercial gain. But it was hard to finance records at that time and Ivo would release demos if they were good enough. Though you could only keep releasing records if they got reviews.'

By comparison, Peter Kent had more old-fashioned ambitions: 'I wanted to be commercial,' he says. 'To have money to spend on bands.' It would have been very interesting if, as Kent claims, Duran Duran – soon to become costumed New Romantic flagwavers alongside Spandau Ballet and Adam Ant – had been available. 'We nearly signed them,' says Kent. 'I played their demo to Ivo, who really liked it, but they'd just signed to EMI.'

Ivo denies ever having heard any Duran demos, but says that journalist Pete Makowski (who had commissioned Ivo to write two album reviews for the weekly music paper *Sounds* before Axis/4AD had begun) had played him demos by The Psychedelic Furs. 'I liked it, but the band had already signed to CBS,' he says. Looking back, the Furs and Duran's ambitions would have clashed with 4AD's developing ethos. Much more aligned was a young band that could combine the commercial aspirations that Kent sought with the musical spirit that Ivo understood.

The Lepers were a down-the-line punk band from Colchester in Essex fronted by singer Robbie Grey (who called himself Jack Midnight) and guitarist Gary McDowell (a.k.a. Justin Sane). Bassist Wiggs and drummer Civvy were soon respectively replaced by Mick Conroy and Richard Brown, but they'd already changed the band name to Modern English before Stephen Walker arrived, whose keyboards accelerated the shift to post-punk. 'Punk's fire had gone out, so we started listening more to Wire and Joy Division,' says Grey. 'Ivo could see what could become of us with a bit of development.'

Wire and Joy Division were two of the best, and most creative, bands to provide an alternative to punk rock's single-speed, two-chord setting. London-based Wire were punk's most artfully oblique outsiders, yet they also wrote clever, melodic pop songs. Manchester's Joy Division had transcended their punk roots as Warsaw and taken on a more rhythmic and haunting shape, embodied by its enigmatic, troubled singer Ian Curtis. Post-punk was a sea of possibilities.

With a sense of adventure, Modern English had followed Mick Conroy's older brother Ray to London where he was squatting in Notting Hill Gate, near Rough Trade's offices. Grey describes a time of sleeping bags in the basement, meagre unemployment benefit, suppers of discarded vegetables from the street market, and bleeding gums as the price they had to pay, but out of it came the debut single 'Drowning Man' on the band's own label, Limp. A Wire-like hauteur over a blatant Joy Division pulse was too slavish a copy, but after Peter Kent had booked Modern English to support Bauhaus at central London's Rock Garden in March 1980, he and Ivo saw just enough reason to commission another single.

'Their demo had stood out, but initially, Modern English weren't great live,' recalls Ivo. 'They couldn't win over an audience like Bauhaus, who were fantastic on stage. And like Bauhaus, the British music press didn't enjoy Modern English. Coming from Colchester, they weren't necessarily considered cool but they weren't, thank God, the kind to hang out with journalists anyway. The first time I saw Gary, he had a huge stegosaurus haircut!'

The band's 4AD debut 'Swans On Glass' was a lashing version of the Wire model of nervous punk-pop. Ivo's faith in Modern English highlighted the gulf between his intuitive belief in raw talent and Beggars Banquet's nose for commerce. 'Martin [Mills] might not have seen what Ivo saw,' says Conroy. 'We were still pretty ropey then. The Lurkers, for example, had songs. We just had bits of music stuck together.'

Nevertheless, Beggars Banquet still wanted to sign the band to a long-term label and publishing deals. But unlike Rema-Rema, Modern English shared Mills and Nick Austin's commercial instinct: 'A five-year contract gave us the chance to grow,' says Grey.

Ivo: 'Long-term contracts were unnecessary, but Peter and I were just two employees for Beggars Banquet Limited, trading as 4AD. But I learnt quickly, and up to 1988, Modern English was the last band we signed long term without doing one or two one-offs with the artist first. Martin could see that even without deals, Bauhaus had immediately started making money for us.'

Bauhaus' quotient of gothic camp was turned down several notches by its second single for 4AD. 'Terror Couple Kills Colonel' showed a stripped-down restraint for a similarly curt lyric inspired by newspaper headlines about the German terrorist unit Red Army Faction. It wasn't as successful as 'Dark Entries', reaching 5 in the independent chart and not hanging around for as long; if the press didn't like goth, there was a swell of public support for the sound. The band played a thirty-date tour and retired to record their debut album, confident enough to produce it themselves.

As Ivo began to mentor Modern English, so Peter Kent's relationship with Bauhaus strengthened when he became the band's tour manager.* 'Peter was charming and witty with great taste, though we discovered he had a very fragile ego,' David J recalls. 'Ivo was very interesting too, with sartorial style. He wore exquisite shirts buttoned up to the top, and you'd discover how knowledgeable he was about music, and what good taste he had as well. To me, he was the ultimate hipster.'

The next arrival at 4AD didn't seem like an obvious fit for either Ivo or Kent, though it was the latter who introduced In Camera, surely the toughest, bleakest sound on 4AD, that came from one of the toughest, bleakest parts of 1980 London.

In Camera's singer, David Scinto, sits in the downstairs bar of nineteenth-century art nouveau landmark the Theatre Royal in Stratford, one of the few survivors of the regeneration that has swept through this part of London's East End. The Olympic Games of 2012 was held only a few minutes away, where former barren stretches of land used to be. But other landmarks have been wiped away, or buried,

---

* Kevin Haskins Dompe: 'Peter Kent tour managed us when we got an offer to support Magazine. We didn't know that Peter was gay, and he booked the band into gay bed and breakfasts around the UK. One had *Playgirl* centrefolds stuck on the walls! We had some funny interludes. All of us wore make-up then and flirted with our feminine side, so after the gig, with all our gear on, down in the bar … the clientele made some assumptions! There were bums pinched. Peter found it very funny.'

in the name of modernisation and the area's former industrial working-class heart has been re-clad in shopping-centre glass and steel. 'It's no longer the Stratford I knew,' says Scinto.

Scinto cuts a burly stature now, but during In Camera's time, he was a lean, intense figure, who called himself David Steiner after James Coburn's character Sergeant Rolf Steiner in Sam Peckinpah's torrid war movie *Cross of Iron*. He's more than a movie buff, he's a bona fide screenwriter, having co-written two acclaimed films, *Sexy Beast* and *44 Inch Chest*, that psychologically dissected a particularly East End kind of gangster. 'I keep trying music, and acting too, but I always come back to writing,' he says. 'Always have done, since I was a kid.'

Born to Maltese immigrants, Scinto was captivated by funk, soul and soundtracks, from *Mission Impossible* to Ennio Morricone's work. 'But then punk did to me what it did to others, a complete inspiration. I fear my options without punk could have been unbearable. Just before punk hit, I was fifteen, and my friend and I were going to rob a shop. I had a replica pistol, but as we walked towards the shop, a police car stopped right outside, so we just kept on walking and then bolted.'

From the Sex Pistols through to his post-punk rebirth fronting Public Image Limited, John Lydon – 'for his courage, and how he spoke what I thought' – was Scinto's key inspiration. 'Siouxsie was important too. But the first band I loved was The Pop Group. They pricked my social conscience. They instigated thought, which people are afraid to do nowadays; we're all bullied into behaving.'

At school, Scinto began to articulate his conscience with two school friends, but both fell by the wayside as In Camera's line-up initially gelled around bassist Pete Moore, drummer Derwin and guitarist Andrew Gray.

In a pub overlooking the Thames, this time in Bermondsey on the south side of the river, the diminutive figure of Andrew Gray sups a beer next to his much taller and imposing friend and former bandmate Michael Allen, of Models and Rema-Rema fame. The pair was to unite in 1983, alongside Mark Cox, in the band The Wolfgang

Press; but in 1980, Gray was experimenting at home with his guitar, seeking potential bandmates that also valued feeling over proficiency.

Like Scinto (the two were born just two days apart), Gray grew up primarily as a soul and funk fan, but he appreciated theme tunes too: he cites the sensual wah-wah lick of 'Theme From Shaft' as his gateway to making his own music. 'But the first time I heard a guitar through loud amplifiers, that was it,' Gray recalls. And Berlin-era Bowie, punk and post-punk changed the way he approached the guitar.

Scinto recalls that, of all the applicants to In Camera's advert, Gray was the only one to fit the bill. However, Derwin's flailing Keith Moon-style drums proved to be an awkward fit, so Pete Moore's friend Jeff Wilmott replaced him as In Camera's drummer. 'Jeff looked like one of the Ramones, but he just locked musically with us,' says Gray.

Wilmott, who is now a financial IT advisor living on Tierra Verde, an island in Florida's Tampa Bay, says he only now drums for fun, preferring cave-diving, which makes him something of a rarity in 4AD circles. But in his teens, he and Moore had followed the Banshees all over Britain, and found themselves as the supporting rhythm section to Scinto and Gray's intense blueprint. Moore also thought up the band's name. '*In Camera* was a play by Sartre, but we were aware of its courtroom association, and it could be a lens or prism,' Scinto explains. 'We liked its in-private feel. We wanted to reach as many people as possible but we felt entitled to our inner sanctum, to put our minds together and see what we'd come up with next.'

The intellectual rigour reached as far as Scinto's flattened vocal. 'Singing suggests a manipulation of the voice, and saying "please like me",' he explains. 'A voice simply suggests an expression. It's not pretentious; it's presenting a fact.' On stage, says Gray, 'Dave was very upfront and confrontational, in the Ian Curtis vein, dancing across the stage, angular like the music. Pete's bass was like Mick Allen's, distorted and hard.'

'Gray,' says Scinto, 'used feedback, syncopation before we knew what that meant, and chopped things about. He was brilliant at sound.'

One of Malcolm McLaren's associates, Jock McDonald, another former stallholder who had a pitch near to Peter Kent's at Beaufort Market, was running Billy's club night at Gossips in Soho. McDonald had heard of this forceful new band, and asked In Camera to support Bauhaus. Peter Kent was impressed enough to visit their dressing room after the show. 'He burst in, and asked if we'd like to make a record,' Gray recalls. 'I was a bit shocked; we'd been going less than six months. Ivo was there too but he was apparently too drunk and obliterated to focus on us.'

Ivo: 'Actually, I had a blinding headache that night, and another the following time I saw them. In Camera were very much Peter's signing, but I grew to like them, and I really, *really* liked the Peel session we released later on.'

In Camera's debut seven-inch single 'Die Laughing' blended staccato vocal, guitar frazzle, high lead bass line and martial drum attack. The rhythmic swish of the flipside 'Final Achievement' lurched in the direction of PiL's 'Death Disco', as Scinto laced the monochrome sound with oblique images of social dysfunction that he'd witnessed across his patch.

Scinto says he could see the difference between introvert Ivo and extrovert partner Kent: 'Peter was more adventurous and outgoing, hanging with the bands.' As a part-time concert promoter, Kent was bound to mingle with musicians, and one night at a mutual friend's in Notting Hill, before Axis/4AD had even been conceived, he had got talking to Graham Lewis, one quarter of Ivo's beloved Wire. 'I later told Graham about 4AD,' says Kent, 'and introduced him to Ivo. They got on like a house on fire, so it was Ivo that ended up working with him.'

On the phone from Uppsala in his wife's home country of Sweden, Lewis recalls how Wire was seeking a way out of their EMI deal. Like many of the early punk bands, Wire had signed to a major, which is why independents such as 4AD were so urgently required. Lewis and Ivo – born a year apart – found much common ground.

Lewis's air force family lived in Germany and the Netherlands but also the English seaside town of Mablethorpe in Lincolnshire, where in the early 1960s, he had first experienced rock'n'roll, blasting through giant speakers at a fairground. 'You'd find strange places between loudspeakers playing different songs, united by a common acoustic, which probably explains my obsession with dub,' says Lewis. Pirate radio – 'unmediated, straight out of the sky' – introduced him to Jimi Hendrix and similar psychedelic voyagers; a cousin gifted Lewis 'an incredible collection of soul music', and at art school at the start of the Seventies, Roxy Music and pub rock's oddballs Kilburn & The High Roads further widened his tastes.

Lewis' musical ambitions were temporarily thwarted: 'I couldn't find anyone to form this fantastic group, as you were meant to at art school.' Eventually, through his college friend Angela Conway, Lewis met Bruce Gilbert, an abstract painter working as an audio-visual aids technician and photography librarian at Watford College of Art and Design, just north of London.

Gilbert, Conway and fellow student Colin Newman were playing together as Overload: 'I intimated that I played bass, which wasn't strictly true, but I owned one and had ideas,' Lewis recalls. Ideas were enough for Gilbert, and after Conway had gone her own way, and Newman had met drummer Robert Gotobed (a former Oundle public schoolboy) at a party, Wire's four components were assembled. Though Wire had made its recording debut on EMI's *Live At The Roxy WC2* compilation, the band was older and more taken with experimental art and design than their punk peers. Over three trailblazing albums (*Pink Flag, Chairs Missing* and *154*), Wire had redrawn rock's boundaries with all the abstract ideas their inquisitive minds could muster.

After their trilogy, Wire decided to subvert the traditional four-piece band unit. 'Bruce and I had become interested in the idea that the studio was the instrument, and we wanted to work with different people to see what might happen,' Lewis recalls. 'We formed Dome to connect with our art background – installation, performance art, video. Rock music wasn't the be-all and end-all of our lives.'

Initially, Dome took their experimental songs to Geoff Travis at Rough Trade, who suggested they release it themselves; *Dome 1*, *Dome 2* and *Dome 3* subsequently appeared on the duo's Dome imprint. Seeking to finance a soundtrack they'd written for a performance piece by the artist Russell Mills, the pair approached Ivo, who eagerly took the chance to work with such respected and influential artists. A twelve-inch single, 'Like This For Ages', was released in 1980 under the new alias of Cupol, a reference to the dome-style cupola inspired by Arabic mosaics. On one side, the title track's shorter, mechanical clangs were layered behind Lewis' urgent vocal; on the other was the 20-minute instrumental 'Kluba Cupol', a slowly evolving mosaic of percussive electronica inspired by seeing the legendary Sufi 'trance' Master Musicians of Joujouka play in London.

'It was nothing to do with Wire, but it was a damn good record,' Ivo reckons. 'Was I disappointed? Yes and no: Graham and Bruce were doing what they were doing. Though I didn't realise until I met Wire that they didn't sell many records, maybe 20,000 each. We struggled to sell 5,000 with Cupol.'

Ivo's relationship with the duo quickly led to a more musically satisfying liaison. Gilbert and Lewis had met a young singer-songwriter Matt Johnson through their friend Tom Johnson (no relation), a cartoonist who was playing bass in Matt's band, The The, while acting as its manager.

Over the past thirty years, Matt Johnson has defied categorisation in any given era, trend or sound, concentrating on a pensive, brooding, progressive fusion of soul, rock and pop. With nine studio albums made by varying line-ups, Johnson has also embraced soundtracks, film itself, and most recently book publishing as Fifty First State Press, with the 2012 book *Tales from the Two Puddings*. This was not Matt's story but that of his father Eddie, who ran Stratford pub The Two Puddings for thirty-eight years. The site has been revamped and renamed, another casualty of merciless town planning.

In its heyday, says Johnson, The Two Puddings was, 'one of east London's busiest and most fashionable music houses'. The large backroom staged regular shows: 'The sound was continually drifting up through the floorboards, and during daytime closing hours, my brothers and I would play the equipment the groups had left set up. It's quite possible the first guitar I ever played belonged to The Who's Pete Townshend or The Kinks' Ray Davies.'

The Beatles' *White Album* was Johnson's treasured album: 'There was something so warm, inventive and free about it. I still marvel at its diversity and originality.' He was only eleven when he formed a covers band, Roadstar, and by fifteen had left school to work at Music De Wolfe in central London, a family-run studio specialising in soundtracks. Johnson admits to a very brief flirtation with punk, but believes most British punk was drab and derivative. 'And the way they dressed identically and yet crowed on about wanting to be different cracked me up. The real weirdos, of course, were the ones who tried to look normal to fit in. So I became part of the "long Mac brigade" and found my spiritual home within post-punk.'

Johnson had begun selling home-made cassettes of a suitably off-kilter solo album, *See Without Being Seen*, before being introduced to Gilbert and Lewis. Johnson shared common ground with the duo, and with Britain's synth pioneers, such as Thomas Leer and Robert Rental, who, he says, 'epitomised everything punk had promised but failed to deliver. It's an incredibly rich, inventive and diverse time in British music history that's been overlooked.'

Lewis was impressed by 'the unusual harmonics of Matt's voice, his ambition and drive'. However, Lewis also says that he and Gilbert had only gone down to the studio, 'in an unofficial capacity', while The The recorded its 4AD debut single 'Controversial Subject', and its B-side 'Black & White'. But, as Ivo notes, 'the sound was heavily manipulated by Graham and Bruce, very much like Cupol and Dome records'.

Gilbert and Lewis' studio of choice was Blackwing, housed in a deconsecrated church in Southwark, just south of the Thames. Ivo discovered that its owner, Eric Radcliffe, 'was an incredibly smart scientist with a musical background. It was inexpensive, and Eric let us do what we liked.' Blackwing was to become 4AD's home from home for years to come.*

Peter Kent agreed that 'Controversial Subject' was good enough to release, and Johnson began piecing together an album. Ivo enjoyed the rough, raw sound of the single, and as a fan of demos with a similar fresh energy, decided to pull tracks from the increasing pile of demos that had caught his and Kent's attention. As Ivo says, 'I had a feeling that every independent single coming out was worth listening to, so I had a pride in everything we released during that time.' A spare Modern English track, 'Home', was added to a twelve-inch EP that became 4AD's first compilation and the label's sole attempt at show-casing a batch of demos. As Ivo says, '*Presage(s)* was hardly prescient of what was to come. It wasn't an original idea either; Factory had released the *Earcom* compilation. But it was fun to do. I designed the dreadful sleeve, which featured Steve Webbon's naked arse on the back cover. But there was no intention of working with the groups.'

A sunbathing Webbon had been captured while on holiday with Ivo; on the front was a repeated image of a child against a lurid lime green backdrop – not exactly 4AD's finest piece of artwork. Musically too, *Presage(s)* is only a footnote in the 4AD story, an experiment that was never repeated. The EP appears not to have been reviewed at the time. 'At its best,' *All Music Guide* concluded many years later, 'these bands sound like second-rate versions of flagship acts like Bauhaus ... at its worst, these bands sound just plain bad, like failed art school experiments.'

For all its drawbacks, *Presage(s)* remains a fascinating document of several musical tributaries of the day, and the demo nature adds an endearing naivety. Of Ivo's two favourite tracks, the floating, haunting mood of C.V.O.'s 'Sargasso Sea' was surely down to co-producer – and German krautrock legend – Conny Plank, while Last Dance's turbu-lent 'Malignant Love' was a messily inspired Banshees revision. Of the

---

* Daniel Miller, who ran Mute Records, also regularly used Blackwing – from his elec-tronic-pop pastiche *Music For Parties* under the alias Silicon Teens to sessions for his two most popular acts, Depeche Mode and Yazoo, whose debut album title *Upstairs At Eric's* referred to Blackwing's owner Eric Radcliffe.

rest, Spasmodic Caress's 'Hit the Dead' (like Modern English's 'Home') had a sinewy Wire-like tension and Psychotik Tanks' 'Let's Have A Party' had a spiky urgency. Red Atkins' finale, the music hall turn 'Hunk Of A Punk', was simply the most bizarre and – in retrospect – unsuitable track that 4AD ever stuck its logo on.

'That was completely and utterly Peter. I thought it was silly,' says Ivo, referring to the two-minute track by Red Atkins, a.k.a. forty-five-year-old Frank Duckett, a home studio enthusiast that, for reasons still unknown, had penned a daft homoerotic ode ('*yes he's a hunk of a punk and you know that he's my kind of man*'). Peter Kent's verdict? 'It's hilarious.'

A 1982 interview in the British fanzine *Blam!* confirmed that the Spasmodic Caress track wasn't actually a demo, but a third re-recording after the first two were deemed 'shit' and 'absolutely terrible', by singer Pete Masters. Promised what drummer Chris Chisnall called 'a single of our own', the Colchester quartet nevertheless had to suffice with *Presage(s)*. Kent did find them support slots to Bauhaus and on a Modern English/In Camera bill, but the band's next release wasn't until 2004's self-released posthumous compilation, *Fragments Of Spasmodic Caress*.

It was a good thing 4AD wasn't staking its reputation on *Presage(s)* because, like three-quarters of the Axis clan, most of these bands went the same ignominious way – but then 'presage' did mean a sign, warning or omen that something typically bad will happen. In 1980, Psychotik Tanks self-released 'Registered Electors' (subsequently added to *Presage(s)*' digital download version) but nothing more; Atkins would only ever release one more EP (including the original, and a second version, of 'Hunk Of A Punk'), and that was twenty-five years later. Both Last Dance and C.V.O. would never release another record.

One of the most anonymous artefacts in the 4AD catalogue was followed by one of its most prized, with Ivo's A&R antennae finely attuned this time. If Bauhaus supplied the foundation and Rema-Rema had shown what heights could be scaled, The Birthday Party was the real beginning of 4AD's inexorable climb. It's been so long since the band was on 4AD, it's generally forgotten that this is where Nick Cave first landed outside of his native Australia.

Hailing from Melbourne, the capital of the south-eastern state of Victoria, The Birthday Party had only been on British soil for a handful of months when Ivo first saw them live in 1980. According to founding member Mick Harvey, the band were in a state of flux, aware that they were having to start again at the bottom of the ladder, as they'd had to in Melbourne five years earlier when they were known as The Boys Next Door.

As Harvey recalls, the band had outgrown their home city and set their sights on conquering the northern hemisphere, taking the usual Antipodean route to London. Given the quintet's original, discordant brew of rampant blues, garage rock and Stooges-style punk, London had never seen anything like The Birthday Party. The reverse was equally true.

'I don't feel that way anymore, but I originally developed an intense, blind, boiling hatred for England,' Cave told me in an interview for the Dutch magazine *OOR* in 1992. 'Everything was so mediocre. All the bands were weak and limp-wristed, and I was so pissed off.'

Harvey is more ambivalent about the experience. 'Yes, it would have been horrible for an unemployable drug addict,' referring to singer Cave (and guitarist Rowland S. Howard, who died of liver cancer, aged fifty, in 2009). 'It wasn't the same experience for the rest of us, but London was a pretty tough, draining place. It felt severe and a bit hopeless.'

Swapping Australia's relative stability, sunshine and wide open spaces for the bitter resignation and winter blues of Britain only drove Cave and the remaining Party members to more agitated states, though they didn't persist with the kind of songs that attempted to address Melbourne's own stifling conservatism, such as 'Masturbation Nation'. It was one of the few original songs by The Boys Next Door, formed by teenage friends Harvey, Cave and (drummer) Phill Calvert, one half of a school band at Caulfield Grammar that had split off to form a new union with bassist Tracy Pew after school was out in 1975. The band had mostly churned out covers of rebel anthems from the glam and punk songbooks, but Howard's addition in 1978 brought a choppier, scything style of play and a bluesy, expressionist mood to match Cave's increasingly oblique lyrics.

'We incorporated punk and new wave into our sound, but we weren't interested in being The Damned,' Harvey recalls. 'We were more Pere Ubu, Pop Group, and The Cramps. By 1979, we'd found our own direction.'

That year's debut album *Door, Door* was followed by a change of name, to The Birthday Party, and of location, to a squat in west London's budget-conscious Antipodean stronghold of Earls Court. 'We arrived in London on a wing and a prayer, completely unknown,' says Harvey. 'It was difficult to get gigs, and we spent a lot of time working out how to.'

The Birthday Party was the first band Ivo signed after seeing a concert, and there wasn't to be another for eleven years. He'd seen them by chance, at their second ever UK show, at north-west London's Moonlight Club; he'd gone to watch The Lines, whose manager was Steve Brown, Ivo's travel companion from the Moroccan trip. German synth duo D.A.F. was top of the bill; the Australians had played first. Ivo was captivated by the uncompromising dynamic sound, especially Harvey's Farfisa organ sound on 'Mr Clarinet', though, he noticed, 'nobody else was paying any attention to what someone described to me as "some bunch of Aussie weirdos".'

It turned out that Daniel Miller had been paying attention. Miller, who had started Mute Records to release his own records (The Normal's 'T.V.O.D.'/('Warn Leatherette'), had expanded the label by signing D.A.F., and was responsible for The Birthday Party opening the show. 'We'd gone to see Daniel because he'd sunk money into getting D.A.F., and also Depeche Mode, going,' recalls Harvey. 'Daniel was very encouraging but said he couldn't take on anything else. But Ivo expressed great interest. We'd heard of 4AD, and it was obvious that we weren't a commercial prospect, so we knew his interest was genuine.'

Harvey invited Ivo down to The Birthday Party's next show; afterwards, Ivo discovered that his favourite song in their set, 'The Friend Catcher', had been recorded back in Melbourne, and 4AD could have it for a single. 'The band came into the shop with the tapes and a grainy black-and-white photo of a cake they'd bought and stuck a candle in, and that was the artwork,' Ivo recalls. 'There weren't many great sleeves in that first year.'

In September 1980, the band recorded a session for BBC Radio 1 DJ John Peel, who had given Bauhaus the same accolade. In October, 4AD released 'The Friend Catcher' though not the album that had been recorded in Melbourne before moving to London (the Australian label Missing Link released it in November 1980), as The Birthday Party preferred to concentrate on their new material, fuelled by the hardships of London and the bile of their response.

PR Chris Carr set to work promoting 'The Friend Catcher', starting with a slew of live reviews. 'The initial reaction was, "What's with the stupid name?"' Carr recalls. 'I told journalists that The Birthday Party was a Harold Pinter play, and they'd say, "I know, but it's still a stupid name for a band." It was like some unwritten rule.'

Carr could see that part of the problem lay with 4AD itself, being associated with the vehemently disliked Bauhaus. 'In those days, your roster was your advertising and it took a long while for 4AD to get the same kudos that Mute or Factory had,' Carr says. 'People didn't like Bauhaus' artistic pretensions and Modern English, for example, were seen as too fey for what was going on around them, and so they could never get established.'

With a proven audience and earning power back home, and an album to promote, The Birthday Party returned to Australia in late November for the summer. Funded by Missing Link, they began recording a new album. In the meantime, 4AD had just released its first ever album.

Bauhaus' *In The Flat Field* had been recorded at London's Southern Studios: 'It was like a bunker, which made things very intense,' recalls David J. 'We had formed in isolation, and the album reflected that we felt like outsiders.' The sound of the album mirrored the claustrophobic conditions, and without any objective input from 4AD, who respected the band's wishes to go it alone, they'd failed to record a defining debut. It had a defining opener in the stentorian 'Double

Dare', but this was the licensed Peel session version as they hadn't managed to match its quality by themselves. 'The album wasn't that good a representation of Bauhaus, unlike their singles, which were always great,' says Ivo. 'The situation over "Double Dare" underlined what was wrong.'

The album showed that Bauhaus was not to be swayed by criticism. 'Terror Couple Kills Colonel' may have changed tack but the album tracks 'St Vitus Dance' and 'Stigmata Martyr' could not have been a more resolute renewal of goth tendencies, with Murphy in the central crucified role. Their resolution was rewarded when *In The Flat Field* topped the independent charts and reached number 72 on the national UK chart. This was despite an unusually vindictive reaction from the music press. 'Nine meaningless moans and flails bereft of even the most cursory contour of interest,' said *NME*. 'Too priggish and conceited. Sluggish indulgence instead of hoped for goth-ness,' claimed *Sounds*.

That *Sounds* wanted more 'goth-ness' was an irony that Bauhaus' fragile ego was unable to appreciate. 'We really had our backs to the wall,' Haskins Dompe recalls. 'We got slammed for the Bowie influence, and the press also felt we were really pretentious. It took me twenty years to accept we were, to a degree, but at the time I wouldn't hear of it. It was us against the world.'

'The zeitgeist was dark and intense, but I thought "gothic" was the antithesis of Bauhaus,' claims David J. 'We felt more eclectic, with influences like dub and early electronics like Suicide, Can and disco. Out of our peers, we felt most empathy with Joy Division. When [Joy Division singer] Ian Curtis said he liked Bauhaus, it meant a lot. He came to see us play and told us he had our singles.'

Retrospection has been kinder to Bauhaus. Simon Reynolds, author of the seminal post-punk history *Rip It Up and Start Again*, claimed that Bauhaus were the exception to the rule that goth bands 'didn't live up to the image'. Reynolds also favourably compared Bauhaus' early singles to Joy Division. 'If we had dressed like Gang of Four or Joy Division we wouldn't have been hated,' Pete Murphy told *Stool Pigeon* writer John Doran in 2008. 'And there was a really strong homoerotic element to what we did – a glamorous element; a very Wildean element.'

Ivo didn't care either. He dismissed labelling and ideas of what was perceived as cool or not – all that mattered was music and an artist's self-belief. 'I never understood the gothic association,' he says. 'If people think the music was dark, that's fine by me. I was just respond-ing to things I enjoyed, that I emotionally connected to, that had possibilities.'

'The music fitted Ivo's character, dark and personal,' says Martin Mills. 'The pop world was on a completely different shelf.'

Disappointed by the Bauhaus album, Ivo was also struggling to fall for Rema-Rema's successor, Mass: 'I liked them enormously as people, but musically, they were an anomaly.' With Max departing alongside boyfriend Marco Pirroni, the remaining nucleus of Mick Allen, Mark Cox and Gary Asquith found a drummer who was already looking for them: Danny Briottet, a schoolboy who would hang out in Beggars' Ealing shop. 'Danny said he really liked Rema-Rema, and to tell them that he'd like to be their drummer,' says Ivo. 'The next thing I know, Mass had formed and Danny – who couldn't play drums! – was in. Was he going to ruin it?'

'The one thing about Mass I don't like is the stiff drums,' says Asquith, who nevertheless went on to form Renegade Soundwave with Briottet (who proved to be a much better programmer than drummer). 'And we didn't have Marco's brilliance. But Mick was a great bassist. And the source of songs was just as good.'

Cox had been Marco's number one fan but could see Mick Allen had come into his own. 'Picture this super-slim guy with unkempt hair, kind of quiet, who had flowered into this multi-faceted personal-ity. And our sound was completely uncompromised. We wouldn't mould anything for anyone.'

Mass' 4AD debut was a seven-inch single that rivalled In Camera for dark and personal, with a side serving of bleak. 'You And I' followed in the eerie slipstream of Rema-Rema's 'Fond Affections', laced with an organ drone, background cries and only an occasional tom-tom roll to lend momentum. The thick bass pulse, layered vocal extortions and thumped drums similarly recalled the old band but the feel and mood was more leaden, without the same degree of liberation. Not even John Peel was on side. 'He thought it some of the most consciously morose music he'd ever heard,' Cox sighs. And, as Ivo recalls, 'Peel's support made all the difference in those days.'

Mass was the perfect example of a band driven by a fearless self-will, in the truest sense of punk's do-it-yourself mentality. As they walked on stage for their first show, third on the bill to Bauhaus at the University of London, Cox recalls Asquith facing the audience and announcing, 'I fucking hate students!' At the Moonlight Club, Ivo remembers Mass receiving no applause after a song and Asquith yelling, 'We've never been loved!' But at the same show, Ivo adds, 'I was mesmerised by Mick crooning "You And I" quite beautifully.'

'We used to call Mass "Mess" because they lacked direction,' says Richie Thomas, whose instrumental band Dif Juz had supported Mass at central London's Heaven nightclub. 'But they had a really interesting look: Germanic, like Bowie circa *Low*, but upmarket. Gary looked edgy and dangerous, like a tightly coiled spring.'

At least Mass had style. Modern English had a guitarist with a stegosaurus haircut, but fortunately their second single 'Gathering Dust' showed a noticeable progress in dynamics, structure and impact. 'It's one of the most underrated of post-punk anthems,' Ivo reckons, who gets credit from the band for his contribution.

Mick Conroy: 'Ivo was quiet at the beginning of our relationship, probably because he was focused on 4AD. But he got stuck in to "Gathering Dust". The studio was as much an adventure for him as us. For example, he really liked Steve's synth noises, which Steve couldn't easily control, so Ivo had the idea to put it all through an Eventide harmoniser.'

Ivo: 'Fucking hell! It was my first taste of influencing a recording, and I loved it. But the only reason I got a producer credit was that the band were practically asleep under the desk, and the engineer had to get approval from someone, so I'd say yes to things.'

After the haphazard art direction of 4AD's early sleeves, including the unsuitably fey figurine on the cover of 'Swans On Glass', Modern

English – and 4AD generally – needed art direction as well. 'Ivo told us that someone was coming in with his portfolio,' recalls Conroy.

An exquisitely designed house in Epsom, Surrey, from the furniture and ornamental bric-a-brac to the shelves of hefty art books, framed posters and wooden sculptures – this has to be the property of an artist. The drawers of big, elegant wooden plan chests dotted all over reveal copious sheaves of artwork: proofs of record sleeves, posters, adverts, most of it vintage, all evidence of a rich body of work.

The owner of the artwork, the man responsible for a lot of the surrounding designer detail, is as integral to the 4AD story as Ivo. There for the long run, he worked on endlessly bewitching, beguiling and beautiful images from his own warped imagination and those of his close collaborators; images that have been exhibited nationally and internationally, published in books and catalogues, and with countless dedicated designers and illustrators pledging allegiance to a body of work they claim irrevocably changed their lives.

This is also a man who, for one particular sleeve image, stripped down to his underpants in a suburban London flat, strapped on a belt of dead eels and enacted a fertility dance for the camera. To say Vaughan Oliver is a character is an understatement. Everyone who ever worked for, or released a record on, 4AD during its first twenty years, has their Vaughan story. He might as well get his version in first.

'The first thing I ever wrote on a toilet wall,' he says, 'were the words "To suggest is to create; to describe is to destroy". So said French photographer Robert Doisneau, and it struck me as the perspective that I come from. To keep things open to interpretation.'

In the spirit of Doisneau, Oliver shouldn't really recount the inspiration behind the belt of dead eels, but it's too good to resist. 'It was a reaction to an all-girl band, called The Breeders, their album title *Pod* and the vibrant colours I was getting from the music,' he explains. 'To me, it needed a strong male response. The eels are phallic, but I'd seen an image of a belt of frankfurters that stuck in my mind, so I developed that. When it came to shoot it, I couldn't get anyone else to do the job, so I did it. There was blood everywhere … but I knew one of the shots would work!'

Oliver hails from County Durham in the Wearside region of northeast England. According to Tim Hall, who joined 4AD in the mid-1990s, 'Vaughan is brilliant and mad, he likes a drink, and he was sometimes a big, scary Geordie! [Oliver would like to point out that he is proud to be a Wearsider, a subtle geographic distinction.] The first thing he said to me was, "Do you know who I am; do you know my work, my reputation?" He was just checking that someone who was joining 4AD understood its legacy.'

'That doesn't sound like me,' Oliver contends. 'People didn't always hear the irony and the humour in what I'd say.'

This helps explain why Oliver's recent talk to an audience in Edinburgh about his career, work and inspiration was entitled *What's in the Bucket Daddy?* 'A bucket is a universal symbol, up there with the wheel,' he explains. 'There's humility to a bucket, but put a logo on it and it clashes. The collision of the glamour of a logo and the bucket's humility is funny to me. In 1995, we had an exhibition, and me and [business partner] Chris Bigg were discussing the death of vinyl and the record sleeve, and we thought it would be funny to have under each exhibition piece a bucket with a melted piece of vinyl, like it was thrown away.'

In the days when vinyl was the unparalleled medium and the scope of the twelve-inch format allowed room to create as well as describe, Oliver attended Ferryhill Grammar School. 'Sanctuary was the art room, where we'd talk about art, girls, football and music,' he recalls. The lurid, sexual glamour of Roxy Music's album sleeves, Roger Dean's sci-fi landscapes and the surreal creations of Storm Thorgerson and Aubrey Powell's design group Hipgnosis were his early key inspirations: 'They all used their imagination, rather than put a band on the front. It opened me to ideas.'

Rather than a foundation course in art, Oliver naïvely applied to the nearby Newcastle Polytechnic to study graphic design, 'Even though I didn't even know what "graphic design" meant,' he says, 'until I read the dictionary definition the morning of my interview. I just hoped the course would lead me to sleeve design.'

Oliver was also fortunate to have a wildly creative course tutor in Terry Dowling: 'He showed me the idea of inspiration being all around. He elevated the banal for me, by showing me stuff that was on his wall, things like pasta alphabets, stuff that he'd take from the street. It was a new way of seeing, a new kind of beauty. He basically changed my mind.'

Although painfully shy, Oliver nevertheless moved down to London in 1980 and quickly found work at the design agency Benchmark, where he worked for clients such as model kit manufacturers Airfix. Benchmark also employed fellow designers Alan McDonald and Mark Robertson, who were friends of Peter Kent; Robertson had designed the original Axis and 4AD logos and the 'Swans On Glass' cover for Modern English. When Ivo wanted more art direction for 'Gathering Dust', Robertson happened to be abroad and Oliver was sent in his place.

'The door cracked open,' Ivo recalls, 'and this head just came in, curly hair and a short back and sides, brown flying jacket, and a beetroot blush of a face.'

It helped Oliver's case that his portfolio included a silhouette of a 1967 photograph by Diane Arbus, of a seated naked couple in a deeply suburban living room. Modern English had used the very image for a mock-up, sticking the image inside a TV screen (their debut single had featured a cracked TV screen with the band logo inside). Oliver simply placed the TV screen/logo between the silhouetted couple, gave it a radiant red and black contrast, and hey presto. 'We leapt at it,' says Mick Conroy.

In 2011, *Guardian*'s '50 key events in the history of indie music' put the cover of 'Gathering Dust' at number 23, in between 'Joy Division's Ian Curtis commits suicide' and 'Depeche Mode take their baby steps', and four places below, 'Bauhaus invent goth'. 'The sleeve,' wrote Michael Hann, 'was nothing special, aside from the fact it was designed by Vaughan Oliver, commencing a relationship between Oliver and the 4AD label that rivalled that between Peter Saville and Factory

Records. Oliver's sleeve designs – abstract, dreamlike, elegant – seemed to be a perfect visual representation of the label's music, which was often, unsurprisingly, abstract, dreamlike, elegant.'

At every Birthday Party gig or 4AD show over the next couple of years, Ivo remembers, 'Vaughan talking into my ear about building an overall identity for the label and, ultimately, a trademark, and me giving him a job! It had already occurred to me because of what Peter Saville had done for Factory, providing a continuity that people would come to trust.'

Oliver: 'I'd bump into Ivo at gigs. I had got my foot in the door and wouldn't take it out! I was obsessed with the idea of working for an independent label and I would have told Ivo he needed a logo and consistency, to express identity. The role models were [German jazz label] ECM and before that, [American jazz label] Blue Note. Ivo got the idea straight away. In my mind, he wasn't into selling units; he loved the music and wanted people to hear it, and he cared so much about it that he wanted to package it properly.'

At the time, Oliver was only retained on an occasional basis, as the later pattern of outsourcing to one designer had yet to be cemented. Knowing what Oliver added to 4AD, it's easy to see in retrospect what was missing from the label's early records. Take the next 4AD release: an album housed in overlaid grey squares. It was an accurate mirror of the music's electronic ambient murk, but the artwork had no enticement or intrigue to draw in potential purchasers.

The album, *3R4*, was released under the name B.C. Gilbert/G. Lewis: 'The name changes were helpful for our own sense of what things were,' Graham Lewis explains. It comprised two very brief instrumentals, both called 'Barge Calm', and two much lengthier works, '3.4 …' and 'R', respective Lewis and Gilbert solo pieces. Anyone who appreciated the films of Russia's visionary, impressionist director Andrei Tarkovsky, or animation specialists Stephen and Timothy Quay (who had illustrated posters for the *Dome 1* and *2* albums), could see the same forces at work in these potential soundtracks: they dripped mood and texture, ominous and otherworldly.

It was just as well that Ivo wasn't driven commercially, since *3R4* slotted neatly into the 'Difficult Music For Tiny Audiences' category (also in a sleeve of overlaid grey squares). Compare this to the following 4AD release, with Peter Kent in the A&R seat. Bauhaus' new single was a cover of glam rock icons T. Rex's 'Telegram Sam', deftly reworked as stark, strutting rock-disco. It seemed to say that if Bauhaus could have credibility, they could be loved, or they could at least be rock stars. It couldn't have been a more blatant chart-bothering tactic, not until, that is, they released a cover of Bowie's 'Ziggy Stardust' in 1982.

Ivo: 'The band had changed since I'd first met them. They used to play "Telegram Sam" as an encore, and they said they'd never record it. But in less than a year, it was a single.'

As mentioned earlier, 4AD's original intention had been to provide bands for Beggars Banquet if it made commercial sense. Both band and label could see this was the way forward. '4AD had been the perfect label for us,' says David J. 'They understood what we were about, they were very supportive, and people respected us because they respected 4AD. But it went as far as it could.'

Peter Murphy: 'We didn't want to be consigned to an independent music ghetto, to be sub-Ivo kids; we wanted to be massive. Anyway, as 4AD progressed, Ivo started to magnetise the centre of what became known as 4AD, and then once Vaughan got a hold of the artwork, everyone looked the same to me. Fuck that!'

David J: 'We were crafting what we saw as dark pop singles, and live we put on a show, not traditional but theatrical, while Ivo was going more experimental and introverted. He had told me that Bauhaus was becoming too rock'n'roll for the label, and not obscure enough. Daniel and Peter would take the piss out of Ivo because the music and the sleeves were becoming too obscure, to the extreme, like an in-joke. We wanted to be on *Top of the Pops* and have hit singles – but on our own terms. So there was a natural parting of the ways When Ivo suggested we move to Beggars, we didn't have to think twice.'

Ivo: 'Within a year, Bauhaus had released four singles, and an album, and gone from being spat on by Magazine fans to headlining [London venue] the Lyceum. They needed the push and resources available to them at Beggars. If we'd fought to keep Bauhaus, for me it would've involved far too much chatting with video makers and worrying what the next single would be.' Ivo also counters David J's claim he was keen on obscurity: 'I can't say I ever consciously looked for anything obscure, but I may well have been put off by something too mainstream.'

4AD's next release bridged the gap between obscurity and the mainstream, between Ivo and Peter Kent's tastes and hopes. Ivo recalls Dance Chapter turning up at Hogarth Road, the week that Ian Curtis killed himself. Joy Division's talisman was already a totemic leader, and the shock of his death was almost like the aftermath of the Che Guevara scenario, the loss of a spiritual leader. In the shop, Ivo recalls a girl sobbing at the counter after hearing the news. 'Out of that, we got to wondering who would fill Ian's shoes. Soon enough, Peter buzzed me from downstairs, saying, "Remember that conversation? Well, they've just walked in".'

'I read something on the internet along those lines, but that wasn't verbalised to me,' says Dance Chapter's vocalist Cyrus Bruton. 'Ian Curtis was Ian Curtis, and no one could step into those shoes. I never even entertained the idea.'

Bruton currently lives in Berlin, with a community that follows the teachings of the late Indian spiritual guru Bhagwan Shree Rajneesh. He moved to Germany in 1985, between extended visits to India and, he says, 'I never looked back.' The same can be said of his short tenure as a singer, as he hasn't made music for almost three decades, though he has DJed at various communes. His main concern, he says, is offering 'public satsangs', meaning spiritual teachings.

Heralding from Leeds in Yorkshire, Dance Chapter was on a tour of London's independent labels with their demo cassette when they walked into the shop. Born in Woking, south of London, to mixed-race parents, the young Cyrus, like Marx Cox and Graham Lewis before him, had primarily been a fan of black music swayed by punk rock and what he calls its 'anyone-can-do-it rules'. 'I wanted to be hands-on and form a band,' he says. He soon joined forces with school friends Stuart Dunbar (bass), Andrew Jagger (guitar, later replaced by

Steve Hadfield) and Jonnie Lawrence (drums). Choosing the name Dance Chapter showed Bruton was an unusually questioning teenager: 'A chapter is a collective,' he explains. 'We were punk, but I wanted something more about dance and celebration.'

Bruton says Dance Chapter, 'were pretty focused, given we were four young men who liked to drink and take other things'. 4AD was a natural target: 'They were one of the cutting-edge labels around and it already felt that was the level to reach.'

The self-produced debut single 'Anonymity' is another buried treasure from 4AD's early era, closer to Joy Division's first incarnation Warsaw than the finished article, with a similarly tense, interlocking energy. Bruton was an unusually melodic singer, and his repeated lyric, *'a piece of recognition is all I ask, bring me flowers'*, was delivered with a palpable yearning. 'We were striving for something that you want to get from the outside world,' Bruton explains. 'But if you can't get it, then you can only give it to yourself. Even if it's only flowers!'

The B-side 'New Dance' revealed a more existential valediction. 'I was speaking of knowing that falling down is the only way to truth,' says Bruton. 'That pain and insecurity is needed so an authentic expression can then come through. It was about vulnerability, and the need to find expression, to join together. People needed guidance, which wasn't as forthcoming as it should have been.'

This was the kind of poignant struggle and musical euphoria that could have had an impact on the same level as Ian Curtis and Joy Division – you could see what Peter Kent had meant when he first heard them. But Ivo was unconvinced. 'Peter wasn't right about the Joy Division bit,' he says, 'and I can't say Dance Chapter were a great band because I only saw them play twice. But they had some gorgeous songs, and I loved Cyrus's voice.'

Perhaps if Kent had stuck around, he could have mentored the young and questioning Bruton. But as 4AD's first year drew to a close, the risk of a split vision between 4AD's two A&R sources – who might not truly believe in the other's choices – was quashed when Kent decided he'd change tack.

Neither Ivo nor Peter Kent remembers their relationship getting fractious, even though they were both hugely opinionated. 'Ivo could be a little bit bitchy, and headstrong,' Gary Asquith recalls, 'and no one wanted to play second fiddle, least of all Peter.' Asquith and Kent had become close friends in a short period of time. 'Peter was a strange cat,' Asquith contends. 'Geminis I've known have their own agenda, and they never seem to be happy. He was a very curious person, but he didn't know what he wanted, and he constantly moved on to the next thing. I think he found it hard to live with himself.'

'My attention,' Kent says, 'was elsewhere than 4AD.'

Besides promoting shows (such as his regular Rock Garden slot The Fake Club), Kent was tour-managing Bauhaus and doing some A&R for Beggars Banquet: his first signing there was the London jazz-funk band Freeez, who broke into the top 50 at the first attempt. But most importantly, Kent had met Billy MacKenzie at Heaven: 'We'd gotten on like a house on fire, so I said I'd come and work with him and Alan.'

Alan Rankine was MacKenzie's creative foil in The Associates, one of the greatest bands of that era. Both men were sublimely gifted, precocious and fairly uncontrollable Scottish mavericks, and totally up Kent's alley. Overtly Bowie-influenced (their 1979 debut single was a cover of 'Boys Keep Swinging', cannily released just six weeks after Bowie's own version), they weren't just dashingly handsome but fashion-conscious too. The pair had released an album, *The Affectionate Punch*, on Fiction, an offshoot of the major label Polydor, but they were open to new offers. The Associates' increasing experimental daring, combined with an arch playfulness, would have considerably brightened up 4AD's procession of brooding young men who, to paraphrase Ian Curtis, had 'weight on their shoulders'.

Steve Webbon: 'Peter was exuberant and camp, mischievous, while Ivo aligned himself with the introverts, all the miserable ones!'

Kent had certainly sensed the same schism. On tour with Bauhaus in the States for the first time, he had familiarised himself with the demi-monde underground scene. Back in London, he told Ivo he wanted to license two singles from Chicago's Wax Trax label: the punk-trashy 'Born To Be Cheap' by Divine – *People* magazine's 'drag queen of the century' and star of John Walters' cult transgressive-trash films – and 'Cold Life' by Ministry, a new, edgy synth-pop band (yet to turn into fearsome industrial-metal). When Ivo resisted, 'that's when I realised we had a different idea of where 4AD was heading,' Kent recalls. 'I wanted us to be more eclectic and diverse. So I slipped away from 4AD.'*

'I'm glad Peter didn't stay,' says Ivo. 'Can you imagine Divine on 4AD? The best way to describe it is, I don't like being around people but Peter thrived in those situations, like being backstage after a show. He wanted everything at the label to grow, whereas I found anything beside the finished album was unnecessary. My head is filled with ecstatic memories of the live experience, but the part that's always meant most is the one-on-one relationship between the listener and a recorded piece of work, the artefact that will stand for all time.

'Some people, within bands and the music industry, thrive on the idea of being involved in rock'n'roll. Doesn't [future Creation label MD] Alan McGee say the only reason he got into the music business was to get rich, take drugs and fuck women? I don't even like being around people enough for that to have an appeal. I guess I was the nerdy one at home with headphones on scanning the album sleeve.'

It all worked out neatly, as Bauhaus and Kent departed at the same time. 4AD's first year of business concluded by it being made a limited company, no longer dependent on funds from the Beggars' mother-ship after the release of *In The Flat Field*. There was one more 1980 release to come: In Camera's *IV Songs* EP had been recorded at Blackwing with Eric Radcliffe assisted by junior engineer John Fryer,

---

* Beggars Banquet gave Peter Kent financial backing to start a new label that he called Situation 2 (Bauhaus' original management company was called Situation 1). The label's first releases were an astounding run of Associates twelve-inch singles (later compiled on *Fourth Drawer Down*), one a month, for five months. 'I can't think of a better and more original introduction to a label than Peter releasing those Associates singles in that way,' Ivo reckons. 'It was crazy, because what would have happened if one was a hit? Would you release the next single?' Kent ran Situation 2 for only a year before he started managing Associates and signed them to Warners. At the end of 1982, illness forced Kent to live a quieter life. He moved to Spain to open a restaurant, though he later worked for Brussels-based independent label/distributor Play It Again Sam before relocating to Chicago.

who captured a feeling of weighty oppression. The opening track 'The Conversation' (another film reference) was a particularly solemn instrumental, and the bass line of 'Legion' was another echo of Joy Division, just like 'The Attic' was an echo of Warsaw's primitive dynamic, reduced by In Camera to an even starker, flatter sound.

'The production values were nearer to our live sound; meatier drums and more avant-garde than the PiL and Banshees influences,' suggests Andrew Gray. 'We, and Ivo, were really happy with it.'

IV Songs was more proof that Ivo was content to put out records that were committed, passionate and uncompromising, though, looking back, the cumulative effect of the catalogue – Red Atkins notwithstanding – was fifty shades of black. The gloom was claustrophobic. Where was the light and shade, the fuller spectrum of humanity? 'Musically, that was the era,' Ivo argues. 'And to paraphrase [American pianist] Harold Budd, I was suspicious of anything that is enjoyed by the masses. I don't think pop artists would have come to 4AD in any case.'

Colin Newman, the next Wire member to strike a deal with Ivo, thought 4AD had its limitations at the beginning. 'Everything was in black and white. And I didn't think most of the records Ivo had released were that good. Cherry Red was a similar label: sketchy, a bit homemade, mawkish and interior-looking. Bauhaus was the exception.'

'Back then, I didn't know what I was doing on any level,' Ivo admits. 'Peter and I were learning what running a label involved. We were lucky that Bauhaus effectively funded the next year. I'll always be proud to have released their records, and eternally grateful too, because without their speedy success, despite the British press, 4AD might have struggled to pay for albums the following year. It started a trend that continued for a decade; each year, I was lucky enough to start working with at least one key band or artist. One album a year did pretty well and allowed us to keep going.'

Towards the end of 1980, Ivo did his first interview with Lynnette Turner, who ran the *Station Alien* fanzine. 'She said, "I just want to get to you before anyone else does". She knew something was stirring.'

There was more stirring than just music: 'Lynnette and I pretty much fell in love at that first meeting and ended up living together for the next two years,' says Ivo. This came after another upturn in his life; Beggars had suggested that he should stop working in the shop and concentrate full-time on 4AD: 'It was the first time I'd ever felt truly, giddily happy,' he recalls.

But with Ivo left in sole charge, without Peter Kent's man-about-town demeanour and his greater potential for playfulness, how dark and personal might 4AD become?

4 1981

ART OF DARKNESS
(ad101-cad117)

Axis had kicked into life in 1980 with four simultaneous singles, three of unknown origin. 4AD's first complete year of operation, 1981, began in similar fashion, with three singles from two new bands, one so far unknown in the UK. Though the trio were not released on the same day, each seven-incher in its illuminating sleeve represented the same opportunity, as Ivo saw it, to 'serve their own beautiful purpose. A record for a record's sake.'

And much like the original Axis offensive, with the exception of Bauhaus, and much of the *Presage(s)* collective, none of the singles by Sort Sol, Past Seven Days and My Captains reappeared on 4AD; none were re-pressed after selling out their initial pressing, and only Sort Sol survived to release another record. These false dawns remained immaterial to Ivo: 'The fact that a record was coming out on 4AD meant that it was a success already, which was absolutely at the heart of what I wanted to do.'

The first of the three was 'Marble Station', a sombre, glacial jewel by Copenhagen, Denmark's Sort Sol (which translates as Black Sun), who had recorded two albums as The Sods before shedding its punk identity for something suitably post-punk. Ivo had heard their second album *Under En Sort Sol* and the band agreed to have his two favour-

65

ite songs released as a single. The six-minute 'Raindance' by Sheffield's Past Seven Days adopted an ominous backdrop of synths but represented a chink of light in 4AD's assembled heart of darkness, coiled around a chattering quasi-funk rhythm guitar in the style of Factory label peer A Certain Ratio, and a matching, insistent vocal melody. The self-titled EP by Oxford quartet My Captains restored the generic setting of gloom, and was less exciting for it, while reinforcing the notion that 4AD's core constituents might be reduced to, as the cliché had it, those shoulder-weighted interlopers in long raincoats with Camus novels under their arm.

Stylistically, all three singles were reminiscent in some form of another band from Sheffield, The Comsat Angels, which had signed to Polydor in 1979. But the Comsats' smouldering style eventually lasted for nine albums; Sort Sol never released another track in the UK; My Captains simply vanished; and Past Seven Days were, Ivo says, 'lured away' to Virgin offshoot Dindisc. However, there were potential perils in joining a major label – Dindisc founder Carol Wilson once said, 'I never signed a band unless I thought they could be commercially successful.' Soon enough, the band asked Ivo if they could return to 4AD. 'I was a bit of a bitch and said, no, you went away,' he admits.

Yet just as The Birthday Party's debut 4AD single 'The Friend Catcher' had followed *Presage(s)*, so the band's debut 4AD album *Prayers On Fire* swiftly counteracted the mood of short-term disappointment. The Birthday Party had started recording the album within a month of landing back in Melbourne at the tail end of 1980, and when they returned to London in March to headline The Moonlight Club (supported by My Captains), Ivo was shocked. 'I wasn't expecting an album, or how it sounded. Where had these Captain Beefheart influences come from?'

Cave claimed his inspiration was, 'the major disappointments we felt when we went to England'. There was a sense of a channelled energy for one of gleeful vitriol and anger; Rowland S. Howard's guitars humped and splintered around Cave's brattish authority, tackling religion and morality with a drug-induced fever; as they phrased it in 'King Ink', this was a world of, *'sand and soot and dust and dirt'.*

Ivo may not have cared that 4AD's releases weren't making an indelible impression, or that the bands were often petering out, but if Bauhaus' previous success had paid for the label's next handful of releases, what might pay for 1981's next batch? What he did have, finally, was a 4AD artefact that he could build into something – and how ironic that Ivo's interest in The Birthday Party had been lit by that old-fashioned instrument, the Farfisa organ. The UK music press unreservedly embraced *Prayers On Fire*: 'A celebratory, almost religious record, as in ritual, as in pray-era on fire, a combustible dervish dance, and another Great Debut of '81,' claimed *NME*'s Andy Gill.

'The Birthday Party started to swing it for 4AD,' says Chris Carr. 'One by one, through word of mouth, journalists got on board.' With John Peel already on side, Ivo recalls, 'Birthday Party gigs started getting very well attended, very quickly. And the more frenzied audiences became, the more frenzied Nick Cave became.'

The band and singer alike were being driven on an axis of disgust, keeping itself one step removed from the UK scene the band despised. They might have been secretly impressed by the jazz/dub/punk verve of Bristol's The Pop Group, but frequent comparisons to the Bristol band had annoyed Nick Cave so much that he studiously avoided mentioning them in interviews. He referred to Joy Division as 'corny', only talking up Manchester's ratchety punks The Fall and California's rockabilly malcontents The Cramps, whose singer Lux Interior had mastered the unhinged, confrontational performance. Mick Harvey admits he'd enjoyed Rema-Rema and Mass, but says that though he liked Bauhaus as people, 'I just didn't get them musically. Being preposterous was part of their charm, but Peter running around with a light under his face, I was just laughing. You couldn't take them seriously.'

Nevertheless, The Birthday Party had a pragmatic core and set off on tour around the UK with Bauhaus in June. The Haskin brothers' testimony to their rakish support band's penchant for alcoholic breakfasts confirmed the Australians were willing to act out the fantasies implied by their songs, as each city and town was taken on as an enemy to be conquered. Yet in Cambridge, the support act joined the headliners for a show of solidarity during the encore of 'Fever'.

'It was good exposure for us,' says Harvey. 'Some of the audiences hated us – they just wanted to see Bauhaus – but others got us. By the end of 1981, we'd gone from playing to 300 people to 1,500. 4AD was helping on a daily basis, though not so much with funds, which Ivo didn't have. We ran things ourselves as we'd done back home.'

But Ivo willingly offered friendship. Mick Harvey wasn't spending his down time trying to score, unlike some other Birthday Party members, and he and his girlfriend Katy happened to live around the corner from Ivo's west London flat in Acton, not far from the old Ealing shop, so they would periodically visit him and girlfriend, Lynnette Turner. It gave Harvey the opportunity more than most to see Ivo from a closer and more personal angle. 'He had an underlying sensitivity that was inscrutable to me,' Harvey recalls. 'Australians tend to blurt stuff out, but the English tend to not let on about what they think or feel, until you get to know them well, and sometimes not even then. Ivo was very forthcoming about ideas, but you could sense something in there that bothered him, that nagged away, that he found difficult to put somewhere. The depressive tendencies, I could sense, were being covered with him getting on with everything and by his enthusiasm. He was very earnest and it was obvious how incredibly important the music was to him. It defined him.'

The Birthday Party only needed 4AD as a production house, while bands such as Modern English needed mentoring. As the youngest in a big family, perhaps Ivo enjoyed adopting the older, wiser role in a relationship, and he was far more knowledgeable about music than Modern English, even though he couldn't play a note. But Ivo didn't feel qualified to bring out a musicality in a band the way a producer could, and so following a Peel session for the band, he paired them with Ken Thomas, who had midwifed two Wire albums and similarly quintessential post-punk landmarks by The Au Pairs and Clock DVA.

Ivo joined the band for part of the fortnight's session at Jacob's residential studios in Surrey – confirming a budget beyond previous

4AD releases. He didn't try and impose himself. 'You got carte blanche with Ivo,' recalls Robbie Grey. 'He let us roll and evolve.' Mick Conroy recalls Ivo would say what he liked and what he didn't. '"Grief", for example, sounded amazing, but apparently not at nine minutes, so he suggested we shorten and restructure it. He wasn't a person who'd say, "Play G minor after E, play that section four times, move on to the middle eight". But none of us were amazing musicians anyway.'

Ivo, however, thought the album had the same problem as Bauhaus' debut; it didn't capture the energy via the spontaneity of the Peel session. In Modern English's case, he blames the lack of budget available to hire an engineer familiar with the studio, as he saw that Ken Thomas was unfamiliar with the mixing desk: 'It wasn't entirely Ken's fault by any means,' he adds.

Teething problems, at least at this stage, were not going to bring a band down, and in any case, the album was recorded mostly live, to keep the desired level of urgency, most notably on the opening 'Sixteen Days', which bravely began with an experimental stretch of guitar and sampled voices (about the only audible words were 'atomic bomb'), and 'A Viable Commercial'. But with four songs around the six-minute mark, more trimming would have helped, as the band's dedication to mood building rarely led anywhere. More melodic ingenuity would have helped too: 'Move In Light' had the best, perhaps only true hook, to counteract the densely packed arrangements.

That The Birthday Party's *Prayers On Fire* was 4AD's first album of 1981, and it was already April, showed that Ivo – without Peter Kent's speedy momentum – was pacing himself. But at least the finished Modern English debut album, *Mesh & Lace*, was scheduled for the same month. Perhaps The Birthday Party had warmed up *NME* writer Andy Gill, as *Mesh & Lace* was also favourably reviewed by him, and in the same issue as *Prayers On Fire*. After establishing that Modern English 'exist in the twilight zone of Joy Division and Wire – a limbo of sorts as both bands are now effectively extinct', he acknowledged it was 'a worthwhile place to be … in some respects, this *is* the modern, English sound, Eighties dark power stung with a certain austerity'.

Gill also nailed where 4AD had positioned itself by claiming the band had 'an edge of sincerity which sets Modern English apart from the new gloom merchants'. He summarised *Mesh & Lace* as, 'not an essential album by any means, but certainly one of the more interesting offerings at the moment', adding, 'And if we must have groups deeply rooted in the Joy Division sound … then I'd just as soon have Modern English as any other.'

If the sound wasn't uniquely arresting, the cover of *Mesh & Lace* certainly was. The full-frontal male nude tooting a long horn on the cover of Bauhaus' *In The Flat Field* showed 4AD was prepared to be provocative: it's impossible to imagine such an image in this paranoid age of sex-ploitation. Modern English's cover star was again male, but partially clothed this time, in a kind of toga, with blurred hand movements that inferred the motion of masturbation to anyone with even a limited imagination, especially, as Robbie Grey admitted, the dangling fish 'represented fertility'.

In a converted south-east London warehouse very near the Thames River in Greenwich where Nigel Grierson combines home and work, images that will be included in a forthcoming book of photographs line the walls. But though Grierson is also plotting a 4AD-themed book, there is no visible evidence of his role in creating the label's visual portfolio, alongside his former partner-in-crime Vaughan Oliver.

Grierson also hails from County Durham, and was one year below Oliver at Ferryhill Grammar School. The pair had bonded over music ('a Jonathan Richman album sealed our special friendship,' says Grierson), literature (he introduced Oliver to the novelist Samuel Beckett; Oliver later christened his first son Beckett) and sleeve design. Grierson followed Oliver to study graphic design at Newcastle Polytechnic, where the pair bonded further over anatomy books – 'old books, intriguing images, strange, static forms' – and collaborated on projects. For example, a photographic series of the nude figure in nature, influenced by American photographers Bill Brandt and Wynn Bullock, but featuring the pair's own bodies: 'We couldn't get any girls to pose naked!' Grierson grins. 'But the masculine figures gave the work another edge.'

After college, Grierson secured a work placement at album art specialists Hipgnosis, where he was mentored by co-founder Storm Thorgerson. 'Storm was an inspiration, though he was heading in a more conceptual, less impressionistic direction than my own work was beginning to take,' says Grierson. But while Oliver took full-time work, Grierson changed tack to a photography degree at London's Royal College of Art; he later took a film degree but photography remained his preferred medium. At the RCA, he conceived of images 'from the viewpoint of imagination over reproduction, more concerned with the inner world, in my head. The work Vaughan and I did was all about the "feel", and an abstraction, reflecting the feel of the music itself. An "idea" often recedes into relative insignificance in the finished cover.'

Visual influences that Grierson and Oliver shared included vintage Polish poster design, artist – and Gilbert and Lewis collaborator – Russell Mills, and the Quay brothers Stephen and Timothy, who, Grierson feels, were 'purveyors of the dark and intriguing'. He recalls, 'We were a generation of people brought up on monster movies, and Hammer horror films on TV every Friday night, which I'm sure had a profound effect on our childish imaginations that manifested in the dark, macabre yet romantic feel of much of Eighties popular culture – and not just goths.'

Grierson's approach to music took the same course, as his tastes shifted from rock to country and swing, 'forever searching for something new', before punk and post-punk was fully embraced, especially Siouxsie and the Banshees' 'Germanic atmosphere'. A few months after moving to London, Grierson had met Ivo at Oliver's suggestion. Grierson instantly approved of 4AD's core roster, bands like Modern English. 'And I must have ended up seeing The Birthday Party ten times – they were the best thing I'd ever heard, so hostile and breathtaking, especially live.'

Ivo used two of Grierson's photographs for the front and back of the Sort Sol single but the sleeve for *Mesh & Lace* was the first venture under a new partnership that Oliver and Grierson christened 23 Envelope. 'It was in opposition to the egotistical way advertising agencies used a list of surnames,' Oliver explains. '23 Envelope was more fun, a lyrical bit of nonsense, which also suggested a studio with a number of people and a broad palate of approaches. I didn't want to get known for a certain style. How naïve we were!'

Mesh & Lace's surreal composition benefited from Modern English giving Grierson the same freedom as Ivo had given the band. 'To describe the image as sexual is too blunt,' Grierson argues. 'I agree the fish is a phallic suggestion, but the lace is simply feminine, and I was into [British figurative painter] Francis Bacon and movement in photos. So there's this slightly strange context and a whole bunch of influences.'

It would have been interesting – if not a ramping up of the homo-erotica – if Oliver had managed to see through his original idea for the album's working title, *Five Sided Figure*. 'Vaughan had this draw-ing of a fifty-pence coin with five blokes around it with their knobs hanging out on the table,' Mick Conroy recalls. 'I don't think we'd have gone with it!'

Ivo remains unconvinced by the finished cover. 'I don't think Nigel would argue that it worked. But 23 Envelope's work was done on faith, and my ignorance. Vaughan and Nigel brought character and taught me how to look at things, to position things, and to contrast between fonts. But at that point, besides Modern English, all the artists 4AD worked with were doing their own artwork.'

What might 23 Envelope have imagined, for example, for the B.C. Gilbert/G. Lewis seven-inch single 'Ends With The Sea'? The duo's chosen seascape, the water flattened and calm at the edge of the sand, was restful but a far too literal interpretation. Just like the pair's Cupol intro 'Like This For Ages', the new single was more of a song than soundscape, its nagging little melody buffeted by some electronic undertows, which converged to a mantra for the flipside 'Hung Up To Dry While Building An Arch'.

'Ends With The Sea' was a reworking of 'Anchor' from the duo's improvised Peel session. 'We asked Ivo, "Can we make a single? We have this top song"', recalls Lewis. 'But we couldn't recapture it in the studio.' This was becoming a pattern for post-punk artists, whose energies and ideas were more suited to short, sharp turnarounds, not deliberation. The single turned out to be the ex-Wire men's 4AD swansong, as Gilbert and Lewis began a project with Mute Records' founder Daniel Miller, and gravitated towards his label, but Ivo values their short residency at 4AD. 'It's easy to dismiss those works as just doodling, but they were a really important part of the freedom people had, after punk, to experiment. Bruce and Graham showed a lot of bravery.'

Mass was a classic illustration of this ingrained liberation. Peter Kent's last task at 4AD had been to organise the band's debut album, *Labour Of Love*, recorded at The Coach House studio owned by Roxy Music guitarist Phil Manzanera. 'Mass took a very loose approach to recording and there was a lot of improvisation,' Kent recalls. But not, it seems, to positive effect. 'There were a couple of good tracks but overall the album was disappointing.'

'A collection of great ideas but poorly executed,' is Mark Cox's similar conclusion. 'Part was down to our attitude that we wouldn't be produced, or let anyone in. Wally Brill, who had produced the Rema-Rema EP, took his name off it after an awful row.'

There was certainly no middle ground with *Labour Of Love*. Its shivering, dank and claustrophobic aura was the fulcrum of 4AD's 'dark and intense' origins, a take-no-prisoners expression of border-line madness, from the opening ten-minute track's musical embodiment of howling rain and fog. Mick Allen's first declaration, which arrived four minutes in, was, '*help is on its way*'.

'Mass frightened people,' claims Chris Carr. 'We had some press support early on from the greatcoat brigade, writers like Paul Morley, but it was too heavy for general consumption.'

Even so, the *NME* ignored *Labour Of Love* for four months, and then accused Mass of being one of the countless Joy Division imitators: 'They parade angst, guilt and all the other seven deadly sins and just leave it at that: a charade … this album represents one emotion, one dimension, one colour, that of greyness.'

The album only struck a chord in America. Punk/new wave authority *Trouser Press Guide* called it: 'dark and cacophonous, an angry, intense slab of post-punk gloom that is best left to its own (de)vices'. On its eventual CD release in 2006, the website Head Heritage claimed *Labour Of Love* was 'the Holy Grail of British Post-Punk', but also highlighted why Mass were hard to swallow: '... drums sounding like things being thrown downstairs, and a bitter and plaintive Cockney vocal by Michael Allen barely masking severe disappointment and contempt.'

According to Cox, 'something dark and serious lay at our core. It wasn't encouraging. Gary told me his relationship with Mick was often tense, and went off to Berlin and sort of didn't come back. And Danny followed Gary.'

'Mick and I were both stubborn, and things had started to fracture and stagnate,' says Gary Asquith. 'Looking back, I still held a lot of disappointment with Rema-Rema, which had been the most important stage of my sordid career so far. Mark was desperately hanging on to Mick, and it felt like time to go our separate ways, to see what happened. Berlin had a great little club scene, and I was hanging out with this all-girl group, Malaria.'

Back in London, says Cox, 'Mick and I were still making sounds, but the energy fell apart. Mick needed to stop smoking spliff, which he eventually did. But he had a bad acid trip, which I think left a bit of a legacy.'

The night of his LSD misdemeanour, Allen had turned up at Ivo's home, showing that even a renegade such as Allen trusted in Ivo's company. 'He was a strange, sometimes awkward, shy fellow,' Allen recalls, 'but I liked him. I saw Ivo as an older brother, and we'd talk about music in the same way, though I'd take the piss out of what he listened to! He was obviously from a certain background, and we were working class, but we connected.'

Mass' unencumbered liberty was mirrored by 4AD's next release, the most esoteric to date: an instrumental album, snappily titled *Provisionally Entitled The Singing Fish*, from a vocalist by trade – Gilbert and Lewis' former Wire sparring partner, Colin Newman.

Newman had been raised in the thrills-free province of Newbury, 60 miles west of London, and attended art school in the marginally more engaging city of Winchester and near to the capital in Watford, which had London pretensions without its credibility. Newman thought he'd be an illustrator, but admits, 'I wasn't very good. I was at art school to join a band.' After being asked to sing in an end-of-term performance by the college audio-visual technician, Bruce Gilbert, Newman had found his vocation, adding pop nous and oblique lyricism to the Wire formula.

When the band had fractured, Wire's manager Mike Thorne had approached Martin Mills at Beggars Banquet, who used some of the Gary Numan profits to fund Newman's album *A–Z*. Newman didn't arrive at 4AD via his Wire bandmates or even Beggars, but after meeting Peter Kent at a party. Kent had, in turn, introduced Newman to Ivo, knowing they'd have much in common: both were the same age (twenty-seven), they both loved Spirit and the late British folk rock singer-songwriter Nick Drake – to Newman's surprise, 'as I thought nobody else knew him then'. The musical conversation had turned to an instrumental record that Newman had in mind, and Ivo was happy to have another Wire representative on board. 'I liked Colin, and I'd loved *A–Z*, which to me was the great lost fourth Wire album. And I thought he would do something good again. And he did.'

On Newman's side, Ivo felt he'd benefit from having access to the independent charts. 'That was one of his lines,' Newman recalls, 'and I'm sure it was true. But that wasn't why I made the record. I wanted to do an alternative to a "song" record.'

Newman recorded all twelve impressionistic tracks – titled 'Fish One' to 'Fish 12' – of *Provisionally Entitled The Singing Fish* by himself (except for 'Fish Nine', which featured Wire drummer Robert Gotobed). 'It was ahead of its time,' he feels. 'People would later do the same with sequencers and sampler, fiddling with varispeeds, flying stuff in off different tapes, building music by layers and extemporised in the studio.'

There was an appreciation for Newman's 'wealth of nuance in such a stripped structure', according to *NME*, in a review that concluded by noting 'surreal dreamscapes whose icy beauty is unusually attractive'. But the only instrumental, filmic exercises that had more than a limited esoteric appeal came from former Roxy Music synth magus – and inventor of ambient music – Brian Eno. *Singing Fish* was too rarefied to compete.

'It upsets me greatly that what Colin did on 4AD is written out of our history,' says Ivo. 'But not as upset as when it happened to Dif Juz.'

Few bands set an agenda that would be barely acknowledged at the time, and yet emulated by so many in years to come, as Dif Juz. While Colin Newman had been experimenting without voices, the London-based quartet was instrumental from the off, laying the groundwork for what became known as post-rock during the mid-Nineties, a genre that eschewed the rhythm and blues-based recycling of rock'n'roll cliché for a more striking, freeform approach. Shorn of words, Dif Juz's only point of view was an exploratory fusion, which pinpointed 4AD's willingness to allow artists to exist in worlds only of their own making.

The saga of Dif Juz is uniquely mesmerising if only for what came after – or what didn't. So total is the disappearance of the band's creative hub, guitarists and brothers Alan and David Curtis, that not even their former bandmates Richie Thomas and Gary Bromley know of their current whereabouts. Neither does the band's music publisher, who cannot send royalty cheques without personal details. There isn't one lead online either. When 4AD released the Dif Juz CD compilation *Soundpool* in 1999, a website had temporarily appeared displaying the words, 'By us about us' and 'more soon'. Since Dif Juz was imbued with mystery, from its name to its sound and song titles, it all has a rational, if sad, logic.

'David and Alan were nice people. Quiet, reclusive, and great guitarists,' is the memory of Dif Juz bassist Gary Bromley. The last time drummer Richie Thomas saw the Curtis brothers was in 2002 at his mum's funeral: 'They liked my mum. Alan was working as an electrician, and they'd do painting and decorating. They were just different. Your first impression of Alan was of a university graduate, very well spoken, and an intellectual. But he was a working-class kid, like me. David was cool, edgy, interesting, a great sense of humour, amiable, but volatile too. Things could go a bit crazy if he was pushed in the wrong direction. I saw him on stage once; his guitar kept cutting out, so he kicked the amp and punched out the stage light above his head. There was glass and smoke everywhere.'

The other curious aspect to the Curtis brothers, who hailed from Birmingham in the Midlands, was that the classically trained David Curtis was even, briefly, a member of the embryonic version of New Romantic icons Duran Duran (Andy Taylor took his place in the final, famous line-up). Legend has it that Curtis vanished one night, fearing for his safety, after Duran hired local nightclub owners as their managers.

Down in London, the brothers formed the punk band London Pride. Richie Thomas saw them play at the Windsor Castle pub. 'I told the singer, "Your drummer's shit". He said, "OK, give me your number". After we rehearsed, I joined.'

Raised in the same north-west London area as the Models/Rema/ Mass boys – though being younger, he only crossed paths with them years later – Thomas tells a familiar tale of glam, hard and progressive rock habits surrendering to punk. He was just thirteen when he discovered the Sex Pistols: 'They had so much energy, and when I bought a Damned album, that was it, I was gone.' He even customised his own clothes, which got him vilified. 'I always felt like an outcast, with everyone having a go at me,' he says.

The same year, Thomas began drumming for a local band, Blackout. When he joined London Pride and met the Curtis brothers, he'd hang out at the band's squat in nearby Alperton. 'This north London gang had been after me so I went to live there, this druggy madhouse.' Under the influence or not, Thomas embraced the brothers' new plans, to make instrumental music, which began with a demo of 'Hu' that was re-recorded for the opening track of debut Dif Juz EP *Huremics*. 'It sounded completely new and tantalising,' Thomas recalls, 'out of the Roxy Music school, but unlike anything I'd ever heard.'

No one is sure of the origins of the band's name Dif Juz. Was it a variation on Different Jazz? Years later, Ivo heard it was to be spoken with a soft Hispanic accent, like, 'diffuse'. Thomas's memory is vague, but he says everyone was stoned at the time. 'Someone asked about our name, which we didn't yet have. Something was suggested on the spur of the moment, and later on, someone said, "What was that name again? Was it Dif Juz?" It was onomatopoeic, and it stuck. When people said it meant "Different Jazz", we'd go along with it.'

Gary Bromley was another admitted stoner, who had also seen London Pride and met the Curtis brothers. Bromley now lives in Louisville, Kentucky (from where his wife hails), but he was raised in west Ealing, where a strong Jamaican community had given him an early taste for reggae and marijuana. Punk was just around the corner: Bromley says he spiked and dyed his hair, and joined a band, Satty Bender And The Gay Boys: 'Homophobic, I know, but we didn't know better back then,' he says. Adulthood arrived alongside post-punk, and Bromley – a regular customer at the Beggars shop – took great interest in PiL bassist Jah Wobble's adventures in dub. 'But only after joining Dif Juz did I take the bass seriously,' he admits.

Dif Juz's lack of a singer, Bromley says, 'was down to the necessity of the situation'. According to Thomas, the band auditioned some vocalists, but says, 'It was hopeless; too much ego going on.' In any case, a voice would have competed with the brothers' musical foraging. It didn't hold Dif Juz back; at only the band's second show, at the west London pub The Clarendon, EMI's progressive rock imprint Harvest, which had had a rebirth, made possible by signing Wire, offered to release an album – if they'd accept a producer of the label's choice. 'A few labels were interested, actually,' Thomas confirms. 'But we didn't think anyone else would know what to do with our music. We felt very protective of it.'

Ivo attended the following Clarendon show a month later. 'Word had got out,' says Thomas. 'I'd bought "Dark Entries" and "Swans On Glass", so I knew who 4AD were. Back then, Ivo had a little ponytail; I'd never seen a picture of Eno at that point and I imagined that Ivo was what Eno looked like! I wasn't far off. He was arty, genuine, and very interested in us.'

Ivo: 'Dif Juz had this husband-and-wife management, who brought me the tapes, and I really, *really* liked it. They were an interesting bunch. Gary had been at school with [Mass drummer] Danny Briottet, and he did the best Robert de Niro impression! He looked a bit like de Niro too.'

'Ivo wanted us to make an album, but we didn't want to be in debt, so we agreed on an EP, to see how things went,' says Thomas. 'Ivo was willing to take a chance and let us produce ourselves. The engineer said, "You can't do that, you can't move things around on the [mixing] desk, the EQ and faders". I replied, "Is there a rulebook that says so?" I was adding reverb, making it quieter, and the guy started getting into it and suggested tape loops, extra echo and other effects.'

Recorded at Spaceward studio in Cambridge, 'Hu', 'Re', 'Mi' and 'Cs' made up the four-track EP *Huremics*, an imagined word that hinted at something indefinable, like the music, which stretched between rock, dub and ambient. Today, Dif Juz would be lauded by the tastemakers of the blogsphere, but in 1981, not even John Peel got it. 'And as you know, you've got nowhere to go without Peel,' says Ivo. 'They never got off the ground.'

Undeterred, Dif Juz released a second EP, *Vibrating Air*, only months later. Thomas recalls rehearsals taking place religiously every Sunday: 'We'd smoke pot and jam for hours, making the music we wanted to hear because no one else was.' Recorded at Blackwing with John Fryer, who was now engineering a succession of 4AD recordings, the four new tracks were called 'Heset', 'Diselt', 'Gunet' and 'Soarn', all anagrams, spelling out These Songs Are Untitled. It was a dubbier affair than *Huremics*, setting it even further apart. 'Dif Juz was ahead of its time, like so much of Ivo's A&R,' says Chris Carr. 'Look at what happened to Modern English, and to Matt Johnson. Ivo went where others would eventually go. His view was, it may take time but it will flourish.'

Modern English had also been visitors at Spaceward and subsequently upped their game after *Mesh & Lace* with 'Smiles And Laughter', a sharper and sleeker single that restored Ivo's faith: 'The sound was again appropriate,' he says. Yet Carr still found it hard to raise the band's press profile. 'Modern English were caught between two stools, on the edge of experimentation, but with a pop angle.

Independent music was beginning to take off on radio, and while Daniel Miller employed radio pluggers for bands like Depeche Mode, Ivo wouldn't do the same. He wasn't willing to play that game. It was a judgement call, but also financial.'

Among Mute's growing stable of synth-wielding acts, from cutting edge to pop, Depeche Mode gave the label daytime radio exposure and a profile that didn't depend on John Peel or the music press. Ivo wasn't even looking for pop acts, and pop acts weren't looking for 4AD. Not that the label wasn't a repository of great singles, such as The Birthday Party's 'Release The Bats', recorded after the band had returned to London, and the perfect lurching anthem to make the most of the band's burgeoning popularity.

The single topped the independent charts for three weeks in August. With the lyric concluding, *'Horror bat, bite!/ Cool machine, bite!/ Sex vampire, bite!'*, Nick Cave may have intended a withering parody of the goth theatrics he'd witnessed close up on tour with Bauhaus, but 'Release The Bats' is considered a genre classic, making number 7 (one place behind 'Bela Lugosi's Dead') in *NME*'s '20 Greatest Goth Tracks' list in 2009, claiming, 'Here was a compelling sonic template for goth's lunatic fringe.'

A month later, in September 1981, The Birthday Party made their maiden voyage to the USA. It was literally a riot by all accounts, with interrupted and cancelled shows, blood spilt and audiences riled. According to band biographer Ian Johnston, at the band's US debut in New York City, Cave weaved the microphone lead around a woman's throat and screamed, 'Express yourself', and the next night, he repeatedly beat his head on the snare drum (both shows got cancelled). It was followed by a debut European tour and a short UK tour, where the hostility didn't let up. Ivo was starting to have doubts. 'The shows were very exciting but it had got too rock'n'roll for me, too grubby. I'm not interested in violence and someone on stage kicking a member of the audience in the face.'

Ivo was on more comfortable ground with 4AD's next single, an oddity that came from a meeting between Bauhaus' David J and René Halkett, the only surviving member of Germany's original Bauhaus school of Modernist craft and fine arts founded in 1919. David J had recorded the octogenarian Halkett in the summer of 1980, at the latter's cottage in Cornwall, supporting his frail voice with a cushion of electronics, upbeat on 'Amour', soothing on 'Nothing'. Despite Bauhaus' shift to Beggars Banquet, David J had stayed in contact with Ivo: 'I told him about the project. He heard it just the once and said he'd release it on 4AD. It was where Ivo was heading with the label: off-the-wall, arty projects.'

Bauhaus' profile would have ensured enough sales to pay for something so left-field, but as Ivo notes, 'It was a lovely thing to do. The single could be described as dreadfully pretentious but who gives a fuck? Halkett was a nice man, and it meant a lot to him that David wanted to do this.'

Ivo's affection for his friends, even those that had left 4AD, was clear, and delivered much more satisfaction than sales-based decisions. 4AD was growing into a little family, and Ivo recalls he felt like an older brother to Matt Johnson during the making of his debut album *Burning Blue Soul*. 'I was shy and introverted, then, still a teenager,' Johnson concurs. The relationship had strengthened when Johnson was unhappy with new demos he'd recorded with Bruce Gilbert and Graham Lewis, and had turned to Ivo, who got more involved with the recording.

As Johnson recalls, 'I was recording a couple of tracks at a time, in different studios with different engineers and co-producers. Ivo wasn't there for a lot of it and his role was more as an executive producer, but he became far more hands on with a couple of tracks at Spaceward [studios]. He'd suggest ideas but wasn't precious about them. I liked that he'd test you to make sure you believed in what you were doing. If he thought differently, he'd strongly argue his case, but ultimately he'd ensure power resided with the artist. He liked working with artists who had a clear vision and self-belief and saw his role as facilitating unusual projects no other labels would take a chance on.'

Given free rein, *Burning Blue Soul* was raw and adventurous, with an unusual blend of bucolic British psych folk and Germany's more fractured krautrock imprint, bearing only distant traces of the sophisticated blend of subsequent The The records. The opening instrumental 'Red Cinders In The Sand' was almost six minutes of ominous churning, and even calmer passages such as 'Like A Sun Rising Through My Garden' sounded infested with dread. Johnson's vocals were often electronically tweaked, boosting the alienation. Johnson recalls: 'It was considered the most psychedelic album in many years when it came out.' (No doubt aided by the sleeve design's heavy debt to Texan psych pioneers The 13th Floor Elevators' album *The Psychedelic Sound of ...*) 'In reality,' Johnson concludes, 'it was almost virginal in its innocence, and unlike some albums I made afterwards, it was made on nothing stronger than orange juice.'

'It's an unusual record, a real mish-mash that works,' Ivo rightly asserts. 'Maybe Matt hates it now, but I'd like to think we had a lot of fun, in the studio and driving back and forth. Watching Matt work was fantastic; he was so fast, and he had that wonderful voice, like [Jethro Tull's] Ian Anderson.'

Actually, Johnson reckons *Burning Blue Soul* still sounds great: 'It was made for all the right reasons; I was just a teenager when I wrote and recorded it so there was not only a fair degree of post-pubescent anxiety but a real purity and unfettered creativity. I didn't know the rules of songwriting then so I wasn't bound by them, but I was able to put into practice a lot of the studio techniques I'd learnt at De Wolfe. It's also the only album where I play all the instruments. So I'm proud of it.'

The post-pubescent anxiety that Johnson describes gave *Burning Blue Soul* a rare burst of politicised anger to match In Camera's David Scinto (coincidentally, both hailed from Stratford, though had different social circles). An upbringing in an East End pub would have borne witness to the volatility of crowds and Johnson says the summer riots across Britain that spring and summer, from London to Birmingham and Liverpool in protest at Margaret Thatcher's economic squeeze on industry, employment and taxes, fed into the album's levels of stress. Likewise the assassination attempts on the Pope and US President Ronald Reagan, specifically on 'Song Without An Ending'.

In its own way, standing apart from all other singer-songwriter records of the time, *Burning Blue Soul* wasn't much less of an oddity than Dif Juz, and with few exceptions, the UK press was very cool (and Peel again didn't bite despite initially supporting 'Controversial Subject'), at least to start with. 'Ivo and I really believed in *Burning Blue Soul*,' says Chris Carr. 'And we couldn't understand why it wasn't clicking with people. It took six months to get a review, but when we did, that's when The The took off, and I'd get calls from journalists asking for a copy of the album. I asked Ivo for more stock, and he said, "Fuck off, they can buy it back from Record & Tape Exchange, where they've sold their original copies".'

Johnson says how much he enjoyed his time at 4AD, but another figure took control of his career in a way Ivo would have categorically avoided. The singularly named Stevo, the founder of the Some Bizzare label and a committed student of Pistols manager Malcolm McLaren's method of major label-fleecing, had become Johnson's manager and solicited a very sizeable offer from CBS, which was raised by competing bids by other majors. 'There was no advance for *Burning Blue Soul* and no royalties for quite some time, so I was always broke,' Johnson explains. 'At certain times of your life, it is very hard to resist these kinds of siren calls. In some ways, I regret not staying on 4AD for another couple of albums. Ivo warned me against CBS – he said it was too soon for me to make the switch and that I could fulfil myself on 4AD. He was extremely gracious and didn't guilt-trip me about it. I've no regrets as I was with CBS [which turned into Sony] for eighteen years and I was allowed a huge amount of artistic freedom, but I sometimes wonder how it would have panned out if I'd stayed with 4AD. Ivo was one of the big influences on my career.'

'I don't remember being disappointed,' says Ivo. 'I was totally committed to the idea of one-off contracts, and if someone didn't want to be with 4AD, that was fine by me. But I wish we'd stayed in touch for longer because I really enjoyed Matt.'

Johnson: 'One last example of Ivo's integrity was that when I decided to change the artist title of *Burning Blue Soul* from Matt Johnson to The The (when the album was re-released in 1984), Ivo didn't want to, despite the fact that it would result in more sales as it would be stacked with my other The The albums. He insisted we put a disclaimer on the cover to explain that it was my decision to change the name. Can you imagine a major label resisting selling more copies on a point of principle?'

Points of principle, however, were a mark of the times. Commerciality meant selling out; integrity and authenticity were the presiding philosophies. After playing shows with The Birthday Party and In Camera, Dance Chapter had also recorded at Spaceward, producing the prosaically named *Chapter II* EP, inspired by the pursuit of beliefs that eventually led Cyrus Bruton to the spiritual comfort of the Bhagwan community. Parts of *Chapter II*, particularly the clotted tension of the eight-minute 'Attitudes', matched the first Dance Chapter single. The track tackled, says Bruton, 'how prejudices build walls, kill love and create pain, which was obvious but I felt it needed to be said in a song'. 'Backwards Across Thresholds' and 'She' addressed desire and relationships while 'Demolished Sanctuary' tackled the suffocation of individual needs within the crowd.

'Punk was cathartic in the sense you could scream and jump, and out of it came a lot of creativity,' he concludes. 'But I felt that people needed to have more faith in their own perception, about how to find their way, in relationships, sexuality, drugs and alcohol, handling money, aspirations and rebellion. I was myself trying to find a way through the impressions and inputs. We all were.'

However, in Ivo's mind, this struggle had manifested itself in the studio, where he'd driven to survey proceedings. 'No one seemed in the mood, so I just left,' he recalls. 'I'd heard the demos, and anyone who has released records based on demos knows that proper recording can lose something. *Chapter II* is OK, but there was no real direction, guts or energy. So for those reasons, I started to get involved more in the studio after that. If things were going wrong, at least I'd know why.'

'It wasn't my impression that things weren't going well,' says Bruton. 'Either way, being on the edge was part of the creative process.' The problem was, Dance Chapter's collective spirit was fast dissolving, over money, or the lack of, and personal ambition. 'We were also going in different directions. Steve [Hadfield] was still studying, and he left soon after the recording. I wasn't looking to make a career from music, though I'd have gone on. But I didn't have a way to hold a group together, or rebuild it. Ivo suggested I move to London and see what happened, but by then, I'd reached the places I needed to go, and I had the freedom to look at things in another way.'

Dance Chapter was the first of 4AD's artists to fall at the second fence, and again, its four constituents didn't make inroads into other music. If the band's demise was a downbeat conclusion to the year, there was enough achievement to end 1981 with a compilation, which Ivo assembled for the Japanese market via major label WEA Japan, which was distributing 4AD in the Far East. Housed in a photo of two wrestling male nudes from one of Vaughan Oliver's medical journals, *Natures Mortes – Still Lives* was a personal inventory of 4AD highlights, including the early Birthday Party single 'Mr Clarinet' that Ivo had reissued on 4AD, and tracks from Rema-Rema, Modern English, Matt Johnson, Mass, Sort Sol, In Camera, Cupol, Past Seven Days, Psychotik Tanks and Dif Juz. Gathered in isolation, 4AD's formative years sound distinctive, predominantly original and, with hindsight, undervalued, though only in light of what was to follow.

In a letter to the American fanzine *The Offense* towards the end of 1981, Ivo said he thought he was 'moving away from rock music, even in its broadest sense, as much as possible'. There was even talk of Aboriginal chants. He concluded, 'I'm confident of change and a very valid and varied output – but my search for something far removed from anything I've ever done will continue.'

Ivo already had something in mind that fulfilled that brief. Driving back home from Spaceward after abandoning the Dance Chapter session, he stuck on a demo that he'd been given at the Beggars shop that week. 'I got called upstairs and whoever was behind the counter said, that's Ivo, and this cassette got stuffed into my sweaty hand,' he recalls. 'Something was quietly said, and the couple left. When I listened, I immediately enjoyed it. It sounded familiar, like the Banshees, though with a drum machine. And a voice you could barely hear. There was no indication that she was great or bad. But the power of the music made me call them to suggest they make a single.'

When Ivo called, he discovered his visitors that day, guitarist Robin Guthrie and vocalist Elizabeth Fraser, had come down from Grangemouth in Scotland to see The Birthday Party. 'We first saw The Birthday Party open for Bauhaus, and we started to follow them around on tour,' recalls Guthrie. 'We were just teenagers, and painfully shy, but we started talking to them after shows. Eventually they said, are you in a band? Yeah, we said. They said they'd met these people in London – which was 4AD.'

Nothing would be the same for 4AD after Cocteau Twins.

5 1982

THE OTHER OTHERNESS
(cad201-bad15)

Sorry for the delayed reply. I've been somewhat affected, in a truly
depressed sort of a way since you came here. Not your fault, buddy, just
a barrel load of worms wriggling about in my consciousness which I'm
not dealing with too well. Apart from that, well, I'm OK.

Someone much wiser than me once told me that I had to make
peace with my past in order to enjoy the present, but what if one's past
becomes one's present.

And that, my friend, is where I am at.

Worms, Can, Opened.

(Robin Guthrie, email, July 2012)

Rennes, to the east of north-west France in the region of Brittany, is
an hour by plane from the southern tip of England. It's where Robin
Guthrie met his French wife, but it's a convenient location, near
enough to keep in touch with his past, far enough to keep out of
reach.

Fifteen minutes' drive from Rennes city centre, the house where the
Guthrie family (they have a daughter of eleven) live is elegantly aged
and comfortably spacious. The vast attic doubles as home studio,

office and storeroom for his solo career, which is predominantly about albums but also occasional touring. Posters, photographs and record sleeves, detailing triumphs from Cocteau Twins and solo eras, line the walls.

These days, Guthrie sports a beard, the significance of which will become apparent. He once claimed to be 'too fat to be a goth', and given the cooking skills he displays over the weekend, he won't be dieting any time soon. Cheerful and broody in equal measures, Guthrie keeps the conversation flowing, but the can of worms lies open, kicked around, its contents spilling out. The past still lives, heavy, bewildering and threatening, in his head, especially since he's recently heard that Elizabeth Fraser, his Cocteau Twins partner, and his girlfriend for seventeen years (the couple have one daughter, born in 1989) was to play her first ever solo shows, a full fifteen years after Cocteau Twins had split. The problem wasn't her belated return, but her plan to sing Cocteau Twins material, music that Guthrie had written and arranged, for which he says he will receive no credit during the expected adulation for the singer.

Fraser, on her part, has admitted that she finds Cocteau Twins too difficult to talk about; since 2000, she has only discussed it twice, and passes up the opportunity to recall her side of the story for this book, a story stained by dysfunction, vulnerability, substance addiction, childhood trauma and astonishing music. 'You take each other's breath away by doing something or saying something they never saw coming,' she told *Guardian* in 2009 when she released her first solo single 'Moses' (a tribute to her late friend Jake Drake-Brockman). 'They were my life. And when you're in something that deep, you have to remove yourself completely.'

Guthrie's memories are clearly torturous as well. Long after midnight on the first day of recollection, Guthrie disappears upstairs, returning five minutes later, beaming, with a box full of memorabilia, of cuttings, stickers, leaflets, tour laminates, letters. The next morning, Guthrie's mood appears to make it more likely he'll burn the box's contents. 'And then, I found that big bag of stuff,' he wrote in an email a month after we'd met. 'Goodness, some revelations were made which have left me feeling, if possible (!!), less comfortable with my past than even I could have imagined. My wtf? turned into a WTF? I feel like I've had surgery performed but the surgeon forgot to sew me back up.'

Earlier in the afternoon, he'd sat down to recall his and Fraser's first visit to Hogarth Road. 'I don't remember meeting Ivo, but we already knew 4AD because we'd collected their records. We were enthralled by The Birthday Party and also Dif Juz. I quite liked Bauhaus, Elizabeth more than me, though I loved "Bela Lugosi's Dead", and Rema-Rema. We'd hear things on John Peel and read the music papers. I wasn't into Cupol but I'd been a bit of a Wire fan. *Burning Blue Soul* was one of the best records of that decade, right out of the mould. But The Birthday Party was the most exciting thing I'd ever heard. And Rowland Howard's approach to guitar – I didn't realise you could do that and still be taken seriously.'

Equidistant from Glasgow and Edinburgh, on the banks of the Firth of Forth, 'Grangemouth was a village around an oil rig,' claims Ray Conroy, who was to become Cocteau Twins' tour manager after first taking on Modern English through his brother Mick's connection to 4AD. Guthrie and his schoolmate Will Heggie were among the town's punk renegades, making stroppy, noisy protest in bands such as The Heat. 'Punk to us didn't mean your clothes, but doing what you want,' says Guthrie. 'Self-expression. A teenage cry for help.'

Guthrie had worked as an apprentice for BP Oil, with a talent for electronics, which he put to good use by building effects pedals for his guitar. 'The aim was to make music with punk's energy but more finesse and beauty, and that shiny, dense Phil Spector sound. I was trying to make my guitar sound like I could play it, so I was influenced by guitarists who made beautiful noise, like The Pop Group, or Rowland S. Howard.'

The new band couldn't be complete until they'd found a singer. They vaguely knew a girl, Elizabeth Fraser, two years below them at school, who they'd see dancing at the Hotel International, a local club where Guthrie would sometimes DJ. His playlist included The Birthday Party and The Pop Group: 'Most people weren't happy with my choices, but Liz was, as she kept dancing,' Guthrie smiles. 'We struck up a bit of a friendship.'

Colin Wallace, one year above Guthrie and Heggie at school, recalls Fraser as, 'This little vision in fishnet tights, leather mini-skirt and shaved head, smoking cigarettes, playing truant until lunchtime. Shy and quiet too. She was ostracised at school, as a weirdo, but to me she was unbelievably brave.'

Wallace recalls Guthrie saying, 'If she's that good a dancer, I bet she can sing. Robin asked her, and she said yes, but she wouldn't even sing in front of Will. But I'd hear them rehearse, above some shops, and in the old derelict town hall, and she was astonishing.'

Guthrie: 'Liz was insanely shy but as her mum later told me, she always sang as a child. We just assumed that she'd be brilliant, like I thought we were all great. We were very naïve and idealistic then.'

The name Cocteau Twins came via the Glasgow new wave band Simple Minds, who The Heat had once supported: 'They had a song called "Cocteau Twins", so we nicked it,' says Guthrie. This wasn't any reference to the fact that the band initially had a second vocalist: 'Carol, a friend of Liz's,' Guthrie recalls. 'But she only stayed two weeks. I forget why she didn't last.' There was also a drummer, John Murphy, though his request for travel expenses encouraged Guthrie to choose the cheaper and more manageable option of a drum machine. The band even broke up for a couple of months: 'Liz and I probably fell out with Will, or he was busy elsewhere,' Guthrie thinks. 'But a friend asked us to support his band, so we re-formed.'

Fraser's memory, in an interview with *Volume* magazine, was that she'd got fed up: 'I didn't feel like [the band] was for me at all … I think it was more the lyrics that I didn't have the faith in. But I started going out with Robin, so I came back into the band.'

During rehearsals in the local community hall, Communist Party office and a squat the trio developed their nascent sound, and after just two shows, they recorded a demo of 'Speak No Evil', 'Perhaps Some Other Aeon', and 'Objects D'Arts' (Guthrie says Fraser purposely spelt it wrong). Fraser's buried voice, Guthrie recalls, 'wasn't done on purpose, we just couldn't record it any better. We only had one microphone and one cassette recorder, so we had to record the songs twice [Wallace says more than twice, as he has a copy too], once for a tape to give to Ivo, the other to John Peel when we met him [at The Birthday Party show]. We had no phone so I wrote down the number of the phone box down the road and "call between five and six" on the cassette box, and I'd wait outside every night for a call! There wasn't a doubt in my mind that they'd both ring.'

Ivo initially sent the trio to Blackwing to record a single, where he was astonished to hear a voice rise out of the music's shivery dynamic: a powerful, plaintive, hair-raising cry of a voice. Recording the new versions of 'Speak No Evil' and 'Perhaps Some Other Aeon' went so well that Ivo suggested Cocteau Twins record an album instead. The band readily agreed. 'We got very handy at the night bus, up and down from Scotland, sixteen hours each way,' says Guthrie. 'No one would take us seriously in Scotland, or give us any shows, because we weren't hipsters from Glasgow or Edinburgh, and we weren't on Postcard Records.'

The Glasgow-based independent Postcard had been started in 1980 by nineteen-year-old Alan Horne as a vehicle for the band Orange Juice, fronted by his friend Edwyn Collins, whose knowing and inspired marriage of The Velvet Underground with The Byrds initiated the Sixties revival that was eventually to redefine the British underground sound, from The Smiths to The Stone Roses. Adding Josef K, a cooler and droll version of monochromatic post-punk, and the exquisite folk-pop of Aztec Camera, Postcard operated with a lightness of touch and irony – each record had the logo 'The Sound Of Young Scotland', a pastiche of Motown Records – with Horne more of a media-savvy, plotting figure in the mould of Factory's Tony Wilson than reticent Ivo. As a result, Postcard had instantly been championed by the press in a manner withheld for the more heavyweight and less conceptual 4AD.

Ivo appreciated Josef K's 'It's Kinda Funny' but saw 4AD 'as an alternative to Postcard', though he says he understood Postcard's dedicated following. Ivo would not have deviated from obeying his A&R instincts for a similar concept or status, yet it's a curious coincidence that 4AD's next find – via a demo – involved members of Josef K and a spindly, hyper-literate Postcard-ian pop that broke the conventional 4AD mould.

The Happy Family wasn't the most satisfying or productive vehicle for the band's singer-songwriter Nick Currie – or Momus, the alter ego he subsequently chose for his solo guise, after the Greek god of satire and mockery. Having lived in London, Paris, Tokyo, New York and Berlin over the years, Currie's current home is Osaka, Japan, where he continues to fashion spindly, hyper-literate albums but in a electronic/folk fusion he calls 'analogue baroque'. He also writes novels and essays, teaches the art of lyric writing and gives, he says, 'unhelpful' museum tours.

Currie was born in Paisley, to the west of Glasgow, a centre of printed wool manufacture that gave its name to the Indian pattern so popular among Sixties flower children. Currie was no hippie or drop-out, taking an English Literature degree at Aberdeen University while leaving time to study John Peel's radio show at night. At a gig in Glasgow, he'd given Josef K guitarist Malcolm Ross a demo with instructions to pass it on to Alan Horne at Postcard, but Ross kept it, and after Josef K's surprise split, Currie found himself in a band with Ross, Josef K bassist Dave Weddell and local drummer Ian Stoddart.

Currie christened the quartet The Happy Family. 'It was tongue in cheek,' he declares. 'I already had a concept for an album, about two children in the [German terrorist organisation] Red Brigade who assassinated their lottery-winning fascist of a father.' The anticipated album would be called *The Man On Your Street*: 'It was about totalitarianism, the idea that your street equals the whole world, with fascism as a global threat, and mapping that with the oedipal dynamics of the family. My mother had just run off with a wealthy accountant with very conservative views. I was working through the break-up of my actual happy family.'

Currie hoped that his perception of Josef K's 'star power in the press' would rub off on The Happy Family – 'People were shocked by Josef K's early demise and interested in what would come out of it,' he says. Ivo admits he was one of them: 'I never had any intense involvement with any of the band, but Nick was a smart fellow, and I liked his concept.'

Currie agrees that he and Ivo never bonded. Both men were shy, though Currie's droll, intellectual way of compensation was more Alan Horne than Ivo. At their first meeting, Currie suggests, 'To Ivo, I probably looked extremely young, skinny and chinny, and not like a pop star.' Such criteria weren't deal-breakers at 4AD, so Currie is probably more accurate when he adds, 'I was probably an opinionated and prickly kind of fellow', which also described Ivo to a point. But Currie did feel some connection: 'Ivo was kindly and avuncular, a very good teacher and indoctrinator, with a very strong aesthetic, and he knew all this music.'

Currie also got a glimpse early on of Ivo's home when The Happy Family stayed at his flat: 'It was awful, suburban hell on the outside but aesthetic and tidy inside, painted lilac and everything filed away beautifully, with fine art coffee table photography books like *Leni Riefenstahl in Africa* and Diane Arbus. He drove us around in his BMW – the cheapest model [only leased, Ivo says], but still a BMW. So he resembled a playboy entrepreneur to me. But in his mild English way, he talked about his childhood on the farm. I said, "That's great, all the family together like that", and he looked at me strangely, like it was my ideal and not his.' Which was true: a happy family wasn't how Ivo remembered his past.

Before any album was recorded, Ivo wanted to release a Happy Family single. A three-track seven-inch headed by 'Puritans' was recorded at Palladium Studios, 'a weird pixie-like place in the hills outside Edinburgh, a bungalow with a studio inside,' Currie recalls. Ivo didn't know it but Palladium would soon become as crucial to 4AD's fortunes as Blackwing, handy for any local Scots and for bands that needed a residential wing for extended visits. Palladium was cheaper than Jacob's Studios, and run by Jon Turner, a musician whose accomplishments were far in advance of any 4AD artist – he'd even regularly backed Greece's psychedelic hero turned MOR entertainer Demis Roussos.

Blackwing was still the preferred choice for 4AD's London-based acts, though Colin Newman preferred Scorpio Sound in central London, where he hoped to begin another solo album, this time of songs. But Beggars Banquet was less keen: 'I'd got a good advance for A–Z and it hadn't sold as many as they'd wanted,' Newman recalls. 'Beggars also wanted me to tour, which I didn't. Because I wasn't playing ball, they wouldn't give me another advance.' But Ivo was eager for a record of Newman's off-kilter, Wire-style pop, and after agreeing a more modest budget, the album was finished, and even featured three-quarters of Wire, with Robert Gotobed and Bruce Gilbert among the guests.

If A–Z was the missing fourth Wire album, Not To was the fifth, and represented yet another diversion from the cornerstone sound of 4AD's sepulchral origins. But the label's reigning masters of foreboding were hardly down and out. A concert by The Birthday Party at London's The Venue in Victoria had been recorded in November 1981, and though it would have been a bigger money-spinner as a whole album, the band didn't think the recording was good enough to be released in its entirety, only picking four tracks (including a cover of The Stooges' 'Loose') for a budget-priced EP. In reality, it was a mini-album since the band had had the idea to feature the evening's support slot, Lydia Lunch.

From Rochester in the northern part of New York State, by her own admission, Lydia Anne Koch was a precocious child. She told 3:AM magazine that, when she was just twelve years old, she'd informed her parents that she needed to attend 'rock concerts until well after midnight, for "my career"'. By fourteen, she was taking the train to Manhattan with 'a small red suitcase, a winter coat, and a big fucking attitude'. At nineteen, she was fronting Teenage Jesus and The Jerks, a prominent part of America's own post-punk response, known as No Wave, an experimental enclave marked by dissonance, noise and jazzy disruption. Lunch's confrontational howls chimed with The Birthday Party's own, and after she'd attended the band's third New York show in October 1981, a budding friendship led to Lunch being added to the Venue bill with an impromptu backing band that included Banshees bassist Steven Severin.

The vinyl's Birthday Party side was called *Drunk On The Pope's Blood*; the title of Lunch's side, the 16-minute *The Agony Is The Ecstasy*, nailed the essence of the semi-improvised atonal festival of dirge. A month after its release in February 1982, The Birthday Party once again returned to Britain after another profitable summer's break in Australia, both touring and recording a new album. Only this time, bassist Tracy Pew had had to remain behind, detained in a labour camp for three months following a drink-driving offence. His deputy was Barry Adamson, bassist for Manchester new wave progressives Magazine, who had befriended The Birthday Party after marrying one of their Australian friends. Bottom of the bill at The Venue was a band playing only their third show – Cocteau Twins. 'Talk about being propelled into it,' says Guthrie.

The Cocteaus had returned to Blackwing to record an album, which Ivo had scheduled for September, leaving time and space for a series of less pivotal 4AD releases. Daniel Ash was the next escapee, after David J, from Bauhaus, collaborating with school friend (and Bauhaus roadie) Glenn Campling for a four-track EP, *Tones On Tail*, whose unusual rhythm and ambience was more Cupol than Bauhaus. 'I was pleased that Daniel contacted me about something outside Bauhaus, and I liked him, and said yes,' Ivo recalls. 'No offence to Daniel, but for me, it's one of the least essential of 4AD releases.'

Ivo considered In Camera's latest release to be one of the more essential of 1981, certainly among the band's own records. But the band's three-track Peel session, which had been recorded at the end of 1980, was named *Fin* because it was their epitaph. The 11-minute 'Fatal Day' suggested a band at the peak of its powers, but like Dance Chapter, In Camera had fallen apart after one seven-inch single and EP, finding that ethics had become an insurmountable barrier.

A fear of compromise had eaten away at the band's soul. Contracts were the first issue. 'We signed one [for the EP], which wasn't a very good deal,' says Andrew Gray. 'But what terrified us was that if we sold x amount of units, Beggars could nab us, as they'd done with Bauhaus, and we'd have had to strike up new friendships.'

Ivo says they shouldn't have been worried. 'In Camera wasn't a group to make the same transition as Bauhaus. We were only doing one-off contracts by that point. Beggars had decided very quickly to let young, or independent, people get on and work.'

Other personal pressures were present as well. There was an intensity to In Camera's mission: David Scinto recalls one drunken moment when he and bassist Pete Moore did a blood-brothers ritual, 'Pete with a knife, me with a Coke can ring. That was nasty. But that's the sort of thing you did.' So no decision was ever taken lightly. When Ivo had requested an album, and Moore and drummer Jeff Wilmott felt ready, Scinto decided they needed more songs while Gray was again 'terrified' a producer might corrupt the band's fiercely protected sanctum of unity. 'Any ideological flaws,' says Gray, 'meant we couldn't carry on.'

'For the band,' Scinto muses, 'we'd tried to remove our egos. But ego drives you on. I guess we didn't have the ego to fight for the band.' Scinto certainly lacked the ego of a frontman, a rock star. 'I would have given anything to be a rock star!' Wilmott laughs. 'But we'd all sat back and let things happen, rather than drive things ourselves. We almost expected 4AD to do the work. Most gigs were arranged by Peter [Kent], and we should have been gigging every other night. We were jealous of Bauhaus' relationship with their tour manager, who pushed and assisted them in achieving their goals. But I still wouldn't change a thing about how we interacted. In Camera was more like an art club than a band.'

The variety of personalities trying to make headway in post-punk times – art school experimentalists, musical terrorists, career opportunists, politically driven ideologists – ensured that most independent labels of any stature would represent a menagerie of interests. For every aesthetically rigid In Camera, there were more pliable types like Modern English, who happily accepted Ivo's suggestion of a producer for their next album who, says Mick Conroy, 'could make more sense out of us'. Hugh Jones had produced Echo & The Bunnymen's panoramic 1981 album *Heaven Up Here*, which was widely admired by both Ivo and Modern English. Jones provided an instant reality check. Conroy recalls asking him what he thought of their songs: 'Hugh replied, "There aren't any".'

But Jones says he was still attracted to the project. 'I liked bits of Modern English's music, but more, I just liked them, which is my chief criteria, along with having chemistry with an artist. I also thought I could contribute a lot.'

Jones had engineered Simple Minds and Teardrop Explodes albums before stepping up to produce the Bunnymen; all had been major-label commissions. Ivo was, he recalls, 'the first record company person I'd met that didn't come across as brash'. The pair also bonded over favourite albums: for example, both believed The Byrds' *Notorious Byrd Brothers* was a contender for the best album ever made. In the process of working with Modern English, Jones says he introduced them to the delights of British folk rock luminaries Nick Drake and Fairport Convention, and American pop-soul prodigy Todd Rundgren, to give them an insight into chorus-led songwriting and arranging.

Out of it came a distinctly altered Modern English. When Ivo had reckoned that pop bands were unlikely to approach 4AD, he wasn't expecting it would come from inside the 4AD camp. The band named the album *After The Snow*: '*Mesh & Lace* had been a very cold, angry record,' says Robbie Grey.

Just as Echo & The Bunnymen and Orange Juice had bypassed punk's disavowal of music of a radically different hue by respectively resuscitating The Doors and The Byrds, *After The Snow* had adopted a broader, defrosted outlook. There was even a flute on 'Carry Me Down'. 'Ivo thought Gary's guitars sometimes resembled The Byrds, whereas he'd previously sounded like he was kicking a door in!' says Conroy. 'I think making the album in the Welsh springtime meant that we ended up sounding like the countryside.'

By comparison, The Birthday Party resembled a night in a city gutter. The band had returned from Australia with a virtually complete new album, *Junkyard*, on which Barry Adamson had played most of the bass given Tracy Pew's incapacitated status. The artwork by the cult cartoonist and hot rod designer Ed 'Big Daddy' Roth featured his Junk Yard Kid and Rat Fink characters on a journey towards, or from, mayhem, and the album was rife with exaggerated figures such as 'Dead Joe', 'Kewpie Doll' and 'Hamlet (Pow Wow

Wow)', and pulp-fiction violence – for example '6" Gold Blade' and 'She's Hit'. The band drove the point home with exhilaratingly malevolent moods, with Nick Cave acting the snorting and dribbling despot. If only the Mass album *Labour Of Love* had managed to articulate their own drama and tension in the same manner.

By having both Modern English and The Birthday Party at the label, 4AD showed it could handle dark *and* light: from Ed Roth's craziness to Vaughan Oliver's graceful design for *After The Snow*, with dancing horses on a backdrop of crumpled tissue paper inspired by a line on 'Dawn Chorus' (*'strange visions of balloons on white stallions'*). 'That was a breakthrough, graphically, my first extensive use of texture to create a mood,' Oliver says. 'It was an act of perversity but also of tenderness, given it was tissue paper.'

While The Birthday Party was giving the impression of heading further out of control, Hugh Jones had guided Modern English to a newly minted pop levity. 4AD adapted accordingly, acting like a major label by taking a single from an album before the album was released. 'Life In The Gladhouse' was sleek and gutsy with a busy funk chassis, a musical advance but also a commercial retreat, losing the band the post-punk audience cultivated via John Peel without replacing it with a mainstream audience. It reached 26 in the UK independent chart, ten places lower than even 'Smiles And Laughter'.

The Birthday Party had made no such alterations, plunging further onward, on tour through the UK and Europe with Tracy Pew back in the ranks. It wasn't a surprise that the wheels were falling off this careering bus, the first instance being the sacking of odd-man-out drummer Phil Calvert, with Mick Harvey taking his place both on stage and in the studio. What's more, the bus was leaving town for good. The Birthday Party decided they were over Britain, and having met Berlin's industrial noise fetishists Einstürzende Neubauten, the Australians chose the divided city as its new base.

Ivo had funded new recordings at Berlin's famous Hansa Studios (where David Bowie had recorded his *'Heroes'* classic), but before the band departed, Lydia Lunch and Rowland S. Howard (who had formed an alliance and played several of The Birthday Party shows as the support act) offered Ivo a cover of Lee Hazlewood and Nancy Sinatra's 1960s psychedelic oddity 'Some Velvet Morning' that they'd recorded in London. 4AD duly released it as a twelve-inch single, with the original 'I Fell In Love With A Ghost' on the B-side, and much the better track; Ivo's fondness for the A-side is perplexing given his love of singing, and given the Lunch/Howard duet features a man who couldn't sing and a woman who gleefully sang out of tune, desecrating the song's magnetic allure.

'Some Velvet Morning' showed that although Ivo's own taste might lean towards the extended listening experience of the album format, he remained committed to singles, a collectable and affordable format that could sell in tens of thousands. Following the pattern of Gilbert and Lewis, Colin Newman followed up an album with a new seven-inch, 'We Means We Starts'. However, he didn't intend it to be his last 4AD release.

Ivo recalls Wire's re-formation as the reason it was: 'I don't remember turning down more of Colin's demos,' he says, though the band's reunion was still two years off. Newman says he did submit demos to 4AD, which, he says, 'Ivo didn't think were pop enough'. But the singer's dissatisfaction went deeper. 'I didn't have a way forward at that point. Independent labels tended to live on a wing and a prayer, and if things work out or not, it's fine either way. I didn't feel part of how everything worked at that time, and so I disengaged myself. I'd been to India for fourteen months and I'd had enough of the beast of the music industry. I did vaguely talk to Ivo about another project, but we drifted apart. I don't feel close to those records I did on 4AD, or that part of my life.'

Newman also admits to other frustrations with Ivo: 'He didn't want me to produce his bands, even though I'd produced an album for [Irish art rockers] The Virgin Prunes that had done really well. And I think I'd have been more honest with his bands than he would have. I think he had his eye on producing himself.'

Ivo does recall a conversation with Newman about production, but says the only outside producer in 4AD's first three years was Hugh Jones. 'Most bands wanted to produce themselves and we didn't have the budgets that Colin was used to with EMI and [Wire producer] Mike Thorne. It's lovely to fantasise about what, say, the Mass record would've sounded like had they been interested in input and Colin had been keen to get involved.'

As Newman suggests, Ivo did take a more active role in Cocteau Twins' debut album. *Garlands* was recorded at Blackwing, with Eric Radcliffe and John Fryer engineering and Ivo given a co-producer credit alongside the band. Guthrie recalls they had quickly regarded Ivo as a mentor: 'He was very intelligent, one of the first grown-ups we'd met, with a car and a flat; we didn't know anyone like that! He was switched on to music, and he was listening to us! We were enthralled by him.'

Ivo, however, downplays his role. 'I might have suggested an extra guitar part, or sampling a choir at the end of "Grail Overfloweth" in the spirit of [krautrock band] Popol Vuh's music or sampling Werner Herzog's masterpiece, *Aguirre, the Wrath of God*, but it was minimal stuff. I also suggested, stupidly, extending the start of "Blood Bitch". But I was there because someone had to say yes or no, and the band lacked the confidence to do so.'

Elizabeth Fraser was an especially vivid example of deep-set insecurity. Back in Rennes, Guthrie paints a picture of a girl who left home at fourteen, with Sid Vicious and Siouxsie tattoos on her arms, self-conscious to an almost pathological degree. In the mid-1990s, after becoming a mother and having therapy, Fraser told me about the sexual abuse she suffered in her youth, from within her own family. In 1982, she was still a teenager, her issues still fresh and unresolved, and facing not just decisions about her life but being judged on her creativity.

'When we mixed the album, you'd isolate an instrument or voice to concentrate on it,' says Ivo. 'Whenever we'd solo Liz's vocal, she wouldn't let it be heard, or she'd have to leave the room. She had very low self-esteem. On stage, she'd wear a very short mini-skirt and bend over, showing her knickers, and she'd strike her bosom. She was a striking presence on stage, doing all this stuff with her fingers, and you'd see the pain on her face.'

Guthrie later told the *NME* that *Garlands* sounded 'rather dull compared to what we know we're capable of', but it was a promising start. 'In the same way as 4AD hadn't yet proved its individuality, the Cocteau Twins didn't with their first album,' says Ivo, but both label and band could be proud of creating an uncanny and original template with such extraordinary potential. *Garlands* may have drawn some comparisons to Siouxsie and the Banshees, but it had its own enchanted and anxious tension. Heggie's trawling bass and Guthrie's effects-laden yet still minimalist guitar was rooted to a drum machine that occasionally lent a quasi-dance pulse. It gave Fraser a restlessly inventive backdrop for her melodic incantations and lyrical disorder, for example: *'My mouthing at you, my tongue the stake/ I should welt should I hold you/ I should gash should I kiss you'* ('Blind Dumb Deaf') and, *'Chaplets see me drugged/ I could die in the rosary'* ('Garlands').

The sleeve dedication to Fraser's brief singing cohort followed suit: 'Dear Carol, we shall both die in your rosary: Elizabeth.' There were thanks to Ivo, Yazoo's Vince Clarke, who lent the band his drum machine, and Nigel Grierson, whose photo graced the cover. Robin Guthrie disliked the Banshees comparisons, so it's good he didn't know the original inspiration behind the photo, which Grierson says the band selected from his portfolio; it had been part of a college project on alternative images for Siouxsie and the Banshees' own album debut *The Scream*. 'I didn't hate it, but I didn't want it, and I wasn't asked,' Guthrie counters. 'It looked really gothy, and we had enough trouble with that as it was, with our spiky hair! We quickly got a goth audience but we never wore black nail varnish.'

Ivo disputes Guthrie's statement that the band weren't consulted; Grierson suggests that the trio's chronic shyness meant they never articulated their own views or verbally disagreed. The mercurial Guthrie takes another view: '[The band appreciated] everyone was helping us make this record, but the underlying attitude was, what do you know about art? You never went to art school. You're not an aesthete, you're from Scotland.'

But Ray Conroy confirms Grierson's summary. 'Cocteau Twins would stay at my flat. I was their translator; they were so shy and timid,' Conroy explains, adding: 'Liz had her head shaved all round the side, with a long ball on top of her head, like a pancake or a bun had landed on there. With Robin and Will, it was all about hairspray! Boots unperfumed. And the amount of speed they did! A ton of it. It was all part of the fun.'

Yet amphetamines didn't loosen anyone's tongues. Chris Carr was entrusted with the duo's first press coverage. 'Liz and Robin were so incredibly shy, I thought that if anyone was to interview them, could the journalist hear them speak? How could we overcome this? But Ivo had faith. And he knew that, musically, something was there.'

As it turned out, Guthrie did speak up in interviews, and was hardly shy; more headstrong and even comical. 'How can we be stars when we're so fat?!' he asked *NME* journalist Don Watson. Guthrie also expressed shock at *Garlands'* extended occupancy in the independent charts despite 'hardly any reaction from the press,' he claimed. John Peel's role could never be underestimated.

The interview made up in part for the fact that *NME* hadn't reviewed *Garlands*, though *Sounds* praised, 'the fluid frieze of wispy images made all the more haunting by Elizabeth's distilled vocal maturity, fluctuating from a brittle fragility to a voluble dexterity with full range and power'. Even so, Guthrie felt the trio were much better represented by the sound – and art – of the *Lullabies* EP that followed just a month after the album. For this, Grierson chose two complementary images of a dancer and a lily, illustrating an elegant beauty over any overt angst and darkness. 'At least they asked us about that one,' Guthrie concedes.

Lullabies' three tracks – 'Feathers-Oar-Blades', 'Alas Dies Laughing' and 'It's All But An Ark Lark' – were written specifically for the EP, and initially recorded at Palladium where Jon Turner's newly purchased and expensive Linn drum machine added a crispness and a drive to the Cocteaus' base sound. Overdubs were added in London, the petrol for the trip from Grangemouth paid for by shows in Bradford and Leeds along the way.

A measure of how quickly Cocteau Twins' popularity grew is that all three *Lullabies* tracks made John Peel's annual Festive Fifty listeners' poll. Added to The Birthday Party's unnerving charisma, Cocteau Twins' mercurial charm upped 4AD's profile and credibility. According to John Fryer, '*NME* would review 4AD like, "another shit record on 4AD", but after the Cocteaus, it was, "this amazing label that signed this amazing band; the future of music".'

'You knew something was happening,' Chris Carr agrees. 'And Ivo had great faith in Cocteau Twins. They weren't out there like Mass, but left of centre enough for things to develop. There was a new wave of music journalists arriving, and discovering their own music, and from here on in, 4AD started being taken more seriously. You could identify Ivo's vision, his mission statement. He knew what he wanted to sign, and it wasn't going to be the next whatever, but things that had their own individual fingerprint. And everything had to be as right as possible, down to the artwork. His vision was different. It wasn't sexy but people were getting seduced.'

This growing profile included a newly expanding audience in the States, where this strange, enigmatic parade of records housed in often oblique artwork, culminating in *Garlands* and *Lullabies*, had struck a chord.

'My friend Leo said, "If you like David Sylvian and Japan, you need to hear Cocteau Twins",' recalls Craig Roseberry, a New York-based producer, DJ and record label owner who was a deeply impressionable teenager at the time. '*Garlands* was fantastic, and I asked another friend who worked in a record store if he had more records on 4AD. He mentioned Modern English and Bauhaus. I bought "Dark Entries", and after that I needed *everything* on 4AD. I'd heard all this British music at [New York club] Danceteria, yet nothing on 4AD sounded like anything else.'

Fronted by David Sylvian, Japan's sound was austere and romantic, a world unto itself. Roseberry found 4AD similarly fascinating: 'It defied definition, but evoked the same feeling, what I'd call an "other otherness". It was an esoteric version of music like Siouxsie and the Banshees, music to the left of what was already left of centre. By then, I'd discovered lots of art, like Bauhaus and Dada. I understood from 4AD artwork, which was just as left field, that 4AD was coming from an art aesthetic more than simply music. It was informing me how to see the world.'

Roseberry began collecting every 4AD release, right back to Axis. 'It was something to obsess over, even more than with Prince or David Sylvian. It was more obscure and niche and when you found it, you cherished it because it seemed to appear out of nowhere. It had such mystique. But what struck me the most was the catalogue numbering! So I had to own it all, and file everything in sequence. 4AD was more than a record label or art house; it became a culture.'

The attention to cataloguing aided the collectability of 4AD (the prefixes extended to DAD, GAD and HAD). It was all part of the bespoke detail that set independent labels apart from the majors. It created an identifiable culture that had grown big enough to support its own distribution system and trade magazine. The Cartel was a new association of independent regional UK distributors, which was partly funding the monthly title *The Catalogue*, which was based in the Rough Trade distribution offices, with listings and features covering the ever-expanding alternative movement of labels and artists.

The Catalogue's Australian-born founding editor Brenda Kelly had first discovered 4AD while working at Melbourne's alternative radio station 3RRR. 'The Birthday Party was a key and radical Melbourne band, and any label that signed them had to be interesting, but what first attracted me to 4AD was Cocteau Twins,' she says. 'All of the four big UK independents – 4AD, Rough Trade, Factory and Mute – had maverick qualities, but, more so even than Factory, 4AD was special because it created an atmosphere around beauty. It was art for art's sake. The artwork gave 4AD the most clearly articulated and uncompromising identity, which was crucial to the independent movement at that time – things were more complex and subtle than "do it yourself".

'People forget that art is a part of youth culture rather than just a succession of trends or an attitude, and such a consciously arty label like 4AD meant the independent scene was enriched and broadened. It created a space for bands and labels to build a roster and create a strong identity and base for their bands. Some independent labels, particularly 4AD, didn't talk much about the politics of independence, but Ivo understood and supported the space that independent distribution created.'

If enough people responded with the same belief and support as Kelly and Roseberry, 4AD had a fighting chance of creating something bigger than an esoteric cult. If there could be songs that US or UK mainstream radio responded to, there might even be hits, to match Depeche Mode at Mute or New Order at Factory. Modern English were 4AD's best hope, and in the major label tradition, a second single was plucked off *After The Snow* after the album had been released.

'I Melt With You' had a simple structure, breezy timbre and matching chorus, which *Sounds* writer Johnny Waller described as, 'a dreamy, creamy celebration of love and lust'. Yet the single barely broke the indie top 20. The video showed 4AD's inexperience in catering to a broader demographic: 'It was one of the most awful we ever did,' Ivo recalls. 'It was filmed in a dingy basement with two hired dancers, and Robbie bleeding from a scab after a cat had scratched his face.'

If Modern English's new identity had lost John Peel's patronage, The Happy Family never had the DJ on side to begin with. This was despite the fact that Peel had always supported Josef K, and line-up changes increased the number of former Josef K personnel; though Malcolm Ross and Ian Stoddart had left (the former, to join Orange Juice), their respective replacements were Josef K roadie Paul Mason and drummer Ronnie Torrence. New keyboardist Neil Martin made five).

Nick Currie recalls that The Happy Family had effectively ambushed Peel at the BBC Radio 1 offices, to hand over the debut album, *The Man On Your Street*. 'I saw [Altered Images singer] Claire Grogan in the lobby, who Peel was famously besotted by, and when John emerged, my first words where, "Oh, we just saw Miss G", with a saucy grin on my face. He looked really embarrassed, as if he'd been consorting with her. It was embarrassingly awkward. Peel never did give us a session.' Despite his very public profile, Peel was as shy as Ivo (whose approach in the past had been to send the Cocteaus-besotted DJ his own acetate of *Garlands*, letting music alone do the talking).

The album didn't find much press favour either. The album's brittle, wordy atmosphere was always going to be divisive: Don Watson at *NME* – reviewing it two months after release – seemed divided himself, referring to the album's 'flat sound that borders on dullness', but also saying, 'It barbs your brain with a bristle of tiny hooks.' Currie says Josef K supporter Dave McCullough at *Sounds* was more certain: 'He gave it a bit of a trashing, saying it was too verbose, and the time wasn't right for the return of the concept album.'

Indeed, *The Man On Your Street* was the least popular album in 4AD's early years, selling just 2,500 copies. Currie thinks Ivo wasn't that keen on the record himself: 'The song he liked the most of ours was "Innermost Thoughts", which to me was the musical equivalent of 23 Envelope sleeves, a delicate object, with a fully-flanged bass line that was the hallmark of miserablist bands at the time. But the album had moved away from that style. I'd got sick of all the long raincoats, the Penguin Modern Classics book poking out of the pocket top, the Joy Division scene. [*NME*'s] Paul Morley was *the* critic of the time, and he was promoting this new, shiny, happy pop music [meaning the likes of ABC, and also Orange Juice] after turning his back on miserablist Scottish pop. The Happy Family was going with that tide, moving away from 4AD's aesthetic.'

Currie had also declined Vaughan Oliver's input, going for his own bizarre mish-mash, a Sixties retro layout that included the subtitle *Songs From The Career Of Dictator Hall* and an out-of-place primitive folk art drawing to the side of a colour photograph of the earth. 'I stubbornly wanted to do the cover myself,' he admits. 'The photo of the globe cost Ivo a lot more than Vaughan!' It was more expensive, actually, than the album's recording budget, which illustrated 4AD's commitment to packaging.

Currie thinks *The Man On Your Street* would have fared better if Oliver had taken over, giving it an identifiable 4AD cachet: 'We were an anomaly on 4AD. I was deliberately trying to undermine their image, to show 4AD could go to other places. I think Ivo was flummoxed by our brash, alienating irony and a narrative music hall sensibility that was at odds with him, and we didn't have that sense of beauty that he liked. It also had this Puckish, communist streak, and I don't think we saw eye to eye politically. But I'm very grateful to Ivo. It was a terrific adventure.'

Currie also saw Ivo's patronage and 4AD's early achievements as part of a watershed era for British music. 'It was the first generation of record label bosses who were creative themselves, and trying to shape a sensibility. Though in the end, I found it easier dealing with old-fashioned record labels that were just a marketing department and a bank!'

As Momus, Currie thrived, but The Happy Family didn't. 'Ivo wasn't interested in another album, nothing was happening in Scotland, and I felt guilty about being the band's dictator, even though the others wouldn't write their own parts. The more we rehearsed, the worse we sounded, so I returned to university before moving to London.'

If Ivo's intuition had failed him on this occasion, his next discovery was another maverick mould-breaker in the Happy Family tradition, albeit in a radically different form. Coming at the end of the year, it finally put paid to the idea that 4AD was a repository of Stygian gloom – even if the title of Colourbox's debut single was 'Breakdown'.

From his home in the Regency seaside town of Brighton on England's south coast, Martyn Young seems to have as many reasons

---

* In 1983, Currie signed to London independent Cherry Red's artful imprint él and released his first recording, *The Beast With Three Backs* EP (catalogue number EL5T), under the name Momus. Currie's new baroque folk sound felt more like 4AD than *The Man On Your Street*. Currie sent Ivo an advance copy of the EP. Inside was a sheet of paper with a limerick that gently mocked 4AD, as well as the label's system of catalogue numbering that has assisted in its collectability: '*There was a songwriter so glad to be given two sides of a CAD/ That his blatant good humour carried dangerous rumours/ That life was more funny than BAD/ But when he composed EL5T consistent in perversity/ He slowed and depressed it, dear Ivo you've guessed it–/ He out 4AD'd 4AD!*' Sadly, it never reached Ivo, or he never realised the sheet was inside before selling it. The EP, with sheet of paper still inside, was eventually bought in a second-hand store and its purchaser revealed the limerick in an online blog.

as Robin Guthrie to consider his past in a someone regretful light. The fact is he is the driving force behind the only act in UK chart history never to have attempted a follow-up to a national number 1 single. In fact, Young and his younger brother Steven haven't released one piece of original music since Colourbox's spin-off project M/A/R/R/S scaled the charts with 'Pump Up The Volume'.

Not that Young cares: he admits that he never truly wanted to make music to begin with, preferring the technical aspects of music, the manuals and the mixing desk; a boffin at heart rather than a musician, who has spent his ensuing years computer programming and studying music theory. In any case, he now has twins (two years old at the time of writing), and though his first course of anti-depressants (he and Ivo have exchanged emails about brands and effects) have lifted him, he doesn't imagine he will make any more music. Given its association with depression, anger issues, creative blocks, writs and extreme food diets, why would anyone choose to return?

Young was born Martyn Biggs, which, he says, 'sounded like "farting pigs", so I used my mother's maiden name of Young'. Home life was dysfunctional; his father had been sent to prison before Martyn was a teenager. At school in Colchester in the East Anglia region, he was two years above his brother Steven and Ray Conroy (whose brother, Modern English bassist Mick, was a year below them). Young's musical path is familiar: a Bowie obsession led to a wider appreciation of art and progressive rock before punk's conversion. 'It immediately made me want to play guitar,' he says.

Young says his first band, The Odour 7, was only a half-hearted teenage exercise, but the following Bowie/Devo-influenced Baby Patrol released a single, 'Fun Fusion' on Secret Records. 'We were particularly crap and I destroyed every copy of the single I could find. I'm singing and the lyrics are so embarrassing. But I was still young.'

After dyeing his hair following Bowie's blonde/orange rinse, Young was labelled a 'pouf' by his father and told he couldn't sleep in the same room as his brother. 'So I started squatting with Modern English in London.' In this new world, Young borrowed a synthesiser and drum machine and spent a year unlocking their secrets.

His next move was a band with Steven (known as Scab because of the scabs on his knuckles that he kept picking, Ivo explains) and Baby Patrol's Ian Robbins; *Colourbox* was the title of an animated film from 1937. Mutual friends introduced female vocalist Debian Curry and the quartet recorded a demo that included 'Breakdown' and 'Tarantula'. As Ivo recalls, Ray Conroy – acting as the band's manager – came to Hogarth Road in 1980 to give the more dance-conscious Peter Kent the Colourbox demo, 'because why would 4AD put out a dance record? I guess Peter wasn't around, so Ray played me the tape. I liked "Breakdown" but I loved "Tarantula". It's such a sad song.'

Musically, 'Tarantula' resembled the moody cousin of Yazoo's synth-pop ballad 'Only You', but unlike Yazoo singer Alf Moyet, Debian Curry's cool delivery reinforced the withdrawn mood at the song's core: '*I'm living but I'm feeling numb, you can see it in my stare/ I wear a mask so falsely now, and I don't know who I am/ This voice that wells inside of me, eroding me away ...*'

'I've only recently come to understand that I've always suffered from depression,' Young says. 'I used to think my strange mood swings were caused by something like food, so I'd try and eat raw salad for months. But anti-depressants mean I'm no longer wallowing in misery and pent-up negativity.'

Ivo and Martyn Young's bond wasn't just musical, but personal, united by their shyness and sadness. 'Ivo had a reputation for being dour, but he wasn't with us,' Young recalls.

Ivo: 'I really liked Martyn. He looked like he was chewing gum and smiling at you at the same time, which was charming. Scab was younger and quieter, and the best drum programmer I'd ever met.'

Steve Young was also a good pianist and arranger, with Ian Robbins making a trio of strong contributors to the Colourbox sound. They were also interested in the new electro-funk sound that had succeeded disco as the prevailing club soundtrack in America's clubs and street scenes, led by Mantronix and Afrika Bambaataa, which filtered into 'Breakdown', making the A-side of Colourbox's debut single a brighter and more pulsing affair than its flipside 'Tarantula'.

The single stood at odds with 4AD's last release of the year, a compilation title released by Warners' Greek office that was named *Dark Paths*, which undermined the fact that Ivo had begun to shed the gothic image. Only seven acts were selected: Bauhaus, Rema-Rema, Modern English, Mass, Colin Newman, Dance Chapter and the David J/René Halkett collaboration. In fact, over three years, 4AD had released more than fifty records by thirty acts; a pattern that Ivo recognised was unsustainable in the long run.

'It took a few years for me to find my focus, and my confidence, and to get a feel for what the label might become,' he recalls. 'And to be absolutely happy to not have many releases. The less, the better, I thought! I was constantly counting our artists, and if we had more than six, I'd get nervous. But that hadn't been possible in the first few years. We had no long-term contracts, no real careers. Besides Modern English, everyone was contracted record by record.'

The haphazard nature of 4AD's development – the one-offs, the artful projects, the short shelf life of bands that promised much more, and both Bauhaus' defection and Modern English's slow progress – confirmed that Ivo really had no game plan to speak of. Things could either lead nowhere in particular or could build to something tangibly greater than the sum of its parts. In any case, Ivo had imagined 4AD would only be an interlude in his life, though it wasn't true, as an offhand comment of Ivo's had claimed, that the four in 4AD stood for the number of years he anticipated it would last.

But while it did last, Ivo could only follow an intuitive, personal path, one that paid no notice to the social and political traits of the staff at the *NME* who thought large swathes of post-punk had reneged on punk's revolution. Sex Pistols manager Malcolm McLaren – who had continued to ruffle feathers with his new puppets of outrage, Bow Wow Wow – mocked what he saw as a return to, in the words of writer Simon Reynolds, 'student reverence and cerebral sexlessness'.

But, in light of music's powerful effect beyond polemic, there was another way to view 4AD's anti-manifesto. In January 2013, for a profile of Bosnian singer Amira Medunjanin in *The Observer* newspaper, journalist Ed Vulliamy also interviewed a law professor,

Zdravko Grebo, who had begun an underground radio station, Radio Zid, during the Serbian siege of Bosnia's capital Sarajevo during the Nineties. 'The point was to get on air but resist broadcasting militaristic songs,' explained Grebo. 'Our message was: remember who you are – urban people, workers, cultured people. We thought the situation called for Pink Floyd, Hendrix and good country music, rather than militaristic marches.'

Nick Currie, one of 4AD's most articulate observers, could also see what 4AD had achieved, and what might come:

I saw 4AD as a coffee table label, with a mild bourgeois aesthetic worldview, which appealed to other tender-minded people. Ivo seemed attracted to suburban places to live in or an office slightly out of the centre of town, with these semi-detached English houses, but then you'd notice some of those very houses had an Arts and Crafts sensibility, with stained glass windows, which opened my eyes to the possibilities of being an aesthete, and importing those sensibilities into people's lives. Indie labels were not so well known or established at that time, yet labels like 4AD and Factory were already so refined, in a new hyperglossy manner, with top-flight art direction. It was at the peak of postmodernism, and it felt distinct from what had come before. In my mind, Ivo and Vaughan were very much going to define the decade.

6 1983

THE FAMILY THAT PLAYS TOGETHER
(bad301-mad315)

The conversion of a large dry cleaning and laundry service gave the Beggars Banquet and 4AD labels the chance to leave the Hogarth Road shop for a standalone office. Alma Road was a street of Victorian houses in London's south-western borough of Wandsworth, an anonymous suburb six miles from central London's entertainment hub where every major record label occupied office blocks or stately mansions. The Slug and Lettuce pub was conveniently located on the opposite corner of the road from their building, at number 17–19.

Alma Road also symbolised the difference between 4AD and its independent label peers. Mute was based over in the west London enclave of Westbourne Grove, near to Rough Trade's shop and label, deep in the heart of Notting Hill, the heartland of West Indian immigration, reggae, Rock Against Racism, carnivals, riots and streets of squats, a thriving low-rent bohemia that had made the bumpy transition from the hippies to the punks. Wandsworth had its less salubrious quarters but carnivals and riots were in short supply.

With room to breathe, and enough funds, Ivo also took on his first employee: Vaughan Oliver, who had previously been designing in a freelance capacity. Ivo knew design and packaging was part of 4AD's identity, a visual language that gave 4AD an extra dimension of

113

distinction. He could also see that many of 4AD's artists were producing sub-standard images when left to their own devices.

It was a mutual admiration society between the two figures; strongly opinionated, stubborn and deeply involved with their particular line of work. 'Ivo had this whole world of musical knowledge that enthralled me, and I looked up to him, and adored him, from the start,' Oliver recalls. 'And I think he had a secret admiration for me, educating him visually.'

Ivo: 'Vaughan singlehandedly opened my eyes to the world of design. In his portfolio, he had samples of Thorn EMI light bulb sleeves. It hadn't occurred to me that behind every object, utensil or drainpipe was a designer and I never saw the world in the same way again. Maybe I didn't show it at the time, caught up in the sheer business and joy of watching this thing called 4AD blossom, but it was a privilege that I still cherish, sitting four feet away from this outpouring of creativity. Nigel [Grierson] was around a lot too and Vaughan and Nigel at full throttle was an experience to remember.'

The friendship was firmly based around work: 'We didn't talk about anything but music, and we didn't have a drink together – Ivo didn't go to pubs,' Oliver says. 'Whereas one reason I took the job was the pub over the road!'

As Ivo discovered, Oliver was not one to dirty his hands with anything but ink. 'I seriously expected Vaughan, like any other employee when they later joined, to help unpack the van when it arrived with records. But you'd always have to track him down. I saw very early on, for example, that he'd take two weeks to design, by hand, each individual letter for the Xmal Deutschland logo. Design was a full-time job for Vaughan.'

Oliver's first task as staff employee was The Birthday Party's new four-track EP, *The Bad Seed*. The band had handled its own artwork to date, with mixed results, and Oliver was forced to work with supplied ideas: the band's four faces and realistic illustrations of their core subjects, a heart wrapped in barbed wire, a cross and flames. The contents were much more inspiring, 'Deep In The Woods' tapping a newly smouldering vigour (perhaps because, for the first time,

Rowland S. Howard didn't write anything on a Birthday Party record), though Cave's opening gambit – '*Hands up who wants to die!*' – on the thrilling 'Sonny's Burning' was as much a self-parody as anything he could accuse Peter Murphy of.

The Bad Seed had been recorded in West Berlin after the quartet had decamped there two months after *Junkyard*'s unanimously strong reviews. Though Ivo considers the EP the band's 'crowning glory', the cost of maintaining The Birthday Party overseas was prohibitive. 'Ivo was disappointed but pragmatic about not being in a position to provide financial support,' recalls Mick Harvey. 'That's when we switched over to Mute. They'd had worldwide hits with Depeche Mode and Yazoo and were pretty cashed up.'

Chris Carr: 'I think Ivo was miffed, but he realised there was nothing he could do, given the financial structure that Beggars could then cope with.'*

As one band departed 4AD for Germany, taking their testosterone-fuelled fantasies with them, so a band departed Germany for 4AD, bringing a jolt of oestrogen, but with as much energy and discipline. If anyone thought Ivo's penchant for dark paths had diminished, Xmal Deutschland would make them think again.

Living again in her native Hamburg after several years in New York, Xmal's founding member and singer Anja Huwe has abandoned music for painting, but she describes herself as a synesthete (a stimulus in one sensory mode involuntarily elicits a sensation in another) who paints what she hears. 'I had a wonderful time playing music, and achieved everything I wanted,' she says. 'But colour is my ultimate music.' It's why she turned down the chance to go solo when Xmal

---

* The Birthday Party turned out to only have one more EP left in them, the four-track *Mutiny*, which, in 1989, Mute allowed 4AD to add to the CD reissue of *The Bad Seed*, ensuring that every Birthday Party release did end up on 4AD. *Mutiny* rang the changes for The Birthday Party as Rowland S. Howard didn't turn up for sessions and Einstürzende Neubauten's Blixa Bargeld stepped in on guitar, lending a more controlled, less jagged aura to the sound. Harvey confirms that communication between Cave and Howard had broken down, and the band had 'no new direction'. Even before *Mutiny* had been released, Harvey had proposed the band split up; Cave and Howard instantly agreed, paving the path to the formation of Cave's solo career with his Bad Seeds backing band, which changed over the years but started off with Bargeld, Harvey and Barry Adamson.

Deutschland finally split in 1990. 'Music was art to me; I didn't want to be a pop star,' Huwe says. 'I knew the price would have been me. It's why 4AD was perfect at the time. I saw it as a platform or a nest. People there understood what we did.'

Huwe was destined to be a model, but she turned down an offer to move to Paris when she was seventeen after visiting London in 1977 and seeing The Clash and the all-female Slits at the London Lyceum. 'The bands were our age, whereas even Kraftwerk felt like old guys to us,' she recalls. 'I also saw Killing Joke and Basement 5 on that trip, bands that had this fantastic mix of punk, ska and reggae. I started buying this music, cut my hair very short, and started seeing every band I could in Hamburg.'

The original Xmal Deutschland line-up had joined forces in 1980. 'We weren't in either punk or avant-garde camps, and we had a keyboard. No one could label us,' says Huwe. That didn't stop the German press from trying: 'We were repeatedly told we sounded more British than German. A friend recommended we move to London, which wasn't meant in a nice way. But we thought, why not?' Once there, their black garb, nail varnish and song titles such as 'Incubus Succubus' (the second of two singles that had been released in Germany) had Xmal tagged as goth. 'That drove us nuts. The Sisters of Mercy, The Mission – that all came later.'

A foothold in London was established after sending 4AD a rehearsal tape. 'It was the label we wanted, because of Bauhaus and The Birthday Party,' says Huwe. 'Our English wasn't that good, and we were aliens really. But Ivo respected what we did.'

Ivo says he had instantly enjoyed what he heard: 'They were boiling over with energy, and Manuela Rickers was an incredible, choppy rhythm guitarist. I flew to Hamburg and agreed to an album.'

Xmal Deutschland became 4AD's first European act, but didn't record anything until their line-up settled on Huwe, Rickers, Scots-born keyboardist Fiona Sangster, new drummer Manuela Zwingmann and the first male Xmal member, bassist Wolfgang Ellerbrock. The German contingent found London a marked contrast to Hamburg, where people had 'health insurance, affordable apartments and heating', says Huwe. 'Many British bands we met were very poor, and desperate for success. I spent a summer with Ian Astbury [frontman of Beggars Banquet's similarly goth-branded Southern Death Cult), spending his advance. He'd say, I will be big one day, a pop star, and he did everything he could to get there. That wasn't our goal.'

That was clear from Huwe's decision to sing almost entirely in German, which she saw as a much harsher language than English and which suited the band's pummelling mantras and Huwe's chanting style. 'I was like Liz Fraser,' she recalls. 'British audiences couldn't understand us! But they got the spirit of it. Ivo sometimes asked what I sang about. Oh, this and that, I'd reply! Relationships, loneliness, emptiness ... what young people sing about. But I saw my voice as an instrument and myself as a performer, not a songwriter. The performance and the sound was the most important.'

Xmal Deutschland's debut album *Fetisch* – 'a word in both German and English, and a word of the time,' says Huwe – was a faster and harsher take on the cold, black steel of Siouxsie and the Banshees, Joy Division, Mass and In Camera. John Fryer engineered the session at Blackwing, where Ivo was again co-producer with the band, but the album could have sounded less dense and flat. 'I did them a disservice by producing,' Ivo reckons. 'I don't take all the blame, as John wasn't the best at that time at micing up a drumkit, which then hinders positioning the guitars around it.'

On stage, Xmal was freer to pull out the stops. The memory of the band's debut UK show, opening for Cocteau Twins at The Venue, is etched in Ivo's memory: 'I'd never seen an audience, clustered around the bar, run so fast to the front of the stage when Xmal plugged in. You could see the audience think, who *are* these women? They looked really striking.'

Both bands set off on tour, sharing a base in London. 'Because of their Scottish accents,' says Huwe, 'only Fiona could understand a word they said – and the other way around too!' Xmal later supported Modern English. At that time, Huwe says, '4AD felt like a family'.

Oliver expanded the 4AD family by briefly dating Xmal drummer Manuela Zwingmann, who Ivo says he alienated by hiring a Linn drum machine for his lengthy remix of *Fetisch*'s opening track 'Qual'. 'What Manuela played on *Fetisch* was fantastic, but she struggled to get good takes, and the drum sound was the weakest part,' he feels. Ivo's remix remains his favourite Xmal recording, though at the Venue show, Ivo recalls John Peel DJing between sets: 'After he played the "Qual" remix, he said, "That's another interminably long twelve-inch single". And he was right.'

The *Qual* EP was still fronted by the original album version, but longer remixes were to become a permanent fixture of singles and EPs, as the newly expanding synth-pop, New Romantic and electro sounds accentuated the dance element across both mainstream and alternative scenes, leading to an increase in club audiences and more specialist radio stations. Post-punk's monochrome palate was slowly receding. Even a resolute rock band such as Xmal got the twelve-inch remix treatment. The apotheosis of the medium was New Order's single 'Blue Monday', released in March, which was to become the biggest selling twelve-inch single of all time; it had only been just under three years since Ian Curtis died, but Joy Division felt like gods from a past age.

At least the twelve-inch format gave Vaughan Oliver the opportunity for a larger canvas for singles. Ivo encouraged every 4AD signing to use the services of 23 Envelope, as it made both artistic and financial sense. The finished image might result from Oliver's interpretation of a demo or a finished track – for example, his book of medical photographs for 'Qual'. However, Nigel Grierson was responsible for the layout of Cocteau Twins' new single 'Peppermint Pig', as well as the photo of a woman (shot from behind, submerged in water) in an outdoor Swiss spa bath. 'That was more for the texture of the hair and the soft misty feeling,' Grierson explains. 'I can't recall why the band chose it. Maybe they didn't have much input.'

Robin Guthrie approved of the image for the single, but not the music. The Cocteaus had accepted Ivo's suggestion of taking on, in Guthrie's words, 'a pop producer'. Alan Rankine of The Associates was dispatched to Blackwing. 'That was a huge mistake,' says Guthrie. 'Alan just sat at the back and read magazines. I did all the work.' Guthrie also claims that Ivo suggested the band 'write something upbeat for a single'. According to Guthrie, 'We had a tour coming up supporting Orchestral Manoeuvres in the Dark and we needed a record out. "Peppermint Pig" is absolutely terrible, but we didn't have the strength of character to wait for the right song to come along. It was an early indication of the power of the music industry, and of too many cooks.'

Contrary to Guthrie's view, Ivo recalls he was very happy with the single, though says it does sound too much like The Associates. 'But if I was interested in a "pop" producer, I'd have chosen someone like Mike Hedges [who had produced The Associates' 1982 masterpiece *Sulk*]. I know Robin wasn't happy with the single but it's silly to suggest that I was trying to commercialise their music. It's not my interest or one of my strong points. But accepting a producer actually did Robin a favour. By imposing myself on *Garlands* and *Lullabies* and then foisting Alan Rankine on them, he was so pissed off that he took control from then on.'

'Peppermint Pig' was only kept off the top of the independent singles chart by 'Blue Monday'. But it's easily Cocteau Twins' least memorable single for a good reason: none of its assets – the melody, the production, the cover – are special. That all was not right in the band's camp was underlined by the departure of Will Heggie. The OMD tour had been fifty-two dates long, a huge number for an inexperienced band such as Cocteau Twins, and the bassist left the band as the band itself left the tour two shows before the end. Guthrie says it was Heggie's decision: 'Maybe he had more integrity than me. He didn't want to tour that much, or to move away from Scotland as we had planned.'

Ivo also suggests that Elizabeth Fraser felt Heggie had come between her and Guthrie, while Guthrie wonders if Heggie was himself keen on Fraser. Ivo only knows for sure that it was Guthrie and Fraser's choice, and that he was asked to tell Heggie. 'They all returned to London, but only Robin and Elizabeth stayed with me. I remember Liz doing some ironing in the living room when they said they no longer wanted Will involved. The next day, he and I met at Alma Road.'

'I didn't know that,' says Guthrie. 'To my knowledge, Will said he was going home – and I'd suddenly lost my best mate, so what the fuck's happened there? But every cloud has a silver lining, because that's when Cocteau Twins started to really happen for me.'

By bringing the core down to two members, Guthrie and Fraser closed ranks to create a strong unity and, it seems, more confidence. That touring had meant a dearth of new material only inspired the pair. As Guthrie recalls, 'We were in a chip shop, unable to eat because of the speed we'd taken, and Liz said, "Let's make the next album, just the two of us, get money off 4AD and say we have lots of songs, and then produce it yourself." We wrote it all in the studio, and everything just fell into place. It felt like the chains had been taken off.'

It was still a big step to allow Guthrie to take charge, so Ivo sent John Fryer up to Palladium to assist. 'John and Jon [Turner] were happy to play pool and let Robin get on with it,' says Ivo. 'This is where his courage to do these huge reverbs first appeared.'

'I'd leave Robin on his own, and if he needed help, obviously I was there,' Turner recalls. 'Liz was another story. She had to be in the right mood to sing, so it was better if I walked out. I'm amazed how it all came together. I was used to people knowing exactly what they were doing, and on what budget, but I learnt from the Cocteaus that it doesn't matter how you get there, the end result is what counts, and they got great results. But it seemed a stressful way to work if you were in a relationship.'

Ivo also felt that Colourbox needed objective input, enlisting Mick Glossop (whose post-punk CV included PiL) for a re-recording of both 'Breakdown' and 'Tarantula': 'The band wanted another go, and we thought it was worth using a successful producer,' Ivo explains. If this was a step up, it was also a worrying step; didn't Colourbox have new songs they wanted to record?

Martyn Young was more interested in perfecting the editing tricks he'd heard from the pirate radio tapes that Ray Conroy and Ivo had started to bring back from trips to New York. 'These incredible mixes, which would sound nothing like the twelve-inch single,' says Ivo. 'Nowadays, you press a button and it's done for you, but back then, you'd bounce down fifteen snare hits and edit them together to get a repeat sound. Mick [Glossop] and John Fryer would do the actual cuts amazingly fast, with Martyn to guide them, but he became an incredible editor.'

The new 'Breakdown' ('Tarantula' was only remixed in the end) wasn't radically different, just sharper and fuller. The single even got interest from the States. Before the licence deal with major label A&M, Ivo had been exporting every 4AD record, in limited numbers. This helped financially but also built an aura of enigma for this UK imprint with the atmospheric underground sound and artfully enigmatic sleeves that rarely featured the artists. Who were these bands? What was their story?

Ivo's introduction to major label culture had not been auspicious. A&M in America was already licensing Bauhaus from Beggars Banquet, so Ivo had accompanied Martin Mills to a meeting. 'Martin introduced me as 4AD, Bauhaus' original label, and the A&M guy said, "Listen to the radio, get an idea of what works here or doesn't." It turns out he thought I was Kevin Haskins. I gave him copies of "Breakdown" and by the time I'd got to the airport, Martin had paged me to say A&M told him they *had* to license "Breakdown". Yet they never again licensed anything by Colourbox.'

A&M would have clocked a cool-Britannia take on American influences – a winning combination. But neither A&M nor 4AD had any success with 'Breakdown', though the twelve-inch mixes went down well in the clubs, where the edits came into their own. After a period that might be kindly referred to as 'research', Gary Asquith and Danny Briottet were to begin their own dance project, mixing hip-hop, sampling and electro as Renegade Soundwave, with Mick Allen and Mark Cox closing ranks as a duo to become The Wolfgang Press, named after German actor Wolfgang Preiss. 'We added "The" to the front, which conjured up an image, something massive, a big machine,' says Allen. 'I thought it was funny.'

Ivo had agreed to go halves on funding new Allen/Cox demos, and on the evidence of two songs, 'Prostitute' and 'Complete And Utter', asked for more. It was partly an altruistic act, and one of faith: 'I liked

Mick and Mark so much, I wanted to support them,' Ivo says. 'They were the only people ever on 4AD I worked with that wasn't just based on enjoying their music.'

Mark Cox: 'I never asked Ivo how many records Mass had sold. He was slightly frustrated, almost dismayed, that we had no ambition and were still asserting our right to be free. Compare that to Modern English – they had a dream that Ivo could relate to, but he wasn't sure what to do with us. We weren't interested in playing live, and we lived in short-life housing with no phone, so things could take days or weeks to happen.'

Mick Allen: 'Rightly or wrongly, we were left to our own devices because Ivo had confidence in us. I wanted to make music that you hadn't heard before, although drawing from the past. I was aware of PiL, the bass and the drums and the simplicity and the space, and I think we achieved that.'

The PiL comparison was to dog them: *NME* claimed The Wolfgang Press's debut album *The Burden Of Mules* could be marketed as a collection of PiL studio out-takes. But freed from accommodating a guitarist at the start, Allen and Cox had begun to explore a wider remit, sometimes gravitating towards a mutant funk that unfolded through a shifting landscape, as though Mass had opened the doors and let in some light and air. But the mood was still oppressive, such as the opening and typically provocative 'Prostitute' (*'Prostitute/ Spice of life'*) with Allen's slightly creepy delivery, while the title track – too closely – tracked the 'death disco' aura of PiL. 'Complete And Utter' wore more urban-tribal colours but 'Slow As A Child' was six minutes of unsettling and shifting ambience, and 'Journalists' (a soft target, though Allen says his lyric was aimed at anyone in his path) and the ten-minute finale 'On The Hill' were as uncomfortably intense as the Mass album.

Ivo still wasn't won over. 'It's a very difficult record and I didn't like it deeply at all. Like Mark said about *Labour Of Love*, it had great ideas, badly executed.'

Cox: 'We were still determined not to be produced, or to be open to guidance in case it meant compromise. But we still didn't know how to achieve our aims.' Even so, the duo had agreed with Ivo's suggestion to add some guitar, and to use In Camera's Andrew Gray – they had all met when Mass and In Camera had shared bills in London and Manchester – whose oblique approach fitted their own better than Marco Pirroni or Gary Asquith's heavier style. Dif Juz drummer Richie Thomas and In Camera's David Scinto (on drums, not vocals) also chipped in.

Gray also signed up for a handful of Wolfgang Press shows, supporting Xmal Deutschland. Allen says it was a frustrating experience: 'We were not easy listening. It affirmed what we were doing was either bad or unheard.' Gray soon stepped down. 'The crowds wanted a particular industrial punk sound, and I didn't. I'd become more interested in photography at that point.'

Ivo: 'My take on Mass, *The Burden Of Mules* and the first live experience of The Wolfgang Press is that people were scared away from them for life. It was impenetrable to some, a different type of music.'

While the nocturnal sounding The Wolfgang Press had been recording an album during the cheaper night shift at west London's Alvic Studios, Modern English had been taking the daylight shift for parts of *After The Snow*'s pop levity. The band hadn't had much success in Britain but the album had been licensed to America by Warners subsidiary Sire. Seymour Stein, the label's savvy and experienced MD, claims to have been the first to re-appropriate the cinematic term 'New Wave' for the new breed of bands after he'd felt that the punk rock tag was putting people off before they'd even heard the music. He had signed the Ramones, Talking Heads and The Pretenders, and after snapping up an unknown local singer called Madonna, he had turned his attentions back to the UK and added Modern English to his stable of UK licensees (The Undertones, Depeche Mode, Echo & The Bunnymen), to be joined by The Smiths.

Stein was especially keen on Modern English's 'I Melt With You'. 'I knew within the first eight bars that it was a smash, it was so infectious and strong,' he recalls. 'I also knew I had to grab the band there and then, without hearing any other songs, or someone else would take them. Other things Ivo signed were too experimental for me, though you could always expect the unexpected from 4AD.'

Ivo's A&R ears weren't attuned to unearthing or spotting hits, though his brother Perry Watts-Russell – now working as the manager of the fast-rising LA band Berlin – says he'd instantly recognised the value of 'I Melt With You.' 'It struck me as really catchy and a definite hit, which didn't sound much like 4AD but could take 4AD into a different space.'

Modern English had played just a handful of US dates in 1981, and when *After The Snow* was initially on import, Sire had licensed 'I Melt With You' at the end of 1982, becoming the first 4AD track to be licensed in America. Sire followed it by licensing the album in early 1983 when the band returned for an east coast tour. But the breakthrough turned out not to be via a show, or even radio, but a film soundtrack. Stein secured 'I Melt With You' a spot in what became that spring's rom-com film smash *Valley Girl*, and MTV began rotating the video despite its alarming absence of merit. American audiences simply saw Modern English on a par with Duran Duran, without any of the post-punk image baggage that might have been hindering them in the UK. 'It all went haywire from there, in a Beatles and Stones way, with all the trappings that went with it,' says Robbie Grey. 'We played Spring Break in Florida to thousands of kids going bananas.'

Ivo: 'I had the bizarre experience of seeing Modern English one afternoon, with screaming girls throwing cuddly toys at them. The band's name moved to the top of the film poster when "I Melt With You" kept selling.'

The single reached 78 in the national US charts in 1983, with *After The Snow* making number 70 and also selling half a million. But the breakthrough could, and should, have been even greater. 'Warners didn't open their cheque book to help move things to the next level,' says Ivo, 'such as the top 40. "I Melt With You" is still one of the most played songs ever on American radio.'

For Modern English, the joy of popularity was tempered by the reality of where they'd landed. 'We played San Diego baseball stadium to 60,000 people, with Tom Petty top of the bill,' recalls Mick Conroy. 'The change was immense and the pressure got insane. Ivo hooked us up with an American manager, Will Botwin, who gave us practice amps, and said to start writing the next album, between gigs. It was so different to 4AD's approach.'

That didn't stop 4AD from joining in marketing the band, with a view to breaking them further. As Sire did in America, 4AD released 'Someone's Calling' in the UK, its first attempt to take a single from a preceding album – though the twelve-inch version had a new, booming remix by Harvey Goldberg and Madonna associate Mark Kamins – and a similarly amped 'Life In The Gladhouse' remix by Goldberg and Ivo with additional edits from Martyn Young. The latter was a reasonable success in American clubs but 'Someone's Calling' reached a miserable 43 on the UK indie chart, barely higher than 'Swans On Glass' three years earlier.

One thing Modern English did achieve was a knock-on shift in profile for 4AD. Even legendary Asylum and Geffen label head David Geffen, who had worked with several of Ivo's American west coast icons, 'was sniffing around, wondering what the story was,' says Mick Conroy. The story for Modern English turned out to be a typical one, of success breeding pressure. Tour manager Ray Conroy was the first to bail. 'I'm very cynical about arrogant singers – once they start believing it all, it's not worth the bother,' he explains. 'Nick Cave, for example, I found full of shit. And Robbie turned into an asshole. We had a flaming row in New York, and when we got home from America, they went off on their merry way.'

Robbie Grey: 'We were pushed too hard. I especially didn't like soundchecks, standing around for hours, only to go on stage and the sound would be all different anyway. I was probably snappy and distant, but I was in my own cocoon, protecting myself.'

Ray Conroy was now tour-managing any 4AD band that required help, such as The Wolfgang Press, Xmal Deutschland and Dif Juz, but he singles out Cocteau Twins as the stand-out live act of the time, even without Will Heggie. 'Robin had just one guitar pedal and a drum box, but as they got more popular, he got the biggest FX rack ever! It was pretty raging stuff, with Liz screaming her head off. Robin loved noise and our mission was to make them the loudest band in the world.'

The personnel of Modern English and Cocteau Twins became entwined in a project of Ivo's instigation. He had flown over to see Modern English play New York's The Ritz in December 1982, where the band's encore conjoined two tracks, the 'Gathering Dust' single and *Mesh & Lace* cut 'Sixteen Days'. Ivo liked the version enough to ask the band to re-record it in that segued form, but they turned it down: 'We were more interested in recording our new material,' says Mick Conroy.

Trusting in his own judgement, and in John Fryer to press the right buttons, Ivo decided to create his own version. He asked Elizabeth Fraser to sing 'Sixteen Days/Gathering Dust' accompanied by Cocteaus' pal Graham Sharp, who had sung the high, delicate vocals on the band's second Peel session and was now fronting his own band, Cindytalk (Sharp now likes to go by the first name of Cindy). Martyn Young and Modern English duo Mick Conroy and Gary McDowell were on hand to create the backing track. 'Ivo was so much into music and creativity that it seemed a natural step for him,' says Conroy.

Ivo: 'I loved the experience of affecting the sound of a record, but it wasn't my place to impose anything. I couldn't play music and I wasn't technical. So I needed to create a situation where people gave me sounds that I could have ideas about, that could be manipulated in the studio.'

With Sharp woven around Fraser's lead, the vocals had power and presence, but the speed of the recording and Ivo's inexperience of direction showed in the stiff and overlong (at nine minutes) result. 'The programming is boring and I'd rather forget about it,' Ivo says. 'But obviously I thought it was good enough at the time to release as a single.'

Ivo now needed a B-side. He had a brainwave: to conjoin his new vocal crush, Fraser, with the song that Ivo had told the pro-4AD American fanzine *The Offense Newsletter* 'was probably the most beautiful song ever written by anybody', and to UK music weekly

Melody Maker, he said, '[It's] probably the most important song ever … it's moved me more than anything.'

Today, Ivo still holds the track, and the singer, in the same regard. 'If anyone wanted to demonstrate what's so special about Tim Buckley,' he says, 'I'd play them "Song To The Siren", because he *soars*. His voice is the closest thing to flying without taking acid or getting on a plane.'

Though he had first recorded 'Song To The Siren' in 1968, Buckley didn't release a (re-recorded) version until 1970, after being stung by a comment poking fun at the song's lyrics, written by his writing partner Larry Beckett. In either incarnation, 'Song To The Siren' had that uniquely, uncannily eerie lull, using metaphors of drowning to allude to what Ivo calls, 'the inevitable damage that love causes'.

Fraser agreed to record Buckley's ballad a cappella, and Ivo gave her a tape of his version so that she could familiarise herself with it. 'Liz never went anywhere without Robin at that time, so he came along to the studio too,' says Ivo.

This turned out to be a godsend for Ivo. 'I couldn't think of what to do between the verses,' he recalls, 'so Robin had, very reluctantly, put on his guitar, found a sound, lent against the studio wall looking decidedly bored, and played it once to Tim Buckley's version in his headphones.' He, Guthrie and John Fryer sat in the garden as Fraser – who hated being watched, worked out what to sing.

Ivo: 'I couldn't bear the suspense so I crept back inside and listened to what she was doing! I probably only heard her sing it once before I let her know I was there and thought what she was singing was brilliant. But because I couldn't make the whole thing work without any instrumentation, and because what Robin had spontaneously done was so gorgeous, it was easy to forget my original a cappella idea. Three hours later, the track was finished. I tried to think of ways of taking away the guitar, but I just couldn't get away from that swimming atmosphere, which is a tribute to Robin's genius.'

John Fryer: 'A-sides of singles can involve tension and stress but B-sides like "Song To The Siren" have less pressure on them. This was one of those times, and the B-side totally outshone the A-side.'

Bucking the trend of cover versions paling in comparison to the original, this new 'Song To The Siren' was exceptional, casting its own and equally haunted spell. 'Buckley got so close to the edge of a loneliness and yearning that's almost uncomfortable and stops you in your tracks, whereas Fraser's version floats in your ears and washes over you, like the sea that's constantly represented,' reckons singer-songwriter David Gray (who covered 'Song To The Siren' in 2007). 'Each time I hear either version, I'm transported somewhere else, outside of myself.'

'Jesus Christ, I made that happen!' was Ivo's reaction. 'And I wanted to do more.'

On the same September day in 1983 as Modern English's 'Someone's Calling' and Xmal Deutschland's re-recorded version of 'Incubus Succubus' – prosaically called 'Incubus Succubus II' – 4AD released a twelve-inch of 'Sixteen Days/Gathering Dust'. An edited version on the seven-inch became the B-side to the lead track 'Song To The Siren'. The name that Ivo gave to this collective adventure was This Mortal Coil, a phrase that had originated in William Shakespeare's most famous play, *The Tragedy of Hamlet, Prince of Denmark*, whose themes centred on treachery, family and moral corruption. The play's most famous speech, beginning with 'To be or not to be', contained the lines, '... *what dreams may come/ When we have shuffled off this mortal coil, must give us pause.*'

The word 'coil', derived from sixteenth-century English, was a metaphor for trouble, or in the Oxford English Dictionary's view, 'the bustle and turmoil of this mortal life'. Not being academically minded, Ivo hadn't known the provenance of the phrase; his source had been Spirit's 1968 track 'Dream Within A Dream', specifically the line '*Stepping off this mortal coil will be my pleasure.*'

'This Mortal Coil somehow suited the music,' Ivo explains. 'I didn't take long to decide. I can't say I still love the name, but I became comfortable with it.'

Less comfortable with the affair was Fraser, who was mortified to discover after the recording that she'd got a lyric of 'Song To The Siren' wrong. The promised sheet music from the publishers had never arrived, so she'd tried to decipher the words from Buckley's version. 'A few mind-bending substances were involved along the way,' recalls *Sounds* journalist Jon Wilde, whose flat Fraser and Guthrie stayed in for several months. 'By the time they had to go to the studio, one line continued to elude us.'

Fraser eventually sang, '*Were you here when I was flotsam?*' instead of the correct line, '*Were you hare when I was fox?*' which was an understandable error given the context for Beckett's lyrics was water and not earth. The mistake compounded Fraser's already self-conscious view of her performance; she'd felt rushed into the recording and was unhappy with what she'd achieved. But this was just for a B-side so it she let it pass.

The *NME*, while featuring Depeche Mode on the cover, buried its review low down on the Singles page, citing, 'a respectable job on "Song To The Siren" and that's about it – no revelation'. But if the leading UK music paper was still being sniffy about 4AD (*The Burden Of Mules* had been reviewed six weeks after release), 'Song To The Siren' entered the independent chart, and Fraser and Guthrie were asked to perform it live on BBC TV's late night show *Loose Talk*. 'I've never been more nervous in my life for anyone as I was for Liz that day,' says Ivo. Fraser was visibly shaky but still cut a mesmerising figure.

The duo also agreed to make a video, and by the end of its run on the UK independent singles chart, 'Song To The Siren' was to rack up 101 weeks, the fourth longest ever in indie singles chart history, behind Bauhaus' 'Bela Lugosi's Dead' (131 weeks), New Order's 'Blue Monday' (186 weeks) and Joy Division's 'Love Will Tear Us Apart' (195 weeks). 'Song To The Siren' also reached number 66 in the UK national charts, selling in excess of half a million copies, without the film soundtrack or major label marketing that had launched 'I Melt With You'.

Only a reissue of Bauhaus singles on the *4AD* EP separated the release of 'Song To The Siren' and new Cocteau Twins records, which had been recorded before the This Mortal Coil sessions. Having had one-off contracts for *Garlands*, *Lullabies* and *Peppermint Pig*, the band had signed a contract for five albums, or to run five years, whichever condition was fulfilled first. Colourbox signed the same kind of deal.

'Both bands wanted a wage and I thought they deserved a certain standard of living,' says Ivo. 'I also wanted to carry on working with them. We all recognised we were part of something that was becoming quite special.'

Cocteau Twins' second album *Head Over Heels* was released at the end of October, followed just one week later by the EP *Sunburst And Snowblind*, a collective hit of newfound freedom, expressed in a lush, panoramic drama that far exceeded *Garlands'* stark origins. The album cut 'Sugar Hiccup' also fronted the EP with an equally new-found commerciality, while the album's serene opener 'When Mama Was Moth' further extinguished all convenient Banshees and goth comparisons. Equally, 'Glass Candle Grenades' fed in a graceful, rhythmic imagery and 'Musette And Drums' was a magnificent finale.

Ivo: 'Robin and Liz's relationship and their music had just blossomed. *Head Over Heels* showed an extraordinary growth, especially Elizabeth's singing. The Peel session recorded shortly after includes my favourite ever Liz vocal, in the version of [*Sunburst And Snowblind* cut] "Hitherto". It's the track I play people if they've never heard Cocteau Twins. She sounds completely unfettered and it still gives me shivers.'

If Cocteau Twins could magic this up on the spot, what could they do with a little planning? Part of the music's magic was down to the euphoria between the duo, bound up in the album title's expression of love and Fraser's new engagement ring. 'We were young and in love,' Guthrie recalls. 'We'd just moved to London, people were saying how great we were, which fuelled us. As did loads of speed!'

23 Envelope mirrored Cocteau Twins' huge pools of reverb with a silver-metal pool of ripples (inspired by a key scene in Andrei Tarkovsky's 1979 film *Stalker*) and a fish disappearing, stage right, from the photo. 'That was a mackerel,' Nigel Grierson explains, 'in coloured ink, in a bath of water, into which we'd thrown flower petals. Everyone at 4AD went nuts over the image, and from there, we were directing operations more, trying to create a connection between the music and the visuals, without narrowing the interpretation, but to let the imagination work.'

Yet Guthrie again didn't find 23 Envelope's choices suited his own image of the band. 'Some of Nigel's other photos were joyous and beautiful but the one they chose was dark, dull and ugly. We'd say what we didn't like, but they still did what they wanted. We had this joke, that Vaughan put fishes on everything, and we'd say, "No fish!" So I think he'd put it on there to piss us off. But I liked the *Sunburst And Snowblind* cover.'

Guthrie also resented the sleeve credits. 'John Fryer only came in towards the end and listened to the mixes, but got a co-producer credit, which I didn't know until I saw the sleeve. Best of luck to John and I'm sure he got some work out of that, but he had nothing to do with it.'

His mood would have lifted when John Peel played all of side one of *Head Over Heels*, and all of side two on the following night's show. Like 'Peppermint Pig', the *Sunburst And Snowblind* EP fell just one place short of topping the independent chart, while reaching 86 in the UK national chart. But *Head Over Heels* was 4AD's first record to top the indie charts, and only fell one place short of the UK national top 50. This wasn't Depeche Mode-level success, but it added to 4AD's tangible sense of arrival.

If would be a perfect end to the year if Colourbox could make similar advances. At least the new EP, called *Colourbox*, had a new direction: Ivo knew Martyn Young's reggae/dub predilections and had suggested reggae specialist Paul Smykle as a producer. New singer Lorita Grahame was a reggae specialist too, in the ballad-leaning area of lover's rock, despite the band's advertising for a soulful singer. Grahame had a more expressive soul than her predecessor Debian Curry, but she didn't have enough to bounce off apart from 'Keep On Pushing'.* The problem was, Young's obsessive edits and mixes were

---

* Without Ivo's knowledge, Martyn Young had recorded a phone conversation with him, and part of it was spliced into one of the *Colourbox* EP tracks: 'It was one of Ian's,' Young reckons, which makes it either 'Nation' or 'Justice'. Yet the only audibly sampled phone call appears to be 'Keep On Pushing', even though the accent sounds more like Ray Conroy than Ivo. 'When Ivo found out, he wasn't pleased,' Young adds. 'It's still on there, but we had to disguise his voice.'

wearing down the sonic quality of the music. 'Nation' had a memorably funky synth-bass riff but it had been as arduous to make as it was to listen to, at ten minutes long.

'Some tracks were created with three Revox machines, cutting and pasting sound from the TV, which pre-dated sampling,' Ray Conroy recalls. 'One track might take three days, chopping it about. Martyn was so anal at getting it finished. But Ivo gave them a lot of time and space.'

'The record was a real hotchpotch,' Ivo concludes, 'and not the most likely thing to progress their visibility and popularity.'

The EP cover wasn't designed to make it an easy sell, and the fact it didn't create a stir showed Colourbox's low profile. Among fans, the *Colourbox* EP was known as 'The Shotgun Sessions' after the lead track, but also 'Horses Fucking' after the chosen image, a photo (in reversed negative, so that the horse's red penis turned green) taken by Vaughan Oliver years earlier while working a glamorous summer job at a local sewage works. In a manner more befitting a provocateur like Mick Allen, Colourbox had requested 'something revolting', says Oliver, who was encouraged by the EP song title 'Keep On Pushing'. From the pretty horses on *After The Snow* to the rutting equine couple on *Colourbox*, Oliver could never be relied on, he says, 'to take the easy road. I like to provoke, to be perverse.'

'We thought the cover was funny,' recalls Martyn Young. 'You could discuss things with Vaughan, and then he'd go and do his own thing, but they were better than our ideas.'

It was a temporary lull in a year that had seen 4AD on an upward trajectory that climaxed with Cocteau Twins' first American visit, playing two shows in New York interspersed with a show in Philadelphia on New Year's Eve, 'to about twelve people in the audience,' recalls Ivo, who flew over to celebrate. In the heat of excitement, he even suggested he could manage the band, and give up 4AD in the process: 'I was so proud to be involved with them,' Ivo recalls. 'I felt total commitment. I'm truly grateful they never responded to that particular idea!'

In the meantime, there was a shared sense of love, pride and excitement – and tour profits to revel in: 'I have a picture of Ivo with three grand in his hand!' Guthrie grins. Grangemouth and Oundle would have felt a long way in the past.

Another band in the giddy heat of ascendancy was The Smiths, who happened to be on the same New York flight as the Cocteaus, to make their own US debut. But Smiths drummer Mike Joyce fell ill and had to return home after one show, so their dates were cancelled. At a consolation party in promoter Ruth Polsky's tiny New York apartment, Guthrie recalls, 'being cornered in the kitchen by Johnny Marr – a lovely guy but all he wanted to talk about were Rolling Stones records! I was more, "OK, let's have more drugs!"'

7 1984

DREAMS MADE FLESH,
BUT IT'LL END IN TEARS
(bad401-cad412)

The scenario of 4AD as a family, drawn together by associations at school or shared aesthetics of sound and vision, expanded further with the arrival of Deborah Edgely, 4AD's third full-time employee, following Ivo and Vaughan Oliver. Edgely started as general assistant but quickly graduated to 4AD's press officer – and Ivo's partner.

In the historic city centre of Exeter, three hours south-west of London in the county of Devon, Edgely is understandably anxious about revisiting the many scenes of her past, complicated by her severed relationship with Ivo, the lost friendships with the artists and other friends at the label. She's lived in Devon since the mid-1990s, after escaping London and the music business. Though Edgely's current job running a nursery school might, in some ways, echo that of looking after musicians, there are far fewer phone calls after midnight. In any case, her two sons keep her extremely busy.

Edgely first met Ivo at a Bauhaus show. She was dating the band's drummer Kevin Haskins while both were studying at Northampton College; she was taking a foundation course in art. 'We were Jam fans, travelling around the country to see them,' Edgely recalls. 'I suppose we were mods. Kevin had a mohair suit and winklepickers and I had a lamé suit.'

With Edgely moving to Kingston for a fine art degree and Haskins' tour commitments, their relationship fizzled out. Ivo later bumped into her at The Camden Palace; they had a couple of dates, 'but things didn't click,' Ivo says. 'That influenced my decision to hire her – because we wouldn't then get involved.'

Edgely was planning a course in theatre design, but following lunch with Ivo and her flatmate Stella (then Pete Murphy's girlfriend), she changed her mind. 'I don't think Ivo even offered me a job, but just said, What about working with me? He needed help, and didn't have anyone else.'

Ivo: 'I was spending a lot of time in the studio, and physically packing AND unpacking boxes. And occasionally I needed letters typed. I needed an assistant.'

One of Edgely's first tasks was to write a press release for Modern English's *Ricochet Days*: 'I didn't know what press was all about, though my sister had always bought the *NME*,' she admits. Slowly, she took on more press duties, as Ivo increasingly felt that Sue Johns, an associate of Chris Carr's who was handling press for both Beggars Banquet and 4AD, was underachieving. 'I never got back to doing my own art but I don't regret what happened,' Edgely says.

Initially, she and Ivo shared a desk and chair, 'which might have something to do with the fact things quickly got sparky between us,' she says. 'One day as we were driving, Ivo said, Deb, I have to tell you something, I'm in love with you, let's go to the mountains in Switzerland. It was a real outpour! We were too busy to go away, but suddenly we were living together. And on a mission with 4AD.'

Thirty years after Edgely joined 4AD, Vaughan Oliver was able to tell her that he was initially jealous of her presence. 'Beforehand, it had just been Ivo and I, and Deb took his time and attention. I never quite clicked with her at the time. But I was also in my own world. I just wanted to make the best record sleeves ever.'

The family atmosphere at 4AD was further underlined by the addition of a new rehearsal studio in the Alma Road basement. '[It was] like a youth club for musicians,' says Mick Conroy. 'There was no daytime television in those days, or the money to do much, so we'd just hang out in the studio, making noise and talking to others.'

Modern English needed to rehearse as they'd returned from America with no songs, 'just bits of music,' Conroy admits. Their level of success meant the band was prematurely thrown into recording, again with Hugh Jones, who recalls the sessions without much fondness. 'They'd done something absurd like a hundred shows in eighty-two days. They were better musically this time around but it was a much harder record to make. We stitched bits together and got it organised, but their management was always looking for another "I Melt With You", so the mood was fraught.'

It wasn't just the band's management. While visiting Warners' LA office, Perry Watts-Russell overheard a conversation where an executive was suggesting Modern English put 'I Melt With You' on their next album as well, 'so they could have another crack at it,' he says. The idea was mercifully nixed, and a new single, 'Chapter 12', was released instead, a passable facsimile of 'I Melt With You' that subsequently ended up on the album *Ricochet Days*. 'It was a more produced and thought-through album than *After The Snow*, and not as raw,' says Robbie Grey, but in reality, it was a passable facsimile in itself, sounding more forced and less intuitive. If Ivo says he was a fan of the album, it wasn't enough to prolong his relationship with Modern English.

Robbie Grey's lyric for 'Breaking Away' had already identified a need for change, and on returning from America, the band's original core sacked drummer Richard [Brown] and keyboardist Stephen Walker. 'We'd shifted gears musically and they couldn't keep up,' Grey says. A streamlined Modern English had demoed 'Breaking Away' as a potential single with a new producer, Alan Shacklock, who had form with the much rockier 'Welsh U2' The Alarm. 'He changed the song completely and turned it into a pastiche of Bowie's "Let's Dance",' says Ivo. 'It was awful.'

Grey: 'We were miffed that Ivo didn't want to release "Breaking Away". Sire said it would sign us worldwide, so encouraged by our manager, we told Ivo things had run their course. He didn't say, please don't leave!'

Ivo: '*Ricochet Days* didn't make any more impact in the UK than *After The Snow*, and everything with Modern English was focused in America and having hits. Of course things had to develop and grow, but that wasn't where 4AD was going. It wasn't a betrayal to let them go. I knew Sire would pick up their option.'

Grey: 'Afterwards, I felt like we were people that Ivo used to know. But we were probably an expensive band to have on 4AD. To get on MTV, you needed £20,000 for a video and that was a large outlay for what was still a small independent label. And though people have had hang-ups about 4AD over money, Ivo had been quick to put us on a weekly wage, a hundred quid a week, when we'd started to do well. It had really taken off for us in America so it seemed a natural progression to sign direct to Sire. Our publisher [Beggars Banquet's sister company Momentum] was pushing for more sales too. I think Ivo thought it wasn't a bad thing for us to sell lots of records. And for the next two years, we were a very big band in America.'

Commercial success meant the band had to sacrifice their sanity. 'We slogged our way across America, without a hit single this time, and got seriously frazzled,' recalls Mick Conroy. 'And incredibly poor. We never received royalties from 4AD until the end of the Eighties.'

Contrary to the behaviour of typical record executives, Ivo had passed on 4AD's two biggest money-spinners Bauhaus and Modern English. Discussions regarding promo videos, choice of singles and chart strategies were not how he wished to spend his day. That didn't mean Ivo didn't try and help his bands do their best, and to have a chance to realise commercial as well as creative ambitions. His attention turned back to Colourbox, though this was going to be a tricky project as the trio was determined not to play live. 'I didn't think we could carry it off,' Martyn Young admits. 'Nowadays, people sequence all the music, but at the time, we'd have felt a fraud.'

Young admits that Colourbox was suffering from songwriter's block, both in general and to suit Lorita Grahame's voice. 'I really like songs, I just don't think I'm good at it,' Young shrugs. 'We were more concerned with production and messing around in the studio, so we began to consider cover versions.'

After enjoying U-Roy's lilting 'Say You' on one of Ivo's reggae compilations, Colourbox recorded a version at Palladium for a single, where Jon Turner's watchful approach allowed Martyn, like Robin Guthrie before him, to gain valuable production experience. This new 'Say You', minus fiddly edits, added clarity and a bounce to Colourbox's rhythmic stash, and was the band's first UK independent top 10 hit and helped secure a second BBC Radio 1 session for the Kid Jensen evening show that preceded John Peel's slot.

The paucity of songwriting was laid bare: all four Jensen session tracks were covers of pop legends, such as Burt Bacharach's 'The Look Of Love' and a horrible throwaway version of Dion's 'The Wanderer' sung like a pub entertainer by manager Ray Conroy. By this point, Young admits, he and Ian Robbins were working separately instead of as a team, and when Robbins chose to take a holiday over recording the session, he was out for good.

As Cocteau Twins had found, a reduced core unit helped to focus creativity. Three months later, the A side of new seven-inch single showed a change of tack. 'Punch' was Colourbox's first direct, upbeat pop song, though the track only reached 15 in the independent charts; it was as if Colourbox fans – and 4AD collectors – didn't want anything remotely cheery. There was little to celebrate either in the B-side support: 'Keep On Pushing' made another appearance and 'Shadows In The Room' was a drum track in search of a song. Altogether, it seemed a waste of Lorita Grahame. The soul/funk root of 'Punch' was also spoilt by the kind of production bluster that typi- fied the Eighties, for which Martyn Young blames producer Bob Carter: 'He wanted to play everything himself, so it wasn't a nice expe- rience. We didn't even like what he did and the samples were clichéd. But we had to release it as money had been spent.'

Colourbox's presence on 4AD is always wheeled out as proof that Ivo wasn't only driven to release music that fitted compilations enti- tled *Dark Paths* – what Bradford Cox, of current 4AD signing Deerhunter, calls, 'hyper-ethereal, borderline-goth'. But as Ivo's first signing in over a year showed, he also wasn't to be deterred from proceeding down the path if the music inspired. And the band's name alone, Dead Can Dance, seemed like the very last word in goth.

Anyone who knows the work of Lisa Gerrard and Brendan Perry can vouch for the group's dedication to rhythm, but a club was not the place you were destined to hear Dead Can Dance; a church, perhaps, or a grand hall in a stately home, or an amphitheatre, to bring the best out of their classically infused, hyper-ethereal ethno-fusion.

In summer 2012, sat around a modest conference table in a plush hotel in Dublin's city centre, Gerrard and Perry were about to release the first Dead Can Dance album in sixteen years – and their first not on 4AD. The photograph on the cover of *Anastasis* features a field of sunflowers blackened by the sun, their seed-heads drooping, exhausted. But once the heads and stems are chopped down, the roots will ensure that life, and flowers, will return. As Perry explains, *anastasis* is Greek for 'resurrection', as Dead Can Dance's ongoing worldwide tour – at the time of writing, it's been going for over a year – proves.

Perry also explains that *anastasis* also means, 'in between two stages', an appropriate term, as Gerrard and Perry are two very distinct characters. One is female, blonde, Australian, possessing a glorious, mournful, open-throated contralto and a penchant for speaking-in-tongues, or *glossolalia*, who later made her mark in Hollywood with film soundtracks, yet sees improvisation as the key: 'That's when I have that initial connection and everything seems to unlock,' she proclaims. 'If I try to refine that, I start thinking as opposed to feeling.'

The other character is male, bald now but once dark-haired, of Anglo-Irish stock, possessing a gorgeous, stately baritone, and a penchant for a painstakingly prepared music inspired by the distressed heartbreak grandeur of 1960s-period Scott Walker and Joy Division's late talisman Ian Curtis, tinged with the Gaelic ballads absorbed via his Irish roots. After meeting in Melbourne in 1979, these apparent polar opposites were to strike up a formidable alliance, traversing not just genres but centuries and continents, bound up in a uniquely visionary sound. *Anastasis* shows how age, and time, hasn't withered their cause.

Gerrard was raised in East Prahran, one of Melbourne's melting-pot neighbourhoods, largely Greek but with Turkish, Arab, Italian and Irish communities. She recalls, 'Exquisite, dark, arabesque voices that would blare out of the windows. It was so sensual and moving.' By the age of twelve, Gerrard was playing the piano accordion and able to sing in her own sensual, arabesque style. 'It was the most alive I'd ever felt. This sounds arrogant but I felt I could change things because of this great gift.' Only a few years later, she was bold enough to perform, on her own, in pubs, 'Some of the most insalubrious environments on earth,' she says, 'with broken bottles and fights, and people screaming, "Get yer top off!"'

By the end of her teens, she'd joined a local band, Microfilm, and mastered the yang ch'in (Chinese dulcimer), which resembled a metallic harp: 'There was no concept of tuning, you just wound it up, and off you went,' she says. When Brendan Perry first saw Gerrard play with the yang ch'in, he says, 'It was frightening! Lisa was singing a song about taking a man home ...'

Gerrard obliges with the lyric: '*I found a man in the park, I took him home in the dark/ I put him in the cupboard, can I keep him for a treat?*'

Perry's background had been equally eventful. Born and raised in Whitechapel in east London, he left for Auckland, New Zealand with his whole family when in his early teens. He learnt guitar at school and after considering teaching or the civil service, he sensibly changed course to play bass in the local punk band The Scavengers. He called himself Ronnie Recent. When original vocalist Mike Lesbian left, Perry began singing too, but feeling New Zealand was too small a scene, the band moved to Melbourne and changed its name to The Marching Girls. After a year and one minor hit single, 'True Love', Perry had re-adopted his real name and was investigating electronics and percussion with bassist Paul Erikson and Marching Girls drummer Simon Monroe as Dead Can Dance.

The first time that the pair had met, Gerrard taught Perry how to cheat on Melbourne's tramway system. Gerrard had already seen a

Marching Girls show: 'I'd never heard bass guitar played that way, with a classical, anchored approach. Brendan was a brilliant musician.'

Gerrard joined Dead Can Dance, and the pair became lovers. The first piece the new line-up attempted, she recalls, 'didn't sound like anything either of us had done before, which drew us close together'. That first demo, 'Frontier', didn't resemble much else on earth. Mixing yang ch'in, Aboriginal rhythms and the duo's hypnotic vocals, it sounded both ancient and modern. Perry says audience reactions were very positive, adding, 'But there was no future in Australia, just like New Zealand. We kept playing to the same crowds. But bands like The Cure, who we supported in Melbourne, showed that this kind of music was appreciated overseas, so we had to go where it was happening.'

Monroe chose to stay behind, so only Erikson joined Gerrard and Perry on the flight to London in 1981. For three months, the couple stayed with Perry's parents (who had also returned to the UK), in east London. Craving independence, they had accepted a hard-to-let flat on the seventeenth floor of Bowsprit Point, a council housing block on the Isle of Dogs, near to the now bustling business district of Canary Wharf but in 1981, one of London's most derelict districts (Stanley Kubrick's war film *Full Metal Jacket* was partly filmed there because of the available wasteland in which to stage explosions).

When I visited the couple in 1986, Perry admitted that his unemployment benefit had initially sustained them and Erikson alike, with odd jobs on top. Showing her propensity to roll up her sleeves, Gerrard also sold houseplants, door to door. What little spare cash they had after buying instruments and seeing concerts was spent on beer, the odd piece of hash and an art-house movie every Sunday. Music was really their sole driving concern. 'There is so much negativity in London, one is inspired to do something positive here, something untainted,' Gerrard said that day. 'You put your ear to the ground, and describe what's lacking.'

'It was incredibly tough,' she says today. 'We'd eat just bread and water sometimes, and the venues we'd play were fashionably filthy and it wasn't unusual to get food poisoning. But we knew people would love our music if we could just get it out there.'

One technical tool was a cassette player with built-in drum machine, and on their rickety second-hand bicycles, they took their demo to a select number of independent labels across London. 'We knew from import copies of the British music press who to approach. Factory was our first choice because of Joy Division – they changed my outlook on music, and their incredibly atmospheric qualities that mirrored Ian Curtis's wonderful lyrics, and the industrial sound by [producer] Martin Hannett. I knew 4AD from The Birthday Party, though I wasn't a fan of their big, cheesy American gothic. Bauhaus' first album, though, was very forward thinking, mixing guitars and percussive rhythms. I only heard Cocteau Twins when we got to London. I'd tape John Peel's show every night.'

Yet Ivo initially turned them down: 'He said he had a full roster,' recalls Perry.

'Ivo had a bit of a phobia about signing acts,' recalls Deborah Edgely. 'It's a big commitment taking on people's lives, and he wouldn't sign long-term deals because then you'd be responsible for their future, and have to maintain a band's income. These young kids would pitch up, and who was going to look after them? If you have a relationship built on one album at a time, there is less responsibility. You release something and hope for the best and then make a choice whether to carry on.'

Though both Mute and Cherry Red reacted positively to Dead Can Dance, the trio carried on without signing a deal. A new drummer, Peter Ulrich, was found living in one of the neighbouring tower blocks, and more demos recorded. Perry says Ivo eventually called again: 'Two tracks, "The Fatal Impact" and "Frontier", had captured his imagination, and he said he hadn't been able to stop thinking about the tape. But he wanted to see us play live.' 4AD helped by finding them two support slots to Xmal Deutschland. 'Ivo was so impressed we'd got it together, and really enjoyed it [the gigs],' says Gerrard. 'That turned things around.'

Ivo: 'It was Lisa's voice that initially did it, which is odd because of how much I love Brendan's voice too. Live, they were really powerful and tight, and Lisa was at her most raw. She sang in a non-lyrical way, using her voice almost like a weapon.'

Ray Conroy remembers meeting Gerrard and Perry in the pub across from the 4AD office: 'This weird hermit-like bloke with a pointy beard and the willowy, ghostly, porcelain figure that was Lisa. She really had something.'

'Ivo,' Perry recalls, 'had a little ponytail, but about seven or eight inches long. I thought he was Buddhist or Krishna.' Gerrard feels that Ivo was a figure of divine intervention. 'He provided a way for artists to express themselves in ways they'd never otherwise be able to, and to reach their potential – which is what This Mortal Coil was about. Bands didn't feel that they were absolutely brilliant, so there was no real conflict or threat. He attracted that kind of energy, of quite shy people, like he was looking for musicians hidden under stones, making this fragile music. Without Ivo, I don't think I'd have developed my own voice – given our circumstances, I don't know if I'd have had the strength to keep going. We were so driven to reach our own idea, this passionate purity about the work, and if we'd been confronted by anyone who put us under pressure to do otherwise, we'd have buckled.'

By November 1983, Dead Can Dance had recorded a John Peel session and a debut album, *Dead Can Dance*, recorded with new musicians – James Pinker, the band's New Zealand programmer (and live soundman) and English bassist Scott Rodger (though the departing Paul Erikson was also on the record). *Dead Can Dance* was instantly gripping, leading with a re-recording of the instrumental 'The Fatal Impact' (the title alluded to the colonial invasion of Aboriginal territory), with haunting chants taped off a TV broadcast of the 1964 film *Zulu*. The equally revamped 'Frontier' was an aural equivalent of the New Guinea tribal mask on the album cover, the idea of 'dead' wood being brought back to life by the carver representing the spirit behind the band's name rather than the goth label tied around Dead Can Dance's neck.

Of course there was a clear gothic element to Dead Can Dance. Not long after they'd arrived in Britain, Gerrard and Perry had gone on a cycling tour of Gothic cathedrals and their sound was tailor-made for such spaces. But just as much, Perry agrees, the album bore the influence of life from a fourteenth-floor eyrie: 'Sparseness, darkness, shadows,' he says. And Joy Division was gothic too, a music debt that the duo paid by the album homage 'Threshold'.

The only disappointing aspect of *Dead Can Dance* was the production, which managed to come through as both dense and thin. Following a now familiar path, Dead Can Dance had been designated John Fryer and Blackwing: 'Every day a different band or a different album every week, no one had money and we'd turn things round very fast,' Fryer recalls. However, though Fryer was (unusually for an engineer, says Ivo) willing to give artists room to experiment, Brendan Perry already had years of experience, and they immediately clashed.

'We fell out with John from day one,' says Perry. 'We only had two weeks for the entire album, which was really hard work. He thought he knew more about the recording process than we did, and came over arrogant and unhelpful when he should have been a bridge for us to get down what was inside our heads. We told Ivo it wasn't working, but we couldn't change it, so as a result, the production was really poor.' Fryer says he didn't like Perry's domination of Gerrard in the studio, and, 'how we had to replicate what he had played on the demos, but without any of their personality'.

Without Fryer's involvement, Dead Can Dance made a sizeable leap with the EP that followed. *Garden Of The Arcane Delights* (named after *Garden Of Earthly Delights* by the medieval Dutch painter Hieronymus Bosch) had a much clearer, warmer sound. It was the first clear sign of two distinct styles: 'Carnival Of Lights' and 'Flowers Of The Sea' profiled Gerrard's ecstatic vocal and yang ch'in, while Perry responded with the ballads 'Arcane' and a magnificent 'In Power We Entrust The Love Advocated'.

Like Fryer, Vaughan Oliver had discovered Brendan Perry wasn't happy to cede control. Perry had chosen the album cover, but for the EP he had supplied his own ink drawing inspired by the artist William

Blake, laden with biblical metaphors. 'It was absolutely dreadful, like something a kid would do,' says Oliver. 'My role was to protect against something like that, by gently persuading the artist that something else might work better, in design and typography. Hopefully it doesn't sound pompous and pretentious, but I was trying to educate.'

Perry: 'There was a big argument, but we stuck to our guns and said if they didn't like it, we'd call it a day. We always had great self-belief and we weren't prepared to throw it all away for someone else's impression of what our music looked like. They eventually admired us for that and we had greater freedom than many other artists on 4AD.'*

Buoyed by the confidence gained from over five years of live performance in both former bands and their present incarnation, Dead Can Dance toured Europe with Cocteau Twins and easily held their own. Surface comparisons between the bands were obvious: on the same label, with ethereal identities, formed by two couples; the two female singers preferred emotional impact over bold lyrical statements, and both male counterparts were perfectionist and controlling. It made sense to join forces, to form a spearhead for a sound that was unique in the UK, and across the globe.

But it was a made-up press concoction that the bands were enemies, or deadly rivals – the fact that Perry and Guthrie toured together in 2011 says as much. 'Dead Can Dance was fucking brilliant when they first arrived, just their energy live, and this huge sound,' Robin Guthrie recalls. 'They blew me away.'

Guthrie helped mix 'The Fatal Impact' before giving Perry the guitar he'd used on *Garlands*. 'It was really sweet of Robin,' says Perry. 'And I still have it. They helped in various ways. But we didn't hang out with Cocteau Twins, or any 4AD band. Everyone else lived in west London, and we were in east London, and miles from the nearest tube

---

* Oliver recalls a memorable night in Brendan Perry's company: 'I gave Brendan my bed after he'd totally gone on some sort of fucking weird trip – not drugs, just Guinness – and he went into this whole one about Lisa and throwing herself out of a building, and the police arriving, which felt all designed to freak me out. And then he started calling me an idiot, and ignorant, in my own flat!'

station, which we couldn't afford anyway. But there was mutual respect, and we felt part of an extended family. If there was competition, it was healthy, not backstabbing jealousy. The concept Ivo had for This Mortal Coil couldn't have existed otherwise. We all wanted to be part of a factory enterprise, a co-operative.'

But of course sparks could fly. Ray Conroy recalls one event, at the Trojan Horse in The Hague, Holland: 'Dead Can Dance had finished their set, blowing everyone away. They came backstage, uncharacteristically giving it a load of, "Let them follow *that!*" But they didn't realise that the dressing rooms didn't have ceilings, and the Cocteaus next door heard it all. Liz and Robin were really fucked off. They were probably thinking, they're stamping on our turf, we're the ethereal ones here!'

Perry confirms the incident, but says, 'It was the other members of Dead Can Dance, not Lisa or me. We'd got an encore that night, our first ever, and we were on a real high. The sad thing was, it really affected Liz and Robin. They sounded fantastic but they overdid the dry ice at the start so you could hardly see them. When the smoke cleared, all you saw was them and the wheels turning round on the tape recorder playing the drums and bass, and I think the audience was a bit shocked and disappointed. Liz broke down and came off stage and they cancelled the rest of the tour. She was fragile at the best of times.'

Mindful of the shortcomings of operating as a duo, Cocteau Twins decided on a new bassist. 'I wanted a balance playing live, and to expand our sound,' Guthrie explains. 'Simon brought a lot in terms of melody and piano and what we could do musically.'

In the kitchen of his house in Twickenham, not far from Wandsworth's Alma Road, Simon Raymonde sits surrounded by cabinets of not just crockery but twelve- and seven-inch vinyl. A Neil Young album plays on the newly installed turntable. A grand piano stands in the next room. Raymonde still makes music, under the alias of Snowbird, but his main job is to run Bella Union, the label that he and Guthrie co-founded in 1996 for the purposes of Cocteau Twins that then developed into an internationally acclaimed independent label, showing the same attention to artists as 4AD had done.

Music also dominated Raymonde's youth. His father was the late Ivor Raymonde, a major figure in Sixties British pop as the arranger for classic hits by the likes of Dusty Springfield, Cilla Black and The Walker Brothers. 'The house was filled with music, but I wasn't starry-eyed about it,' Raymonde recalls. 'But I do remember Scott Walker coming for tea. I didn't know who he was but I knew it was significant.'

Born and raised in south London, Raymonde and his family had moved further south to the tended lawns of Surrey by the time the legendary Walker came to visit. Raymonde says he loved glam rock icons such as Marc Bolan but says he wasn't much interested in music 'until punk, and I became completely obsessed. I'd tape Peel's show every night.' At Charterhouse boarding school (where the members of Genesis had met), Raymonde survived the abusive regime run by the school's prefects: 'Anything bucking the system was attractive to a small rebellious minority. We'd wear bondage trousers, spike our hair and hang out on the Kings Road at weekends.'

Despite his indifference to music, Raymonde was the first violinist and so the leader of the school orchestra. When his older brother Nick bought him a bass from Woolworths for his fifteenth birthday, he learnt to play in one afternoon and formed the school band Disruptive Patterns. Leaving school, Raymonde moved to Earls Court with his best friend Stan and began to see concerts every night: 'Wire, The Teardrop Explodes, the Bunnymen and Joy Division, it could all be in the same week. It was the best time to live in London that you could possibly imagine.'

The Beggars Banquet shop was just down the road, where Raymonde got a job while he played in the instrumental band The Drowning Craze, which was comparable to Dif Juz (who remain Raymonde's favourite 4AD band). Peter Kent had enjoyed their live performances but suggested they try out a singer – first was New York art school student and promising jazz singer Andrea Jaeger, then another American, Frankie Nardiello. The band had released three singles on Situation 2 before splitting up. At the same time, Ivo told him that Cocteau Twins was looking for a bassist.

By this time Raymonde had become Ivo's regular gig-going companion, so the Cocteaus had heard the Drowning Craze releases. Raymonde was no longer working at Beggars after the shop suddenly closed in 1983 – 'a huge shock – Nick Austin came in one day and told us not to come back tomorrow' – (Martin Mills says he had no memory why it happened, or why so drastically), and he was balancing two part-time jobs: for music chain store Our Price and a recording studio in Camden.

'I told Robin and Elizabeth, if they ever needed somewhere to record, they could use it for free,' says Raymonde. 'So they accepted. When they came in, and as I prepared to help them record, Robin said, "Have you got some music, then?" He thought I wanted to write with them! But when Elizabeth went to get chips, I had this bass line I'd been working on, and Robin and I wrote what became "Millimillenary". Robin was great like that, not at all "this is my band, my way", and Elizabeth said it was one of the best things she'd heard. The day after Our Price sacked me over a stock issue, Robin said they were recording next week in Edinburgh, did I want to come?'

At Palladium, Raymonde says he initially found the session, 'daunting and strange, walking into an established group, and a couple at that. And do I just play bass, or suggest other things?' He saw up close Robin and Liz's intense relationship. '*Head Over Heels* had a spikiness but it's a romantic record and they did love each other quite deeply then. Robin seemed worldly-wise to Liz, who was still super-shy and reserved, and Robin looked after her. The first few years were hard work but superb fun.'

The new trio's first session produced an EP, which, like This Mortal Coil's single, had different lead tracks: the euphoric 'Pearly-Dewdrops' Drops' and the brooding 'The Spangle Maker' fronted the seven- and twelve-inch versions respectively. Guthrie again claims that 'Pearly-Dewdrops' Drops' was a response to Ivo's request for something radio-friendly. 'That's rubbish,' Ivo retorts. 'Hadn't they already written and released "Sugar Hiccup"? It was always my least favourite track on the EP but it was also the obvious A-side to a single.'

Commercial aspirations versus purity of motive is always the potential flaw in any relationship between an artist and his or her conscience, and between a musician and record label; the post-punk and independent label movement was partly a response to the fact that most of the pioneering punk bands (Wire included) had signed to major labels, with indie options severely limited at the time. Guthrie was proud of his punk roots, and found this new world of opportunism a vexing experience.

'We wanted to make "The Spangle Maker" the single, as a statement, but Ivo said he couldn't use it and did we have other tracks?' he recalls. 'A twelve-inch and a seven-inch with different A-sides was the compromise. Ivo wanted a video too, for MTV – all the things we didn't want. But that's the way forward in business; you reach a certain level, and you have to feed it, to be in the game to win it. I can't diss Ivo, but what he needed from us at that time was a hit, to get on *Top of the Pops*.'

Guthrie also claims Ivo offered to remix 'Pearly-Dewdrops' Drops' to make it more radio-friendly, by making the drums and the hi-hat louder. 'I did, and I've regretted it since because it sounds out of balance,' he adds. 'But had I not done it, I feel Ivo could have turned his back on us and moved to the next band. That's human nature. What I didn't understand then was that everyone wants to make their mark on something, and to push people away was really alienating. If I'd had more people skills, I'd have embraced their ideas and then carried on and done exactly what I wanted, which I learnt to do much later on.'

Ivo denies adding commercial pressure, but a video was made for 'Pearly-Dewdrops' Drops' and a radio plugger hired to boost its visibility. All combined, the single became both Cocteau Twins' and 4AD's first independent chart topper, and for both the first national top 30 hit. The band was asked to appear on *Top of the Pops*, which they snubbed. 'We were vehemently against it,' says Guthrie. 'The show had become terrible with balloons everywhere and audience noise over the songs.'

At least John Peel remained on board. As Ivo recalls, 'On air, he said he first heard "Pearly-Dewdrops' Drops" when driving and he had to pull over to the roadside because it made him cry'

Deborah Edgely also cherishes the memory: she and Ivo had just bought a flat together, near to Wandsworth in neighbouring Balham. 'We bought an art deco radio and the first thing we heard on it was "Pearly-Dewdrops' Drops", and this was during the daytime.'

But the track's ubiquity was to spoil it for some. 'I've heard "Pearly-Dewdrops' Drops" too many times, it doesn't give me chills anymore,' says Ivo. 'I liked "Spangle Maker" more, which is one of their best ever tracks.' In Simon Raymonde's view, 'The EP was brilliant, but we played "Pearly-Dewdrops' Drops" so many times, it turned into this silly pop single. Actually, it's probably more the video. It's so po-faced and hideous.'

Robin Guthrie: 'I don't mind it now but people dwelt on it so much at the time because it got us a wider audience.' When Cocteau Twins played Channel 4's music TV show *The Tube*, they pointedly played *Head Over Heels* tracks 'Musette And Drums' and 'From The Flagstones' instead.

Xmal Deutschland was also navigating the art of compromise. They'd experienced another line-up change, with Manuela Zwingmann replaced by Peter Bellendir, 'a much more professional drummer, which made a huge difference,' recalls Anja Huwe. 'Peter said we needed to move on as a band. Manuela [Rickers] was improving, and I tried as well. We knew more about writing songs; before the second album, verse-chorus was an unknown language, but we found it could be a fascinating language too.'

Language was a prickly issue with Xmal Deutschland, singing in German to audiences that expected to hear English. The band named its new album *Toscin*, after a storm bell: 'Better that than calling it *Toxic*, so that people will look and listen,' says Huwe. 'If journalists understood it wrong, we'd stop talking to them. Those were the times!'

The most problematic language breakdown for Xmal proved to be with Ivo. *Tocsin*, produced by Mick Glossop, was more forceful and gleaming than *Fetisch*; the re-recorded 'Incubus Succubus' had shown the way. But the band's advance in song construction didn't make enough difference, and Huwe recalls Ivo's disappointment. 'But then he wasn't an open person, who explained himself,' she says. 'He didn't really say why he didn't like it. I think Ivo saw us a certain way, like the new Wire, and he didn't like the direction we were going in. It did feel like a family at 4AD, for some time, but you don't fit anymore when you have your own ideas. Other companies wanted to sign us, so we separated.'

Which faces more closely fit the 4AD community was confirmed by Ivo's unwavering support for The Wolfgang Press. The trio were allowed to control their artwork, such as for their new three-track EP *Scarecrow*, which came with a garishly coloured illustration of the title character that resembled a child's drawing even more than Brendan Perry's recent offering for Dead Can Dance, and setting the image on its side to create a more expressionist image didn't compensate. Fortunately, the music was more adult, showing the benefit of accepting an outside producer for the first time: Robin Guthrie.

Mark Cox explained that the band and Guthrie had bonded in an unusual manner, not via shared musical ideals but during the time that Mark Cox and girlfriend Shirley stopped their car to offer Guthrie and Elizabeth Fraser a lift: 'Shirley had drunk too much, so they had to stop the car so she could be sick, and Robin said he could relate to that! We all got on, and had mutual respect, Robin for our creative force and us for his ability and technical possibilities. He trod the eggshell line between not changing our ideas and organising them, which we hadn't tried before. He knew about drum machines, which we didn't. He got us counting bars, whereas before we'd been a bit jazzy.'

The seven-minute 'Ecstasy' – a smouldering ballad marked by a wandering mariachi trumpet – and the more rhythmically staccato 'Deserve' explored this new balance between experimenting and convention. 'We began to gel as a band,' Mick Allen claims, but the closing cover of 'Respect', the Stax soul classic perennially associated with Aretha Franklin, showed execution could fall short of ambition. Colourbox provided the programming, and Liz Fraser, with Mark Cox's support, sang the *'just a little bit'* refrain. As Allen admits, 'Our version was too rigid. I should have been thrashier, heavy, more tribal. It was almost comical by the end.'

Collaborations between The Wolfgang Press, Cocteau Twins and Colourbox members were put to better use in the 4AD family gathering that was This Mortal Coil's debut album. Ivo had also called on Robbie Grey, Manuela Rickers and Cindy Sharp. Two prominent guests outside the 4AD family were cellist Martin McCarrick and his sister, violinist Gina Ball, both members of former Soft Cell singer Marc Almond's backing band the Mambas. But the crucial cohort was John Fryer. 'He's still the only person I've ever made music in front of,' Ivo says.

'It worked between us because we were both depressed mother-fuckers at the time, and he trusted me in the studio,' says Fryer. 'We got along from day one. We were in the same headspace and he knew that if he put new bands in the studio with me, he'd get a good album out of it.'

Ivo had initially drawn up a shortlist of songs to cover, and invited people to the studio, like a film director conducting auditions and feeding the actors their lines. 'When I was younger, I had a guitar and all the time in the world, but I had never tried to write songs or play, I wasn't meant to do that.' he says. 'I'd seen Bruce Gilbert and Graham Lewis create sound, and here's me, I can't play anything but I can change how a sound sits in a track, and how a song can grow. But I needed source material to manipulate it. I didn't want to impose myself on bands' records, so I created a situation that technology afforded me. I loved being responsible for a piece of music, to embellish or improve it. From ears to heart to head to mouth, and back to the ears – that's magic.'

Ivo says he only let Fryer become involved in This Mortal Coil 'to disguise the fact I didn't know what I was doing!' Of their relationship, he says, 'It's astonishing that John and I didn't become close friends given how much time we spent together, but we did develop this incredible dialogue that mostly involved facial expressions. And he never rolled his eyes when I asked him to mic up a kettle. He wasn't one of those jaundiced, bored engineer types.'

The pair would bastardise the recordings. 'Ivo would say, I want the vocal to sound like it's coming through a waterfall, and I'd try to create it,' says Fryer. 'Every track was an aural movie. It was all about the feeling that we could drag out of the music.'

In Mark Cox's mind, 'Ivo had a sound in his head that nobody else was making, so he had to make it for himself.' Ivo's response: 'That suggests I knew what I was doing. I knew what I was *hoping* to do.'

None of This Mortal Coil's collective players recalls specific instructions. 'I don't remember, but Ivo says I was lying back on the floor playing guitar chords while he messed around with a space echo unit,' says Martyn Young. 'He wanted to see what we'd come up with.'

Simon Raymonde: 'Ivo might use an adjective or two, like, "This should be melancholic, slow and dark", or, "This is almost right but it needs to be less perfect". He'd lead you down the right path but leave room so that you weren't following something parrot-fashion.'

Ivo drew on the palate of sound that had made the most impression on him over time: Steve Miller and Randy California's spacey guitars, Martin Hannett's drum sound, the huge reverb of Guthrie and also Frankie Goes to Hollywood producer Trevor Horn, the collage mentality of The Mothers of Invention's *We're Only In It For The Money*. 'But This Mortal Coil sounds the way it does because of the ideas everyone brought along,' Ivo contends.

Martin McCarrick thinks Ivo is being too humble. 'I know some excellent musicians who lack natural raw talent, but Ivo, who couldn't play, had it. He could manipulate sounds with effects, and he knew what he wanted, like vocals that sounded like memories of songs from long ago. Some of the music still sounds quite insane – baby cries, birdsong over foghorns, beautiful strings, and then a dog barking … it was dreamlike and surreal.'

Ivo told *Melody Maker* that the effect he had wanted was 'the beauty of despair', and cited Lou Reed's 'desperate' *Berlin* as a benchmark to aim for. 'Somehow,' he said, 'when you're depressed, and listen to it and it sounds right, it almost *helps* if that's possible.'

Two songs that were more chilling than depressed came from Dead Can Dance after Ivo had allowed the project to morph by freeing the duo to record original pieces. 'Lisa was invited to sing a cover, but she didn't like that idea so she stuck her neck out and asked if she could do an original,' recalls Brendan Perry. 'That became two tracks, which Ivo really liked. Lisa asked me to help, and Ivo gave us total free range. He and John re-worked the treatment on "Waves Become Wings" but they left "Dreams Made Flesh" intact.'

Ivo says he didn't ask Gerrard to sing a cover until 1985, but states that he had heard tracks that, 'weren't suitable for Dead Can Dance. I was giving her an outlet'. He also denies Cindy Sharp's claim that he was initially asked for three Cindytalk original tracks to accompany three apiece from Cocteau Twins and Dead Can Dance, with the remaining tracks to be cover versions. 'Ivo specifically asked for one of our earliest tracks "Everybody Is Christ",' Sharp elaborates. 'It's a fairly searing and dark piece, but I said no because it was in line to open our own first album. It's utterly unlike what This Mortal Coil became. Ivo was flying blind, and slowly everything took shape.'

In the process of recording, more originals were fashioned by Ivo and Fryer out of the raw material. Sharp added vocals and lyrics to 'A Single Wish' whose melody came from an instrumental idea of Colourbox's Steve Young, and of the three instrumentals, Simon Raymonde's 'Barramundi' featured his own guitar and synth plus Gerrard's accordion. 'The Last Ray' had Ivo stabbing rudimentary keyboards to Raymonde and Guthrie's sombre arrangement, while Cox and Steven Young combined for a muddy swirl that Ivo named 'Fyt': 'It stood for "Fuck You Too" because it was the first piece of music I'd ever assembled, this little moron who couldn't play anything.'

A *Montreal Gazette* review later made reference to the album's atmosphere: 'phantasmagorical, inchoate and machine-tooled all at the same time'. But This Mortal Coil will always be remembered for the direct, often unadorned versions of the cover songs. Two came from 4AD's own catalogue: Rema-Rema's 'Fond Affections' was squeezed of all its drama by a tremulous Sharp vocal, and a taut arrangement of Colin Newman's 'Not Me' – the album's sole rocker – was sung by Robbie Grey with a dream team of Robin Guthrie and Xmal Deustchland's Manuela Rickers on guitar.

This left four covers, from the songs-that-saved-my-life compart-ment of Ivo's mind, to form the centrepiece of the record. 'Song To

The Siren' was included, and Fraser also sang 'Another Day', an exqui-sitely aching ballad written by folk rock renegade Roy Harper. Fraser's version sounded perfect, but she disagreed. 'The Cocteaus were a strange bunch,' Raymonde sighs. 'We never liked anything much after we recorded it. But "Another Day" is absolutely beautiful, and Roy Harper thought so too.'

It turns out that Ivo *didn't* unreservedly love Fraser's take on 'Another Day', but he blames himself. He'd encouraged the singer to get more confidence by seeing voice coach Tona de Brett: 'All Elizabeth practised was scales, but that night in the studio when Cocteau Twins were recording "Pepper Tree" [the third track on 'The Spangle Maker' twelve-inch], I heard the new, higher Elizabeth voice, the start of her not pushing and straining from the throat. I considered taking out the Kate Bush-isms in "Another Day" but decided against it.'

That left two truly anguished ballads from Big Star's *Third/Sister Lovers*. The album had been recorded in 1974, unreleased until 1978, and by 1984 was only worshipped by the few. The Memphis-based rockers were long forgotten and its lynchpin Alex Chilton was recover-ing from a self-destructive decade of alcohol and sedatives. 'He must have been in a very dark and despairing frame of mind and shit … I'm moved by that in music,' Ivo was quoted in a press release for the album.

Depressed motherfuckers certainly could have a field day. The more wretched of the songs, 'Holocaust', was sung by Howard Deveto, with a mixture of iciness and exhaustion at odds with the rest of the vocal performances. Ivo not only admired the former Magazine (and Buzzcocks) vocalist but had met the post-punk figurehead after Devoto had married his friend. 'I knew the name Big Star, but not their music,' says Devoto. 'But I'd loved the version of "Song To The Siren", which sold me on the idea of singing "Holocaust".'*

---

* Ivo wasn't alone with his concept and tastes. Around the same time, David Roback, the core songwriter of LA band The Rain Parade, had put together a similarly styled collective drawn from the city's psychedelically inclined bands (such as The Dream Syndicate, The Bangles and The Three O'Clock) that had been grouped under the label The Paisley Underground. An album of covers was also released in 1984, under the band and album name *Rainy Day*. The nine tracks included 'Holocaust', sung by Dream Syndicate bassist Kendra Smith.

For 'Kangaroo', which Ivo once likened to 'a cross between The Velvet Underground and Syd Barrett on heroin', he envisaged just Sharp backed by bass and cello, which Simon Raymonde would arrange, to accentuate the lyric's desperation. 'I know those songs should never be covered,' Ivo acknowledges, 'but they came out just mad and perfect, and completely different to the original, something of our own.' Enough for 'Kangaroo' to be the lead single from the album, reaching number 2 on the UK independent singles chart in August.

The only task left was to name the album and choose the artwork. The title *It'll End In Tears* had been percolating in Ivo's brain since 1980, when Mass was visiting his new flat, and he'd taken them to the empty flat below to take some press photos. 'I'm useless at that side of things, and I was throwing around confetti and stuff,' Ivo recalls. 'Danny and Gary started getting a bit physical, and Mick shook his head and said, "It'll end in tears!", which I mentally filed away.'

The image was also borrowed. Nigel Grierson had taken a black-and-white photo, out of focus, of a dark-haired woman named Yvette who he'd met through mutual friends. 'She was very attractive with great features,' Grierson says. 'I was trying to create an intriguing image, influenced by the subconscious and scenes from [David Lynch's] *Eraserhead* and [Luis Buñuel's] *Los Olvidados* – eyes closed, hair pulled back.'

Yvette – she doesn't disclose her surname – now goes by the name Pallas Citroen, and works as an artist: 'I specialise in arty-serious sculpture, installation and film,' she explains. 'It's hard to explain but it's about surfaces and transparency and façades,' which sounds suitably 23 Envelope. In 1983, she was taking her final school exams and eager for arty-serious collaboration. It didn't necessitate much: 'We went outside, Nigel pulled some branches down from a tree, waved them in front of the lights, and took the shots.'

One image had been offered to Modern English for *Ricochet Days*, but the band had turned it down: 'Yvette was a friend of ours who lived in our house, and it was tricky with our girlfriends, who were suspicious of other girls on our covers,' admits Mick Conroy. But Ivo saw something that resonated for This Mortal Coil, and took it for his own purposes.

Inovatively fusing a melancholic footprint of both pre-and post-punk eras, in October 1984 *It'll End In Tears* followed *Head Over Heels* into the UK top 40, and settled down for an extended run in the independent charts. Ivo tried his luck again in America by licensing the album to Atlantic Records, encouraged by comments that 'Song To The Siren' would get used in a film. 'Atlantic only sold eight thousand copies and deleted it after a year,' he recalls. 'Afterwards, I immediately sold three thousand copies on import.'

What every purchaser got was, most likely, an introduction to the likes of Tim Buckley, Alex Chilton and Roy Harper, the kind of artists that a post-punk generation had been programmed to consider the work of the enemy – hippies at best. Even most contributors to *It'll End In Tears* didn't know the originals that Ivo had plucked out from memory. 'Coming from a classical background, I'd have considered all that stuff acoustic nonsense,' McCarrick admits. 'But Ivo wanted to keep these names alive, and he was chuffed when he got a credit on a Big Star compilation for doing just that.'

According to Sharp, 'It was a brilliant education in this great British and American folk and country music that had got lost in the mist.' Raymonde describes Ivo as, 'A pied piper, with extraordinary taste, who opened me up to all sorts of things, like Tim Buckley, Tim Hardin and Scott Walker, which was strange because my dad had worked with Scott. It was movies with Ivo too. I remember him taking us to a double bill of Tarkovsky films.'

Ivo later told *Melody Maker*, 'I was so pleased that six months after the first This Mortal Coil album, all of the covered songs were available again as either UK releases or US imports … the third Big Star album, the Tim Buckley retrospective.'

In the same interview, he also said, 'I do feel that the strongest feeling from music comes from desperation. I think it's all about intense feeling, and whether it's about an intense high or an intense low doesn't matter. It doesn't hurt to embrace any extreme of feeling, rather than just carry on in some limbo.'

Ivo's words help towards explaining why *It'll End In Tears* appears to have made a palpable impact on gay men in their impressionable teens, drawn by the strong female voices – Sharp as much as Fraser and Gerrard (the only 'masculine' singer being Robbie Grey) and the music's dreamlike and frankly desperate mood. For example, Michigan-born singer-songwriter John Grant, whose 4AD crush in the Eighties would eventually lead his Colorado-based band The Czars to sign to Bella Union in 1999, recalls the days when his emerging sexuality was being outlawed by his strict religious upbringing in a particularly conservative corner of smalltown America. 'My high-school friend Greg introduced me to *It'll End In Tears*, and I was deeply in love with Greg, and terrified of being found out, so This Mortal Coil – and the Cocteaus and Dead Can Dance – gave me – they still do – the feeling of a most intense longing, sadness and confusion,' Grant says. '"Not Me" was so dark and sexy, like black leather and understated cool. I even covered "Song To The Siren" years later. I didn't even know half the words to those songs at the time. I just sang along to the parts that I knew, that I could apply to my own life. It sounds cheesy but they helped save me.'

The love of Antony Hegarty (of Antony and the Johnsons) for This Mortal Coil didn't stop at 'Song To The Siren'. 'My friends and I all found *It'll End In Tears* weirdly hopeful and with an air of gentleness, humanity and spirituality that accompanied me through my adolescence,' he recalls. 'It was taking a risk by being poetic and using piano and cellos as well as lush, ambient Eno-esque sound. I didn't realise they were cover versions until years later! When I moved to New York City in the early Nineties, all the punk drag queens who'd listened to This Mortal Coil in their teens were lip-synching to those songs in late night clubs.'

This appreciation wasn't restricted to sexuality any more than gender. In the Nineties, Martin McCarrick recalls, 'This dark-haired guy came over and said, "Are you Martin from This Mortal Coil?" It was Trent Reznor [of the electronic band Nine Inch Nails]. There's an unusual collection of people touched by those records, but the music was so unusual at the time, just bare bones and voices, and minimal and ambient, before those terms were used commercially. There was something dreamlike that sucked you in, like in a film.'

Ivo: 'The records that have affected me the strongest have created their own space, and taken me on a journey. And most of those albums, like Big Star's *Third* or Lou Reed's *Berlin*, exist in a less than happy atmosphere.'

At that point, Ivo hadn't even figured out his depression, though John Fryer seemed to realise. 'It was very morose music so we'd have to have been miserable, to make it work,' he says. 'It was just a period in our lives, in the music industry, and the world, that it worked out like that. We couldn't have made *It'll End In Tears* today.'

Any tendency to wallow in misery was outweighed by Ivo's relationship with Deborah Edgely, the speed and range of 4AD business, and the exhilaration of achievement, not just with This Mortal Coil but those closest to his heart, such as Cocteau Twins. He could also see 4AD's critics finally accept what he was trying to achieve, and a fan base that was buying every release. Cocteau Twins' imminent third album, *Treasure*, was to extend the feeling, topping the UK independent charts and breaking the national top 30, to become 4AD's highest selling album yet.

After the immaculate conception of *Head Over Heels*, the new album had a troubled delivery. It had begun with Ivo's suggestion that Brian Eno produce the Cocteaus: 'Liz and I thought it was a decent idea, Eno being one of the great producers of our time,' recalls Simon Raymonde. 'But when we met him, Robin was in one of his particularly antagonistic moods. Eno finished by saying, "You don't need a producer, you know exactly how your music is meant to sound like, you should do it yourself". Robin was like, yup, told you so! He wasn't ready to relinquish control of his baby, and he was probably right.'

Ivo: 'Eno and this guy Danny sat on the carpet, and Eno said, "I'm really flattered that you've asked, but I'd never have had the courage to use the size of reverb that you used on *Head Over Heels*! You know what to do. But if you want a good engineer, work with Danny" – who turned out to be [engineer and future producer] Daniel Lanois. The band returned to Palladium, Robin produced the album, and it sounded fantastic.'

The band again began with no songs in hand, and snowbound in a particularly harsh winter. 'The recording,' says Raymonde, 'was half enjoyable and half stressful, up to the last week booked when we didn't think it was finished. We don't work best under that pressure, but we knew our future was being determined by that record. I always hear *Treasure* as half-finished.'

The Cure's Robert Smith would disagree with that verdict, since he admitted he'd become obsessed with *Treasure*. '[It was] the most romantic sound I'd ever heard,' he said when interviewed for the documentary *Beautiful Noise*, and confessed he'd played the album while getting dressed on his wedding day. 'It always intrigued me how they made it sound so effortless,' he concluded.

Many Cocteaus fans that consider *Treasure* is the band's finest album would agree, but not Guthrie. 'I feel the early stuff we did with Simon was fumbly and only a stepping stone on the way to something. *Treasure* has a great atmosphere but it's a bit devoid of content because we ran out of time. And it sounds so 1984, what with the drums and the DX7 [synth], instead of sounding timeless. That's the drum sound that made Tears For Fears famous!'

Elizabeth Fraser was also feeling the clock ticking. 'I got a call from Robin: "You gotta come up and help, Liz has got no words, she's completely dried up",' Ivo recalls. 'I went up and sat with her, with a dictionary, and wrote some fourth-form poetry – I wasn't seriously suggesting lyrics but I tried to kickstart it. But it was so awful and inappropriate and not what she wanted. There, for the first time, Liz started using words more phonetically than lyrically.'

Guthrie: 'Liz was never comfortable with being judged on what she'd done. The more she got comments like, "the voice of God" [coined by reviews editor Steve Sutherland for *Melody Maker*], the less confidence she had in what she was writing. I agree that no one had a voice like her, but it built such huge expectations. So she started to disguise what she wrote, or split the words up in the wrong places. But Liz should have realised that people loved it. She couldn't let the good in.'

But then neither could Guthrie, who can't enjoy the numerous rapturous episodes such as 'Pandora', 'Donimo' and 'Ivo' – the last formerly titled 'Peep-Bo' but renamed in tribute to her mentor and friend. If the production and drum sound does date *Treasure*, it can't nullify the vocal overlaps, breathless tone and hypnotic flow of 'Lorelei', the uncanny madrigal 'Beatrix' or the tour de force 'Persephone'.

And Guthrie also couldn't see the beauty of 23 Envelope's striking image for *Treasure*, a dressed mannequin shrouded in lace that mirrored the intricate layers of the music. This came after the use of Gertrude Käsebier's 1904 photograph *The Crystal Gazer (or The Magic Crystal)* for *The Spangle Maker* EP, with its aura of unknown and wondrous forces given a more precious and retro feel when set against a backdrop of combed marbled paper. 'They pushed the packaging in a Pre-Raphaelite art direction, all flowery, arty-farty and poncy, but thankfully no fish this time!' says Guthrie. 'The album cover also cost a fortune. Special dresses had to be hired, from a plush shop in Richmond, whose owner's husband happened to be Martin Mills.'

Vaughan Oliver: 'It was a chiaroscuro effect, light and dark, with attention to detail on the typography. But boiled down, it's a bloody mannequin with a few bits of lace around it! I liked that the subject matter of *Treasure* was so banal but you could create something special from it. It went with the music, not against it. That's why 4AD was so outside the times, so un-post-modern. We were romantic and poetic.'

Guthrie clearly kept his feelings of dissatisfaction from Ivo, whose memory of this time is one of harmony. The camaraderie of the times had seen artists guest on one another's record, sharing tour managers, holidays and even, in the case of Modern English and Colourbox, a house. In July, three couples – Ivo and Deborah, Guthrie and Fraser, and Cox and girlfriend Shirley – had even flown to the Greek island of Corfu for a two-week holiday together. One particular memory abides for Ivo, of driving to the airport, 'bonkers in love' with Deborah, listening to The Wolfgang Press's EP *Scarecrow* that Guthrie had produced the previous week. 'Everything intermingled,' Ivo recalls. 'Creativity and friendship. Everything was positive at that time.'

But as Modern English knew, success can bring its own problems. Though all three Cocteau Twins had contributed to *It'll End In Tears*, Guthrie was nursing some grievances that would seep into his friendship with Ivo, complicated for Ivo by the fact he was the guitarist's friend, mentor and financial provider.

It was 4AD's fortune to have discovered Cocteau Twins first, and its misfortune that the band with the most unique talent was also the most difficult to contend with. Guthrie's punk rock principles made him an inflexible and oppositional force to be reckoned with: 'Robin was an antagonistic kind of chap, very opinionated, with a very strong vision of his band,' says Simon Raymonde. 'He liked to take a stand, often to put people on the back foot. But he did believe in most of what he was saying, and nine times out of ten, he was right.'

Guthrie admits he had chronically low self-esteem that would flare up when he felt a lack of recognition, especially regarding a fair financial deal commensurate with what he felt he was worth. Another bone of contention with 4AD had been over contracts. Guthrie, who knew nothing about them as a naïve punk rocker, feels he was misled when Cocteau Twins signed a contract for *Garlands*. 'We asked, "Should we take it to a lawyer?" and I was told, "No, it's standard", and we listened to them. The contract we signed for *Head Over Heels* was the first time we got any money, £50 a week each.'

Contracts highlight another marked difference between 4AD and Ivo's label peers at Mute, Factory and Rough Trade (whose founder Geoff Travis ran the company as a co-operative, and had almost gone out of business in 1982) who offered deals on a 50–50 profit split between label and artist. Martin Mills, who was in charge of business rather than Ivo, was a more old-fashioned profiteer who had worked in the civil service and run retail and promotions businesses. According to Fredric Dannen's 1990 book *Hit Men: Power Brokers and Fast Money Inside the Music Business*, music business lawyer Don Engel said that standard artist contracts through the Seventies were, 'the most onerous, impossible, unfair'. Nothing had changed by the

Eighties, especially given the restricted budgets of independent labels. Mills employed the services of media and entertainment lawyers Harbottle & Lewis to establish the standard contract that Beggars Banquet, 4AD and Situation 2 would issue.

'I think it's unfair for Martin to take all of the blame for the contracts,' says Ivo. 'I'd been keen to work on a 50–50 basis from the start because it seemed more transparent, though Martin didn't agree. He did, however, point out one myth of the appeal of such a deal, which was overseas royalties. On a 50–50 deal, an artist would earn 50 per cent of a royalty rate as low as 12 per cent, which is less than they would earn on a direct percentage royalty rate. In my defence, I did constantly try to improve the basic royalty rate on a one-off contract and would often ask James Wylie at Harbottle if our contracts were fair. He assured me that they were better rates than most record companies and that I was paying the right level of session fees.

'That said,' he continues, 'I understand why, in order to survive, the scales are tipped in a record company's favour. But even if we'd worked on a 50–50 basis, that wouldn't have stopped Robin's complaining. Nothing was ever good enough. But we all put up with that side of him because he was also such a sweet and generous man and we realised that sort of insecurity just went with the creative territory.'

But Guthrie's big bone of contention was the very nature of creative territory, and he remains furious that he was initially paid a £250 session fee for 'Song To The Siren', and hadn't been rewarded for the income – and boosted reputation – that had come 4AD's way as a result.

Guthrie: 'Initially, we treated "Song To The Siren" as one of our own, and I'm very proud of it. Liz's vocal was extraordinary, and it was all so simple and flawlessly executed. And I did more stuff for *It'll End In Tears*, as a favour to a mentor and a mate. At that point, I'd have done anything for Ivo. But I shouldn't have been paid as a session musician, because that record wouldn't have existed without us. Liz and I gave it that sound. We were starting to stand up and grow up and have our own ideas, and I wanted to take credit for what was ours.

There were big incomes on records like *It'll End In Tears* and make no mistake, the money coming into This Mortal Coil wasn't shared. And that's wrong because it's exploitation under the guise of art. Imagine if I did a show with my band, and I get £10,000 and I give the band £25. You just don't do that.'

Ivo maintains that he and Guthrie did talk after the recording of 'Song To The Siren', and says that 'Robin insisted that he didn't want to be paid anything, but that I had to promise to pay Liz royalties, which I did.'

Simon Raymonde: 'Our fault was that we didn't ask [for royalties] at the time. For all Ivo's amazing A&R and creativity, he wasn't brilliant at business. But rather than talk about it, which as a band, we never did, we retreated to lick our wounds. I'm sure Ivo did what he felt was right at the time. My irritation is with Martin Mills, who sorted out the contracts.'

Brendan Perry shares Raymonde's opinion. 'The contracts were woeful, really antiquated deals that should have been thrown out years ago. I don't blame Ivo; it's more Martin. But that was the scale of our ignorance back in those days.'

Guthrie also claims, 'that Ivo agreed, after I'd hammered the point home: constant sales of This Mortal Coil, if "Song To The Siren" was ever requested for use in a movie, he would split the royalties three ways. But he won't let it be used in a movie. You know the scene: when your record company boss is driving around in a Mercedes and you're on the cover of the *NME* but still taking the bus. Chuck Berry or Motown artists will tell you the same story.'

Deborah Edgely had a ringside view of Ivo and the Cocteau Twins' relationship while retaining an outsider's perspective. 'Ivo had the mindset and mentality from a privileged background, with a start in life, like the money to buy his flat, for example, so you can afford to be slightly romantic about where your future lies and what it holds, which is not the same for a band without money and prospects,' she says. 'I feel it was partly my fault, as Ivo had this old BMW, and I said, go buy yourself a new car, so he did, and I'm sure a lot of bands didn't like that. You always see in life those that share a bit of the cake and those that don't, and some would have felt more deserving than others.'

The problem was made worse by the fact Guthrie never raised these issues at the time, so resentment festered, while Ivo was oblivious to the existence of it. Looking back at their friendship at the time, Ivo recalls a comment by Pink Floyd's drummer Nick Mason: 'He said, "Things got so bad that we almost spoke about it". The Cocteaus and I never did speak about things.'

The band, for example, was resentful of how, as Raymonde put it, 'We were foisted with this image of what 4AD thought Cocteau Twins was, the Victorian gothic imagery, or us playing in a church, which made us look like a bunch of cunts. 4AD had become such a strong brand at that point and we had become part of what 4AD had become rather than our own thing.'

Nigel Grierson says, 'I'd always wondered why I never followed David Bowie, even though I liked a lot of his music, and I realised I was put off by the degree of idolisation, where something becomes a cult, almost a religion. In the same way, it irritated me when I met people who were more 4AD than 4AD – I didn't want to be part of some little club. It's an interesting subject, to want to be a part of something and yet apart too. The stronger the identity, the more specific it is and the harder it is to feel that it sums you up. Like no one wanted to be associated with "Goth", because it's too simplistic. So is saying "it's very 4AD". None of the bands seemed to have some big idea about themselves or what 4AD was; it was more what it bred, and yet ironically, that was a measure of its success.'

Brendan Perry: 'Robin and Liz wanted to maintain their uniqueness and individuality as much as possible and not have it diluted, psychologically, and lose themselves within a common herd or a stable within 4AD. We saw how every album was pushed in Vaughan's direction to get this homogenised look, which we railed against. Those were the cracks that appeared in the general goodwill towards 4AD's command centre.'

Perry may have been a more confident personality than Guthrie; certainly he was more secure and unafraid of confrontation. He also wasn't Ivo's close friend and holiday companion. Like Guthrie, he recognised the implications of being part of the 4AD brand, and had withheld permission for Peter Murphy to cover Dead Can Dance's 'In Power We Entrust The Love Advocated' for potential inclusion on *It'll End In Tears*. 'Our own EP had only been out a couple of months, and it needed a life of its own, to be associated with Dead Can Dance and not This Mortal Coil,' Perry explains. 'This Mortal Coil was also selling way more than we were, so our decision was solely pragmatic.'

A stubborn individualist like Guthrie would never have felt comfortable as part of any family collective, happy or otherwise. 'I hated the illusion that 4AD were a bunch of mates,' he says. 'The backstabbing that went on between the bands was incredible!'

That's not how Perry remembers it. 'If there was competition, it was healthy, not backstabbing jealousy, and there was definitely a sense of mutual consideration between acts. We loved the idea of a central crucible, like a hub, where all acts intersected and cross-referenced. It was refreshing to see a record company boss being involved creatively and seeing the process from our point of view. We did feel part of an extended family.'

John Fryer had a more objective view: 'I was working with lots of 4AD bands, and Ivo would bitch about them and they'd bitch about him, like they had to use Vaughan for the artwork. And Ivo could have tunnel vision, like it was his way or the highway. But that's why 4AD sounded like it did. 4AD was like a club that you bought into and people would buy 4AD because it was on that label.'

Vaughan Oliver could also see both sides. 'I was a layman where business was concerned, but my impression was that it [the scenario with Cocteau Twins] was less financial and more about ego and status and resentment about this concept of branding for 4AD. We were growing at the same rate, at the same time, and Robin could never see how the success of 4AD could help them.'

But Guthrie didn't want to be part of anything communal, especially the musical identity of This Mortal Coil. He says he hated the original songs that *It'll End In Tears* covered: 'All these earnest, bearded men with acoustic guitars. I was trying to take Cocteau Twins to new places, sonically, and I found This Mortal Coil pretentious and miserable, and I now wish I'd never done it. Thirty years on, it still follows me around and it's nothing to do with anything I've ever done.'

The tension was further compounded by the times that 'Song To The Siren' was erroneously attributed by parts of the music press to Cocteau Twins – that the Cocteaus *were* This Mortal Coil, and had even changed their name. Nor did it help that Cocteau Twins had played 'Song To The Siren' in their live set.

'I know now I should have released "Song To The Siren" as a Cocteau Twins song,' says Ivo. 'I loved them virtually unconditionally, more than anyone. I loved their music, their attitude, and I felt protective towards them. But had they themselves recorded "Song To The Siren", it would never have sounded the way that it did. I know it hurt them that the track got more attention than "Sugar Hiccup", that it stuck around the indie chart for ever, and that Robin grew to resent that 4AD became more important than the names of the bands on it.'

Guthrie: 'I was really sick when I heard it ['Song To The Siren'] played on the radio all the time and the Cocteaus had never been played,' Guthrie told *The Offense Newsletter* in late 1983, as if there had been a conspiracy against the band. 'So the only way we could get played on the radio was to do somebody else's song under a different name.'

Deborah Edgely: 'When "Song to the Siren" was released, Cocteau Twins hadn't had that much exposure, so to record a song that wasn't theirs, under a different mantle, was very hard for them to cope with. Bear in mind how Robin and Elizabeth were totally in control of their own musical destiny. It was their world, they made music without anyone else influencing anything, and then they agreed to this thing that Ivo had chosen, a vocal performance that was the most obvious that Elizabeth had ever sung in terms of words. Whatever she thinks, it sounded fantastic, and Robin produced something spellbinding. But it wasn't theirs. Their unhappiness was never spoken at the time.'

It wasn't only Cocteau Twins who had its doubts. 'I could tell that This Mortal Coil was difficult for some people to bear,' says Edgely. 'It caused issue with Mick Allen, for example, with Mark [Cox] being part of it and getting close to Ivo. He had a hold over everyone, to a greater or lesser extent. It would have had some emotional impact, because he was the boss who would be shaping and influencing their futures.'

Ivo was not just Guthrie's friend, mentor and boss, but also his artistic peer, and a perceived rival potentially drawing interest away from his own band. More than one 4AD artist recalls being approached by fans with the question, 'Who is this Ivo?' And Cocteau Twins had inadvertently contributed to the growing cult of Ivo by naming a song after him, which showed their admiration for him.

The cult of Ivo, and the advancement of a 4AD brand – and a 4AD 'sound', with Cocteau Twins, This Mortal Coil and Dead Can Dance at the core – was no different to that of Tony Wilson at Factory, who also signed bands of a similar nature, in the slipstream of both Joy Division and New Order. But Wilson was much more the self-promoter than Ivo, and was interviewed almost as often as his artists. At least Ivo was trying to keep a low profile; he didn't know that This Mortal Coil would take off, in the same way as he hadn't planned for 4AD to be in such a strong position by the end of 1984.

To celebrate the achievements to date, and to tie up the artistic venture that was dividing the artists, 4AD's last release of the year was a catalogue of releases, designed by Oliver. Like most everything on 4AD, it was bought by the growing legion of fans.

Without knowing the depth of Guthrie's discontent, Ivo remembers this period as 'glorious'. In his words, 'Everybody liked each other, they were mostly happy to work with Vaughan and Nigel, and people helped each other, like Robin produced The Wolfgang Press and Dif Juz too for their new album.'

There was a triumphant end to the year in December when Cocteau Twins played a one-off show at Sadler's Wells Theatre, London's premier home of ballet, supported by Dif Juz, certain members of whom subverted the grandeur of the occasion by sticking their bare arses through the stage curtain. There was a palpable sense of arrival in the air, reflected in the label's standing in John Peel's third annual Festive Fifty listeners' poll, where Cocteau Twins had seven entries

('Pearly-Dewdrops' Drops' at number 2, 'The Spangle Maker' at 4, 'Ivo' at 15), as many as poll-toppers The Smiths. This Mortal Coil had two ('Kangaroo' and 'Another Day').

'It was impossible not to be affected by the creativity around, and everyone was sharing in it,' Ivo concludes. 'I'd always loved the tail end of the Sixties and the early Seventies when artists such as David Crosby would record with Paul Kantner and Grace Slick and other musicians, and their record labels didn't tell them that they couldn't. We were young and everybody was being creative, we all hated "the man" and it all felt real. It felt fantastic to be at the helm of all that. But that was before things changed.'

 1985

THE ART SHIT TOUR AND OTHER STORIES
(bad501-cad514)

With Cocteau Twins' grievances unaired, Ivo and Deborah paid a New Year visit to the band at Jacob's Studios where the trio was recording a new EP. 'The pattern was to record an EP after an album,' says Simon Raymonde. 'Four tracks were easier than ten, and we loved the format.'

After basing most every *Treasure* song title on a person's name and singing in her own indecipherable private language, Elizabeth Fraser further expanded her wordplay with a dictionary and an encyclopaedia – from 'Rococo' and 'Kookaburra' to the imaginary 'Quisquose' and the title track 'Aikea-Guinea'. One of Cocteau Twins' finest recordings, reactivating the levity and joy from *Head Over Heels*, *Aikea-Guinea* saw Robin Guthrie eradicate the problem of Eighties production clichés, Simon Raymonde appeared settled in the mix, and the manner in which Fraser broke into 'Quisquose' nailed the mercurial sound that *NME* described as, 'a cross between Piaf and a bird sanctuary'.

The indefinable alchemy of Cocteau Twins' music continued to mask the unhappiness that seemed to fuel the band, with Guthrie increasingly prickly and unpredictable. Ivo recalls the mixing session at Blackwing for *Aikea-Guinea*: he and John Fryer were making subtle adjustments without Guthrie – 'I think he was packing up some gear, before a tour,' says Ivo – in order to make Fraser's vocal clearer. As the band was going on tour, Ivo was elected to approve the mastered version in their absence: 'Robin said, "Use whatever version you think is best". So I used our mix, but when Robin heard the test pressing, he burst into tears! Of course we changed it back to his mix.'

Another example of his contradictory behaviour was that his resentment towards 'Song To The Siren' didn't mean that he wasn't prepared to allow the track a longer shelf life. When David Lynch unexpectedly requested permission to use the song – as well as Guthrie and Fraser – in the anticipated prom scene to *Blue Velvet*, Ivo informed the pair about the offer. 'I said that if they didn't like the idea, I wouldn't take it further. But they said, "Yes, absolutely". I pleaded my case to the lawyers for Buckley's estate, saying it would give Tim's music exposure, but they didn't give a fuck about art, they just wanted their $20,000. I was heartbroken. In the end, the prom scene wasn't in the film either.'

Guthrie also had a strange relationship with the press, wanting attention but then being difficult once he got it. Ivo had seen him rip into inexperienced journalists, such as a reporter for a Manchester newspaper who ended up in tears, telling Ivo, 'All I asked was how Robin got the name for the band and he said it was none of my business.'

The guitarist equally invited trouble when *NME*'s Danny Kelly turned up at Ivo's flat to interview Guthrie and Liz Fraser for a potential front cover. Deborah Edgely left them to it – Ivo stayed on, in the kitchen – and later returned to find, 'Robin and Danny red in the face, with real hostility in the air. Danny took me aside and said, "If you'd only told me, I've just wasted my time, I've got nothing out of them". I don't know what he expected as they usually didn't communicate.'

Ultimately, Guthrie was on much safer ground when he was creating music, and Ivo's trust in his blossoming studio skills had reunited Guthrie with The Wolfgang Press to produce two more EPs. With someone else handling the technical burden, the Wolfies could attend to refining their sound, and the four-track *Water* showed a marked advance over *Scarecrow*. There was more breadth, from filmic instrumental 'The Deep Briny' and delirious ballad 'My Way' to tribal waltz 'Tremble (My Girl Doesn't)', while 'Fire Eater' rectified the stiffness that blighted the duo's 'Respect' cover with a stealthier fusion of artful London and Motown rhythm.

The four-track *Sweatbox* was even better, benefiting from the return of Andrew Gray, this time for good. 'I could hear a funk element coming into The Wolfgang Press and more movement, like in reggae,' he recalls. Gray's addition meant there was another opinion in the mix, and as the band grew increasingly confident with their greater rhythmic stealth, they found Guthrie returning to his intransigent ways. 'Robin was very controlling and forthright in what he thought was right,' says Mick Allen. 'For example, I was adding various vocal layers on *Sweatbox*, to find out what worked, and he'd say, "No, that's the mix and we don't touch that". But he did bring things round to make it sound more palatable.'

'That was me being an idiot,' Guthrie recalls. 'I wasn't mature or experienced enough to allow other people to make their own record, so I was very much putting my stamp on it. It was me thinking that The Wolfgang Press was left field, and Mick's attitude would have stopped them at times. He was an old punk, and angry all the time, at everything.'

Guthrie could so easily have been talking about himself. In any case, *Water* and *Sweatbox* – and Gray's permanent addition to the ranks – indicated that Allen was able to subjugate his headstrong nature, to collaborate freely and remove the darkest elements of Mass and *The Burden Of Mules*.

Guthrie wasn't the only one taking time out to produce; Ivo had been at Palladium studios overseeing his new signing, Xymox. Nothing showed more than the arrival of the Dutch band that Ivo didn't care for categories, or that goth was unfashionable. The band, as they now exist, with only founder member Ronny Moorings remaining, are even more goth than they were upon signing to 4AD – all black clothes and hair, and po-faced expressions. These days, goth is called darkwave (one online site describes Xymox as, 'goth industrial electro', but it's clear where Moorings' roots lie – the band's

2012 covers album *Kindred Spirits* includes Joy Division, New Order and Cure songs.

Moorings (born Moerings) has been the band's driving force since he conceived Xymox in the late Seventies. More than thirty years later, he still persists, without a single break between line-ups. His driven personality is revealed via an email (his choice) response to questions for this book that totalled over twenty-one thousand words. 'I know I wrote a bit more than I should have,' he emails again, with classic understatement. 'It was also good for me to put things in order before I really forget all :).'

Born in Roosendaal in the south of Holland, Moorings says that, even at the age of six, 'I was a very opinionated little munchkin concerning music.' He formed his first band at twelve; his second was named Zymotics after an ancient medicinal term referring to acute infections. Clearly Moorings was not your average teenager. He only changed it to Xymox, 'because it looked better on paper, with a logo that resembled barbed wire'.

This suited the era: 'Economic depression, distrust in government, the fight for social justice and the need to create and take possession of affordable homes,' says Moorings, blighted Holland in the late Seventies and early Eighties.

Moving up the country to Nijmegen to attend university, Moorings studied the social sciences and formed a new band, LA Ruin, which he then renamed Lace: 'We were almost heavy metal but with melodies,' he says. But as his political views led to demonstrating for nuclear disarmament and squatters rights, and squatting himself, he turned to Joy Division and the 'Neue Deutsche Welle' ('New German Wave'), which he describes as, 'the new industrial music from Germany that set the mood perfectly for total nihilism and cynicism … soundtracks for all the people dressed in black. It fitted the lifestyle of most young people, mainly students and drop-outs in this period.'

Working as a barman at a local venue, Doornroosje, Moorings saw countless shows, including Bauhaus – 'the ultimate goth band' – and The Birthday Party: 'Nick Cave was swinging like a monkey from left to right using the light rig frames. I wanted to be part of things which were happening in front of my eyes. I wanted a band instead of just making things late at night on my own that no one else would hear.'

The chance came after he'd met Anka Wolbert in a Nijmegen bar, 'hair up, backcombed. I had to talk to her. We ended up spending the night together. She said she wanted to play bass on the tracks I played for her. I released the tape under the name Xymox.'

Living in Highgate in north London since returning to London in 2009 after extended periods in New York and Amsterdam, Wolbert now spells her first name Anka; unlike Moorings, she has retired from music, and now designs websites. 'In the Eighties,' she says, 'it was so exciting experimenting with music technology, as it was in the Nineties with the internet.'

Born 50 miles east of Roosendaal in Eindhoven, Wolbert had moved to Nijmegen to study Psychology. 'But I got corrupted by music,' she says. 'It was all new wave, and I saw Bauhaus too, Siouxsie and the Banshees, New Order. Dutch bands were desperate to get out of Holland, and I was always looking at England. I started playing bass and guitar, and I wanted to be a singer, but I bought a keyboard and started playing around with tapes and loops.'

Following Cocteau Twins and Dead Can Dance, Xymox's dynamic also depended on a male and female couple, but Moorings and Wolbert were particularly competitive. Moorings says that the lovers would test each other by sleeping around, adding, 'yet for a long time, we could not let each other go'. What made this equation more interesting, and trickier, was a third prominent band member, Pieter Nooten. Moorings had met him while squatting: 'Pieter was a funny guy with short, punk-like red-blonde dyed hair who shared the same passion of making music.'

Another southern Dutchman, Nooten was also another precocious child, 'nervous and restless,' he says. To help pacify him, his parents bought him a home organ, which he became obsessed with: 'No lessons, no notes, no chord structures, just random searching for harmonies and melodies.' He was eventually diagnosed with ADHD (Attention Deficit Hyperactivity Disorder), which, he says, 'brought on annoying side effects such as isolating myself from people and situations'.

In his university student years, Nooten shared Moorings' outlook on life. (He also asks to respond to questions by email.) 'The early Eighties were a time of pent-up panic, when we were constantly exposed to the threat of war, a further economic decline and no positive perspective,' he writes. 'The trend was "black" and "gloomy" and the regulatory mood was "depressing". I felt at home in this culture, but I longed for a glimmer of beauty, something more aesthetically satisfying, and I found it in Joy Division's *Closer*, which had an immediate transformative impact on my life.'

Nooten and Moorings had shared musical equipment but composed separately, and Xymox's debut EP *Subsequent Pleasures* featured just Moorings and Wolbert after they'd both moved to Holland's capital, Amsterdam. Returning to Nijmegen to distribute copies of the EP, Moorings discovered that Cocteau Twins was playing at Doornroosje. Before the show, he saw who he thought were Robin Guthrie and Elizabeth Fraser: 'Without hesitating, I started asking them questions. They said they were the support act, Dead Can Dance. They put me on the guest list and I gave them a copy of *Subsequent Pleasures*. Both bands blew me away that night.'

Sensing his chance, Moorings called Nooten. 'After severe persuasion, Pieter also moved to Amsterdam and the band was now complete. We only needed more songs.' Moorings and Nooten began co-writing – pale, sad, dreamy, gloomy songs that mirrored the need for a glimmer of beauty in troubled times. The politics of squatting or anti-nuclear protest were conspicuously absent.

Wolbert was also writing. 'Xymox was an intense band,' she recalls. 'Three songwriters didn't make it easy. But we worked towards a common goal, and we wanted to grow. And it was fun at first to explore.'

Dead Can Dance asked Xymox to support them on a UK tour, and Brendan Perry told Moorings about 4AD, and gave Ivo his copy of *Subsequent Pleasures*. Moorings delivered a second demo: 'It was melodic but very experimental, as we weren't good songwriters yet. Everything was about atmosphere.'

As with Dead Can Dance, Ivo was initially guarded. 'I told Ronny I really liked it, because it's important to say well done, but that I wasn't looking to get involved. But Xymox had a sadness that I really enjoyed. Their influences were apparent but some things didn't sound like New Order or The Cure. Pieter's ballad "Equal Ways" was absolutely gorgeous.'

Unfortunately, touring worsened Nooten's ADHD and he'd already left Xymox, so it was Moorings and Wolbert that had turned up at Ivo's house, in full make-up and hair extensions, 'our gothic extravaganza', in Moorings' words. He says that he told Ivo they wanted to visit 'the notorious Batcave club', London's centre of goth subculture. 'But Ivo was dismissive and said goth was over in the UK and The Batcave had become a tourist attraction.'

Goth was indeed floundering as a scene, but that wasn't important; what was key was Ivo finding Xymox's heart-rending tunes hard to resist, and offering Xymox a one-album contract. Nooten's replacement Frank Weyzig, and drummer Jos Heijnen had joined the band, but Moorings claims Nooten suddenly reappeared after he'd found out about the 4AD deal. 'Pieter said he was feeling relaxed, and he had his priorities straight ... he could always charm people when he needed something off them,' Moorings claims. 'I had no problem because he was part of the songwriting team. I was glad he was giving it one more try.'

Nooten remembers it very differently. 'I was asked back by Ronny and Anka, for obvious reasons: I wrote a lot of the music and owned the synthesiser and drum computer, and most importantly, I knew how to make them work!'

On a modest budget, and buoyed by the experience of It'll End In Tears, Ivo took the (unpaid) producer's role at Palladium for a ten-day stint at recording Xymox's album debut. The pressure and the band's inexperience immediately showed, with Heijnen effectively sidelined for the more trustworthy Linn drum machine. This only reinforced the New Order comparisons: remove the inspired mellotron intro and 'Stranger' was a dead ringer for 'Blue Monday'. But the predominantly crepuscular mood of the finished album, Clan Of Xymox, more closely mirrored *Movement*, New Order's own debut album that had preceded the Mancunians' electro-pop rebirth, a despondent dance through the ruins.

Moorings felt that a Dutch band wouldn't be taken as seriously, so he didn't put the band's individual name credits on the album: 'It was better just to hide our identity, giving us a degree of mystery and the benefit of the doubt with reviews.' True, there was little precedent for Dutch bands, alternative or otherwise, in the UK; Moorings claims the majority of UK reviews reckoned the band was Scottish (was it the Palladium connection, or the 'Clan' suggestion?). In any case, reviews were positive: 'a nervous and brilliant record' (*Melody Maker*), 'a strange and wonderful debut' (*Sounds*). 4AD's roster seemed to protect any new signing from adverse press … the wheel had turned.

Ivo even believes, '*Clan Of Xymox* was a much better record than New Order could ever dream of making.' This lofty claim, favourably comparing his nascent pretenders to a band that were loved as much as their former incarnation Joy Division, was not atypical, this being a man whose tastes did not dovetail with popular opinion. For example, Ivo says, 'all the fuss around The Smiths, I never got over. And I never liked Morrissey's voice. Apart from "How Soon Is Now", I've never enjoyed a Smiths song.' As for New Order, 'I really hate them,' he says. 'That's an extreme reaction, but I respected Ian Curtis so much, it's ridiculous that Joy Division would carry on with someone who couldn't sing or write lyrics.'

Following John Fryer's mix of Xymox's album, he and Ivo remixed and extended two of the strongest tracks for a twelve-inch single. Ivo has mixed feelings about what he and the engineer had achieved: the nine-minute 'A Day' remix, for example, 'is nuts … there's even a didgeridoo on there. But it doesn't really work.' Regarding 'Stranger', 'it wasn't much different to the album version but it's one of the best mixes I was ever involved in.'

John Peel was on side, particularly enjoying '7th Time', with Wolbert on lead vocals, leading to two Peel sessions in June and November. But though 'A Day' was 4AD's most concisely commercial single since Modern English's 'I Melt With You', it only sold 3,500 copies, compared to 45,000 for Cocteau Twins' *Sunburst And Snowblind* and even 13,000 for Xmal Deutschland's 'Incubus Succubus II'. But in America, the video to 'A Day' (in which Nooten didn't even figure and Wolbert was a peripheral figure next to Moorings) got valuable exposure on MTV, despite the fact the track was only available on import. Before *Clan Of Xymox* became the second 4AD album to be licensed to the States, by the US independent Relativity, 'Xymox contributed to the growing popularity of 4AD on a global scale,' says Ivo.

4AD and Beggars Banquet's profile in America had been further raised by working with British exporters Windsong and American importers Caroline, with three to five hundred copies of each release serviced to Rockpool, a marketing company with its own newsletter and alternative chart. By 1985, American college radio had gathered momentum alongside the spurt in independent record labels, with the likes of 'A Day' striking radio programmers as adventurous *and* commercial, and a modern, gleaming alternative to the guitar-centric homegrown scene spearheaded by bands such as R.E.M., Sonic Youth and Hüsker Dü.

Given the small amount of staff, the workload in the 4AD office must have been considerable, but Ivo also found time to initiate another round of This Mortal Coil sessions. The idea of a trilogy of This Mortal Coil albums had taken shape as *It'll End In Tears* came to fruition, so in March 1985, he had booked five days at Palladium and taken Martin McCarrick to score a series of string arrangements. 'At Palladium with Xymox, I'd realised what an incredible musician Jon Turner was, and that he really wasn't precious about how his work might end up distorted, manipulated or simply abandoned,' says Ivo. 'I also wanted to establish a blueprint for working that wasn't reliant on 4AD musicians and friends, and I also enjoyed the relaxed residential aspect that everyone I'd sent to Palladium had enjoyed. We'd work from 11am until 11pm and finish off with a few hands of poker with whoever was around.'

One poker player who hung around the studio was Turner's friend Les McKeown, the former singer of the Scottish Seventies pop stars

The Bay City Rollers, an obsession of many a pre-pubescent and teenage girl. 'Late at night,' Ivo recalls, 'I'd often play a cassette with David Sylvian's *Brilliant Trees* on one side and Scott Walker's *Climate Of Hunter* on the other. Les would say, "Who's this, then? Do people make a living out of this kind of music?"'

Ivo had a good reason for not relying on the immediate 4AD family: the fact that the term 'family' could even be used. 'I hated the fact that people described This Mortal Coil as a band,' he says. 'There was never any rehearsing and other than Gini [Ball] and Martin [McCarrick], no two musicians ever played together in the studio. Some never even met each other. It was a studio project.'

Yet the news would draw on label allies Mark Cox, Steven Young, Andrew Gray, David Curtis, Richie Thomas and Peter Ulrich. Ivo had not invited Robin Guthrie: 'He'd been no fun on *It'll End In Tears*. He'd played on "The Last Ray" and afterwards he disowned it, saying I'd taken out all his good bits.'

But Ivo had approached Elizabeth Fraser and Lisa Gerrard, and been turned down by both, albeit for different reasons. Fraser's refusal wasn't down to Robin Guthrie's negativity but a common cold; the Cocteaus singer had felt it had spoilt her attempt at singing Judy Collins' 'My Father' and she declined to try again. Gerrard was offered Pearl Before Swine's 'The Jeweller'. 'It was a song that Ivo connected to but I couldn't,' she says. 'Music is so elusive, and you either get it or you don't. I needed an internal connection, from the source of the work itself, and these weren't even my words. I felt like I'd have had to reinvent myself, which would have been too difficult.'

Ivo was also turned down by a trio of iconic singers: Scott Walker, David Sylvian and Robert Wyatt, the former drummer and co-vocalist of UK progressive rock icons Soft Machine who carved out a rich and varied solo career that included his own notable series of covers. 'I only got a direct response from Robert Wyatt – who I'd asked to try Pearls Before Swine's "Rocket Man". He said, "My days for singing funny little pop songs are over". That was a massive "FYT" and I never again asked more established singers, for fear of being turned down again.'

Simon Raymonde was a principal part of the second, and longer, session of recordings at Blackwing with John Fryer. '*It'll End In Tears* had been super-rushed, like a production line of people,' Raymonde recalls. 'This time, I could come into my own.'

Raymonde wrote and played the piano parts for Van Morrison's 'Come Here My Love', Pearls Before Swine's 'The Jeweller', and Colin Newman's *A–Z* cut 'Alone' and his own 'Ivy And Neat'. This was one of several instrumentals that Ivo and John Fryer began to stockpile, supplemented with their own compositions, to help, Ivo says, 'the whole thing flow, to feel like four separate sides to an album that would also work as a single CD'.

As the music took shape, prototype versions of 'Rocket Man', [ambient pianist] Harold Budd and Brian Eno's 'Not Yet Remembered', The Comsat Angels' 'Total War' and The Boys Next Door's 'Shivers' were abandoned, as Ivo strived to find the best blend. 'For example,' he explains, 'the vocal I had for "Come Here My Love" was beautiful but it didn't gel with Simon's arrangement, so the music evolved into "Red Rain", which I named after the slice of French film dialogue hidden in the song.'

Other music samples were buried in the mix, while the second half of 'A Heart Of Glass' was inspired by the spectral foghorn effect from Steve Miller's 'Song For Our Ancestors' and its parent album *Sailor*, 'a crash course in really interesting, unpredictable crossfades'.

Ivo clearly favoured the similarly progressive actions of his art-rock-leaning hot house of artists, and taking the producer's role to help shape the outcome advanced the aspect of what truly engaged him – the music. But it inevitably left less time for the business side of running a record label, which Ivo admits was neither his strength nor his interest. Contracts, for example, he calls, 'about as interesting to me as Chemistry classes had been at school'.

It turned out that Dif Juz had felt sufficiently perturbed to leave 4AD – a first for Ivo – after 1981's twin EPs, releasing a full-length album *Who Says So?* for another independent label, Red Flame. But by the time the improvised performance *Time Clock Turn Back* was released by the cassette-only label Pleasantly Surprised, Dif Juz were back in the fold and recording a new album, *Extractions*.

Ivo feels the band had abandoned 4AD because they thought they were being ripped off. 'There was absolute mistrust, but I don't know why. Maybe we didn't give them enough of an advance.'

'It was more that we were scared of being typecast as a 4AD band,' bassist Gary Bromley admits. '4AD wasn't fully recognised that way back then but it had started to get like that, or so we believed. We just wanted to be Dif Juz.'

Unlike Cocteau Twins, Dif Juz had had the courage of their convictions to move away from the label. 'We had played a show in Italy, where people thought we all lived in a 4AD house, with Colourbox and Cocteau Twins, this big, happy family, and had asked what it was like,' recalls drummer Richie Thomas. 'We didn't want to get pigeonholed, but equally, Ivo didn't show us a great deal of encouragement, to record again, or even say he really liked us – not to me, anyway. So we made our own way, and we did a deal with Red Flame where we paid for, and owned, the music. But *Who Says So?* came out disjointed and not very professional.'

4AD and Dif Juz had become reacquainted in late 1984, when Thomas bumped into Ivo on the morning of a Dif Juz concert, and invited him along to the band's matinee show. Robin Guthrie and Elizabeth Fraser, who were cutting a Cocteau Twins record around the corner, also came along. 'Dif Juz was exciting, different, rhythmic, outside the box, and very powerful,' Guthrie recalls. 'They blew me away.'

At Ivo's suggestion, Guthrie took the band to Palladium to record the new album. When Fraser visited the studio, she agreed to sing on a track that Thomas – suffering from a busted relationship – had named 'Love Insane'. 'I think Liz agreed to cheer me up,' says Thomas. 'She said, "Do you think I'll do it justice, do you *really* want me to sing?" Yeah, I said, give it a shot! She used her voice as an instrument anyway. But we didn't ask Liz because we were trying to sell more records.'

Extractions was another glorious and indefinable excursion into Dif Juz-world, albeit through a sonic Guthrie filter. Thomas recalls the Curtis brothers didn't like the guitar sound that they were given:

'A syrupy, chorus reverb honey … like Cocteau Twins. David and Alan wanted to remix it, but Robin wouldn't. He'd do things to the drums, and I'd say not to, but he would anyway. He acted like he was captain of this ship, though very persuasively! It was about control for Robin. He said, "I want to do the best for you", and naïvely, I think he meant it. And we really did like him.'

Guthrie: 'I don't think Dif Juz sounded too much like me, but it was the first time I'd worked with them, and I was in complete awe of them. Looking back, I do cringe a bit.'

The friendship survived, and following the aforementioned Sadler's Wells show in December 1984, Dif Juz joined Cocteau Twins for a full UK tour, including a climactic night at London's prestigious classical showcase the Royal Festival Hall.

'We called it the Art Shit tour,' says Richie Thomas. 'Everything was very beautifully done, with theatrical light effects and props. We'd drive up and down the motorway during the miners' riots, England in revolution – I was working on a building site at the time! One minute, I was digging a deep trench for a sewage pipe and the next I was playing a theatre. Robin was in the dressing room saying, "Have you ever tried caviar?" He asked me to play sax on "Lorelei" before Liz started singing, and at the end of the tour, he gave me £200 [£550 by 2013 levels], which was unnecessary, but a lovely gesture.'

Thomas also witnessed, at close quarters, how Elizabeth Fraser was a jumble of nerves. 'She always found it very difficult to go out there and sing, and some days it looked like she was in torture, madly pulling at her fingers. But she always sang absolutely beautifully and she never had a bad night.'

There was one drawback on the tour: Dead Can Dance bassist Scott Rodger had to step in to replace Gary Bromley in Dif Juz. 'I'd been diagnosed with schizophrenia when I was twenty-one, and I'd got ill, brought on by taking speed,' Bromley admits. 'The band stuck by me, but it was a continual battle, and I just had to muddle through.'

Richie Thomas: 'We were trying to learn new stuff and Gary couldn't seem to remember anything. Dave would have to have long conversations with him. I was more light-hearted, with Alan stuck in the middle. But it wasn't the same with Scott. The original four had been together since the start.'

Gary Bromley: 'It was good to hear I was missed, but I'd stopped enjoying it anyway. David was very strong-willed and had taken the leader role, and they'd all started to tell me what to do, which became a chore rather than the labour of love we'd experienced when we'd written our own parts from jamming. So I left the band for good.'

Bromley was still a member for one extended, extraordinary session that Dif Juz recorded but Ivo rejected, and the tapes remain unreleased to this day, 4AD's very own holy grail. Thomas had met reggae legend Lee 'Scratch' Perry through an ex-girlfriend; she had courageously invited Perry to stay at her mother's house, and invited Thomas to meet the legendary certified space cadet.

'There were about ten of us in this council house, and Lee came in, threw a bottle of nail varnish removal on the electric bar fire,' says Thomas. 'It made this massive flash of flame, high up and across the ceiling, and he shouted, "FIRE!" At one point, I slipped on a Dif Juz record, and Lee said he liked it. He exuded this barrier, which was a way of protecting himself, but he was fun to be around, and we hung out for couple of months.'

Perry and Dif Juz soon agreed to record together. 'We said we'd do one of his, then one of ours,' Thomas recalls. 'Lee started singing Bob Dylan's "The Mighty Quinn", so we did that and called it "The Mighty Scratch". But we ended up only doing three more tracks that we'd written. Lee thought we were a modern version of what he used to do, so he wrote words for our music, about the IMF [International Monetary Fund], McDonald's and Stonehenge, just before the ban on walking over Stonehenge. It was really prophetic stuff.'

The band considered the session some of their very best work, but Ivo asked Robin Guthrie to, in essence, rescue it, which included editing 'The Mighty Scratch' down from nine minutes. 'This was despite Lee saying you couldn't edit out one word of what he said because everything that came out of his mouth was intentional!' says Ivo.

The iron wills of Guthrie versus Perry resembled the immovable mountain meeting the irresistible force. 'I'm mixing Lee fuckin' Perry, so no pressure there!' Guthrie recalls. 'He sat around being intimidating and weird, laying little coins around so the lights would bounce off them. But he let me get on with it.'

Richie Thomas: 'Robin's talent includes his powers of persuasion, and he managed to get his way, and he did make things more concise and create a sense of space. What we did with Lee was still Dif Juz, but more guttural and raw, and Lee's lyrics were very real. It didn't fit the 4AD doctrine, which was much artier, prettier music, with lilies on the artwork, beautiful objects, quite precious. If Lee hadn't been singing on it, I'm sure the session would have been released.'

'I thought it was worth releasing,' says Guthrie. 'But Lee wasn't as malleable as a young band gagging to be on 4AD. He wouldn't have given a fuck. Ivo liked to control the situation.'

Ivo's comments concur with this claim: 'I knew Lee would be a nightmare to deal with. The first time we met, he was spray-painting the walls, and intensely looking at the spray in the air. His eyes, when they paid attention, were like a very young child, trying to understand an adult for the first time. But ultimately, I didn't think it was very good. I was a huge reggae fan, and Dif Juz, especially Gary and Richie, had dub aspirations. I would have loved to release a collaboration that actually worked. If I heard it now, perhaps I'd realise how wrong I was.'

Perry subsequently asked Dif Juz to back him at a show at London's Dingwalls. 'Lee liked us because he didn't want to just do the same thing again,' says Thomas. 'We never got paid for the show, but we didn't want anything from him, he was someone we just loved.'

The reggae element to 4AD would have to remain in Colourbox's hands, the only exponents on the label beside The Wolfgang Press and Dif Juz to meaningfully tap any black music tradition. The problem was none of them showed the ability to nail a swinging groove. On top of this Colourbox suffered from songwriting block: it had been three years since debut single 'Breakdown', and they'd still not released an album or something that truly defined them. 'It was a chore,' Martyn Young admits. He says that Sixties (and Morrissey) idol Sandie Shaw had asked for a song, 'but we declined because it would have been too hard to come up with something'.

Ivo remained patient and indulgent; he liked the Young brothers and sensed their potential; Colourbox was also signed to a five-album deal so he had a vested interest. For the time being, the duo's safest passage was another genre revamp, and at least the new single, 'The Moon Is Blue', was the band's best yet, a slice of Fifties-slanted doo-wop, by way of Sixties northern soul, fronted by Lorita Grahame's fulsome vocal and massed harmonies in support. 'A good song with iffy lyrics,' is Martyn Young's conclusion, but it was infinitely preferable to the B-side cover of the Motown classic 'You Keep Me Hanging On', that they'd first attempted for 1984's second Kid Jensen radio session. At least Colourbox were now selling records, about 10 to 12,000 of every single, arguably aided by the 4AD roster surrounding the band, and 'The Moon Is Blue' made number 3 in the UK independent chart.

A debut album finally materialised in May, though *Colourbox* (self-titled, like their EP) resembled a depletion of the store cupboard rather than a record proudly conceived as a unified statement. The ten tracks included 'The Moon Is Blue', 'Say You', 'Punch' and even 'You Keep Me Hanging On'. Of the two older tracks, 'Just Give 'Em Whiskey' was more a string of samples over a driving beat than a song, and 'Sleepwalker' was a brief piano instrumental in search of a film soundtrack. This left four reasonably adept pop-funk songs.

Ivo was disappointed enough with so much old material to demand that Colourbox give away a bonus EP with the first thousand copies of the album. Young duly assembled a similar random collection of edits, remixes and the vaguely new 'Hipnition', which ex-member Ian Robbins had written. The barrel-scraping was antithetical to the 4AD mark of quality, and Young knew it. 'A lot of the album is unlistenable,' he confesses.

Cocteau Twins had no such problems, creatively agile and continuously recording. 4AD released two new EPs, *Tiny Dynamine* and *Echoes In A Shallow Bay*, two weeks apart, 'to break the mould a bit,' Robin Guthrie explains. Using a makeshift studio rented to them by musician/producer William Orbit, the Cocteaus benefited again from not thinking about having a chart hit or the clock ticking, and with no expectations of them from within band or label camp to record a follow-up to *Treasure*: 'No outside influences at all, in fact,' Guthrie asserts.

The EPs were two halves of a whole, with matching covers – 'like a brother and sister,' says Guthrie. The sleeves from another Nigel Grierson paint/water experiment were of a piece, this time shot through layers of glass to lend the images a three-dimensional glow. They're Guthrie's favourite Cocteaus sleeves, and among his favourite Cocteaus records: 'They're fucking gorgeous,' he grins.

Simon Raymonde agrees: 'They're really beautiful and really under-valued.' The reason for the latter, Ivo suggests, was the absence of an obvious lead track that reviewers and radio could grab hold of, which didn't make for a cohesive album. 'But I'm extremely fond of both records and I agree with Robin that they're the best Cocteaus sleeves.'

The consensus of fans and critics is that neither rank among the band's all-time greats. Perhaps releasing both as one mini-album would have made more impact. In retrospect, *Tiny Dynamine* sounds slighter than its clearly underrated counterpart; 'Pale Clouded White' and 'Eggs And Their Shells' deserve a place on any Cocteaus compila-tion. Both titles sprang from Fraser's latest encyclopaedic raid, on butterflies and moths (also see 'Great Spangled Fritillary' and 'Melonella'). A modern-day treat is to read online lyric sites attempt-ing to articulate Fraser's glossolalia. Try singing along with the chorus of 'Sultitan Itan' from *Tiny Dynamine*: '*sultiapollanella-nella cossus cossus abillatoeya stroemella ...*' Yet Guthrie insists that Fraser always sang discernible lyrics. 'How else do you think I could double-track Liz's vocals?' he asks.

Between the release of *Aikea-Guinea* and the twin EPs, the Cocteaus had played five shows in America, including the Newport Music Hall in Ohio's college town Columbus, as a favour to Tim Anstaett, whose fanzine *The Offense* (renamed *The Offense Newsletter*) had been so supportive to 4AD since its simultaneous launch in 1980. The show had a proper sense of occasion, as if royalty was visiting, and in one sense, Guthrie and Fraser resembled the king and queen of this myste-rious new world across the water. Anstaett's latest issue had the cover headline 'Cocteaus Fever', and local TV station WBNS had run a story where the excited reporter talked up, 'one of Britain's number one bands … who will be influencing mainstream rock'n'roll music for years to come'.

The WBNS coverage extended to a live report from the venue, where Cocteaus fans, hair primped and teased to match the finery of their outfits, gathered, they said, 'from hundreds of miles away' to pay homage to their bashful idols.

Between Cocteau Twins' *Aikea-Guinea* and the release of the twin EPs, Dead Can Dance had been finishing their second album, intent on proving that they could overcome the relative disappointment of the debut album. Brendan Perry says those songs had arrived with him and Lisa Gerrard on the plane, pretty much formed in their minds: 'Now we had to find our musical vision.'

Choosing to record as a duo instead of a band, Perry and Gerrard's guiding principle was that rock'n'roll had begun to exhaust itself, recycling rather than reinventing, and refusing to acknowledge, says Perry, 'that all musical forms are basic hybrids or fusions by nature. And that the essence or attitude within the form itself must progress.'

These were lofty ideals, conceived in a lofty flat fourteen floors up from the ground, as the couple consumed the records they borrowed from a nearby library. 'I became obsessed with classical music,' Perry admits. 'But baroque music, Gregorian chants and film music too.'

Gerrard: 'I saw John Barry and Nino Rota influences immediately turn up in Brendan's arrangements and choice of instrumentation, like the cimbalom [hammered dulcimer]. We'd gone shopping with the first advance from 4AD, and bought a sequencer and a Mirage [sampler] so Brendan could access all these keyboard sounds.'

Abandoning John Fryer and Blackwing, the pair worked with producer John Rivers (who had made a mark by producing the suitably precious guitar mavericks Felt) at his studio in the Midlands 'John was to Brendan what Jon Turner had been to Robin,' says Ivo, namely someone supporting, rather than leading, the chance to learn the ropes. Perry never again needed an outside producer.

The leap that Dead Can Dance made matched that of Cocteau Twins from *Garlands* to *Head Over Heels*, beginning with the startling opener 'De Profundis (Out Of The Depths Of Sorrow)' on a startling album called, a little less startlingly, *Spleen And Ideal.* Gerrard's voice cut through the massed choral drift like a galleon emerging through the fog, in a way that Scott Walker used to do in the Sixties, except Gerrard was singing what sounded like Latin but was actually her own language, Fraser-style. 'Enigma Of The Absolute' was Perry's chance to shine, in the kind of time-suspended drama that fancifully repositioned Scott Walker to the eighteenth century. The lyrics were more Homer than rock'n'roll: *'Through darkened doors, her aspect veiled with indecision/ Gazing out to sea, she craved lucidity.'*

Nothing quite like this classically infused solemnity and vaulted ambition was to be heard elsewhere for at least a decade, in the instrumental era of Godspeed You! Black Emperor and Stars of the Lid. For the time being, Dead Can Dance was operating in a field of one, which the album cover to *Spleen And Ideal* made plain, ramping up the enigma with a figure in a hooded red cape holding a cut-out white star in front of a huge, half-demolished building. It looked like a still from a Tarkovsky film, shot in some forgotten corner of Estonia. In fact, it was staged by photographer Colin Grey, in Salford on the outskirts of Manchester's city centre, outside an old dock warehouse that explosives had failed to bring down. The white star in the outstretched hand of a mysterious hooded figure was a piece of rubbish discarded on the ground.

The striking image, in saturated colour, was perfect for Dead Can Dance's newfound poise and ambition; the butterfly emerged, in saturated colour and spectacle, from its cocoon. And they were bound to leave some behind, people such as Robin Guthrie. 'They were no longer the same people we knew,' Guthrie says. 'They turned from normal to cerebral people quoting Sartre in interviews.'

On the contrary, believes Simon Harper, who was to join 4AD's international department in 1987: 'Lisa Gerrard is one of the funniest, most un-pretentious people I've ever met.'

Dead Can Dance continued to reinforce 4AD's identity as a repository for sensitive, rarefied, idealistic and introverted souls, their music lacking in the kind of humour, playfulness or cultural comment that provided other entry points to artists on the likes of Factory, Mute and Rough Trade. 'There was a sense of self-importance about 4AD and artists that some would have hated, and some would have loved,' says Deborah Edgely. 'Some people hated bands on principle because they didn't like the label, which was hard to deal with. But the band was most important; if you didn't represent them fairly, and treat them individually, you might as well not bother.'

Ivo naturally, 'didn't give a damn' if anyone found Dead Can Dance pompous, pretentious or aloof. 'They were absolutely brilliant, and I was so proud to represent them. Everything released on the label was extremely important to me but Cocteau Twins, Dead Can Dance and This Mortal Coil was the shape of 4AD for me, as it proved to be for many others. They were as good and as important as all the music that had influenced me as a child and that had led me to this place of running a label.'

The year 1985 ended with two band compilations, which showed Guthrie's continuing impact on 4AD. Under his watch, The Wolfgang Press had beaten a path away from their impenetrable past, and the majority of the last three EPs *Scarecrow*, *Water* and *Sweatbox* made up *The Legendary Wolfgang Press And Other Tall Stories*. The second was Cocteau Twins' own collection, *The Pink Opaque*, their first album to be released in America, specially compiled for the independent label Relativity, and the first 4AD album to be pressed in the new Compact Disc format.

True to form, Robin Guthrie had been unhappy about how the American market hadn't been open to Cocteau Twins sooner. 'Ivo had the opportunity to license us quite early on but instead he made a lot of money exporting us, until *The Pink Opaque*. We just picked the songs that we played live; the album is a set list.'

According to Beggars Banquet's Martin Mills, 'Licensing was the only way to survive long-term, by picking up big advances from American labels for long-term contracts. For example, A&M paid a £75,000 advance for Bauhaus, and Sire paid £60,000 for Modern English. They were huge amounts at the time, and you ran your business on those advances. Beggars had over ten licensing deals going at any one time.'

'I'd love to know what my opportunities to license Cocteau Twins were,' Ivo responds. His experience with A&M and Colourbox hadn't endeared him to major labels, and his reticence beforehand was due to safeguarding quality – 'I didn't enjoy working with licensees who all expressed an opinion and wanted to influence the records that we were making,' he says.

The second issue, according to Ivo, was even more problematic. 'One questionable aspect about signing to 4AD at the time was that your [band's] record wouldn't be available domestically in America, because I wasn't signing bands long-term, and most American licensees wanted at least a five-year contract on the table,' Ivo explains. 'American indie labels weren't a serious option for licensing as they couldn't offer an advance, but we thought it was worth experimenting with Relativity. In the meantime, the exports had helped 4AD create a mystique and loyalty from the fans. The real glory years for me were those years, when everything 4AD did was sought after, and got a very good reputation.'

4AD's arrangement with Relativity had a spin-off benefit, as it meant Ivo could import copies of *The Pink Opaque* back to Britain and then export them out again to different territories, turning a profit on each copy. If 4AD was shipping British music to America and around the world, the label's next phase would see 4AD bringing American music to Britain for the first time. It wasn't planned; in fact, Ivo resisted it for a while. But when he accepted the challenge, it was to change the face, direction and future of the label from which there was no turning back.

9 1986

LE MYSTÈRE DES DELICATE CUTTERS
(bad601-cad613)

There were enough musical oddities in 4AD's catalogue, from The Wolfgang Press's beat fusion to Clan Of Xymox's synthetic dance, to counter the idea that the label's identity was limited to Cocteau Twins, This Mortal Coil and Dead Can Dance. But Ivo could not have under-lined the hyper-ethereal any more than he did by releasing a single by Dutch vocalist Richenel – especially given it was a grand ballad about a crush on a slave boy written by an operatic French diva and sung by a man of Dutch Suriname extraction considered the Netherlands' version of Boy George.

In its remixed form, 'L'Esclave Endormi' remains one of 4AD's lost treasures. The man helping to sustain the label's measured and spellbound attempt to transcend mortal form for something more divine was Hubertus Richenel Baars, born in Amsterdam. He now lives in the south of France, his base for an ongoing career as a jazz singer.

'I have had a crazy life,' Richenel declares. 'I never planned to make music, or sing, but music was always in our house.' He was neverthe-less already twenty-one years old when he was invited to replace the departing singer of the band Luxor Funk. The one potential issue was that the (female) singer's boyfriend was a Hells Angel, and the bikers made up the band's core fan base. 'The strange thing was that the Angels loved me too!' he recalls, even when he dressed up. 'I wasn't always in drag, but I always wore heels and lipstick. That was still a big deal in those days.'

Richenel knew he wasn't destined to spend his life working as a translator for an Amsterdam bank and moonlighting for Hells Angels. At art school, he befriended the multi-media collective Fetisj, who backed him on his 1982 debut album *La Diferencia*. The title was ambitious, less so his pedestrian soul-funk. Salvation came in 1984 after hearing 'L'Esclave Endormi' (which translates as 'The Sleeping Slave') on the radio, sung by the sublimely camp French-Turkish singer/actress Armande Altaï.

The track was from the album *Nocturne Flamboyant*, produced by Martin Hannett, Factory Records' crazed and genius in-house producer, the man who had turned Joy Division's base metal into gold. Altaï's album attempted the same kind of vaulting classical/ electronic hybrid as the outrageous German singer Klaus Nomi; Richenel instantly wanted to cover the song, and after he rejected the request for a disco version from his new label, Dutch independent Megadisc, he aimed for the same exalted spirit of Altaï's original. He concocted a mood as exotic and precious as any Dead Can Dance quest, though the way Richenel entwined the styles of choirboy and soul boy against a backdrop of suspended synths was in line with Eighties synth-pop, more Art of Noise than Art of Goth.

Megadisc had sent Ivo a copy of Richenel's next album *Statue Of Desire*, which he hadn't enjoyed, except for 'L'Esclave Endormi'. 'It had an absolute purity and beauty, so I asked for the multi-tracks so that John and I could remix it – which I think we did beautifully.' The remix, released on a twelve-inch single alongside Richenel's original version, drew out the singer's superlative technique across seven giddy minutes.

'It's one of my all-time favourite releases on 4AD,' Ivo says. 'Beautiful image, logo, beautiful singing by a beautiful man. It's possibly my favourite sleeve credited to 23 Envelope. Nigel and Vaughan were collaborating at their best.'

23 Envelope's pursuit of beauty reached an apotheosis on 'L'Esclave Endormi'. Nigel Grierson's photograph of a naked boy, lying in a bath of milk, was posed like Michelangelo's twin statues L'Esclave Mourant (The Dying Slave) and L'Esclave Rebelle (The Rebellious Slave), but Vaughan Oliver says the image was more inspired by nineteenth-century German photographer Baron Wilhelm Von Gloeden, whose images of naked Sicilian youth – and the sleeve of 'L'Esclave Endormi' created ninety years later – are fragments of a very different moral age. 'Nigel kept asking the boy to get in a cold bath of milk,' Oliver recalls. 'You're working as an artist; you're not thinking it's naughty. These were two heterosexual men working on this. It's a lovely sleeve.'

'L'Esclave Endormi' became a one-off; Ivo saw no evidence in Richenel's other material to release anything else. But he could see what Richenel could bring to a song, and invited the singer to London, to join the ongoing sessions for the new This Mortal Coil album. Ivo paired him with two songs – Tim Buckley's 'I Must Have Been Blind' and Quicksilver Messenger Service's 'Fire Brothers', another of Ivo's west coast acid rock memories.

The singers that ended up on the second This Mortal Coil album all had the same undiscovered, untapped potential, with a talent for conveying the sadness and drama that the collective's music embodied. They also shared an androgynous aura. Though no one's sexuality was on Ivo's radar, the album's other male voice, Dominic Appleton, was also gay, like Richenel.

Appleton was discovered via a demo, by his band Breathless. The press release for the band's 2012 album *Green To Blue*, their first in nine years, began with a quote from Ivo: 'Without exaggeration, Dominic Appleton is by far my favourite living male vocalist. He has such a beautiful, sad voice and comes up with melodies that do the same.'

Appleton admits that *It'll End In Tears* had been a big influence on the London-based quartet. 'It was exactly what I was looking for at the time and something I hadn't heard before; unbelievable beauty,' he says. 'People focus on the gothic tag with 4AD but to me it was such delicate music, with fantastic textures. I'd immediately invested in

Tim Buckley and Roy Harper's catalogues and got pushed in all these lovely directions. Ivo pulled in a lot of people in the same way.'

Breathless had released its earliest singles on the band's own Tenor Vossa label; the 1985 EP *Two Days From Eden* had been recorded at Blackwing with John Fryer and Wolfgang Press engineer Drostan Madden. Hearing one track, 'Pride', was enough for Ivo to contact Appleton to say how much he'd liked it – but in this case, he didn't take it further by signing Breathless. A version of 'Pride' was even attempted for the new This Mortal Coil album, but Dif Juz guitarist David Curtis was unhappy with his accompaniment and Ivo scrapped the idea, saving some of Curtis's part for the instrumental 'Meniscus'.

Compensation for Appleton came in the form of an invite to sing on the album. Ivo matched Appleton's sorrowful baritone to three lyrics of unreserved melancholy: 'The Jeweller', Colourbox's 'Tarantula' and former Byrds member Gene Clark's 'Strength Of Strings', which Ivo says still never fails to reduce him to tears.

Ivo: 'Someone said to me that Dominic had the kind of voice that would have sung a lot of these songs in the first place. My experience of him in the studio was he was shy and a bit flustered, but such a wonderful voice. There were moments when he felt he couldn't hit a note, and then it would just build.'

Ivo also singles out Scottish sisters Louise and Dee Rutkowski, the vocal frontline of the white soul band Sunset Gun that Ivo had unearthed via a compilation cassette. 'More than anyone, they got what This Mortal Coil was about. Their voices took me back to the era of Emmylou Harris with Gram Parsons, or Linda Ronstadt, those wonderful, capable, pure voices that understand how to harmonise with each other as easily as breathing.'

The Rutkowskis co-sang 'I Want To Live' (from Gary Ogan and Bill Lamb's soft-rocking *Portland*), a second Tim Buckley cover 'Morning Glory', and provided back-up vocals to Appleton's trilogy. 'Ivo had wanted Scott Walker, but we managed to get our foot in the door instead!' says Louise Rutkowski. 'At the time, I was listening to Chic and Philadelphia soul, but listening to This Mortal Coil's originals, I realised that it was more "me" than the commercial stuff. I didn't find those songs dark or depressing, just interesting and beautiful, and Ivo pulled that out of me. Dee agrees that, singularly or together, This Mortal Coil has been the only thing we've ever done that's had any class or enjoyment. The rest has been hell!'

This female side of This Mortal Coil's vocal collective also included Jean, who had released a single and the EP *Lady Blue* under the name Jeanette, who Ivo paired up with 'Come Here My Love'. Introduced to Ivo by Bauhaus singer Peter Murphy, Alison Limerick sang 'My Father' and Talking Heads' 'Drugs' while 'Alone' was sung by Caroline Seaman, another discovery from a demo. Ivo also added Seaman's Elizabeth Fraser-style wordless vocal to the needling guitars and solemn backbeat of 'Red Rain'.

Compared to their own nascent solo careers that had yet to bear much fruit, the singers were part of a bigger event: a new family, all united by Ivo's obsessive vision. 'It was just the best experience because of Ivo, the combination of the music he was making and pulling together,' recalls Dee Rutkowski. 'There was something beautiful and real and true about it, because the real truth of life is that it's dark. Ivo was eccentric in the best way, with a passion for all things creative. And at the same time, he was running a record label!'

Ivo's capacity for overwork had already been proven, driven by 4AD's success and, perhaps, subconsciously, from a need to fill the spaces in his life. But he did have valuable office back-up – from Deborah Edgely to Rob Deacon, who had been working part-time in the label's warehouse since 1984. Deacon (who was killed in a canoeing accident in 2007) had been publishing *Abstract*, a vinyl-based fanzine that was as loyal to 4AD as *The Offense Newsletter* had been. In 1985, he had also begun his own independent label, named Sweatbox after The Wolfgang Press EP. Freed of the daily hassle of warehouse duties, Ivo had more time to spend in the studio, including an offer from Peter Murphy to produce the former Bauhaus singer's first solo album.

Bauhaus' shift to Beggars Banquet had paid off: a cover of David Bowie's 'Ziggy Stardust' reached number 15 on the UK national chart in 1982, getting them on *Top of the Pops*, and their third album, *The Sky's Gone Out*, had subsequently reached the UK national top five. Bauhaus had also broken into film. Where Cocteau Twins had been thwarted by Tim Buckley's lawyers, Bauhaus had successfully made it to celluloid by miming to 'Bela Lugosi's Dead' for the opening night-club scene of Tony Scott's vampire melodrama *The Hunger*, in which Bauhaus idol David Bowie had a modest role as a centuries-old bloodsucker.

Murphy also had a significant role in a dramatic TV and press advertising campaign for Maxell cassettes, playing the imperturbably cool figure pinned to a chair as the supposed crystal-clear tape wrecked the room but only ruffled his hair and tie. The image went around the world, no doubt expanding an already sizeable ego, and after one too many confrontations between stubborn factions within the band, Bauhaus split up after their fourth album, *Burning From The Inside*.

As the other three members regrouped around Daniel Ash's side project Tones on Tail – which was eventually renamed Love and Rockets – Murphy recorded an album with ex-Japan bassist Mick Karn under the name of Dalis Car. For Murphy's first solo album, he called on Ivo, impressed by This Mortal Coil and knowing that Ivo would not be the usual kind of overreaching producer who might stand in his way.

Not that Ivo thought Murphy had made the right choice. 'Peter had unstructured songs and jams and needed someone to help arrange it all,' Ivo recalls. 'He should have made it with John [Fryer] as I'm not a musician, but I was flattered that someone was asking me.'

Over five weeks at Blackwing, Ivo discovered that Murphy had left his ego at home. 'Though I'd never got close to Bauhaus, I'd really enjoyed them as people. Those weeks with Peter were nothing but gracious and fun, with lots of self-deprecating humour. There wasn't the hint of a tantrum. I'd go into the 4AD office every morning till midday, and once Deborah was there too, everything was safe and I could head to Blackwing.'

Working on Murphy's album *Should The World Fail To Fall Apart* made no difference to Ivo's standing as a producer, as he received no other such offer. But the collaboration had the most extraordinary payoff. Every night after recording had finished, Murphy and company would wind down to a cassette that he'd been given. For fifteen years, Swiss musicologist Marcel Cellier had recorded the Bulgarian State Radio & Television Female Vocal Choir, and in 1975 had released a selection of their recordings on his own label Disques Cellier – hence the French name *Le Mystère Des Voix Bulgares* on the cassette that Murphy insisted they enjoy every night.

So it wasn't the Aboriginal chants that Ivo had once talked about that became a possible direction for the label, but the Bulgarian choir's uncannily piercing, resonating timbre developed from the open-throated technique of singing. For Ivo, schooled by Elizabeth Fraser and Lisa Gerrard in the art of female vocal supremacy, it was a defining moment. 'It simply buckled my knees!' he recalls. 'The solo piece "Prïtourïtze Planinata" first did it. The more I listened to the album, the less interested I was in finding out how old the music was, or if any of the singers were still alive. The sound was all you needed, these incredible singers making sounds with lyrics that I couldn't understand.'

Ivo insisted Murphy help track down the origin of the tape, which led to him making an offer to license the album from Cellier. 'I had to own the album rather than a fourth-generation cassette, and to make it available so that others could have the same emotional experience,' Ivo says. 'And, of course, to be part of 4AD's catalogue. I'm so extraordinarily proud of having released that record. The circumstances are a reflection of the absolute purity that exists outside of the music industry.'

Ivo also had permission to license *Le Mystère Des Voix Bulgares* on to Virgin France and 'most beautifully' to Japan: 'That made it a Bulgarian recording, through England, and to Japan, just because they'd heard a 4AD-sounding record! It was so quickly jumped on everywhere else too.'

The album had no precedent outside of folkloric collections; the so-called 'World Music' movement hadn't yet been conceived, with only African music making a dent in Western tastes. The Bulgarians simply fit the 4AD aesthetic of sound, but its uncanny and sublime power was enough to reach consumers and media outlets alike unaware of 4AD.

The UK breakthrough came from DJ and former TV newsreader Richard Baker on BBC Radio 4, who had a much older and conservative demographic than BBC Radio 1. Baker had received one of the five thousand copies of a seven-inch single – 'Prïtourïtze Planinata' backed by 'Polegnala E Todora' – that 4AD had pressed for promotion. BBC Radio 2 subsequently playlisted the album and the choir – suddenly fêted outside of their usual domain – began to perform live, kickstarting a career that still thrives, albeit without the same media overkill.* The result was that 4AD had suddenly, unexpectedly, crossed over. 'It was such an exciting time,' Ivo recalls. 'You didn't know what could happen next.'

What did happen next was a surprise turn from Cocteau Twins: an acoustic record. With Simon Raymonde on This Mortal Coil duties, Robin Guthrie had decided to embark on a project that he says was less about Raymonde's position in the band than his own desire to record with just Elizabeth Fraser: 'To see if what we did worked without the drums and the huge reverb and the big wall of sound. Did we have substance?'

'I wasn't particularly bothered,' says Raymonde. 'My pride might have been dented for a few minutes. But it was strange because I didn't realise it was going to be released as Cocteau Twins. They could have asked if I minded. Of course I would have said no. It was their band, not mine. But people did start asking if I'd left the band.'

Guthrie was also occupied in establishing a studio for the Cocteaus, so 4AD put them in a residential studio outside London, where the duo cut just 32 minutes of material. After teething problems at the

---

* The first public performance of *Le Mystère Des Voix Bulgares* was as the soundtrack to the all-female dance troupe The Cholmondeleys for their support slot to Dead Can Dance at London's prestigious Barbican arts centre. The troupe's founder Lea Anderson was the singer of the band Temporary Title, who had been considered for one of the first Axis releases. One composer that Anderson commissioned to score her dance pieces was her boyfriend at the time, Drostan Madden, who would later produce tracks by a momentarily-reformed In Camera and also The Wolfgang Press.

cutting plant where the reverb distorted, the album had to be cut at the faster speed of 45rpm, 'to satisfy "Bat Ears" Guthrie, as the mastering engineer called him,' says Ivo.

'It's fucking gorgeous, that album,' says Bat Ears.

Fraser named it *Victorialand*, a region in the Antarctica that also inspired many of the song titles, from places ('Oomingmak') and animals ('Whales Tails') to the elements ('The Thinner The Air'). There was a third musician involved, with Richie Thomas's occasional saxophone and tablas woven into the fabric of the album's gentle serenity. It was obvious to anyone but the band that Cocteau Twins could work on a more intimate scale. '*Victorialand* is absolutely beautiful,' Ivo agrees. 'I also loved the fact that it didn't sound acoustic, or like any other Cocteau Twins record.'

Guthrie continued on a roll, accepting other offers of production, such as ex-Orange Juice frontman Edwyn Collins, British indie-pop artisans Felt and the American punk-blues band The Gun Club. But his increasing self-esteem, from recognition of his studio prowess and the money he was paid for production work, record sales and tours, was to give him the confidence to afford better drugs, and one effect of cocaine is an increased sense of confidence and bluster. As witnesses saw, Guthrie had the capacity for taking an awful lot of it, spurring him on to more work but also more dependency.

Guthrie admits that he got carried away during this period, especially in the company of The Gun Club's hellraising leader Jeffrey Lee Pierce, who was to die in 1996, aged thirty-seven, of a brain haemorrhage; he was also HIV positive and suffering from cirrhosis and chronic hepatitis. Guthrie wasn't that kamikaze-minded, but the manic schedule he set himself was compounded not just by cocaine but Thunderbird wine, 'the stuff that winos drink,' he admits. 'Cocteau Twins records were getting more beautiful and my lifestyle was getting more dangerous.'

One of the few 4AD bands that Guthrie didn't have a hand in was Colourbox, who had Martyn Young in the role of studio savant. It had been a year since Colourbox's debut album, and given Young's confession about depression and anger issues, it's easy to see him buried in his machine manuals and his reliance on samples, not wanting to play live, and struggling to find a way out of this vicious circle. A sliver of hope was bound up in not one new single, but two, released on the same day.

Granted, the first single was yet another cover, albeit a sterling version of Jamaican roots reggae singer Augustus Pablo's 'Baby I Love You So', which Lorita Grahame was born to sing. The equally unadventurous B-side, 'Looks Like We're Shy One Horse/Shoot Out', laid samples ripped from the 1968 spaghetti western *Once Upon a Time in the West* over reggae beats. The second single showed a spark of imagination. Young had composed a pumping instrumental based on a horn-style synth riff over massive drums that he envisaged would work well in a baseball arena. Football fan Vaughan Oliver suggested it could alternatively be used for the summer's approaching global football tournament the FIFA World Cup being held in Mexico, and that Colourbox should submit the track to the BBC.

With a cover star of the era's BBC football pundit Jimmy Hill in his younger, playing days, 'The Official Colourbox World Cup Theme' was a joyful and strange addition to the 4AD catalogue, and reputedly came very close to being chosen by the BBC for its theme music. The B-side 'Philip Glass' was another instrumental, this time a dreamy interlude named after the New York minimalist composer who had inspired it. Without any sense of what the young brothers were creating, the two tracks were identifying the elements that would mould the whiter side of popular British dance music – samples, ambience, the diverse terrain between all factions of dance rhythm, even the concept of behind-the-scenes producers eschewing the idea of an identifiable 'band'.

Emulating the success of 'The Moon is Blue', 'Baby I Love You So' and 'The Official Colourbox World Cup Theme' reached the UK independent top 10 (4 and 6 respectively), and Martyn Young says he was feeling positive. 'We started to feel more in control. We'd recorded at Palladium with Jon Turner who would only step in if you had a problem that needed fixing. It was a good atmosphere to learn in. Les McKeown was there too!'

John Fryer and Jon Turner's role guiding the likes of Robin Guthrie and Martyn Young to take charge themselves can't be underestimated, and even The Wolfgang Press accepted the idea that Fryer could be the answer after the controlling Robin Guthrie. Andrew Gray could already vouch for Fryer's accommodating ways during In Camera sessions. 'John was ideal,' says Mark Cox. 'He had technical knowledge, he was open to experimenting and I didn't think he'd contradict us, which was ideal.'

The whole band agrees with Ivo's view that the resulting album, *Standing Up Straight*, 'was The Wolfgang Press shaping up to be what they became'. Namely a contemporary outfit plying a sharp post-punk-funk, bruised and theatrical in a similar vein to Nick Cave's Bad Seeds (especially 'Hammer The Halo') with the dexterity of Talking Heads' taut, crisp rhythm and some of the knife-edge friction from Rema/Mass days, such as the lengthy 'Rotten'. 'It wasn't a sound that anyone else was making, so we had to make it ourselves,' says Cox. 'I thought what The Wolfgang Press were making was soul music, an expression from the heart.'

'I Am The Crime' was a fine example, a delirious ballad graced by backing vocalist Elizabeth Fraser, still granting favours to friends. Mick Allen saw how the relationship that drove Cocteau Twins was panning out. 'Robin came along to that session, and to be frank, he was a bit of a bully with Liz. She was terribly uncomfortable, so lacking in confidence with her own ability, which was unbelievable. She'd do these incredible things and then she'd stop halfway and wouldn't do any more. She said she couldn't sing the second part that we'd asked her to do. Liz was pitch-perfect, and because my vocal wasn't, maybe she found it difficult to put her vocal to mine.'

4AD had reached a peak, with Cocteau Twins, The Wolfgang Press, Colourbox and Dead Can Dance all making progress, the return of Dif Juz, the immediate impression made by Xymox, This Mortal Coil's imminent second album and the shock addition of *Le Mystère Des Voix Bulgares*. 'At that point, 4AD was relatively safe and straightforward,' recalls Deborah Edgely. 'Cocteau Twins was great, the centre of everything, the most demanding emotionally, but life was good. And then Throwing Muses walked in.'

There is no better example of Ivo's method of curating a label based on nothing more than gut instinct than the Rhode Island band, Throwing Muses, 4AD's first American signing. In 1985, The Smiths' uniquely slanted update of Sixties pop mores had swept over the UK, and for all Morrissey's quintessentially English guise, Sire Records in the US had its most popular UK import since Modern English. In Britain, a back-to-basics movement had gelled behind them and the similarly Sixties-indebted The Jesus and Mary Chain, around a phalanx of guitars, pop melody and new independent labels such as Creation, Pink, Fire and Ron Johnson. These strands were woven together in a movement christened C86 after the cassette of the same name compiled by the *NME* and released on Rough Trade in the summer of 1986. In the States, R.E.M. – a repository of Sixties and roots influences – had similarly spawned a mini-movement, such as the LA-based Paisley Underground scene of Sixties rock renegades.

Released in August 1986, two months after *C86*, *Throwing Muses* didn't resemble a single sound, band or faction associated with either scene.

November 1986: Time was up for my interview with the band, as they had to travel from west to north London in order to soundcheck at The Town & Country Club, where they were supporting Cocteau Twins that night. In order to keep talking, I drove Throwing Muses singer Kristin Hersh there. Kristin sat in the back, holding the tape recorder, next to her, her boyfriend Andrew was holding their nine-month-old son Dylan. It wasn't your average interview, and Hersh wasn't your average interviewee.

Not yet twenty years old, Hersh was not just a mother but a Philosophy and Psychology graduate, and the rhythm guitarist and principal songwriter of an album that, three months earlier, had received the best reviews of any 4AD album to date. For example: 'The finest debut album of the eighties … a very beautiful, contorted mystery' (*Melody Maker*); 'This album is one you've got to listen to about a hundred times before singalong comfort sets in, simply because it's so unpredictable. The beauty is that you can listen to it a thousand times. Easily' (*NME*).

Sounds reviewer Chris Roberts claimed *Throwing Muses* was the most promising American debut album since Patti Smith's *Horses*, adding, 'I despair that I live in a city where this music does not come out of taps.' He also compared the music to 'a thousand pea-green seahorses floating past your window, upwards'. It was that kind of album, uncannily haunting and jarring, a whole new strain of 'other otherness'.

Twenty-six years on from that first interview, Hersh connects via Skype from her home in Newport, Rhode Island that she shares with her husband/manager Billy O'Connell and their three boys. Her extraordinary tale is partly encapsulated in her 2010 autobiography *Paradoxical Undressing* (retitled *Rat Girl* for North America: 'the publishers thought *Paradoxical Undressing* was too many syllables for the American audience,' says O'Connell), named after a medical condition where sufferers of hypothermia start to undress as if they're too hot. Why does someone who feels overwhelmed by the world put herself in the spotlight by writing and singing songs, and playing them on stage? Hersh felt she had no choice. As a teenager, she was knocked off her bicycle by a car, and suffered a double concussion: one bizarre side effect was she began to hear music in her head that she says forced itself to be written down, otherwise the unbearable tension made her feel suicidal. So it had been through three decades.

Hersh's restless spirit has doubtless contributed to her family's nomadic lifestyle. Home is currently split between New Orleans, where O'Connell has been teaching, and during those stifling southern summers, back to Newport on the east coast. Born in Atlanta, Georgia, Hersh was raised on a commune on Aquidneck Island off the Rhode Island coast. Throwing Muses guitarist Tanya Donelly, who became Hersh's stepsister after Kristin's mother moved in with Tanya's father when the girls were eleven, lived there too.

Best friends as well as step-siblings, the girls had each been given a guitar by their respective fathers, and both had been converted by punk and new wave: Donelly by New York's CBGBs scene, Hersh by the diverse clout of Los Angeles' X, Athens' R.E.M. and Milwaukee's Violent Femmes. Donelly recalls some British music had also filtered through, such as London's all-female post-punks The Raincoats, whose raw, jerky folk influences – alongside X's pungent declarations, fronted by the untamed, poetic female singer Exene Cervenka – provided the building blocks of Throwing Muses' uniquely fevered sound. 'It still seemed novel that women played instruments, so we were bolstered by their example,' says Donelly. 'But anything you love gets into your blood.'

'We initially sounded like other people,' Hersh recalls. 'There was no magic yet. That fell into place after I got hit by a car and everything turned strange.'

Throwing Muses' identity was as much shaped by the military-trained style of drummer David Narcizo, who still resides in Newport where he runs the graphic design agency Lakuna, Inc with his wife Misi. His parents were friends of Hersh's and Donelly's family; thus he knew Kristin and Tanya, and had a similar musical outlook. 'Punk,' he says, 'made me want to throw away everything I'd been listening to, but I had no aspirations to join a band. I'd never played a drum kit until I joined Throwing Muses.'

Forming in 1981, the band had originally called itself The Muses, an all-female four of Hersh, Donelly, bassist Elaine Adamedes and drummer Becca Blumen. Narcizo was in a rehearsal room, practising for an all-State marching band audition, when he heard a piano playing next door. 'It captured my attention, and I discovered it was Kristin. I was intrigued that they had a band, because they were such interesting people. They had a drummer but Kristin called to say they'd lost her and they had a session booked, could I play? I borrowed a kit, but the owner had lent the cymbals to someone else, so that was a statement by accident. After about a year, all the songs started pouring in. Tons, every day.'

As Hersh wrote in *Paradoxical Undressing*: 'All the strangeness seemed to find a sound body and Throwing Muses imitated that. Every day I wonder if I ever wanted that to happen, I don't like strangeness, but I'm attracted to it in art.'

Narcizo: 'When Kristin brought in "Hate My Way", I remember thinking, holy shit! How did you do that? It taught me the value of sticking with something and the reward can be huge. One song, "Cowboy", had a million parts in about five minutes. Leslie [the band's new bassist] would say, "We can't catch up, slow down!"'

Leslie Langston had been discovered working in a drugstore-cum-delicatessen after Adamedes' departure. Langston was a bit of a legend around town, having played bass guitar in punk, funk, reggae, hardcore and Portuguese polka bands, plus an orchestra. 'We were surprised Leslie said yes,' Narcizo recalls. 'It was like she came from another world, an adult world. She was more of a technician than us, but she was really excited by what she could sink her teeth into.'

The band had taken the name Throwing Muses as they were no longer an all-female band, and while still at high school, had released a five-track seven-inch EP on their own Blowing Fuses label, led by the track 'Stand Up'. The local university campus at Rhode Island School of Design (RISD) quickly adopted them and Hersh and Donelly were interviewed for the school newspaper, 'by these two Amazonian sisters, or lovers, I wasn't sure!' Hersh laughs. 'They asked if we'd heard Cocteau Twins and they said, "This is the label you need to be on, talk to 4AD".'

Donelly and Hersh hadn't heard of Cocteau Twins. 'But we discovered they were all over RISD,' says Donelly. 'I'd never heard anything like them. It was like … heaven music. I'm sure Elizabeth found any "voice of God" comments annoying but it was true! And the band stood out so starkly. So did Dead Can Dance. And of course, "I Melt With You" had been everywhere.'

After being courted by Gary Smith, who ran Fort Apache studios in Cambridge, Massachusetts, he produced ten tracks that were turned into *The Doghouse Cassette*, which the band's new manager, former lawyer Ken Goes, sent to 4AD.

Ivo played the cassette in his car. 'I'd got stuck in traffic, and I listened to it three or four times in a row. It was an odd experience. There was something so exciting about it, which reminded me in a way of The Birthday Party – the energy, the lyrics. But I wasn't looking to get involved with anything else. I always felt we were too busy and not giving enough attention to every individual record. Ken said he'd only had one other response, from Stiff.'

Ivo called and left a message for Hersh: her flatmate wrote down, 'IVO called', and she didn't know any IVO: did it stand for the International Voting Organisation? But he called back. 'I was confused,' says Hersh. 'I thought the only help that record labels offered was signing bands! But Ivo and I would talk about everything but the music industry, which was easy because that didn't interest either of us. We'd discuss rose diseases, interesting animals, crazy shit that we saw. He was essentially a child in a man's body and I was still a child. We were both quirky people that didn't need many other quirky people around, so we got along great.'

Deborah Edgely: 'I was in the car when Ivo played the tape, and I'd never heard anything like it, just spine-chilling. To me, we could have the most fantastic band that ever walked the planet after The Birthday Party, and Ivo so did not want to sign them! Was it commitment? Finance? That they were American? Too complicated? There were lots of reasons, but we kept talking about them.'

Eventually, Ivo capitulated. 'The music was hard and aggressive but the more you lived with it, the more their beauty came through. But my main caution was that 4AD didn't have guaranteed American distribution and I was concerned we wouldn't do them justice. If I'd actually got on a plane to meet the band, I'm sure the offer would have been made a lot more quickly, because I'm still not sure how such incredibly original talent existed in four such smart, young and super-nice people.

'There was also something quite different about American musicians back then. They really took what they did very seriously, constantly rehearsing and improving. I'd not experienced that much before as so many of the bands I'd worked with had pretty much made things up in the studio and only rehearsed when they were about to tour.'

Ivo was also captivated by Throwing Muses' conspicuous gender. Since the masculine clamour of Bauhaus, In Camera and Matt

Before 4AD and 23 Envelope, the four Axis singles: The Fast Set's 'Junction One', Bearz' 'She's My Girl', Bauhaus' 'Dark Entries' and Shox's 'No Turning Back'

RIGHT: Bauhaus and Peter Kent, O'Hare airport, Chicago, 1980: (left to right) David J, Daniel Ash, Peter Murphy, Peter Kent, Kevin Haskins

ABOVE: Peter Murphy of Bauhaus, 1980

RIGHT: Rema-Rema, Royal Albert Hall, London, 1980: (left to right) Mark Cox, Mick Allen, Gary Asquith, Marco Pirroni, Max

LEFT: Modern English, South Bank, London, 1981: (left to right) (back row) Stephen Walker, Robbie Grey, Richard Brown, (front row) Gary McDowell, Mick Conroy

BELOW: Flyer for a 4AD night at Clarendon Hotel, London, October 1980

ABOVE: The Birthday Party's creative core, 1982: (left to right) Rowland S. Howard, Mick Harvey, Nick Cave

clarendon hotel presents...

the
BIRTHDAY PARTY

MASS

IN CAMERA

thursday 30th october   7.30pm
advance tickets £1.75 from this shop

the clarendon hotel
on the roundabout hammersmith

ABOVE: Cyrus Bruton of Dance Chapter, The Africa Centre, London 1980

ABOVE: The cover of In Camera's EP *Fin*

LEFT: Matt Johnson, aka The The, 1981

BELOW: Colourbox, 1983: (left to right) Steven Young, Lorita Grahame, Martyn Young, Ian Robbins

ABOVE: Xmal Deutschland, London, 1983: (left to right) Anja Huwe, Wolfgang Ellerbrock, Manuela Zwingmann, Manuela Rickers, Fiona Sangster

ABOVE: Dif Juz, 1985: (left to right) Gary Bromley, David Curtis, Richie Thomas, Alan Curtis

ABOVE: Cocteau Twins mark I, 1982: (left to right) Robin Guthrie, Elizabeth Fraser, Will Heggie

RIGHT: Cocteau Twins mark II, 1985: (left to right) Simon Raymonde, Elizabeth Fraser, Robin Guthrie

ABOVE: Cocteau Twins – *Garlands* cover, 1982

ABOVE: Cocteau Twins – *Treasure* cover, 1984

ABOVE: Cocteau Twins – *Echoes In A Shallow Bay* cover, 1985

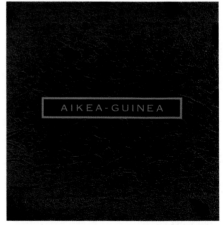

ABOVE: Cocteau Twins – *Aikea-Guinea* cover, 1985

ABOVE: Vaughan Oliver, 4AD office, 1983

ABOVE: On holiday in Corfu, 1984: (left to right) Robin Guthrie, Mark Cox, Elizabeth Fraser, Shirley, Deborah Edgely, Ivo Watts-Russell

LEFT: 23 Envelope, 1990: (left to right) Nigel Grierson and Vaughan Oliver

LEFT: Ivo on the cover of *The Offense Newsletter*, December 1986

RIGHT: Ivo and Deborah, 1984

RIGHT: Cocteau Twins/Wolfgang Press European tour, 1985: (left to right) Mick Allen, Elizabeth Fraser, Andrew Gray, Colin Wallace

LEFT: Dead Can Dance, 1984: (left to right) Brendan Perry, Lisa Gerrard

ABOVE: Xymox, 1985: (left to right) Ronny Moorings, Anka Wolbert, Pieter Nooten, Frank Weyzig

RIGHT: Poster for The Carnival Of Light tour, 1986

BELOW: The Wolfgang Press, 1988: (left to right) Andrew Gray, Mick Allen, JFK impersonator, Mark Cox

LEFT: Throwing Muses, 1986: (left to right) David Narcizo, Tanya Donelly, Kristin Hersh, Leslie Langston

BELOW: A.R. Kane, 1987: (left to right) Alex Ayuli, Rudy Tambala

ABOVE: M/A/R/R/S – without A.R. Kane: (left to right) Martyn Young, Steven Young, CJ Mackintosh, Dave Dorrell

RIGHT: Piixies, 1989: (left to right) Charles Thompson, Kim Deal, Joey Santiago, David Lovering

1. Rema-Rema - *Wheel In The Roses*
2. Modern English - *Mesh & Lace*
3. Various Artists - *Natures Mortes - Still Lives*
4. Colourbox - *Colourbox*
5. Dead Can Dance - *Spleen And Ideal*
6. Richenel - 'L'Esclave Endormi'
7. Clan of Xymox - *Medusa*
8. This Mortal Coil - *Filigree & Shadow*
9. Various Artists - *Lonely Is An Eyesore*
10. Pixies - *Come On Pilgrim*
11. Ultra Vivid Scene - *Ultra Vivid Scene*
12. The Wolfgang Press - *Bird Wood Cage*

Johnson's *Burning Blue Soul* in 4AD's formative days, the label had transitioned to a more feminine and androgynous spirit, but shot through with a tenacious streak (no wonder gay men were drawn to 4AD). Ivo wasn't gay, just mesmerised by women – their presence, shape, energy and sound. No other A&R man or woman, before or since, has given so much opportunity to female artists.

'It wasn't just about the number of women on 4AD,' says *The Catalogue* editor Brenda Kelly, 'but the female voice. You never thought, "Oh, 4AD, all those chicks", because it wasn't about being pop stars or even their personalities, but about the music. And Kristin Hersh made total sense on 4AD. There was something wide-eyed and extraordinary about her, something emotional and visceral, something basic and yet complex.'

Hersh was hugely relieved when Ivo changed his mind. 'We were about to sign some shitty deal with an American company, but the 4AD deal was so exquisitely fair compared to that. Ivo was a real hero. He'd still call me and talk for hours, in long, beautiful circles, which I loved. He was just like me, except he could talk. Music was the only language in which I was fluent.'

Hersh's language problem emerged when it came to negotiating the recording of Throwing Muses' debut album. As a purist, she beat Ivo hands down: Hersh wanted nothing that came between the material and the listener. Her yardstick was the first Violent Femmes album, 'a raw, attractive piece of work that didn't insult the material,' Hersh says. 'I only wanted that we become professional without being ruined, to stay raw without being unlistenable. That was a way of saying leave us alone, but clearly our craziness needed to be reined in.'

Having felt exposed by his technical and instrumental lack, Ivo had begun to count himself out of the producer's role. For something as complex and unusual as Throwing Muses, he turned to Gil Norton, who'd partially helmed Echo & The Bunnymen's baroque masterpiece *Ocean Rain*. The Muses trusted Ivo's judgement, but the fastidious Norton proved a challenge, especially as Hersh was putting forward new songs, such as 'Delicate Cutters', an unnerving acoustic portrayal of self-harm. Plus she was pregnant. Hormones raged.

Ivo: 'Kristin was just nineteen when she gave birth to, and lived through, these songs, and Gil had to guide her. Colin Newman once told me that the most important thing a producer can do is know when to make a cup of tea. But most producers feel that they have to change things, and that's why they're hired. But I still think Throwing Muses' album is true to the arrangements on the demos.'

'Throwing Muses always had an art school angle, which we always tried to deflect, but 4AD embraced it,' claims Narcizo. 'And because of This Mortal Coil, Ivo had a greater affection for production. But we genuinely still felt that 4AD got what we did, which drew us closer to the label.'

Donelly: 'We were so concerned about artifice. In some ways, it was our generation's aesthetic – don't mess with the roots, don't dress the skeleton. Even reverb sounded slick to us. Of course, we can hear now that the album's not that over-produced. There was nothing cluttering or getting in the way and at the end of the day, we did work well with Gil.'

Still, Hersh says, 'Ivo should have produced us. Gil was going places we weren't going to go. Producers need to discern a style within the material and exaggerate it, and that's what didn't work for us. I adored Gil but to ask him to rein in Throwing Muses just wasn't fair. He didn't understand why we wanted it to be raw.'

With Hersh resisting every suggestion from Norton that she 'sing', the band used up its allotted time in the American studio, so Norton had to mix the album back in the UK. Narcizo flew over as the Muses' representative. 'Gil and I had little battles along the way, like he wanted a string section on "Hate My Way". I'd say I wanted things to sound amateur, and he'd say, "That's because you are amateur". I love that album, but it felt so different to how we felt about ourselves. I was so nervous coming home with it, thinking the others would be so disappointed.'

Ivo: '"Hate My Way", "Delicate Cutters", "Soul Soldier" – it's the freedom in Kristin's voice, the naïvety of her rhythm guitar and Tanya's lead guitar, the absolute brilliance of the rhythm section. David was such an extraordinary and unusual drummer. It's a real shame that

Kristin wasn't happy with the way it sounded and it's probably little compensation that it got such unanimously positive responses.'

Hersh: 'I eventually made peace with the album, but it's hard when it's you that's sounding nuts. Ivo chose our most harrowing songs and left out the fun ones that had been a relief to us. Ivo didn't want any relief! I thought, that's just mean, no one will want to listen.'

There was another tussle over the artwork, where the band, for all their youth, dug their heels in. 'Everything else [on 4AD] was so smooth and wispy and gauzy and pretty,' Hersh recalls. 'Poor Vaughan, he wanted it to be beautiful but we said, we're not beautiful, we're not nice! He said, "Why would you fuck it up on purpose?" That's what being the first American band on 4AD was about. It was certainly a shift.'

David Narcizo: 'We should have just let Vaughan do what he wanted, but we had a desperate need not to come across as pretentious. We know our music sometimes evoked surreal and strange feelings, but we wanted it to be normal, a result of regular work, and not scare people away.'

The finished artwork – against 4AD/23 Envelope tradition – even featured small photos of the band at their request, floating in a sea of exquisite calligraphy that ushered in a new era for 23 Envelope. The lettering and design was the work of Chris Bigg, who admits his chronic dyslexia had held him back at school but had had an accidentally beneficial effect: 'I like the shape of words rather than what they're saying,' he admits. 'I look at shapes and where the word sits against an image.'

Bigg was a perfect fit at 4AD and alongside Vaughan Oliver, who would take the role of art director when Bigg took on the role of designer. He was a fan of the original Bauhaus art movement and of The Birthday Party, Wire and beautifully designed album covers, back to his father's record collection, he says, 'all the old classics, Santana, The Beatles, all the inner bags and lyric sheets … I used to dream of doing it myself one day.'

Born in Brighton where he also studied graphic design at the local university, Bigg wrote his dissertation on post-punk sleeve design with a focus on 23 Envelope. Vaughan Oliver had been the only one of the leading sleeve designers that Bigg approached during his research to respond. Bigg later visited Alma Road to hand out home-made *Head Over Heels* T-shirts. And when Oliver was deskbound after breaking his foot playing football and had an impending dead-line for Colourbox's album, Bigg had been temporarily summoned to do the legwork between art desk and darkroom. 'And I've been running around after Vaughan for the last twenty years,' he sighs.

Bigg had become a semi-permanent fixture at Alma Road to assist Steve Webbon on Situation 2 projects, but, 'under heavy direction from Vaughan,' says Bigg, he gravitated to 4AD, starting with Throwing Muses after Oliver had baulked at the band's insistence on photos. Bigg mirrored Oliver's pioneering design, starting with Xmal Deutschland's *Qual* EP, of putting song titles on the front cover. 'I didn't want an obvious front or back, but something more anony-mous,' Bigg explains. 'For me, it harked back to the feel of Birthday Party sleeves. It's a bit naïve for my tastes now, but it suited the project.'

Ivo: 'Chris's jagged yet flowing logo referred to the unborn Dylan heartbeat in Kristin's belly while she was recording the songs. It suited their music perfectly.'

Throwing Muses was also significantly the first 4AD project to be actively promoted in America. Sheri Hood was working in the college radio section of the New York-based promotions company Thirsty Ear when Beggars Banquet bought into the company. Hood was designated 4AD's releases, with *Throwing Muses* something of a trial by fire. 'They were so unbelievable and different,' Hood recalls. 'Listening back, the album fit really well, in that edge-of-madness, crazy-great way, but it caused a lot of head-scratching at college radio.'

John Peel also found the band a challenge. He'd remained support-ive of 4AD, and Ivo was convinced he'd respond to Throwing Muses – after all, the similarly angular and jerky The Fall was his favourite band. But he didn't respond to a test pressing, and when Ivo eventu-ally tracked Peel down, he admitted he'd been listening to the album when his producer, John Walters, had enquired, 'Who's that then, Melanie?' The American singer-songwriter best known for her flower-power whimsy had once visited Peel in hospital when he had jaundice and, to the DJ's eternal embarrassment, serenaded him from the end of his bed. Peel would never give Throwing Muses another chance, but then Ivo knew all about judgements based on emotional reactions.

While Throwing Muses were doing the Cocteau Twins tour in the UK, the band was persuaded by its album reviews to re-try Gil Norton. Four more, equally sublime tracks were recorded at Blackwing for the *Chains Changed* EP, plus a new version of *The Doghouse Cassette*'s 'Fish' for a forthcoming 4AD compilation. Hersh admits she still battled with Norton, though Ivo is adamant that the EP 'was their best ever recording'. He believes that 'It's unpolished and unembellished, and it's what it was like to hear them in a room, with no loss of energy. It was still the final nail in the coffin of them and Gil.'

It was so much easier to be artist, producer *and* label, a luxury that This Mortal Coil had afforded Ivo, with no risk of communication breakdown. After nearly two years of plotting, accumulating and mixing, the collective's second album, *Filigree & Shadow*, was ready. By the time Ivo had called a halt, he had 74 minutes of music, 25 finished pieces including 13 instrumentals, with five the proud work of Ivo and John Fryer alone. It was enough for a double album, 4AD's first, an act of hubris given this privilege was being granted to himself.

In 1985, double albums were still considered relics of a wasteful age, but with the painstakingly stitched mood flowing over four individual sides of vinyl (and one single CD), *Filigree & Shadow* promised an immersive experience and a timely reminder of a style of rock music that was to come back into fashion, unencumbered by punk's didacts. The album expanded the midnight mood of *It'll End In Tears* with only 'Drugs' (like 'Not To' on the first album) interrupting the slow, dream-like descent down a dark path that began with the album title, named after a favourite track by the Texan psych-pop band Fever Tree (also, incidentally, Ivo's favourite band name). The artwork drove the point home, a stark black-and-white close-up of a returning Pallas Citroen, her face half in shadow, looking more disturbed than the sleepwalking state she'd portrayed on *It'll End In Tears*.

Ivo's original choice for cover star had been his first proper crush, actress Maria Schneider, most famously Marlon Brando's degraded foil in *Last Tango in Paris*. 'She was beautiful then and still so in her final days,' he says. 'The problem was that Maria did not trust men one bit. I knew she was a lesbian because she, very publicly, checked herself into an insane asylum to be with her partner. It was a difficult conversation, I explained I was a fan and that This Mortal Coil was a personal project and it would mean so much if she'd grace the sleeve. We agreed I'd send her *It'll End In Tears*, a tape of *Filigree & Shadow* and a copy of Nigel's recent book of photos, but I must have done little to convince her that I wasn't a pervert as I never heard back. So we decided to use Pallas again.'

Pallas Citroen was also the face of 4AD's first ten-inch single, a double A-side of 'Come Here My Love' and 'Drugs', which preceded *Filigree & Shadow*. 'We did endless shoots,' Citroen recalls. 'Nigel [Grierson] built a huge sandpit on the studio roof that I sat in for a couple of days, or he uses infra-red lighting with me naked, or I was rolling down a mountain. I didn't get paid much, but it wasn't about the money, I just liked seeing what came out of it. And I loved the music, so it was great to be involved.'

Beautifully chilled, swathed in texture using the full extent of the FX toolbox, the mood of the album was described by *Pitchfork* when reviewing the This Mortal Coil box set in 2011 as 'spooky and woozy'.* Given it was made in batches, shaped by a man more used to signing bands than directing them, it was a substantial achievement. Without the unique slant that Elizabeth Fraser and Lisa Gerrard had brought to *It'll End In Tears*, the new album did resemble a collective more than any preceding 4AD gathering. And without an obvious spearhead such as 'Song To The Siren', and spun out over 74 minutes, it also felt more like a cohesive piece of work. At the same time, *Filigree &*

---

* When 4AD trailed the This Mortal Coil box set via a brief video posted on YouTube, Ivo was frustrated to discover that the soundtrack chosen was the instrumental 'At First, And Then', written by former Dead Can Dance collaborator Peter Ulrich. 'It was given to me by Peter, and so it was the only piece on *Filigree & Shadow* that I didn't commission, write or play on! I was told it was the only piece that fit the trailer.'

Shadow lacked those incredible voices, and a song to rival 'Song To The Siren'.

The press reaction was decidedly mixed. 4AD aficionado Chris Roberts made 'Come Here My Love' single of the week in *Sounds*, and rightly pointed out how 'Drugs' was 'very Colourbox' – and should have added that Colourbox should sound more like this, with some of The Wolfgang Press's sharp edges. *Sounds* also gave *Filigree & Shadow* five stars: 'The pain and love it's soaked in drip like nectar onto a thirsty tongue … the perfect soundtrack for evenings spent alone with just self-doubt and love as company.'

But one man's 4AD is another man's indulgence, and the two traditionally weightier opinions from *NME* and even the perennially 4AD-supporting *Melody Maker* were anti as they could be. Both had reviewed *It'll End In Tears* favourably, with *Melody Maker* unreservedly behind Ivo's vision. Now, though finding five tracks to recommend, *Melody Maker* called the album, 'dull, lifeless, profoundly uninteresting … mannered hymns of hollow sorrow', as if doubting Ivo and John Fryer's ability to authentically feel pain.

Sounds had called Dominic Appleton's vocal, 'haunting … chanting such sweet sorrow'. *NME* called him, 'posturing'. Underneath the headline 'Coma Lilt or Shit (anag.)', *NME* suggested, 'If Cocteau Twins rule this amorphous hinterland, then This Mortal Coil are the court jesters … TMC are an idea that mutated into a monster.' The comment, 'I heard the ghost dance of dinosaurs; a music that reeks of old muso values', would have particularly appealed to Robin Guthrie.

NME's sentiment pinpointed exactly why *Filigree & Shadow* created such antipathy. Nineteen eighty-five was clearly too soon for this return to yesteryear, to the values of progressive rock (musicianship, production, double albums), the devotion to music of the past, made by those 'earnest, bearded' types that had so offended Robin Guthrie (whose beard today is worthy of Old Father Time). Ivo had made it much harder to embrace by unleashing something so particular, detailed and singularly immersive on a scale of 74 minutes, but there was no A&R man to hold him back, so This Mortal Coil was judged as a folly to one man's self-indulgence.

The title of the first album was indeed prophetic. Deborah Edgely recalls Ivo scanning both reviews, 'and bursting into tears'.

Ivo: 'I virtually stopped reading the music press after they tore into the album. But if you're going to read the good, you have to accept the bad. But it still really hurt. I'm still immensely proud of that record.'

At the time, Ivo typically saw music and its emotional force as the only criteria, telling *Melody Maker*, with admirable prescience, 'I like the idea that the records we release aren't just for the moment, but will sound valuable in ten years. And I think the groups on 4AD share this aim.'

As Bauhaus well knew, vindictive reviews didn't harm sales, and reaching number 2 in the UK independent charts with *Filigree & Shadow* would have been some consolation. Antony Hegarty says he wore out his cassette version, and for those that hadn't yet discovered *It'll End In Tears*, *Filigree & Shadow* was another vital lifeline.

One such devotee was John Mark Lapham, who, born and raised in Abilene, Texas (once voted America's second most conservative town), would in the Noughties form Anglo-American folk-tronic quartet The Earlies and the TMC-influenced 4AD signing The Late Cord. 'A friend said, "You have to hear this", and he stuck in a cassette and played Colourbox's "Tarantula". I felt speechless, just bowled over,' Lapham explains. 'I must have played *Filigree & Shadow* almost every night during my teenage years, and even in my twenties, I was listening to it regularly. I've since grown to love *It'll End In Tears* more but you can never erase that early connection.'

Of course, if there had to be one dissenting voice beside factions of the music press, it would be a Cocteau Twin, bothered by the financial aspect of the This Mortal Coil arrangement.

From Ivo's perspective, 'Simon was one of the sweetest people I'd ever met, but then he started to develop a similar attitude to Robin, which was less fun. John Fryer's working title for "Ivy & Neat" was "Moody Simon".'

Perhaps if Raymonde had spoken his mind at the time, Ivo might have understood the cause. 'Much good came out of This Mortal Coil, and creatively, I had a great time on those This Mortal Coil albums,'

Raymonde says. 'But the effect it had on our relationships – mine and Ivo's, and Robin, Liz and Ivo's – all of the good we had going with him, were damaged by how it panned out. It's only when I look back and I wonder why I didn't say, am I not getting paid? Not even for me to get home at night?

'I don't know how Ivo remembers it, but I did a fuck of a lot of work on *Filigree & Shadow*, which I loved doing. But if it was me, I'd have said, "Here's a grand". I was doing it out of love for Ivo, but when you think of the money going through This Mortal Coil's coffers ... did Howard Devoto not get anything? Did he put in as much effort as me? I came to the conclusion that I should be more cynical about our relationship. That maybe Ivo wasn't as cool a bloke as I thought he was.'

Ivo claims that Raymonde, like every This Mortal Coil contributor, was paid a session fee for each track that they contributed to. Had Robin Guthrie's grievances rubbed off on Raymonde? It's interesting to note that only Cocteau Twins had such grumbles over This Mortal Coil; maybe as the closest members of the 4AD 'family', Ivo had begun to take them for granted.

Ivo: 'Simon created the template for so many of the cover versions, and contributed a couple of gorgeous instrumentals to those first records. Like Jon Turner, he wasn't remotely precious about how his work was used or ended up sounding. He really was as happy with how we worked together as I was. Take "Kangaroo". It was an almost impossible song to cover, yet he extracted the heart of the thing, sticking to the brief of bass guitar and cello, creating the ideal backdrop for Gordon [Sharp] to float over. He was brilliant every step of the way. I'm amazed he didn't get more frustrated with my vagueness.'

Ivo says he is sure Raymonde was paid. 'Maybe it wasn't enough. Maybe I should've paid everyone royalties. But at no point did I try and pay people as little as possible in order to maximise 4AD, and ultimately my own, income. Money has never been a motivating factor in my life and, frankly, anyone who suggests otherwise doesn't know me at all. Peculiarly, and beautifully, it has been my experience in business that if I ever did make a decision that I thought might work out financially, it was a guaranteed failure, whereas everything that we did that really was from the heart seemed to do really well.'

'If Ivo says I was paid, that's good enough for me,' Raymonde responds. 'Though I don't recall and I don't tend to be upset about things for no reason. But it doesn't dwarf the good memories or the pride I have in that work.'

Yet Raymonde also expresses the same feeling as Guthrie of feeling Cocteau Twins were taken for granted. 'Our success seemed to pave the way for other bands to be signed and have money spent on them,' Raymonde contends. 'That was fine, but it never felt like we were rewarded for the success we brought. We were selling hundreds of thousands of records. For example, I know *Treasure* sold a hundred thousand really quickly. I run a label [Bella Union] now and I know how much money is generated by selling that amount. And we recouped on every record. *Garlands* cost about £900 to make! But we were always busy and never checking our bank account.'

From unofficial 4AD figures discovered in the vault dating to March 1985, *Treasure* had sold 85,000 copies, though Cocteau Twins had sold a total of 463,000, with 'Pearly-Dewdrop's Drops' selling 100,000. (*Garlands* had sold 45,000 and *Head Over Heels* 76,000.) 'Song To The Siren' had sold 90,000, and *It'll End In Tears*, 63,000. These sales far outstretched any other bands – for example, Birthday Party albums sold 25–30,000 copies, Xmal Deutschland's *Fetisch*, 23,000, the first Dead Can Dance album sold 15,000 and The Wolfgang Press's *Burden Of Mules* not even 5,000.

The underlying point that Raymonde, and Guthrie, were making was that Ivo couldn't just have had a purely musical agenda: 4AD was a business as well, sustainable only through making a profit. Guthrie's view, whether deeply cynical or simply realistic, was that 'Ivo and Martin Mills had sewn everything up and were making a shitload of money, exploiting bands because there was a premium to being on 4AD, so the deals were shit,' he claims. 'What pissed me off even more was that they hid behind the art of the whole thing. It *was* business. Martin stayed very much in the background – we knew and respected him, and we were a bit scared of him too. His agenda was ruthless.'

Perhaps if Ivo hadn't got so close to Guthrie, there wouldn't have been the same sense of betrayal. Maybe the most revealing opinion comes from Guthrie himself. 'Being stubborn and spiteful are two of my hugest influences when making music,' he admits, grinning at the same time.

Cocteau Twins kept up an exhausting schedule, away from business matters; after a run of three EPs and the acoustic interlude of *Victorialand*, they recorded a new EP and another album, albeit a more spontaneous side project that hadn't required the same extended commitment as a band album.

The four-track EP fronted by 'Love's Easy Tears' suggested the old force of nature from the *Treasure* era had been stored up and the dam had been breached. '"Love's Easy Tears" is beyond belief,' reckons Ivo. 'I'm not sure what was going on in Robin's head. All three tracks were fantastic but I found the sound impenetrable. The guitars were out of phase and seemed to compete with the likes of The Jesus and Mary Chain. They never again released anything that resembled it.'

'That was about pushing the sonic envelope as far as we could go, louder and fatter,' Guthrie says. 'I'd found the button on the mixing desk marked "more" and I wanted to see if I could go there.'

Another possible reason for the outpouring of sound was another record, which had reactivated Cocteau Twin' gentler side. Ivo had been contacted by Britain's TV station Channel 4 about a series that would unite musicians from different genres. He says he suggested Cocteau Twins and that Simon Raymonde had in turn suggested the band approach Californian pianist Harold Budd – though Raymonde thinks Budd was Ivo's idea. 'Harold had made a beautiful record with Eno [*The Pearl*] and we thought it could be amazing with him,' says Raymonde. 'I'm not sure Robin agreed at the time.'

On the contrary, Guthrie says, who has since recorded several albums with the ambient-leaning Budd. The TV series never evolved but both parties still rendezvoused to record *The Moon And The Melodies*, released as Harold Budd, Simon Raymonde, Robin Guthrie,

Elizabeth Fraser. 'Harold was very like us,' Raymonde recalls. 'He arrived unprepared, we started playing together and then we pushed the record button.'

Budd told journalist Dave Sexton that he hadn't heard of Cocteau Twins, but had contacted a friend in the music industry who told him he'd like them, and put a tape together for him. 'And he was absolutely right. As musicians, I found them immensely interesting people to work with. And in spite of my inclination to work alone, it's great to get into the studio with someone else and pick each other's brains – very satisfying.'

'Sea, Swallow Me' – scored by Budd's refracted piano sound, which did indeed sound as if it was emanating from underwater – even harked back to the imagery of 'Song To The Siren', and showed Elizabeth Fraser's ability to conjure up a compelling melody was undiminished – the Cocteaus were sufficiently taken with the track to play it on tour later that year. 'She Will Destroy You' was another cool beauty, with Richie Thomas's saxophone blowing mellifluously over the coda.[*] 'It's a lovely, lovely record,' says Ivo. 'It wasn't the best work by either the band or Harold, but I was extremely happy to release it.'

Guthrie's only regret was that *The Moon And The Melodies* wasn't a true collaboration: 'it was either Harold produced by us, or us with a bit of piano. Harold isn't even on the last track – the album was too short and we had to write something new after he'd left. Sorry, man!'

After loving the *Tiny Dynamine* and *Echoes In A Shallow Bay* covers, Guthrie was back to his usual tetchy self with criticism of the band's artwork. 'Love's Easy Tears' wasn't that different from the preceding EP, while *Victorialand* had been taken from the same session as *Sunburst And Snowblind*, so to call the former 'much of a muchness' and the latter 'a beautiful photo but not much more' wasn't harsh. But

---

[*] 'Ooze Out And Away, Onehow', the instrumental finale on *The Moon And The Melodies*, got its title from a lyrical phrase in the *Head Over Heels* cut 'My Love Paramour', while the title of one of Budd's contributions, 'Bloody And Blunt', came from the same album's 'The Tinderbox (Of A Heart)'. 'Melody Gongs', another Budd composition, reappeared on his 1986 album *Lovely Thunder* under the title of 'Flower Knife Shadows'.

to say *The Moon And The Melodies* was 'ordinary … I never liked it' just sounded bitter.

'Robin would get intense and instead of embracing the positive, he'd go full tilt into rucks in the office, like with Vaughan, several times,' Deborah Edgely recalls. 'He seemed so frustrated. The angry man kept coming out.'

'With any journalist, Robin would slag off 4AD and particularly Ivo,' says Ray Conroy. 'It was awful. He was coked out of his mind, and very aggressive. He really relished it too, sometimes staying up for three days. He turned into a nightmare.'

After one too many rows, Oliver had already handed over the Cocteaus to Nigel Grierson. 'They developed more of an issue with Vaughan than me,' says Grierson. 'Robin didn't like anything in boxes, and he kept going on about "Vaughan and his boxes"! And they had an issue with Ivo that I could never work out.'

With Grierson dictating events, the iridescent paint/water impressions had become predictable, and perhaps in recognition of change – or because Harold Budd's presence necessitated it – Grierson's cover for *The Moon And The Melodies* was a black-and-white photo of a hawthorn hedge: 'a really intense abstraction,' says Grierson, 'almost Jackson Pollock-like, and twisted so that it looked like it was spiralling.'

Guthrie's friends in Dif Juz were on the edge of their own spiral. The band's *Huremics* and *Vibrating Air* EPs were remixed and reissued as the vinyl-only *Out Of The Trees*, with the unnecessary novelty of having Richie Thomas's friend Hollis Chambers sing, in a jarringly soul-jazz style, over the dub-fractured 'Heset'. The handsome pelicans on the cover – being 23 Envelope, no one was expecting trees – fulfilled their brief of masking the problems spilling over from Gary Bromley's departure; Richie Thomas says he was also feeling the heat of Dave Curtis's controlling manner, and that touring had adversely affected the guitarist's health. 'It was how we were living, touring around Europe, not eating and living well,' Thomas recalls. 'Dave was a bit older than us and it took its toll. He was on painkillers and he had to have an operation, after which he said he didn't want to carry on.'

There was dissent in the air too with 4AD's last record of 1986, another band-family feud, though 4AD was not involved. Xymox had survived the recording of *Clan Of Xymox*, but the dream come true of an association with 4AD was not enough to prevent the fragile relationships between Ronny Moorings and Anka Wolbert, and between Moorings and Pieter Nooten, from pulling the band apart.

Living in the Netherlands, with their only familial connection to 4AD being Dead Can Dance, and being the most peripheral members of the established clan, Wolbert says that Xymox felt very isolated. '4AD was a weird bunch, solitary, individual and hypersensitive. Maybe we were too. Maybe it was just the age. But we just kept to ourselves.'

The band had returned to Palladium in the summer, sidelining guitarist Frank Weyzig to only live performance, meaning one less ego to contain. Ivo had met Xymox at Palladium but felt he was no longer the right producer. 'Their songs needed a lot of rearranging, which I couldn't do, and I thought I was one cook too many.'

Talking of cooks, studio life didn't denote glamour, and Moorings' memory of Palladium includes the frugal catering by Jon Turner's wife Anne: 'chips, frozen peas and some sort of schnitzel, every day. And Jon habitually re-used tea-bags, and was now charging for a second cup of tea or coffee.'

A more serious source of tension was the aftermath of the explosion at Russia's Chernobyl nuclear reactor three months earlier, as Scotland was in the pathway of the radioactive cloud that was floating westwards, throwing the memories of anti-nuclear protests in the Netherlands into sharp relief. But more immediately threatening was what Moorings calls, 'the volatile situation in our own band'. He says, 'The recordings were even more unpleasant than before.'

Whatever creative milestone the new recordings were setting was overshadowed by the cloud that settled over Xymox, with clashing testimonies as to the severity of the scenario. Moorings claims that Wolbert and Nooten fought over her lack of contribution while she still claimed an equal share of the band's earnings. 'Pieter belittled her input constantly in the studio. I was not too happy about that considering she was still my "partner",' Moorings writes.

Wolbert and Nooten deny this was ever the case. Wolbert had her first Xymox song on the album, with the potentially revealing title 'Masquerade', while Nooten wrote three outright – 'Theme 1', 'Lorrentine' and 'After The Fall' – and the music for the title track 'Louise', and 'Backdoor', for which Moorings wrote and sang the vocal melodies. He also wrote the remaining three songs. The trio collaborated on arrangements that Moorings says created, 'terrible scenes and arguments, tears and a mish-mash of ideas'.

Neither Wolbert nor Nooten recall such drama. 'I think I'd remember,' says Wolbert. 'It was a typical second album. It took a long time to get together, it's darker, there were no club hits, but we got better at songwriting. Ronny was trying to be more commercial but he was also afraid to go commercial.'

Moorings claims that Ivo was unhappy with what Xymox had recorded at Palladium, and had asked the band to keep recording. Ivo doesn't recall this, but what is agreed is that Xymox returned to Blackwing to mix the album with John Fryer. Moorings also claims that he'd recorded new parts on his own, to which Nooten had agreed, 'because Pieter was already working on his solo project … That might explain the little input he gave to Xymox in those days.'

Wolbert insists that Moorings was never in the studio without her (unless he went behind her back), so was this trauma all Moorings' invention, to create the idea that only he was working towards the final goal? The move to assume full control of Xymox seemed clear from his admission that he now wanted the band to be called Clan Of Xymox, 'like on the artwork of the first album. I had read the book *Clan Of The Cave Bear* and I liked the ring of "Clan Of". When I saw it in print, it made sense: I was Mr Xymox and the Clan was the rest.'*

---

* Moorings was at least willing to play a subservient role to Vaughan Oliver, who chose to out himself on the cover of *Medusa* – with a plaster cast of his head, based on the mythological Greek character of Medusa who could turn people to stone turned to stone herself. Nigel Grierson recalls that he took the head, in a bag, to various locations for filming; one was a wood outside London in East Grinstead, where he later heard that a headless body had been found in a plastic bag …

The album, *Medusa*, was eventually completed to everyone's satisfaction. 'Sometimes the most difficult album is also the most interesting one,' Moorings concludes. For some, it was a better record than *Clan Of Xymox*: despite its painful genesis, it sounded rounded and atmospheric, nailing a particular European melancholy, all faded grandeur and downtrodden fortune.

Nooten: 'People still tell me *Medusa* is a masterpiece, combining ambient and early gothic electronica.'

The album's standout, Nooten's 'After The Call', came decked in woodwind, timpani (kettledrums) and a choir, bearing an uncanny resemblance to both Breathless and various Factory label bands, especially Belgium's The Names, in the old Joy Division manner. Moorings' 'Back Door' mined a similar mood, haughty and, yes, gothic. Crossing Kraftwerk with OMD and Ultravox's 'Vienna', Wolbert's 'Masquerade' was an elegant ballad with her bass high in the mix and scored with strings, but even when the track momentarily sped up and a sequencer was added, it was much less obviously indebted to The Cure and New Order.

If anything, it shared more common ground with early Dead Can Dance records and with This Mortal Coil's moods; there was a more pronounced sadness to the new album, with which to seduce Ivo. In reality, however, Ivo admits, 'I didn't connect with *Medusa* the same way as I had with the first album.' The UK coverage was very positive for the rebranded Clan Of Xymox: 'An overriding achievement ... every track sounds like the finale to a brooding epic overture ... in their prime passages, they brush with a sexy breathlessness,' ventured *Sounds*.

The Xymox experience had been a tumultuous end to a frankly tumultuous year for 4AD – extraordinary music, unpleasant fall-outs, divisive press reactions, and even an astonishing piece of fortune: Ivo and Deborah had been forced to cancel a holiday to the Maldives after *Filigree & Shadow* had been released in September because they felt things were still too busy. During the plane's stopover in Sri Lanka, the flight that they would have taken was subsequently blown up by the separatist militant organisation the Tamil Tigers.

The demands of running a label saw Ivo continue to keep a firm hand on most aspects of the business. 'I saw different sides to Ivo,' Vaughan Oliver recalls. 'How could one man pick up the phone to a band to talk about artistic direction, then talk to a producer, and then to a distributor, saying, "Where are my fucking records, and why aren't you selling any?" He juggled it all.'

As 4AD grew in size and profile, Oliver could see that aspects of this dream opportunity – as Ivo once said, 'I take music very seriously' – had begun to wear him down. 'We had one conversation where Ivo said he was jealous of me, because I didn't have the business and political sides to deal with. I could just be creative. I didn't get it at the time, because I thought he was happy with what he was doing.'

It was late December before Ivo and Deborah flew to the Maldives, accompanied this time by Vaughan and his girlfriend Ginny – but not, on this holiday, by Robin Guthrie and Elizabeth Fraser; manic work schedules on both sides had separated the two couples' orbits, reducing the chance for consolidating friendships. With what was to come in 1987 – from epic highs to miserable lows – the holidaying couples would value the chance to snatch some moments of peace.

10 1987

CHAINS CHANGED
(bad701-bad711)

M/A/R/R/S was the best and worst thing that ever happened to 4AD.

(Simon Harper)

In the Maldives, 4AD's four holidaymakers had shaved their heads. It was Vaughan's idea: 'I enjoyed the idea of a pretty face with a shaved head, so I used to shave my girlfriends' hair.' Ivo and Deborah joined in, and Ivo and Vaughan both kept a shaved head or a close crop for the next twenty years. 'They created a look for the label,' claimed an ever-cynical Robin Guthrie. 'They wanted the same celebrity as the bands.'

Kristin Hersh of Throwing Muses was typically less judgemental. 'My strongest memory of visiting the 4AD office was the shaved heads. And that their tea was like cocaine.'

Throwing Muses' *Chains Changed* EP instigated 4AD's 1987 offensive with the same dizzy charge as the band's debut album, especially the manic rockabilly slant of 'Snail Head' and the flat-out charge of 'Cry Baby Cry'. The EP was a faultless mirror of the band's capabilities – and never to be repeated, as Gil Norton would never again get his hands on the Muses.

Also rather fond of a shaved head, The Wolfgang Press was on its own persistent path of evolution. The four-track EP *Big Sex* accentuated four facets of the modern dance: pop ('The Great Leveller'), tribal ('The Wedding'), mantra ('That Heat') and funk ('God's Number'), which put it closer to the elements of the Talking Heads' *Remain In Light* model, with guest backing vocalist Ruby James adding soulful lustre to the feeling of liberation.

Another reason why Ivo had been unable to take time off was a project that was finally coming to fruition, providing all the proof needed that the toil was worthwhile. Ivo hated the idea of compilations, of tracks conceived for one purpose being re-packaged for another, so instead of raiding the back catalogue as most every major or indie did, he had issued instructions to every 4AD artist 'to record one song that they'd be happy to release as their next single. Or a single on 4AD terms.' The way he saw it, 'A purpose-made compilation was a celebration of what the label was doing at that time.'

A Hersh lyric, from Throwing Muses' typically-pulsating contribution 'Fish', lent the album its beguiling title: *Lonely Is An Eyesore*. 'I knew it would confuse people, unless you heard it in the context of the song,' says Ivo. 'I was also thinking of Gene Clark's line in "Life's Greatest Fool": "*… too much loneliness makes you grow old*".'

On the back of the cover, Oliver listed the acts that had passed through 4AD's doors. Yet the compilation was only nine tracks long, and even then, two were from Dead Can Dance, one each from the diverging Lisa Gerrard and Brendan Perry. Ivo was intent on keeping 4AD a select, boutique operation, with the core constituents being those affiliated to This Mortal Coil, a core family with Clan Of Xymox the overseas relations and Throwing Muses the new, adopted children. 'In many ways, *Lonely Is An Eyesore* was a line in the sand, the end of an era, of relationships within 4AD, and graphically too,' says Ivo.

With an equal dislike of videos, or rather the growing necessity to have one attached in the competing marketplace, Ivo wanted a visual version of *Lonely Is An Eyesore*, 'though not with the view to get it on TV,' he says. 'This was fucking art!'

Two years earlier, Nigel Grierson had made the thirty-minute film *Maelstrom* for his postgraduate degree, a *noir*-styled depiction of what Grierson calls, 'a relationship between a man and woman, seen through the murky subjectivity of the man's memory. An internal reality'. The imagery struck an even better balance of 'filigree' and 'shadow' than Grierson's most recent This Mortal Coil sleeve, with a suitably impressionistic soundtrack of Brian Eno, Harold Budd, Colin Newman and Duet Emmo (a musical alliance between Bruce Gilbert, Graham Lewis and Mute's Daniel Miller). *Maelstrom* was part of the *Six Nix Hix Pix* season of promising young British filmmakers at London's Institute of the Contemporary Arts the same week that it was shown at Dead Can Dance's 1986 concert at The Town & Country Club – a 4AD carnival with The Wolfgang Press, Dif Juz and The Heavenly Bodies (an alliance between This Mortal Coil contributor Caroline Seaman and Dead Can Dance's James Pinker and Scott Rodger) also on the bill. Ivo subsequently commissioned Grierson to make the *Lonely Is An Eyesore* video. The only limitations on Grierson's brief were meant to be time and money; he had to farm out Throwing Muses' video, as the band was in America, but some artists (he doesn't name them) resisted the idea, as they had 23 Envelope's efforts to freely interpret their music. Grierson's treatments often involved grimy water in the style of Tarkovsky's *Stalker*, and grainy monochrome, creating a shrouded, solemn mood, rarely detouring from the 4AD vernacular.

Ivo singles out Dif Juz's 'No Motion' for two reasons: it's his favourite ever Dif Juz track – 'finally they captured themselves' – and the video is the only known visual evidence of the band. 'There's one moment where Alan Curtis looks up and gives a deep sigh, he's so bored,' Ivo recalls. It's also the most poignant Dif Juz track, as it was the last recording that the band ever released. Dave Curtis's health had improved and so Ivo had funded some rehearsals, but the guitarist quickly backed out, hoping to record a solo album instead. Ivo still hoped that this effort would turn back into a Dif Juz record, but there was to be no album, band or solo.

Ever since Steve Miller's *Sailor* and Neil Young's eponymous debut, Ivo had been fond of albums that set the scene with an instrumental.

In retrospect, 'No Motion' would have been a suitably moving intro for the album, and the right scene-setter, but Ivo elected to start with Colourbox's 'Hot Doggie', a red herring as far as the rest of the album was concerned, being yet another slim, punchy TV-style theme, littered with samples, from *2000 Motels* and *Star Trek* to *Supergirl* and *The Evil Dead*. Grierson's treatment thankfully eschewed water and sobriety for film samples spliced between the sight of the Young brothers driving a mock car in a fabricated, neon-drenched version of London's Soho district, with a rare dose of camp on 4AD – cartoon gangsters, a close-up on a cleavage, messy kissing, terrible wigs.

Cutting from 'Hot Doggie' to This Mortal Coil's 'Acid, Bitter And Sad' was like swapping sugar for salt. Ivo's first entirely self-composed track was partly an inspired case of plagiarism that improvised a haze of synths over a rhythm borrowed from Cocteau Twins' 'Musette And Drums' and Colourbox's 'The Moon Is Blue'. Alison Limerick's phased vocal briefly emerged towards the end with a desperately sad lyric: *'The half-moon is aching, bitter and sad/ We are bare, we are stripped to the bone/ It's out of our hands, a dream without a dream/ We are bare, always alone.'*

It's unlikely that Ivo would have chosen 'Acid, Bitter And Sad' as This Mortal Coil's next single. Besides 'Hot Doggie', 'Fish' and Clan Of Xymox's synth-rocking 'Muscoviet Musquito', *Lonely Is An Eyesore* failed to fulfil Ivo's original remit of potential singles, from The Wolfgang Press's slow-burning 'Cut The Tree' to Brendan Perry's lengthy, Philip Glass-esque instrumental 'The Protagonist'. Lisa Gerrard wasn't involved until Ivo suggested a remixed version of 'Frontier' from the first Dead Can Dance album, diluting the concept of imagined singles even further.

Next to Perry and Gerrard's protracted approach to recording, Cocteau Twins were much more adept at creating new bespoke pieces, providing the new and exquisite 'Crushed', an extension of the relaxed *Echoes In A Shallow Bay* sound. The track was to be the trio's sole recording in 1987; after an intense five years, they were taking a breather while Robin Guthrie assembled a proper home studio, housed in a warehouse in Acton, aided at the start by the technically proficient Young brothers – for the Colourbox boys, any distraction from writing and recording a song was preferable.

Mention *Lonely Is An Eyesore* to Guthrie and his response is typical: 'I've never had a royalty statement for that album,' he claims, 'which is interesting.' Guthrie also says he never received one of the hundred limited edition versions, a wooden (American beech) box designed by Vaughan Oliver to house vinyl, CD, cassette and video versions plus a booklet and two art prints by Terry Dowling: 'All this by little 4AD,' says Oliver, whose commitment to design was second to none. (One of them can be found in London's Victoria and Albert Museum's permanent collection, evidence of 4AD's place in British design). Guthrie takes pleasure in recounting that Martyn Young – who *was* sent a box set – turned his into a cat litter tray. 'I saw it round his house!' Guthrie smirks. 'But then Martyn is a very obtuse character.'

Like the V&A, *Melody Maker* treated *Lonely Is An Eyesore* as a landmark, honouring the occasion by putting 4AD on its cover and profiling every artist on the compilation. Press coverage might not always have been favourable, but at this point 4AD was guaranteed blanket coverage. TV and radio were another matter; Ivo decided, after *Le Mystère Des Voix Bulgares* and the specialist dance coverage given to Colourbox and The Wolfgang Press, that he needed to look at getting broader media coverage with more than the piecemeal freelance plugging that he'd previously commissioned.

For the post of running 4AD's TV and radio promotions, Ray Conroy suggested his friend Howard Gough, another Colchester lad who had been working at Island Records. Colourbox's songwriting was signed to Island's in-house publishers Blue Mountain, so Gough had already worked on 'Baby I Love You So' and 'The Official Colourbox World Cup Theme'. He could bring experience, and contacts, gained from working for a major label, to change the perception of 4AD's esoteric appeal. 'Radio 1 would need to know there was a possibility a single could be a hit, and that the machinery was in place for that to happen,' says Deborah Edgely. Gough was to bring much more: energy, chaos, distress.

According to Conroy, Gough is currently living back at his parents' house, without a working email account or mobile phone, which doesn't paint an encouraging picture. The only feedback from requests for an interview – via Conroy – are that Gough reckons he has nothing interesting to say. And this from a man who reputedly never stopped for breath.

'Howard was a motormouth,' says Brendan Perry. 'But not in a good way. He was a coked-up train run amok, full of braggadocio. He didn't even need coke. His arrival felt like things were changing at 4AD.'

Ivo: 'I can understand why Brendan might say that. Howard was an extraordinary character, a really positive person who loved to party. No one could ever say he and I had much in common or operated with a shared vision, but he did an enormous amount to raise the profile of most of our bands. I wanted to unify 4AD's representation on the radio, and that Gough did that really well. And he was great at taking care of visiting bands. He could make them feel special, and he was the go-to person to fix stuff. He could get anything done. I remember Howard once parted the crowd leading into the Glastonbury festival, like Moses and the Red Sea, so that Throwing Muses' van, which had broken down earlier, could get through.'

There was an instant clash of personalities between Gough and 4AD's resident party animal, Vaughan Oliver. 'We had absolutely no connection, besides taking drugs,' says Oliver. 'I think Ivo brought Howard in to shake things up, because he had such a different mindset. He was going to take us somewhere else. Whenever we talked about music, he'd say, "Yeah, this band sold this many units." What the fuck was he doing at 4AD?'

The question was instantly answered by a release that would make the best of Gough's motivation and bravado, and test the foundations of this music-centric label forced into competition with the majors. Gough's first 4AD assignment involved Colourbox, 4AD's newest signing A.R. Kane, and a collaboration that tilted 4AD off its axis and into a thrilling and uncertain present.

A.R. Kane had been formed by two east London school friends, who took their initials from their first names Alex (Ayuli) and Rudy

(Tambala). With bassist Russell Smith as the silent partner in the relationship, the trio timed it well: their swirl of guitar FX chimed
perfectly with the tenor of the times, as bands such as Dinosaur Jr and
the emerging My Bloody Valentine signalled a further shift from
social and political engagement into the realm of beautiful noise.

'We borrowed from rock and soul and jazz and blues,' Tambala
explained when I first met him in 1987, citing jazz trumpeter Miles
Davis's fusion masterpiece *Bitches Brew* as the band's benchmark.
Today, Tambala lives in the old Roman town of St Albans north of
London, a semi-rural contrast to A.R. Kane's urban roots, while Ayuli
has lived on the west coast of America since the early Nineties. The
pair no longer talk, not even when the band's *Complete Singles
Collection* was released in 2012. Everything the pair touched seemed
destined to implode. 'We weren't on 4AD for long,' says Tambala. 'We
were extremely disruptive everywhere we went.'

A.R. Kane's debut single 'When You're Sad' had been the second
release on One Little Indian, an independent label formed by Flux of
Pink Indians, an anarcho-punk band associated with punk rock's
continually committed agitators Crass. Iceland's Sugarcubes, fronted
by the inimitable Björk, was soon to follow, showing A&R supremo
Derek Birkett was casting the net wide.

At the time, says Tambala, '4AD was our favourite label, esoteric
and out there. Cocteau Twins and This Mortal Coil records were like
pieces of God; you put them delicately on the turntable, and you felt
God touching you! We were really into that ethereal world, being from
east London, and trying to escape from the shit. But neither of us had
a clue how to approach a record label.'

They had only made contact with One Little Indian after Tambala
had been introduced to Derek Shulman, a former member of the
progressive band Gentle Giant who had been producing Sugarcubes.
Birkett came to see A.R. Kane rehearse: 'He said, "You're fucking shit,
let's do a record together!"' Tambala laughs. 'That was Derek's way of
talking, like a hard man.'

A.R. Kane's debut single 'When You're Sad' had been favoured by
the music press, who saw an angle in that Tambala and Ayuli were

black, and had labelled the band 'the black Jesus and Mary Chain' (even though bassist Smith was white). Ivo was equally a fan of the single, which he considers better than anything they recorded for 4AD. They had contacted Ivo after growing increasingly frustrated with Birkett delaying a follow-up – most likely he was distracted by Sugarcubes' impending debut single 'Birthday', which was to be received by the music press as another piece of God. 'It was funny,' says Tambala, 'because Derek had told us, "You'll do a few songs with me, but eventually you'll go to 4AD"'.

A.R. Kane duly sent Ivo a demo of 'Lollita': 'He loved it and suggested we record a single and asked who we wanted to produce it. Can we have that bloke from Cocteau Twins? Yeah, he'd love to, Ivo replied. It was like a dream come true.'

Ivo already knew Ayuli, from his job as the copywriter responsible for the Thompsons Holidays advert that had used a version of 'Song To The Siren', sung by Louise Rutkowski after Ivo and Cocteau Twins had vetoed This Mortal Coil's version. But One Little Indian didn't share the dream – Ivo had wrongly assumed that A.R. Kane had told Birkett of their imminent move.

'Derek and his crew marched down to 4AD's office for a confrontation with Ivo and the 4AD gang,' says Tambala. 'Imagine a room full of middle-class skinheads; 4AD's effete skinheads and One Little Indian's anarcho-punk skinheads! I wish I'd been there. Eventually, I hear it fizzled out and Derek's lot went off. We thought it was great that they were fighting over us.'

Ivo didn't agree. 'He loved the demo but he didn't love us,' says Tambala.

'It's true, I didn't enjoy them,' Ivo recalls.

Tambala: 'It was a culture clash between us and 4AD and we made Ivo a little nervous and edgy. 4AD believed their own press to an extent; it was all very beautiful and precious, everyone wore black and had their heads shaved. You'd call it Zen, but it wasn't the rough-and-tumble Kerouac Zen of living the money, but the aesthetic, bourgeois idea – that everything must be very carefully done, that we're all sensitive individuals.'

A.R. Kane weren't impressed: 'We thought, this is fucking bullshit, we're not buying into it! You have to take the piss out of that stuff. Alex would say, "Ivo, you look really hip. The last time I saw you, you were wearing pixie boots with your trousers tucked in." I guess he [Ivo] wasn't pleased to be called on his pretensions. At the same time, they were really nice and unthreatening people.'

The twelve-inch *Lollita* EP, comprising the title track 'Sado-Masochism Is A Must' and 'Butterfly Collector', was audacious and thrilling, especially the middle eight of 'Sado-Masochism Is A Must', with Ayuli hollering, *'and this hurts and that hurts and this hurts and that hurts'*, the staccato guitar/drum slash resembling a knife or the impact of a punch. This was duly illustrated by the artwork, of a naked girl – borderline-underage in homage to the controversial novel *Lolita* by Russian novelist Vladimir Nabokov – holding a knife behind her back, which the band had commissioned from the emerging (and now world famous) photographer Juergen Teller.

Producer Robin Guthrie played his part by amplifying the trio's violent, bruising take on dream-pop, his finest hour outside of Cocteau Twins. He was probably revelling in working with a band that he knew were mocking his pet peeve, 4AD. 'The way Robin and Liz would talk about Ivo was unbelievable,' Tambala recalls. 'But Robin could also be incredibly warm and magnanimous. He let us use his guitars and effects; we could even borrow them. But then he could flip into darkness at the drop of a pin, the most cynical bastard around. Working with Robin was a trip! He was extremely exacting, and harsh, like, "What's the fuck's that shit? Do it again." But to go from a scrappy first single to something good enough for 4AD, you needed someone like Robin.'

Tambala says he identified with Guthrie's working-class mentality and his view of 4AD. 'Neither Robin or us had time for all that effete stuff about 4AD. It was all about making good music. So there was that edge between us and 4AD, but that kind of relationship *should* be edgy. They're exploiting you, in the sense of, "We'll make money out of what you create, we will take a big cut and give you some back, and without us, you don't exist". As much as you need them, you hate them, so you try to tear them down.'

As the newest outsiders to the 4AD clan, A.R. Kane had a perspective on how Cocteau Twins and the label were perceived. 'When we played in Europe,' Tambala says, 'fans appeared to love Ivo more than Cocteau Twins, as if Ivo was some god. I think he liked to play that Svengali role; not Ivo Watts-Russell, just Ivo. The Cocteaus even wrote a song called "Ivo". You kept seeing his name on 4AD's record sleeves, like Manfred Eicher on [European jazz label] ECM. Like, who's this guy, who seems to be touching all of this amazing stuff and making it happen? I could imagine there might be a lot of envy around that.'

Justifiably proud of 'Lollita', A.R. Kane wanted to show the breadth of their tastes and ambition, informing Ivo that they wanted to make a dance track. 'We'd been clubbing since we were about twelve, and we knew [On-U Sound label head/producer] Adrian Sherwood, who was an East End boy like us,' says Tambala. 'He'd show us what he was doing with samplers, and he was working with the Sugarhill label guys, Doug Wimbish and Keith LeBlanc, the world's best rhythm section at the time, so we asked Ivo if we could work with them too. His reaction was, "I don't really like that lot, this is what I'd like you to do, Colourbox haven't worked for two years, I want to get them out of retirement and re-energise them, you've both got eclectic tastes". Who were we to say no to God? We were massively grateful to be in the studio, and on what we thought was *the* best indie label.'

Ivo: 'Some would argue, as with Robin, you knew what you were getting with Adrian Sherwood, meaning his white man dub. I thought it would be more interesting to work with Martyn Young, who liked the idea of following a suggestion instead of having to come up with a new track.'

Young hadn't heard of A.R. Kane but accepted the challenge. He also had the root of a new track after meeting British DJ/journalist Dave Dorrell, who had taken Young clubbing on London's rare groove scene, a fusion scene of old jazz, funk and disco. Dorrell also gave Young bootlegs of rare groove breaks by the likes of Double Dee and Steinski. But the new track didn't just flow; this being Colourbox, it had to be expertly measured.

The Young brothers began at Blackwing, with engineer John Fryer, to make programmed beats have the same swing as rare groove breaks. 'This didn't work with just straight drum beats,' Young explains. 'We also wanted things to be sample-based with a narrative, so we started using vocal snatches mainly influenced by James Brown. John had a new sampler, the Akai S900, loaded with samples that he flicked through as I played them on a keyboard, which is how we got the piano sound that crossfaded into a backwards snare. Once we had that, we knew we had a track.' He was to call it 'Pump Up The Volume'.

When Tambala and Ayuli joined them at Blackwing, Young changed tack. 'I suggested a slow instrumental that I thought would be good with melodic feedback. But they weren't up for it. I found them very student-y and arrogant, in it for what they could get out of it. I always had to bite my tongue with them, which is why we started working on "Pump Up The Volume" without them. We only got A.R. Kane in to put down some guitar feedback to keep Ivo happy as it was supposed to be a collaboration.'

Tambala: 'There are so many stories about "Pump Up The Volume" and they're all wrong! Mine too, probably. My memory is that we turned up with a four-track demo of our track, "Anitina", and started messing around. We had an idea for a vocal, a drum machine groove, a twelve-string guitar and echo. It just needed a massive production. Martyn, however, had been seduced by the dark side and he came in with this ambient piano piece, which was dreadful new age shite. I told him that if he put that down, I'd cover it in layers of feedback. He went a bit moody and started working on our track. Martyn was really hot on drum programming, and he lifted our track into the dance area, with a big fat bass and loads of space and echo. It sounded like a smash hit, with all the elements of what was percolating on both the dance and indie scenes.'

Once the studio version of 'Anitina' was finished, says Tambala, 'Martyn wanted to do this dance track that they'd started. He was totally hyped up, so we started pissing around, playing that stupid bass line, which was spoofy and filmic more than funky or rocky. At one point, Alex and I were on the drum machine, and it all started to gel. At which point, Martyn suddenly didn't want us there anymore, a complete turnaround. We didn't care; we'd had a good laugh and got "Anitina" done. Then Martyn's mates turned up, this used car sales-man guy that turned out to be Dave Dorrell, and his mate, CJ Mackintosh, who brought out his records and started scratching them, and then he was pushed to one side as well. But the backbone of that track was nothing without CJ. He lifted the whole track off the floor.'

One of Dorrell's records had unearthed an Eric B. & Rakim sample (from 'I Know You Got Soul') with the phrase *'pump up the volume'*, which Mackintosh's scratching laid neatly into the track. Young also concedes that A.R. Kane did get 'unique and unusual sounds out of their Roland space echo unit, which worked well with the James Brown samples'. Whatever the level of each contribution, the whole was greater than the sum of the parts, and fulfilled a potential more than Colourbox's own tracks.

As Howard Gough got to work servicing the first round of white label test pressings of 'Pump Up The Volume' to the clubs, 4AD released Dead Can Dance's third album. Brendan Perry and Lisa Gerrard had also seen the creative benefits of personal tension; Ivo could tell from meetings with the duo that their personal relationship wasn't built to last, though they'd gone ahead and dispensed with other musicians after realising they could record everything them-selves using programming and synthesised sound. *Within The Realm Of A Dying Sun* was even split into separate sides: Perry's tracks on side one, Gerrard's on side two.

The duo may have been living in a depressed part of London but when they looked out the window, they saw Europe. The new album reflected the pair's latest obsessions with nineteenth-century roman-tic classical music and French symbolist poetry; for example, the title 'Anywhere Out Of The World' was borrowed from Charles Baudelaire. Gerrard had been as spellbound as everyone else by the Bulgarian choir and had the raw talent to train herself to sing in the same open-throated style. 'We'd heard and seen and read such an exotic and extraordinary weight of treasure that crossed all boundaries, and we realised that we had the right to do the same,' she says. Perry adds, 'I also wanted to reclaim ceremonial music from the special preserve of religious music', as if this was a normal activity.

The duo's Euro-centricity was being rewarded by growing audiences across the continent, whereas Perry says Dead Can Dance's UK concerts might only draw a handful of people outside of London. They seemed ready to move on again, like The Birthday Party, seeking new inspiration and not tied to Britain by sentiment or roots. They also found London's dense concentration of media stifling, as well as the labelling that came with it. 'When we worked on "Dawn Of The Iconoclast", Gerrard recalls, 'Brendan said to me, "I really want this piece to break the image that people have of us, this gothic punk stereotype that has no value".'

'Dawn Of The Iconoclast' opened the 'Lisa' side by torching the idea of stereotypes, with an opening rally of horns, Gerrard's Bulgarian-style incantation, swelling strings and timpani. On 'The Summoning Of The Muse', Gerrard's voice overlapped in madrigal form, framed by church bells. This was not even of the same planet as Batcave goth staples Sex Gang Children, sounding more like the film soundtracks of epic European cinema. Perry's side hit a similar mood. 'Anywhere Out Of The World' and 'In The Wake Of Adversity' joined the dots between Scott Walker's lonely voyages and the mood of the Ingmar Bergman films that had so inspired him. For all the separation of the two sides, the album formed a magnificent whole.

Throwing Muses had also persisted with dogged intuition, searching for a producer that could capture the band as they really were. This led to Mark van Hecke, who had produced the first two Violent Femmes albums, and a new mini-album. *The Fat Skier* also had two distinct sides: playing at 33rpm, six new tracks (including a re-recorded 'And A She-Wolf After The War' from *The Doghouse Cassette*) sounded lean, stripped back; playing at 45rpm on the flip, the debut album's 'Soul Soldier' pointlessly bookended with ambient noises, from percussion to Kristin Hersh and Tanya Donelly in a park with a gurgling baby Dylan.

The re-recorded track was not the band obeying intuition but the influence of Throwing Muses' new American label, Sire. Label boss

Seymour Stein wasn't only interested in British bands: he clearly wanted American bands on British labels. Someone at Sire, or parent company Warner Brothers – no one can recall who – had singled out 'Soul Soldier' as a possible route to success. The additions were a bizarre way of refreshing it for fans that already owned it. It felt like a forced move, and Van Hecke's production didn't feel right either. 'Mark erred on the other side of what we were shooting for,' says David Narcizo. 'We were disappointed because we expected the sound to get bigger. I preferred it to the first album, but Ivo wasn't too happy.'

Ivo: 'I can't help it, I like reverb and texture. I thought *The Fat Skier* sounded horrible and I probably only listened to it a handful of times. But things were beyond my control by then, because Sire had taken over the A&R. I really, *really* tried to persuade [manager] Ken Goes that it might be great for Sire to sign the band for America, but to let us represent them for the rest of the world and so not condemn them to the Warners system in Europe. But Sire had given the band money and we hadn't, so we ended up with Throwing Muses only for Britain.'

On paper, Sire was a valid option. It wasn't uncommon for American bands to sign to a major label; the size of the country meant that US independents struggled to fulfil the needs of the larger alternative bands such as R.E.M. (the band's record label IRS was an independent distributed by a major) and Hüsker Dü (Warners); even Sonic Youth would go the same way with Geffen. And Throwing Muses wouldn't have fitted in with the punk/hardcore-minded indies such as SST, Touch and Go, Homestead and Dischord.

Money was also the motivation behind the conflicting factions as 4AD got ready to release 'Pump Up The Volume'. After the white label got an emphatically positive reaction, the collaboration had needed a name, so Tambala suggested M/A/R/R/S, after the first name initials of the five principal members – Martyn, Alex, Rudy, Russell, Steven. Tambala's reasoning was that 'Even though Steven was never there, he was part of Colourbox and therefore M/A/R/R/S'. This implied a meeting of equals, but given what the Youngs thought of A.R. Kane's limited contribution to 'Pump Up The Volume', which they could see had commercial legs, this was not the case. Sensing they could have publishing on both A- and B-sides, Ray Conroy informed Ivo that Colourbox wanted the current B-side, 'Anitina (The First Time I See She Dance)', removed, to be replaced by a new Colourbox B-side. Ivo wouldn't agree, 'for two reasons. One, to honour the original idea of the collaboration. If A.R. Kane hadn't appeared, we'd probably still be waiting for Martyn to go into the studio. Second, I had no idea how long it would take Martyn to come up with a new B-side. Ray would have known that. I had to stick to the original plan.'

Deborah Edgely: 'I was on a train with Martyn, who was really angry about this marriage with A.R. Kane. From his perspective, "Pump Up The Volume" was nothing to do with Alex and Rudy, they'd just made the B-side, and he didn't want it on his record. Something Ivo had instigated for all the right reasons had become something else. If he'd stood back and thought about what was happening, perhaps he could have done something different, like release the tracks separately.'

Tambala: 'If they'd removed "Anitina", we'd have sued. We were brought in to fire Martyn up, and it totally worked. "Hot Doggie" compared to "Pump Up The Volume" is a shambles! Martyn didn't have that street element in his music, so where do you think it came from? Sorry to be corny, but it came from the street. We were East End boys and West End clubbers. We mixed up every element that we'd heard and you can hear that mash-up spirit in "Pump Up The Volume". That's what Ivo picked up on, the naïve, aggressive feel. If you hear Martyn's ambient track that he wanted us to work on, you'd understand.'

The elephants in the room were Dorrell and Mackintosh: given how the pair influenced the sound of 'Pump Up The Volume', they, and not A.R. Kane, were arguably the sound of the street. Even so, Young now agrees with Ivo's reasoning. 'We may not have done "Pump Up The Volume" without A.R. Kane. We might have missed the boat, even if we'd done "Pump Up The Volume" eventually.'

The track was an irresistible slice of what had been christened 'hip-house', a blend of house's sleek mobility and hip-hop's rougher energy, chock full of sample hooks (James Brown, Tom Browne, Pressure

Drop, Trouble Funk, the list goes on), but little noticeable guitar. 'Anitina' was a mind-bending treat for anyone expecting more of the A-side's dance/club purity, with a spacey mood swirled with guitar haze over a shifting palate of programmed drums that was beyond A.R. Kane's abilities at that point. If anything could be called a true collaboration, it was here.

Young's next step was to return to the studio to improve the mix. Ivo refused to pay for it so Colourbox paid to use Cocteau Twins' studio; the resulting version became the first 'Pump Up The Volume', released on white label, explains Young, 'so that DJs wouldn't prejudge a record on 4AD, which was Howard Gough's good idea. I'm not sure if it would have taken off otherwise.'

Though 4AD had nothing to be ashamed of, this was a pragmatic decision; dance DJs valued authenticity and 4AD's 'white' and solemn image would detract from the music. Ivo was content to let Conroy and Gough take control: 'It was a way to get a buzz going in clubs, and in the process of that, things just exploded. I'm sure both Ray and Howard, like the rest of us, made it up as they went along, but it went like clockwork.'

The timing was perfect. Dance music pouring out of American clubs was predominantly house and techno but with the funk-based rare groove as part of the stew. 4AD, bastion of hyper-ethereal border-line-goth, was about to reap the benefit. 'Dance and 1987 was like 1977 and punk rock, the start of something completely new, for 4AD as well,' recalls Conroy. 'Deborah and I were in New York for the [annual music industry conference] New Music Seminar, and we handed out copies of "Pump Up The Volume" and people went bonkers. We thought it was going to be huge. And that's when it all went wrong.'

'Everything was fine and dandy as the record started to take off, but we got totally sidelined,' says Tambala. 'No one mentioned us in interviews, which I don't accept as decent behaviour. I'd read about Dave and CJ and the Youngs being M/A/R/R/S, though Alex and I were there through the drum programming, the bass sounds and the samples as a team. M/A/R/R/S should have had equal footing on both sides.'

But the decision had been taken that Tambala and Ayuli were no longer part of the makeshift M/A/R/R/S. The first interview, in *Sounds*, had included them, but not the interviews in *Melody Maker* and *NME*, where Dorrell – an *NME* contributor himself – took centre stage alongside the publicity-shy Young brothers. The press shots followed suit. Tambala also points out that when *Supersonic* – commercial channel ITV's equivalent to the BBC's *Top of the Pops* – gave 'Pump Up The Volume' a slot, Ayuli recommended some dancers for the visual presentation, 'but then they all fucked off and did the show without us!' he says. 'And there's CJ and Dave representing us! After we'd helped them organise it. That was a turning point. I loved 4AD up till then, but they changed radically. It went legal. But as they say, where there's a hit, there's a writ.'

But the first writ came from an unlikely source. When 'Pump Up The Volume' first charted, Martyn Young had done a remix that helped the single climb ever higher, into the UK top 10, but at a price. 'The furore over stealing other people's records had begun, so there was a definite sense of wanting to push the envelope,' says Young. Pete Waterman, one third of Stock, Aitken and Waterman (SAW), the savvy factory-line pop producers behind the restricted talents of Kylie Minogue, Bananarama and Rick Astley, had remixed Sybil's 'My Love Is Guaranteed', replacing the original backing track with M/A/R/R/S's own and throwing in the same *'pump up the volume'* Eric B. sample.

'They've sampled us, let's sample them,' was Young's motivation. The problem was, Young told *Record Mirror* that he had 'bunged' SAW's track 'all over our track'.

Waterman disingenuously claimed to *Q* magazine that his name was on the Sybil label credits by mistake, '… only last week Stock Aitken Waterman were credited on six records we had nothing to do with.' SAW's next move was to take out an injunction on 'Pump Up The Volume' for not seeking permission – it didn't seem to matter that Sybil and cohorts hadn't sought M/A/R/R/S's permission to sample them. The truth was, SAW's action was more about putting a spanner in the works and preventing M/A/R/R/S from potentially knocking Astley's 'Never Gonna Give You Up' from the top of the UK singles chart.

SAW's considerable wealth meant they could sue M/A/R/R/S for copyright infringement, but M/A/R/R/S and 4AD's limited resources ensured that they couldn't respond in kind. 'We had problems with 4AD, A.R. Kane and Stock Aitken Waterman and it felt like we were talking to our lawyers every day,' says Young. 'We had no money anyway, but Steven and I were in the firing line for every infringement. The legal position in those days concerning sampling was very unclear and if everyone had sued, we might have owed money every time our track was sold or played.'

As quickly as they'd slapped it on, SAW withdrew the injunction; Waterman claimed that he'd discovered the 'Road Block' sample was only on the twelve-inch of 'Pump Up The Volume' and he didn't want to harm the sales of the seven-inch. Even so, says Young, 'We agreed to pay their [SAW's] choice of charity thousands of pounds and had to settle a big lawyer's bill.'

SAW's injunction had put the brakes on 'Pump Up The Volume', but it couldn't stop the momentum. 'The demand rose as the chart placing did and there were four of us packing vinyl all day long at the warehouse,' recalls Ray Conroy. '"Pump Up The Volume" was at number 2 for two weeks, stuck behind Rick Astley, including the week where we agreed we wouldn't distribute more copies and we'd take off the offending sample.'

But 'Pump Up The Volume' did manage to climb one more place. From a band devoid of 'pop' personality, that wouldn't play live or even regularly release records, 4AD had its first number 1 single, the first such British house track to reach the pinnacle, where it stayed for two weeks. It was also the first number 1 for independent distributors The Cartel. The single went on to sell three million copies worldwide, all on vinyl, and became the year's best-selling twelve-inch in America after being licensed by Island Records subsidiary 4th & B'way.

'I'm very proud to say 4AD never ran out of stock, though we couldn't press it fast enough,' says Ivo. But the residue of the dissent from all sides had soured the occasion, despite it being the biggest record that 4AD might ever have. Ivo recalls The Cartel's London team based at Rough Trade turning up at Alma Road with the most enormous bottle of champagne he'd ever seen. 'I embarrassingly joined them for five minutes,' he remembers, 'but I not only didn't feel comfortable around a lot of people, I didn't feel like celebrating.'

Justice was served when Eric B. & Rakim's publishers Blue Mountain Music took SAW to court over its sampling 'theft' of the M/A/R/R/S track. No one even got an advance from 4th & B'way as the US label behind the Eric B. & Rakim track had only given permission to use the sample if it didn't have to pay up front for 'Pump Up The Volume'. But the damage had been done, and the repercussions were considerable.

First, Ray Conroy had decided to sever his ties with 4AD. 'I'd work at 4AD all day and then Ivo and I would have a very bad meeting,' he recalls. 'This went on for weeks. Finally we'd had enough and it was best that I left. At the end of the day, with indie record labels, it's thievery in terms of the contracts they give out, and I share Robin Guthrie's view on that. They tie you up for ever, and don't pay you properly. And the money they made out of it funded the next five years for 4AD. Martin [Mills] wasn't helpful – they still can't find the original contract that was signed. We liked Ivo and thought he was our friend, so it felt like a big betrayal.'

'With hindsight, I made a massive mistake not supporting Colourbox over M/A/R/R/S,' says Ivo. 'I didn't know what success would mean – I had no concept of "Pump Up The Volume" selling so many copies, of which A.R. Kane got half of the profits. My sales forecast had been ten thousand! Being friends with Rudy and Alex wasn't remotely important, but Colourbox and Ray were. Ray called me a cunt, and said I wasn't supporting them. But then he managed a band that never played live, or did much, and all of a sudden there's potential huge success.

'If there's one redeeming feature to all this, it was proving that Rough Trade Distribution could have a number 1 single. It was also a concrete way of saying thank you to [Rough Trade's] Richard Scott and Geoff Travis for the unbelievable support they had given 4AD, especially early on. Without them, many labels would never have had the opportunity to start or to have the ability to continue.'

Conroy was followed out the door by A.R. Kane. 'Things got nasty after Ivo put a contract on the table and said we had to sign,' says Tambala. 'Alex signed, but I wanted to read it first, and I found they were trying to cut us out of the deal. My parting conversation with Ivo was him saying that if I didn't sign, he wouldn't put A.R. Kane's next single out. I told him to fuck off and put the phone down – end of our 4AD story. We were taking a risk, but there's only so much crap you can take. Ivo's angle was that Colourbox had been on 4AD and in the industry longer than us, and so deserved more than us. I spoke to a lawyer, who spoke to theirs, and a deal was struck where we got five times more in terms of the royalties Ivo was trying to pay us.'

Ivo: 'I'm not sure what contract Rudy is referring to. There was already a signed M/A/R/R/S contract for "Pump Up The Volume" and "Anitina" and I certainly didn't want to work with them again, so I didn't want a new contract. It made no financial difference to me, or 4th & Broadway in America, whether "Anitina" was on the American version. The lawyers finally agreed how to split the US royalties, with A.R. Kane getting a fifth as there were four versions of "Pump Up The Volume" and one of "Anitina".'

Encouraged by Conroy, Colourbox decided that they should also leave 4AD. Conroy played off two major labels, Polygram and EMI: 'I negotiated one of the best deals I could have got, about two million pounds for M/A/R/R/S and Colourbox. We were still contracted to 4AD, but Ivo wouldn't let us go for nothing, which felt like blood money. I credit him with being patient with Colourbox but it really soured things.'

Adding insult to injury, A.R. Kane had put an injunction on Colourbox over the use of the name M/A/R/R/S, and to ensure any version of 'Pump Up The Volume' would have 'Anitina' on the B-side. 'Until that was sorted,' Young says, 'none of the money from "Pump Up The Volume" could be released. We couldn't even do remixes as M/A/R/R/S without them. On the publishing side too, they tried to get as much as they could, which hinged on that B-side. So we had to settle with them too.'

'It became all about the money,' Conroy declares. 'M/A/R/R/S was outside of Colourbox's original deal, and we felt it was a collaboration gone too far. A.R. Kane got a £30,000 publishing deal on the strength of that B-side! We looked after Dave Dorrell and CJ Mackintosh too. It felt like we were being royally shafted.'

'If we hadn't fallen out with everyone, [M/A/R/R/S] would have gone on to do a load more, and that's sad,' Tambala concludes. '[Subsequent UK number one acts] Bomb The Bass and S-Express came on the tail end of "Pump Up The Volume", which was miles ahead of them. But they slew the goose that laid the golden egg. It was absolute greed. If they'd really been M/A/R/R/S on their own, why didn't they make another M/A/R/R/S record? Because Martyn had burnt out.'

The Young brothers were also legally unable to be M/A/R/R/S without A.R. Kane's permission. Tambala and Ayuli knew that M/A/R/R/S was dead in the water, and with a publishing deal and pride intact, the duo's next move was to send new demos to Geoff Travis at Rough Trade, who responded favourably with the offer of an album. 'After everything that had happened,' Ivo says, 'Geoff phoned to say A.R. Kane was calling, and what should he do? Which made me feel even worse not calling Derek Birkett to begin with! I told Geoff to do whatever he wanted. For me, Alex and Rudy's personalities had got in the way of enjoying the music that they might make.'

Now all Martyn and Steve Young had to do was sign a deal that Ray Conroy had negotiated. 'And they could leave as extremely wealthy people,' says Conroy. 'But they decided not to. When a massive cheque for M/A/R/R/S finally arrived, Martyn spent it all on a studio, taking over Cocteau Twins' old studio in Acton after they moved out – where he proceeded to not make another record!'

'Ray's ambitions were so much greater than either Martyn or Steve's, which didn't do them any favours,' Ivo says. In 1985, he had attended a meeting that Conroy had organised with Island Records founder Chris Blackwell, hoping Island, who owned Colourbox's publishing, would license them in America. 'But CBS [now Sony] had wanted to license Colourbox for the world,' Ivo explains. 'I told Martyn that I wanted nothing to do with CBS but that Colourbox was free to go. It wasn't the first time that I'd told them either. Martyn and Steve probably would have enjoyed a large advance that we couldn't afford, for Colourbox or anyone else, but they were comfortable on 4AD. It hurts that Ray complains that Colourbox was tied up for ever by a 4AD contract. We had done at least two separate one-off contracts to test the waters before they signed anything long term.'

This was borne out by Martyn Young's decision to stay with 4AD, 'even though, in the end,' he says, 'we didn't do any more music. Ivo lived around the corner from me, so we'd see each other occasionally and talk.'

Ivo managed to coax Young into remixing some tracks for The Wolfgang Press, and he later produced a cover of The Isley Brothers' soul classic 'Harvest For The World' for the Liverpool band The Christians (released on Island) and remixed West African star Mory Kanté's 'Yeke Yeke', but it was a tiny return for someone with the technical skills of the Youngs. But this was his choice. 'I turned down other things because I didn't like the offers,' he recalls. 'I became disillusioned after "Pump Up The Volume". It made me question if I ever wanted to do music in the first place. Would I have to go through the same shit again?'

Ivo might have been asking himself the same question as Young. The aftermath of the M/A/R/R/S debacle, on top of the ongoing tension around Cocteau Twins, was leaving profound and potentially damaging traces. 'I put a shield around my heart and didn't let people in because of what happened with friends and relationships that I had valued,' he admits. 'Before, I was the good guy in the white hat, and afterwards I was the baddie in the black hat. I never felt different inside because of my motivations, and because people were enjoying the fruits of our labours at 4AD, I couldn't be all bad. But I felt I was being judged in a different, suspicious manner. It deeply affected me and I see it as the first sign of depression starting to take over. It wasn't healthy to separate myself from such intense feelings, positive or negative, from that era, but it was easier to push them away.'

One positive result from the M/A/R/R/S scenario was that the public profile of 4AD was forever removed from the re-peddled cliché of goth, despite *NME*'s initial, risible review of 'Pump Up The Volume' as, 'more dark offerings from the goth label 4AD'. This was retracted and the record re-reviewed after the mistake was pointed out.

A second boon was the arrival of Simon Harper, ostensibly to take Ray Conroy's place, but whose job soon encompassed running 4AD's international department, liaising with licensees. As Ivo's friend and confidant, Harper became a much more integrated part of 4AD than Conroy was ever likely to be.

Harper had worked for Rough Trade Distribution for five years, handling labels such as Mute, Creation and 4AD. 'Ivo and I had got to know each other pretty well when M/A/R/R/S was all going off, juggling all that stock, and through the injunction,' recalls Harper. 'Our relationship blossomed through adversity and hilarity.'

Ivo. 'I fell in love with Simon during that awful M/A/R/R/S period! In terms of physically managing our first hit single, he seemed like the only one that understood the kind of pressure I was experiencing, because he was experiencing it himself in terms of getting stock out there, feeding this insane machine. He was a great sounding board. Martin Mills was also solid as a rock.'

After the storm, came the calm, even if the lull was only to last for one single. Instead of the usual guitar/bass configuration, Brighton's Frazier Chorus harnessed flutes, clarinets and strings behind singer-songwriter Tim Freeman's fey, breathy delivery. Fans of Cocteau Twins and Dead Can Dance, they had sent a demo to 4AD. 'Our wildest dreams of appearing on the label were nothing more than optimistic fantasy,' says Freeman. 'So hearing from Ivo was, to put it mildly, unexpected. Chris Bigg had noticed from our demo that we were from Brighton, same as him, and his curiosity led him to play "Sloppy Heart" while Ivo was in the office.'

'Frazier Chorus were old school,' Ivo says. 'I liked "Sloppy Heart" very much, and I also chose the two B-sides ['Typical' and 'Storm']. As a demo, I had played "Sloppy Heart" on a bullet train to Osaka to Robin Guthrie, who said it was a great song, but a pity that The Velvet

Underground had already written it! They went into the studio to specifically record the EP knowing there wouldn't be another record with 4AD, as I didn't feel quite the same about their other songs. It was clean, tidy and honest on both sides.'

The folk-pastoral 'Sloppy Heart' was as much an aberration – and a commercial contender – in 4AD's catalogue as 'Pump Up The Volume'. Likewise, the artwork, a simple design of a woman in a print dress that could have doubled as the cover of a womenswear cata-logue. But it wasn't a hit (neither would Virgin's marketing budgets get Frazier Chorus's next six singles any higher than 51 in the UK national chart).

'Sloppy Heart' was ultimately more memorable as the bridge between 4AD's most successful single in 'Pump Up The Volume' and the band that rocked the label off its comfortable axis even more than M/A/R/R/S: the Pixies, who would have the same effect on the whole of alternative rock – as well as rock mainstream.

'Nineteen eighty-seven was a very good year to arrive at 4AD,' Simon Harper recalls. 'Cocteau Twins were established, the label's profile had risen on the back of M/A/R/R/S, and after Throwing Muses, Pixies exploded very quickly.'

'Name someone who has had more influence over the flow of modern rock – where noise and rhythm meet mystery and beauty – over the last twenty-five years,' online site BlogTalkRadio asked in 2012. The answer was a man they described as an 'Alt Rock Demigod', who has referred to himself over time as Black Francis and Frank Black. He now lives in Los Angeles, but in 1986, he was plain Charles Thompson, born and bred in Boston, Massachusetts.

'I have mostly pleasant memories about 4AD,' says Thompson. 'And those that weren't, time has put them into perspective.'

Thompson, the main creative force behind Pixies, who adopted the alias of Black Francis in the spirit of punk rock idol Iggy Pop, says his life was changed at the age of six: 'I heard loud sounds coming from a basement on my street, which turned out to be drums. I was afraid but I knew I wanted to have something to do with that.' His mother's folk records (*Donovan's Greatest Hits* was a favourite), The Beatles and new wave developed Thompson's love of song: fed by both noise and melody. Pixies' unique dynamic range would chop merrily between quiet and loud. The band's musicianship was equally both electrifyingly taut and gleefully unpolished. 'I wasn't the best player but I knew from bands like the Violent Femmes that it wasn't only about prowess,' he says. 'Boston has a huge student population, so there were lots of people about flying their flag of independence.'

One of them was Joey Santiago, Thompson's next-door neighbour at Amherst's University of Massachusetts. Born in Manila, capital of the Philippines, and raised in Longmeadow, Massachusetts, Santiago had absorbed his older brother's Beatles, Velvet Underground and Hendrix records, which chimed with Thompson's love of melody and noise. 'Out of boredom,' recalls Santiago, the pair turned to surf music: 'It didn't have any lyrics but it conjured up these images through the song titles, like "Link Wray Rumble" and "Run Chicken Run"'

When Thompson returned from six months studying Spanish in Puerto Rico, he persuaded Santiago to start a band. They placed a hilarious classified ad: 'Band seeks bassist into Hüsker Dü and Peter, Paul & Mary'.

Kim Deal would have known both trios – the former hardcore rockers and the latter winsome folkies. Even though she played guitar and had never played bass, Deal still applied for the post, and was the only one to do so. 'Kim wasn't just cool and enthusiastic,' says Santiago, 'she was perfect because we wanted a female bassist who could sing harmonies.'

Kim Deal and her twin sister Kelley came from Dayton, Ohio. Kim recalls them, aged four, singing along to their mother's tape of her singing 'Second Hand Rose': 'Mum sounded like a real hillbilly! Dad had a guitar, a microphone and sheet music, and we soon learnt "King Of The Road". Later, we started making up our own songs.'

Kim strummed guitar; Kelley, inspired by Karen Carpenter, played drums. As precocious teens, they'd both experimented with drugs, 'but then so did everyone else,' insists Kelley. Legally underage, they'd played covers sets in local bars and truck-stop restaurants. 'It was

great, because the old drunks would buy us sloe gin fizzes,' remembers
Kim. 'We covered Hank Willliams, Everly Brothers, Delaney and
Bonnie, blues songs. But I was scared to death too. It took ages for me
to figure out how to sing into a microphone.'

The sisters' musical evolution needed outside assistance. 'Punk
rock passed Dayton by,' says Kim. 'Still has, I think. But this friend of
Kelley's on the west coast was sending her mix tapes, stuff like Elvis
Costello, The Specials, rockabilly.'

In 1983, Kelley moved to LA to work as a program analyst for
Hughes Aircraft while Kim stayed in Dayton, taking cleaning jobs. Two
years later, Kim and new husband John Murphy moved to his home
town of Boston. While working as a doctor's receptionist – maybe
that's where she perfected her ebullient charm and Cheshire Cat smile
– Deal replied to Thompson and Santiago's advert. Once on board, she
suggested Kelley for the post of drummer. 'I hadn't touched drums in
ages,' says Kelley. 'I flew in and we tried some songs, but I knew I could
fake lots of things, just not drums. I think Charles would have dug a
girl drummer but Pixies were exactly what they needed to be.'

Dave Lovering, born in Burlington, Massachusetts and John
Murphy's work mate at a branch of RadioShack electronics stores, got
the job instead. Like Throwing Muses' David Narcizo, Lovering had
been a member of his school marching band. He'd studied electronic
engineering at Boston's Wentworth Institute of Technology, followed
by the RadioShack job. The completed band just needed a name.
Santiago suggested Pixies – they all enjoyed the idea of being 'mischievous little elves', he says. They got to work on Thompson's songs, as
savage and unusual as they were mischievous, and lyrically surreal. 'I
thought we were too strange to sell records,' Santiago recalls. 'All I
knew was I was having fun, and it was better than school.'

Pixies started playing around Massachusetts. 'It wasn't about big
commercial success and mainstream moves, more these scrappy little
bands pressing up records in their basement and touring,' says
Thompson. 'To this day, Pixies aren't good at the flash.'

None of Pixies had heard of 4AD, which speaks either of the label's
select appeal or the band's restricted knowledge. Thompson had been

a Birthday Party fan but hadn't noticed the band's records were on 4AD, but he was a regular at the local club Spit: 'It had a goth and a gay night that played that big, booming, British-based stuff, so I would have heard 4AD by osmosis,' he says. 'But we did know this hip band, Throwing Muses, and this producer, Gary Smith, who was into them and then us as well. We went on tour, and in Ohio, Tim Anstaett [of *Offense Newsletter* fame], 4AD fan *numero uno*, picked us up, and his car licence plate read "4AD". It was my first realisation that 4AD itself had fans, its own concept and sub-culture.'

Santiago: 'Our dream had been to sign to a label overseas because we didn't want to be seen as a local band. Before we had a manager, we sent a demo to New Rose in France, but they'd rejected us. We were happy when one Boston club advertised us as, "Pixies from England".'

Gary Smith introduced Pixies to Ken Goes, who began managing them alongside Throwing Muses. When Ivo visited the latter in Newport, Goes gave him a cassette of seventeen Pixies demos, which Kim says was recorded in a three-day rush, fuelled by nothing more than Jolt Cola.

Ivo flew to New York: 'My first memory of Pixies was walking around playing the tape on my Walkman, enjoying Joey's guitar on "Vamos", a great, wild sound. But the impact faded over seventeen tracks and some songs weren't their greatest. On "Here Comes Your Man", Charles's voice was almost like Willy DeVille. Plus I was still nervous about getting involved with another band managed by Ken, and an American band, because of the frustration of taking a major like Sire into consideration.'

Deborah Edgely saw how the 4AD office had a different atmosphere: less precious, more combative. 'M/A/R/R/S did feel like a sea change, but that was as much to do with the people we were associated with,' she says. 'Howard, for example, loved to party, and he was very good at it. He injected oomph into a label that had been fairly backward in looking forward. Ivo was always reticent, but I encouraged him to be more embracing.'

Ivo: 'Apparently Pixies had been turned down by every American label. Peculiarly for me, because I'd just sign what I wanted, I started playing the Pixies tape to others, asking what they thought. I really liked that 4AD had created a genre of its own, and I thought Pixies were, frankly, quite rock'n'roll. It took Deb saying, "Don't be so bloody stupid, of course we have to get involved". Howard, Vaughan, Simon, everyone liked the band, so I called Ken. Charles and I ended up working very closely together, and for the most part, very easily. I'd always credited Deb with having given me the kick up the backside to get involved but it seemed weird, and hurtful, when Charles later referred to me as, "the guy at the label didn't even like Pixies".

'If there's a myth about Ivo not liking us, then I'm a victim of the myth,' says Thompson. 'It was hearsay from Ken because Ivo and I never discussed it. From our point, we didn't care. And I don't think there was anyone that cared as much about us at 4AD as Ivo.'

Ivo: 'I love all of Pixies' albums and I compiled the track listing for most of them, and I chose the A-sides and B-sides too. I thought that we worked together brilliantly, even if we weren't ever the closest of friends.'

Ivo's ideal plan was to release a mini-album, taking eight songs from the cassette, known as *The Purple Tape* after its coloured cover. Ivo wanted to call it *Come On Pilgrim* after a Thompson lyric (*'come on pilgrim, you know he loves you*', from 'Elevate Me'), a phrase that Thompson had lifted from actor John Wayne. 'It reminded me of Billy Pilgrim from one of my favourite books, Kurt Vonnegut's *Slaughterhouse-Five*,' says Ivo. 'And Charles agreed.'

Thompson: 'It was an opportunity to be signed to an artsy-fartsy label with an odd name, what was there not to like? I remember seeing Vaughan's artwork for our record, of this incredibly hairy man in sepia tones, which to my eye was straight out of a David Lynch movie. We didn't know we wanted to be like this, but it was right, and I never questioned what Vaughan gave us after that. The day I saw the artwork, I quit my job at the warehouse of The Windsor Button Shop, to go on the road, where I've been ever since.'

The photograph of a man, facing away from the camera, his head bald but the top half of his body carpeted with thick hair, was a suitably arresting image for a record that felt like an uncanny surprise. It had been taken by English photographer Simon Larbalestier of a mutual friend, Sean Bolton: 'Vaughan purchased a print at my degree show in the summer of 1987 and then persuaded the Pixies,' Larbalestier recalls. 'I was experimenting with themes of alienation and a sense of loss but in essence this image was evoked from reading *The Temptation of St Antony* by Gustave Flaubert. A lot's changed in the years since but essentially my preoccupation with decay and texture is still there.'

Like French author Flaubert's novel, Thompson's lyrics embraced lust, death and decay, yet the music of *Come On Pilgrim* was not the usual textural stuff of vintage 4AD but a thrilling, rollicking charge, interspersed with gentler moments and seasoned with surf rock and Puerto Rican spice. Thompson's often coruscating vocals were reputedly inspired by a Thai rock star who told him to 'scream it like you hate that bitch'.

The first time Ivo actually met the band was when they opened for Throwing Muses in Hoboken, New Jersey, but as a trio because Kim Deal was attending a funeral in Ohio. 'I'll never forget Charles walking towards me to shake my hand, with a big smile, a lovely bloke,' Ivo recalls. 'Joey was a man of few words but he said, "Make me famous in the Philippines because I love Filipino girls!" None of them had any attitude.'

Deborah Edgely was at the same show. 'Pixies were gobsmacking, even without Kim. I told Ivo, if you don't pull your finger out, you'll lose them, you need to offer them a proper contract. And he did in the end, thank God, or the whole shape of 4AD's future would have been different.'

If purist Brendan Perry had had any say in the matter, 4AD would have remained the preserve of a rarefied commodity. 'I wasn't that keen on 4AD's commercial side, like I couldn't understand why Colourbox was on the label,' he says. 'Ivo played me Pixies' demos and I didn't get it. But obviously there was a lot more money around, and more acts got signed. Ivo was a rock to us but I could sense the whole promotional spin aspect of things was becoming more like a major label, like the way singles began to be hyped. 4AD's expansion, and into America, brought it more into the corporate sphere. It didn't impact on Lisa and I – we only saw it when we went to visit 4AD, to have lunch or a few beers across the road.'

One supporter of the change that the visceral Pixies represented was none other than Rudy Tambala: 'Pixies had an edge, and 4AD turned into a proper record label, no longer stuck in Zen land,' he says. 'They hardened massively, and the music got tougher.'

As ever Ivo wasn't thinking so conceptually, or commercially; he'd just discovered another band that didn't fit any obvious category. And he was still pushing bands away if he didn't feel the connection with the music, with Xymox becoming the latest band he let go despite their popularity.

Two Xymox-related records had been scheduled side by side: *Sleeps With The Fishes* was Pieter Nooten's solo project that had turned into a collaboration with Canadian ambient maestro Michael Brook, and the *Blind Hearts* EP was by Xymox – Moorings had restored the original name after Nooten had again left the band, and that was enough for Ivo: 'For me, Pieter was the heart of Xymox, and taking him out, they became much more like their influences. Pieter was more interested in classical music at that point.'

Moorings claims Nooten had chased Ivo about the demo that he'd given him, 'moaning about touring, how unhappy he was, how he did not like to be in a band, the whole sob story'. Nooten's memory is that Ivo asked if he had any solo material. 'I said I had some basic, but still intimate, melancholic material. Apparently Ivo loved it because he asked if I wanted to record an album. I couldn't believe my ears. But we were very apprehensive about how to approach it.'

Ivo had decided to produce the album at Blackwing: 'But I realised I couldn't bring anything fresh to it,' he says. 'We needed new blood.' As an enormous fan of recent ambient work on the Editions EG label, Ivo thought of Canadian guitarist Michael Brook, whose pulsing ethno-ambient fusion *Hybrid* had featured Brian Eno and Daniel Lanois. Brook accepted the Nooten job, 'and as things evolved, Michael's input was so large, it became a joint record,' Ivo recalls. 'I was really enjoying [Brian's brother] Roger Eno and Michael's first albums, so I loved releasing something in that vein, combined with Pieter's melodies.'

Three years older than Ivo, Brook had followed a similar musical trajectory, through psychedelia – he'd seen Jimi Hendrix, The Grateful Dead and Jefferson Airplane in concert – but admits that he'd bypassed punk and glam for an appreciation of synthesisers and Indian music, refining a musical palate.

Nooten: 'Michael was the ultimate producer – calm, thoughtful, highly skilled and, above all, a brilliant guitarist. We shared the same approach to the material: subtle, sensitive, thoughtful, intimate and intense.'

'*Sleeps With The Fishes* is an amazing record,' Brook thinks. 'It was a magic moment of ambient music but not ambient songs, with a rare mix of electronics and strings. It still sounds modern.'

Sleeps With The Fishes was an instrumental extension of the ambient-classical haunts of Nooten's choicest Xymox contributions. 'Equal Ways' from *Clan Of Xymox*, and 'After The Call' and 'Theme I' (renamed 'Clouds') from Xymox's *Medusa* were even re-recorded for the new record – beautiful, but with no noticeable improvement. However, with instrumentals floating in between, the alluring effect was of murky oceanic depths, a world of luminescent fauna living in unquiet slumber alongside all those bodies tipped overboard (Ivo suggested the album title). Nooten's austere, tremulous vocal matched Dominic Appleton for aching sadness, icing an album that should be more widely celebrated for its underrated part in the vintage mid-Eighties 4AD period.

Ivo: 'Among the forum world of 4AD followers, some people think it's 4AD's best record. I'd place it in the top ten. It's absolutely beautiful. So is the sleeve, with Chris Bigg's embossed calligraphy.'

Back in Xymox's camp, Ronny Moorings wasn't happy: 'Pieter had defected. Again. But I understood *Sleeps With The Fishes* was closer to his heart. I wanted more driven songs like "A Day" and "Back Door" anyway.'

Moorings and Wolbert turned *Blind Hearts* into a more electronic Xymox, successfully so, as the EP topped the US import charts. But it was the tipping point for Ivo, although Xymox's departure from 4AD was also triggered by the band's new manager, Raymond Coffer.

'Ivo wasn't trying to keep us,' Anka Wolbert recalls, 'and Ray kept saying we should tour America, where we'd had the most success, and to sign with a major label.' Xymox would follow Xmal Deutschland to the Polygram major conglomerate and so close 4AD's chapter on European signings.*

There was one more conclusion to the year: the twelve-inch *87 Anthology*, a fifteen-track CD compiled for Japan, which summarised a cataclysmic twelve months, for better and worse. There were also the promising growth spurts of the *Big Sex* and *Chains Changed* EPs, but all of the A- and B-sides of the 'Pump Up The Volume', 'Lollita' and 'Sloppy Heart' singles represented premature dead ends for 4AD and relationships within the label. Not that it mattered; 1987 was not a year that would end in tears. 4AD was in a very healthy position, and by releasing so many of its albums on CD (Ivo the audiophile had loved the crackle-free format) and adding hard-to-find singles and EPs, the label was selling more copies and encouraging new consumers to investigate the back catalogue.

Lonely Is An Eyesore had also become the first import album to top the Rockpool college radio chart in the US; one week, it was supported by Dead Can Dance's *In The Realm Of A Dying Sun* at number 2 and A.R. Kane's *Lollita* EP at number 3. The immediate future would be driven by a bunch of mischievous little elves, and one increasingly green-eyed monster.

---

* Just as Moorings and Wolbert couldn't sever their emotional bond, so Nooten couldn't let go either, returning for the band's third album *Twisted Shadows*. 'Pieter smelt major wages,' says Mooring, 'but I let him back.' In another twist, the album's third single, 'Imagination', written and sung by Wolbert, became Xymox's biggest hit, making the Billboard Hot 100 and MTV's playlist. But she lasted one more album and left in 1991 after a violent confrontation with Moorings following the label's suggestion that she sing half the songs on the next album. 'I got a lot of energy out of being on stage,' Wolbert shrugs. 'Ronny loved it too. It's a shame he didn't allow anyone else to stand next to him.'

11

TO SUGGEST IS TO CREATE;
TO DESCRIBE IS TO DESTROY

'*Lonely Is An Eyesore* was a watershed moment,' Vaughan Oliver recalls, 'putting to bed everything we'd done so far, and into the Victoria and Albert Museum in a wooden box.'

Whereas Ivo had to negotiate the potentially delicate terrain of signing bands, and even negotiations with managers, studios, producers, engineers and contracts, the 4AD art department didn't have to be waylaid in quite the same way. In the main, Oliver's role as 4AD in-house designer – to maintain a consistency of design approach, and to counter what he felt were lapses of judgement on behalf of the artist – had Ivo's full support. If Dead Can Dance, The Wolfgang Press and now Throwing Muses were proving resistant to 23 Envelope originating ideas for the bands to (hopefully) approve, Oliver mostly enjoyed the freedom to interpret the sound of 4AD in whatever way he felt appropriate. As his only true peer, Peter Saville, once said about his similarly close relationship with Factory Records, 'I had a freedom that was unprecedented in communications design. We lived out an ideal, without business calling the shots. It was a phenomenon.'

'It's true there were no record company demands,' says Oliver. 'Though I was working with all the artists' desires; I took everything on board. That was the whole concept of the independent movement: that everything was in the hands of the musicians, and you had to respond to their requirements rather than the record company's. I was just trying to give them creative direction, to show them something else. You want to do something different. Not just another record sleeve.'

For Oliver, the root of inspiration had to be music, 'or the work is worthless,' he says. 'And in terms of reflecting music, texture has always been there for me. You can see music as textures, colours, ideas, or the words that pop out at you.'

He cites his 'breakthrough moment' as the crumpled tissue of Modern English's *After The Snow* in 1983, which launched a series of groundbreaking images and ideas. These included use of his own photos, from the copulating horses of *Colourbox* to the Lynchian aura of 'Song To The Siren' that he had captured by camera on a cross-country trip of America. He would also use found images, such as an evocative, discarded 'Make Ready' print found on the floor of a Japanese printer's studio, with multiple images pressed on top of each other to test the correct weight of ink for the final version, to match Colourbox's sample-based sound.

Oliver was especially keen on the technical process becoming art in its own right. For example, the crumpled black texture of Xmal Deutschland's *Fetisch* saw Oliver, as he describes, 'abusing the camera in the darkroom, fucking up the process, with underexposures and old chemicals'. He enjoyed placing the common mistakes at the edges of artwork into the centre. 'My love affair with the PMT machine started there,' he says. The process of Photo Mechanical Transfer involved using a large and unwieldly camera to enlarge and reduce typesetting in scale, in the days of chemical fumes and the heat of the lens before Apple Macs and Photoshop became the tools of the design trade. 'It was the idea of abusing a controlled system, something that you're not supposed to do. To not know where you're going, but to create mistakes and to enjoy them, like feedback on a guitar.'

Oliver's PMT affair continued through Modern English's 'Someone's Calling' and *Lonely Is An Eyesore*, where he showed a small section of his PMT baseboard, the scalpel scratches providing the texture alongside carefully selected typefaces, some invented by Oliver, and later by Chris Bigg. Sometimes Oliver would put song titles and/or lyrics on the front cover, such as Xmal's *Qual* or Modern English's *Gathering Dust* EP, so, he explains, 'typography becomes the subject matter. The information becomes the illustration and text becomes image.'

Oliver occasionally returned to other points of fascination, such as the male nude, as seen in *Gathering Dust*, which featured a skeletally thin torso. Similarly, in *Nature Mortes – Still Lives*, Oliver says the anatomical image of two wrestling men was intended to isolate the image's homoerotic potential, years before such imagery entered the mainstream.

The designer would often go to unexpected places, such as the cast of his own head used for Clan Of Xymox's *Medusa* – pre-dating British artist Marc Quinn's blood-filled heads – or the unsettling postures of 'Life In The Gladhouse' taken from an encyclopaedia that Oliver felt suggested the in-patients of an asylum ('Gladhouse'/'madhouse'). 'There are two ways of re-appropriating images,' he contends. 'If you just take an image that's recognisable for its beauty, then what are you really doing? For me, Peter Saville would re-appropriate old Futurist designs, and put them on New Order sleeves, which is too easy. Post-modernism is not my thing, which I railed against at the time. It was a new kind of awkward beauty that I didn't subscribe to. But put an image in a new context, one which you were never meant to look at from that point of view, is when it's valid. That's what my work was about.'

Oliver's work also took inspiration from filmmakers David Lynch and Andrei Tarkovsky, a fevered dream of 'relics and remnants and memories and mementos, things that evoked other things, that touched people,' says Oliver. 'There is some art that confirms your aesthetic, or thought, or view of the world, and some art that takes you somewhere totally new.'

Searching for clues to Oliver's game plan, he says one key moment was in Tarkovsky's *Mirror*. 'I'm not a great one for plot; it's more moments. In *Mirror*, a doctor walks across a field of long grass, to speak to a woman, who is missing her husband. She had two kids, both with shaved heads. It's all very gentle and lovely. But something has happened between them [the adults], and as he walks back across the field to leave, he looks back at her, and over his shoulder out to the field, the grass between them is flattened by the wind. Forget CGI; how did that happen? It was pure visual poetry.'

David Lynch's *Eraserhead* made the same kind of startling impression. 'It was daring, this constant industrial soundtrack, the desolation, but the humour too. Like a moment in a film, such as Nicolas Roeg's *Walkabout*; a girl dives naked into water – how beautiful is that? It's very hard to find that point again, like you did in your formative years, like when I first read Samuel Beckett or saw *Blue Velvet* – can that happen again? To find something new, which touches your central core, that confirms your inner meaning, and another strand that says, what the hell is going on there?'

That might well have been the reaction of an artist on 4AD seeing the finished sleeve for the first time. Though Oliver denies this was the case, more than one artist claimed he feigned collaboration, and then conveniently ignored their wishes in the pursuit of better art and design. For example, Xmal Deutschland wanted a black wash of raven feathers for *Tocsin*; instead, Oliver gave them a purple wash of pigeon feathers. 'You'd discuss with Vaughan and when it was done, it's different to what was agreed!' says Anja Huwe. 'That was Vaughan. But he was great, and unique.'

Oliver denies that he ever got entirely his own way. 'Nothing was forced on anyone. Everything had to be approved by the band,' he maintains. 'Working independently wasn't my role, but I was in a position to show them other stuff that we hadn't talked about. With *Tocsin*, for example, I was trying to evoke the stormy sea, so whether it was ravens or pigeons didn't matter. But we always tried to create something fresh that was unique to the artist rather than use an already generated image. So where do you get ravens from? Instead, Nigel shot these amazing photographs of pigeons.'

Oliver says he had to be careful about imposing himself. 'Their [a band's] work was the centre of it, so you didn't want to take a line of conversation outside of what they were doing. It's more the ideas of their work, in the lyrics and music. If I did bring my influences, it was intuitive. Photographers would show me their work but I might wait two years until a piece of music came in that suited a particular photo. If anything, my skill was about putting the right photograph with music, and then I would put the commission into the hands of the photographer, to explore whatever they were into at the time, and I wouldn't instruct them. That's an unusual way of art directing.'

In general, so was the idea of an in-house designer, with only Factory and ECM having the same arrangement. (In the 1950s, Blue Note mostly used artist Reid Miles, but others too, including an as-yet undiscovered Andy Warhol. In German jazz label ECM's case, the artists were predominantly instrumentalists who didn't have the same hang-ups about profile.) Oliver concedes that the artist's identity could be subsumed by that of 4AD, or as BBC TV's youth culture show *Rapido* put it, 'be absorbed into a unified 4AD graphic mush'.

Robin Guthrie was a prime critic of that approach, and of what he read as Oliver's arrogance. He describes the way the designer treated Dif Juz's *Extractions* as 'abominable', adding, 'Dave Curtis did a beautiful sculpture, like a rock face, with gold leaf inside and the letters Dif Juz to look like nuggets. Instead of taking the picture of the actual work, Vaughan shot the artwork and included the baseboard. The band hated it, but their opinion wasn't respected even though Dave knew a lot about art.'

Oliver says that if there was some shared insight into the creative process, some knowledge of art theory or history, the collaboration could be very productive. Xymox's Anka Wolbert, for example, had worked in design and screen-printing and she had supplied images and ideas. A further discussion with Oliver had led to a screenprint of caged puppets by Oliver's former tutor Terry Dowling for the cover of *Clan Of Xymox*. Oliver only really had problems when the likes of

Brendan Perry and Mick Allen resisted collaboration and then supplied sub-standard work. For example, he calls The Wolfgang Press sleeves of the mid-Eighties, 'a huge disappointment'. 'Perry had learnt stuff himself, but had no context, Oliver says. 'Education in a real way gives you context.'

Perhaps Oliver wasn't free of blame. In the 1985 BBC TV documentary *23 Envelope Presents*, Oliver was asked why the band wasn't happy: 'Graphic design is about communication and we're not graphic designers, so we aren't very good at communication,' he replied.

Perhaps that was Guthrie's complaint – that Oliver saw himself as an artist too. He and Oliver certainly butted heads over Cocteau Twins artwork. 'The hoops that we had to jump through to get where we did with Robin,' says Oliver. 'He'd say, "No, that's not us", but he'd never offer a positive alternative. All we wanted to do was reflect their music.' One Oliver concept that Guthrie did adore was for *Aikea-Guinea*. The piece of Japanese rag paper screenprinted with a gold font in a grey box was inspired by the Chanel perfume logo, the colours purposely unaligned with the PMT camera to give added texture and relief.

But when Oliver chose an image by British photographer Simon Larbalestier for the cover of *Come On Pilgrim*, it felt like another leap of imagination, just like Pixies music. It mirrored a leap from Grierson's expanding homage to Tarkovsky's *Stalker* to David Lynch's more brutal *Eraserhead*. Oliver admits that, by this point in 23 Envelope's collaborative venture, he was feeling restricted by Grierson: 'His working methods, his going back and forth. At times, I felt the relationship was stifling, like how many more times can you go back to a pool of water? And Nigel was becoming increasingly frustrated with me. He wondered why I was leading things.'

The answer, says Oliver, was that he was 4AD staff and Grierson was freelance. 'Nigel would say, "Why are bands always coming to you?" Because that was my job and the office was a meeting place for bands. Nigel was still studying and, anyway, he didn't want to be employed. But he wanted to be equal, which I thought we were, to a degree. For example, he would art direct projects like This Mortal

Coil. In the beginning, we'd hidden behind the 23 Envelope name that had blurred the boundaries of our disciplines, but over time, Nigel wanted more credit. At the same time, it was a huge relief to work with different photographers.'

Grierson: 'There was a power struggle between us. I started asking for credit on some of the photos, which I didn't see any issue with, as in, "Design by Vaughan Oliver, photography by Nigel Grierson". It was a reaction to Vaughan manipulating the situation to suit himself. He was in the 4AD office taking phone calls that concerned both of us, including commissions outside of 4AD. If it was to do with design, he'd do it himself, and if photography, he'd do it with me, so everything I did had him involved. Vaughan was always in more of a position of power.'

This was also the period that Chris Bigg became a full-time member of staff at 4AD. 'I was incredibly fortunate to work with Chris,' says Oliver. 'He'd confirm my ideas and finish my sentences. He didn't ask many questions of me but he confirmed where we wanted to go. He enhanced my confidence. He also brought something wonderful and personable to the design table, which enhanced our work together. It was a different kind of energy, a neurotic approach to typography, a very clean and lyrical approach to his calligraphy. And in terms of how he talked to bands, and got information out of them. He had a different way of working than me; he's a selfless character that allows people to come towards him and give them space, and I learnt a lot from that, in life as well as work.'

It surely was not a coincidence that Bigg's arrival clashed with the breakdown of communication within 23 Envelope, a relationship summed up by a photo of Oliver and Grierson wearing the same outsized hat. 'They were the funniest couple of people, like a precursor to [comedians] Vic Reeves and Bob Mortimer,' says Bigg. 'But I never got to the bottom of what went on between them, and I was with Vaughan 24 hours a day for all those years. Vaughan has a big ego, Nigel too, though his was more unusual and self-destructive.'

Grierson maintains that the fall-out had begun once he'd completed the *Lonely Is An Eyesore* assignment and started shooting videos for

265

bands outside of 4AD. 'Vaughan said something about keeping the 23 Envelope name for projects he'd do with other people, such as, "sleeve by 23 Envelope and photo by Simon Larbalestier", which didn't seem right. Vaughan didn't like the idea of using a different name, so the vibe was maybe that we shouldn't work together, which we didn't, for about a year.'

The pair did collaborate on David Sylvian's album *Secrets Of The Beehive*, released by Virgin Records in October 1987. But Grierson was conspicuously absent from 4AD artwork. Oliver himself went freelance at the end of 1987. 'I'd asked Ivo if I could become a director of 4AD, as I was so much a part of everything. But neither Ivo nor Martin went for it; they said that a director had to put money into the label, which I didn't have.'

Ivo doesn't recall this request or suggesting that Oliver needed to inject funds: 'I thought Vaughan just wanted to become part-owner, which was not a decision that I could make alone. For years after, at the end of a night, the subject, and his disappointment in me, would inevitably reappear.'

Oliver: 'Ivo said he'd give me freelance status and I'd be kept on a nice, fancy retainer at 4AD, and I could do outside work using the facilities of the office, which was a fantastic deal. It suited me financially and creatively.'

In 1985, the BBC documentary *23 Envelope Presents* had talked up the collaborative spirit of the venture. By 1989, a four-minute feature by *Rapido* on Oliver didn't even mention Grierson's former contributions; neither would SNUB TV's piece in 1990, when Oliver staged his first exhibition. In 1987, 23 Envelope was quietly retired, and Oliver's new enterprise was given the more personal title of v23.

However, as Bigg points out, the tension surrounding the art department didn't end there. 'Ivo's big beef with Vaughan was wondering why something he was working on was late, and blaming his freelance work,' says Bigg. For all the freedom that Oliver had enjoyed, the art of business began to increasingly interfere in the business of art.

12 1988

WITH YOUR FEET IN THE AIR
AND YOUR HEAD ON THE GROUND
(cad801-cad810)

Vaughan Oliver's newly liberated freelance status was temporarily expanded thanks to the short joint European tour of Throwing Muses and The Wolfgang Press where he projected slides behind the bands on stage. 4AD's newest recruit Simon Harper came along, driving them in Ivo's old BMW.

4AD's European trip briefly extended to the east for the second licensed volume of *Le Mystère Des Voix Bulgares*. 'It wasn't quite as beautiful as the first,' Ivo contends. 'I turned down volume three because it was the scraps, but it got licensed [to Warners] and the name still lives on.'

However, in 1988 4AD was less about the ecstatic aura of old rural Bulgaria and more about the ecstatic buzz of modern urban America. The double whammy of having Throwing Muses and Pixies on the label was a thrilling way to kickstart a closer relationship with the States, and a side effect was that it encouraged more demos to be sent from across the Atlantic. To celebrate the union, Throwing Muses' second album, *House Tornado*, and Pixies' debut album, *Surfer Rosa*, were released on the same day: 21 March.

In their continuing search for an honest reflection of their sound, the Muses had turned to *Doghouse Cassette* and *Purple Tapes* producer

Gary Smith: 'We should have worked with him all along,' reckons Kristin Hersh. David Narcizo remembers how Smith raised their comfort and confidence levels: 'Gary made us feel part of the process. We still felt we didn't truly capture our ideas until later, but the songs survived.'

'With tracks like "Colder" and "River" ... *House Tornado* was a great album,' says Ivo. The title was Hersh's acknowledgement of the contradictions of domesticity, a rare feminist statement for the label even if the lyrics weren't recognisably political. Sonically, the album was more indicative of the band's energy than *The Fat Skier*, denser and more insular than *Throwing Muses* but equally electrifying. The band also made peace with their artwork. Sire's under-designed choice of cover featured a black-and-white band photo with album and band name in red type. Vaughan Oliver was still determined to portray some representation of the music that wasn't like the abstract paint splotches (by Hersh's dad Dude) reconstructed as a child-like scribble on *The Fat Skier* cover. 'Finally,' says Narcizo, 'Vaughan said he'd found us the perfect person, who was Shinro Ohtake.' The young Japanese artist's multi-coloured scrapbooks of drawings and found images fused the surreal with the all too real, the twin properties of Hersh's songs.

This negotiated arrangement was the opposite of Pixies' relationship to artwork; they were simply intrigued to see what Oliver would conceive next. For a singer-songwriter, Charles Thomspon was unusually open to suggestion: the suggestion of a producer for *Surfer Rosa* even came via Colin Wallace, 4AD's new warehouse manager.

Wallace had progressed from Cocteau Twins' driver to driver-for-hire for any 4AD artist in need. When he was busted for possession of hashish while helping Robin Guthrie and Elizabeth Fraser move house, he decided he needed more stability and accepted Ivo's offer to run the warehouse. He joined just before 'Pump Up The Volume' had exploded, a real test of his abilities that he passed with flying colours. He settled down, taking on the additional role of casually dealing drugs to interested parties at work when the need arose. One of Wallace's favourite bands was Big Black, the pummelling hardcore trio fronted by the uncompromising, freely argumentative bassist-vocalist Steve Albini: 'I loved Steve's production sound,' says Wallace. 'I don't know why I thought it would work with Pixies.'

The band, and Ivo, agreed, and Albini and Pixies were in Boston's Q Division studio by December 1987. Albini reported that they'd finished the album in a week but used up their allotted booking time to see what else might happen. Albini's trademark anti-production style – he insisted on being credited as 'recorded by' in the style of an engineer – nevertheless gave Pixies a wicked, heavyweight bottom end for extra brunt, which gave songs such as 'Where Is My Mind?' and 'Cactus' the feeling of a juggernaut.

Ivo's first reaction to *Surfer Rosa* was that it sounded 'incredibly raw'. The album also didn't sound like any other American rock band, due to Pixies' meld of offbeat influences and the way Albini had recorded them. Thompson's innate sense of musical drama was heightened by a fascination with internal dysfunction: song titles included 'Break My Body' and 'Broken Face', two of the four songs the band had revamped from *The Purple Tape* alongside 'I'm Amazed' and a second stab at *Purple Tape* cut 'Vamos' after the *Come On Pilgrim* version, with Thompson regaling in both Spanish and English. 'Vamos' was Joey Santiago's showpiece, with dizzying runs and tyre-squealing turns.

If Kim Deal's bass played the album's anchoring role, her lead vocal on 'Gigantic' helped transform it into the album's most euphoric turn. Deal's precocious delivery made the most of Thompson's ode to voyeurism and sexual prowess, a mood that Oliver's cover for *Surfer Rosa* made explicit – a Simon Larbalestier photo of a topless flamenco dancer posing next to a crucifix. The figure was Oliver's idea – 'it's about debasing a Spanish tradition in the flamenco,' he says – with Larbalestier adding the cross. Deal initially didn't like the bared breasts on show, thinking it encouraged people to sexualise her own role in the band, but the image was quintessential Pixies: lustful, provocative and subversive. Thompson's parents were, after all, committed Pentecostal churchgoers.

It turned out that Albini wasn't as on side as people might have thought. He described *Surfer Rosa* to *Forced Exposure* magazine in

1991 as, 'patchwork pinch loaf from a band who at their top dollar best are blandly entertaining college rocks'. About Pixies, he said, 'Their willingness to be "guided" by their manager, their record company and their producers is unparalleled. Never have I seen four cows more anxious to be led around by their nose rings.'

'If a band was desperate to be successful,' Ivo retorts, 'it wouldn't be an obvious choice to work with Albini to make your debut album.' Albini later apologised for his comments. Ivo, however, was spared his savagery; Albini thought 4AD's boss was 'a good guy' who had Pixies' 'best interests at heart'.

Ivo may have conceived the title *Come On Pilgrim*, and he compiled the track listing for both albums, but *Surfer Rosa* was Thompson's title (from his lyric to 'Oh My Golly!': '*besando chichando con surfer rosa*', which translates as, '*kissing, fucking with surfer rosa*'). 'Ivo's suggestions and Vaughan's artwork, no problem, it was all coming from a good place,' says Thompson. 'It wasn't that we couldn't form our own opinions or that we didn't care or we were scared of disagreement. We just trusted 4AD.' End of controversy.

Surfer Rosa would spend sixty weeks in the UK independent charts, though it only peaked at number 2 even when Pixies joined Throwing Muses for a UK and European tour in May. 'That was the most exciting time to be working at 4AD,' Ivo recalls. 'The Muses were at their musical peak, just phenomenal every night I saw them, likewise Pixies. As mental as audiences were for Pixies, the Muses rose to the challenge. The audiences sang along to both bands' songs. It was both incredible and intimate.'

Deborah Edgely's abiding memory is of Throwing Muses: 'Their fingers bleeding from playing their guitars so busily and passionately, this noise coming out of these little girls, Leslie in all her glory and beauty, dripping with rhythm, and Dave, the drummer boy. The venue in Birmingham was this little, low-slung Sixties disco, which had a stage riser, and when Pixies played, the place went absolutely mental, and the riser came to pieces. Dave Narcizo was hanging off the edge of it, trying to stop Dave Lovering's drums from slipping between the gaps, and then they swapped when the Muses played.'

The band's shared memory is of one tour bus – chaperoned by 4AD's resident tour-managing couple Chaz and Shirley Banks – having the atmosphere of kids on a summer holiday, except that when they got into town, there would be screaming, capacity crowds to greet them. Santiago recalls getting 'shitfaced' in Frankfurt and being chased around a lamppost – for reasons unknown – by an incensed fan. In Greece, he handed out Pixies T-shirts to anyone within sight. 'But we were the only ones drinking,' he notes. 'The Muses kept it straight. They were intellectuals. Well, they read books.'

Throwing Muses weren't party animals, but the band's lack of hi-jinks had more underlying reasons. As the more established band, they'd begun the tour as headliners, but their complex mosaic of songs was less conducive to crowd pogoing than Pixies' boundless rock'n'roll; subsequent record sales and crowd reactions meant that, as the tour continued across Europe, it made sense for Pixies to head-line instead.

'The tour was awesome and also complicated,' says Narcizo. 'We all got along really well, and shared a cornucopia of experiences. Though we could play up the loud side of ourselves, we were different to Pixies and not everyone appreciated that. I honestly didn't have a problem with Pixies headlining, but it was awkward at times, not between bands but within our band. The Muses was Kristin's baby and she struggled with it.'

Hersh remembers things differently: 'It's true that to follow Pixies, it's hard for audiences to get down and listen to subtleties when they want to crash some more. But it was such a great high to see a band that you love before you play yourself. We were tiny, goofy babies who'd sing folk songs in the van about being far away from home. My big problem was that being away from my baby tore me up. Charles was a great friend then. We'd walk in botanical gardens and he'd let me be sad where I had to be happy for everyone else. That Pixies got more attention than us was actually a relief. It meant I had the afternoon off or had more time for my songs. Pixies were driven and ambitious; they wanted to be rock stars. I guess Tanya was too, though I didn't know it at the time.'

Hersh was also experiencing the gulf between the way 4AD and Sire operated. Across Europe, Pixies was handled by 4AD's licensees while Warners attended to Throwing Muses – or rather, didn't. To start with, each of Warners' individual territories had to be persuaded to release *House Tornado*. Ivo could see the marked difference in effort. 'I'd call Seymour [Stein] and scream, "You must do something for your band!" A chimp on acid could have done a better job than Warners did for the Muses. Ken [Goes] didn't recognise that he'd failed them. It gave me the confidence to sign non-British bands to long-term deals because I felt 4AD could do a better job.'

Tanya Donelly admits that the Muses, not their manager, had the final say on choosing Warners, believing the corporation's European network was more advanced than that of 4AD. In Amsterdam, Narcizo remembers that the Warners representative didn't even turn up. 'The guy from [4AD's Belgian licensees] Play It Again Sam even said, "I'll do everything to make sure Pixies succeed and you don't". In another territory, a Warners guy said it was either our record or Prince's. I remember thinking, we're from Boston, we're not thinking about Belgium! A lot of what we came to love about 4AD was our experience with other labels when we realised how unique and nurturing 4AD was.'

Hersh: 'Warners was like a million people, in their own little offices, and I'm trying to get my little memos in there. At 4AD, you talked to one person and they leant over the desk and asked the other person if it was true.'

Pixies had no such issues, and revelled in the fact they were with sympathetic people who could out-party them. 'It was the record label that was crazy!' Kim Deal insists, recalling an inebriated Vaughan Oliver chuck a TV out of a Paris hotel window. '4AD looked more like rock stars than we did,' says Santiago. 'They had crew cuts, they wore black. Vaughan was just out there and Howard made you feel like you were the most exciting, important band in the world. They were serious, though, and hands on. We knew we were in the right place.'

'Howard [Gough] was definitely one of the twenty-four-hour party people,' says Thompson. 'To him, no one could be better than

The Clash, but we were a close second. If you were looking to party, he'd facilitate that. He'd be the guy at the Italian restaurant after the gig, rolling a giant spliff, acting like a rock'n'roller, and introducing us to rock'n'rollers like The Jesus and Mary Chain, like a traditional hustling publicist. His younger brother sold T-shirts for us for a while.'

As for Ivo, 'He was this older gentleman, classy, never loud, always polite,' recalls Deal. 'But for the longest time, I didn't know what kind of person he really was. We played a show in Rhode Island and people came up after, saying "What's Ivo really like?" They'd heard of him but not us! Simon Harper was like the nice uncle, in a Nehru jacket, very sharp-looking. Vaughan was the perverted uncle you wouldn't leave the kids with. Deb was the heart of the label that everyone relied on, warm-hearted, happy to see everyone, sensitive and empathetic, with those big eyes and a desire to listen.'

Kim Deal: 'I remember The Wolfgang Press getting back off tour from Poland, all wearing their huge fur hats with shaved heads underneath, and all in black too. They looked like a faction. I liked that people at 4AD had artistic temperaments too. I'm sure some people wouldn't think that was a good way to do business, but they had something other than living through each band and sale. They were doing art of their own. It was life-and-death stuff to them, and there could be tears over stuff.'

Kristin Hersh would sometimes call Ivo and Deborah 'Mum and Dad'.

The thrills and spills of life with the new east coast family that was Throwing Muses and Pixies was a chance to forget issues with M/A/R/R/S and Cocteau Twins, and Ivo could afford to be more relaxed. He was also finding that 4AD's newfound chart success, and the kind of people now employed at 4AD, had changed the mood. 'One of my biggest regrets is that I didn't turn into the kind of fascist that a lot of people thought I was, and say, we're not releasing singles, we're just an album label,' he recalls. 'But I ended up playing the game. I was making a commercial decision. From *Victorialand* onwards, we were having top 20 albums, but singles were a different matter, and we wanted to get Pixies on to the radio. I'd also seen the impact of M/A/R/R/S on the staff, of the pleasure that success had given them, which was followed very quickly by Pixies' explosion of popularity. It would have been absurd, me being this one person, not to do so.'

At least Ivo wasn't planning to return to the strategy of plucking singles off albums as he'd done during the Modern English era. In 1987, Gil Norton accompanied Ivo to Boston to talk to Throwing Muses about the possibility of producing what became *House Tornado*, and was excited enough after seeing Pixies play to pitch for their next album too. To try Norton out with the band, Ivo commissioned him to re-record 'Gigantic' and 'River Euphrates' from *Surfer Rosa* and a version of 'Here Comes Your Man' from *The Purple Tape*, with a view to making Pixies 'more polished'.

Santiago: 'Gil wanted everything tight, which we liked. But I still don't like his version of "Gigantic". I thought it sounded too perfect, which defeated the purpose.'

If this move resembled the kind of commercial compromise that major labels encouraged, it was balanced by the fact that the most obvious commercial choice, 'Here Comes Your Man', was shelved for 'Gigantic' to be the new single. The new 'River Euphrates' became a B-side alongside live versions of 'Vamos' (again!) and a cover of 'In Heaven (Lady In The Radiator Song)' written by the American composer Peter Ivers for *Eraserhead*. Both Pixies and Muses sets had been recorded at The Town & Country show the same night, but Ivo felt the overall quality wasn't high enough: 'I wasn't going to bung out records for the sake of it,' he says.*

Vaughan Oliver could always be relied on to deliver an anti-commercial blow. For the twelve-inch 'Gigantic' he chose a close-up photograph of a naked, screaming baby. It was actually Howard Gough's son Josh, neatly following the man on the cover of *Come On Pilgrim* and the woman on *Surfer Rosa*. Oliver rendered the photo in such stark contrast it looked like Josh hadn't washed for weeks (Oliver

---

* Only Throwing Muses' 'Mania' and a new Pixies song, 'Hey', were subsequently released, on a seven-inch flexi given away with the weekly *Sounds* magazine.

says he didn't touch the photo). Kim Deal didn't know whether to smile or be appalled: 'People said to me, this is child abuse! Vaughan made it look awful, I'm sure.'

In any case, 'Gigantic' still sounded too bold for daytime radio. Despite Gough's efforts, the single stalled at 93 in the UK national charts, substantially lower than the likes of 'Pearly-Dewdrop's Drops', as if Pixies fans already had the definitive version of the song on *Surfer Rosa.*

4AD released another twelve-inch single on the same day, 22 August, which more definitively rang in the changes – the success of 'Pump Up The Volume' and the increasing domination of dance music had increased the numbers of remixes for any given single. The Wolfgang Press's 'King Of Soul' came in three different mixes; a separate DJ promo version was to end up as the new album's opening track – the first time that 4AD had followed the traditional industry procedure. Even the three singles found on Modern English's *After The Snow* had been released *after* the album.

The rise of independent labels, in dance music as well as the supposed sound of 'indie', showed the majors no longer had a monopoly on the mainstream. 'Everyone was doing it – singles before albums, twelve-inch remixes, different B-sides, plectrum-shaped singles ... all this formatting so that labels could compete,' says Ivo. 'Bands were under pressure to record extra tracks for B-sides, but sometimes it felt like I cared about the quality of those extra tracks more than the artist did. But it shows how traditional 4AD started to become.'

4AD had made enough profit to hire another name producer besides Albini. Flood (real name Mark Ellis) had worked with Mute acts such as Depeche Mode and Nick Cave & The Bad Seeds, and had stepped in when The Wolfgang Press's original sessions with the classically-trained Simon Rogers came to nothing. Rogers – who could proudly boast of being part of The Fall and South American folk troupe Incantation (one of Nick Austin's stranger success stories at Beggars Banquet) – had just completed Pete Murphy's second solo album *Deep*, but Andrew Gray says he didn't suit them: 'We spent too much, experimenting, which is the only time Ivo commented, saying it was extravagant. Flood remixed a couple of tracks and we realised we had to make the whole album with him.'

It showed Ivo was still willing to support his friends, not a traditional record company manoeuvre this time. He also knew what potential still lay in the trio, and there was a sentimental reason: only Mick Allen and Mark Cox had been along for the ride since the very beginning. 'Thanks to Ivo, those boys had a career,' says Deborah Edgely. 'I think part of him felt that if he took it away from them, what would they then do? But Ivo was pretty shrewd and he didn't often indulge people with money. He knew when to take a risk or not.'

'Ivo knew we had the potential, but was still scratching his head about how to open things up for us,' says Mark Cox. 'He was this constant connector, putting people together. But we benefited from the fact budgets had gone up because of the success 4AD was having.'

The band's third album, *Bird Wood Cage*, again showed a slowly unfolding picture of deft songwriting, uncluttered arrangements, brusque tension and more contributors – among them Steven Young, Gini Ball, Peter Ulrich and Ruby James, all adding telling little details, from the bluesy sweat of 'King Of Soul', the nervy pulse and chorus chant of 'Kansas', the slow reggae skank of 'Hang On Me'. It received great reviews in the press, even nine out of ten in *NME* ('their songs are layered so deftly, each one a new gateau of ear-bending rhythm, silly words, Mick Allen's MAD voice and irreverent noise from outer space'). And still the album didn't shift public perception of the band, or increase sales.

'Journalists want to know what's coming next, rather than what's not been successful,' says Edgely. 'And very few journalists supported The Wolfgang Press to begin with. We'd get a review here, a column inch there. Their gigs were never well attended, and they didn't sell any records.'

Perhaps America would be the land of opportunity? Rough Trade's new US wing, based in New York, had taken the plunge and licensed *Bird Wood Cage*, as it had Pixies' *Come On Pilgrim* and *Surfer Rosa*.

But the album might still have a limited appeal if American retail or radio was unprepared to embrace an album dressed in a toilet bowl.

Mick Allen's tribute to Marcel Duchamp on the cover of *Bird Wood Cage* addressed the album's themes of domesticity and taste, but it was still a toilet bowl on the cover, and an old, used model at that. 'Vaughan wouldn't have anything to do with the toilet bowl,' says Chris Bigg. 'And unlike Robin Guthrie, Mick Allen couldn't be persuaded otherwise. He didn't buy into what he saw as this ethereal wishy-washy stuff on 4AD; the band wanted to be more on the edge, to stand on the outside.'

'Vaughan saw a record as his next sleeve,' says Mark Cox, 'whereas we saw it as what went around our music. Chris could entertain the fact that we had our own ideas.'

Bigg: 'Mick was complicated. He was gentle with me, but he could be very confrontational and angry, though I never worked out about what. He just didn't want to join in, and that's what most of his lyrics were about.'

While The Wolfgang Press always struggled with critical acclaim, other bands were instant press darlings, like The Sundays. Ivo, usually highly suspicious of hype, didn't even find out about the London-based quartet from the usual demo, concert or industry word of mouth, but from a salivating review in *Melody Maker* of the band's second ever concert.

The core of The Sundays was yet another couple. Vocalist Harriet Wheeler and guitarist David Gavurin had met at Bristol University and quickly found a signature sound; every major and independent label was drawn to check out the band based on the description of them fusing Cocteau Twins to The Smiths, though Wheeler's wistful voice had nothing in common with Elizabeth Fraser's, except for a beautiful tone.

Ivo invited Wheeler and Gavurin to Alma Road and offered them a one-off album deal: 'As they left the office, to visit Geoff Travis at Rough Trade, Simon [Harper] said, "How could you let them go? You know Geoff will do anything they ask." The Smiths had split up so he didn't have them anymore. Harriet and David were very cautious

277

people and so they signed to Rough Trade for a single to begin with. It was the first time I'd been turned down and I was gutted.'*

Ivo also acted out of character by not hesitating when he was confronted with another American artist to his liking. With The Sundays lost, Kurt Ralske, who called himself Ultra Vivid Scene, became 4AD's third US signing in a row.

At the time Ralske posted his demo, he was living in London. He's now back in New York City, where music is a hobby again while he teaches video at the School of Visual Arts in the MFA (Master of Fine Arts) computer art department. He is also a visiting professor and artist-in-residence for the MFA Digital and Media department at Rhode Island School of Design. 'I've always been interested in visual art, and I was always active in it on some level,' Ralske explains.

Raised in North Bellmore on Long Island, Ralske had inherited his parents' musical nous, learning piano and trumpet when he was just five. A diet of jazz and classical appreciation had left little room for pop, 'Which I wilfully decided was not for me,' he says. However, his sister (ten years his senior), Jimi Hendrix and Jefferson Airplane changed his mind, and at the age of fourteen, he took an adult decision: 'The suburbs felt like death, a void, so I started going by myself to New York City, which was something like the Wild West then. I walked straight into jazz clubs and nightclubs, and no one would say a word.'

Ralske was in time for the city's No Wave post-punk craze, playing what he calls 'messy avant-garde guitar' among a crowd of older jazz musicians. As Ultra Vivid Scene, he pressed up a hundred copies – with expensive covers in silver leaf – of a seven-inch single while living in New York. He also befriended singer-songwriter Mark Dumais and formed Crash, a more conventional C86-style guitar band imbued with a dark, dreamy and sad core. Ralske's guitar drew from The

---

* When I interviewed The Sundays in 1990 after the release of their debut album *Reading, Writing And Arithmetic*, the band denied they were opposed to signing to 4AD, only that they were concerned that 4AD had Pixies. 'One Little Indian were interested too,' said David Gavurin. 'We couldn't make our minds up. It's hard without hindsight. It partly helped that Rough Trade were nearer to where we lived, down the road.'

Velvet Underground and Jesus and Mary Chain songbook: 'It was incredibly intelligent, but as simple as pop music,' he says. 'I felt this incredible wash of noise, which I can now describe as [German playwright and poet Bertolt] Brecht alerting the audience to the idea that all is not what it seems on the surface. It was like putting quotation marks around the music, which I found very exciting. I wanted to make music that seemed simple and direct but wore its intelligence on its sleeve.'

With the support of Rough Trade distribution manager Dave Whitehead, who had started his own label Remorse, Crash moved to London in 1985. The band lasted three singles and an album, then Dumais went solo and signed to Creation while Ralske resuscitated Ultra Vivid Scene (or UVS). A demo got offers from One Little Indian and Cherry Red. 'But 4AD was my first choice,' Ralske says. 'I really enjoyed Cocteau Twins, other groups less so, but the label put a huge importance on the packaging. It was the complete artistic project that interested me.'

Ivo was particularly struck by Ralske's 'The Mercy Seat'. 'But once Kurt was back in New York,' he explains, 'I got a completely different version, like slow Suicide instead of fast Velvets, which suggested how good the song was to begin with. Kurt wore his influences on his sleeve but he had a great understanding of melody.'

Ivo could sense something in Ralske of the sharp, inventive psychedelia of his youth, and he subsequently lent him albums by Fever Tree. 'Ivo thought I used guitar sounds similar to theirs,' Ralske recalls. But Ralske was looking beyond psychedelic; the B-side of his new-wave-jittery 4AD debut single 'She Screamed' was a cover of 'Walkin' After Midnight' – made famous by Fifties country queen Patsy Cline – turned into a slow, druggy dirge with the sense of ironic quotation marks around it.

Vaughan Oliver, meanwhile, was wearing his naughty hat for the occasion, lining up a series of centrefolds from the porn magazine *Hustler*, though you'd need a sharp eye to see the row of clitorises down the spine of 'She Screamed'. The head of current British monarch Queen Elizabeth II on the front is much more obvious. 'I think that's the first time those images have been juxtaposed,' he says. 'Yes, it was a laddish sense of humour but exciting too, to disguise it except to those who know it's there. But we eventually all grow up.'

Ivo quickly organised a two-week session at Blackwing for an Ultra Vivid Scene album with John Fryer co-producing, but like Brendan Perry, Ralske was too experienced for guidance. 'I was used to working by myself, in total control,' he says. 'The experience of collaborating, and working so quickly, fell apart after just two days. I told Ivo that the demo he'd liked so much had been recorded in a friend's New York studio, which I could do again, and make the record I wanted. The sonics aren't those of a commercial pop record, but I was never anxious for commercial success.'

Rough Trade US licensed his debut album, perhaps anticipating Ralske would emulate Pixies' success and Throwing Muses' profile after both American bands had first broken in the UK. *Ultra Vivid Scene* warranted the attention, full of melodic nuggets, all quicksilver guitar and drowsy moods, particularly the serpentine 'The Mercy Seat' and the delicate 'The Whore Of God'. For all his clear influences – the Velvets, the Mary Chain and the adenoidal tone and narcotic ballads of Peter Perrett (frontman of Britain's brilliant new wave rockers The Only Ones*) – Ralske fulfilled the 4AD brief: Ultra Vivid Scene didn't seem to belong anywhere.

Cocteau Twins was the next in line to benefit from 4AD's increasing presence in the States. Having taken time out to build a recording studio, the trio had recorded an album without any limitation of any kind, except their own exacting standards. There had been time for Elizabeth Fraser to fall pregnant, and for the band to hire its first

---

* Coincidentally, at the same time Kurt Ralske signed to 4AD The Only Ones guitarist John Perry approached Ivo on his and singer/songwriter Peter Perrett's behalf. 'I was a huge The Only Ones fan,' Ivo recalls. 'John was trying to get things going for them and was really enthusiastic. I financed some demos but they just managed to add a bit to two songs already demoed and roughly sketch a couple more. It was clearly going to be a long road with no guarantee that anything would get finished. It was such a shame because Peter seemed very sweet but very lost. He had a childlike look in his eyes, just like Lee Perry had had.'

manager, Raymond Coffer, who had negotiated a new long-term contract with 4AD.

As Ivo has pointed out, if Robin Guthrie had truly felt undermined by 4AD's 'conniving and thieving', Cocteau Twins should never have re-signed a long-term deal with 4AD. Yet the new contract did give the band larger advances and an improved royalty rate.

Coffer was a former chartered accountant with a background in intellectual property law through running a soccer merchandising company. A friend of Bauhaus' David J, Coffer had entered band management with Love and Rockets and then Xymox. He had been recommended to Cocteau Twins by the band's American booking agent Marc Geiger after, Guthrie claims, they discovered a £100,000 bill (the details are not divulged) that he manages to blame on 4AD. 'They allowed us to accrue it without any help in terms of management or accountancy,' he says.

When Cocteau Twins played Amsterdam in 1986, Guthrie had contacted Xymox's Ronny Moorings, less out of friendship than necessity. According to Moorings, 'Robin needed some "energy powder".' He assumed that, because Moorings lived in Amsterdam, he'd know where to get it. 'And indeed, I did,' he says. 'Before their soundcheck, Robin asked all sorts of questions about Raymond. He was interested in getting management as he did not get along with Ivo anymore. I heard him shout at Ivo on the phone a few times and he seemed very agitated.'

The punk rocker in Guthrie had initially baulked at the idea of Coffer. 'I took one look at him and thought, "No fucking way, he's from another planet". But a real businessman is what we needed. He said, "You know why you're in trouble; look at the difference between what your record company is making and what they're giving you. You can do so much better." Ivo would be the first to admit he wasn't much of a businessman, and he should have had someone else look after our business. We couldn't articulate what we needed in business anyway.'

Cocteau Twins had spent seven years without a manager. 'You wonder now how that's possible,' says Simon Raymonde. Ivo's experience of managers meant that he had never encouraged artists to find one, finding that they got in the way, especially the likes of Coffer. 'Raymond wasn't someone who expressed a musical opinion or had any musical preferences,' Ivo claims. 'He was hired to be a businessman.'

Cocteau Twins had earned money; that much was clear from the band's brand new twenty-four-track studio, a huge step up for their operations. 'Any money we got, we spent on equipment, never on ourselves, so we could make better records,' says Raymonde. Whether from the band or his other production work, Guthrie was also able to fund an increasingly expensive cocaine habit. Brimming with confidence from both sources, he had assembled a new album, *Blue Bell Knoll*, Cocteau Twins' first full band album since *Treasure* three years earlier, that showed another creative leap: more relaxed, subtle, grown up. It was obvious from the first few notes of the opening title track, with a harpsichord or synth equivalent behind Elizabeth Fraser's simmering glossolalia, a lattice of tiny details over two minutes and twenty seconds that suddenly unfurled into a hair-raising burst of colour.

'*Blue Bell Knoll*,' Guthrie says, 'is where things finally gelled with Simon.' The bassist puts this down to the fact he was also playing more piano, 'and being more confident in the band, because I'd been around longer'.

Ivo also saw a marked change in Fraser. 'It's got her best singing since she discovered her higher range,' he says. '"Carolyn's Fingers" is absolutely beautiful, and still gives me the shivers.' Curiously, the track wasn't released as a single in the UK, only by Capitol in the US, with a video that showcased Fraser's bird-like demeanour, head bobbing and eyes darting, looking anywhere except into the camera as her wondrous vocal escaped from her mouth.

'Cico Buff' – released as a US-only promo single with an accompanying video – was more evidence of a newfound accord, applying some of the restraint imbibed from *Victorialand* and *The Moon And The Melodies* to the baroque architecture of *Treasure*. Guthrie was right: as his personal life got more ragged, so the music got calmer.

'Suckling The Mender' and 'Spooning Good Singing Gum' were an altogether different Cocteaus, slim and dreamy, and on 'For Phoebe Still A Baby', the slow lullaby could have been written for the couple's unborn child. Enchanting melodies and elaborate titles ('A Kissed Out Red Floatboat', 'Ella Megalast Burls Forever') tumbled out.

With a second five-album contract in hand, Coffer had taken *Blue Bell Knoll* around the US majors and Ivo and Martin Mills negotiated a licensing deal with EMI subsidiary offshoot Capitol. The label was resolutely mainstream – its idea of alternative was Duran Duran and The Motels. But they'd signed Canadian electronic act Skinny Puppy and there was a new A&R team, including Claudia Stanton. 'She did the right thing by wooing Robin and Liz,' says Ivo. 'She hung out with them in England, bought them cuddly toys and befriended them.'

One problem with licensing deals was the risk of losing control, over artwork, promotions material, and the needs of the artists. With The Wolfgang Press, Ultra Vivid Scene and Pixies, Ivo had begun dealing with people working for independent labels that should understand what he was looking for, but Cocteau Twins involved one of the majors. At least Ivo had someone who would represent him and his exacting standards: 4AD's first US employee on the payroll, Sheri Hood.

Promoting not just 4AD releases at press and radio for Thirsty Ear, Hood had become frustrated with aspects of the job. 'I'd gotten into trouble for being too honest with some of the major labels,' she says. 'I was always on the artist's side.' Hood had decided to leave, and, she says, 'Ivo's response was that 4AD would leave too. I was stunned that someone would take a chance on me just because I was excited about music.'

Hood now lives in Portland where she makes wine, comfortably removed from the music industry that initially enthralled and eventually infuriated her. It's clear why Ivo was so supportive of Hood and wanted her input. 'Ivo and I are very different people in many ways but we share an affinity with being alone, and not dealing with all the bullshit,' she says. 'Dealing with major labels meant this huge disconnect, and it could be a waste of time and energy, knowing that this was the real world.'

Hood's involvement with 4AD began when her parents returned from London with a pair of Doctor Marten boots and the first Dead Can Dance album for her. 'I wasn't a true 4AD fanatic but I loved the label for its sense of purity and truth. Working with Ivo taught me a work and life ethic, and I still believe art is for art's sake, and though it's beautiful when it happens, no one should expect to make money from it.'

Hood was given a desk in Rough Trade's New York office before progressing to a 4AD cubbyhole of her own, single-handedly running promotions, retail and video for the label, beginning with *Come On Pilgrim*. With Dead Can Dance finally touring the States in 1987 and the various licensing deals in place, Hood found herself on a mission. 'I had to explain to people what 4AD was about, and I was a little overzealous about how particular we would still be with licensees,' she says. 'Major labels were used to running with stuff, but we wanted to stay involved with marketing and promotion and presentation, like if the licensee wanted to make a Frisbee with the artist's name on it. We might have quelled some enthusiasm, but we needed to keep the 4AD aesthetic, to make people understand why it was special, and worth the extra effort to run things by us. And that was hard. Toes were stepped on.'

Robin Guthrie would have admired Hood's principled stand, being himself more than happy to step on toes. With the exquisite creation that was *Blue Bell Knoll* as the bone of contention, Guthrie had won his ongoing tussle with Oliver over the artwork, insisting that he use Juergen Teller's photo of a hand of the band's friend Carolyn (hence 'Carolyn's Fingers'). Not even Chris Bigg was involved, with Oliver handing over the design to Paul West, like Bigg another former student with a dissertation on sleeve design. The vinyl version of *Blue Bell Knoll* was a special three-part gatefold sleeve, 'which we'd never allowed anyone to do before because it was so very 1970s,' says Ivo (something that hadn't stopped him making *Filigree & Shadow* a double album). 'But we didn't want to stop Robin doing stuff. We were bending over backwards to please him. Robin was going through a very difficult stage and was very difficult to deal with. The mood had changed.'

After all that had gone on, Ivo says that he still hadn't realised the full extent of Guthrie's unhappiness, as it was never expressed to him: 'I knew from the first time that I laid eyes on him, sitting on the pavement outside the tube station, that this quick-witted man had some chips on his shoulder. But Robin was amusing too, and none of us took the other side of him seriously as it was always balanced with something tender and real. I feel guilty now at having enabled him to get away with that meanness, because as long as it wasn't directed at me, or those close to me, nothing was said. It now appears that he was saying really cruel things about me after all.'

Having the band's finances on a more secure and rewarding level, Guthrie simply transferred his aggression to the fact that Ivo was now ignoring Cocteau Twins in preference to Pixies. Never mind that the Cocteaus had taken 1987 off and disappeared. But all the money in the world wasn't going to cure Guthrie's self-esteem issues – now with added feelings of abandonment to complicate matters. Raymond Coffer's role thus came into sharper focus.

Simon Raymonde: 'My dad was to die in 1990 and Robin's had when Robin was fifteen, and Liz's at some point in the Eighties. So we were all yearning for a father figure. We had all looked up to Ivo – people would call him Uncle Ivo, which I now get with my bands. What appealed about Raymond was he was cuddly, and wise, very much like an uncle, and understanding about all the issues. He loved our music, and he liked us. And he was totally apart from the music scene, so he could be objective. But Raymond set the cat among the pigeons, as he and Ivo didn't see eye to eye at all.'

'Maybe I was too busy running a record company to hang out with them socially,' Ivo concedes. 'I was in the studio, and going to America. It could be argued that, with the Cocteaus having been the absolute centre of attention, there was now another band that, if you thought of 4AD, you now thought of Pixies in place of them. It happened so damn quickly. But the Cocteaus did feel unloved, and less of a priority.'

'By *Blue Bell Knoll*, the rot had set in, because Ivo stopped looking after us,' Guthrie claims. 'We weren't the first band to feel it; you're darlings for a while, and then that goes. But we were very aware of not being supported, of being taken for granted, of being a cash cow. Our ambitions were on a different page to Ivo, who had ambitions for 4AD. He was looking at other labels – Rough Trade had The Smiths, Factory had New Order, Mute had Depeche Mode, and he wanted similar success. He had to find money-makers for his label. His focus moved away on to something more malleable with overseas bands. Before, we'd been welcomed in the office, but then we'd turn up, to be told that people were busy. The respect we once had went out the window.'

Guthrie says he was angered by what he saw as The Wolfgang Press draining the coffers. He claims 4AD never advertised *Blue Bell Knoll* because Ivo felt that the album would sell anyway. 'Yet other bands got full-page ads,' he complains. '4AD put so much money behind Pixies, and poured stupid amounts into The Wolfgang Press, fifty or sixty thousand pounds, to make an album, while we weren't getting anything like that because we'd made ourselves as self-sufficient as possible. In any case, Mick Allen's attitude, always angry at everything, would have stopped them from having hits.'

Simon Raymonde took a contrary position. In his eyes, 4AD's American contingent 'was a breath of fresh air, because it got 4AD away from the niche that they'd got stuck in'.

At least the two bands respected one other. Charles Thompson liked the 'mystery' of Cocteau Twins. Guthrie says he liked Pixies' energy. 'But not,' he adds, 'their stop-start weirdness. Lovely people, though!'

Charles Thompson had an experience of what he calls 'the first hint of darkness in this whole record business' at a dinner attended by Pixies, Cocteau Twins and 4AD's top brass. 'Ivo was at one end of the table and Robin at the other. Ivo said something about money and Robin immediately followed up with some snide comment that was obviously aimed at Ivo, that the rest of us didn't understand, that implied he wasn't getting what he was due. Ivo gracefully didn't rise to the bait. It didn't make me feel paranoid; I think I thought that there was a rosy side to all this and we also felt in good hands with our accountant and manager.

'But I realised this happy 4AD family was not so happy. But to be fair to 4AD, as I found out, they were a lot better than other labels in that department. They weren't perfect, but no one was.'

Tanya Donelly had realised much the same. 'I'd thought, what an amazing, big happy family we'd fallen into. A year later, what a big dysfunctional family we'd fallen into … what a bunch of hothouse flowers! I'm sure we all acted like divas. It was a complicated structure, being in a band, working with a label, all sharing a love of music, with fragile trusts. It's quite a lot to navigate emotionally. Every band I've ever been part of involved siblings, and families, which sets an atmosphere.'

Without tension, argument and axes to grind, with no issues of dependency, abandonment or addiction, Dead Can Dance had made similar headway to Cocteau Twins; and they had continued to thrive creatively even when Brendan Perry and Lisa Gerrard's rocky domestic scenario threatened to capsize everything they had.

Perry had also built a home studio, funded by a £10,000 advance from 4AD to record their fourth album. Royalties had started to arrive, enabling regular trips to the supermarket – 'still on our bikes, though,' Perry smiles. If London was opening up to the duo, new influences from Europe continued to seep in, this time mostly indigenous folk music from Hungary and Ireland. Gerrard continued her open-throated odyssey, proudly leading off the new album *The Serpent's Egg* with the spectacular 'The Host Of The Seraphim'. 'That's my favourite ever piece that Lisa sang,' says Ivo. 'And the album as a whole was wonderful. Maybe it was down to the balance between Lisa and Brendan.'

Gerrard's progress slightly tipped the balance on *The Serpent's Egg*. 'Song Of Sophia' was another Bulgarian-influenced epic, and her take on Hungarian folk lament 'The Writing On My Father's Hand' even had decipherable lyrics. Perry delivered two of his strongest ballads, 'Severance' and the processional 'Ulysses'. It was an epic way to round off 1988, which Ivo cites as his favourite single year of 4AD releases.

There was one crowning glory to come: Pixies' *Surfer Rosa* was voted album of the year by the writers of *Melody Maker* and *Sounds*. *NME*, which had awarded the album nine and a half out of ten at the time, put it at number 10 in its annual list, with rap giants Public Enemy's *It Takes A Nation Of Millions …* on top. Both albums are now recognised as being seminal influences on artists and audiences alike; in Pixies' case, Kurt Cobain of Nirvana was paying close attention, as was a teenage Polly Jean Harvey, to name but two. In America, *Spin* named Pixies the magazine's musicians of the year.

Both the title and the subject matter of the documentary *1991: The Year Punk Broke* – which followed US hardcore band Sonic Youth on tour with its various grungy disciples such as Nirvana – would come from an American perspective: Britain had succumbed to punk a full fourteen years earlier. But although it would be Sonic Youth that encouraged Nirvana to sign to Geffen, Pixies would more closely influence the sound of Nirvana's *Nevermind*, seeding the revolution in the States from Pixies' adopted base in south London. By the end of 1988, punk and new wave had already mostly been and gone in Britain, to be replaced by a sprawling hybrid of influences, such as Sixties pop, Eighties dance and the new offspring of Robin Guthrie, making beautiful noise, such as the newly fêted My Bloody Valentine.

The scene in both countries echoed those of the Sixties, when artists were unafraid to strike out in any direction. Having admired Elektra Records' unique imagination and diversity, Ivo and 4AD had finally arrived at much the same place – and they had Vaughan Oliver's bold tendencies as well. M/A/R/R/S may have provided a momentary crisis, but it had been successfully countered by Pixies' runaway success.

13 1989

AN ULTRA VIVID BEAUTIFUL NOISE
(cad901-jad911)

Hit-makers of the Sixties were expected to churn out albums every six months. By the Eighties, the speed of life wasn't any less hectic, but studio-based schedules were replaced by global tours, video shoots and other promotional duties, filling gaps between recording sessions. No one was taking three years between albums, unless it was Pink Floyd.

For example, there were only ten months between Throwing Muses' *House Tornado* and the follow-up *Hunkpapa*. The album at least had the benefit of being released on a different day to Pixies' own latest, which was also ready to go. After the joint offensive of the 1988 tour, the Muses needed to be appreciated as a unique entity rather than the more sensitive half of a sensational double act.

Having re-employed Gary Smith as producer, the band had begun to further assert their independence with David Narcizo's emerging interest in graphic design. The drummer's chosen primitive motif on the album cover was inspired by the album's title, *Hunkpapa*, named after the tribe of Native American chief Sitting Bull. Where Kristin Hersh felt *The Fat Skier* and *House Tornado* had been, 'based on strength and subtlety', she saw the new album as 'more solid and spacious'.

Ivo wasn't overjoyed. '*Hunkpapa* was patchy,' he says. 'And it's still hard to forgive Gary for slowing and smoothing out the language of "Mania".' The track was the Muses' most frenzied episode yet, as if Pixies' energy had driven Hersh to respond. Or maybe it was simply the mania of her increasing mood swings and fractured personal life.

The band had found manager Ken Goes as exasperating as Sire, and he was now being assisted by Billy O'Connell, Seymour Stein's former assistant, a firm Muses ally and also Hersh's new boyfriend. Three-year-old Dylan's father was fighting for custody, painting Hersh as an unfit mother, mentally fragile and a rock singer too, forever travelling, and writing lyrics, as Deborah Edgely saw them, 'of spine-chilling madness'.

Perhaps that explains Hersh's need to shift towards a more accessible sound. She was convinced that her songs – which she was also convinced had minds of their own – were struggling to find acceptance. 'I have songs The Bangles would die for but I try and stay away from straightforward writing as much as possible,' Hersh told me when *Hunkpapa* was released. 'But I don't have anything against trying to make it easier for people to listen to us. It's not a good thing to be seen trying to keep people out.'

Hersh was only trying to protect her songs, as she would her children, against a culture that was willing to exploit them as well as her. It was an unenviable paradox that the more the alternative scene that had nurtured the Muses succeeded, the more it was coerced into competing with the mainstream it was trying to overturn, via promotion, marketing, video and the shift in formatting of singles, with two versions of a single and varying B-sides, to encourage more sales.

'Sire would say, "Don't take this as anything to do with your creativity, but …",' Hersh recalls. 'We were starting to see some of our peers making stupid slips through the cracks, and Sire's implicit and often explicit message was that we should dumb down our product, not to succeed, but just to continue working.'

Throwing Muses' new single was 'Dizzy', by no means a sell-out but it could have been a smash hit for The Bangles. Hersh felt grubby by association. 'Ivo agreed that singles could be radio-friendly, and yet they didn't have to be stupid, which wasn't the opinion shared by anyone else in the record industry. For "Dizzy", I took one of my father's old songs, made it dumb and added a hook, some sex and PC crap and we just laughed, it was hilarious. But it backfired instantly because Sire liked it! 4AD played along so that we could carry on. But it was the beginning of the end for me. I started to give up around that time, and I think Ivo did too.'

'Dizzy' and even – bizarrely – its B-side 'Santa Claus' were taken from *Hunkpapa*, so to give it some cachet the single was issued on ten-inch with a gatefold sleeve and two live Town & Country recordings ('Downtown' and a correctly manic version of 'Mania').* 'It was a potential crack at getting them on the radio,' says Ivo. 'But it didn't work.'

There would be no second single pulled from *Hunkpapa*. If 4AD had been truly mercenary, 'Angel' would have done the trick, Tanya Donelly could match Hersh for jigsaw-shaped melody, from 'Green' on the debut album to 'River' and 'Giant' on *House Tornado*, while *Hunkpapa*'s 'Dragonhead' sat comfortably among Hersh's jagged rockery. But Donelly had begun to write with a more honed approach; The Bangles would have murdered to have the Sixties-girl-group swoon and bounce of Donelly's 'Angel' at their disposal.

The pressure to conform combined with the overdue need for a breakthrough ensured that The Wolfgang Press would continue down the road of formatting. At least this time they had the right tool: 'Kansas' might have been pulled from *Bird Wood Cage* but the insidiously taut and springy mood, hissed chorus and Andrew Gray's guitar stabs lent a danceable, Stax-influenced mobility. The promo video was equally distinctive, with the band – and supporting characters such as Simon Harper – wearing JFK and Jackie O masks, careering around an isolated wooden shack. There was no toilet seat on the

---

* A manufacturing fault meant that the sleeve to Throwing Muses single 'Dizzy' didn't close properly, but awkwardly sat open. Ivo: 'We covered our arses by highlighting it in a slogan in the adverts as a "self-opening ten inch single"!'

album cover, and the title 'Kansas' would have appealed, but mainstream American audiences might have been dumbfounded to see such cherished icons thrown into some kind of Lynchian universe.

Mick Allen's vocal was also still too dark for daytime radio. The confusion over what to do next was reflected in the next single being the slower, swampy 'Raintime', slightly re-tweaked from the *Bird Wood Cage* version, to no discernible point. Remixes for both singles were now adding to the growing overload of tracks aimed at the clubs. 'We weren't forced into them [remixes], but we didn't like most of what came back,' Allen admits. 'It diluted a lot of what we did because the remixes were more about the remixers than about us.'

Ivo felt just the same. Remixes also inflated budgets, which the band would have to recoup, and the originality of the music became of secondary importance. 'Remixers didn't care if there was nothing of the original piece as long as it could be a hit,' he says. 'I'm all in favour of collaboration, a different pair of ears to bring something new to the mix, literally. Though it was rare that anybody we hired improved the original version. But closing the barn door was also pointless; the horse had bolted.'

An illustration of how hard it was for left-of-centre artists to compete in the UK singles chart, Pixies' 'Monkey's Gone To Heaven' only reached number 60, and disappeared from the top 100 after just three weeks, despite the band's first promo video and three new B-sides on the twelve-inch. It was a proper single too, with a fantastic chorus hook, though like The Wolfgang Press, Pixies didn't make enough concessions; the tempo was slow, the mood was bristling and the middle eight culminated in the line, *'If man is five, and the devil is six, then God is seven!'* with Charles Thompson repeating the last part in his finest lung-busting manner.

It was now taken for granted that 4AD singles would set up an album, and those with their expectations raised by 'Monkey's Gone To Heaven' were not disappointed by *Doolittle*. Despite reservations over his polishing of 'Gigantic', Gil Norton had got the job of producing the album. Thompson says he liked how *Doolittle* turned out, though he'd also experienced a tussle with Norton as Throwing Muses had, 'to keep things simple, and to keep to the same set of Pixies rules,' he says. 'Steve Albini was more, "Yeah, let's make a record" as opposed to playing the songs for Gil for three weeks, eight hours a day, fine-tuning every niche and cranny. We got more into playing a groovy kind of rock as opposed to sounding hyper.'

Albini wouldn't have considered adding strings to 'Monkey's Gone To Heaven' as Norton was driven to do, but Thompson's new songs still sounded pretty hyper, as well as groovy, especially the opening salvo of 'Debaser', 'Tame' and 'Wave Of Mutilation'. But 'Here Comes Your Man' finally made it on to record after being shelved the last time. Thompson admits he felt embarrassed about the track's pop conceit, but he allowed it through because of Norton's affection for the song: 'I threw Gil a bone,' he says.

That a track both Pixies and Ivo weren't particularly fond of became the band's next single indicates that a white flag of creative surrender had been raised. Ivo admits 4AD was engaged in playing the game of a major label: 'You release the lead single – what a horrible expression that is – then follow it with the album, which supposedly goes wallop! And then you follow with the radio-friendly single or a remix. But our track record of failing with hit singles remained intact.'

Pixies' new American licensees Elektra, another arm of the Warners conglomerate that had taken them on after 4AD had signed Pixies to a five-album deal, would have been subtly (or otherwise) pushing the band down a more commercial path. Ivo still A&R'd the band, and he again sequenced the track listing, with Thompson choosing the title *Doolittle* after a lyric in 'Mr. Grieves'. His original title had been *Whore*, which would have had a divisive effect, but Thompson changed his mind. 'I told everyone, I didn't give a shit, *Whore* was the title,' he explains. 'But Vaughan changed the artwork and said he was going to use this monkey and halo, so I thought people would think I was some kind of anti-Catholic or getting into naughty-boy Catholic stuff. So I changed the title.'

Thompson says this was not a corroboration of Steve Albini's claim that the band would do anything for success. 'To me, it's a lot more fun to see what this guy will send us in the mail, like, "Oh, *that's* what he did with the artwork!" like it's somebody else's album. Vaughan never represented us in a corny or bad way.'

With its multiple oddball images in a ten-page booklet, *Doolittle* remains Vaughan Oliver's favourite 4AD artwork: 'For the power of music and graphic design combined. When that works, it's fabulous.'

If Pixies answered to Oliver, they didn't answer to Elektra, Thompson told me in 1989. 'Maybe after we sell some records, the pressure will be on, but they pretty much let us do what we want. It's good for us because at least in America, 4AD has the Cocteau Twins kind of image, and we're not. We aren't too hip [in America]. They think we're some stupid underground college band.'

Even so, Elektra helped *Doolittle* (just) break the Billboard Hot 100 and both 'Monkey's Gone To Heaven' and 'Here Comes Your Man' respectively reached numbers 5 and 3 on Billboard's Modern Rock chart. The Pixies' irresistible momentum seemed on course, and *Doolittle* wasn't only a flagship for Pixies but 4AD as well. The band was a new wave in itself, broadening the idea of a 4AD sound and vision. Beyond the converted markets of North America and Europe, fan cults had continued to blossom in Japan and South America, as more records, media opportunities and the growth of alternative music further spread the word.

In the Eighties, says Colombian writer José Enrique Plata Manjarrés, '4AD records were so scarce and expensive. We treated them as precious things. But one time, I saw a promo for a group called Pixies, with a cover with a little monkey on an orange background. It was interesting – a record called *Doolittle*, like the doctor who talked to animals. The guy in the shop said it had just come in. What's more, it's, "For-Ey-Dee". I didn't understand, and I was told it was the name of an amazing English label. The records were expensive but people bought them – Cocteau Twins, Dead Can Dance, and some others the shop got in, but not so much because not everybody was into them. Cocteau Twins' *Blue Bell Knoll* was first for me. It was like hearing an angel sing, and I'd got the bug. "For-Ey-Dee" made sense to me now.'

Manjarrés continues, '4AD became soldered into my brain with each record, each one a piece in a puzzle that stood out as distinctive and completely original, a pure essence but an uncertain reality. There was no internet to guide me so I had to build my puzzle with the pieces as they came to me, without an image. The aural coherence of the label wasn't based on the styles of the groups; it was more the work and efforts of exquisite taste. And it was Ivo who had it. But he wanted great design too, and in that way, the music entered through your eyes and the images got into your ears. That's how I started to understand 4AD's logic.'

Of course, behind the ecstatic reception for everything 4AD released, disharmony could always undo the good work. The one thing that could derail the Pixies, to throw the band off that irresistible course, was the band itself.

Deborah Edgely had managed to keep the news from the press, but it was no secret among the inner circle that Charles Thompson and Kim Deal had fallen out during the otherwise triumphant Pixies/ Muses European tour. Edgely recalls the Pixies tour bus returning to London, where Charles's girlfriend had turned up as a surprise, and the atmosphere being extremely frosty. There hadn't been any defrosting by the time of *Doolittle*, and though 'Gigantic' was a *Surfer Rosa* highlight, *Doolittle* didn't feature a single Deal lead vocal.

Was Thompson simply jealous of his sidekick? Perhaps the problem was that Pixies' most popular song was perceived as Deal's own – the credit on *Surfer Rosa* said as much; Pixies superfan Kurt Cobain later said, 'I wish Kim was allowed to write more songs for Pixies, because "Gigantic" is the best Pixies song, and Kim wrote it.' But it wasn't really true: 'I wrote the chords, suggested the title "Gigantic", and Kim did the lyric and melody,' says Thompson. 'That's my memory of it anyhow.'

On *Doolittle*, Deal co-sang 'Silver' (and got a co-writing credit) and various backing vocals, and by making her song 'Into The White' the B-side to 'Here Comes Your Man', 'Charles threw Kim a bone,' says Ivo (something that Thompson was getting good at). But *Doolittle* otherwise sidelined her. For example, the album's delightful oddity 'La La I

Love You' sounded tailor-made for Deal's voice but was instead sung by drummer Dave Lovering.

Surely this could only harm the band's brilliant chemistry. 'When you think about great teams, the creative spark is almost doubled as they bounce ideas off each other,' says Edgely. 'Kim brought charm, melody and sex appeal to Pixies and she was emotive, honest and open, and so easy to get along with. Charles was more the type to stand in your face, not shouting or being intimidating, but brusque and talking loudly. It was hard to know where he was coming from. He could be adorable too, but the way Kim stood on stage, grinning from ear to ear, she almost became the reason you smiled at them. You just warmed to her. Her harmonies with Charles were the dynamic duo that just worked.'

As Edgely says, you can't be in a band and be on your own, which is what she believes happened to Charles. 'He had found touring tedious. He didn't like to fly, so he'd take the [cruise ship] QEII when he could, or he'd drive across Europe with his wife, while the others were in the van. The magic and the glory of Pixies wore off relatively quickly for Charles and the rift evolved. I don't know, maybe it was because Kim was a girl. It was tough on her. Kim is a creative cookie, and she wanted her voice.'

Santiago agrees. 'Kim was headstrong and wanted to include her own songs, to explore her own world,' he explains. 'I think Charles saw it as the band made pizzas, not cookies. We were even going to fire Kim, after a gig in Frankfurt, where we found her hanging out in her hotel room, with no intention of playing. But our lawyer convinced us to try and work it out, to give her a warning. I'd blocked that incident out of my head – it was too heavy for me. Kim couldn't believe I'd be party to it but I told her that she didn't seem happy, so why hang around? In the end, she realised it was Charles's bag, and that he was the singer. But they kinda stopped talking after that.'

Ivo recalls he'd met up with Pixies the last time they'd come to London, and instead of the traditional get-together meal, 'Charles and I got into my car, where he played me demos of *Doolittle*, clearly agitated about Kim, and defensive about his apparent decision to use

Kim less, and the parts that she contributed. I'm sure Gil encouraged Charles to let Kim sing lead on something but it didn't end up happening. But *Doolittle* turned out quite good, didn't it?'

A provocative member of the touring party christened Pixies' 1989 US tour, 'The Fuck or Fight Tour', after which Thompson moved house to Los Angeles. Santiago and Lovering were soon to follow, leaving Deal alone back east, and wondering what would happen next. A pattern was emerging: another male-female dynamic under 4AD's aegis – another fall-out.

What a relief it must have been for Ivo to work with one singular talent such as Kurt Ralske. Still, at this stage of 4AD's development, there were tough decisions to take. Ivo was pondering how to get the best out of his artists; budgets (boosted by licensing deals) and expectations (and managers) dictated that it was hard to produce them himself, or to offer the John Fryer/Jon Turner option. And having tasted chart success, the temptation was to see if an Ultra Vivid Scene album could be a hit. Ivo tried for a hit single first by having Ralske re-record 'Mercy Seat'. 'It deserved to be isolated from the album, and it was preferable to re-record it. But it was the first time Kurt had worked in a proper studio with an engineer, and I didn't like it. It was too clean and lacked Kurt's basic, distorted guitar.'

Returning to basics, Ralske quickly followed it with 'Something To Eat', a free seven-inch single recorded in a trial session with young, unproven British engineer Ed Buller (who'd go on to produce Pulp and Suede). For the second UVS album, Ivo put forward Hugh Jones, the producer's first 4AD commission since Modern English's *Ricochet Days* in 1984. It was a beguiling choice. Ralske didn't like being controlled or care much about success; Jones was a fastidious producer who liked helping reorganise songs to expand their appeal.

Ralske nevertheless took Ivo's advice, and while he and Jones settled down to recording at London's Protocol Studios, Ivo was contemplating the fact that, incredibly, he had not signed a British artist since Colourbox in 1982. He'd tried with The Sundays, of course, and the provenance of a signing was immaterial to him, but Ivo felt swayed by his co-workers. 'The 4AD staff wanted to get their teeth into something, to be involved with bands here, who could hang out in the office. Cocteau Twins had drifted away, Dead Can Dance never hung out to begin with, so the mood was, let's get involved with someone that we can follow all the way through, that we don't have to always wait for them to tour.'

Since 1980, alternative music in Britain had evolved through post-punk, synth-pop and punk-funk to a more retro- and psyche-delic-tinged – albeit still dog-eared and punk-minded – pop and rock. By the end of the Eighties, two distinct factions had developed: one was the dance-and-Ecstasy brigade that made its home in Manchester – or, 'Madchester', as the music weeklies christened it – after the Acid House revolution, with the valedictory anthems of The Stone Roses and the mutant funk of The Happy Mondays. The other was a much noisier concoction that followed in the slipstream of the latest alternative rock sensation, My Bloody Valentine, which had used Cocteau Twins and The Jesus and Mary Chain as a base for its own freakish experiments in sound on the landmark album *Isn't Anything*.

Given the influences, and a collective surrender to the tingling and blissful moods created by the heavy use of trippy effects, it made sense that Ivo might be interested in this particular sound. However, it wasn't like him to be at all interested in any aspect of a 'scene' – for example, the sound of 1986 had had elements of the Sixties psyche-delia he loved as a teenager, but he remembers the C86 crowd as 'fey and jingly-jangly, not interesting nor original. And give me one good voice out of any of those people. Primal Scream made me angry during that period. They'd already copied The Byrds and then turned to The Rolling Stones.'

It wasn't until the following year of 1990 that this new coterie of Cocteaus- and Mary Chain-smitten bands were given a label – the music press settled on 'shoegaze', first coined in a *Sounds* review of the band Moose. Like goth, shoegaze was more of a criticism than a sound, based on the way that young musicians were relying so heav-ily on effects pedals at their feet that they were forced to gaze down instead of facing the audience. It helped disguise the fact that these bands were often lacking in arresting personalities, strong vocalists and brimming confidence. To use all the clichés that surrounded shoegaze, the sound was swirly, fuzzy, dreamy, narcotic, distorted and billowing – dreamy, escapist music played by breathy-voiced students who followed Ivo's view of music as an interior landscape and not an articulated viewpoint. Shoegaze seemed almost in denial of the cultural or musical revolution happening around those bands.

In the pile of demos that had landed on his desk in 1989, Ivo unearthed two bands that had a rippling, swimming approach. He especially liked the track 'Sight Of You' by Leeds-based trio Pale Saints, for its melodic and anthemic aspects. 'The singer was fantastic too,' he adds. As for Lush, he says, 'Neither of the two singers had beautiful voices, but "Thoughtforms" and "Ethereal" were good enough for me to get in touch.'

Coincidentally, Pale Saints and Lush were sharing a bill just a few days later, in the tiny backroom of The Falcon Pub in Camden Town. The entire 4AD office went along. 'Neither band was very good,' Ivo recalls. 'They were still young, and both drummers had problems keeping time, which affected everyone's performances. The singing wasn't good either. But I still wanted to work with both. Everyone at 4AD thought I was crazy, but they had real potential. A lot of English bands at that time, like Slowdive and Ride, suggested that things could develop, that they were experimenting, taking influences from the Sixties but being just as experimental from one album to the next, like The Byrds had done.'

Coming from the same scene, signing to 4AD at the same time and later going on tour together, Pale Saints and Lush became as entwined as Throwing Muses and Pixies in 4AD folklore. But the bands were to experience contrasting fortunes with their music, different levels of success, stress and eventually, catastrophe.

Pale Saints beat Lush to a 4AD release by three weeks. By all accounts, the band's founding singer and principal songwriter Ian Masters is another maverick character that prefers to communicate by email, citing the fact he lives in Japan as a good enough reason to communicate digitally – or at arm's length.

Masters has been in Japan for the last eleven years. 'I got bored with England – London became incredibly predictable. So I decided to find out what it would be like to be a foreigner. I wasn't intending to stay so long. It's a more naturally psychedelic experience. I needed to shake things up. It worked. Japan is like an immature, obstinate teenager, but on balance, I prefer it here. The beer's dull but the food's incredible.'

This was probably not the case in semi-rural Potters Bar in the county of Hertfordshire where Masters was raised. However, the music he was exposed to growing up was incredible. Early on, he showed unusual musical tastes, being 'obsessed' with jazz singer Ella Fitzgerald's 'Ev'ry Time We Say Goodbye' and 'bewildered', he says, by the eerie electronic theme to the BBC TV sci-fi series *Dr Who*. With basic piano skills, he'd joined the school rock band but switched to guitar at the same time he saw American new wavers Blondie in 1976: 'I knew then I'd need to go to live gigs until I died. The unexpected nature of a gig and the thought that something might go terribly wrong was too inviting. That extended into the time when Pale Saints started playing live. If things started to go badly, we'd just concentrate on having a good time. Whenever music has stopped being a pleasure, I've stepped away.'

Masters had also immersed himself in Blondie's more sophisticated NYC pals Television and their Sixties antecedents The Red Krayola and 13th Floor Elevators. Cocteau Twins' first Peel session 'blew my head off', while seeing Dead Can Dance live 'was a real Eureka moment … tears poured out of my body'. Masters was a late starter, only releasing his own music when he was twenty-five. He'd been studying at Birmingham University when he met the C86-era band Yeah Yeah Noh and followed them further north to their home town of Leeds in Yorkshire. The advert he placed in a local record shop unearthed two schoolmates, drummer Chris Cooper and guitarist Graeme Naysmith. With Masters switching to bass, the trio called themselves Pale Saints after a song by the Leeds duo Eyeless in Gaza. They began practising in a rehearsal space on a farm, only interrupted by the mooing of cows.

Early Pale Saints demos had been included on three UK compilation albums, but Ivo never listened to compilations. It was the band's
third demo cassette that had reached him, with two of the three tracks
re-recorded for the band's debut EP *Barging Into The Presence Of God*.
'Sight Of You' was an angular, wiry version of the Paisley Underground
sound over in America, while 'She Rides The Waves' drew from the
same Byrds-slanted camp as Primal Scream and The Stone Roses. A
third track, the slow and suspenseful 'Mother Night' produced by Gil
Norton, was equally assured. The EP wasn't brilliant, but it was hugely
promising, and they already sounded fully formed.

Lush, however, was anything but.

In the Victorian house in north-west London that she shares with
her partner Moose (formerly of the band that took his nickname) and
their two children, Miki Berenyi has just cleared up lunch. Her ten-
year-old daughter watches TV; her seven-year-old son is straining to
play football. Minus her trademark luminous red hair of the Lush era,
fans might struggle to recognise her, and that's how she likes it.
Nowadays, Berenyi works full-time as a magazine sub-editor. Moose
keeps pressing her to do some recordings together but, she says, music
must be all or nothing – so it's been nothing since Lush ended, bar the
very occasional guest vocal.

Berenyi's background is one of the most fascinating of all 4AD's
artists. Her Hungarian father had immigrated to London in 1956 and
was working as a sports journalist when he met, and later married,
model and actress Yasuko Nagazumi at 1964's Tokyo Olympics. She
subsequently landed a minor role in the 1967 James Bond film *You
Only Live Twice*. They divorced when Berenyi was four, and when
Nagazumi moved to the USA eight years later, Berenyi decided to stay
behind, though her father's poor parenting skills saw her camp out in
her school's music room one time when she was only fourteen.

Ska and Abba – who wrote songs about divorcing couples – were
her favourites until she met Emma Anderson at a north London
school. Anderson was equally into Abba, but had latched on to the
new wave bands on *Top of the Pops*, from The Teardrop Explodes to
Siouxsie and the Banshees. At thirteen, they'd bonded at a concert by

pop upstarts Haircut 100, but their tastes spanned The Smiths and the resolutely goth Sisters of Mercy. 'We'd go to gigs and share half a cider all night,' says Berenyi.

Across town, the pair would sell their fanzine, *Alphabet Soup* (tag line: 'It may be shit but it's only 5p'), which contained irreverent interviews; one was with Xmal Deutschland, on whom they modelled their glamorous look. They temporarily joined different bands, Anderson The Rover Girls and Berenyi The Bugs – that emphasised their differences. 'Emma was artier than me, more *NME* and The Smiths,' Berenyi recalls. 'I was more into garage bands like The Milkshakes. But we were really geeky about record labels, so we'd both buy Factory and 4AD records. We played Throwing Muses' *The Fat Skier* to death and saw the Muses and Pixies tour in 1988. We liked that they were overly cerebral, geeky and intense, not loud and rock'n'roll.'

Anderson is also a mother (her daughter is nearly three) and is about to leave London for the south coast. 'I was the 4AD obsessive,' she says. 'Factory, too, though less so. I really related to 4AD's artwork – it had such strong imagery. I'd buy records without hearing them, like the *Natures Mortes* compilation and Rema-Rema. And I loved Throwing Muses. But Miki and I were both goths. We wore black lipstick and blusher, which didn't look as good on me as I was chubbier, and had wavy hair.'

Anderson and Berenyi finally joined forces in Baby Machines, which they named in the same spirit that was driving the emerging feminist punk movement riot grrrl. Their new name of Lush made a point too: 'It was used in a derogatory way to describe a drunken woman, so we wanted to champion it,' says Berenyi. But Lush's lyrics turned out to be more introvert, with airy-fairy titles such as 'Thoughtforms', 'Babytalk' and 'Scarlet', the tracks that made up the demo that Ivo had heard.

'To call Baby Machines riot grrl is to dignify it with an insight and direction we didn't really have,' says Berenyi. '"He's A Bastard" was a song about an ex – "*He's a bastard, can't you see, he's not good enough for you*", and "Female Hybrid" – "*Boys look at me, hybrid queen, on page three*". Just garbage! We later realised that it wasn't just a case of writing something – anything – so we could do a gig, but that the quality of the songs also depended on writing to the band's strengths, and the more oblique lyrics were part of that. "Scarlet" was still about why boys like slutty girls, and "Etheriel" was still about a break-up of sorts, but there were extra levels of meaning. The sounds of the words were as important as what was being said, and that made them a lot more enjoyable to play as well as listen to.'

Neither Berenyi nor Anderson intended to sing. Meriel Barham, Berenyi's friend at North London Polytechnic, was Lush's original vocalist, with a rhythm section of two fellow students – the inexperienced bassist Steve Rippon and drummer Chris Acland, who had played in various punk bands in the Lake District region, which was nearer to Scotland than London. 'Chris turned out to be a very good drummer, but the turning point was Emma writing "Thoughtforms",' says Berenyi. 'I knew I had to get my arse in gear and practise more.'

Another turning point was Barham's sacking, for a lack of commitment; 'Etheriel' was named in her wake. 'My experience of Lush was in its early, thrashy days, which was great fun among mates, and much more Emma and Miki's project than something that I was as focused on, so I understood our different standpoints,' says Barham.

When auditions for a new singer turned out to be 'a disaster', Berenyi reluctantly took over. 'I totally did not want to sing – I never did think I could. But it was a needs-must scenario.'

Anderson had taken responsibility for posting demos out and booking gigs. Geoff Travis at Rough Trade had also liked Lush's tape, but like Derek Birkett had done with A.R. Kane, told the band he thought 4AD was a more natural fit, if Ivo was interested. Howard Gough in 4AD promotions had tried to persuade Ivo otherwise. 'Howard had seen us live, when we were shambolic, and said we were shit,' Anderson recalls. 'But Ivo said he couldn't dismiss the songs and wanted John Fryer to record some more demos.' One condition of Ivo funding it was that Berenyi and Anderson take singing lessons from Tona de Brett, the same coach Elizabeth Fraser had studied with. 'I think it was to placate Howard, who was obsessed with the idea we were crap,' says Anderson.

303

Miki Berenyi: 'Hand on heart, what Ivo could find in that live mess was beyond me. And John Fryer had to organise everything because we were very timid.'

Ivo says Fryer worked his magic, 'because no one, Lush included, had any idea they could sound that powerful'. Instead of just re-recording the same three songs from the demo, Ivo suggested Lush record three more with Fryer and release it as a six-track EP. *Scar* followed Pale Saints' debut to become 4AD's last release of the decade.

Scar wasn't a groundbreaking statement, with Berenyi's tentative vocals slathered in effects, but it was a suitably sparkling testament to new beginnings and ethereal melody, with a more pop sensibility than Pale Saints. The press reaction to *Scar* was positive, likewise to the image, with Anderson's jet-black hair contrasting with Berenyi's scarlet rinse. Interviews revealed that Lush weren't shy, shoegazey types, and indeed they liked to celebrate the alcoholic connotations of their name. The band also had strong connections to the music press; Anderson had previously worked as an assistant to former Creation PR Jeff Barrett, 'so at least people had heard of us,' says Berenyi.

But familiarity brought the risk of contempt. 'Our interviews were all about Tottenham [football club], red hair and drinking, which jarred with 4AD's image,' Berenyi recalls. 'Ivo didn't give a shit, but it did feel like people were saying we were on the wrong label. No, we were on the right label. Otherwise, we'd have been written off as a bunch of alcoholic chancers. I hated having to tell journalists what the songs meant, so being on 4AD made people concentrate on our music, to take the music seriously without us having to.'

Lush and Pale Saints were young, didn't bring history and baggage, and they were British: if unconvinced by the new signings, most of the staff were on side. And 4AD had the chance to further shed the solemn, arty and dark image. In return, the label's new charges viewed them with affection and amusement.

'Ivo was kind and patient and I did rather hang on his every word,' says Berenyi. 'So when things went wrong, if he didn't agree with a decision or was revealed to not be doing absolutely everything for your benefit, there was that similar wail of injustice that spoilt teenage kids have about their parents. But he never made me feel silly or naïve. He was funny, too, and not at all sombre and serious. Chris used to call him Uncle Ivo and would do a rather fussy, owlish impersonation of him! He'd do impressions of all of them. Simon Harper was the boarding school house master and Debbie was Alice in Wonderland.'

This eccentric parade of fairytale-like characters were about to have a brand new and heavily designed modernist office to work in. The building next door – 'a very run down convent,' Ivo says – to 17–19 Alma Road had been bought, and was being revamped by Deborah Edgely's friend and architect Sandra Douglas at Ben Kelly Design (the company that had overseen Factory's Hacienda club in Manchester). 'That's where the M/A/R/R/S money went,' says Ivo.

Staff numbers were now in double figures. With Lush and Pale Saints combined, and combined again with Throwing Muses and Pixies, it was a very different 4AD that closed the Eighties compared to the 4AD that had started the decade with such modest hopes 1990; forward.

14 1990

HEAVEN, LAS VEGAS AND BUST
(cad0002-cad0017)

It wasn't an ideal way to celebrate the transition from one decade to the next. Over the Christmas period, while 4AD's outlook appeared seamless and positive, the label's future was under threat.

During the Eighties, Beggars Banquet co-founder Nick Austin had taken a different A&R path to his business partner Martin Mills. In 1985, Austin had launched the Coda label, a new Beggars subsidiary mostly dedicated to New Age music, the bland and commercial version of the ambient minimalism associated with Brian Eno and Michael Brook. This was the influence of Austin's new wife, former folk-rock singer-songwriter Claire Hamill, who was now busy creating overlapping layers of chanting voices in the fashion of Irish MOR starlet Enya. Coda peppered its New Age brief with jazzier and world-musical tones, such as Incantation's *Panpipes Of The Andes*, one of 1987's biggest hit albums.

'I couldn't say no to Nick, because that's what he wanted to do,' says Mills. 'But we were uncomfortable bedfellows. We were still friends and business partners, but he was becoming isolated in his own company. So we decided to split it in two.'

Mills' half was worth more than Austin's, and the pair had agreed a split of assets to ensure things were equal. The legislation that allows a company to de-merge (without paying tax during that period) took a year to come through, by which time Austin had bankrolled the New Age music channel Landscape TV and spent the majority of his share. 'Nick then decided our agreed deal was unfair,' says Mills. 'I had to sue to force him to commit to our agreement.'

The process took eighteen months: 'It was extremely painful, hugely stressful and expensive,' Mills recalls. Three months alone were spent in court as the case dragged on into 1990. Since it was an argument between shareholders of Beggars Banquet, the company could not fund the costs of either partner, so Mills was forced to fund his legal case from the 4AD side of the business, of which he was the principal shareholder, while Austin resorted to legal aid. To do that, Mills had to restructure 4AD's shareholder agreement to allow the label to pay dividends to himself, and in the process, Ivo was made an equal partner in the label, which, says Mills, 'was the right thing to do anyway'.

If Mills had lost, it's interesting to speculate about the impact on 4AD. But Austin lost the case, and had to declare bankruptcy. 'We became sworn enemies, but Nick has since apologised,' Mills concludes.

The outcome was that Ivo was in a much stronger financial position, though daily business didn't change; Mills had never interfered in the running of 4AD, and Ivo's way of running a record label had created something much more recognisable than Beggars Banquet. There was the attention paid to every detail, from the big architectural stuff, such as the basement of the new office with its glass ceiling (planning laws meant the building couldn't be built up, so they just dug down instead), down to the bespoke design of v23's calendar. Oliver had always relished the free rein that came without having account for the wishes of artists that, at the very least, wanted their name, or the album title, on the front of their records. The calendar's limited run of 5,000 copies quickly sold out, confirming that no other label put as much importance into the visuals, and that 4AD collectors had to have everything.

After the watershed moment in 1967 with The Beatles' *Sgt. Pepper's Lonely Hearts Club Band*, designed by British pop art painter Peter

Blake, record sleeve design blossomed. However, the Eighties had taken it to new heights; record sleeves became worthy of being framed, or becoming the subject of an exhibition. Thirteen years before Saville's show at London's Design Museum, Oliver was awarded an exhibition of 4AD design drawn from both the 23 Envelope and v23 periods, to be staged between 1 February and 11 March 1990 as an inauguration of a new gallery, the Espace Graslin in the French city of Nantes.

4AD made it a bigger occasion, flying in Lush, Pale Saints and The Wolfgang Press to play shows alongside UK print, radio and TV media. Interviewed by BBC series *SNUB TV*, the first television show to showcase independent music (three series ran on BBC2), Oliver discussed his efforts to keep re-contextualising the work; for example, putting album covers inside baroque frames 'to exaggerate their preciousness'. A feature in France's national newspaper *Le Monde* certified the importance of the event, even if the writer's tone was suspicious, or, as Oliver mimics, 'this exhibition is all very well, but what is graphic design doing in an art gallery?'

Oliver remembers it as, 'one of the best experiences of my life'. But once more, the dazzled visuals hid upsetting undercurrents and the Nantes exhibition put an end to the friendship between 23 Envelope's founders.

After an uneasy truce through 1988 and 1989, Nigel Grierson says that he and Oliver had re-established friendly contact, but that was before Oliver mentioned the Nantes exhibition. 'Vaughan said something like, "It's nothing big, it's in Nantes, not Paris", playing it down,' says Grierson. 'It turned out to be very big, and he'd left me out. We were still collaborating in 1987, and, bearing in mind most exhibitions of this magnitude are planned two to three years in advance, it's unthinkable there could be an exhibition just about Vaughan planned at that point, when all our work had been a partnership under the 23 Envelope banner. After all, no one knew who Vaughan Oliver was at that point. Of course, by the time the exhibition did happen, he could add a couple of years work with other people so that it didn't look quite so obvious.'

Grierson continues: 'I was credited in the catalogue, but not on the exhibition walls, and he did every interview. I flew over, and on the night of the gig, Vaughan started crying on my shoulder, saying, "I'm aware of how much of this work is yours", which was more salt in the wound. There was also no mention of me in any coverage back home. I called one TV programme, saying, "Didn't you research this? You're using my videos." Someone must have called Vaughan, because he called me, and said, "It's Vaughan. I'm sorry." I hung up and we've never spoken since.'

Grierson says that an article about Oliver in 1991 used his *Filigree & Shadow* poster on the cover, with no reference to Grierson. 'You'd think he'd be ten times warier after Nantes but it didn't happen. I initially refused to be involved in a book [*Visceral Pleasures* by arts writer Rick Poyner], but Ivo and others said, "It can't do any harm, set the record straight, make sure you get credit". But why is the book about Vaughan and not 23 Envelope? I see it as insecurity on Vaughan's side, but now he's world-famous, hopefully he's past that point now. Maybe he wanted a bigger share of the pie.'

Unsurprisingly, Oliver has another view. 'About fifteen per cent [a figure Grierson hotly disputes] of the [Nantes] show was our combined work. I'd invited Nigel to take part, and to contribute ideas, but he never came up with anything. I invited him to the show, and when he saw it, he said, "I didn't know it was this big". My problem was that the show had to open without captions on the sleeves, which was the curator's fault. The bands were coming over to play, so we couldn't delay it. Nigel was incredibly pissed off, but he wouldn't take anything as an explanation. I thought I'd bent over backwards, to open the door to his influence on the show, to mediate and get us back together, because we used to get on so amazingly well. When *Visceral Pleasures* came out, our roles were identified, and he got the credits he wanted, which I thought would appease him.' *Visceral Pleasures* was published in 2000, which meant Grierson was to stew for a decade, and even then, he still didn't pick up the phone.

'Of all the break-ups of intense working and personal relationships, and there were many, that between Vaughan and Nigel is the saddest for me,' says Ivo. 'They were like two peas in a pod, bouncing ideas off each other and, for a while anyway, seemingly devoid of ego in terms of job description. Whilst working with both of them, separately, on the This Mortal Coil remasters in 2011, I was constantly trying to provoke a softening, an understanding or simply forgiveness in either one of them. I came to realise that would never happen.'

'Nigel was an inspiration to me,' Oliver concludes. 'He brought something wonderful and personable to the table, he had a fantastic eye, and we gave each other strength. We had an amazing time together, from school onwards. It was a real shame that we fell out over business.'

'It's difficult to work around what Vaughan did to me, his best friend and creative partner, something that has never been properly addressed until now,' Grierson concludes. 'But I don't begrudge an ounce of his success. He deserves it all. It was obvious to me, even at the age of fifteen when we first met, that Vaughan had something quite exceptional.'

As 23 Envelope dissolved, v23's relationship prospered in the converted basement of 4AD's new office. 'We were driven,' Oliver says. 'The split with Nigel opened up so much as Chris [Bigg] and I worked together with all these different photographers, and had all these new ideas.'

Bigg says he feels privileged to have worked at 4AD during what he remembers as a golden age. 'It was all go,' he recalls. 'One weekend, we'd see Primal Scream live, My Bloody Valentine the next week, then Pixies, then off to The Wag Club to see Big Audio Dynamite ... But then it changed, when people started going to weird places to get drugs at weird times of night, in tow with a few hangers-on.'

Compared to the likes of Creation's all-weekend parties, 4AD showed a modicum of restraint. But if the label's music didn't tap the revolution of dance after 'Pump Up The Volume' anymore than it did before, there was still a mood of celebration and inebriation – no one was exempt in the music industry. Lots of creative work was undertaken in the art department, but according to eyewitnesses, it hosted its fair share of drugs, around Oliver's plan chest, especially the

'Fourth Drawer Down', named after the 1981 compilation of Associates' singles on Situation 2.

'I love Associates but that's poppycock,' says Oliver. 'I used to call it, "old artwork". As in, 'Do you want to come and see some old artwork?' It was a framed Cocteau Twins poster, and you'd get a line [of cocaine] on that. For me, drugs got in the way of productivity and creativity, but when I look back at the drugs taken, it must have had some influence on the work, at least in a naïve way.'

'The Cocteaus poster was in the fourth drawer down,' Bigg recalls. 'It did get a bit out of control at times. I thought it helped get you focused, because there was lots of work and stuff happening all at the same time. We had deadlines but Ivo made sure everything was right before it was ready to go.'

Ivo kept his distance from the excess, especially as he was steering clear of getting friendly with the artists for fear of repeating the sapping experience with M/A/R/R/S and Cocteau Twins. His reticence reinforced his shyness, and to late arrivals such as Miki Berenyi, he cut an enigmatic figure. 'I didn't really know what to make of Ivo,' she says. 'People in the music industry had this large-and-in-charge attitude, to show they were as much a rock star as any band, but not Ivo. He was quite proper. On odd occasions when he'd swear, it was almost jarring, like hearing the Queen swear! He was very avuncular, as others have said, like there was something elderly and doting about him. But that sense of control was part of his character.'

It seemed fitting that 4AD's first release of the decade was named *The Comforts Of Madness*. Pale Saints' debut album matched Ultra Vivid Scene for fashioning new dreams out of psychedelia that the album's two producers exploited in their own particular style. 'Gil Norton was always excited and aspirational,' says Ian Masters. 'John Fryer was playful and open, more of a super-imaginative engineer. He was up for anything, like, "How about using this tape loop of dogs shagging?"'

At guitarist Graeme Naysmith's suggestion, the album included a cover of 'Fell From The Sun', written by David Roback, the lynchpin of Paisley Underground contenders The Rain Parade, for his new outfit Opal. *The Comforts Of Madness* even ran as one continuous piece of music, with instrumental links based on stage improvisations to plug the gaps between songs when there was barely any audience applause.

The album title seemed a good bet for one of v23's most virtuoso covers, but Pale Saints wanted to be involved from the start. After American artist Cindy Sherman refused permission for use of her image, the band settled on a photo by Sarah Tucker, one of the Bournemouth University students that v23 was mentoring. The cat lying among flower petals, rendered in green and red, was marginally psychedelic, but far too decorative and soft, and it's one of Vaughan Oliver's least favourite 4AD sleeves.

Lush was much more accommodating. Oliver had loved photographer Jim Friedman's diffused colour Polaroids but didn't feel they were appropriate for a 4AD cover until the band's six-track debut *Scar*. 'Jim reminded me of [American painter] Mark Rothko, all blurred colour and long songs of sound,' Oliver explains. 'Talking to Lush, I saw walls and waves of colour. Jim's work almost became Japanese pictograms, like images in a shape that has meaning.'

For all the band's musical and visual swirls, Lush was not part of any psychedelic renaissance; the band's vice was alcoholic, not pharmaceutical, and they were more prone to saucy humour than semi-mystical bravado – the run-out grooves on the vinyl version of *Scar* read, 'Fanny tits delight' and 'I'll still fondle you'. And the first cover version the band had recorded was Abba's 'Hey Hey Helen'. It was one of three tracks recorded for a Peel session. Sadly, Peel's patronage lacked the impact it had once had; he'd lost his Thursday night slot as early as 1984, and instead of broadcasting three nights a week (he had never done Fridays), Peel's show was moved to the weekend in 1990, starting an hour later than usual, so that he'd finish at 2am. In many cases, people were either out having fun – or asleep. The old post-punk order that had launched 4AD had effectively disappeared.

The same could be said for Cocteau Twins' original sound, even if Robin Guthrie hadn't retired his effects pedals. He'd even turned into an indie-pop producer for Lush's studio version of 'Hey Hey Helen' after picking out the band as his favourite of all the shoegaze kids following in his footsteps. Emma Anderson had sent Guthrie an early demo, and he, like Ivo, could hear so much potential. 'The performances were bad and the guitars were out of tune, but I could hear songs, harmonies, melodies, and I wanted to get my hands on them,' he recalls. 'Ivo knew I'd expressed an interest, but he'd used John Fryer for *Scar*.'

Fryer had been a logical choice at the onset of Lush's career, but Guthrie was the means to lift them higher. Ivo was understandably wary of involving Guthrie in more 4AD business and tried to put the band off. 'Ivo was very diplomatic and didn't say why he thought using Robin was a bad idea,' says Berenyi. 'Maybe he thought we'd be the wide-eyed innocents and Robin would take the piss and be a pain to manage. Maybe he thought we'd sound like the Cocteaus, which became one of the main criticisms we had afterwards. But we were incredibly flattered that Robin was interested.'

Berenyi says that Guthrie had singled out an unrecorded Lush song, 'Deluxe': 'Robin said he could do great things with it. We said we were crap but he said not to worry. We needed that, because we couldn't have dealt with a producer rolling their eyes and tutting. It was almost like we were so grateful that anything sounded fine that we didn't want to express an opinion, because we could so easily be shot down.'

Lush's first Guthrie recording to emerge was the *Mad Love* EP, which sounded bolder and brighter than *Scar* (contrast the two versions of 'Thoughtforms'). Guthrie was spot on about the cascading 'Deluxe', and neither 'Downer' nor 'Leaves Me Cold' revealed them as a band with self-esteem issues to rival the producer's. But Berenyi says that Lush was always insecure about their abilities, and that the instant press attention had increased the pressure. 'We were on the cover of *Melody Maker* six months after we formed, which became a nightmare because we weren't prepared – we'd only played about four gigs. We didn't even have a long enough set to be able to headline. And we were awful live, so we were forced to become good in public.'

Since The Falcon Pub show, Lush and Pale Saints had only shared a stage twice – Leeds in November 1989 and Norwich in March 1990. It made sense to use 4AD's profile to co-promote both bands, so a co-headline tour in the UK and Europe began in the Netherlands in March. The bands alternated the top slot each night, but from the start it was clear the two bands didn't share a bond as Throwing Muses and Pixies had, especially the two lead singers.

Berenyi recalls an unspoken rivalry: 'They [Pale Saints] didn't like the fact we'd got more press, and we were threatened by the fact they could play their instruments and could show us up, even if they didn't have much charisma. It got narky over who was headlining which cities. It was still good fun, but Ian was sneery and I couldn't bear him. I know I could be annoying when I got drunk, but on the last night in Brussels, he kept making nasty comments. Finally, I said, "You really don't like me, do you?" and he slapped me around the face! I was so shocked, I didn't respond, and he just smiled and walked off. In those times, there were so many people you could row and fall out with.'

'Ian Masters, or Master Masters as I used to call him, was incredibly intelligent in a wonderfully dysfunctional way,' recalls Simon Harper. 'He used to send really long postcards from tours, all written in back-to-front writing so you had to read them in a mirror, which, of course, was his whole point – to annoy.'

Chalk up one more confrontation that was never resolved. It was as if 4AD, from its avuncular leader to the Cocteaus and on down to the new breed, sought out artists whose creative imaginations ran in direct proportion to their inability to express their emotions in any other way, feeding all that buried tension into the music.

Kurt Ralske's reaction to his new Ultra Vivid Scene album sprang from the exact same source. Even though he valued control and independence, he had allowed Ivo's choice of producer, Hugh Jones, to pursue his usual dedicated effort to make the music as palatable as possible. Years after the fact, during which he remained silent, Ralske feels that the situation had served 4AD's interest more than his own.

'I adore Ivo and am eternally grateful to him,' he starts off, 'but it all came at the moment when 4AD had had huge success, this feeling of, I can do anything, including taking me, this very shy kid from New York City, and pushing him over the top. Hugh was wonderful, so I blame myself for allowing a record to be completed that had nothing to do with my vision, sonics, structure and tone. To me, it sounds slick, English and complacent, which was so far from my concept of music that had a slightly dangerous, uncomfortable edge. And it was very slowly, painstakingly made. But decisions get made, and when the money runs out, the album's finished and being released. I haven't listened to it once since it was finished.'

Ralske's album title, *Joy 1967–1990*, was intended to read like a tombstone. Regarding his disillusionment, he recalls someone at 4AD suggesting he shouldn't bring it up with Ivo because it wouldn't do anyone any good. 'So,' he says, 'I bit the bullet.'

'Kurt must have done some fine acting, because it's difficult to hide displeasure with your producer over such a long, intense period of time,' Ivo feels. 'I remember Kurt being incredibly complimentary about Hugh, but maybe that was more about his work ethic than the end result. I remember thinking Kurt was extremely happy with it. The album proved not to be very commercial-sounding anyway! But it sounded commercial to Columbia's ears.'

Ralske at least stands by the songs on *Joy 1967–1990*, which might explain why Ivo places the album in his all-time 4AD top 10. Few might agree with such a vaulted opinion, but for all Jones' audio polish, it was still a finely honed version of Ralske's signature narcotic allure, with the occasional great pop melody. It gave 4AD and Columbia the chance to adopt the lead-single-album-pop-single strategy, starting with 'Staring At The Sun' (the B-side 'Three Stars' was another album cut), and following *Joy 1967–1990*, the album's poppiest and best track 'Special One', the one most deserving of Jones' diligence, and one of the finest singles that 4AD ever released. It didn't even make the UK independent chart, though either Columbia's muscle or 4AD's American profile got 'Special One' to 14 on the Billboard's Modern Rock chart.

Or maybe it was the presence of Pixies' Kim Deal, after Ralske had asked her to sing the chorus for 'Special One'. 'I thought, "Oh crap, I don't want to sing on other people's shit, I don't even want to sing on Charles's shit", says Deal. 'It was really awkward, but OK, I agreed.'

Deal also agreed to appear in a video, which helped make 'Special One' one of the few 4AD promos to warrant repeat viewing. Ralske claims the video took all of 15 minutes to film. The pair sat side by side on bar stools, 'like in those old country videos, where people look into each other's eyes, super creepy!' Deal says. As Ralske mimed as nonchalantly and twitchily as the camera would allow, Deal nodded away appreciatively, grinning all the way before she started to nuzzle Ralske. After she'd sung the first chorus, she waited patiently – even smoking a cigarette – for Ralske to finish his verse before she knocked him off his stool and took centre stage herself for the chorus coda. When Ralske eventually walked around to sit on Deal's vacated stool, she smacked him across the face – all of this improvised.

'It was either kiss or hit him, so obviously I was going to slap him!' Deal says. 'I'm sure I hit him harder than he was expecting.'

Ralske was on more solid ground with the artwork, sending Oliver into rapture with Fifties ad cuttings. On the first UVS album, Oliver had blown up the image of a toothbrush and mimicked around it the embossed gaffer tape that held together the package Ralske had posted his images in. For the new album, Oliver isolated a drill, juxtaposed images of tyres, stars and the Virgin Mary for a slice of Warholian kitsch pop art. 'They're amongst the most original and sympathetic sleeves that v23 ever did,' says Ivo. 'It's another example of sleeves that sit in the Victoria and Albert Museum.'

Perhaps if Ralske had been happy with his album, he would have been a happier, more confident frontman. 'I wasn't into being a performer,' he admits, which Ivo says wasn't a problem: 'If performing was considered, I wouldn't have signed half the bands that I did.' Ralske says he only grudgingly assembled a touring band after *Joy* … had been released, and cites the band for his feeling of losing 4AD's support when he most needed it. 'I know Ivo was very happy with the album, but it got very little promotion,' he claims. 'Someone at Rough Trade later told me that when we toured the UK, we were so awful that no one would give any more music a chance. That's understandable. Pop music isn't about second chances, it's about delivering.'

Two people who clearly believed in second chances were Kim Deal and Tanya Donelly, who had joined forces in the hope of escaping the shadow of their bands' principal songwriters. The root of this unexpected union was a bonding on the Throwing Muses/Pixies tour of 1988, both as women (Deal being the only female Pixie) and partly as the clan that were playing rock by day and sometimes clubbing by night. It turns out that not every Muse preferred reading books to hi-jinks. It was a Boston nightclub where Deal and Donelly first hatched the plan, in a drunken conversation, 'to write a disco song and make a lot of money,' says Deal. This had gone as far as recording Donelly's track 'Rise' in a disco fashion with Narcizo on drums, but Deal and Donelly's schedules weren't to coincide for another eighteen months. During that time, while Deal was caught up in dysfunctional Pixies business, Donelly became distracted, possibly because of the company she was keeping, she says, referring to her then boyfriend, 4AD promotions man Howard Gough.

Donelly admits that they were 'like oil and water', but under the euphorial of Ecstasy – and presumably the music – something had blossomed; something that gave Donelly an outlet from the pressure cooker of Kristin Hersh's emotional trauma. 'Howard [Gough] was a handful,' Donelly admits. 'It was too crazy and chaotic for a real relationship, but he brought along this novelty element, the idea you were allowed to have dumb fun. It demystified the sanctity of the overall vibe. Kristin thought it was funny and fun for me too – until I weighed ninety pounds and needed vitamin shots in my ass! That's when the fun ended.'

'Howard was totally smitten with Tanya,' recalls Miki Berenyi, 'but being a coke-addicted meathead, he fucked it all up.'

While the fun lasted, Donelly had been sharing it with Pixies' rhythm section and occasionally David Narcizo. By the time she'd reconnected with Deal, the conceptual jape of a disco collaboration had worn thin. But Donelly's commitment didn't waver: 'Kim was one of my heroes and an incredible songwriter and I wanted to see if I could do something else besides the Muses.'

The opportunity arose when Charles Thompson announced he was going on a solo tour. 'I thought that we were a band, and I didn't get the solo thing,' says Deal. 'So I thought I'd do something solo too. I told Tanya to come over and write some songs.' Deal says she suggested each write one side of songs, which Donelly doesn't recall. What they do agree on was that neither planned to quit their main band. 'That would have been disrespectful,' says Deal, 'even though I knew Tanya did want to start her own band.'

Ivo recalls that he loved the demo that the pair recorded with American violinist Carrie Bradley, which had a country music flavour. He responded with an offer to fund an album. 'I wanted to encourage Kim to reveal to the world that she could make simply beautiful music,' he says.

The band name The Breeders could have been some sly feminist statement along the lines of The Baby Machines, but it was actually an in-joke between Kim and sister Kelley, being homosexual slang for heterosexuals: 'That they saw a straight couple's goods as disgusting was so funny to me!' says Kim. 'Later, the meaning became more layered, like one man saying to another, "He's a breeder, too bad".'

The Breeders needed a rhythm section as Deal wanted to play some guitar – it was easier to combine with singing on stage, she says. For the bass, she called on Josephine Wiggs of The Perfect Disaster, a British equivalent to the Paisley Underground sound that had supported Pixies in London. 'She was musically intelligent, self-deprecating, and easy on the eye,' says Deal. In return, Wiggs found Deal complex and entertaining company.

'I was in Frankfurt when Pixies were playing in 1989, and we got to hang out,' Wiggs recalls. 'We sat in the railway station next to the venue, where Kim insisted there was enough clearance between the train and platform to dangle her knees over, which didn't seem a good idea! She was hilarious on that level, a risk-taker, who liked to live in the moment. At 3am, everyone else had left and she had no

Deutschmarks for a taxi, and no other way to get back to the hotel, which was out at the airport! My friend had to pay for her.'

Deal had wanted twin sister Kelley to play drums, but she couldn't get leave from her current job (as a program analyst), so Steve Albini – Deal's choice of producer for his no-nonsense approach to analogue sound – had brought along Britt Walford, a member of the Louisville, Kentucky band Slint, whose Albini-engineered debut album *Tweez* had mastered a slow, stark sound at total odds with the fast, FX ear-bashing of alternative rock. As the only male Breeder, Walford insisted that he adopt a pseudonym, settling on Shannon Doughton when Deal rejected his original suggestion of Mike Hunt. Walford was a very different, minimalist drummer to the likes of Dave Lovering, and with Albini stressing live performances and quick takes, the album only took two weeks to record at Palladium. It didn't sound like a country music record for one moment.

The title 'Oh!' suggested something upbeat but the track was more Slint-like in its funereal pace and barren arrangement, with a stark drum tattoo, Carrie Bradley's lonesome violin, Deal's surprisingly raw, cracked vocal. There was clearly much more to Deal than the 'cookies' that Joey Santiago had described, something more savoury, something more vulnerable behind the wide grin.

The album turned out to be Deal's deal. She sang and wrote all the songs, with the idea that Donelly would take over when a second Breeders album got made. The sole Deal/Donelly co-write 'Only In 3's' didn't break with the record's stripped, wired dynamic; seven of the twelve songs were closer to two minutes than three, some were mercurial ballads and others had angular Hersh-style twists. On the surface, 'Hellbound', 'Limehouse' and 'Opened' mirrored Pixies' bouncy momentum (the closing 'Metal Man' had similar melodic parts to *Doolittle* cut 'Cactus'), but under Albini's watchful eye, there were no busy rock heroics; Ivo's suggestion to cover 'Happiness Is A Warm Gun' resulted in one of the most inventive Beatles covers in years.

Deal denies she felt liberated by the experience. 'I didn't think, Charles won't let me shine, now this spirit's come over me, I've been given a chance to sing my songs, like TV Moment of the Week. All I cared about was it sounding good. And I didn't know how the songs would go. One moment, I thought it sounded awesome, the next minute not.'

A surprise studio guest was Mick Allen, who had spent a reputedly riotous night at Manchester's Hacienda club with the Boston brigade and later added murmured backing vocals to 'Oh!' Deal liked Allen, from his bass lines to his bolshie character. 'Mick had a big fucking mouth,' she says, meaning it as a compliment. 'He'd talk trash constantly and destroy everyone in front of him, but not in a mean way, more very funny, all snotty with disdain.'

Pod – the album's title inspired by a painting Deal had seen in Boston – 'and it's a good word' – was given one of Vaughan Oliver's most memorably surreal images with the aforementioned belt of dead eels attached to his underpants. Albini considered the album one of his best sessions, and John Peel was smitten enough to allow The Breeders special dispensation to record a session at Palladium rather than the BBC's west London studio. Kurt Cobain was such a fan that, according to his posthumously published journal, *Pod* and *Surfer Rosa* were in his top three favourite albums, just below Iggy and The Stooges' *Raw Power*. In 1992, he raved to *Melody Maker* about the main reasons he liked the band and *Pod* as being, 'for the songs, and the way they structure them, which is totally unique, very atmospheric'.

Pixies didn't sell that many singles but they did albums, and *Pod* reached 22 in the national UK chart. Santiago says that the other Pixies supported Deal all the way: 'Especially Charles.'

Deal subsequently recorded a new Pixies album, though Ivo wisely kept the two records apart to avoid any conflict of press duties and reduce the number of unavoidable comparisons. Ivo also kept the two albums separate in terms of licensing, thinking that *Pod* was more suited to an independent label. He managed to persuade Elektra of this thought, and licensed *Pod* to Rough Trade America.

Pod was released at the end of May, to be followed six weeks later by Pixies' single and the band's third album a month after that. Two releases acted as convenient buttresses in between, one from another of 4AD's circle of distressed male-female relationships.

Despite being two hot-headed individuals who made music and toured together, Brendan Perry and Lisa Gerrard had continued with Dead Can Dance after moving to different countries. Gerrard was in Barcelona where she had taken her first film role, in Spanish director Agustí Villaronga's fantasy *El Niño de la Luna*, for which Dead Can Dance had written the soundtrack. Perry had reconnected with his family's ancestry by moving to rural Ireland, where he had rented a six-bedroom house and bedded in a home studio. Two vocals arrangements, 'The Arrival And The Reunion' and 'The End Of Words', had been completed at John Rivers' studio in the Midlands, with guest singer David Navarro Sust adding Gregorian choral support, but the rest of *Aion* made up the first Dead Can Dance album to be recorded outside of the UK.

At twelve tracks and just 36 minutes, *Aion* was a precise and focused adventure. Such was the speed at which the duo was evolving that Gerrard had already bypassed the Bulgarian influence, and Perry was less intent on ceremonial settings than mining folk music of the very distant past. There were hallmarks of the band's own past with Perry's 'Black Sun' and Gerrard's 'The Promised Womb', but 'Radharc' had Middle Eastern strings and much of the album reflected their new locations. 'Saltarello' and 'Song Of The Sybil' were respective covers of a fourteenth-century Italian instrumental and a sixteenth-century Catalan ballad, while Perry sang 'Fortune Presents Gifts Not According To The Book' with lyrics by seventeenth-century baroque poet Luis de Góngora. That Gerrard sang the traditional Gaelic ballad 'As The Bell Rings The Maypole Spins' showed that each of the pair was willing to cross into the other's spiritual comfort zone.

To complete the historical mood, the cover of *Aion* was a small section of the triptych *The Garden Of Earthly Delights* by sixteenth-century Dutch painter Hieronymus Bosch. It was taken from the earth section, flanked by representations of Eden and hell. If Perry and Gerrard sang separately, Dead Can Dance was still a shared voyage, and Perry's chosen image was the 'flower' of a plant in the shape of a transparent bubble. The naked couple inside, says Perry, 'reminded me of myself and Lisa transported back to the past in a kind of alchemical, alembic time machine'.

Aion's cover was also the first time that Perry had relented his artistic autonomy. Despite his claims that Dead Can Dance would rather leave 4AD than surrender total artistic control, Ivo says that he rejected outright Gerrard's primitive pencil drawing of an angel. Perry says he can't remember the image, or that, as Ivo recalls, he was furious. 'I'd have been embarrassed for that [drawing] to exist on any record,' Ivo says. 'Probably within a day, they'd picked the Bosch image.'

Artwork had been the only hiccup in the relationship between Dead Can Dance and 4AD; otherwise it had been a total and unified joy. But Ivo's next signing was the label's most co-operative venture of them all, offering Vaughan Oliver complete freedom, and Ivo the chance to take a creative role beyond This Mortal Coil, within the context of a similarly cinemascopic sound.

Warren Defever was born to Canadian parents in Livonia, a small suburb of Detroit, Michigan. His grandfather was a musician who had taught Defever and his brothers not only guitar but bass, slide guitar, banjo, accordion, saxophone and fiddle. The Defevers had subsequently worked up a repertoire of polkas, waltzes, country and western and Fifties pop, to which Warren added Fifties rock'n'roll and rockabilly. 'And then I heard punk rock. WOW.'

Defever also chooses to communicate by email. Much like Ian Masters and his backwards-written postcards, Defever would often send haikus. Taking the name of His Name Is Alive, his music was similarly infused with both darkly ruminative and distinctly playful trails. As a teenager, he recalls a litany of lonesome yet comforting voices that would float, like apparitions, from his radio, the kind of anguished beauty that had bewitched David Lynch, such as Roy Orbison and Bobby Vinton, whose crooned 'Blue Velvet' had given Lynch the title of his film.

Over the years, Defever writes, he has specialised in what he describes as a kind of interior music. 'I used to listen to music primarily with headphones because my father worked nights and would often sleep during the day,' he explains. 'I wasn't going to parties or school dances, so things developed on a very personal level. I think I probably got into "weird sounds" from that. Eyes closed, headphones on – anything can happen.'

His Name Is Alive's interior world of electro-acoustic, digi-organic fusions was topped with exactly the same kind of towering female vocal that Ivo had used on *Filigree & Shadow*. Unsurprisingly, 4AD had been a strong influence on Defever. He was fifteen when he bought Cocteau Twins' *Aikea-Guinea* just because of the cover: 'But it sounded so good, so different from anything I'd heard before. I tracked down *The Pink Opaque* and other 4AD records. They were so mysterious and weird, as were the covers. Instead of telling a story, they were vague enough that the listener could fill in the blanks with their own experiences, thoughts and feelings.' He singles out *Le Mystère Des Voix Bulgares*, *Sleeps With The Fishes* and 'Song To The Siren'. 'Twenty-five years later, they still seem just as important, inspirational, bewildering and mystifying.'

His Name Is Alive's very first tracks were recorded with vocalist Karin Oliver, released on a cassette that Defever sold locally and also posted to 4AD under the hand-scrawled title '*I Had Sex With God*'. In contrast to the usual demos Ivo received, this was a bolt out of the blue. 'I enjoyed the simplicity, and the prettiness of Karin's voice offset against some crazy guitar playing,' Ivo recalls. 'It was very rough and done quickly.'

Once again, Ivo contacted its maker to say that he'd enjoyed the tape, but wasn't looking to get involved. 'Then a week later, another version of all the songs turned up. Warren did that for a third time! Each time he remixed them, the structure became more abstract until he finally went too far. Eventually I asked if I could mix it myself. I thought I could make it sound better, to stop this deconstruction.'

Defever blames his obsessive behaviour on circumstances. 'Karin lived in Ypsilanti, about 40 minutes' drive away, and she didn't have a car, so it was a big deal to get her over. I'd rather work on the same song than write new ones, just so I could hear her sing.'

Defever says no specific contract was discussed with Ivo in advance, adding, 'other than being gently reassured that if I was uncomfortable with anything, I could pull out'. He says it seemed like a dream come true, especially as Defever's only previous experience had been with an American label: '[Their] every interaction devolved into shady dealings and outright deceit. It was also very promising to work with a label [4AD] that I enjoyed and respected.'

Shaped by Ivo and John Fryer's mixes, His Name Is Alive's 4AD album debut *Livonia* was a perfect marriage of Karin Oliver's pure, precise tone, Defever's feverish constructions and Ivo's 'golden ear'. Defever says, 'He took these incoherent ramblings and musical jibber-jabber and fixed them up, polished them and helped put them in a place where people might be interested.'

Ivo was equally pleased. '*Livonia* and the second His Name Is Alive album sit just below This Mortal Coil in terms of how close I feel to them, because of how I could affect the way they sounded, what tracks to include and in which order. Warren was abnormally generous to let me do all of that.'

Ivo told Defever that *Livonia* would be a 'sleeper', in the style of Nooten and Brooks' *Sleeps With The Fishes*. But 4AD exported more copies of *Livonia* than any other 4AD debut, 'and without an American licensee,' Ivo adds. 'It's an illustration of where 4AD was as a label, for which huge credit has to go to Sheri Hood who'd represented us in the States at college radio and retail for the previous four years. We'd been Label of the Year in the *College Music Journal* for years, and people continued to trust our releases because they were on 4AD.'

Defever only travelled to London to meet the 4AD team after *Livonia* had been released. He found the shaved heads the only weird or cultish thing about the office. 'I sometimes stayed in the little apartment above the office, and at Ivo's place,' he says. 'But if I'd been there a few days, someone would let me know I had to move on. Ivo seemed to need a lot of privacy and alone time. But whenever I was in London, he'd put money in my pocket and he'd take me to unbeliev-able concerts, like Philip Glass doing a live *Koyaanisqatsi*. We saw Indonesian gamelan, Slowdive, Lush.'

Few people were allowed inside Ivo's private space, which showed how comfortable Ivo felt about Defever. At Ivo's flat in Balham, Defever recalls, 'A grapefruit-sized lump of hash by the bedside. Ivo caught me staring at this enormous shiny brown ball and admitted, "My music is drug inspired". Later, he explained that all his decisions were made while super-high and the next day in the office, no matter how ridiculous they seemed when sober, he'd stick by them.'

Ivo finds Defever's memory more amusing than accurate. 'Warren is writing the way it felt for him. I'd never owned a piece of hash that size! But as to the final approval of a mix after smoking a joint, the track always later sounded as good as when I'd made that decision.'

Ivo's kinship with Defever was starkly contrasted by his ongoing relationship with Charles Thompson, who was keeping his distance from most everyone at the label, and in the band. It turned out that Kim Deal had very nearly not been included on Pixies' third album – was this why Thompson had been so supportive of her alternative career?

Deal had found she was the only Pixie left on the east coast, and after her (amicable) divorce from John Murphy, she found no reason to stay in Boston, and so moved back to Dayton, Ohio. She had enquired about the next round of band rehearsals, only, she says, to be told by Thompson, '"I don't want you there". I was so confused. There'd never been any talk about them wanting to do something different, or not wanting me in the band.'

It was another glaring example of the seemingly preferred strategy among 4AD associates of avoiding communication and confrontation. When Deborah Edgely heard from a panic-stricken Deal, she told the bassist to immediately get on a plane to LA. 'It hadn't occurred to me,' Deal says. 'Even Ken [Goes] had flown out there, so it had to be a big deal. I arrived to find a meeting in the lawyer's office. I don't think they said it was to fire me, but more to air stuff. They said that they hadn't given me a warning, so they were going to give me another chance, and I just burst into tears. It didn't matter if they were just or right, or how they went about it – all that mattered was they were in agreement, so it must be right. What assholes! Joey and David have since apologised.'

Deal's surprise appearance ensured that any real confrontation would be avoided. SNAFU, in other words: Situation Normal, All Fucked Up. 'David Lee Roth once said, "Two words will ruin a band – band meeting", says Santiago. 'The problem was, we'd toured so much and so quickly after we formed that we never really gelled as a unit. We might go to a bar after practice but then we'd quickly move on. And we'd always brush stuff under the rug. Man, there was a lot of shit under that rug, and I thought it might explode one day.'

Pixies had settled into recording in Los Angeles with Gil Norton. If there was a time for Pixies to explode, it was now. After being on his solo tour, Thompson had far less prepared material than usual, and in addition, Santiago recalls, 'Charles felt more pressure because *Doolittle* had been so popular. People wanted another goddamn "Monkey's Gone To Heaven".'

In a roundabout fashion, one of those people was Ivo. Thompson recalls playing him some new guitar riffs, and Ivo responding by asking, 'Can you write some anthemic songs?' Rather than be insulted, Thompson says, 'I got a kick out of it. I don't think Ivo was trying to get us to sell out; he just wanted us to capture the ear of the audience. He was good at not meddling and he trained me well because I've never accepted any meddling since from anyone. You'd hear other bands talk about how the label made them do this or that, but why let them? Tell them to fuck off, or tear up the contract.'

This was Ivo's only attempt at A&R; the rest had to be left up to the producer. Santiago says that Gil Norton's expertise was called on during the making of the album, meddling with only the best inten-tions: 'Gil's a great producer and arranger, but a great psychologist too. He knew the band's psyche like no one else: the singer, the girl in the band, all that stuff. He'd say, "Let's just make a record, please".'

It was no surprise that *Bossanova* felt like a backwards step after *Doolittle*. Thompson admits that writing music and lyrics 'sometimes five minutes before they were recorded' wasn't a way to guarantee brilliance, while Santiago says Pixies had only rehearsed for two weeks instead of the regular practices they had when they all lived in the same city. There was no new equivalent to 'Monkey's Gone To Heaven' either, though 'Velouria' was conceivably another 'Here Comes Your Man'. *Bossanova* included the first cover on a Pixies album: the instrumental 'Cecilia Ann' (originally by the Sixties California surf band The Surftones), which opened the album with an adrenalin burst prolonged by the following song, 'Rock Music'. 'Is She Weird' and 'The Happening' helped make *Bossanova* one of the era's most compelling, fiery rock records. But the likes of 'Blown Away' and 'Hang Wire' showed Thompson was now also writing by numbers.

Perhaps the whole band was tired of the rigmarole. Even the artwork – a Simon Larbalestier photo of a Saturn-like globe – was far less intriguing than previous Pixies artwork, though you could wonder which band member was represented by the four little drop-ins – a doll, a frog, a mole and a piece of barbed wire. The band's real faces were in the CD booklet, but the beautiful portrait of that gorgeously grinning Kim Deal was a mere cover-up to those in the know. Once again, she had no lead vocal, and no writing credit.

Pixies would have had a profound impact on modern rock music, yet *Doolittle* only reached 98 in the Billboard chart, and *Bossanova* only reached 70. The two singles, 'Velouria' and the relatively average 'Dig For Fire', only reached 4 and 11 respectively on Billboard's Modern Rock chart. Dave Lovering thinks Elektra was to blame: 'They dropped the ball as far as promotion went,' he claims. 'The A&R guy, Peter Lubin, had vision but not compared to 4AD. It was no hardship but we just didn't catch on in America.'

An example of Charles Thompson's vision was the unique, though prohibitively expensive video for 'Dig For Fire'. In a pronounced satire of sexiness, the band were shown getting dressed in combinations of leather before being driven on motorbikes by Hells Angels to an empty football stadium (in the Netherlands) where they performed a live version of 77-second *Bossanova* cut 'Alison'.

If Thompson didn't appear to respond productively to tension, Cocteau Twins certainly did, judging by how the trio responded to the continuing pressure of moving into a new studio and continuing to write while having Robin Guthrie and Elizabeth Fraser's baby Lucy Belle on the scene. Like Ivo, Robin Guthrie appeared to be making creative decisions while high, and whatever state the guitarist was in hadn't harmed his creativity. In early 1990, the band had moved from their Acton warehouse to leasing the first floor (and later, the whole studio) of a beautiful building owned by The Who's Pete Townshend, overlooking the Thames by Richmond Lock.

'It was like a rock star's paradise, with a thousand-square-foot balcony,' Simon Raymonde recalls. 'The only problem was that it was seriously expensive. But we justified that by reckoning that we'd have paid the same with album advances if we were to use another studio.'

Townshend had named the studio Eel Pie after the nearby islet that could be seen from the balcony, though the Cocteaus re-christened it September Sound, after the month that Lucy Belle had been born in 1989. In their new plush surrounds, a new album had been started, whose sound was clearly influenced by the joy and release felt by the couple at having their first child, but Simon Raymonde recalls that it wasn't all sweetness and light given the effect Guthrie's continued drug-taking was having. Fraser named the album *Heaven Or Las Vegas*, a suggestion of music versus commerce, or perhaps a gamble, one last throw of the dice. 'It was a great, very symbolic title,' says Guthrie.

'I think the act of giving birth and becoming a woman, of having her daughter, can be heard in Liz's vocals and lyrics,' says Raymonde. 'There was salvation in there too, in terms of helping save her relationship with Robin, the joy of bringing a baby into the world that they could love. It did give them a new lease of life, and it gave the album an energy and vibrancy. But my dad had passed away very soon after Lucy was born: I wrote the piano part to "Frou-Frou Foxes In Midsummer Fires" the day after he died, so writing songs about birth, and also death, gave the record a darker side that I hear in songs like "Cherry Coloured Funk" and "Fotzepolitic". It was an inspirational time to be in the studio, and an absolute joy to make that album, but Robin deteriorated afterwards. Maybe being a father was a responsibility he found hard to handle. But, of course, we never talked about it.'

'Robin was very good at hiding his insecurities,' says his old Grangemouth pal Colin Wallace, who knew Guthrie well enough to judge. 'He was doing more and more drugs when Lucy came along. I remember one time, he wouldn't come home from the studio, and Elizabeth had to send a taxi, even though Robin was 500 yards from the house.'

Guthrie admits he had become paranoid: 'I got security cameras fitted so I could sit all night watching to see who was coming in and out of the building. I was so fucking high, I wouldn't even let Simon in the studio. That's coke for you. I played half the bass on that album, though Simon brought an awful lot in terms of melody and piano, and he expanded what we were doing musically.'

Raymonde remembers 'a wild old time, a legendary session' with Echo & The Bunnymen singer Ian McCulloch in regular attendance due to recording his first solo album *Candleland* at September Sound (Guthrie wasn't producing, but Elizabeth Fraser guested on the title track). 'We were hanging out with some of the greatest British music hedonists,' says Wallace. 'Pete Wylie, Mal from Cabaret Voltaire, Jim Thirlwell, Shane MacGowan. A lot of people came and went.'

Raymonde: 'Robin was taking several grams of coke a day. It was all he lived for. Liz was looking after Lucy Belle. It was very hard being part of the band at that point. It affected the relationship with my wife too. I felt torn, between my own marriage and this other relationship. I didn't want to abandon either. But in hindsight, I spent too much time trying to heal the band.'

Guthrie: 'I was in a very dark place. I didn't party with cocaine; I was a drug addict and I was slowly killing myself. Things got progressively worse from *Victorialand* onwards. I was in a successful band, touring around the world and, on paper, I should have been happy. But I was tormented by this need. Years later, after I'd gone to rehab, I worked out what was making me so self-destructive, and working myself into the ground. I felt I had been fucked over, and whose fault was that [at the time]? Ivo. So I'd use more drugs, which would make things worse. It was a vicious circle.'

That Guthrie could subconsciously heap all the blame for his deterioration on Ivo showed how the relationship had plummeted. But then Guthrie was estranged from everyone. Raymonde says he was a relative outsider since managing to stem his own daily drug-taking. 'I didn't like what I'd become, miserable and depressed about things, and all the arguments,' he says. 'That affected our relationship, because those who keep taking drugs, like Robin, feel they're being judged by you not doing them.'

It seems impossible that an album as magical and timeless as *Heaven Or Las Vegas* transcended all the strife. Fraser's luscious, dreamy hooks even came with odd articulated words – a baby had freed her from her self-imposed interior prison of what could be regarded as a baby language in itself. On record anyway, Cocteau Twins was united, even healed, by the experience. In August, the album had been followed, rather than preceded, by its most obvious, upbeat track, the ecstatic 'Iceblink Luck'. *Heaven Or Las Vegas* followed in September.

Guthrie prefers *Head Over Heels* and *Victorialand*, 'for emotional reasons', but he knows why fan forums think *Heaven Or Las Vegas* is Cocteau Twins' finest hour. 'I was showing off, to people who'd written us off as some unintelligible, ethereal and weird art rock. And it was evolution. A lot fell into place, like our relationship with Simon had matured, and we'd got better at recording. I know drugs made it slower to make, but *Heaven Or Las Vegas* was made despite the drugs.'

Not only does Ivo say it's his favourite Cocteaus album, but his all-time 4AD album – 'by a long shot,' he says. 'It's a perfect record.' And yet what personal memories come attached with it. It would be the last Cocteaus album on 4AD after Ivo kicked them off the label in October.

By which time, he was also no longer in a relationship with Deborah Edgely.

Ivo: 'In 1979, I had been given the opportunity to start a record label. A decade later, I was running a record company and I'd always hated record companies. I might have been good at certain aspects of it but I found it really hard, and the pressure was building. An earlier collapse, or a breakdown, was probably prevented because of splitting up with Deb. I very quickly fell in love with someone else, which saved me through this crazy period.'

Like Ivo, Edgely is understandably wary of discussing the end of a six-year relationship, not just romantically but the effect on her working life too, having shared with Ivo, on a daily basis, the highs of friendships and music, and equally united when it came to handling the lows when it was necessary. But enough time has passed, and Edgely is now comfortably settled with her partner and their two sons.

She admits that children had been 'the fundamental flaw' – she wanted them, Ivo didn't – and being together 24 hours meant no release. 'It was too painful to get out but too painful to stay, and I dragged things on far longer than I should have,' she recalls. 'When it did end, it felt so catatonic and raw that I had a breakdown and went home to my parents for six months.'

Ivo had hidden his depressive tendencies from his closest ally, and though Edgely finds it hard to blame the mental condition rather than the man, she acknowledges his troubles with a degree of equanimity. 'He had to be tough and deal with those people annoyed or frustrated by his responses, but he wouldn't waver once he'd made a decision,' she says. 'And he was being pulled in all different directions. It took its toll, but not just on him. He never gave much out of himself – a lot of bands probably didn't know him at all, because he didn't let them in. But from what I knew of his background, he was prone to an insular, self-obsessed world due to his family, all the reasons he's ended up the person he is.'

Guthrie and Fraser were equally in a daily bind, even more so after having a child. 'We were very much an entity, but it was a very personally disruptive relationship, working and living together, like two concentric circles,' says Guthrie. 'But that's another story.'

Under all sorts of stress, Guthrie's behaviour had reached breaking point. 'Robin would go AWOL a lot of the time,' recalls Simon Harper. 'When he was clean, he was the nicest guy, with a fantastic, friendly twinkle in his eye. When he was using [drugs], he was a pain in the arse for everyone. *Heaven Or Las Vegas* was a fantastic record, one of their most colourful, and commercial, but once they'd given birth to it and they had to do the promotion and all that entails, that's when it fell apart.'

One witness to Guthrie's mood swings was journalist John Best, who had forged a working friendship with Ivo. 'I used to be in thrall to 4AD,' Best admits. 'All the main indie labels in the UK had a very strong and different aesthetic, dominated by one well-educated, early-to-middle-aged man, but 4AD had a particularly original and hermitically watertight aesthetic that became the template for many imitators, and 23 Envelope had clearly thought about everything. Ivo was a decade older than me, and into pre-punk stuff that I knew nothing about. This Mortal Coil was like an education, with Pixies bringing something completely different, which 4AD managed to bring into the fold very effectively.'

In January 1990, Best had changed tack and started his own PR company, Best In Press. Ivo hired him to run 4AD's press department while Edgely was away. Once on board, he started dating, and living with, Miki Berenyi of Lush (the band's drummer Chris Acland was their flatmate). Best also spent time with Pixies after *Bossanova* was released. 'I didn't see any rows but I didn't see any warmth either,' he recalls. Then there was Ivo's apparent lack of warmth. 'He could be so undiplomatic when it came to artists, but he was very straight up, and it was useful for both sides if someone did speak their mind. I learnt from Ivo not to be mealy-mouthed around people.'

Best also recalls Kristin Hersh, 'very unhappy, in bits, crying after an interview'. But the most searing memory of his tenure at 4AD was of a Cocteau Twins press trip, where *Melody Maker* had flown to Las Vegas to write a cover story. 'Robin came over and said, "What are you doing here, to do press? What fucking press? No one told me", and walked off. Liz said, "I can't talk to him, you have to". Their manager wasn't around either. Robin then agreed to do the interview after the show. Well, Robin hated the show and then said he wouldn't do it. At 1am, he finally said, "I'll do it if you give me $200", so I did – we'd spent thousands so far anyway! Robin was such a difficult client. He could be affable, and funny, but also bitingly harsh.'

It was another press interview that finally forced Ivo's hand, even though the Cocteau Twins' contract stipulated that the band owed 4AD three more albums. 'Everybody had seen Robin rip someone to shreds with words,' Ivo recalls. 'He didn't mention Deborah by name, but his comment in an interview was obviously about her, and it was just unacceptable.'

A meeting was quickly called at 4AD's lawyers between Martin Mills, Raymond Coffer and Ivo, who told the Cocteaus' manager of his decision. 'I can still see Coffer trying to stop himself from smiling,' Ivo grimaces, 'because he knew he could now go and get a load of money off a major label for the band.'

Simon Harper: 'Friendship-versus-work can be a cloudy entity, and Ivo and Cocteau Twins' personal and business relationship suffered. With all fairness to Ray Coffer, he tried to make the best of a bad lot. But it was an ironic own goal to hire Ray, who totally misunderstood the relationship between Ivo and Cocteau Twins and their true personalities, and he furthered the band's perceived feeling of aliena-tion, in part due to the fact that he'd barrel into meetings with an appallingly misguided sense of optimism about what he'd get his artists to do, regarding touring and promotion. He was trying to twist their arms into doing what he wanted them to do and not asking what they wanted.'

Guthrie: 'On many occasions, Ivo made the right call, but he made a bad call on letting us go. We could have gone on indefinitely if he'd approached things differently. But he was so uninterested in us by then. We'd been so close before. We'd go on holiday together, to shows, we lived with him for months, and he let that all go because he got into something else.'

Guthrie also insists that denying v23 the chance to design the *Heaven Or Las Vegas* cover (Paul West again took over) contributed to the problem. 'That was wrong in Ivo's eyes. That was me undermining his label. I know others didn't use Vaughan but they hadn't been mentored like we had. I think Ivo had given us so much that we had a sort of debt to him. As we slowly, but surely, grew in confidence and focus, he moved on to the next people he could play God with.'

One step removed, Simon Harper could see the problem: 'It's going to be tricky when a label is presented with young American bands who are so excited to be in Europe, and so optimistic with what they can achieve, to play music and be in such a lucky position. If I were a British band, I'd feel confused and possibly hurt, and scratch my head – are we doing something wrong, does the label not care? A huge factor was that Robin was a drug addict, and with that comes the consequences of addiction.'

'When I heard they'd parted company with 4AD, I was so shocked,' says Colin Wallace. 'Ivo and Robin weren't even talking by then. Maybe both sides were as stubborn as the other.'

In November, Cocteau Twins were on tour, and Ivo decided he would attend the London show at The Town & Country Club; after all, he still loved the band's music and felt a deep attachment. 'Over the years,' he recalls, 'there'd been a gaggle of extraordinarily dedicated Cocteaus fans who attended every gig. At the Town & Country, I was approached by a pair of them, who said, "Hi, Ivo, how are you, how are Robin and Liz, how's Lucy?" And then they realised I couldn't answer their questions. I hadn't been involved in their lives for a couple of years. When the band started the first song, I had to leave, in tears. I felt I was living a lie. Here was this group that had meant the world to me – it demonstrates my love for their music because I remained pretty oblivious to the extent of Robin's apparent longstanding mistrust of me for such a long time. They should've just come to me, called me a cunt and said they never wanted to work with me again. Now I was just this record company person that they didn't get on with anymore, and that was not why I'd got involved with them, or with the business of music.'

Ivo baulks at the suggestion he could have approached them: 'It might involve talking about feelings! I'd had to have had a bucketload of group therapy in order to do that. But it's absurd to think now about the what-ifs.'

In the context of the split, the title of 4AD's subsequent release was just too ironic – Lush's new single 'Sweetness And Light'. Guthrie had not been involved, with Tim Friese-Greene, the producer of (and collaborator with) the rarefied and elegant Talk Talk, taking charge. 'We were so un-formed that we thought it would be good to try something else, to not get entrenched in one direction,' Miki Berenyi explains. 'And Tim had a different perspective.'

Friese-Greene was even more of a perfectionist than Guthrie, and spent six weeks with Lush recording just three tracks. 'Robin had such a clear, sharp sound whereas Tim's was more nebulous and suffered in comparison,' Berenyi concludes. 'But I'm glad we had the experience.'

Ivo wasn't so sure. 'I loved Talk Talk's space and clarity, but "Sweetness And Light" sounded thin, distant and woolly, and so unrepresentative of Lush's live sound. Yet it was a fantastic song, and the record served its purpose by accelerating the band's popularity.'

A debut album would have sped up the process, but Lush was still lagging well behind Pale Saints, whose own album debut was almost a year old, with a new four-track EP ready to go. The difference between the album and *Half-Life* was the contribution of former Lush member Meriel Barham. Pale Saints needed a permanent second guitarist for live shows, and Berenyi, still feeling guilty over sacking Barham, 'busted a gut' to introduce her to Pale Saints: 'I told them, she can sing, she can play, she can write!'

Ian Masters: 'Meriel fitted in perfectly. We weren't that proficient, and she was as able as any of us. She was a good songwriter too and she made it less of a lads' band.'

The daughter of an armed serviceman, Barham had been born in Yorkshire and raised in Yemen, Singapore and Germany. She doesn't recall any early musical epiphany, but says, 'After I drifted in my late teens and early twenties, one day I heard myself announce to my mum that I was going to make music and that was absolutely what I wanted to do. My first song "Skin" was on the first Lush demo.' She says Pale Saints was a better fit: 'Guitar had always been my musical form of expression rather than vocals, so it was a natural move. I doodled experimental guitar-constructed soundscapes purely for enjoyment.'

Lush did eventually release an album, in December, but *Gala* was only a compilation of all their releases to date, plus the 'Hey Hey

Helen' cover and an extended version of 'Scarlet'. The album had been assembled for Warners subsidiary Reprise, whose A&R man Tim Carr had fallen heavily for Lush and set up a licensing deal.

Carr had also been involved in Cocteau Twins' licensing deal by helping overcome Reprise's traditional demand to own the global rights for an artist. 'Before, 4AD had been just another label to me: I hadn't got what it was all about,' Carr admits. 'But I flew Robin and Liz over to America, and I met Ivo too. It was like meeting the Samuel Beckett of the music industry – tall, gaunt, and the opposite of our goofy dress sense and too much hair mousse. And Cocteau Twins gave me chills each time I heard them. It was also a way to compete with Seymour Stein at Sire who was bringing everything else over from the UK. And I'd wanted to sign Throwing Muses but every record that mattered seemed to be on Sire.'

Ivo had been wary as he suspected Carr and/or fellow A&R source Claudia Stanton would leave Capitol long before Cocteau Twins ever left the label: 'Otherwise Ivo said that he would just be signing with the building,' says Carr. 'He never acted like he was my friend, and he was always distrustful of America, the Madison Avenue business guys on the other side of the world. People thought Capitol was too big and monolithic.'

While Carr was on holiday in Thailand, Capitol did indeed have a major staff reshuffle, and after an extended absence, Carr returned and began working for Reprise. Warner's head of creative services, Steven Baker, asked Carr if he was going to sign Lush, but Carr admits he hadn't then heard of the band. 'In my time away, I'd lost contact with everything, so I flew to England to see Lush play Glastonbury, and drove up with Howard Gough to see them in Leeds. I wanted to sign Pale Saints too. I flew Lush and Ivo to LA to meet Warners, which was a real record label, run by real music people, and it was the first time Ivo had met American label people he said he could trust.

'After that, I was forever in England trying to license bands. On Beggars Banquet's side of Alma Road, Martin [Mills] sat among a stack of albums higher than his head, like a college newspaper, and two doors over at 4AD, it was pristine, like a monk's quarters –

incredibly white, polished wood, and only Vaughan's art on the walls. Everything was as clean and crisp and quixotic as their record covers.'

To onlookers, 4AD would have resembled a cohesive, composed, forward-moving operation, with an immediately identifiable image, rounded off by the wonder of *Heaven Or Las Vegas*. But insiders knew of the ructions that had seen the album's creators, the label's original flagship band, depart, and the new American vanguard, Pixies, dangerously divided. Yet out of ashes, phoenixes rise. With Ivo already in a new relationship and the shadow cast by Robin Guthrie now removed, there was a chance of a new era, personally and profession-ally, and an outbreak of renewed peace and happiness might reign again.

15 1991

FOOL THE WORLD
(bad1001-cad1017)

In Ivo's mind, the turning point of his disillusionment was discovering that running a record label had evolved into running a record
company. But 4AD was unable to release music in a vacuum. There
was the nature of relationships – between artist and label, artist and
manager, label and manager, between band members, everyone with
their own agenda, and complicated by the lure of filthy lucre. Money
didn't have to ruin everything: it could help move an artist out of a
squat, or build their own studio for greater independence, or buy time
to write and make the perfect record. However, in the independent
music sector, where principles were treated as part of the art, and the
business, money was often a corrupting force.

Outside of the hot house of egos, ambition and self-esteem issues,
larger cultural and technological changes were afoot. Ecstasy and the
less quantifiable desire for something more hedonistic and escapist
after the often-bruising Eighties saw a new generation turn to clubbing as well as gigs. Sampling and the art of the remix attended to the
needs of that crowd, while in America, grunge was providing a head-
banging kind of freedom. The climate of 1991 was unrecognisable
from that of, say, 1981, when 4AD could almost operate without such
considerations, or even 1986 when Throwing Muses had first emerged.

The band was trying to steer a path that was as open, authentic and artistic, and the relationship between band and 4AD was uncomplicated and mutually beneficial. Yet in almost every other department, Kristin Hersh was struggling. The custody case over her son Dylan had forced her to share parental duties with his father, and her fevered mood swings had finally been diagnosed as bipolar disorder.

At least the business end was in better shape. The band had separated from manager Ken Goes after they'd suggested he handle the contractual side while Billy O'Connell act as the 'people person'. 'Ken was socially strange,' says David Narcizo, 'whereas Billy could sell you your own shoes. Ken freaked out when we suggested it. We weren't sad to see him go.' Part of the agreement was that the band couldn't talk freely about Goes, who continued to manage Pixies.

They were much sadder to accept Leslie Langston's resignation. 'Leslie didn't pursue the band as much as the rest of us, so it wasn't a huge surprise,' says Narcizo. Fred Abong, a friend in Newport, took over on bass, and joined the Muses in LA to record the band's fourth album. Pixies was recording *Bossanova* in a nearby studio, and both bands stayed at the same apartment complex, swapping stories by the pool.

Perhaps the Californian heat was wilting these east coast kids, because as *Bossanova* was relatively undercooked, so was Throwing Muses' *The Real Ramona*. While Pixies had settled down with Gil Norton, the Muses had been trying out yet another producer. On paper at least, Dennis Herring had seemed a good fit, having worked with folk-punk renegades Camper Van Beethoven.

'I was trying to make a record with this evil producer and I swear Warners was trying to break up my band, telling me we needed Eighties drum sounds, even though this was the Nineties!' says Hersh. 'I didn't even like them in the Eighties! Some guitar sounds got changed too. I love a lot of those songs but they were so flat without their sharp edges. I felt like I was sleepwalking, until I didn't want any part of the band any longer.'

'Red Shoes', 'Hook In Her Head', 'Two Step' and Tanya Donelly's 'Honeychain' were fine songs given a solid, unexceptional sound.

Punchy lead single 'Counting Backwards' had the right momentum to match the way Hersh's head would sway from side to side, steely eyes forward, as she sang on stage. Even when Hersh was melodically direct, serving up pizzas, Donelly was mining something sweeter, more like cookies. Her second *Ramona* song 'Not Too Soon' had a distinct Sixties Spector backbeat with a chorus that had been donated by, of all people, Hersh's dad Dude. 'Tanya wanted a hit,' says Hersh. 'And I was holding her back.'

'Not Too Soon' was the campaign's second single; it couldn't have been more radio-friendly, but it wasn't even a small hit. 'Pump Up The Volume' had proved that 4AD could physically shift units, and theoretically many more people were now aware of the label; they even had a committed radio plugger. So why did so many 4AD singles undersell? Perception counts for a lot, and 4AD's carefully cultivated, curated image was the 'manic depressive Motown', as *Sounds* put it, the 'by-word for melancholia' Singles, as Motown boss Berry Gordy knew, were generally upbeat and celebratory missions to thrill, to make your feet move. 4AD was simply an albums label, serious and artful, and even if Pixies made great singles, Ivo tended to sign artists who didn't practise the art of the standalone single; the lack of radio support seemed to say as much. Nothing 4AD released as a single after 'Pearly-Dewdrops' Drops' was destined to stir the same interest as its long players.

Hersh was really against the idea of a blatant commercial lunge: 'I'd rather be dead than suck in order to get a million people to listen to you,' she says. It meant that Donelly's 'Gepetto', her most gleefully charged melody yet, hadn't even been recorded for *Ramona*. 'Kristin couldn't tolerate it,' says Ivo. 'That was the final straw for Tanya, so she started making her own demos.'

'The only person I'd really talk to was Ivo,' says Hersh, 'He said, "Don't you think Throwing Muses is essentially you and Dave?" Yup, but it didn't matter. So we took time off. Dave got a day job, Billy was bartending, and I got pregnant again. Tanya was the only one who was still attracted to the music business. She knew my relationship to music was very intense, and it was obvious I had no place in the world of pop. First and foremost, she and I are friends and sisters, so we'd spend time playing with the baby instead of being in a band together, and I walked away from all the garbage.'

Donelly knew it was the right decision. 'Dennis Herring told me that when Kristin or I were in the studio individually, things were very musical, but together, we totally sucked the music out! Being sisters, we were so careful with each other that things had become almost static. Once the tension went, things were fine and the next Muses tour was one of the happiest, because I knew it was over. Only after the fact did I realise what a rare situation we had as a band, with the kind of joy that we shared.'

Leslie Langston was recording demos too, which Ivo says were reggae-fied, and not something he wanted to pursue, 'even though I believed she was the most natural, individual bassist I'd ever heard'. But Langston was all over 4AD's next album – from The Wolfgang Press. As usual now, a new Wolfies album sounded more accessible and open; once they'd been closed off, now they had eleven guests, such as Dif Juz drummer Richie Thomas, chipping in. Langston was the most involved of all, playing keyboards on top of bass and co-writing 'Fakes And Liars'. Mark Cox says Langston nearly joined full-time, 'but we had this impenetrable funny-old-mates thing going on. I also think Leslie wanted a more equal contribution, which she hadn't experienced with Kristin.'

But the greatest change was the use of computers and samples organised by producer Drostan Madden and programmer Rew. The key was the recent album *3 Feet High And Rising* by the free-flowing American rappers De La Soul, whose 'daisy age' sound was the antithesis of angry old Wolfgang Press, but which the band had listened to relentlessly. 'Honey Tree', patched with the synth mantra from the opening of Kraftwerk's 'Europe Endless', sounded light on its feet – happy even. 'We were conscious of the darkness that we can put across to others, and being seen as po-faced, so we wanted people to realise that we made music because we loved making music,' says Mick Allen.

But Allen's choice of album title – *Queer* – showed that he didn't think for a moment of changing face. He says he meant it in the original sense of the word, but he knew the double meaning. 'Back then, queer was still an insult,' says Cox. 'Over dinner, Claudia Stanton from Capitol had told Mick that the most offensive thing you could say in America was "cunt", so he started saying cunt all the time. The more I complained, the more he'd say it. His view was that if you're going to take offence, look at yourself first. One of Mick's enjoyable aspects was his love of contrary possibilities. He could say something, and then the opposite, both with the same total conviction.'

The Kraftwerk sample aside, *Queer* was The Wolfgang Press's New York album, from De La Soul's influence to the presence of street-smart singer/poet Annie 'Anxiety' Bandez (a starlet in her own right, she had recently married Dif Juz guitarist Dave Curtis) on 'The Birdie Song', and The Velvet Underground samples ('Waiting For The Man' and 'I'll Be Your Mirror') on 'Birmingham' (which more likely referenced the town in Alabama than the British city). It felt like three British men on a tooled-up trip to Manhattan, an aural sample of simmering tarmac, taxi horns and midnight games. *Queer* is both Cox and Gray's favourite Wolfgang Press album (Allen prefers the preceding *Bird Wood Cage*). 'We spent years figuring out how to realise our ideas, and finally captured them,' says Cox. Ivo agrees: 'They were finally making the music that they were hearing in their heads.'

Which made 'Time', a Martyn Young remix of the album track 'A Question Of Time', a strange choice for a single, sounding more like the old-fashioned, swarthy Wolfgang Press, with Andrew Gray's snaky 'Shaft'-style guitar and his old In Camera bandmate David Steiner's ominous snatches of spoken word. 'Time' turned out to be a taster as it was followed only six weeks later by the album's cover of American songwriter Randy Newman's 'Mama Told Me Not To Come'. The distance between the trio's stiff cover of 'Respect' and this lithe and funky version showed how far they'd come, and the way the team had made digital rhythms swing should have made Martyn Young envious.

Could Newman's classic paranoid fable be the crossover hit The Wolfgang Press needed, and deserved? After all, it had been a number

1 US single in 1970 for AOR giants Three Dog Night. It didn't even reach the UK top 75 for The Wolfgang Press, despite at least five 'Mama Told Me Not To Come' versions available, including one on the free limited edition twelve-inch of Martyn Young remixes packaged with *Queer*, which was partly motivated by Ivo's plan to coax Young back into working again. It sounded like he was having fun; his remix of 'Sucker' (on the album, more rhythmic grind than mellifluous melody) added a mammoth boom-box beat. But didn't Mick Allen dislike remixes? Maybe this was his contradictory nature in full flow. 'Time' had also been available in five versions. On top of the samples (unlike Colourbox and M/A/R/R/S, 4AD was now having to seek permission and pay up), this was both expensive and, frankly, a bit desperate, like a major label flogging its wares.

'With The Wolfgang Press, we clearly went with the method of launching a band with two singles and an expectation of hits,' says Ivo. 'At that point, the route to success was the indie charts and *The Chart Show* on TV, which could get you into the *real* charts. So we played the format game in case things took off. With Howard's TV and radio connections, there was a good chance we might get some exposure, but it was very half-hearted. I was in charge, so it was my fault.'

Ivo admits that The Wolfgang Press campaign was when he started to really not enjoy what 4AD was doing. 'We had the best of intentions, to expand the popularity of our friends and charges under long-term contracts. The singles and EPs we released were fantastic and stood up in their own right, but they were tools, and expensive tools at that. They weren't the artefact, the legacy, the work.'

In light of *Queer*'s influences, America could be a viable way out of the cul-de-sac that The Wolfgang Press were in at home. 4AD artists didn't have to sound American to see the opportunities in the world's largest marketplace. And with American labels feasting on 4AD with licensing deals, the structure was in place. But having artists with an increasing number of licensees was tricky to co-ordinate, from Capitol (Cocteau Twins) and Reprise (Lush) to Columbia (Ultra Vivid Scene), Elektra (Pixies) and Rough Trade America (The Breeders, The Wolfgang Press), as Sheri Hood had discovered. When offers came in to sign a licensing deal for the entire label, it was too good not to investigate first.

In a Mexican restaurant on West Pico Boulevard in Los Angeles, two British ex-pats sit reminiscing about their time representing 4AD in the USA. Both still sound as English as the day they swapped continents – Robin Hurley in the late Eighties, Chris Staley in the mid-Nineties.

Staley had been the first to join 4AD, in 1990. In 1986, he was working for British exporters Windsong. Mindful of Ivo's interest in Bulgarian voices, Staley had sent him some recordings of Russian choral singing, which Ivo had sampled for This Mortal Coil's 'Acid Bitter And Sad' and the pair had struck up a phone friendship. Staley was working at Mute when Ivo offered him a job, handling 4AD's video production, which quickly evolved into overall production duties, freeing up Ivo from liaising with The Cartel's hub of regional distributors.

Hurley had been running Nine Mile, the Midlands member of The Cartel. Ordering stock from 4AD, Hurley had also struck up a friendship with Ivo. In 1988, Hurley's business nous and even-tempered charm had made him the ideal candidate to launch Rough Trade's new US operation, first from San Francisco and then New York.

As the main instigator of UK independence, first with a shop, then a label and finally a distribution company, Geoff Travis at Rough Trade was a tireless pioneer. Like Ivo, Travis had found the business side tricky – and coping with the success and personal issues of its flagship band The Smiths was a full-time job in itself. Rough Trade was a much larger operation than 4AD too, and beset with financial worries. The cost of expanding into the States was draining resources from Rough Trade Inc, which had already written off £1m from a bad debt. A move to new London premises with a new and inefficient computer system costing £700,000 crippled them further, as did a sizeable tax bill that Rough Trade Germany was suddenly presented with.

At a crisis meeting at the suitably depressing site of a motorway service station, Cartel members were asked to use the company exclusively, but there was not enough faith in the operation; 4AD, among others, was also using The Cartel's rival Pinnacle for UK distribution. In 1991, The Cartel soon filed for bankruptcy, owing the likes of Mute and 4AD – the biggest creditors – a substantial amount of money. After the Mills–Austin court case, 4AD's survival was under threat again, but a financial arrangement with the auditors allowed the label to keep trading, and both 4AD and Mute were both eventually repaid by the company that took over, run by Pinnacle MD Steve Mason. Rough Trade America was one of the casualties. Robin Hurley was out of a job, but Ivo swiftly moved to ask him to run 4AD's US operation alongside Sheri Hood, because 4AD itself was going to sign a licensing deal.

As Ivo recalls, 'It was a nightmare working with different majors. Every time, you had to go through the process of explaining who, and what, 4AD was, and to dozens of people, all these departments within each major label, to ensure that things like the 4AD logo were on every press release or photo.'

'The Breeders never got any money for *Pod*,' recalls Kim Deal. 'We were told that the money Rough Trade America made [by licensing *Pod*] was reinvested in Butthole Surfers' [album] *piouhgd*, and then the label went bankrupt. When Robin [Hurley] joined 4AD, I asked if he was going to bankrupt this place too!'

One suitable licensee could end the time-consuming task of finding empathic partners for individual 4AD artists, letting Ivo get back to the role that suited him best: handling the music. But in terms of the diplomacy and the experience to guide 4AD to find the best label in the States, Ivo could see that Sheri Hood was not the right person. Enter Robin Hurley.

Hood knew Hurley from dealing with Rough Trade America; now they would be equals. Four months after Hurley joined, Hood quit. 'I'd seen Rough Trade step up to play the game, to be more visible by spending money, and I thought that wasn't the way to do things,' she says. 'Grass roots are still very important for artists. Also, I couldn't see a place for myself in the new 4AD set-up. I enjoyed working with the bands but I'd felt so much resistance from the majors.'

Ivo: 'Sheri had represented the label so fearlessly. The bands and 4AD were in safe hands with her when it came to aesthetic over exploitation. But this confused some people at the majors. She could be confrontational and did upset people, and herself, in the process. Like me, she wasn't cut out to explain herself to these people. Robin was far more pragmatic and flexible. And I needed someone who could get along with them.'

The main offer for 4AD came from Warners, driven by its new A&R man, former Capitol Records employee Tim Carr. 'I'd already fallen in love with Lush, and then Pale Saints,' he says, 'so I told Ivo, "You saw that I came after you with Cocteau Twins and Lush; have you thought of putting all your eggs in one basket?"'

Hurley met with every American major label, but Warners still proved to be the best option, with industry veterans Mo Ostin and Lenny Waronker at the helm. Ostin had run the esteemed Verve label, where he'd signed Ivo's beloved The Mothers of Invention as well as The Velvet Underground. Then Frank Sinatra had hired him to run Reprise where he worked with legends such as Ella Fitzgerald, Jimi Hendrix and Neil Young – a peerless CV. Waronker had produced numerous sessions with the likes of Randy Newman, Rickie Lee Jones and James Taylor, and had helped Ostin build Warners' reputation as a musician's label. R.E.M., for example, had chosen Warners for its first major label deal.

It also helped that the son of Warners' in-house producer Ted Templeman was a huge 4AD fan. Warners employees Steven Baker and Jeff Gold were equally committed fans, with Tim Carr the active cheerleader. Carr says he saw Warners president Waronker as the main draw for Ivo, and paints an image of a consummate music professional that put music first, like Ivo. 'Lenny wouldn't move while he was listening to a record,' Carr recalls. 'He'd have his head in his hands, and his eyes closed, tapping his foot, and he'd say, "Who's the artist in the group?" Ivo fell instantly in love with Lenny, and with me as the point man, 4AD could accept the deal.'

Ivo was also considering an offer from American Recordings, the label founded by Rick Rubin, the former co-founder of the pioneering rap label Def Jam. Rubin's current roster spanned Slayer, The Black Crowes and Andrew Dice Clay, which didn't seem to fit with 4AD, but Rubin's right-hand man Marc Geiger was a 4AD obsessive. American Recordings was also distributed by Warners, so as far as Geiger was concerned, 4AD would get the best of both worlds.

As a student, Geiger had run the independent record store Assorted Vinyl on the university campus in San Diego. He later became a booking agent for tour specialists Triad, snapping up New Order, Echo & The Bunnymen and The Smiths in their infancy, and had won huge respect from every UK independent for his knowledge, enthusiasm and efficiency.

Out of all of those labels, says Geiger, 4AD was his favourite. 'My tastes had dark sensibilities – I was a prog rock kid, which was very unfashionable at that time, and also of southern Californian goth, which was treated as a joke in Britain,' he explains. 'A lot of what Ivo did mixed up all of that. 4AD not only had the world's best A&R man, they had the best graphic artist in Vaughan. They held their ground over what they believed and they didn't follow any trend other than personal taste. Ivo saw things earlier than others, looked deep into the artists and the music. There were only three or four acts on 4AD that I didn't absolutely love. I didn't get His Name Is Alive, and maybe Pale Saints. But once you have that many goals or home runs, it's clear that the bands are incredible but that the guy anointing them is the real talent.'

Wanting more personal input into the cultural growth of the alternative scene, Geiger had already assisted Perry Farrell in creating the Lollapalooza festival, conceived as a farewell tour for his band Jane's Addiction. Seeing 'how record companies were having more influence in music', he had just moved into A&R with American Recording, licensing The Jesus and Mary Chain and British Eighties psych rock loon Julian Cope, but 4AD was the deal he truly desired. 'In my head,' Geiger recalls, 'there was no other person in the picture for the licensing deal besides me. I loved 4AD, and Ivo, and I wanted to help.'

As he had with Capitol, Ivo doubted the wisdom of a deal based on one individual. 'If Marc left American, who would champion the likes of The Wolfgang Press? Warners was the best option.'

Warners' offer was built on a two-tier system. Tier A was reserved for the more commercial releases, such as The Wolfgang Press, which would be distributed through the main Warners distribution network. Tier B was for 4AD's more esoteric artists, such as His Name Is Alive, through the Alternative Distribution Alliance that Warners co-owned.

But into which tier would Spirea X fit?

The Scottish trio was proof that 4AD was building a mini-wave of neo-psychedelia. Spirea X's frontline was Jim Beattie and his co-singer/ girlfriend Judith Boyle, but unlike Pale Saints and Lush, Beattie was no ingénue, having co-founded Primal Scream with his school friend Bobby Gillespie. Like Ivo, Beattie had been a Byrds and Syd Barrett-era Pink Floyd fanatic; Spirea X also performed a cover of 'Signed D.C.' by west coast legends Love. Primal Scream had been signed to Creation, run by another school friend, Alan McGee, who had got his break by signing The Jesus and Mary Chain (Gillespie was their drummer at the time). Primal Scream's jangly Sixties revivalism had ridden the C86 wave before they'd hardened up with a pseudo-Rolling Stones raunch on the 1988 album *Sonic Flower Groove*, released on McGee's second label Elevation, a pseudo-indie funded by Warners UK.

The inflated cost of the album and the apathy of its reviews inflamed band dissent, and Beattie had quit. He took his new band name from the B-side of Primal Scream's 1986 single 'Crystal Crescent': 'Spirea X' was a surf-rocking instrumental in a Pixies fashion. A new demo, 'Spirea Rising', followed suit, which had snared Ivo's interest alongside the Byrds-influenced 'Chlorine Dream' that was eventually re-recorded for its 4AD debut. The band's follow-up single 'Speed Reaction' aped the same Sixties west coast pop dream.

There was enough promise in Spirea X's streamlined, shimmery pop/rock sound to suit both 4AD and Warners, but there were caveats. 'I couldn't sing to save my life, and to sing and play at the same time made it worse,' Beattie confesses. Ivo agrees: 'They weren't at all good live, but on record, it worked beautifully. And remember, Lush's initial live form didn't get in their way. And Kurt wasn't great live until after the third Ultra Vivid Scene album.'

It didn't matter that Beattie also wasn't the first 4AD signing since the former Wire members to have got his start elsewhere; he was the first to sound like he'd taken his influences from a current trend. Just as Primal Scream had absorbed (with great success) acid house influences, Spirea X singles rode the same beats lifted from James Brown's 'Funky Drummer' that typified many indie rock bands of the time, such as The Stone Roses and The Charlatans. In other words, Spirea X was an unusual signing for 4AD. Still, Beattie recalls, the advance for the one-album deal was 'hefty' especially for a band signed on the strength of two demos. But 4AD could afford it, and Ivo's gut instinct hadn't let him down yet.

Times had clearly changed, as Beattie is the first signing to praise a 4AD contract. He says it was just two pages long. 'We were used to sixty-page contracts, with everything itemised like, "We'll rip you off here, here and here". This one had short clauses: "We will release records, this is the advance, you have total artistic control, you don't have to work with Vaughan, you can record where you want". I now teach music industry law, and I always use 4AD as an example of how simple contracts should be.'

4AD's commitment extended to the artwork. The neon logo centrepiece that featured on Spirea X's covers cost nearly £17,000 to make. 'A huge thing, at huge cost, for a band that we had signed for one album,' says Ivo. 'How bonkers we were! It looked great, though.'

It had been Beattie's idea, inspired by the neon sign on Big Star's first album. 'Ivo let Vaughan get carried away,' says Beattie. 'Vaughan being Vaughan, he took it twenty steps too far. It had three different mirror backgrounds and about forty coils, which took two engineers to set up. I asked if I could take it on the road, and Ivo laughed and said, "If you can get it on the train!" It was about sixteen foot high.'

Oliver, Beattie claims, was a lunatic: 'On Friday afternoons, the art department liked to get out their heads. At one of the early meetings about "Chlorine Dream", Vaughan suddenly disappeared, and all of a sudden, on this really sunny day, it went dark, because Vaughan had spread himself across the office's glass roof, naked. He was hammering on it, out of his head on Ecstasy.'

It seems that the cause of Oliver's spontaneous and speedy reaction was Beattie himself. 'Jim was difficult and annoying,' Chris Bigg recalls. 'Everything had to be referenced to look like something else, like a Daz logo, or pop art. And he was obsessed with The Byrds. Vaughan just got so fed up, he took his clothes off and slid down the roof. On his front!'

The logo made for some inspired artwork; the music proved to be less spectacular. Ivo thought Spirea X's debut album *Fireblade Skies* 'was disappointingly inconsistent'. And, he adds, 'it didn't flow beautifully. But I did like "Chlorine Dream", "Spirea Rising" and "Signed DC" enormously.'

Spirea X felt like a misstep – a snap judgement that lacked Ivo's usual intuition and care. But for someone distracted by the Cartel and Cocteau Twins disasters, Throwing Muses' hiatus, Pixies on a plateau, The Wolfgang Press ignored, the impending Warners deal and his own encroaching depression, the simple rhythms, chiming guitars and evocative melodies with the flavours of yesteryear would have been a suitable comfort.

Ivo had also been putting the finishing touches to a third This Mortal Coil album that he'd assembled, piece by piece again, over the last five years. This project, so close to his heart, had never been a source of stress, more of an escape, a cathartic opportunity to turn pent-up emotion into beautiful art, on his own behalf and that of the 4AD followers of his crusade. More than before, Ivo had chosen to work with even fewer 4AD personnel and more of an outside cast of old friends, some new to the collective. 'I only worked with people I felt very comfortable with,' Ivo recalls. 'The studio atmosphere, with one or two contributors at different times, was very relaxed. I don't remember any tension, more adrenalin rushes from the beauty of a spontaneous idea or performance.'

Ivo had grown in confidence too, writing a handful of lyrics, melodies and instrumental passages, such as the Hendrix/Pink Floyd-influenced guitars of 'Ruddy And Wretched'. The lyrics, understandably, mined the acid, bitter and sad, on the frontline of depression, and he named the album *Blood*. 'In 1987 alone,' Ivo admits, 'my cat had died, my father had died, I'd fallen out with Colourbox, we'd released Pixies records and my relationship with Deb had fallen apart. Everything that was happening to me is on *Blood*.'

To articulate his state of mind, Ivo had drawn his lyrics from fragments he'd either read or overheard. 'They weren't autobiographical in the sense that they came from my brain to illustrate a period of my life,' he contends. 'But they expressed emotions that were really common to me. I've been depressed my whole life, so it's all familiar, like the phrase, "*I carry sadness around like so much small change in my pocket*". When people ask me how I felt about certain things, I'd reply, "Don't ask me, I wasn't there". I didn't feel present. I was doing everything to avoid the sadness that was continuing to grow.'

The outside world crept in too. The otherwise instrumental 'Loose Joints' sampled the voices of a mother and daughter from a clan of Puerto Rican junkies that Ivo had found in a documentary about struggling New York City families.

The only other family on *Blood* were the returning Rutkowski sisters Dee and Louise, unless you counted Kim Deal and Tanya Donelly, the only 4AD artists on the record. 'It's a testimony to how much I enjoyed the Rutkowski sisters,' says Ivo, 'because there weren't many people I carried over from *Filigree & Shadow*. Louise and Dee were the heart and soul of *Blood*.'

'All the music on *Blood* went straight to your soul, like being punched in the stomach, but in a good way,' says Dee Rutkowski. 'Creativity is a product of a diseased mind – when you're not right in the head, that creative force is what keeps you right. If you're not right, it comes back with a vengeance. I most enjoyed singing Ivo's songs because of his words. They were extremely dark, which, as I got to know him, made sense. But he was so together and professional in the studio. If he was having a bad time, he wouldn't let that get in the way.'

Louise Rutkowski: 'It was all so effortless and enjoyable. We laughed a lot in the studio. But like comedians, we were dark in our private life.'

Of the five lyrics that Ivo had written, 'D.D. And E.' consisted of only one line: '*Daylight, dreams and echoes*.' 'Baby Ray Baby' was two short statements – '*I needed you/ I trusted you/ I wanted you*' and '*but you'll never, ever, change my mind*'.

'I was talking directly to Ray [Conroy] about how I felt about him during the "Pump Up The Volume" fiasco and how he was behaving,' Ivo explains. 'Ray was represented by the [sound of the] nonsense babbling baby.'

The remaining trio of lyrics were more fleshed out. 'Bitter' was an expanded version of 'Acid, Bitter And Sad' with a sample of Alison Limerick's original vocal and Dee Rutkowski's phased, ghostly addition, with Ivo's friend Ikuko Kozu providing spoken word Japanese translation. It included the lines: '*Now pardon me for trying/ Trying to tear apart/ And pardon me for lying/ It's just easy, so easy, to start.*'

Dee's controlled, chilled sadness was equally suited to 'Dreams Are Like Water' ('*When you were a child/ Unhappiness took the place of dreams/ Dreams are like water/ Colourless and dangerous*') with a strangely contemporary beat that pre dated trip hop (it was based on tracks by London collective Soul II Soul). She also laid down the overlapping vocal parts for the album's finale '(Nothing But) Blood'. The album's last words resembled an elegy: '*Now's the time to draw the line/ It's time to say goodbye.*'

Ivo: 'Goodbye to who, I wonder? Cocteau Twins, Deborah, 4AD, life? Perhaps This Mortal Coil. We'd made three albums, which had always been my intention.'

John Fryer had remained Ivo's cohort, with Jon Turner assembling the backing tracks for the new cover versions and Martin McCarrick and Gini Ball embellishing the sketches. Frazier Chorus singer Tim Freeman was marginally involved, lending vocal support to the Rutkowskis on a version of 'I Come And Stand At Every Door', The Byrds' adaptation of Turkish poet Nâzım Hikmet's heartbreaking poem about a child killed in the atomic bombing of Hiroshima, now walking Earth in search of peace. Pieter Nooten was also present in spirit, having written 'Several Times' during the solo session that Ivo had produced before Michael Brook became involved.

Ivo remembers several vocal highlights. Caroline Crawley was the lead singer of Shelleyan Orphan, a duo that Ivo might have signed if

Rough Trade hadn't beaten him to it in 1986. Like a softer version of the Rutkowskis, Crawley had a controlled, even subdued approach that was the perfect conduit for Ivo's repressed nature, as opposed to Lisa Gerrard's liberation or Elizabeth Fraser. Yet like Fraser, Crawley had been crippled by a lack of self-confidence, and she had repeatedly turned down Ivo's requests. 'I could accept singing my own songs, but otherwise I felt like an imposter,' she recalls. 'Eventually, I got so fed up with Ivo asking, I agreed. After I sang a first take, he was like, that was it, off you go! It was a bit mean of Ivo, but I can see he was right. It felt uncomfortable for me but he could see the beauty and vulnerability in that, and he was very skilled at getting that out of people. I remember Ivo saying, "You're so lucky, to be able to feel so much".'

Ivo recalls that Crawley's final version of 'Late Night' had left her shaking. 'I asked what was wrong, and she said, "I just feel really good",' he told *Melody Maker* when *Blood* was released. 'And to me, the thought of being able to do something as pure as sing, and make yourself feel that wonderful, is way beyond anything I could hope to possibly achieve in my life.'

Crawley became as involved as the Rutkowski sisters, fronting three *Blood* covers: Syd Barrett's forlorn 'Late Night', the tender 'Mr Somewhere' (co-sung with Dee Rutkowski) by the Australian band The Apartments, and 'Help Me Lift You Up' by the uniquely affecting Canadian singer Mary Margaret O'Hara. Gordon Sharp, who had sung on *It'll End In Tears*, says that Ivo had commissioned him to sing O'Hara's exquisitely exposed original, 'a more emotive version that Ivo wasn't happy with, so he went with Caroline instead, which from my perspective sounded more detached'.

Crawley and Dee Rutkowski's voices were sampled for the intro of Ivo/Fryer's 'The Lacemaker', for which Martin McCarrick's string arrangement was the saddest sound on an album of crushing melancholia.

Ivo had named the track after one of his favourite films, starring one of his favourite actresses, Isabelle Huppert. In her 1977 debut, based on Pascal Lainé's novel *La Dentellière*, Huppert's character

Apple eventually falls into a catatonic depression living among other psychiatric patients. The Wikipedia entry for the book tellingly concludes, 'Apple is surrounded with characters who believe they know how to express themselves, while Apple never succeeds in saying anything. Her silent suffering is the central light of the book.'

Another voice, Heidi Berry, who had just signed to 4AD, sang American country singer-songwriter Rodney Crowell's 'Till I Gain Control Again', which Ivo knew from Emmylou Harris' brilliant rendition. The pairing of Deal and Donelly – both underrated, charismatic vocalists – on the same track was another highlight. 'You And Your Sister' was an exquisite ballad written by Chris Bell, Alex Chilton's creative foil in Big Star, who had died in a car crash in 1978, the same year the track had become the B-side of his debut solo single 'I Am The Cosmos' on – would you believe it? – the Car label.

Bell's song was more intensely yearning than tragic, so the mood of the session wasn't downbeat; a good thing too, as Donelly recalls that she and Deal couldn't sing together because of their uncontrolled laughter, though listening to their version you'd swear that they'd been enslaved by the song. 'Internally, I was thinking, what kind of shit have I got myself into?' Deal recalls. 'I like rock'n'roll but to me music is played, not sampled. I'd never even heard [the backing track] before I got to the studio. So I was very out of my comfort zone. But I really enjoyed it. The music was so perfect, and the song was so gorgeous, I choked up.'

Tanya Donelly: 'Kim sings it so beautifully, she makes it so sweet and sad and gorgeous. And there was something so nice about that lyric sung by a woman.'

Tribute was also paid to Byrds founder Gene Clark ('With Tomorrow'), to Spirit ('Nature's Way') and David Roback (Rain Parade's 'Carolyn's Song'). There was also a version of 'I Am The Cosmos', sung by the sole male voice on *Blood*, the returning Dominic Appleton. Over two decades later, he still doesn't enjoy his contribution, though he says, 'Ivo said he liked that it was pedestrian.' Nothing spoke louder about the way 4AD's label owner preferred burying emotion instead of displaying it.

At 76 minutes, ebbing and flowing in the same style as *Filigree &
Shadow*, *Blood* was another double album. The criticism that had
greeted the length of the preceding double album didn't affect Ivo's
judgement call. Nor the idea that the kind of music it featured was too
interior, too removed from the more ragged and expressive forms of
emotion, too shrouded in a glacial mood, like the eponymous blood
had not only fatally spilt, but congealed.

Appleton, who had unreservedly loved This Mortal Coil's first two
albums, felt the same. 'I loved "You And Your Sister", the instrumentals and Caroline's voice, but I felt that Ivo was going for purer singers
rather than more interesting singers. I wasn't surprised that it was the
last This Mortal Coil album. It didn't feel as good. It felt a bit past its
sell-by date.'

Mark Cox also thinks that *Blood* suffered in comparison. 'It got a
bit serious for me. The melancholy was weighty, and though there
were times when I could immerse myself in parts, This Mortal Coil
had evolved away from where I was at.'

Ivo is also critical of the end result, though for different reasons. 'I
don't like *Blood* as much as *Filigree & Shadow*, which for me exists out
of time. *Blood* still feels like the most personal record I was ever
involved with, but it doesn't sound as natural. It suffered from some
stiff programming because I was flirting with the rhythms of the day.
For example, the Soul II Soul beat on the end of "Bitter" sounds pretty
inappropriate now.'

Cox's reference to a sell-by date inferred that music was only of its
moment. Its Soul II Soul inspiration aside, *Blood* was out of sync with
1991's cultural charge that was shaped by the euphoria of dance
music, shoegaze and Nirvana's new single 'Smells Like Teen Spirit', but
being its antithesis only made This Mortal Coil all the better. It also
stood for a measured comedown following the heightened drama of
the preceding decade. The album's hermetically sealed mood was
undisputedly moving, a luminescent walk on the dark side that would
come to life through headphones.

'I do think music is an incredibly important tonic, more than
anything,' Ivo told *Melody Maker*. 'And it's incredibly relevant in a lot

of people's lives to go and stand at the front of a Swans gig and have your head blown off by the sheer volume … and for even larger quantities of people to go to a disco or club every night to dance. Equally, though, I think it's important to disappear into music, and if that directs you to a degree of introspective meditation as well, I personally find that quite healthy.'

Against the odds, *Blood* received far better reviews than *Filigree & Shadow*. With C86, shoegaze and grunge, Sixties influences were a fact rather than the supposed embarrassment of old-fashioned taste. 'I bought *Melody Maker*, expecting a slagging, and it was so completely the opposite that I screamed,' recalls Caroline Crawley.

Blood was another milestone for Ivo, a reminder of how music could feel unspoilt, uncomplicated. Pixies records used to be like that too. The conflicting desire of Charles Thompson and Kim Deal wasn't enough to derail the momentum of Pixies selling out auditoriums and there was a public appetite for more records. The trusted Gil Norton had overseen a new album, which again Thompson had prepared little for. 'Charles said he liked the pressure,' recalls Ivo. 'But he was also under extra pressure to write different B-sides for different formats.'

Lyrically, *Bossanova* had explored Thompson's sci-fi interests, which he carried over to the new *Trompe Le Monde* – translated, 'Fool The World'. Was Pixies even the same band? One marked change was the hiring of Eric Drew Feldman, a former member of Captain Beefheart's Magic Band who Thompson had met on tour in Europe. Feldman's provision of 'keyboards and synthetics' was a sign that Thompson was looking for textures to mirror sci-fi sound, or simply that he didn't want just another Pixies album. He had already discussed a solo venture with Norton. 'I wasn't shouting it from the rooftops,' Thompson says. 'Even at the end, I was trying to put on a good face, that we were still a band.' Albeit one again without a lead vocal or writing credit for Kim Deal.

Fortunately *Trompe Le Monde* restored Pixies' upward trajectory on record, starting with v23's surrealistic shock for the cover, embedding sheep's eyeballs in bulbous white material alongside an inspired new band logo. Vaughan Oliver had assistance not just from Chris Bigg but new boy Paul McMenamin, a former graphic design student at Newcastle-upon-Tyne Polytechnic where Oliver had lectured. The album's lead single 'Planet Of Sound' was perfect, snorting and snarling with Joey Santiago's expert slide guitar. This was not the sound of a band willing to be led by its nose ring to the nearest point of crossover. Much to Marc Geiger's annoyance.

'I was very close to Pixies, who I represented when I worked at [booking agency] Triad, when I heard they were going with "Planet of Sound"', says Geiger. 'I thought their breakthrough smash for America would be "U Mass", so I told Elektra it was a huge mistake, I can't believe you're going to fuck over my band. They said, "You're the agent, stay in your box", which is the main reason I had left Triad and joined American and gone for that 4AD deal. "Velouria" hadn't been the best single off *Bossanova* either, and commercially both were disasters. I couldn't accept this horrible set of choices for this brilliant band.'

As with all Pixies singles and album track listings, 'Planet Of Sound' had been Ivo's choice. 'My intention was, Here we fuckin' go! You think things have got a bit soft on *Bossanova*? Stick this in your pipe! It was my favourite track on *Trompe Le Monde* and I was really pleased that Charles agreed to make it a single, as he graciously did all my choices, because they seemed right at the time.'

'U-Mass' was even passed over for the second single for 'Alec Eiffel', a middling album track and a baffling choice. 'My choices proved to be pretty poor because Pixies didn't break through with any single in any form,' Ivo shrugs. 'But after Pixies, you had Nirvana. The times had evolved.'

Ivo and Thompson agreed on the subject of singles and track listings, but they only remained work colleagues. 'The final day in the studio,' says Ivo, 'I'd done the running order for *Trompe Le Monde*, which everyone had loved, and only Charles was there with Gil. Rather than join us for the usual celebratory album wrap supper, Charles said, "I'm not coming, I'm going to put the songs in alphabetical order and see what it sounds like". Fair enough. None of the other band members or anyone from 4AD had even come to the studio. It was indicative of how sour things were all around.'

Marc Geiger: 'By all accounts, Pixies had issues that they couldn't resolve. I called Ivo once and said, "What the hell is *with* you? Signing all these groups, the guy and the girl in the lead roles, who have romantic problems, all this baggage, all driven by these maniacal songwriters. What were you doing, following a pattern?"'

Lush and Pale Saints had brought no baggage, only promise, though not yet the brilliance to emulate the successes of 4AD's top tier. Pale Saints were intelligent, elegant, melodic, interesting, as the Japanese-only compilation *Mrs Dolphin* amply proved. But even with Meriel Barham on vocals, the new EP *Flesh Balloon* wasn't the sound of a band grasping for new heights, or even a great single in its own right. The lush, lengthy 'Hunted' led the way, moving between languid verses and euphoric passages of guitar, but it could have come from the band's debut EP. But showing some marketing 'vision', the band's Nancy Sinatra cover 'Kinky Love' was chosen to front the seven-inch version. 'With me banging on about playing the game and commercial choices,' says Ivo, 'and my interest in people recording covers, you'd think I'd given Pale Saints something to do, but "Kinky Love" was the band's own choice.'

'We were never prolific,' Ian Masters says, 'so working on other people's songs helped relieve those tensions and give us something constructive to do.' The gentle, daydreamy ardour of 'Kinky Love' was out of kilter with everything else Pale Saints had done; with Barham on lead vocals, they suddenly resembled Lush. Getting Barham to sing the suggestive lyrics, Masters admits, meant that was 'a bit of sexual harassment going on. But Meriel accepted it fairly quickly.'

This being alternative rock, where a seizure of sexiness or lust had been confused with sexism and exploitation, the band's 'Kinky Love' became the music equivalent of a teenage diary. Shoegazing, as well as the more chart-bothering Madchester sound, were equally afraid of stating desire, from lust to the reality of relationships – druggy bliss replaced sensuality and shapeless baggy clothes hid the body; the video to 'Kinky Love' had the band sitting on a four-poster bed inside some psychedelic garden, giggling away and playing with toys, as if this is all a bed was good for. Only, among 4AD's cerebral lot, Charles Thompson was willing to unleash emotions, sex among them, and he'd gone all sci-fi.

Ian Masters says the video was shown on TV just the once. Not even MTV wanted this innocuous confectionery. Neither did Pale Saints' profile pick up after they supported Pixies in Europe, 'Just like Throwing Muses hadn't when they'd played with R.E.M.,' recalls Ivo. Commercially, as a whole, 4AD was slipping, and Ivo wasn't likely to sign anything attached to a current trend. But could he find the next? 'I hadn't enjoyed the music of the here-and-now,' he admits. 'My attempts to work with bands that fitted in, like Spirea X, weren't successful, artistically or commercially.'

Which made Heidi Berry's arrival so timely: a voice and a style outside any recognisable trend, as far away from the here-and-now as possible, even if there was a connection between Berry and her patron at Creation Records, label boss Alan McGee.

Berry was another American, but living in London and making quintessentially British music. Born and raised in Boston, she had moved to London in the mid-Eighties when her French-Canadian mother remarried. She never went back, and currently lives in Brighton, where she teaches a Master's degree in songwriting, though she says her first album in over ten years is now finished. Music was in her blood: her mother sang, and her father was good friends with music archivist Alan Lomax. 'Making up songs was normal in our house,' Berry recalls. 'My older brother Mark showed me how when I was fourteen.'

It proved to be an essential lifeline. Berry says her family moved between towns and countries, so she'd found it impossible to put down roots. 'I thought there was something wrong with me because I couldn't be like everyone else. It made me withdrawn and depressed, and seeking some kind of beauty as an antidote to the sadness and rootlessness.'

Berry became engrossed in the singer-songwriters of the early Seventies, from confessional Americans Carole King, Laura Nyro and

Tim Hardin to the British folk rock trinity of Sandy Denny, Nick Drake and John Martyn that had more clearly shaped her own sound; Berry recalls having an epiphany, while 'incredibly stoned', when she first heard Drake's third album *Pink Moon*.

This Mortal Coil's cover versions had rescued many important folk and country stylists of yesteryear, but such was the unsullied and particular mood of Denny and Drake that Ivo hadn't attempted a cover. Both had died early – Drake was twenty-six when he took a presumed accidental overdose of tranquillisers (he left no suicide note) in 1974, while the former Fairport Convention singer Denny had died in 1978 following a brain haemorrhage. Drake had finally got the recognition he deserved through reissues and tribute albums, but no one had successfully melded Denny and Drake's rich, heart-rending sound, until Berry. With her tremulous, pure style of singing, Ivo had returned to the source, the introspective font that had nourished and comforted through his formative years.

Berry didn't even have the confidence to record. But while studying painting and printmaking, she'd confessed to boyfriend Pete Astor, the former singer/guitarist of Creation signings The Loft, now leading Elevation signings The Weather Prophets, that she had a stockpile of original songs. Berry had sung a selection for Astor: 'He said I should record them, which scared the living daylights out of me, and I was still so scared that I put on my headphones the first day of recording and thought I'd gone blind! I told the engineer I wasn't ready for anyone to hear it, but of course Pete told Alan McGee. I wish I'd waited, because my ideas outstripped my technical ability on those early records. Each cost about ten pence to make, and then we hoped for the best.'

After her mini-album debut *Firefly* and full-length *Below The Waves*, Berry felt she was languishing, and that she'd only been signed to Creation because Astor was McGee's friend. Meeting Ivo was like being freed, she says. He had seen Berry, third on a bill to Lush and headliners Felt: 'It was a bit like The Birthday Party at the Moonlight, where no one else was paying attention to the support,' he remembers. 'For me, it was almost like *West Side Story*, where Tony sees Maria across the room at the dance and everything goes dark except the spotlight. I watched Heidi, transfixed, and loving her Dusty [Springfield] hand movements. I didn't call up Alan McGee, I called Heidi, as she'd already been dropped.'

Berry recalls first meeting Ivo at London's Old Vic theatre. 'He was suffering from a deep depression and he said he thought he had to get out of the country, go to America, to save himself. He was like this quiet grey cat, with English reserve, in an old man's vintage second-hand tweed coat, but he just crackled. It was all underneath the surface, this amazing person inside, who I still couldn't work out.'

One review described Berry's voice as 'an intimate, misty warble, which shifts from melancholy to desperation with heartbreaking ease'. Ivo's task was to find the right producer for it: 'Alan McGee didn't know what a producer was,' says Berry. 'He also saw me in the vein of Suzanne Vega, who was having hits around then. He really didn't know what I was about. But I felt understood, and nurtured, at 4AD. Ivo put me in touch with the right people.'

Berry and Ivo loved the mood of Scott Walker's 1983 comeback album *Climate Of Hunter*, whose producer, Pete Walsh, was assigned Berry's 4AD debut. The superlative session band included Berry's brother Christopher, Martin McCarrick, bassist Laurence O'Keefe, jazz saxophonist Lol Coxhill and House Of Love guitarist Terry Bickers, who all worked up ten originals plus an unusual and insightful cover of Hüsker Dü's 'Up In The Air', which put into song her Creation experience (*'Poor bird flies up in the air, never getting anywhere/ And how much misery can one soul take?'*).

The finished album *Love* was as finely rendered as v23's cover of lilies against a textured backdrop and delicate calligraphy. There was no single before or after *Love*; no playing the game, just the artefact. '*Love* has the melancholy of a folk record that has had all its signposts removed, like a village in the war,' *Melody Maker* observed. 'Heidi was the perfect example of what 4AD was all about,' says Ivo. 'You love the music, you get on well with the artist, you collaborate well regarding a producer, and you make albums. We did release a single or two later on, but not from *Love*. Take away the singles and I felt great comfort and pride in what 4AD had grown into.'

If only Ivo had successfully added two more unique and stellar female singer-songwriters that he was desperate to sign, he could indeed have continued unknowingly mining the sound of the future. Who then knows what might have been? Ivo had been approached by the management of an unknown Swedish singer, Stina Nordenstam. Her debut album *Memories Of A Colour* was already finished, but Ivo was immediately transported by the delicately frosted melodies, bare-boned arrangements and a voice as beguiling and exotic as Liz Fraser's, albeit in a much jazzier mode of expression, like a Swedish Billie Holiday. Scandinavian sirens are dime-a-dozen now, but in 1991 this was unexplored terrain.

Ivo offered to release the album, but after meeting Nordenstam, whose personality mirrored her beguiling, obsessive music, he changed his mind. 'Alarm bells went off in my head and I came to realise that a working relationship with Stina was going to be complicated, and complex was not what I needed at that time. I don't regret the decision, and I really liked everything she did for a long time, especially her second record *And She Closed Her Eyes*.'

Ivo had no choice in the loss of Polly Jean Harvey as, this time, he was too late on the case. The only artists he had signed from seeing them live were The Birthday Party and Heidi Berry, and nowadays, Ivo was attending increasingly fewer concerts. Generally, artists had to find him. The growing number of independent labels and competing majors meant more offers from rivals, especially those who'd eagerly hung out, wined and dined, and even shared drugs with the artist. Ivo was not Peter Kent.

Hailing from Yeovil in south-west England, Harvey had left the Bristol-based rockers Automatic Dlamini and was now fronting a taut, rough trio that had a bit of Pixies and Nick Cave's Bad Seeds about them, but a bluesy, sinewy brilliance that was purely PJ Harvey, as the band was called. One of her London shows had been promoted by Paul Cox, the co-founder with Richard Roberts of a new independent label, Too Pure.

Cox: 'I was a typical record-buying indie kid, though I didn't collect 4AD; it was known specifically for its house style and, for my tastes, too defined and not rock'n'roll enough. I was more Creation and Rough Trade. But Throwing Muses and Pixies were right up my street. It was still arty, but they swung. By 1990, 4AD was super-cool.'

By early 1991, Too Pure had released vinyl singles by British bands Th' Faith Healers and Stereolab, the compilation *Now That's Disgusting Music* and PJ Harvey's sensational debut single 'Dress'. John Peel instantly rewarded her with a session while the music press reaction was unanimous.

By chance, Too Pure had approached Ivo about signing the London band Moonshake, who Cox and Roberts were managing and trying to find a more sympathetic home than, yet again, Creation. Ivo wasn't keen but suggested Too Pure should release the band's music themselves. Seeing a way to work with PJ Harvey, and feeling protective of this new, energetic label, he proposed buying into Too Pure. Harvey had also enjoyed Too Pure's attitude, and her manager had requested the label commit to two singles and an album, 'though,' Cox recalls, 'we had no money.'

Ivo had been equally infatuated with Harvey: 'Polly was such an interesting guitar player, the songs had so much space, the distorted bass had such power, the drummer was fantastic and was a great backing vocalist. But I'd learnt from my experience with A.R. Kane and One Little Indian, so I talked to Too Pure about what they were trying to do and about me getting involved. I encouraged Polly to stay with Too Pure, and I really liked Stereolab and aspects of Moonshake. The idea was to give Too Pure more muscle.'

Cox: 'Either Ivo saw something in us, just starting out, and wanted to help, or he only wanted to get involved with Polly. He said, "Try everything to make sure you do as much as you can with Polly, because special artists like her don't come along often". I shrugged that off at the time but he was right.'

Ivo subsequently bought a third of Too Pure to get the label going, and so they could afford PJ Harvey. A limited version of the trio's debut album *Dry* was packaged with the original demos, which was

Ivo's idea. But for all Ivo's input and reputation, Harvey still signed to Island Records after the release of the album. 'Polly had stuck with Too Pure for the first album, against her manager's wishes as he'd been totally swayed by Island,' says Cox. 'They'd acted really underhand to prise Polly out of our hands, to the point of mentioning a Too Pure label deal, which was never in the picture.'

Instead, they got Ivo, a much more suitable and hands-off partner. 'We'd only just started Too Pure, so that was hard,' says Cox. 'But in the short period that we'd got to know Ivo, there was no one else in the music industry that I'd have trusted to do such a deal. He came across as so honest, and he had so much experience, so we were convinced to take the step up. He left us to it but he was there to answer questions, and we'd play him stuff and value his opinion.'

At the time, Ivo was also busy advising Warren Defever for the second His Name Is Alive album. *Home Is In Your Head* – a title that perfectly captured Defever's – and Ivo's – Music-For-Interiors mindset. The album followed the same pattern as *Livonia*, Ivo remixing a slew of tracks (twenty-three in total, none listed in the artwork) of ethereal and eccentric dream-song with Karin Oliver out front, though Defever had this time supplied finished pieces instead of sketches. 'I just took the bits I liked,' Ivo recalls, 'things that might ramble or disintegrate. One piece was only forty seconds long. But I didn't think there was anything I could do that would upset Warren. He'd dismantle his own songs anyway. He was the least precious individual about his own music that I'd ever met.'

Defever was also sharing credits, with Karin Oliver on 'The Well', while 'Tempe', a rare acoustic reverie among all the twitchy experiments, was written by guitarist Jymn Auge. Song titles such as 'My Feathers Needed Cleaning' and 'Beautiful And Pointless' were a rare sign of playfulness in the 4AD canon. The closing 'Dreams Are Of The Body' provided the balance with a mood right out of the This Mortal Coil songbook.

Ivo listened to the rough mixes that he and John Fryer had made of *Home Is In Your Head* as he settled in a new, two-level basement flat on Clapham Common. 'I'd bought it for the height of the ceilings, but I was feeling really insecure, thinking why on earth *had* I bought it? The ceilings made me feel so small, I feared that, spiritually, I would never fill the place, which had nothing in it but the stereo, CDs, clothes and a sofa. Late at night, I'd listen to the mixes of Warren's stuff there, very quietly, because I didn't yet know my neighbours, allowing the ticking of my own alarm clock to mingle with those sampled on the mixes. I love that record. It's such an unpredictable, yet fluid, musical journey.'

The chance to work with Defever was such a contrast to the nightmare of Robin Guthrie, but despite everything that had gone on, Ivo didn't stop him from reuniting with Lush to produce the band's debut album.*

Since the release of the *Gala* compilation, Lush had been touring almost constantly, especially in Japan and America where *Sweetness And Light* had reached the heady heights of the Billboard Modern Rock top three. As well as a very supportive producer, they had acquired a manager – Howard Gough, the man who had tried his best to dissuade Ivo from signing Lush.

'Howard had been worn down by the fact we were making good records,' says Emma Anderson. 'And once he'd got to know us, we'd gotten along well and he'd reached the stage where he wanted to leave 4AD and manage us. Maybe he was unhappy there, or he was bored of plugging, or he could see an opportunity. When people get a sniff of America, they just see dollar signs.'

Having once tried to dissuade Lush over Guthrie, so Ivo tried with Gough. 'Ivo again didn't come out and say *why* we shouldn't go with Howard,' says Miki Berenyi. 'Perhaps he should have.'

---

* There was another Cocteaus/Lush connection, a one-off collaboration featuring Miki Berenyi, Chris Acland, Simon Raymonde and Moose members Kevin McKillop and Russell Yates. They named themselves The Lillies, after their favourite football team Tottenham Hotspur, nicknamed The Lilywhites after their all-white kit. The instrumental (with Berenyi's coos and some samples of football commentary) was called 'And David Seaman Won't Be Very Happy About That …' referring to the goalkeeper of the team's London rivals Arsenal. It was released on a seven-inch flexidisc given away free with copies of *The Spur* fanzine.

Gough had the swagger and ambition to go it alone, and after leaving 4AD in 1991, had gone into management with his friend Ray Conroy, who was already managing Moose and their fellow shoegazers Chapterhouse. Gough's first move on Lush's behalf was typically confident, embarking on talks with various major labels about a long-term contract, which would give Lush – and Gough – greater financial benefits. Gough had no sense of loyalty to 4AD, but the band did. 'A major could have dropped us after one album, and we already felt a rapport with 4AD,' Anderson explains. 'Ivo stuck with his bands. He wasn't swayed by our records being slagged off or if they'd only sold five hundred copies.'

Beside a decent publishing deal with his former colleagues at Blue Mountain, Gough was able to negotiate a bigger advance with 4AD than Ivo would usually offer. 'Howard had worked at 4AD so he knew how much he could push for,' says Berenyi. 'Ivo said, "Aren't you lot greedy?" which was a bit rich. We only had enough to put ourselves on a hundred pounds a week. And as I told him, he was getting his money straight back by licensing Lush to Warners – which was money that we never saw.'

Lush and Guthrie started recording at September Sound. 'Robin loved the band and liked our songs,' says Anderson. 'He just wasn't in a state to do a good job.'

Berenyi: 'The recording started fine but dragged on and on. Robin would go on bloody great benders, doing drugs with all sorts who'd turn up at the studio. You'd get [Echo & The Bunnymen singer] Ian McCulloch sitting in the kitchen, completely non-communicative. We might not see Robin for four days and then he'd turn up and say, "Don't worry, stop moaning, come on, plug in". Then he'd want to record all night but we were knackered. We felt we had to stick up for Robin, so we'd paper over the fact he was AWOL instead of complaining to Ivo.'

Unsurprisingly, Guthrie has another view. 'It was one of the hardest records I produced because the girls' ideas were so far ahead of their capabilities. For example, singing in tune. And they were all high as kites too! [Since Berenyi hardly ever took drugs, this wasn't the case.]

And Howard – need I say more? I won't take any shit about that album. I worked my ass off to get what I believed those people were capable of and I delivered.'

The new EP *Black Spring* previewed two album tracks, the pure-pop 'Nothing Natural' and the languid 'Monochrome', which rewarded the faith that Ivo and Guthrie had first shown. Like Pale Saints' 'Kinky Love', the EP's cover [Beach Boy] Dennis Wilson's 'Fallin' In Love' coated a pretty tune in lush layers of gentle vocals and flange guitar. Lush kept up the momentum with a second EP; *For Love*, that 4AD released on the last day of 1991. The title track was again neat, springy and poppy, and made the UK top 40 at 35. It wasn't high enough to get BBC's *Top of the Pops* calling, but 'For Love' was 4AD's first certifi-able hit single in an age. The EP's other tracks – a reverential reading of Wire's luscious 'Outdoor Miner' and the brief ambient-blurry 'Astronaut' – were more proof of a growing stature; as he says, Guthrie had actually delivered.

Two other 4AD releases that autumn had celebrated the stature of past triumphs – a Cocteau Twins box set (which appeared to have no title – the band's own website calls it *The Box Set*), comprising all their EPs and singles on nine individual CDs, from *Lullabies* to 'Iceblink Luck', with a bonus EP of rarities including *Lonely Is An Eyesore*'s 'Crushed'. The crimson box only featured a tiny insignia and the band's name in unassuming capitals – no artwork, no logo, no fuss.

With the Warners licensing deal still not signed, Dead Can Dance's first compilation *A Passage In Time* had been assembled for another independent, Rykodisc. For the first time, Brendan Perry allowed v23 to design the sleeve: 'It was Brendan's picture, of a moth wing,' says Chris Bigg, 'but I'd got his confidence by then, and the logo and text were more considered.'

A Passage In Time also marked the journey that Dead Can Dance had taken: eight years since leaving Australia, seven years since their album debut, or the six centuries between now and fourteenth-century Italian folk dances. There were two new tracks: Lisa Gerrard's percussive incantation 'Bird' and Brendan Perry's 'Spirit', which closed the album with a narrative that potentially marked his and Gerrard's journey, from their curtailed romance – *'I never thought it would be quite like this/ Living outside of mutual bliss'* – to their shared fight for survival: *'I thought I'd found a reason to live, just like before when I was a child/ Only to find that dreams made of sand/ Would just fall apart and slip through my hands/ But the spirit of life keeps us strong/ And the spirit of life is the will to carry on.'*

Ivo could have identified with Perry's sentiment, with his relationship with Deborah Edgely and his dream of a record label challenged by both personal and professional circumstances. Where would he find the will to carry on? In the States, perhaps, as he'd confessed to Heidi Berry at their first meeting? Perhaps even Ivo, the quintessential English gentleman, needed the American dream. The decision to sign a licensing deal with Warner Bros was made between the Christmas and New Year period of 1991–92. So now he even had a reason to go.

16 1992

A TINY SPECK IN A BROBDINGNAG WORLD
(bad2001-tad2019)

'In the end,' American Recordings A&R Marc Geiger recalls, 'Ivo said, "Love you and all your help, but I need to go direct to the Warners mothership". I was crushed. But I understood. And anyway, American and Warners did split up years later.'

Warners victorious A&R Tim Carr recalls how his boss Lenny Waronker reacted to the 4AD deal. 'I was also trying to sign [US alt rockers] Helmet, but they wanted a million dollars and Lenny said no. He also said, "You won't mind in six months. What you should be really happy about is 4AD. That kind of thing happens once every ten years, they're a cool and unique label, and you won't find another one like it".'

The licensing deal was for three years, after which point Warners had the option to extend it for two more years. This was to be celebrated with *Lilliput*, a promotional limited edition (3,000 copies) double CD in book-bound format that was given away to retail and media. Everything 4AD stood for existed in this singular, lavish artefact. As Ivo told me at the time, 'There's precious little originality, identity or experimentalism going on. It's hard to find those people, so you have to grab them, but you have to have the means and ideals and reputation to secure them.'

Bar nudity and surreal shocks, everything v23 stood for was summed up by *Lilliput* – delicate, austere design, fine calligraphy and all the credits listed down the side of the sleeve under a clear plastic binding. The first CD was Ivo's highlights from 4AD's past, from Bauhaus' 'Dark Entries' to Lush's 'Deluxe'. The second CD was an appetiser for the present featuring two tracks each from Pale Saints, The Wolfgang Press, Spirea X and the forthcoming album from Pieter Nooten's former collaborator, guitarist Michael Brook. There were single tracks from Heidi Berry, His Name Is Alive and a new signing, Swallow.

The title *Lilliput* came from Irish novelist Jonathan Swift's classic eighteenth-century satire *Gulliver's Travels* (or to give it its full title, *Travels into Several Remote Nations of the World, in Four Parts. By Lemuel Gulliver, First a Surgeon, and then a Captain of Several Ships*), whose titular shipwrecked hero was imprisoned by Lilliput's race of miniature people. The analogy was clear: '4AD was a tiny little speck next to Warners,' says Ivo. In terms of the deal, 4AD was smaller still since the label's established names – Pixies, The Breeders, Lush and Throwing Muses – were already licensed elsewhere. 'Looking back,' says Ivo, 'the train had already left the station. But logic said it was appropriate to use one label for licensing.'

Much like the next fantasy-human race that Gulliver encountered, the giants of Brobdingnag, Warners was an institution that carried a lot of expectation. But Ivo lived in hope. The last image in the booklet of the *Lilliput* compilation was of a sleeping baby, a tiny Lilliputian figure but also the symbol of what could grow. It would take four months for the deal to take effect, by which point 4AD had charged into 1992 with Lush. Three years since Ivo had watched their faltering show at The Falcon, dotted with a mini-album, four EPs and one three-track single, the band finally released its debut album. *Spooky* came wrapped in one of Jim Friedman's Polaroid 'scapes, of luminescent deep sea creatures overrun with a swarm of Lush logos and scratched lines that scarred the aquamarine beauty.

Musically, Lush had aimed for a similar blend of colour, shape and tension. As singles, 'Nothing Natural' and 'For Love' – and the reappearance of *Black Spring*'s madrigal-style 'Monochrome' – took their expected place alongside an elated 'Superblast', the wistful Sixties strain of 'Untogether'. At 48 minutes, the album was at least two tracks too long, and it felt like repetition had set in: '*Spooky* suffered from what was traditionally referred to as the sophomore slump,' Ivo thinks. 'Lush had already released an album's worth of material in the form of *Gala*, so it wasn't their strongest material. And I don't think Robin [Guthrie] was well by this point.'

Yet at heart, *Spooky* was a pop record, and it topped the UK independent chart and reached number 7 on the national charts – a gratifying sign of affirmation for everyone involved. 'Some of the songs suffered,' Emma Anderson says, 'but it's got this bubblegum pop feel that I really like.' Berenyi is less sure: 'Some bits were great, but the album needed a firmer grasp.' Was it Guthrie, or Ivo that she was referring to?

Despite his worsening condition during the making of the album, Guthrie had boosted Lush's confidence while his space rock coda on 'Laura' showed his sonic trickery could be exemplary. But given the band were idolising ingénues, it was inevitable that the press would again accuse Guthrie of forcing his own sound on an artist. 'Absolutely not,' he responds on this occasion. Ivo's view was, 'Why hire Robin if you don't want that sound?'

Spooky's opening passage – the intro to 'Stray' – was exactly like an excerpt from *Blue Bell Knoll*, but after it the album is much more Lush, a more rocking version of ethereal bliss, something fast and using two intertwined lead guitars. However, sections of the press, usually looking for a stick with which to beat shoegazers, weren't finished there. A more stinging criticism of the band came from a friend of Anderson's, *Melody Maker* assistant editor Everett True. 'He slagged off *Spooky*, saying we were Robin's puppets, and that riot grrrl bands were the real feminists,' she says. 'Years later, he told me he regretted writing that.'

4AD's contribution to the visibility and advancement of women was evidently no longer enough in itself; writers like True demanded some kind of political awareness – a familiar critique of 4AD through the years. The fact that True's housemates happened to be Huggy Bear, the UK's most prominent feminist punk band under the riot grrrl banner, might have egged him on. Colleen Maloney, who joined 4AD's press office in early 1992, says that Lush weren't the only 4AD artists harangued for the same apparent crime of being determinedly non-partisan. 'Bands and writers desperately tried to bring Kristin Hersh and Kim Deal into the riot grrrl ranks and shunned Tanya Donelly because she wore make-up and wrote pop songs, but to me they were all from the same family,' says Maloney. 'Kim sometimes got the same treatment. And people would try to create friction between Kristin and Tanya when it didn't exist.'

Berenyi thinks that Lush's girl-around-town tag did them no favours. *Select* magazine's first feature on the band had the headline, 'Drinks £151.28', referring to the evening's bar tab while the text below threw in the reference 'glamour-afflicted hellbabes'. Such were the hard-fought and often-suspect indie music wars – a similar bar tab for a bunch of men would have gone unreported. Colleen Maloney: 'Lush was so immersed in that scene, hanging out at venues in Camden like The Underworld, and they got really well known, which can cause problems. It's good to have some distance and mystery, plus the band took everything that was written about them too seriously. But they got lots of press, and good press, and they had a very strong dynamic, with two very strong and articulate women. They gave as good as they got.'

Still, Berenyi felt, '4AD liked to have a mystique around their bands that we lacked.' Ivo dismisses her observation. 'Miki forgets that I'd been around Vaughan, Howard and Robin for years. The mystique of our artists was always in the music and enhanced by the packaging. It's interesting that, having been initially drawn to the music, virtually everyone who came to 4AD was pretty shy, which can be interpreted as mysterious or arrogant. Miki herself was extremely shy around me most of the time.'

By comparison, Pale Saints had that layer of intrigue, being based in Leeds outside of London's media menagerie, with Ian Masters as reticent as Lush were gregarious. Given his indefensible slap of Berenyi on the bands' shared tour of 1990, Masters had some sort of unsocial, awkward streak. While Lush was prepared to slog it out on tour, Masters says he disliked the rigour, and could only be on board if it was fun. Clearly that would soon end, given that Pale Saints' first album with former Lush member Meriel Barham was also Masters' last.

Produced by Hugh Jones, *In Ribbons* wasn't at all short on quality or surprise.* Like Lush, Pale Saints could straddle dream-pop and a more muscular clamour, such as 'Throwing Back The Apple', which seemed only released as a single after the album in the hope more people might actually know who the band was. But it wasn't a tailor-made single, outstripped in swarthy melody and mood by the B-side cover of 'Blue Flower', a Velvets-inspired ballad by the Seventies Brit-art-rock trio Slapp Happy.†

Ivo says he was very happy with the album; it wasn't a sophomore slump by any means. But neither was it any tangible leap forward, and Masters must have sensed this. Beside the finest, most luscious Pale Saints track yet, 'Hunted', he sounded most inspired and comfortable in the virtual solo surrounds of two waiflike ballads, 'Shell' and 'Hair Shoes', and the similar skeletal 'Neverending'.

'I left almost entirely due to musical boredom,' Masters confesses. 'I almost left before *In Ribbons* was finished but working with Hugh Jones was calming and it wasn't hard to stick it out. But after we finished the album, Graeme and Chris wanted to go in a more conventional rock direction, which didn't interest me. I knew I couldn't stay and remain happy.'

---

* One of the more maverick contributions to the 4AD catalogue was the free single included with initial copies of Pale Saints' *In Ribbons*, with two band songs covered by the Tintwistle Brass Band, which was based in a small village in the county of Derbyshire. It was Masters' idea, and he knew the band's conductor so was able to set something up quickly, and inexpensively.

† Pale Saints had first heard of 'Blue Flower' from an existing cover by David Roback's new alias Mazzy Star, with new singer Hope Sandoval replacing the absconding Kendra Smith. Around this time, Robin Hurley talked to David Roback about releasing an album that he had previously produced by Sandoval and acoustic guitarist Sylvia Gomez, under the name of Going Home. But Ivo says that Roback's requested $75,000 advance was too high, and the album remains unreleased (though tracks can be heard on YouTube).

That the first release under the new Warners deal was a band that had lost its key member was not an auspicious start. 'There was resentment on both sides, as it left the band in the lurch,' recalls 4AD's most recent staff recruit Cliff Walton. But Ivo didn't panic: 'I was never upset when groups stopped or were unhappy if someone left. Anyway, Meriel was an alternate songwriter. And Graeme was a rare example of a British musician who got better at his instrument.'

As Pale Saints stumbled, Lush strode on. Manager Howard Gough had secured the band the opening slot on the second annual Lollapalooza festival tour that kicked off in July 1992, followed by thirty-seven more dates across the States. 'We were very grateful that someone thought we were good enough to manage us, and he was persuasive and very good at networking,' says Miki Berenyi. 'He buddied up to [Lollapalooza's] Perry Farrell, and to Warners, who all thought Howard was great.'

Lush fanatic and festival organiser Marc Geiger might have had something to do with the booking too. The band had the honour of appearing on the main stage, albeit bottom of the bill, beneath the fast-rising Pearl Jam, with the bill ascending to the headlining Red Hot Chili Peppers. Lush also had a new bass player: Phil King had played with a handful of guitar bands (several associated with Creation) and had been working as a picture researcher for *NME* when he got a call to replace Steve Rippon, who left to devote himself to writing fiction.

Lollapalooza was a very timely invention, providing a kind of travelling circus for America's newest musical youth-quake, led by Nirvana. The Pixies had been instrumental in establishing that scenario, but Pixies were not about to reap the benefits. At the end of February, the band had opened for U2 on the first leg of the Irish band's Zoo TV stadium tour playing the thirty dates, to, according to Marc Geiger, 'really try and break them'. It seemed a strange way to heal a fractured band. Worse was to come when Kim Deal's boyfriend, *Spin* writer Jim Greer, wrote a feature about the tour, claiming that Pixies had been badly treated. Word came through to 4AD via Pixies manager Ken Goes that a furious Charles Thompson had unilaterally decided that Pixies was finished.

The news didn't leak out, and it seems the other Pixies were similarly in the dark: likewise the band's US licensee, Elektra Records. Ivo and Robin Hurley were later summoned to a meeting with Elektra boss Bob Krasnow who demanded Ivo renegotiate a longer deal with Pixies or he'd go directly to the band. 'Having broken Sugarcubes and The Cure in America,' says Ivo, 'Elektra was supposedly the label of choice and Krasnow wasn't happy that Geffen could be stealing that crown with Nirvana, so he was determined to get more Pixies. At some point, the word "Nirvana" passed my lips, and I only found out later that Krasnow had had the opportunity to sign them and hadn't. But he exploded, screaming that Nirvana could have been produced by a doughnut and they'd still have sold millions. It's one of my very few regrets that I didn't just walk out. The problem was that Robin and I already knew Pixies were going to call it a day.'

Ironically, Ivo didn't even think Elektra had done a good job. 'It seemed the right label to license Pixies at the time, as they'd had some great successes, just as Sire had been the most appropriate major label to license to in 1982. But Elektra didn't have the same success with our bands. Getting involved with 4AD was clearly the kiss of death.'

As Pixies simmered with even more unresolved tension, Kim Deal decided to reconvene The Breeders. While on a UK tour with Pixies in late 1991, Josephine Wiggs had received a call from Deal, saying she had a song she wanted to demo called 'Do You Love Me Now?', written by the Deal twins during their truckstop-gigging days. The pair recorded it at Wiggs' home in Brighton and hired Spacemen 3's Jon Mattock to add drums. Months later, the original Breeders plus one met in New York to record three more new songs. Despite being a relative novice on guitar, Kim's twin sister Kelley was set to replace Donelly, who was busy with her own solo plans, yet the latter turned up anyway, making it the one record with five Breeders.

Playing what Wiggs calls 'stream-of-consciousness guitar playing', Donelly's contributions lifted the tracks. But the sensual, prowling nature of 'Do You Love Me Now?' indicated The Breeders would survive without her. The closing cover of The Who's 'So Sad About Us' on the resulting five-track EP *Safari* could conceivably have referred to Pixies, but the truth was, Kim Deal was simply smitten with Who bassist John Entwistle.

As Deal had found her feet because of Charles Thompson's solo tour, so Donelly had been freed by Kristin Hersh's need for change. 'Leaving [the Muses] was really sad, but I was in danger of losing my sense of self to something that had run out of control and that nobody involved had any control over,' says Donelly. 'Kristin and I were too tired and numb, which was dangerous, but we got over it the second I quit.'

Donelly's songs originally bound for the second Breeders album gave birth instead to Belly, 'a womanly word, a lovely and an ugly word,' Donelly suggests. 'Belly means a lot of things to a lot of people.'

Before this new band formed, Donelly had recorded an album of demos that Ivo became familiar with driving through the desert east of LA after meeting Warners. 'Tanya wasn't saying, "I have a band, here we go",' he recalls. 'She'd simply recorded herself with an electric guitar. I loved it and said she should make a record.'

Sire had acknowledged that Warners in Europe would never work in Throwing Muses' favour and had handed back the territory to 4AD – Belly followed this arrangement. Ivo subsequently stepped back into the A&R role. 'He was my sounding board, my comrade in arms,' says Donelly. 'His belief in me was incredible.'

Ivo suggested that Donelly try out a first-time producer in Tracy Chisholm, an engineer that he'd discovered via the Pixies-influenced Los Angeles band Carnival Art. Donelly assembled a team for the session, including Kim Deal (Donelly thinks she's on 'Feed The Tree') and Leslie Langston. But Belly's first permanent bassist was Fred Abong, who had also chosen to leave Throwing Muses along with Donelly. Belly's third and fourth permanent members were brothers: guitarist Thomas and drummer Chris Gorman, Donelly's childhood friends from Newport who'd cut their teeth in the hardcore punk band Verbal Assault.

The interesting aspect of Belly's *Slow Dust* EP wasn't the four tracks of tenderly skewed rockers and ballads but the lack of obvious hits that Donelly supposedly craved. 'As far as songwriting goes, I'm more attracted to straightforward, universal songs,' she says. 'But for me, it's less The Go-Go's or girl groups and more Big Star and Neil Young. And I like intricate guitars.'

By following Donelly's gut instinct, *Slow Dust* surprised both Belly and 4AD by topping the UK independent charts, a feat not even managed by the following single 'Gepetto' – the sparkling pop song that Kristin Hersh had rejected for the Muses. But the song shone much brighter than it might have midway through Muses' *The Real Ramona*. The choice of producer for 'Gepetto' was revealing: Donelly had brought back Gil Norton. 'I liked Tracy's southern, swampy, cool sound, but he was too mellow for us,' she recalls. 'I wanted someone I knew and trusted, and the Belly songs that Gil produced were the ones I knew he'd treat in a poppy way, and I wanted to make a pop album.'

Lush's evolved direction and the advent of Belly injected a new openness and pop consciousness into 4AD, leading to more success in the UK. It was a strong contrast to the publicity-shy enigma that was His Name Is Alive, never playing live and preferring to exist within Warren Defever's studio lair.

4AD's success with exporting *Livonia* and *Home Is In Your Head* had convinced Rykodisc to license both albums and release a promotional compilation drawn from both. *Sings Man On The Silver Mountain And 8 Other Songs* also tapped into the standalone EP *The Dirt Eaters* that 4AD released at home. Defever acted like a strategist, throwing out clues and red herrings: the EP's title track was unlisted, the lead track was an unrecognisable recasting of 'Man On The Silver Mountain' written by hard rock guitar hero Ritchie Blackmore, and instead of promoting it with live shows, a promo video was made for the Ivo/Fryer remix of 'Are We Still Married?'

This last decision was actually down to the videomakers. Ivo had tracked down the Brothers Quay, Stephen and Timothy, identical American twins living in London, creators of eerie and wildly inventive stop-motion animations that resembled a Wallace and Gromit impression of *Eraserhead*. At the meeting, Ivo and Defever informed the twins that they could animate whichever EP track took their fancy. Defever's memory of the afternoon is hilarious.

'On the phone, they wouldn't give out their address. Ivo drove us to where they described, where we found an antique bicycle that seemed to have been locked since the 1800s. We knocked and eventually a dishevelled and groggy man in homemade wooden glasses and no shirt answered. The other twin was still in the bed in the centre of the studio. That was a little weird. They'd finish each other's sentences and stand very close to each other.'

Ivo politely explained about 4AD and His Name Is Alive and gave them posters and CDs. 'They quickly kicked us out saying they really weren't interested in commercial rock videos,' Defever continues. 'It seemed like the worst meeting ever. Ivo was confident, however. The next day, they said they'd use our music for a short film and would we like to see the script or a treatment? Ivo said we trusted their artistic vision fully. The finished video, or film, was insane and beautiful.'

The Quays were an inspired foil for Defever's quixotic vision, and Ivo regards the collaborations (a second video would follow in 1993) as 'the only absolutely essential music videos 4AD was ever involved in', although he adds, 'I'd have preferred never to have had videos but I wish we'd developed a relationship with a visual artist as valuable as the one with 4AD's graphic team.'

Videos commissioned by 4AD otherwise followed the predictable MTV aesthetic of fast cuts and thin narratives. They could be entertaining, but all too often lame, or in the case of The Wolfgang Press's new standalone single 'A Girl Like You', a bit of each. The song itself was slinky and brooding, complete with female gospel voices supporting a sweetly sinister Mick Allen, who sounded like a man that no woman should trust. The video was tailored to the single's mood by featuring a group of pouting women in tight skirts surrounding Mick Allen on a podium, which resembled both a parody of Robert Palmer's iconic 'Addicted To Love' video and a poor sequel. And still the song didn't get the band away.

In the interim, The Wolfgang Press might have hoped that *Queer* would find its natural home in the US, but Ivo's indecision over signing a deal meant the album would be released there a year after it had been released in the UK. It was the first 4AD record Warners could really get its teeth into, but the first sign of trouble was the label's refusal to release 4AD's version until every little audio sample had either been cleared or removed. This followed a precedent-setting court case that Warners had lost. Instantly, 4AD's autonomy had been undermined.

'Sampling was now called theft rather than "having fun with sound"', recalls Mark Cox.* Hadn't anyone at 4AD been paying attention since 'Pump Up The Volume', five years earlier? Warners released a re-tweaked *Queer* alongside a twelve-inch single of remixes, three of 'A Girl Like You' and one each of 'Mama Told Me Not To Come' and *Queer*'s 'Louis XIV'. For Canada, the latter two were replaced by a remix of *Queer*'s 'Angel' by Vince Clarke (Depeche Mode/Yazoo/ Erasure). Welcome to the machine.

The 4AD that wasn't thinking of budgets, formats, remixes and pop videos returned with an album by ambient guitarist Michael Brook. Having stayed in touch with Ivo since his Pieter Nooten collaboration *Sleep With The Fishes*, Brook had asked for advice on the track selection for a new album funded by Brian Eno's label Opal. Ivo had left off some tracks and assembled a running order, 'which Michael agreed transformed the record,' Ivo says. His suggestion to also release the album excited Brooks: '4AD had a wider, rockier audience than Opal, and a unique commitment to visuals and quality. I liked that Ivo followed his instincts for things that he just liked.'

Once Opal had agreed, 4AD launched *Cobalt Blue* at London Zoo's aquarium at the end of May, where Brooks played a live set. 'It was in a lovely setting, surrounded by moray eels, but also noisy, fucking music journalists,' says Ivo. 'We recorded it and in many ways, it's better than *Cobalt Blue*.' The limited edition *Live At The Aquarium* was released at the end of June (and soon packaged with *Cobalt Blue* on a double CD). The studio album was a rhythmic, blues-inflected version of Eno-esque ambience (the man himself was credited with

---

* Beside samples on *Queer*, The Wolfgang Press also couldn't get clearance to use Snowflake the albino guerrilla for the cover, only to find UK dance duo Basement Jaxx use the very same image for its 2001 album *Rooty*.

'structural rearrangements') and a lovely oasis of calm in 4AD's otherwise state of agitation.

That sense of a straightforward, co-operative alliance was to be quickly undone by the band first unveiled on the *Lilliput* compilation – Swallow. The duo of Louise Trehy and Mike Mason brought complications, frustrations and heartbreak. Marc Geiger was right: Ivo did seem to be following a pattern of dysfunctional couples.

Swallow had surfaced via a demo that ticked several boxes: personal and professional male/female partnership, female singer, beautiful noise. Trehy now lives in Aberystwyth, Wales where she teaches Art History at the local university, though she has recently posted online her first recordings in nineteen years. Born in Dublin, Trehy went through various pop crushes – The Beatles, Kate Bush, Blondie, Sugarcubes 'and most 4AD bands'. By 1988, she was living in London – 'Dublin was a provincial shithole when I was growing up' – with then-boyfriend Keith Cullen, who was running the independent label Setanta. One of his early signings was the Bunnymen-influenced Into Paradise, whose touring keyboardist was Mike Mason. 'I'd told Keith I wanted a go at singing, and he shoved Mike and me together,' says Trehy.

Still based in his home city of Oxford, Mason was also a Beatles fan before shifting allegiance to David Bowie. Music was just a hobby, as he worked as a fine art photographer before making promo videos and running light shows for bands such as Spacemen 3 and Spiritualized, until he joined Into Paradise and then met Trehy. 'After doing some music, we ran off together,' Mason recalls. 'On the off-chance, we sent a tape to 4AD, not expecting anything would happen. But very quickly Ivo called, saying he loved it. When we met, he said, could we make an album now? Yes, of course. We then had to write a lot more songs!'

'Swallow fitted in with the times,' says Ivo. 'They weren't extraordinarily original, but Mike was very talented and Louise's vocals were OK.' If that didn't sound like a vote of confidence, Trehy wasn't unreservedly positive about 4AD either. 'It was a very interesting, slick operation, in newly designed offices, and quite pretentious. Though we were pretentious too! But we knew some music journalists and their feeling was 4AD was old hat, and that up-and-coming labels were more interesting. But I liked the fact that Ivo just wanted good records and wasn't out to make money quickly. His one concern was that we [sounded] shoegaze, but he thought we were different enough to stand on our own.'

The problem was that Swallow's beauty/noise aesthetic depended on great songs, which they had to write quickly, and yet they had no experience to speak of. Like Spirea X, Swallow seemed like a rushed judgement on Ivo's part, and the problem wasn't fixed by the default addition of John Fryer. He had recently gone freelance after being denied a share in Blackwing by studio owner Eric Radcliffe, and so he and Swallow had driven to Palladium studios in Scotland. 'On the way,' Trehy recalls, 'Mike asked John if he'd had any thoughts on our songs, and he replied that he hadn't yet listened to anything. That really pissed me off. It was my first time in a studio and I had no confidence. I didn't play an instrument, and I had to trust what John said, including his line, "everything will be all right in the mix".'

Mason: 'As soon as we started recording, John gave it this enormous sound, which we'd never intended. But he was the professional who knew best, and he'd worked with Cocteau Twins, and knew all the tricks.' Mason says Ivo had requested more bass, 'but we'd never intended to have bass. It was a dream to be on this cool label that we'd grown up with, so you didn't want to piss them off, but Louise struggled and got very hurt. We both were. Our dream got pulled away from us.'

Ivo: 'Louise wasn't the strongest vocalist on the planet, and I did everything I could, to the point of rudeness, to suggest what she could do differently.' He even hired Caroline Crawley to assist Trehy re-record her vocals after Swallow had returned to London. 'I felt like that awful record company man, sending what they'd done back and back, and I realised I shouldn't have got involved in the first place.'

Trehy: 'We felt our demos had been immature, but Ivo signed us on the basis of them, and he picked the songs he really liked. So to go to, "You've lost it, that's your fault" was awful, especially since I agreed. I knew I wasn't great, and 4AD had these brilliant female singers, but I got narked at Ivo and we fell out.'

This was written up in a music press article when Trehy was asked why Ivo had signed Swallow. 'I think I said it just appealed to his ego. He went nuts and said he didn't want to work with me again. I was gobby then, and I still can be, but I think I was more pissed off with myself than anything. Looking back, Ivo tried his best, and it wasn't his fault it didn't work out.'

Swallow's album *Blow* can be viewed as one of the more underrated contributions to shoegaze, but it left no lasting trail of brilliance. Ivo says he still likes the album, but surely his truer feelings are reflected in 4AD's release of the instrumental version *Blowback* only months later. Trehy says she knew Ivo had also suggested Mason carry on with another singer and that it went downhill from there: 'Mike wanted to be a pop star and he resented me clinging on.'*

With Swallow and 4AD parting ways, another of the new *Lilliput* offerings was to prematurely stall. Spirea X had yet to release another record after *Fireblade Skies*, which Jim Beattie puts down to his stubborn resistance to advice (shades of fellow Scot Robin Guthrie) and Ivo's odd behaviour. 'He wanted us to sound more like "Spirea Rising", and have Judith singing,' Beattie recalls. 'I hated singing but if Ivo suggested something, I'd go the other way, because I hadn't asked for it. So I left Judith off our new demos. I admit there were lots of drugs involved at the time. Another thing was, Ivo told our manager that the music that had influenced me wasn't the obvious stuff, which I imagined to be a good thing! But Ivo wanted us to be more obvious. How do you do that? I think that was part of the stress he was under.'

Beattie recalls Ivo giving him, 'strange records, lots by German bands, but darker-sounding than krautrock'. He continues, 'Deborah

* Geoff Travis at Rough Trade offered the duo a lifeline, but after one EP for the label, *Hush*, in 1994, Travis lost his financial backer (One Little Indian co-founder Brian Bonnar) and control of the label. 'It was the second big blow to everything we were trying to do,' Mike Mason says. 'Even though [Louise Trehy and Mason] had a daughter by then, our relationship fell apart, and we split up.'

told us that he was going into this awfully dark art phase, like bondage photography by Helmut Newton [Ivo thinks Beattie means Joel-Peter Witkin, who preferred staged tableaux of society outcasts, including amputees and transsexuals: 'I bought Witkins' work around that time. I wasn't a big Newton fan – too smooth']. Ivo kept talking about how he couldn't take Cocteau Twins to the next level, and that's why they'd left. He'd taken it badly, and you could see the strain. But as far as Cocteau Twins went, at least Ivo had put his money into 4AD. He wasn't living it up in Cannes. And he didn't drop many bands. But he dropped us.'

With Michael Brook heading off to make records for the Real World label, that left only The Wolfgang Press, Heidi Berry and His Name Is Alive among the *Lilliput* hopefuls. It was a curator's triptych in the traditional 4AD mould, but how Warners must have secretly wanted a Pixies or a Lush, or any band that could match Throwing Muses' dramatic impact.

Not that Kristin Hersh had ever wanted to play ball with Warners, to the point of packing up completely, but she had decided – or her songs had decided for her – that she could carry on and had recorded a new Throwing Muses album with Dave Narcizo. In the process, Hersh declares, 'We became a band that didn't give a fuck. We were starting over, in a better place.'

The duo had even considered changing the band name. Narcizo recalls one suggestion was Khuli Loach, 'a type of fish, but Billy [O'Connell] talked us out of it!' The old name wasn't dishonest; wasn't Throwing Muses Hersh and Narcizo, as Ivo had said? With Fred Abong joining Belly, former Muses bassist Leslie Langston helped out, and the *Red Heaven* album unveiled the concept of Throwing Muses as a dynamic power trio – a template that remains to this day, with Bernard Georges joining as permanent bassist as soon as the album was recorded. 'That was the band I had been looking for,' Hersh admits. 'I liked the strength of a trio. And I liked not giving a fuck!'

Ivo was again the band's A&R, but he left them alone to produce their own album, which was handed over after completion. The ebullient mood of *Red Heaven* was clear from the lead single 'Firepile' but it was the B-side's pummelling take on Jimi Hendrix's 'Manic Depression' that truly rang in the changes. Another B-side, a revamp of the *Chains Changed* track 'Snail Head', drove the point home – faster, heavier, looser. Four months later, 4AD released *The Curse*, a whole live album of old and current songs; chains not so much changed as snapped.

The album's opening track 'Furious' was well named too, and the blistering feel of 'Dio' was reinforced by the guest vocals of ex-Hüsker Dü guitarist/singer Bob Mould. Hersh's gentler side was framed by 'Pearl' and 'Summer Street' and the bonus limited edition of her solo show at New Jersey club Maxwell's. 'I don't think anyone tried very hard to sell *Red Heaven*,' says Hersh, 'but we were happy because we were kids again.'

Ivo had been thinking along the same lines. As an antidote to all the fuss, he conceived of a project – a new label, in fact – that would mirror the label's original one-off ideals. It would be like a system-restore setting on a computer. 'I was sick of being calculating with our releases, of working with people because it was essential that we sold records,' Ivo explains. 'I wanted to get away from something that was becoming a predictable formula, which would prevent us from having just a successful record, and that just built careers – that's not what I was good at as an A&R person. That's not what I was good at. So no first single, tour, video, and strictly one-off releases.'

This had to be the first time a record label discouraged the possibility of growth. 'When 4AD started, a record was made, given a catalogue number and released,' Ivo continues. 'What happened after that, whether it sold five copies or a million, was irrelevant.'

Ivo named the label Guernica, after Pablo Picasso's painting of 1937, created in response to the bombing of a village in northern Spain by German forces during the Spanish civil war. 'I remember being really affected by the painting at school. The picture was clearly not painted for decorating rooms; it was an offensive and defensive instrument of war against the enemy.'

The plan also included a free seven-inch single with each vinyl version of a Guernica album, to firmly put the emphasis on music. Ivo also sought out another design team, The Senate, 'so it wasn't 4AD-esque'.

Lined up for August, the debut Guernica release, *Imperial f.f.r.r.* by the US trio Unrest, was so strong it seemed Ivo's A&R instinct had been reborn.Unrest was a particularly imaginative, sharp and playful guitar-pop trio from Washington, DC. Today, the band's singer-songwriter-guitarist Mark Robinson still retains the same quirky instincts. For paid work, he designs book jackets for publishers Houghton Mifflin Harcourt while still running his independent label Teen-Beat. He also sings in the a cappella group Cotton Candy, who specialise in Fifties and Sixties commercial jingles, as well as the Unrest-like trio Flin Flon.

Robinson's musical youth had been marked by classic Seventies rock, from Queen to Elton John, but punk and post-punk had wiped that slate clean; while his classmates were playing Van Halen and Rush covers, Unrest was being named after a song by Seventies Brit-art rockers Henry Cow. Robinson and future Unrest drummer Phil Krauth were among his school friends in Arlington, Virginia, a bunch of whom started a label in 1984 to release their school band rehearsals. He'd subsequently started Teen-Beat at college in Boston, where he had met future Unrest bassist Bridget Cross.

Teen-Beat was modelled on 4AD and Factory, creating beautiful artefacts with distinct artwork. For example, Robinson pressed only 1,040 copies of their unofficially self-titled 1987 debut album, each with a hand-decorated cover. Since each one was different, each copy had its own title. Catalogue numbers were even given to the label's Christmas cards. Teen-Beat had also licensed In Camera's CD compilation *13 (Lucky For Some)* that 4AD had just released.*

---

* After In Camera split, singer David Scinto, bassist Jeff Moore and Moore's then girlfriend formed Deflowered, but the trio never released any music. In 1991, Scinto, Moore and In Camera guitarist Andrew Gray reconvened to record four tracks, but without drummer Jeff Wilmott, who had moved to the US. Given Gray's Wolfgang Press commitments in the interim, and the producer was Wolfies associate Drostan Madden (he co-produced the band's last two albums), the new material sounded more like Gray's current band than his old one. 'It was a failed experiment,' says Scinto. 'Jeff wasn't there, and In Camera was the four of us. And Drostan was a lovely guy but he was too anal, fiddling with little bits of tape!'

'4AD and Factory were like mysterious art projects more than record labels,' Robinson recalls. 'I'd been working in a record store, and sometimes 4AD sleeves didn't even have the band's name, let alone pictures. You didn't know what would be inside when you got it home. Even if you weren't going to buy a record, you'd still like it. Those records were all over college radio, and all my friends listened to them.'

Imperial f.f.r.r. was Unrest's fourth album, 'a cleaner and more focused record, with the humour more buried, than what came before,' Robinson reckons. Former 4AD staffer Sheri Hood had recommended the album to Ivo, who fell in love with it during a lengthy drive in a hired convertible up Highway One between LA and San Francisco – even though he admits he was terrifying himself with thoughts of driving off the road and careering down the cliff and into the ocean. Vertigo had become another symptom of depression, meaning he could no longer walk across a bridge, take an escalator or even watch a concert from the balcony.

The second release showed Ivo was not following any particular path with Guernica. Melbourne's Underground Lovers was spearheaded by high-school friends Vincent Giarrusso and Glenn Bennie. Debut album *Get To Notice* was independently distributed by Shock, 4AD's Australian distributor, and when Ivo was in Australia to meet Shock, he was handed a tape of the band's new album *Leaves Me Blind*. By the time he was back in London, a one-off deal was on the table.

Giarrusso: 'All we knew is that Ivo liked the album and wanted to release it, and that's all we wanted to know. The rest is just guff.' Ivo would have agreed with that, but not with Giarrusso's view of 4AD. 'In our small bubble, it was a huge cult label, carefully curated, wanky but generally good. As poor musicians, we would often troll the Shock warehouse and take anything we could get from the 4AD racks. We loved Pixies, Cocteau Twins, M/A/R/R/S, The Birthday Party. The perception was of a stereotypical preciousness and seriousness, but the British [music] I really liked was the wacky, satirical side.'

That included the Madchester sound, which according to Giarrusso was 'uplifting, funny, working class', using 'rhythm loops, samples and repetition to drive the beat and support the song'. Not that Underground Lovers were cut from the same cloth as The Happy Mondays. Giarrusso, who now lectures in film and TV at Melbourne's Swinburne University of Technology, says 4AD's strategy 'often reminded me of the idea of taste and cultural aspirations as a marker of socio-economic habitus, which inevitably led to questions of class division and exclusivity'. Which, couched in less semiotic terms, was similar to what Robin Guthrie thought – that 4AD were a bunch of middle-class snobs.

Giarrusso also claims that one 4AD employee told him that *Leaves Me Blind* was 'the most loved, played and sold the most of all Guernica releases. We never saw figures so it was only his word.' Since it was on Guernica, *Leaves Me Blind* wasn't followed up by another album, and 4AD video commissioner Cliff Walton says the band hoped it would lead to a 4AD deal. In fact, Underground Lovers never released another record in the UK,

By Ivo's reckoning, Guernica's most popular album was the label's third and last of 1992. By the sound of it, Dutch quartet Bettie Serveert was particularly taken by the American post-hardcore trio Dinosaur Jr and similarly molten US bands, but with a real dedication to songs, and the attractively smoky voice of Carol van Dijk to soften the blow. Growing up in the east of the Netherlands, Peter Visser had grooved to hard rock staples Deep Purple and Status Quo: 'Punk rock never reached me,' he claims, so he went looking for it instead.

Visser says his first band De Artsen (in Dutch, The Doctors) was partly influenced by Joy Division, and when the band's singer quit, Visser began a new band with drummer Berend Dubbe and the band's sound technician, Carol van Dijk. New bassist Herman Bunskoeke made four, with Dubbe naming Bettie Serveert after a book (in English, *Bettie Serves*) written by Dutch tennis player Betty Stove. The band later wished they'd made a less flippant choice but the target audience in the US and the UK had no clue to the name's origins.

Bettie Serveert had split up after just one show, but reformed in 1990 and got a deal with the New York independent Matador for the US. Ivo had been sent the demos, and Guernica released the band's debut album *Palomine* in the UK. Visser says the artwork – a simple shot of a toy dog – took 20 minutes to create, but it had something of v23's style of investing everyday objects with a new significance. *Palomine* got great reviews, especially in the US, where Ivo recalls hordes of A&R men at the band's first show outside of Europe. Yet he and Bettie Serveert, he says, 'didn't get on particularly well, and I didn't particularly love them'. But Beggars Banquet did, and Bettie Serveert became the first band since Bauhaus to swap sides at Alma Road.

Guernica might come free of stress and expectation but the label could never really express Ivo's true feelings about music. Unlike his newest signing to 4AD, which combined his core values – beauty, authenticity, emotion, a towering vocalist and an original spin on folk rock's properties in the music's inexorably slow, minimalist delivery.

Red House Painters was described as slo-core, but also sadcore; singer Mark Kozelek sang of the inevitable damage that love – and youth – brought with unflinching realism. 'Lost hope, tortured idealism, love madly unrequited – that sounds about right to me,' Kozelek says. The band quickly became Ivo's favourite 4AD artist of the era, and over time, has succeeded Cocteau Twins as his favourite ever signing. 'Red House Painters was the peak of collaboration between the artist and the record label, with v23, all in harmony, to get the best creative results,' Ivo says.

Born in Massillon, Ohio, several state boundaries from the trend-influenced cosmopolitan centres on the east and west coasts, the band's founding member Mark Kozelek was a classic rock fan, into Led Zeppelin and Pink Floyd, Heart and Peter Frampton. 'Massillon was a football town, and the energy from the Massillon Tigers' high-school football team was always in the air,' Kozelek recalls. 'I didn't like football and so I went searching for something else, and I found a guitar.'

By the age of ten, Kozelek had already found drugs and alcohol, and done a stint in teenage rehab. Now sober, he had channelled his energies into songwriting, though he'd eschewed the formula of classic rock for a very distinct alternative. 'I've liked music that's fast and hard, and I went through a stage of playing punk,' he told me in 1992. 'But I've otherwise enjoyed songs more than riffs, lyrical songs with acoustic guitars, which sound much better when it's slow – anything else feels really forced. I'm a pretty slow-paced person. I keep to myself in lots of ways, and my songs come from spending time in my apartment and in bed.'

His first band, God Forbid, was shortlived, and when Kozelek had his first relationship crisis, in 1986, he decided to relocate to Atlanta. An advert in the local paper found drummer Anthony Koutsos before the pair moved on to San Francisco. 'Atlanta had jobs and a music scene, but it was very redneck,' Kozelek recalls. 'I had visited San Francisco in 1988 and I fell in love the moment I stepped on to Market Street.'

In San Francisco, Kozelek worked as a hotel night clerk, adding bassist Jerry Vessel and guitarist Gorden Mack through more ads and taking a new band name from local painting crew The International League of Revolutionary House Painters. San Francisco already had one sadcore institution, American Music Club, but Kozelek stripped everything right to the bone, with his refusal to hide behind metaphors and his voice etched with the unmistakable mark of depression. Drummer Koutsos ignored any temptation to speed up the tempo even when RHP songs broke the ten-minute mark. Audiences needed patience, and some empathy with a desperate world view.

After seeing American Music Club for the first time, Kozelek invited the band's guitarist Vudi to watch his own band. Vudi brought along AMC's singer-songwriter Mark Eitzel. Soon Kozelek began dating Eitzel's friend, and before long Red House Painters opened for AMC. But in the age of grunge, only small audiences – and not yet one record label – had embraced Kozelek's particular brand of unhappy. Kozelek says he was, 'getting tired of nobody knowing us, copying demos on a boombox' but he'd given Eitzel some Red House Painters tapes and asked him to pass them on to interested parties.

It was in a London hotel room in late 1991 that, during an interview, Eitzel gave me a Red House Painters cassette. It was 90 minutes long. As a piece of music, it was fantastic; given it was a demo, it was better than any other I'd heard. I copied it twice and sent a copy to Geoff Travis at Rough Trade and another to Ivo.

'I'd never had a 90-minute demo to listen to,' Ivo recalls. 'I'd drive from my flat in Clapham to Alma Road, and I'd stick the tape on and hear the first track, "24", and then I'd arrive at the office. When I started again, I'd wind it back to the start and hear "24" again. So it went on. I now think "24" would have been enough for me to pick up the phone straight away, it's such a knee-buckling song. But it took me weeks to hear the whole tape.'

Ivo telephoned Kozelek, who was in the bath when he took the call: 'It was very surreal and caught me off guard,' he recalls. 'I knew nothing about 4AD, or the music business, although I recognised the name Cocteau Twins when he mentioned them. But I knew Ivo was for real. And, within the first ten seconds of the conversation, that we would release a record on 4AD.'

'Ivo told me to go and meet Mark Kozelek,' head of 4AD US Robin Hurley recalls. 'That's when you realise why people like Ivo are so special at what they do, because the music was lo-fi to say the least. But Ivo heard through the surface noise and the rambling to what was underneath.'

'Mark had a self-deprecating sense of humour, and was self-obsessed, which is a compliment, because you'd have to be to make music like that,' says Ivo. 'It was absolutely beautiful and very sad and not like anything else at the time.'

Ivo reckoned the demos were strong enough to release, but told Kozelek (as he had Charles Thompson) that he could re-record any songs for future release. Named after its longest track – nearly 11 minutes – *Down Colorful Hill* comprised just six songs (Ivo's choices). Another lengthy epic, 'Medicine Bottle', very slowly dissected another failed relationship while 'Michael' paid painful tribute to a friend who had slid into the druggy delinquency that Kozelek had escaped, another epic. 'Ivo's choices were perfect,' says Kozelek. 'My only regret is that I remixed some of it, which came out too bright and glossy.' At 43 minutes, *Down Colorful Hill* was longer than most albums, but it was still marketed as a mini-album.

'Chris Bigg described *Down Colorful Hill* as making Lou Reed's *Berlin* sound like a disco record,' Vaughan Oliver recalls. 'It really gets in there.'

The role of v23 was crucial, with Simon Larbalestier's photo of a bed draped in a lace bedspread, given a sepia wash to emphasise the image's solitary power. Kozelek had rejected Vaughan Oliver's first idea – a photo of a dead cow hanging by its hooves. Oliver had also baulked at Kozelek's own choice: 'We'd normally try to go with the flow of a band's suggestion, if they have strong ideas,' says Oliver. 'But Mark's idea was this flattened sunflower in horrible colours, which was so far from the music. I persuaded him that the sleeve should look like the music felt – melancholic, reflective, romantic and slightly desperate. The line, "*We went into a big house/ And slept in a small bed*" ['Medicine Bottle'] was what clinched it for Mark. It's one of the most complete images we ever did. The band was so close to my heart.'

Signing Heidi Berry and Red House Painters suggested Ivo was returning to the singer-songwriter comfort of his formative years, while creating a mirror of his depressed soul, much like signing Spirea X and Swallow resembled an escapist, and ultimately pointless, attempt to engage with the here-and-now. If 4AD's early years had been almost unrelentingly downbeat and the second wave, from Throwing Muses and Pixies to Lush, had broadened the spectrum, for all the new notes of grace and breathing space in Kozelek's and Berry's music, the mood was even darker than those so-called gothic days because the expression of despair was plainspoken for once.

At the time, Ivo wouldn't have been aware of any pattern of behaviour, sunk in depression and suddenly ending his two-year relationship with Ros Earls, who ran the management company 140db. 'Mark Kozelek's lyrics were so raw and real, emotionally unfettered and beautifully descriptive, which reflected my state of mind,' he says. 'The fact that Ros and I had split was a reflection of the confusion in my head. I was starting to get totally lost.

'I'd seen a couple of therapists, for the first time in my life, both useless. I'd always had difficulty gaining access to happiness but now I was in a non-feeling state, interspersed with desperateness, of heightened sadness. Things felt out of control, and I had a responsi-bility to so many people, staff in two offices, people that I feel awful about because I didn't engage with them – or anyone in the business. It was too scary to open myself up to the reality of who I was. I can only liken it to a war situation. The seasoned army marines wouldn't talk to the new grunts, because they might be killed the next day. Why risk pain or hurt?'

The latest 4AD 'grunts' were Cliff Walton and Colleen Maloney. Walton had been editing *Promo News*, 'the only industry magazine dedicated to the pop video industry', when he heard of a job at 4AD in video commissioning, with junior responsibilities in artist liaison. He'd also begun sifting through demo submissions, feeding a shortlist to Ivo: 'He had very particular tastes, and almost everything was rejected,' Walton says. From Ireland, Maloney had been working in regional press for the major-funded label Dedicated. Ivo would sporadically call her for guest tickets to see Spiritualized, and Maloney would reciprocate for requests to see Cocteau Twins and Throwing Muses.

After a six-month absence starting at the end of 1990, Deborah Edgely had returned to replace John Best as 4AD press officer, initially working from home before gamely resuming her role in the office. But over time, working in such close proximity to her ex became intolerable and Edgely decided she had to leave 4AD. Before she accepted the post of head of press at Island Records, she had mulled over Kim Deal's offer to manage The Breeders. 'We got along really well, and after Ivo left, Kim would still visit and stay over at the house,' Edgely recalls. 'I loved The Breeders, but how could I go in the next day to 4AD as their manager? Part of me also knew it would be a real can of worms with Kim and Kelley.'

4AD offered Maloney the press officer's job. 'I told Ivo I was inex-perienced; that I was only twenty-two and did he think I could do this? He said yes. Deb was meant to stay for a month to teach me the ropes, but on the first day, you could cut the mood with a knife, and the next day, she said she wasn't coming back. The mood lifted, and I cracked on.' Maloney's first job was to get acquainted with Belly and

Ultra Vivid Scene's forthcoming albums, but Red House Painters struck her as being 'how things should move on at 4AD. I was gobsmacked by how beautiful their album was.'

Maloney was also entranced by what she calls the 'office bat phone' behind Ivo's desk. 'The only people who had the number were bands and managers, so you'd pick it up with a sense of excitement because it might be Charles, or Kristin. I got thrown in the deep end but all the artists were smart and thoughtful. Ivo was surprised that I worked more than I needed to, staying late and working over weekends. But I was young, and I didn't have emotional ties with 4AD. I was part of the new breed.'

A third new grunt was Tony Morley, Maloney's new assistant. He'd written for a student publication in Leeds, and loved 4AD. 'I was in the right place at the right time,' he says. 'Bauhaus and Modern English were before my time, so it was 4AD's second flowering that I loved, but that included The Wolfgang Press and His Name Is Alive. I've heard people say 4AD was slightly more style over content but it was all integrated to me. The artwork drew you further into this world, but in a slightly elusive way, presenting you with a different way of looking at something. Only major labels were doing what 4AD did, printing inner sleeves, embossing and trying out different inks and typography.'

At Alma Road, Morley sat by the frosted glass, he says, 'to avoid the random freaks that would knock on the door to see the offices'. 4AD fans could be unswervingly loyal, and despite Louise Trehy's suggestion that 4AD's time had passed, Maloney says, 'people still paid a lot of attention to 4AD'. But she also saw how the press would always search for new thrills and stories. Comparative under-achievers like Pale Saints and Ultra Vivid Scene struggled to maintain a press profile, and with Kurt Ralske his case wasn't helped by having taken two and a half years to release a third album.

'I had to make sure I got what I wanted this time,' says Ralske. 'I'd hit bottom with the process being so tightly controlled before, and I'd stopped growing. Before, I'd thought my insistence on total control was based on weakness and not strength, but I decided that if I selected the right people to work with, I could make the music stronger.'

Rev was co-produced by Fred Maher, who had done a sterling job on shaping *New York*, Lou Reed's best album in a decade. Maher brought in bassist Jack Daley and drummer Julius Klepacz to raise Ralske's game, and aligned with his superb and underrated guitar work 'The Portion Of Delight' and the ten-minute 'Blood And Thunder' demonstrated they were a formidable trio. Ralske says *Rev* is his strongest album, and his most underrated. 'It was slightly inconsistent but the record I wanted to make. But I felt *Rev* wasn't listened to properly, because of the timing. A lot had changed on the scene, and Ivo had probably given up on us. He said he was very happy with *Rev* but I felt very little support from 4AD. To me, they were now going through the motions.'

Ivo's memory says otherwise. 'I saw the trio play live at Maxwell's. I saw maybe two people from Columbia there, so I called the label the next day and said, "You have to get everyone involved, they're phenomenal, kickstart something!" That was another example of 4AD being wooed and seduced by a licensee that then did nothing. Columbia didn't even come up with bad ideas.'

Yet Ivo's commitment did end at *Rev*. He claims Ultra Vivid Scene's sales didn't warrant renewing the contract: 'It was traditional record company business, which is not what 4AD was supposed to be about. I only had myself to blame for doing such deals.'

The Wolfgang Press had had continuing support, creatively and financially, but that was before the Warners deal came into effect, bringing in a new fiscal arrangement based on progressively higher advances for each album. Ralske recalls Ivo explaining this, 'And though *Rev* didn't have unreasonable sales in America,' he says, 'the advance required to do a fourth album wasn't worth it, and Ivo said he didn't have the finances either. My guess is that, when he didn't get any validation for his own support, he felt he was beating a dead horse.'

Nineteen ninety-two proved to be the most transitional year in 4AD's life, even more than 1987. For every depressing scenario –

Spirea X, Swallow, Ultra Vivid Scene, Pixies – there was an artistic watermark – Heidi Berry, Red House Painters, His Name Is Alive, the birth of Belly, the return of Throwing Muses, the making of Lush and the delights of Michael Brook – to show something was worth doing for its own sake. The baby with the quiet smile in the *Lilliput* artwork, gazing up at the gargantuan world around, was still a figure of hope, just as Warners could be the way for 4AD to establish a stronger foothold for its artists.

Though no one knew it at the time, part of that story had already been written. In the summer, The Breeders had played some shows, first at Kurt Cobain's request, supporting Nirvana at two Irish shows (Dublin and Belfast) in June 1992. On a short European tour in early autumn, they'd started playing a new song with an irresistible stop-start momentum and layered hooks. Kim Deal had named it 'Grunggae'. 'The name was a joke, combining "grunge" and "reggae",' Josephine Wiggs explains, 'because Kim thought the accented riff resembled the accenting in reggae.'

Though no one knew it at the time, Ivo still had a hankering to spend more time in America. He may have been encouraged to actually make a move by a meeting during that summer, at the Lollapalooza show outside of LA. Backstage, he had bumped into Lush's drummer Chris Acland holding hands with a girl he found incredibly attractive. 'Later on, in the dressing room, we got chatting, and we got on well enough for me to want to track her down in LA.'

Brandi Machado had met Acland at a party in Los Angeles on tour while Lush was opening for Cocteau Twins, and they'd met up whenever he was passing through LA. Beside Warners, Ivo now had another reason to spend time in LA. For now, he was heading off to Thailand, alone, for a dose of hopefully regenerative winter sun, probably feeling like a tiny little speck in a Brobdingnagian world.

17 1993

AMERICA DREAMING,
ON SUCH A WINTER'S DAY
(bad3001-bad3017)

Formed a band and had loads of good songs like
'Love Froth Tuesday', 'Pancake Candy Shoes'
Got a good guitarist, but he's got a sad barnet
'Kiss Cream Carnival', 'Lime Sky Spooky Pills'
It's me 4AD3DCD
And I'm on a foundation course
Playing eerie madrigals
On the campus egg slicer
I'm a pop sensation
I'm an all-round icon
Thank God Cardigan
Laugh Crash Sunday School
Kiss Cream Carnival
Lime Sky Spooky Pills
The flotsam, the jetsam
The cherubim and seraphim
On me foundation course.

('4AD3DCD', Half Man Half Biscuit, 1993)

Returning to London from Thailand, Ivo caught up with 4AD US staffer Robin Hurley. 'He could tell that I was confused and struggling. Robin suggested I work out of LA for a month. He said it would be great for the relationship with Warners and the new 4AD office in LA.'

Ivo was not about to abandon London; at the time, he told me in an interview for the independent trade music monthly *The Catalogue*, 'I'm going to work in LA half the year. But in my mind, it's pretty likely that, after about a year, I'll move there. It's purely personal reasons. I want to get away from England.'

In any case, Ivo had big plans in London for another label landmark, to draw a line under 4AD's achievements to date as *Lonely Is An Eyesore* had in 1987. This time, it would be a live event, staged in the summer, which Ivo had christened *The 13 Year Itch* – being thirteen years since Axis/4AD had started. 'It's like the traditional marriage, "seven year itch", but mine's been going for thirteen,' he said. 'But it's not a celebration, more that it seemed a good time to do this.'

The itch, he'd explained, was a love-hate relationship with the music industry: 'I need a different perspective on my response, and what I believe my position is within it, and whether it has any relevance. I can get that in America for a while. Part of the reason for moving is that I will have to create a "me" in the UK, which will distance me from the industry, and hopefully give me more time and desire to focus on making music, to be more involved with people making music, to be more creative. I still get the same buzz from a demo, a finished record or a great gig, but I get less and less satisfaction from wondering what to do with it, how to market it, if it's appropriate to put a sticker on, or wondering why someone who is a delight to work with suddenly becomes an utter pain in the arse! It's me, probably. Artists probably wonder the same thing about me.'

He talked particularly about the desert to the east of LA: Joshua Tree and Death Valley. 'It's the space there. I feel spiritually more focused there, and therefore happier, and I hope I can get recharged. Since the Cocteau Twins episode, I really have withdrawn from my relationships with artists but I've found it easier to open up in

America, as people are more open. There's that "good day" bullshit but that's far more preferable to grim, oppressive, depressive London.'

He talked of having 'brilliant people' in both offices. 'The only thing missing right now is the person to effectively fall into my shoes here, so that I can be freed up. It's possible the move is happening internally.' He thought 4AD would benefit from somebody who was less of a soft touch than he was financially, who could control it better than he had. 'There are lots of Americans to deal with – His Name Is Alive, Charles, Belly, Throwing Muses, The Breeders, Unrest, Red House Painters, Ultra Vivid Scene, and one or two who may get signed in the future.'

In a comment about how American artists also inspired him, it wasn't hard to imagine Robin Guthrie was still on his mind. 'Rather than a drive and a passion to make music the British generally behave as if it's their God-given right to be in a group, and that working with a record label is potentially a chore, and that the label is potentially the enemy. The majority of Americans I know in groups pick up guitars – if there's one in the room, they'll play it. If groups come over for promotion, they ask for a guitar. The British almost have to be forced to think about writing songs and making demos. It's just not in their blood in the same way. There's an "I'm owed" attitude. Apart from the British musicians I'm working with, of course!'

That didn't mean Ivo only wanted to sign American artists. 'It goes in phases. The period when I enjoyed more English music was around 1989, the whole shoegazing concept with Lush, Pale Saints, Slowdive and Ride,' explained. 'They were taking influences from the Sixties but being as experimental as people were then, from one album to another, a classic example being The Byrds. But it didn't happen here. It seems that those groups very quickly influenced American bands to take the next step, like the Swirlies. They sound too derivative of My Bloody Valentine and Pale Saints, but their album is better than the majority of things I've recently heard. I'll probably hear more British demos when I'm in America because I'll have the time to listen.'

Our interview concluded by Ivo saying he wasn't worried about change. 'My attitude is, things are meant to be. It's got nothing to do with zooming down with twenty-five other A&R men, which puts me off more than anything. I don't see myself as someone with their finger on the pulse. When I got the Red House Painters demo it took me weeks, months, before I called. Fuck the instant thing.'

Throwing Muses hadn't been an instant addition to 4AD either; but were a band that continued to press ahead and break new ground. Tanya Donelly's decision to leave the band to forge her own path was part of that progress, and Belly's debut album was the fulfilment of a decade of the kind of songwriting dedication that Ivo was talking about. 'I think that as long as I'm in somebody else's band, I'll never become a good songwriter,' she told me in 1992. 'I needed to learn the hard way.'

The suitably titled *Star* exceeded the promise of *Slow Dust* and 'Gepetto', with a weighty 51 minutes (though a third of the fifteen tracks were already available) of grit, fragility and classic pop tropes. Donelly says that she wrote most of the songs when Throwing Muses were about to record *The Real Ramona*. She says the solo country lament 'Untogether' was 'a goodbye song' in three verses. She wouldn't say who the second verse was for, but the '*frog who was endlessly testing my faith/ He made out outrageous demands*' could well have been Howard Gough. The last verse was definitely for her old band: '*Now the bird nest on my back keeps me turning and straining to see/ We threw outrageous parties, we were golden/ Now the bird keeps her distance and I keep my speed/ Sometimes there's no poison like a dream.*'

'I felt like I had to dance around my departure from Throwing Muses for a couple of years, because it wasn't a good subject matter for Kristin,' says Donelly. '*Star* was a transitional record for me, representing the time when I was completely revamping my life. New band, new relationship, new everything.'

For once, Ivo's choice of lead single worked a treat. 'Feed The Tree', one of four tracks Gil Norton had produced, became the first 4AD track to win MTV's highly coveted Buzz Bin slot, and off the back of that guaranteed exposure, *Star* sold half a million copies in the US alone. In Britain, it had the same impact, and was only kept off the top of the UK national charts by Beggars Banquet's hard rock renegades

The Cult. 'Nobody expected *Star* to chart so high,' Colleen Maloney recalls, 'or Beggars would have moved The Cult album to a different week.'

A remixed 'Gepetto' was released with six new B-sides split over two EPs. The new cover versions showed Donelly's distinct halves: fizzy Tanya (Tom Jones' Sixties pop belter 'It's Not Unusual') and heart-achy Tanya (The Flying Burrito Brothers' lovelorn country ballad 'Hot Burrito #1'), but it was the kind of marketing ploy that Ivo should have vetoed. 'Formatting was what was needed to keep your head above water during a campaign,' says Maloney. 'And we'd hire a proper plugger for proper pop songs like "Feed The Tree" and "Gepetto". You might want to put all the attention on the album but the media didn't work like that. Bands like Lush didn't want to be known for wonderful artistic albums, they wanted to be in the charts.'

Success by playing the game was no success for Ivo. 'He told me that Belly's success was the beginning of the end of him with 4AD,' says Donelly. 'Our success, and what was to come, meant that everything ballooned out for him. It was exciting for everyone but stressful too. All of a sudden, there were many more employees at 4AD, and as things grew, the experience wasn't as sweet.'

Donelly was one of the sanest among 4AD's club of fragile creatures, but even she struggled with the concept of success. 'It threw everything into turmoil, because Belly was still coming from this position of integrity. Like, what is pure, and what is cool? Do we appear on magazine covers? That stuff fell by the wayside years ago, but back then people still obsessed over doing the right thing – no ads, no corporate sponsorship ... we constantly and agonisingly soul-searched every decision.'

Fred Abong had already left Belly by the time of *Star* (the band photo in the album's booklet suggested Belly was a trio like Throwing Muses), choosing to train as an Ayurvedic astrologer and nutritionist. 'Fred and I were very close at that point, and we'd co-written a song [*Star* highlight 'White Belly'] and I wanted us to write more,' says Donelly. 'I was amazed he'd walk away when it was obvious things were going upward. But he felt it wasn't the lifestyle for him.'

Abong's replacement was Gail Greenwood, a change of sex and of attitude. The artwork that Chris Bigg designed included photos supplied by Chris Gorman (like Throwing Muses, Belly had a drummer with artistic ambitions), there were images of tiny ballerinas and a sea of nuts and bolts; Greenwood, a former member of all-female grunge band L7 in Doc Marten boots, was tough as nuts'n'bolts, right down to her goofy heavy metal stage persona. 'I thought, let's do the opposite of what people expect, let's rub up against the preciousness,' says Donelly. 'Gail was extremely charismatic, charming and fun, and we loved having her on board.'

After *Star*'s ascent, came Ultra Vivid Scene's decline following the release of the *Blood & Thunder* EP. It was only four and a half years since that hugely promising debut album. The sublime trinity of albums he left behind was tainted by the feeling that Ralske didn't appear to enjoy his experience, as he only released a minimal amount of music again, preferring production and then the visual side of art.

Another ending took place before Ivo had even booked a flight to America: news of Pixies' split broke during Charles Thompson's interview by the BBC Radio 5 show *Hit the North*. 'The last show we ever did was in Vancouver, at the end of a tour, and we all just went home,' Joey Santiago told me in 2003. 'Everybody was under the impression that we were taking a year off, like a sabbatical, but it never came to that. Charles started his own album, and Kim had The Breeders. Three or four months later, Charles called, out of the blue, at my girlfriend's house, to say he was splitting the band, and that he'd faxed Kim and Dave [Lovering].'

Ivo says the myth that Thompson informed the other Pixies by fax still annoys him. 'It's true Charles wrote a fax, but also that Ken [Goes] refused to send it, saying he wasn't paid enough to do something like that.'

In 2012, Santiago says the only fax was the one Thompson sent to Ken Goes. Kim Deal recalls getting a call while in the studio recording a new Breeders album. 'I had no reaction other than I wasn't surprised,' she says. 'It had clearly run its course.'

'You'd really have to ask Charles why,' says Santiago. 'But I'm sure the tension between Kim and Charles had something to do with it. Charles hasn't even discussed it: it's not his style to analyse. It wasn't like we ended up fist-fighting or arguing constantly, it was more unspoken tension. Kim phoned me and said, "Did you know that the Pixies just broke up?" and I replied, "I'd be more surprised if we got back together". I was shocked but what could I do? I thought it was premature because I really thought we could do more. Ending that abruptly was weird.'

Thompson says he has had enough therapy since 1993 to be philosophical about Pixies' demise, though he noticeably doesn't refer to Kim Deal: 'Apart from writing anthems, the only other thing Ivo encouraged us to do was make records at a regular pace. I'd say that was one of the factors that ultimately broke Pixies up. I wasn't looking for advice, and I'm not blaming 4AD, but it would have been great if they'd had an A&R guy whose job it was to sit artists down and help plan the next move, or had said, "Slow down or you'll burn out the band". A good manager would have done that too. In the end, it was too much of a treadmill, of being on the road, at that pace. But 4AD was thinking, "How do we sell more records?" And we were one of many bands on 4AD. If Ivo was the father figure, he had lots of children, and he couldn't give all of them the same amount of attention.'

That Thompson felt less important to Ivo would have made Robin Guthrie smile: the more importance an artist felt seemed to mean a bigger ego to be dashed. Thompson also admits that he too had drug issues, albeit of a softer variety than Guthrie's habit. 'I was smoking too much marijuana, and not being clear-headed I'd get wound up by stupid stuff I'd never get wound up by now. I must have been frustrating to deal with.'

Even if Ivo had acted like a career advisor, Thompson thinks it would have been fruitless. 'It didn't seem like we were doing anything wrong at the time. Up until *Bossanova*, people were slapping us on the back and saying Pixies was the greatest thing ever. That had levelled out but enough people were still saying it, so you kept on believing it.

The person who had the best chance to slow us down was Gil [Norton], but I was cocky and full of energy, and wanting to learn, to throw ideas down, to write in the studio. Gil would have been trying to let me do my thing.'

Ivo's first port of call when he left the UK for the States that year was San Francisco. There, he visited The Breeders during the new album's closing session with Mark Freegard, who had engineered the *Safari* EP and progressed to co-producer. Kelley Deal was now a permanent fixture in the band, having quit her job as a technical analyst when denied more leave; and with Britt Walford choosing to stay focused on Slint, Deal had snapped up Jim Macpherson, the drummer of the Dayton band The Raging Mantras. He had regularly posted flyers through Deal's letterbox until she turned up to see one of their shows. Macpherson was a different proposition to Walford: 'Jim was extremely powerful, but also sensitive, which was a very interesting combination,' says Josephine Wiggs.

Driven harder by Macpherson, The Breeders started to resemble a different band to the one that had made *Pod*, especially armed with the new version of 'Grungae', which was now called 'Cannonball'. It also had a new deeper, rippling bass intro. For inspiration, Deal singles out the basslines of Mick Allen, especially the *Queer* cut 'Louis 14th': 'warm and oozing, up and down the fretboard,' says Deal. The actual finished part was down to a mistake: Wiggs had played the last note flat but everybody decided it was better for it.

Freegard recalls the first time he heard Kim's newest batch of songs: 'She was playing them down the phone, her guitar perched on her knee, saying, "Kelley, play the lead guitar I taught you" as I made notes.' But this impromptu approach was drastically altered in the studio, as a three-week booking turned into four long months with Kim painstakingly building a new sound, full of overdubs and treatments.

'All of a sudden, independent music had become a tag word, a philosophy,' Deal explains. 'There had been this college music network across the country, in the early days of R.E.M., and then Pixies, Throwing Muses, Sonic Youth. We're all going overseas, and someone sees this young community that marketing people can reach, so there's sponsorship and advertising dollars, and you've got this thing called Alternative Music, a tag word that I was told market research had shown piqued the interest of readers from the age of fifteen to thirty-two.

'Nirvana just blew it all up. Grunge was in *Vogue* magazine, and bands were signing to majors who were creating indie labels for them. The whole phenomenon was cynical and strange to me, so to have our album sound so produced was a reactionary move. But on "Cannonball", I'm screaming the last line, and we're manipulating my voice all the way. It sounded great, but it wasn't a template for radio.'

'It was an exhausting recording because things were so unpredictable,' says Freegard. 'For "Flipside", for example, Kim wanted it to sound like a bad cassette. The project became one big edit, but no computer in sight. Kim wouldn't have it. It was exhausting and stressful for everyone, but mostly Kim, because of expectations, from management, label and herself. It took its toll.'

The shed-load of pot that Kim was consuming might have made the sessions a lot of fun, but would have only added to the trial. Freegard discovered pieces of burnt silver foil in the lounge area, suggesting harder drugs were also being consumed, but any such use was kept hidden from the other members. The sessions continued in San Francisco, where the band stayed on houseboats as the last pieces of the musical puzzle were slotted into place.

After flying on to LA, Ivo rented an apartment for a month, where he recalls listening to Dead Can Dance's forthcoming album *Into The Labyrinth* for the first time. After that, he planned to spend ten days in LA, at his brother's place or a hotel, and ten days back in London, and repeat. In theory, Ivo could work anywhere in the northern hemisphere and still give the LA office a figurehead, even if his core strengths didn't run to meet-and-greet duties. And he was hardly zooming down to gigs. Live shows of non-4AD artists were largely confined to the likes of San Diego's blues rockers The Paladins: 'It was a relief to see something that made me feel good and I didn't have to give a "professional" opinion afterwards,' he says.

Colleen Maloney: 'There was also a lot of readjustment for the London office to make. Ivo didn't go off the radar and it didn't seem weird that he'd be working from LA, but it was weird for artists who'd had a long-term relationship with him. They'd have gone from getting Ivo on the bat phone to reaching someone else who couldn't provide that kind of assistance.'

Eight weeks after the news of Pixies' split, Charles Thompson had the chance to emulate Donelly's break for freedom. While news of Pixies' split had yet to be announced, he'd recorded a solo album with Eric Drew Feldman, re-engaged as his musical wingman and now producer in place of Gil Norton. Thompson nevertheless re-employed Norton's engineering assistant Al Clay, but Feldman was able to put necessary daylight between Pixies past and solo present. So did Thompson's new alias – inverting Black Francis to become Frank Black.

Thompson had also re-engaged Joey Santiago (credited with 'additional guitar'), one of three guests alongside the core trio of Thompson, Feldman and drummer Nick Vincent. Like *Star*, *Frank Black* made good use of the CD format by including fifteen tracks, stylistically spanning the short, punchy flair of latterday Pixies albums with broader and often sprightlier fare; with chugging saxophones, 'Fu Manchu' was more Electric Light Orchestra than Pixies. A similar surprise was Thompson's cover of The Beach Boys' 'Hang On To Your Ego', the sole survivor of a proposed covers album that Thompson had nixed in favour of his own songs. That Thompson was smitten by his new home city was clear by the album's opener 'Los Angeles', which adapted Pixies' bristling energy with distinctly grungy guitars. The point was gleefully driven home by the hair-metal band miming in the song's video.

Frank Black might have been a liberating experience but it was also a perplexing record. Thompson knew it would be judged, and typically unfairly, by a music press lamenting the end of Pixies. And not surprisingly, the Thompson/Feldman/ Vincent trinity didn't have the same gelled personality as his old band. 'Hang On To Your Ego' was also a strange choice for a first single, as if none of Thompson's originals warranted the job. Hard-headed independence ensured Ivo had had no A&R input; he says he approved of the record without feeling any particular love for it. Relations between them 'were fine' says Ivo, adding, 'but maybe Charles had reasons, as I had, for not wanting to stay close.'

If Thompson had increasingly raised Ivo's anxiety levels, Warren Defever continued to be a paragon of harmony and co-operation. But since Defever had upgraded his studio and His Name Is Alive's approach (including using three singers besides His Name Is Alive staple Karin Oliver), many new songs for the band's third album were more concise and approachable, and he didn't require Ivo's remixing input. Ivo was still asked to compile the track listing, drawn from two albums that Defever had supplied, though he hadn't explained that one of them had been written by His Name Is Alive guitarist Melissa Elliot under the band alias The Dirt Eaters. Defever convinced Elliot to allow three of her songs on the finished album, which helped as Ivo felt that neither of the two albums was strong enough in its own right.

The seventeen tracks of the resulting album *Mouth By Mouth* bridged old and new His Name Is Alive models. From the old, the Middle Eastern-toned backing track to 'Can't Go Wrong Without You' was deliciously warped, as though the hole in the middle of the vinyl was off-centre. From the new, 'Sort Of' juxtaposed power-pop crunch and ethno-ambient passages. The noise-poppy 'Torso' contrasted with a reverent cover of 'Blue Moon', one of ex-Big Star frontman Alex Chilton's rare wistful ballads. The Brothers Quay's second His Name Is Alive video, for 'Can't Go Wrong Without You' – another brilliant animation that would have no doubt again challenged the programmers at MTV – showed that not everything was being formatted to suit current industry standards.

Warners would have appreciated Defever's new fluid approach to sound and structure: 'Proudly eclectic, reflective, and obscure – hell, arty – Warren DeFever's concession to rock normality is mood music for more moods than you'll first believe are there, including plenty of sex for the polymorphously inclined,' Robert Christgau wrote in *The Village Voice*. Warners would also have appreciated Defever's handsome face on the cover – 'just to be different,' says Vaughan Oliver, adding, 'But you don't do a portrait by draping fairy lights all over. And that was Warren's favourite bedspread in the background.'*

If only Warners could encourage Defever to leave the cosseted womb of his studio for the stage. Where the major label did force his hand was to insist he copyright-clear the multiple samples, or delete them. So the voicemail, left by accident by a woman asking to be taken to 'an insane-um asylum', which Defever had added to 'Jack Rabbits' was cut, and the illegal taping of Native American chanting on 'The Homesick Waltz'. 'We used to refer to [the Warners edition] as the "raped and dismembered" version,' says Defever. However, Warners hadn't noticed that 'Lord Make Me A Channel Of Your Peace' was composed of samples from Prince's *Under The Cherry Moon* soundtrack (or so Defever thinks, though Wikipedia claims it was 'Can't Go Wrong Without You' that was composed via samples, from Prince's *Purple Rain*). Neither source can be trusted ...

Like Defever, Ivo was a homebody and isolationist at heart, and he soon came to regret his new transatlantic lifestyle, which compounded a dislike of travelling, and made even worse by daily 2am conference calls to London when he was away. It soon became the worst of both worlds. 'In LA, I didn't feel I had found my place whatsoever in the office, and very quickly, I felt I was losing focus whenever I was in London. And when I wasn't in London, someone still needed to take care of things. Briefly, it had started to make sense, but then came the big meeting at Warners about The Wolfgang Press.'

It had been almost two years since the UK release of *Queer*, but backed by the major's promotions, 'A Girl Like You' had indeed found a place on American radio, and after twelve years of resistance, The Wolfgang Press had itself a nominal hit – a heady number 2 on Billboard's Modern Rock (Alternative Songs) chart. But that didn't

---

* Artwork for Pale Saints' 'Throwing Back The Apple' and Frank Black's 'Hang On To Your Ego' had featured the artists, following other occasional instances through the years – but always on singles. When it came to albums, it was only when the artist made that choice, such as The Wolfgang Press on *Queer*. Vaughan Oliver had never willingly done so until *Mouth By Mouth*.

mean an automatic crossover; Warners needed to expand the budget to pull out the stops for a national hit.

Ivo: 'For the first time, I joined Robin at Warners for a big meeting where the future of The Wolfgang Press was to be decided. I expected certain individuals to rally around 4AD and "A Girl Like You", but no, they decided that they would just let the song run its course. Almost ten years to the day, Modern English had been getting airplay in America with "I Melt With You" and Sire had decided not to open their cheque book and take it to top 40 radio, and here it was happening again.'

Warners head of services Steven Baker was at that meeting. He had begun as an A&R scout for Warners and enjoyed a long association with Beggars Banquet that had begun even before 4AD had started, and he'd been around when 'I Melt With You' had received a humungous amount of airplay but hadn't reached the US top 50. 'The segregation of radio formats and the charts, such as rock, pop and country and western meant that a new wave song like "I Melt With You" would not have been worked by Warners' pop department, but by alternative promotions and marketing,' Baker explains. 'British groups were almost thought of like coming from another planet, and not even New Order or Depeche Mode had pop singles.'

Baker also explains that a label of Warners' size had to prioritise releases. 'Ivo would have viewed his releases in the A and B tiers, but you'd have to take into account how many records we'd released that month, across jazz, rock, pop and alternative, so it could have been the F or G tier to Warners. But I can sympathise with Ivo's state of mind. He experienced what others had at major labels. Records slipped through the cracks that shouldn't have.'

Ivo: 'It dawned on me incredibly quickly that we'd made a massive mistake to commit everything to one label, because here was a single track breaking out and Warners wasn't prepared to get behind it. I felt they weren't on our side.'

Ivo had already told Tanya Donelly that 'playing the game' was the beginning of the end for him, so why was Warners' lack of game-playing such a disappointment? Ivo was upset enough not to return to the Warners office for years – a self-protective measure, but a potentially devastating blow to both 4AD's and Ivo's supposed bright future. But with an independent record *label* forming an alliance with a major record *company*, how did Ivo expect that it would work out?

Tim Carr, however, feels there was an element of retribution to the event, and that Ivo has unwittingly undermined his own efforts. 'Lenny [Waronker] and Mo [Ostin] never said it, but I know that they were upset by Guernica, because they thought they had had Ivo's complete attention.' Not that Warners was giving up on 4AD soon, he says: 'Everyone there loved Robin Hurley, and every single 4AD act had a champion at college radio and alternative radio,' says Carr.

Mick Allen recalls hearing of 'money being pumped into Goo Goo Dolls', American pop-punks with younger, trendier and more malleable looks than the gnarly, maverick Wolfgang Press. And was Warners truly comfortable promoting an album named *Queer*? Tim Carr says that was less an issue than the fact 'A Girl Like You' might have been a natural hit in the UK, but in the world of Nirvana, it wasn't on US radio. 'And it would take six months to make something happen with a song like "A Girl Like You",' he explains. 'How willing would The Wolfgang Press have been to tour America outside of the primary markets like New York, Chicago, Philadelphia, LA, San Francisco and Minneapolis? Even Pale Saints might have broken America if they'd been more willing to tour. Only Lush was prepared to do the work.'

Ivo had interpreted Warners' actions as the latest in a line of major labels 'wining and dining you, and then once they'd licensed your band, acting like they were waiting for something to happen first. My thoughts were, it's clear what 4AD does, who we sign and how we go about things; there's value in the music but also the logo, the graphics and the presentation, so please give us bigger exposure than we've had on import. But things almost diminished because our hipper supporters at college radio switched to another label because we'd lost that indie credibility by signing with a major. I was proud enough to think it a worthwhile risk for Warners to take, but I was wrong.'

Marc Geiger puts things into perspective, explaining that Ivo's pure ideals were impractical in the American marketplace: 'When you don't need to make your bands big, and you can let them be, there's no measurement of whether anything works or not, there's just great music. Ivo fostered the organic aesthetic of people coming to music instead of hitting you over the head with it. But in America, you needed to amp it up, because things had become more about promotion-driven marketing.

'As Ivo will tell you,' Geiger continues, 'I had been the most potent marketing force [in America] for bands like The Wolfgang Press, because I made them show up here by booking them shows, because otherwise you were left with a beautiful cover, or something you had read in the *NME*. Bands wanted success but they didn't want to know the ingredients, they wanted to hide. We'd jokingly refer to "the seven date mega-tour". Artists wouldn't have their pictures taken, and would only do one interview. Nobody to this day knows the name of The Wolfgang Press singer, or Kurt Ralske, artists who'd look down their nose at others wondering why they had more success. If you had great art *and* marketing, you could do it. Pixies could have been a stadium band but two bad single choices in a row, after they were ready to break, didn't help.'

Geiger also believes that things started to go backwards for indie music when it got polluted. 'Lollapalooza was powerful and well-timed,' he says, 'but it opened the floodgates to imitators who competed in the market, a mini-artistic perfect storm where Third Eye Blind were considered a cool band. Bands needed management to survive, and The Wolfgang Press didn't have any early on. Ivo preferred things that way, because it was more organic, but it hurt The Wolfgang Press, because you needed that commitment, hard work and focus in order to succeed in this marketplace.'

Actually, The Wolfgang Press did have management, and their choice was a problem for Ivo. 'Trent Reznor [of Nine Inch Nails] had pointed his manager John Malm in our direction,' says Mick Allen. 'He was aware of 4AD, and liked us. But he said he couldn't handle things in the UK, so we went for Ros Earls.'

Ivo was still in a relationship with Earls, whose management company 140db handled producers rather than artists. 'Ros knew people and was able to make things happen, like organising an American tour for us, which felt very positive,' says Allen. 'But once she and Ivo became an official item, she said she had to choose. It was almost like an ultimatum from Ivo.'

'I definitely didn't enjoy Ros suddenly representing them,' Ivo says. 'Our relationship had been a beautiful oasis away from 4AD, though we obviously had a lot in common.'

At least Warners couldn't influence and shape 4AD's schedule. Ivo released a box set of This Mortal Coil's three albums, with a fourth CD covering as many of the original songs that TMC had covered as he could fit and get the rights for. It was a generous and expensive gesture due to the royalties that 4AD had to pay to the sixteen song-writers over twenty-one songs. But respect, and royalties, were paid, and purchasers of the box set had the chance to share what had origi-nally inspired Ivo.

Those days, when music could be appreciated without being filtered through the demands of the workplace (anyone lucky enough to work in the industry they love will be confronted by how it taints that love) would have seemed very preferable to the shenanigans of business in the post-Lollapalooza world.

Another change was the way major labels on both sides of the Atlantic were now picking off any potentially credible alternative sound, and forming faux-indie offshoots, such as Dedicated (RCA), but using independent distributors such as Pinnacle. Could artists resist bigger major-label advances, or see artists that clearly didn't deserve them take them instead? Unrest's *Imperial f.f.r.r.* had triggered interest from Atlantic and Elektra but fortunately Mark Robinson was committed to the independent aesthetic, preferring to stick with his own Teen-Beat label in America and Ivo's offer to shift from Guernica (it being a one-off shop) to 4AD for the rest of the world. 'The deal was for much less money than we'd get with a major,' Robinson recalls, 'but 4AD were super-nice people, their office wasn't over-whelming, and we would get packaging by v23!'

Robinson was so used to running things that Unrest had completed a new album without consulting Ivo, who had only asked for some songs to be remixed for radio. He hadn't needed to be involved: 'There are great things on *Perfect Teeth*,' Ivo says. 'They did feel like American indie favourites.'

Colleen Maloney: '[*Melody Maker*'s] Everett True wrote that Unrest had sold out by signing to 4AD, implying we were EMI. Come on, get a grip! The band would like to sell records! 4AD was never indier-than-thou.'

Like Warren Defever, Robinson enjoyed playing around with form and credits. 4AD released a seven-inch single 'Isabel' (the B-side 'Wharton Hockey Club' was 101 seconds of ear-piercing electronic squeals) and the *Isabel Bishop* EP, but none of the combined six extra tracks appeared on *Perfect Teeth*, which explored every facet of Unrest's encyclopaedic pop – elegant, abrasive, reverential. Teen-Beat released the album in a numbered limited edition box containing six seven-inch singles, five on coloured vinyl. Robinson also designed the typeface for the band logo, leaving v23's Chris Bigg to design an extravagant sixteen-page booklet. 'I was probably too involved,' Robinson reflects. 'Hopefully, I wasn't too annoying.'

In keeping with the indie aesthetic, 'Cath Carroll', a frenetic rush of spindly guitars, was released after *Perfect Teeth*, with two more new B-sides. Robinson liked to pen tributes: 'Isabel' was for renowned American painter and graphic designer Isabel Bishop, while Carroll had been a busy fixture on Manchester's early-Eighties post-punk scene, co-founding the *City Fun* fanzine, befriending a young Morrissey, contributing to the *NME* under the pen name Myrna Minkoff, and recording as Miaow for Factory Records.

Carroll's crossover with 4AD was ironic as Ivo was convinced (then and now) that it had been Carroll who had penned the *NME*'s savage dismissal of *Filigree & Shadow* (in fact, 4AD's archives reveal the culprit to have been Sean O'Hagan). Ivo wasn't too bitter at the time, however: it was he that had recommended Unrest use late photographer Robert Mapplethorpe's monochrome portrait of Carroll (in her Miaow years) for the cover of *Perfect Teeth*.

Using a host of photographers, rather than relying on Nigel Grierson, showed many different facets of 4AD, though in fairness,

Grierson's portfolio did this too, beside the impressionistic experiments associated with Cocteau Twins. Vaughan Oliver's intention to keep expanding the remit had meant he'd only used Simon Larbalestier once – for Red House Painters' *Down Colorful Hill* – following the Pixies series. The sepia image of an abandoned rollercoaster for Red House Painters' forthcoming debut album looked like another Larbalestier shot, but it had come from a photographic agency. Instead, Larbalestier's image of a Venus flytrap plant adorned Heidi Berry's second 4AD album. The sepia tone Oliver gave both album covers effectively united Berry and Kozelek – the Sandy Denny and Nick Drake of 4AD.

Ivo had simultaneously compiled the track listings for both albums in his Clapham Common flat, while feeling 'single and sad, gradually piecing them together'. *Red House Painters* preceded *Heidi Berry* by two months: Ivo had trusted Mark Kozelek to produce the Red House Painters sessions himself, which the singer admits wasn't easy. 'It was a nightmare, because the initial excitement of recording twenty-three songs became, "one down, twenty-two to go",' says Kozelek. 'And I was nervous that people were now paying attention, but Ivo made helpful suggestions and never demanded anything. If we went over budget, we went over budget.'

And over budget they went. The band had begun to tackle Kozelek's backlog of songs, and by the end of the session had 120 minutes on tape, enough for a triple album. Ivo suggested a double, 4AD's first outside of This Mortal Coil. *Red House Painters* included several of Kozelek's very best songs: 'Rollercoaster', 'Katy Song', 'Mistress' and a pensive, virtually solo 'Take Me Out', which is Ivo's all-time favourite track on 4AD. With a devastating key change towards the end, which fades out at the usual snail's pace, the singer's emotions still trapped and unresolved, the lyric would have nailed Ivo's own predicament: *'That sound coming from those holes/ A voice that soars/ And takes my wounds with it/ To levels unknown/ If only you could take me out instead of back in/ To a relationship I don't understand/ If only you could take me out instead of back in/ To myself that's dying within.'*

'The line "*A voice that soars and takes my wounds with it*" always made me think of both Elizabeth Fraser and Tim Buckley,' says Ivo. 'And the chorus of "Take Me Out" could also apply to 4AD and me looking to someone for rescue.'

The music hit new heights of serene self-pity, and live too the tension could be overbearing. At a solo Kozelek show at London's Borderline, as the singer addressed the crowd with a back story, a voice in the crowd heckled, 'Now I know why she left you!'

On *Heidi Berry*, Hugh Jones was the perfect, painstaking producer, coaxing the best from a singer more generous with her wistful and bittersweet notes than Mark Kozelek was in his blanketing despair – even if the album's opening line was Berry singing, '*I walk through the graveyard/ And a late snow is on the ground.*'

The musicianship on *Heidi Berry* was extraordinary, with her brother Christopher Berry on acoustic guitar/string arrangements and guests including former boyfriend Pete Astor and the legendary Danny Thompson, plucking the double bass, as he'd once done during Tim Buckley's London stage debut in 1968. The ensemble shaped originals such as 'Little Fox' and a tender version of Canadian sisters Kate and Anna McGarrigle's compassionate ballad 'Heart Like A Wheel', expanding the elastic flow and timbre of those fabulous Seventies folk rock records.

Buoyed by what was at their disposal, 4AD and Warners even had a crack at a Berry single with 'The Moon And The Sun', a more upbeat model of rootsy British fusion. If Ivo found Warners' handling of The Wolfgang Press to be lacking, the major label seemed on board – though Berry found she was expected to play the game. She had been offered a choice between being an A or B tier release, 'to be handled by the Warners machine, or solely by 4AD,' Berry recalls. 'B was ideal but my ego said A, so I took that.' Her LA show 'had a nice English vibe', she says. 'But after, a Warners guy with a crowd around him handed me some felt tip pens and a roll of posters and said I was to sign, like I was a performing monkey. He said that he'd be right back, and left. Ivo would never have done that. When we met up, Robin

[Hurley] said, "You know Heidi, there are lots of nice people at Warners", and Ivo snorted, looked at me and said, "Robin is right". He'd become distanced from it all.'

Marc Geiger would have classified Berry as one of the artists that looked down their noses at others, but hawking oneself to sell more records was in another dimension to the artists that Ivo valued. A much more 4AD-friendly live event, one that lived on in the memory of everyone who attended, was staged two weeks after Berry's album was released. For *The 13 Year Itch*, 4AD chose London's Institute of Contemporary Arts, an austere black box of a room but with excellent acoustics and sight lines. Kristin Hersh, making her solo UK debut, headlined the week's opening night, supported by the Meriel Barham-fronted Pale Saints. Subsequent nights included the novelty sight of a His Name Is Alive performance, supporting Unrest and with former Pale Saint Ian Masters in the band.

Warren Defever punctured his retiring image by being the week's stage compère: 'He was hilarious,' says Ivo. A Guernica night show-cased Bettie Serveert and Underground Lovers, while forthcoming Guernica signings, Insides, supported Red House Painters and were the unannounced guests the next evening behind The Wolfgang Press and headliners The Breeders, who were previewing their forthcoming album. On the closing night, Heidi Berry supported Brendan Perry, also making his solo stage debut.*

Limited to 2,000 copies, *The 13 Year Itch* compilation was released on the opening day, 13 July. The thirteen tracks, unique to the album, ranged from demos – notably Hersh's solo offering 'Your Ghost' – with live versions, remixes, and Perry's effortlessly lovely rendition of Tim Buckley's 'Happy Time'. *Melody Maker*, six years after its *Lonely Is An Eyesore* cover, repeated the honour with a photo of Miki Berenyi,

* There was a surprise guest on each of the five *13 Year Itch* nights, such as Babacar – with Caroline Crawley on vocals, her then boyfriend Boris Williams (the drummer of The Cure), guitarist Rob Steen and bassist Roberto Soave of the band Presence, who had also counted founding Cure drummer Lol Tolhurst in its line-up. It turned out to be the only show for this gothic-slanted super-group, and Babacar only released one EP, *Midsummer*, in 1993 and a self-titled album in 1998.

Kristen Hersh, Mark Kozelek and a 4AD birthday cake. Someone evidently thought this was a celebration.

Vaughan Oliver provided a provocative image, a photo (taken by Bournemouth University student Tony Gibson) of a topless, blind-folded woman wearing gloves (a familiar Oliver motif). '[She was] vulnerable and denied her senses,' he explains. 'It was a perverse turn to represent the label this way, with all the festivities. And it didn't look typical of our work.' Turn the sleeve on its side and you can see a faint image of former Stock, Aitken Waterman popsicle Kylie Minogue, 'her head tipped back with her mouth open,' Oliver says. 'I liked the hidden secret.'

Ivo, meanwhile, had asked Chris Bigg to design the commemorative T-shirt with the word, 'shuffle' in brackets after the title, 'as in, "to shuffle off this mortal coil",' Ivo explains. 'It was a cry for help. I thought it was obvious I was having a real problem, but it didn't occur to anyone else.'

'We knew something of Ivo's issues, but I didn't know him well enough to ask,' says Colleen Maloney. Discussions of intimate feelings would have gone against the grain, though during the week, Kim Deal recalls noticing an exhaustion overtaking everyone involved. 'Imagine how it must have been, every day, around all those bands,' she adds. It would have been an especially sensitive occasion with Deborah Edgely attending some of the shows, as did Ivo's new love Brandi Machado, the woman who he had met the previous year at Lollapalooza.

Back in LA, Ivo laid the groundwork for a permanent move by renting an apartment, 15 minutes from 4AD's LA office in the Fairfax district, and Brandi moved in. 'I thought she was extremely good for Ivo at that stage,' says Simon Harper. 'Young, opinionated and honest. They were a good combination.'

Ivo: 'Brandi cheered me up, but it was confusing. She was confused by me. I realise that I should have quit 4AD right then. I'm glad I didn't because of a couple of records we released after that, but I was done. I was exhausted and disillusioned. I guess I could have got a lot of money for 4AD then too. But I didn't let it into my head. And it carried on and I struggled until I went crazy. But I loved that week of shows. I loved the fact we sold out every night before people knew who was playing.'

No one was more surprised that Ivo and Brandi had become an item than Miki Berenyi. 'When we first met Ivo, he was very English and proper, like a public schoolboy, not like most people we knew in the industry, which is what we liked about him,' she explains. 'He'd arrive just before we played a show and leave right after. The next thing you know, he's in LA, and shagging someone who had been going out with someone in our band! One of the side effects of being reserved and enigmatic is that people have their own ideas about what goes on behind the façade. I thought Ivo's shell harboured deep wells of wisdom and profundity and it was a shock to realise that he could be as shallow as the rest of us and as susceptible to a mid-life crisis!'

Over in London, Vaughan Oliver was watching his friend from both near and far and being forced to accept the changes. 'Ivo didn't explain stuff that he was experiencing, and I didn't pry,' he recalls. 'The move was what he wanted, so I couldn't argue with it. But I missed him, and the effect of not having that person around, that someone that everyone listened to, that enigma in the upstairs office, was traumatic.'

Heading the London office in Ivo's absence, Simon Harper was also conscious of the shift. 'I thought it would be good for Ivo, but that it could well become a problem over time, with artists, and certain managers, very concerned. But I'd talk to Ivo every day when he was away, and we'd fax too, so we were at least communicating.'

The timing of the new album from The Breeders, taking the focus off the internal anxieties of the label and back on to the music, cannot be underestimated. The record proved to be an exceptional diversion, and an even bigger hit than Belly's *Star*.

Co-producer Mark Freegard recalls how exhausted the band had been after finishing the album, yet its sound and mood was exhilarating and mostly upbeat, warm and oozing like the 'Cannonball' bass intro. A lyrical snippet from the track donated the album's title: *Last Splash*. With an equally addictive chorus hook and Kim's vocal approximating a loudhailer, 'Cannonball' struck the same balance between left-field adventure and pop accessibility as 'Monkey's Gone To Heaven'. When it was released as a single three weeks before the album, MTV's Buzz Bin programmers were instantly on the phone. Kim Deal could make cookies after all.

'Cannonball' was backed by a cover of Aerosmith's 'Lord Of The Thighs', sung by Wiggs with deadpan detachment, tapping Kim Deal's fondness for dumb American rock. But Kim had cracked the mainstream herself. 'At the end of mixing *Last Splash*,' recalls Freegard, 'Ivo came in to listen, and he said, "Mark, this is going to be the most successful 4AD record ever". I was staggered that he'd say that, but he was right.'

It would have been interesting to see the reception if Vaughan Oliver had got his way over 'Cannonball'; for the back cover he'd suggested the image of a singular testicle 'pushed through a piece of card to ensure its loneliness', as Oliver wrote on a fax to the band, alongside a drawing of said testicle. 'We tried it today and it looked super.' Well, it was one interpretation of a cannonball. 'For the back of *Safari*,' Kim recalls, 'Vaughan had wanted the texture to be an areola. I said, "Can we *not* have naughty bits?"'

Oliver's front cover design, of a fur-covered American football helmet, effectively captured the wolf in sheep's clothing that was The Breeders. With a video co-directed by Kim Deal's pal (and Sonic Youth bassist) Kim Gordon and the fast-rising Spike Jonze, 'Cannonball' topped Billboard's Modern Rock chart and entered the Billboard's national top 50 – Pixies had never achieved that, for all the acclaim and influence. In the UK, the single only reached 44, but *Last Splash* reached the top five. The album was the only time 4AD commissioned a billboard advert, the album cover's vibrant red heart splashed with blood visible on the flyover into Hammersmith, photographed by the appropriately named Bournemouth University student Jason Love.

Last Splash wasn't only about 'Cannonball' or the second, relatively gentler single 'Divine Hammer', or the third, heavyweight 'Saints'. There was a breath of style, from grungy sludge ('Roi') to breezy country rock ('Drivin' On 9', originally by US alt-folk band Ed's Redeeming Qualities, whose violinist Carrie Bradley had become a regular Breeders contributor) to Pixies-style turbulence ('No Aloha'). The album shot past 500,000 sales towards the million mark. Again, Pixies had never had such success.

Following *Star* and *Last Splash*, 4AD's purple patch continued with a Dead Can Dance album, *Into The Labyrinth*, which would go on to sell half a million copies in America and provide Warners with its first bankable return on its 4AD investment. Like The Breeders', Perry and Gerrard's album had crossed over by way of a radio hit, showing that Warners could have tried much harder with The Wolfgang Press.

The fact that Lisa Gerrard – now living back in Australia, in the rural outskirts of Gippsland, Victoria – and Brendan Perry were living so far apart didn't stop them from scaling a creative peak. *Into The Labyrinth* unfolded over 55 minutes of diverse influences, with earthier ethnic strands taking over from more medieval settings, and with every single note played by the duo for the first time. 'Everything blossomed to the point that we took on our signature shape,' says Gerrard. 'The album opened up the most doors for us too.'

No one expected Perry's stately 'The Ubiquitous Mr Lovegrove' to become a radio hit after being surprisingly picked up by LA's influential KROQ, but Warners had done its job. MTV was also on board after Tim Carr had taken one of the station's influential programmers to see Dead Can Dance: 'She couldn't believe a band this artistic and non-MTV had such a huge, young audience. She said she'd never felt more square, and was so glad I'd asked her to come.'

'The Ubiquitous Mr Lovegrove' was Perry's self-portrait, taking its title from an episode of the British Sixties James Bond-inspired *Danger Man*, while 'The Carnival Is Over' and 'Tell Me About The Forest' quoted from Joy Division lyrics ('The Eternal' and 'Love Will Tear Us Apart' respectively). Even this rarefied collection didn't really belong in the world of Lollapalooza and MTV, and the album made no concessions. The title *Into The Labyrinth* referred to the legend of the Minotaur, one of several allusions to Greek mythology. 'The Wind That Shakes The Barley' was an eighteenth-century Irish folk ballad, which Gerrard sang as if she and not Perry had the Irish roots, while the source of her 'Yulunga (Spirit Dance)' was Aboriginal Australia; she was rewarded when the National Geographic TV channel used the track as incidental music for a year.

There was, however, a concession to the preferences of MTV. Ivo says that Perry refused to make a video for 'The Ubiquitous Mr Lovegrove': 'They still had the attitude that videos, and merchandising too, was obscene. Otherwise, they could have taken things to another level.'

Perry doesn't recall a video (much as he didn't remember *Aion*'s rejected artwork), but he did agree to one for the following single, 'The Carnival Is Over', since neither of the duo had to appear. The part-animated circus theme cost £100,000 and 'was a no-brainer' according to Perry. He also thinks the video was 'a wonderful extension of the creative imagination of that piece'. If Perry is happy, who is to say the mish-mash of clichéd ethno-symbolic play-acting wasn't the right choice? But just think what the Brothers Quay could have achieved.

Red House Painters' chosen route to success was not by video but rather hypnotising people into submission. Ivo agreed to release the remainder of the mammoth recording session as an album, only six months after the last – it's why this album was also called *Red House Painters*. 'Ivo was like, "Great!"' says Kozelek. 'Any other label would have said no way.'

The cover – this time of a bridge – led fans to refer to the album as *Bridge* and its predecessor as *Rollercoaster*. Kozelek also initiated what was to become a sideline of cover versions with Simon and Garfunkel's 'I Am A Rock' (inspired by the two months Kozelek spent, 'hiding out in Tennessee, not talking to anyone, because I was so devastated about my life that I couldn't write anything') and the American national anthem 'The Star-Spangled Banner'. 'It was the polar opposite of everything else that we, or anyone else, were doing,' he claims.

There was no slacking-off at Alma Road, with three Guernica releases scheduled for the same November day. All stood apart from the other, and one was good enough to have earnt a 4AD release. Another came from a recognised source.

After leaving Pale Saints, Ian Masters had teamed up with Chris Trout in a duo they originally called The Long Lost, before settling on Spoonfed Hybrid. Trout was a former journalist who had once interviewed Masters and was playing bass in the Sheffield band AC Temple. 'Chris was very creative, playful and peculiarly funny, with a constant stream of good ideas,' says Masters, who still took creative control on an album that recalled a more pastoral Pale Saints, with none of AC Temple's Sonic Youth-style aggression. Ivo enjoyed the self-titled album enough to release it, but only on Guernica. 'Ivo didn't like Chris's voice, which he and I would argue about,' Masters recalls, 'but he offered us the one-off deal and we took it.'

Ivo agrees with Masters' assessment, 'but I still enjoyed Ian, and it was a good album. But a record had to be great or perfect to be on 4AD, so I wanted to let myself off the hook and not be so involved.'

The Brighton-based couple Kirsty Yates and Julian Tardo, who called themselves Insides, also found Ivo both an accommodating and frustrating figure. Once again, Ivo was drawn towards a domestic and creative couple, though Yates and Tardo have bucked the trend by still being together after twenty-five years. The pair had been two-thirds of Earwig with Dimitri Voulis – the trio had all met at Sussex University. 'We were the weirdos that no one else wanted to talk to!' Tardo recalls. 'Dimitri was massively into Cocteau Twins and goth, and Kirsty would be blasting My Bloody Valentine, which I found a complete revelation as I'd grown up with heavy metal. I became obsessed with Pixies too but one of the great unexplored areas of music for me was soft, ambient rock music that had a fundamental crack in it.'

Earwig's album *Under My Skin I Am Laughing* had transcended scratchy guitar roots for a slow, sombre and emotionally racked sound – a rare outbreak of UK sadcore. Earwig fan Tony Morley had played it to Ivo, who called Tardo 'out of the blue, asking if we wanted to make an album. Yes! But it meant writing it really quickly, which took us two months'. After Voulis moved to Spain, Tardo took a risk and bought a sampler to replace their traditional instruments. 'It was *de rigueur* in certain circles to get rid of guitars, which didn't pay off live as venues couldn't cope with new technology and we'd have do things like put the drum machine through a vocal PA, which sounded crap,' he says. 'But we wanted to do something different, which Ivo understood. *The 13 Year Itch* was the first time he'd heard what we were now doing, and he said, "That's the best demo I've ever heard!"'

The night of The Breeders' *13 Year Itch* show, while loading Insides' equipment, Tardo saw lines of Japanese kids outside. 'Only then did I appreciate how much people were obsessed with 4AD,' he says. Yates was equally amazed to see Kim Deal bouncing into their dressing room: 'She said, "Let's talk to these nice Insides people".'

Insides followed Spoonfed Hybrid into Palladium Studios, and the resulting album *Euphoria* was softer, more fluid and disarming than any Earwig record. Ivo loved it, enough to see it released on 4AD in America, though Tardo and Yates never heard this from Ivo; he was out of reach in LA. Tardo recalls that they'd feared *Euphoria* was too smooth, not the out-there album that Ivo had hoped they'd deliver. 'It's probably a universal feeling between band and label, when you worry and second-guess people. We had champions at 4AD, but Ivo wasn't around to push things further, so everything dissipated almost immediately.'

4AD's London office suggested Insides go on tour. 'We agreed to tour with Slowdive, but not with ridiculous noisy bands, because we were done with that,' says Tardo. 'We started to make an animated film, but the money wasn't there. [American film director] Hal Hartley said he liked us and might use something in a film – 4AD at least had connections. But it didn't happen. And Ivo was absolutely against using music in ads.'

Guernica's equivalent of a one-night stand may have fulfilled Ivo's needs but it left the artists uncertain about the next move; Unrest had shifted over to 4AD, so could Insides? 'I didn't have a burning ambition to be a 4AD band but we did want to find a home,' says Yates. 'Other labels were asking why Ivo didn't want us, because the album had done well, critically speaking. But Ivo had said 4AD's roster was full and that he couldn't devote enough time to us.'

No helpful answer was forthcoming until Tardo says their manager finally heard, 'absolutely, for certain, that we and 4AD wouldn't be working together again'. Yet Ivo was to change his mind. Feeling less than euphoric, the band launched *Euphoria* with a show at London's Borderline, composing a 38-minute piece of music to act as the support band. 'It was a single, gorgeous instrumental that they called "Clear Skin"', Ivo recalls. 'I wanted them to record it but I had to stand by my principles of no two releases on Guernica. I said we'd release it on 4AD, and that would be it. They agreed, but they should have told me to fuck off.'

Yates: 'Ivo said that two albums on Guernica would be confusing, so what about a Japanese-only release? It was like he was thinking out loud. One time, he said, "I can't let myself think about it".'

For Guernica's third album of the year, Ivo was in danger of over-thinking; he even offered to manage LA trio That Dog, which, he says, shows how lost he was. 'Management was the last thing on earth I should ever have considered doing,' he says, 'and I withdrew the offer before they could take it seriously. But I was trying to find some meaning, a new direction, and stuff to fall in love with, so the offer also illustrates how much I fell in love with them.'

At the end of 1992, Ivo had been given a That Dog cassette by 4AD LA promotions man Mark Brown. 'I loved it, and wanted to sign them to 4AD,' Ivo recalls. 'But I discovered they'd signed to Geffen two weeks earlier.' He also discovered that That Dog's principal singer-songwriter was Anna Waronker, daughter of Warners boss Lenny. Anna had taken note of her father's productions, such as Randy Newman's *Sail Away* – 'records with a harmonic sensibility and direct lyrics, as if he was speaking to you, and that stuck with me,' she says. She began to write songs after a break-up and formed a band with her friend Rachel Haden, another strong singer who was happy to learn bass guitar. Rachel's violin-playing sister Petra wanted to join, and could sing too, giving That Dog the gift of triple harmonies, which they put to fresh, naïve folk rock with an extra kick. None of the girls had yet turned twenty.

Waronker preferred songwriting to performing, but Rachel Haden convinced her to add drummer Tony Maxwell, with the third Haden triplet, cello-playing Tanya, an auxiliary stage member. It was the five-piece That Dog that Ivo saw play live: 'They had this combination of rackety Throwing Muses-esque guitar balanced by slower songs, and three gorgeous voices working together. I adored them.'

That Dog adored 4AD right back. Rachel Haden idolised Cocteau Twins and Kristin Hersh: 'She sang about feeling crazy, and that's how I felt. I loved the bands that rocked out on 4AD, like Lush and Pixies.'

Pixies had been Anna Waronker's gateway to 4AD: 'They spoke to me the way that Randy Newman did when I was younger. It was their directness, simplicity and untraditional chord changes. And there was Kim Deal! There weren't many women in rock who could sing and have it be pretty without being delicate and too commercial.'

In other words, as Rachel Haden says, '4AD was our dream label.' But Waronker admits That Dog had been too disorganised to post out demos: '4AD was the only label that hadn't contacted us, And Geffen's roster was great.' But knowing of Ivo's interest, Geffen A&R man Tony Berg thought it would be useful, Ivo says, 'if That Dog had indie cred outside of America. They weren't an obvious band to break in America, so they needed all the help they could get.'

After the band's self-titled album was released on Guernica, Ivo brought That Dog to the UK, to play shows and record a Peel session. 'Given the parameters of Guernica, it worked,' Ivo reckons. That Dog reciprocated demonstrative affection. 'He was smart and safe and respectful,' says Waronker. 'We let him into our inner sanctum, and we didn't even let in Tony Berg.'

That Dog's album was well received, and Guernica felt like an ongoing success; sure it had had teething problems, but it served a purpose. The three albums brought the curtain down on another tumultuous year, a time of massive upheaval, unexpected successes, failures and frustrations, and uncertain futures.

In November, Dead Can Dance had made a video much more suited to the duo's image: a simple, recorded concert with a crack team of session players for just 150 invited guests at The Mayfair Theater in Santa Monica, California. It was a rare chance for Lisa Gerrard, living in Australia, to catch up with her old friend Ivo. 'Artists could fall to pieces,' she says, 'but he was expected to be the person who kept everything together, to be grounded and sensible, which was a huge pressure after a while.'

But the other half of Dead Can Dance saw a happier side to Ivo. Ivo recalls he and Brendan Perry had taken a drive, listening to a version of Perry's solo performance of 'American Dreaming': '*I'm in love with an American girl …*'

Ivo: 'You see, Brendan was in love with an American girl, Francesca, same as I was with Brandi. Nineteen ninety-three was a pretty good year for me. Brandi and I got married on New Year's Eve; Simon Harper, Martyn Young and his three-year-old daughter were the witnesses.'

Young's daughter, like the *Lilliput* baby, were unwitting emblems of new hope at the end of a year that saw Ivo strike out to save his life at its beginning. 'As he says, "New wife, new country, fresh start". *The 13 Year Itch*, scratched.

18 1994

ALL VIRGOS ARE MAD,
SOME MORE THAN OTHERS
(bad4001-bad4018)

Ivo made his move permanent by buying a house in LA in February 1994. In order to feed him demos, and assist with artist liaison, Colin Wallace was promoted from 4AD's warehouse to A&R. 'Ivo knew I was passionate about music as I was always listening to new things,' says Wallace. Yet Ivo called the post 'negative A&R', meaning the job entailed sending Ivo any demos that stood out, but to otherwise return the rest with a courteous covering letter, and to log the information in a book. 'I didn't see it as negative A&R,' Wallace maintains, 'but Ivo warned me that he wouldn't like anything, and he was true to his word for years.'*

Ivo also hired a new general manager after he'd failed to persuade Simon Harper to accept the role. 'I'd already drifted too far from what I really enjoyed,' Ivo says, 'dealing with all international licensees, artists and managers, to much more paperwork and business affairs meetings, coupled with managing the increasing frustration and overall bullshit of people in the office. I was burning out.'

---

* Colin Wallace recalls that one of the cassettes that he returned was from Antony Hegarty. 'He told me that I'd rejected his demo. I said I was really sorry, and he said, "Don't be sorry, you sent back a really sweet hand-written letter, which was really touching, and I kept it. It was one of the few letters I did get back".'

The job – with the grand title of Chief Executive Officer – went to Richard Hermitage, the manager of Pale Saints, with Robin Hurley made general manager in LA. Hermitage had put in eleven years as a concert booking agent before switching to artist management with synth-pop survivors The Human League. He'd heard that '4AD's exciting new act, Pale Saints' needed a manager, and was invited to meet the label. 'Practically every staff member turned up, which was very unusual in terms of taking a band on,' says Hermitage. He soon built a shoegazing roster of Pale Saints, Slowdive and The Boo Radleys.

Of all the labels that Hermitage had had to deal with, he says, '4AD had an intelligence and sensitivity towards the artist that I didn't encounter elsewhere, a shared vision. And Red House Painters was the greatest thing I'd heard for ages. Years later, Mark [Kozelek] asked me to manage him, and I refused, saying that if he fired me, I'd never be able to listen to his music again!'

The first record released under Hermitage's charge was one of 4AD'S finest – as visionary and unexpected as the first Throwing Muses album. Outside of her remit of Muses duties, Kristin Hersh had recorded some acoustic songs, as a token of love for Billy O'Connell, after they'd gotten married. 'I thought we had an understanding that he was my husband, but he saw it differently, that he was my manager, and he sent them to my business manager, who gave them in turn to [R.E.M. singer] Michael Stipe,' says Hersh. 'Between all them, this decision was made to release these demos. It was like someone walking into your house and publishing your diary.'

Hersh agreed to let the tracks go public, but, she says, 'only if I could [also] make a record on purpose'. She also agreed to postpone the release of a new Throwing Muses album that was being recorded in New Orleans to make way for her solo album, which she simultaneously recorded in Portsmouth on the east coast. For her own record, Hersh would only be accompanied by cellist Jane Scarpantoni and an inspired choice of producer: Lenny Kaye, Patti Smith's guitar sidekick and learned journalist and garage rock archivist.

'Lenny had wanted to work with the Muses for years,' Hersh recalls. 'He came to our shows, and sent us postcards, when we were still kids.

I wanted to use him as a computer program for pop, or the average listener, to see why people thought I was so strange. I used him as an ear, to sit in the control room so I didn't have to break any performance spell.'

The album ended up with an additional guest. Hersh had called Michael Stipe to discuss her problems recording the cello for what turned into the album's lead single 'Your Ghost'. As the pair chatted, she heard the solution – Stipe's own voice, as a chorus echo to her own. 'I promised Michael it wouldn't be a big deal, or a single, and even if "Your Ghost" was a single, there wouldn't be a video, and it wouldn't get played on the radio – and it became the biggest song I'd ever had! He agreed to make the video, and we had fun.'

Hersh still had her reservations over recording her vocals: 'None of my band training had taught me how to record this gravelly, wobbly instrument that I couldn't control It was like trying to record a horse.' Yet her voice, stripped of extraneous detail, conveyed the honesty of her trials and tribulations. The performances on 'Sundrops' and 'Me And My Charms' were edgier but 'Your Ghost' was typical of the album's softer entry into Hersh's world. 'Luminous, alluring and slightly menacing,' said *Rolling Stone.* 'One of the best records we ever released,' says Ivo.

Something about *Hips And Makers* struck a nerve and the album entered the national UK charts at number 7, considerably higher than any preceding Muses record. 'From *Victorialand* onward,' says Ivo, '4AD got really good chart positions in the first week of release, which spoke of the fan loyalty towards a lot of our artists.'

To prolong the album's shelf life, 4AD staffer Chris Staley suggested scoring four songs with a string quartet (arranged by Martin McCarrick) and double bass, and adding another four tracks. The *Strings* EP that followed three months after *Hips And Makers* is a lovely document, but the real beauty of Hersh's solo performance was the solitude around her vocal.

But it wouldn't be the story of 4AD in the Nineties without a frustrating lapse following a life-affirming success, or vice versa. Ivo had discovered The Swinging Swine through the band's Nick Drake cover version 'Voice From The Mountain'. From Galway in the west of Ireland, the band's folk-influenced jangle preceded the similarly and significantly more successful Cranberries: guitarist/violinist Hugh O'Carroll says that Ivo had found the band 'too straight-up folky' at the time. O'Carroll and singer Joanne Loughman must have felt the same, as they split off to start The Glee Club and emulate their influences – Cocteau Twins, This Mortal Coil, Siouxsie and the Banshees – and releasing a self-titled EP through Setanta.

'Ivo made approving noises about The Glee Club,' says O'Carroll. 'He also enjoyed our brash, boozy and forthright nature, compared to some of the people he was used to dealing with. We enjoyed visiting him in Wandsworth and chatting about music.'

A plan was hatched to re-record the EP and add new songs, to turn it into a full-length album for 4AD. Hugh Jones was hired to produce, and The Glee Club found itself in the same predicament as Swallow – without due A&R care for what they wanted. 'Hugh taught us a lot, but we preferred the less-is-more approach to how he overloaded the tracks,' says O'Carroll. Jones helmed four tracks but The Glee Club wanted the EP's producer Dick Meaney back. 'Ivo was a bit doubtful,' says O'Carroll, 'but otherwise he was on board.'

But Ivo wasn't on board enough to get behind the finished album. At times *Mine* mirrored The Sundays' dreaminess, such as with 'Remember A Day', but other tracks sounded like the shriller Cranberries, without conjuring up the same hooks. 'The Glee Club was another example of being disappointed,' says Ivo. 'We gave the album back to Setanta for the UK, which was embarrassing, but I was just being honest. 4AD released it in America because Robin thought it was worth a shot – he needed to feed the Warners machine, and we needed the £10,000 advance. But I recently bought the original mini-album and really enjoyed it. Joanne had such an amazing voice.'

4AD's popularity and The Glee Club's indie-pop blueprint ensured *Mine* was a college radio hit, but new demos didn't persuade Ivo to prolong the relationship. O'Carroll also decided to start afresh, and moved to San Francisco. Loughman returned to Ireland, and neither have had a similar profile since.

LEFT: Kurt Ralske, aka Ultra Vivid Scene

BELOW: Pale Saints, 1990: (left to right) Graeme Naysmith, Ian Masters, Chris Cooper

RIGHT: His Name Is Alive, 1993: (left to right) Karin Oliver, Warren Defever, Trey Many

BELOW: This Mortal Coil muse Pallas Citroen: outtake from 1990 session

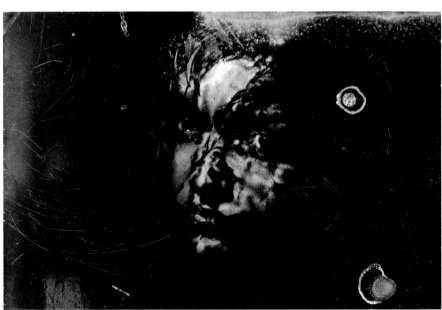

LEFT: Heidi Berry, 1992

BELOW: Mark Kozelek
of Red House Painters

LEFT: Belly mark II: (left to right) Tom
Gorman, Tanya Donelly, Chris Gorman,
Gail Greenwood

BOTTOM LEFT: Unrest: (left to right)
Mark Robinson, Bridget Cross, Phil Krauth

BELOW: *Melody Maker* cover, July 1993

LEFT: The Breeders mark II, 1992: (left to right) Kelley Deal, Tanya Donelly, Josephine Wiggs, Kim Deal, Britt Walford

BELOW: The Breeders mark III, 1994: (left to right) Jim Macpherson, Kelley Deal, Kim Deal, Josephine Wiggs

LEFT: The Amps, 1995: (left to right) Luis Lerma, Jim Macpherson, Nate Farley, Kim Deal

ABOVE: Ivo's 'bitches', 1993: (left to right) Kim Deal, Josephine Wiggs. From Kim Deal's personal collection

RIGHT: The Breeders mark IV, 2001: (left to right) Mando Lopez, Kim Deal, Richard Presley, Jose Medeles, Kelley Deal

ABOVE: Lush and Pale Saints on tour, France, March 1990: (left to right) Chris Cooper, Miki Berenyi, Chris Acland, Graeme Naysmith

ABOVE: Tanya Donelly and Chris Acland, Los Angeles, September 1990

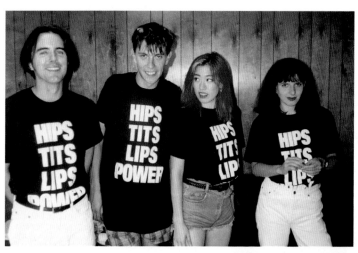

LEFT: Lush mark II, on the Lollapalooza tour, San Francisco, 1992: (left to right) Phil King, Chris Acland, Miki Berenyi, Emma Anderson

ABOVE: Backstage at The Ubu, Rennes, 1994: (left to right) Miki Berenyi, Robin Guthrie, Emma Anderson

ABOVE: Kristin Hersh and Miki Berenyi at the Reading Festival, 1995

LEFT: Lisa Germano

BELOW: Mojave 3, 1995: (left to right) Neil Halstead, Rachel Goswell, Ian McCutcheon

LEFT: Scheer, 1996: (left to right) Paddy Leyden, Joe Bates, Audrey Gallagher, Peter Fleming, Neal Calderwood

BELOW: Paula Frazer of Tarnation, 1996

ABOVE: GusGus, Iceland, 1998: (left to right) (back and middle row) Magnús Jónsson, Baldur Stefánsson, Siggi Kjartansson, Stephan Stephensen , Stefán Árni Þorgeirsson, Birgir Þorarinsson, (front row) Hafdís Huld, Daníel Ágúst Haraldsson

ABOVE: Publicity shot for The Hope Blister, 1998: Ivo and his dog Friday

ABOVE RIGHT: Vinny Miller, aka starry smooth hound, 2004

RIGHT: Ivo with Moke, Lamy, New Mexico, April 2012

BELOW: Ivo with the author, Lamy, New Mexico, April 2012

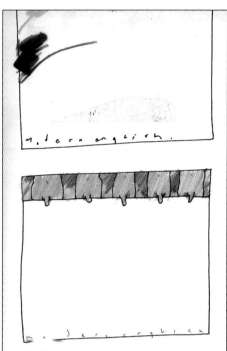

ABOVE: Vaughan Oliver at the *Surfer Rosa* shoot, 1989

RIGHT: Vaughan Oliver sketch for Modern English's debut album, working title *Five Sided Figure*, 1981

Vaughan Oliver sketches for 4AD logos

1. The Breeders – *Pod*
2. The Wolfgang Press – *Queer*
3. Pixies – *Trompe Le Monde*
4. Lush – *Spooky*
5. Heidi Berry – *Heidi Berry*
6. Swallow – *Blow*
7. Red House Painters – *Down Colorful Hill*
8. Various Artists – *Lilliput*
9. Various Artists – *The 13 Year Itch*
10. Scheer – *Schism*
11. His Name Is Alive – *Stars On ESP*
12. Various Artists – *Anakin*

Things might have been different for Loughman, however, had Ivo succeeded in getting the best out of her during a new bout of cover versions on his next musical collaboration. Having retired This Mortal Coil, the new working title was Blood, named after TMC's final album. Ivo took Loughman to Blackwing to sing over arrangements that he'd recorded with Jon Turner at Palladium. Rough versions of Red House Painters' 'Take Me Out' and American Music Club's 'Why Won't You Stay?' were recorded with Loughman, but they never even got around to recording a vocal for 'Need Your Love So Bad', a 1955 blues ballad that Ivo knew via the original Fleetwood Mac featuring another of Ivo's most beloved guitarists, Peter Green.

'Nothing gelled with Joanne,' says Ivo. 'Which had never happened to me with This Mortal Coil before. She was very shy, maybe even nervous around me. Once she'd had a couple of drinks, she did some fantastic singing, but I never did anything more with it. What was happening to me [his depression] was on its way up.'

The emotional detachment that underlined his relationship with The Glee Club was brought into sharp relief by the artist-serving A&R policy that 4AD usually stood for. Yet again, it featured a female singer. The number of women Ivo regularly created an environment free from alpha-male insensitivities for would have been notable in any industry. By the standards of the music industry, it was remarkable. By the end of his tenure at 4AD, Ivo had worked with twenty-six solo or band ventures that featured female singers and musicians, not many fewer than the label's male contingent. But what Ivo achieved for Lisa Germano was also an act of mercy, rescuing her from major label hell.

Born in northern Indiana, Germano – like her namesake Gerrard – had grown up in a multi-cultural neighbourhood with a shared language in music, in her case, largely Irish and Italian brands of gypsy. Her Italian father was a member of the Chicago Symphony Orchestra, and Germano says she appreciated 'melodies and harmonies, mushy stuff like Carole King, Cat Stevens and James Taylor'. She adds that she wasn't cool. 'I'd mostly play piano and write operas and tragic stories, about princesses tortured by the bad queen. I'd lock myself in the closet and wait for the prince to save me.'

Playing violin, that staple of gypsy music, Germano had become a successful session musician, with a lengthy stint with American rocker John Cougar Mellencamp. Her self-recorded, self-released debut album *On The Way Down From The Moon Palace*, however, sounded nothing like Mellancamp's adult-oriented sound, with hushed vocals and pristine, folky arrangements; it sounded as though she had a major label budget behind her. Capitol subsequently signed her, and A&R man Tim Devine put Canadian producer Malcolm Burn on the case to record new demos.

Burn had trained as Daniel Lanois' assistant, and he became Germano's boyfriend. 'Malcolm was a master manipulator,' she claims. 'He brought in some awesome players and we did way more [than demos], spending £75,000. It all sounded great, and I was in ecstasy. But Tim only really liked "You Make Me Want To Wear Dresses" because it could get played on radio, and Capitol could market the violin side of the music. Tim and I constantly fought about the track listing, and my manager sided with Tim. They all wanted to see sales.'

Germano's exasperated and naïve response was, she says, 'To think of the stupidest song I could do, that Capitol would like, so I recorded [Nancy Sinatra classic] "These Boots Are Made For Walking". And they did like it! So that had to go on the album.'

Germano named the album *Happiness* with all the bitter irony she could muster, but another prince was on the way to save her. Ivo had read a review of … *Moon Palace*, and seen her photo. 'Lisa was so attractive, and it sounded like an interesting record, so I'd bought it and primarily enjoyed the instrumentals. I later saw Lisa in concert and got talking to Tim Devine, who suggested 4AD release *Happiness* outside of America, like That Dog's arrangement with Geffen. I agreed, but first I wanted a crack at some remixes.'

Germano had never heard of 4AD. 'But I'd never heard of The Smiths either! I was still in John-Mellencamp-world. Ivo sent me a package of CDs, which blew me away: Pixies, Dead Can Dance, The Breeders, Cocteau Twins, This Mortal Coil, the artwork – it was so much more my world. This atmospheric, weird stuff was much more about music than hits.'

By the time Ivo and John Fryer had done their thing – 'they took stuff out, looped other bits and added bits and pieces between songs' – Germano had been dropped by Capitol. Two weeks after *Happiness* had been released in 1993, most of the label's staff had been fired. She says Capitol's new MD Gary Gersh said to her, "Not to beat about the bush, but I don't like your record". He offered to give it back to me to get out of the contract. Hurray!'

Ivo moved to sign Germano long-term. 'On its own "The Darkest Night Of All" could guarantee Lisa my complete admiration and empathy,' he gushes. Her 4AD debut, the *Inconsiderate Bitch* EP, included four *Happiness* remixes alongside '(Late Night) Dresses' (a renamed version of 'You Make Me Want To Wear Dresses'), remixed by Malcolm Burn. A re-tooled version of *Happiness* followed with a new sleeve design,* and new songs 'Destroy The Flower' and 'The Earth' replacing 'Breathe Across Texas' and the Sinatra cover. 'Ivo had a strong vision,' says Germano, 'but he never acted like I had to do what he said. He knew my situation at Capitol, and worked *with* me.'

Germano started on a new album to be released in October 1994, just six months after *Happiness*. Free of compromise, the irony-free title of *Geek The Girl* fronted a record as haunted and harrowing as anything with Hersh's name on it. 'A psychopath' sampled an actual 911 emergency call by a woman whose home had been invaded by her stalker (he subsequently raped her). 'It was so devastatingly powerful that I almost didn't include the tape, but this was how I felt, as I had a stalker who knew where I lived, and would call me, but the police couldn't do anything until he actually came there,' says Germano. 'I'd lock myself in every night, with mace and a baseball bat.'

Other song titles on the album included 'Sexy Little Girl Princess' and 'Cry Wolf'. The album's sleeve notes explained that *Geek The Girl* was a concept album of sorts: 'A girl who is confused about how to be sexual and cool in the world ... and dreams of still loving a man in

---

* Ivo, who owned the painting by Cathy Fenwick used for the cover of *Inconsiderate Bitch*, also paid extra to have it used on *Happiness*, and subsequently gifted it to Germano, which he regretted, he says, 'Because I love the painting! I also gave the *Livonia* print to Warren. It seemed right for the artists to have the work.'

hopes that he can save her from her shit life … ha ha ha, what a geek!'

Not since Kristin Hersh had an artist on 4AD delivered a bold feminist parable bordering on shock. 'Lisa experienced some dark episodes in her life,' says Ivo. 'Such as being in a successful touring rock'n'roll band, and how women are treated in that situation.'

Germano: 'I didn't mean to make that kind of a record. You just go with what's coming out of your psyche rather than writing music to sell. It definitely wasn't the "pop" record 4AD was looking for. Maybe "pop" isn't the right word, but they felt I had the ability to make more of the left-field hit record like Dead Can Dance or The Breeders.'

She is talking less about Ivo than Robin Hurley, who was busy managing Warners' expectations. Though he thought *Geek The Girl* 'was amazing', he also feels it shouldn't have been her second 4AD album. Ivo, however, is 'totally proud of the album'. He'd even suggested releasing Germano's demos as the finished record, to preserve it 'rough and raw'.

Germano might have seen Ivo as a prince. Yet by the time *Geek The Girl* was released, and getting very favourable reviews, 'that's when Ivo was pulling away and feeling unwell, and he wasn't there for me,' she says. 'He told me later that he couldn't listen to any music at all.'

The mantra of 'New wife, new country, fresh start' had not been enough for Ivo to stave off a now crushing depression exacerbated by new bouts of insomnia. Regular therapy wasn't solving the issue, and Ivo admits to self-medicating in response. In April, it was a case of a full-blown nervous breakdown. 'One night, I started hearing voices. I'd find myself in the shower at 4am, crying my eyes out. Finally, after another five months, on my fortieth birthday, I decided to try anti-depressants for the first time. That was the only drug I could handle. As a psychiatrist had suggested to me months earlier, it was like, "raising the basement". But, sadly, I remained derailed from 4AD. I was now at least aware of where the tracks were but still unable to get back on, and uncertain if I even wanted to.'

Ivo had been keeping daily contact with the London office. 'I'd get to the office at 10am, which was 2am in LA, and we'd run through everything that Ivo wanted carried out,' says Richard Hermitage. 'At

6pm, which was 10am in LA and Ivo had got up, I'd report back. This lasted until about April. And from where I stood, Ivo went missing. No one told me where he was because no one seemed to know.'

Hermitage says it was at least a week before he heard that Ivo was unwell. A four-man board of Hermitage, Hurley, Harper and Martin Mills convened to make decisions while Hurley took over Ivo's daily transatlantic calls, an arrangement that Hermitage says, 'lasted a long time'.

Ivo began to retreat from the LA office, as he had with Warners, for the comfort and security of his home and his wife Brandi. Feeling he should be honest about a worsening condition that isolated him from work and contact, Ivo faxed a letter of explanation and revelation to the London office. He ended it by asking anyone who had any questions to go ahead. 'But not a single person did,' he recalls. 'I'm sure it scared the living daylights out of everyone. I've since learned they were anxious that London would become the satellite to the LA office, and if I'd remained healthy, that probably wouldn't have happened. If I'd managed to sign bands and things had worked well through the Warners system, and that had grown, and everyone had been in love and making money ... But it went the polar opposite way.'

Ivo plugged the time by attempting to learn the latest Cubase computer music software. 'I remember letting the manual instructions drop out of my fingers and crying because it was like Greek to me! I'd never learnt how to engineer a record. I was hopeless!' He still managed two instrumental sketches, one of which Ivo feels chimed with Portishead's debut album *Dummy* that Colin Wallace had sent him: 'It was the space and the sound, except Portishead's was like a polished, finished, vocal version of what I'd done. I can't remember what else Colin sent me, but there nothing I wanted to sign.'

Hurley: 'It's no coincidence that 4AD's flight downwards started with Ivo's withdrawal. He was the one fighting for no remixes, videos or singles, but as head of the American 4AD looking at a bigger view of the world, I was being persuaded, or even doing it willingly, to follow what the industry was doing, hoping it would lead to a new dawn and success to match Pixies, Breeders, Dead Can Dance and Belly. I really believed we could turn it around.'

Hurley's problem was two offices, a combined staff of fourteen people and no idea what was really happening to the label's totemic leader. LA, the heart of the entertainment industry and the epicentre of ego, where success was the most prized commodity, was not the city in which to have a nervous breakdown, triggered by all that it stood for. 'You know what it's like when you watch a band on TV, really going for it, with the sound muted?' says Ivo. 'It looks ridiculous and doesn't make any sense. That's what I felt about the music business.'

'By the time Ivo got to America, he was enjoying the nightlife, drinking like an Englishman,' Tim Carr recalls. 'He let his hair down, even though he still had a monk's crewcut! But he and I went through the same kind of thing, addiction problems, so I was hiding out on my days off, as he did.'*

Ivo recalls a conversation with Miki Berenyi back in London. 'When I told her I was moving to Los Angeles, her response was, "LA, what on earth for? It's so fucking shallow." I assured her that shallow was something I was actually looking forward to. Of course, she was right. Having loved the place for over fifteen years, I found that almost as soon as I bought a house we weren't a match made in heaven. LA spat me out.'

At work, only Hurley was a confidant, but even he didn't know the full extent of Ivo's breakdown. 'He'd disappear for a while, and then call, asking to meet,' says Hurley. 'So we'd go for a walk, like in the Zen garden in Pacific Palisades. He'd say that he was scared and uncertain, but, really, I had no idea what was going on. Brandi was equally confused, this relatively young girl who'd married him, and he'd liter-

---

* Lush had reaped some extra-curricular benefits, by visiting Tim Carr on holiday in the Thai island of Koh Samui. Ivo used the Thai expression, *mai pen rai* – which translates to 'that's life' or 'no worries' – for a 4AD promo sampler for the US market. *Mai Pen Rai* was extravagantly produced in cardboard with a letter-pressed insert available in eight different colours. *Mai Pen Rai* also became highly prized among collectors because it included a Matt Johnson track from *Burning Blue Soul* (4AD was about to reissue the album on CD) and a hidden track of Dance Chapter's 'Anonymity'.

ally gone off the rails. She wasn't equipped to deal with it either. I'd let Simon Harper and Martin know some of what was going on. We all wanted to let Ivo sort through his demons, and then come back as the person we'd known.'

Ivo: 'Robin was just incredible. To paraphrase Mark Kozelek, he didn't judge, criticise or make demands, and he had my back. I was letting so many people down but his quiet, solid support, on a personal level, helped me to at least survive. So many people would've just got the hell out of there but I seriously doubt it crossed his mind.'

For all Hurley's support, he couldn't give 4AD A&R direction. Richard Hermitage says he had signed 'great acts, but as an agent' and had to accept that wasn't his role at 4AD. Colin Wallace, Hermitage says, 'got where Ivo was at, but Colin wasn't Ivo'.

With releases on the schedule, Ivo's absence was only felt by employees and artists used to his avuncular presence, from Germano to That Dog. 'Ivo just vanished,' says Rachel Haden. Anna Waronker adds, 'We were a lot younger than Ivo, but he treated us as equals, and though I don't recall him laying out all his woes, he did say he was disillusioned, and coming out to America had only added disappointment. After he met Brandi, he began to retreat.'

In between Lisa Germano's *Inconsiderate Bitch* and *Happiness*, Red House Painters had released the *Shock Me* EP in the UK. After the clearing exercise of the last two albums, this was the first of a new batch, headed by an electric and an acoustic version of the EP's title track, written by Kozelek's teenage hard rock faves Kiss, revamped with the singer's trademark exhaustion. A new album was in the process of being recorded but Kozelek admits he was struggling again in the producer's role. On top of his indecision – which you might expect from his personality – 'I had horrible fits of insomnia that delayed things for months,' he says. 'I thought the sound of my voice was too nasally and some tracks took for ever to complete.'

Charles Thompson had had no such doubts, and had fired through another session. Apart from the fourteen-track *Bossanova*, every album that Thompson had worked on after *Surfer Rosa* had been fifteen tracks long, showing Thompson's propensity for a speedy turnover of ideas. This time, he'd recorded twenty-two tracks, enough for a double album, inside which a superb single album was screaming to emerge.

Eric Drew Feldman, Nick Vincent and Al Clay had all returned for the session, with Joey Santiago one of three lead guitarists, giving tracks such as 'The Hostess With The Mostest' the same cut and thrust as Pixies. The lead single 'Headache' preceded the album *Teenager Of The Year*, which was as eclectic and sprawling as The Clash's *London Calling*, from the joyful zip of 'Big Red' and the Beefheart-ian 'Two Reelers' to the fond Beatlesy vibe of 'Vanishing Spies' and reggaefied 'Fiddle Riddle', with more fascinating but underwhelming examples of roots music.

Ivo considers *Teenager Of The Year* 'patchy', but reviews were largely positive: 'Black adopts a slightly less sprawling sound but maintains his penchant for turbulent, eclectic pop' (*Entertainment Weekly*). 'Black has loosened up, hunkered down and put together a killer Senior Variety Show … a happy sprawl of an album that holds together even as it offers some wild contrasts' (*NME*).

Given that the *Frank Black* solo debut hadn't sold as much as Pixies records, was it a good idea to follow it with a double album? It would have been difficult to dissuade Thompson when Red House Painters had been granted the privilege. The discussion at the LA studio owned by Eurythmic Dave Stewart was another unpleasant confrontation.

'Charles could be right in your face, literally so, getting his point across, out of excitement or anger,' Ivo recalls. 'I'd always enjoyed the enthusiastic version but this was the first time he got very confrontational. He was really keen to release a double album, suggesting he'd probably never get the chance again. Instead of just telling me that that was important to him, he got incredibly defensive. [Thompson's manager] Ken Goes was also peculiarly confrontational, probably because he wanted to impress Charles.

'Maybe Charles, in his heart, knew the album didn't deserve to be a double and he overcompensated in his effort to convince me or, as I've often wondered, this was a method to get me to drop him, as I had with Cocteau Twins. With Rick Rubin at American Recordings waiting in the wings, should Elektra not choose to pick up the remaining solo album option, it worked, as I left that studio thinking it was best not to work with Charles or Ken again.'

Whatever issues Thompson had, the end of Pixies hadn't solved them, and the aftermath had probably made them worse. 'Charles got most of the blame in the press for Pixies' split, and his early albums got overlooked in the excitement to write about Kim, who was such a popular character,' Ivo feels. 'Charles resented that there was so much good will towards Kim and I'm sure it confused him that his solo records never sold anything like Pixies albums. But a solo Bono record would sell much less than U2. Compare the sales of Brendan and Lisa's solo albums to Dead Can Dance albums.'

Thompson admits that The Breeders' success had negatively impacted on his relationship with 4AD: 'I'm sure I wouldn't have even realised it at the time, but I had lots of self-esteem issues floating around. After all, I was the big poo-bah, Pixies' frontman and song-writer, with important things to say, so I felt I should have been treated with a lot of respect as a solo artist. Kim had a big hit single with The Breeders, bigger than Pixies, and good for her. But it made me feel like I wasn't liked. It wasn't like I wasn't still trying to make creative progress, so it ruffled my feathers for sure.'

Thompson also concedes that the bond between Ivo and Kim Deal had been difficult to endure. 'They had a yin-yang connection, which I now understand, because sometimes the male-female dynamic works better and male-male isn't so good,' he admits. 'I find the idea of talking to a male therapist nauseating, for example. When I think of the women I get along with best, it's not usually romantic. But otherwise, I don't know why I wasn't getting on with 4AD. But Ken wasn't getting on with them either. Sometimes your representatives think they're looking out for you when they're burning bridges instead. It was all too touchy. Maybe between the aggressive style of Ken and my cockiness, it kept people at bay.'

At the time, Thompson claimed his reason for leaving 4AD was that *Teenager Of The Year* didn't get enough promotion from the label. He dismisses that view today, 'but 4AD had a beautiful thing going with Pixies and my solo thing wasn't as beautiful,' he says. 'How could it be the same? Ivo tried to stay interested, and he flew over to hear what I was doing as I was spending lots of money, so they wanted to make sure I wasn't completely off the rails.'

In any case, Thompson thinks that his contract with 4AD had already ended. 'Ultimately, I didn't live in the UK, so I decided to try my luck elsewhere,' he concludes. 'I wasn't beholden to 4AD, and though I felt bad that I didn't stay, I had to move on.'

More than Belly or The Wolfgang Press, the fallout from Ivo's meeting with Thompson was the last straw for Ivo – according to his brother Perry: 'The renown 4AD had achieved was partly down to the twin pillars of high artistry and commercial success that was Cocteau Twins and Pixies, and in both cases, the relationships with Ivo deteriorated pretty drastically. I think Ivo's heart was broken, maybe more than a girlfriend could have broken it, where you feel you've given everything, and yet they will turn and stab you in the back for no apparent reason, so why the hell are you devoting yourself heart, body and soul, with no loyalty or appreciation? But life is seldom simple.'

Life certainly hadn't turned out easy for Kim Deal in the wake of *Last Splash*. A strained touring schedule culminated in the 1994 Lollapalooza tour, fourth on the bill behind The Smashing Pumpkins, Beastie Boys and George Clinton & The P-Funk All Stars. Deal felt that they needed a record to coincide with the festival, and responded to an album that had now sold 1.5 million copies with a vinyl-only ten-inch EP of bristling lo-fi, in case anyone had thought the band had forgotten its roots. Joining the atonal, thrashy title track of the *Head To Toe* EP, written by bassist Josephine Wiggs, and the appeasing presence of *Last Splash* single 'Saints' were covers of songs by lo-fi underdogs Guided By Voices ('Shocker in Gloomtown') and Sebadoh ('Freed Pig').

Josephine Wiggs says that *Head To Toe* was a response to the difficulty of reproducing the layered sound of *Last Splash* on stage. But she also acknowledges that there was more to it: 'Kim would have felt under a lot of pressure to carry on, and that the next album must be even bigger and better.'

Deal had also notably turned down a Levi's ad campaign that wanted to use 'Cannonball'. 'Everyone knew that if Kim had agreed, The Breeders would have been *huge*,' says Ivo. '"Cannonball" was the tune of 1993, but she wouldn't be defined by it.'

The same week in June that 4AD released *Head To Toe*, Lush returned with its second album, *Split*. With former producer Robin Guthrie consigned to the past, discussions with manager Howard Gough about a replacement producer had raised the name of Bob Mould. The former Hüsker Dü guitarist told *Spin* magazine that he'd talked to one of the band – Emma Anderson – but had declined 'because I kept picking the wrong girl's songs … I had to get out before I broke up the band!'

Favouring Miki Berenyi's material might well have been a fatal start for Mould, given the rivalry between her and Anderson, which added internal tension to go with the external pressure. But the two women were united in their view of their manager. Berenyi says Gough also suggested hard rock specialists Bob Rock, Rick Rubin and [Led Zeppelin's] John Paul Jones. 'Howard went nuts with his suggestions, all because he wanted us to break America.'

Eventually, Lush got its way by hiring Mike Hedges, who had worked with The Cure, Associates and Siouxsie and the Banshees. The recordings had gone well, Berenyi says, until Hedges insisted he had to mix the album at his home in rural France. 'We ended up in the middle of nowhere, isolated, with no TV, and everyone homesick. Mike kept disappearing and, again, we were never assertive enough to ask why. Howard and Ivo began to vanish at the same time, and Tim Carr! The three people who were meant to guide us were gone.'

Lush's theory was that Hedges was being badgered into spending time with his family, but either way, the mixes he turned in were universally disliked. Ivo told the band in his usual plain-speaking manner. 'We ended up having a massive row,' says Berenyi. 'I said, "Where have you been? You can't come in at the last minute and just say it's shit".'

Ivo: 'I think Brandi had suggested I start the conversation by being very positive, as my approach was usually to just say what I felt, and I'd take for granted people knew what I liked about something so I could get to what I didn't like. I praised certain songs, but it veered into me saying it needed remixing. Miki said, "It's not your fucking record", and I replied, "It's my fucking record label, you better think about it".

Gough further upset Lush by commissioning remixes from R.E.M. producer Scott Litt, another American, designed to raise Lush's US profile. 'Our opinion wasn't asked, and we got railroaded into Scott, who was up his arse,' Berenyi says. Lush's choice, Alan Moulder, engineer and remixer to the likes of My Bloody Valentine and The Smashing Pumpkins, turned in the incisive mixes that were used on the album *Split*.

With Ivo preoccupied, the risky decision to release two new Lush singles on the same day was Tim Carr's at Warners. It was an undeniable gimmick, but at least the band's two distinct halves equally shone, from Berenyi's buzzing 'Hypocrite' to Anderson's lengthy, languid 'Desire Lines', which Ivo thinks is Lush's best song, and *Split* his favourite Lush album.

The timing of *Split* wasn't great. Gough's ambitions had expanded to running his own label, Laurel, funded by the major label London; it kicked off in March 1994 with Tiny Monroe (who Gough also managed). Howard said he saw himself as an 'Ivo figure', claims Berenyi. 'But he didn't have Ivo's taste – and when Howard started his own label, he wasn't good at picking potentially successful bands, because he was far too swayed by what others thought.'

Laurel's next signing proved Berenyi's point. Menswear was the tragic, youthful wannabes of the new Britpop scene, riding on the coat-tails of far better and more successful bands Suede, Blur, Elastica and the new, brash kids in town, Oasis. Enough time had passed from even post-punk to see influences such as Wire alongside Seventies glam and Sixties pop, a brash and declamatory mix that was shifting the axis of the UK mainstream – as grunge had Stateside – further away from Ivo's introverted model of progressive and folk roots. Even if he had cared, Ivo was too far from the Britpop epicentres of London and Manchester to have a chance of finding fresh bands, while the A&R feeding frenzy would have alienated him.

Next to Oasis, Berenyi says, 'shoegazing was that soft, southern shite'. *Split* was well named, as reviews were both positive and negative. 'One said we were irrelevant because we just sang about fluffy clouds,' says Berenyi. 'Fucking hell! How much darker could the lyrics be?' Anderson says subjects under discussion included child abuse, abandonment, neglect and, on 'When I Die', the death of her father. *NME* recognised the content but said it needed more heavyweight music. 'We shouldn't have paid attention,' says Berenyi. 'But it felt personal, that people wanted to crucify us – and shoegazing.'

The fact that neither 'Desire Lines' nor 'Hypocrite' reached the UK top 50 might have been down to each single halving the chance of the other, but *Split*'s chart placing of 19 – twelve lower than *Spooky* – confirmed that audiences had already transferred allegiances to Britpop. Fortunately, the US wasn't judging Lush by the same trend-based criteria, but Warners decided against releasing either single, preferring that the band keep touring. Having only played two shows in 1993, they would play sixty-four shows by the end of 1994, over half of them in America. 'The Cranberries and The Sundays, even Belly, had sold lots of records, and Howard thought Lush could be the next female-fronted band to suddenly sell a million,' says Anderson. 'Calm down, I said, it won't happen. Or just let it happen naturally.'

On tour in Europe, Lush began to experience Richard Hermitage's budgetary controls in the wake of Ivo's breakdown, one of which was reducing overheads. 'It was a fucking nightmare,' says Berenyi. 'We didn't have a hotel for the first week, just the tour bus, so we'd have to find change at 7am just to use the toilet at a station, and to wash in the sink. Richard asked if we needed a soundman on tour. I'll tell you what – no, and we can ask someone in the audience if they know the songs so we don't need to sing either! That was more of Ivo backing away, saying, "Richard deals with everything now ..." But Richard was an idiot. And Howard was nowhere to be seen either.'

At least Lush had a profile in America as well as Europe, more so than their peers Pale Saints. Without Ian Masters, the band was a more generic and less absorbing entity, though Ivo says 'Henry' (named after the Polish composer Henryk Górecki) is his favourite Pale Saints track, written by the band's new singer and songwriter Meriel Barham. Her influence happened to make the band's new EP *Fine Friend* and its third album *Slow Buildings* sound more like Lush – at ten slowly evolving minutes, 'Henry' was Pale Saints' equivalent to the latter's 'Desire Lines'. The arrival of new bassist Colleen Brown also meant that Pale Saints shared Lush's boy/girl split.

Sessions with Mark Freegard – chosen because of his Breeders sessions – hadn't worked out, so Ivo had rehired Hugh Jones. He was a sensible choice, but Ivo's suggestion that Barham write new lyrics to the melody of 'Poison In The Airwaves' – the B-side of a 1981 single by the obscure Scottish band Persian Rugs – was frankly bizarre. 'This was post-This Mortal Coil,' says Ivo, 'and I was flinging off ideas for covers to people, but not getting involved in the outcome.'

This had turned into the title track of *Fine Friend*, a very pretty slice of what Miki Berenyi calls 'soft southern shite'. Barham told 4AD fanatic Jeff Keibel in 2002 that she did 'Fine Friend' out of a sense of obligation. 'Ivo gave us a lot of freedom and never really pressured us … but I didn't really like the result.'

To have a stranger's melody provide the base of what would become your band's lead single was an undermining gesture to say the least. Barham could conceivably have given Pale Saints a profile to match Lush, but after a European and American tour and a cover of 'Jersey Girl' for the Tom Waits tribute album *Step Right Up*, she left the band, which eventually split up in 1996. 'I didn't really enjoy the last year of Pale Saints,' she told Keibel.

One of Pale Saints' last shows was in September during a California version of *The 13 Year Itch*. Ivo called the week-long event *All Virgos Are Mad* after his and Vaughan Oliver's star sign. Ivo was well enough to attend the first shows, but his rally had come too late to choose tracks for the accompanying compilation. In his place, without the proper planning, Chris Staley had been forced to assemble the CD from 4AD's back catalogue. There was just one unreleased offering – His Name Is Alive's tinny pop collage 'Library Girl' – and a barely noticeable remix of Pale Saints' 'Fine Friend'.

In theory, this was a cardinal sin in Ivo's eyes, but it was no time for adhering to principles. In fact, Ivo had had the idea of releasing compilations, 'not by 4AD artists, but just music I loved. I remember one tape had Miles Davis, Dan Hicks, Fever Tree, Throbbing Gristle, diverse, eclectic stuff. It was a light-bulb moment, and probably my first manic episode. I was charging around, making up C90 cassettes that I gave to Robin [Hurley] and Simon [Harper], but they got steered away from the idea. The tapes ended up being used during the *All Virgos Are Mad* shows, over the PA.'

Warren Defever was master of ceremonies again for the larger shows at the Troubadour, with more intimate affairs taking place at McCabe's Guitar Shop. *All Virgos Are Mad* was timed to coincide with a prestigious exhibition of v23 artwork at the Pacific Design Center in LA. Vaughan Oliver gave his show a separate title: *This Rimy River* (subtitled *Vaughan Oliver and v23 Graphic Works, 1988–94 [peep]*), named after a line in a poem written by his then partner Victoria Mitchell. Oliver says the limited edition of the accompanying book is his favourite ever piece of work. 'There were seventy-two words in the poem, I put one on each page, I then took scraps from the waste bin and used those images to print over the regular edition, so you'd have had to buy that to be able to read it,' he explains. 'It was a perverse thing to do, like running over your favourite child. It took three months and burned out two assistants. The printing cost £16,000. Which other independent record company would finance that?'

Oliver's artwork for the *All Virgos Are Mad* compilation visualised a similar state of madness by turning the song titles into anagrams ('Effin Diner' for 'Fine Friend', 'I Sing Duff' for 'Diffusing', 'Rude Lob Drama' for 'Bold Marauder', etc), while the photograph of a woman's face was covered not in what appeared to be scratches, but in physical slashes that had been carefully re-stitched by hand. 'It was to take something beautiful and slowly destroy it, which was a theme through a number of our sleeves,' says Oliver. The reverse image ladled on the irony with the image of a bowl of cherries.

The *LA Times* paid suitable homage in a feature by journalist Lorraine Ali. 'Some of the most valuable rock'n'roll over the years has been served up by small, independent labels, but few of these indie labels have been as identifiable – aurally and visually – as 4AD. Over the past fourteen years, the London-bred company has coupled spiritual, dark and surreal music with its own style of abstract album art and presented it all with handmade care.'

'Creativity is a gift,' Lisa Germano told Ali. 'But when most labels try to market this gift and make hits, strangely enough, creativity is the very thing that gets destroyed. For me, 4AD's greatest quality is that they promote creativity and uniqueness.'

Ivo was quoted as saying he was both sceptical and appreciative of the respect his label has garnered. 'On the one hand,' he said, 'it's frustrating when people refer to a 4AD sound – is it the Pixies or is it Dead Can Dance? But on the other hand, when people describe something as "4AD-esque" I find it quite flattering, though I'm not sure what it means. It's like they've created a genre that doesn't exist.'

Ivo used the opportunity to again intermingle the UK and US factions; Lisa Germano, Red House Painters, Brendan Perry, Pale Saints, Kristin Hersh, His Name Is Alive, Heidi Berry and Michael Brook all played … though not The Breeders, who were on Lollapalooza duty. There were a handful of surprises too – Ian Masters and Warren Defever playing as a duo, a solo show by Lisa Gerrard. Also playing was Air Miami, the successor to Unrest with new drummer Gabriel Stout. The Wolfgang Press had a surprise guest – Tom Jones, who Ivo curtly viewed as an unnecessary injection of 'light entertainment'.

Jones' presence would come to light when The Wolfgang Press's new album was released in 1995. The other unexpected appearance was Kendra Smith. David Roback's former partner in Opal had been living, frugally and remotely, in a cabin in the northern California woods since 1988, and though she had released a mini-album (*Kendra Smith Presents The Guild of Temporal Adventurers*) in 1992 through the tiny LA label Fiasco, signing to 4AD was a much bigger deal. Both Smith and Air Miami had recorded tracks for the *All Virgos Are Mad* compilation, and were recording albums for 4AD on one-off contracts – hardly the way Warners wanted Ivo to proceed. 'Warners needed me to sign things that would sell and be loved,' he says. 'But I wasn't hearing much I liked, let alone good choices, that would be workable in that environment.'

For that reason, Ivo had surrendered a tentative interest in the jazz-tinged 'O'rang', formed by ex-Talk Talk members Paul Webb and Lee Harris. Cliff Walton had tried to get Ivo interested in Seefeel, whose intricate, experimental and electronically tweaked sound had its roots in the post-rock scene developing around Insides, Bark Psychosis and Disco Inferno. This was the logical progression from shoegaze, but Ivo wasn't in the mood to respond, despite the ambient qualities of the music. Seefeel signed to Too Pure, and Ivo was to let Insides go for a second time.

Guernica came to a premature end with a limited edition of *Clear Skin*, Insides' 38-minute minimalist fusion that Ivo had intended to release on 4AD before he knowingly contravened Guernica's one-off policy. There was also a vinyl-only remix version that turned out to be particularly popular with Italian house DJs. 'It raised our expectations for the future,' says Julian Tardo. 'But Ivo called to say that he'd thought of all the options, and that he'd taken too much on, and that someone always suffers.'

Insides felt rejected all over again. 'We told *NME* we were pissed off that 4AD wasn't going to take us on, or words to that effect,' Tardo recalls. 'Someone from the label said, "What the fuck did you say that for?" But it had been a year since *Euphoria* and things weren't going anywhere. In retrospect, we were creatively spent. And no other label was beating down our door.'*

'Guernica suffered from not releasing enough records and realising its potential,' says Richard Hermitage. But Ivo's LA base made it impractical to front a label that wasn't releasing records in America, and would involve multiple relationships. Ivo had to inform two prospective Guernica bands that the offer was withdrawn: Portland in Oregon's Pell Mell, whose cool, tempered twang would have sounded great while driving through the desert, eventually had their *Interstate*

---

* Insides eventually talked to Acid Jazz and Warp but they didn't release a new album – the sweeter, R&B-influenced *Sweet Tip* – until 2000, on the 3rd Stone label.

album released by Geffen, while the album by Germany's Rossburger Report, a guitar-chestra of up to fifteen players that included ex-Xmal Deutschland members Manuela Rickers and Peter Bellendir, is still unreleased.

The upside followed the down, with the first Throwing Muses single in two and a half years, having been delayed by *Hips And Makers*. 'Bright Yellow Gun' was the first recording to feature bassist Bernard Georges, who slotted effortlessly into the band. It had been a rude comedown for the band's rhythm section: George had been gainfully employed by a bicycle repair shop, while David Narcizo had been working in an antiques shop. But besides raising children (her second son, Ryder, was now three), Hersh had continued to write with the same furious commitment, and a Muses album was due early in 1995.

The hope was that 4AD, and Ivo, could similarly rescue themselves, and keep moving forward. The label had survived Martin Mills' court case and The Cartel's bankruptcy, and the loss of Cocteau Twins and Pixies. Belly, The Breeders and Dead Can Dance were all stars with some of the best music the individual songwriters had ever released. The rich, sad, folk strains of Red House Painters, Heidi Berry and Lisa Germano made for the best downbeat response to Britpop imaginable. Could they, and 4AD, maintain it? Was there even more to come?

As things stood, it might be a while before Ivo could return to work with the kind of A&R force that he had been. In the meantime, Cliff Walton recalls, there was not even a business plan in place. Were Richard Hermitage and Robin Hurley waiting for their prince to return to lead them on? It seems the last thing he was capable of doing.

'After a while, it became obvious that Ivo wasn't coming back, and people in the office slowly started to accept it,' says Simon Harper. 'A lot of our licensees were upset and shocked. Many of them had worked with Ivo since the beginning, and for some Ivo *was* 4AD. I tried to put a positive spin on it but our partners around the world weren't buying it. Even Martin Mills, the master of spin, was struggling to be his usual upbeat self.'

Once upon a time, 4AD had been able to advance via a series of spontaneous decisions, happy accidents. Now the competition was fierce, from the major labels and other independents, such as the insurgent Creation with Oasis leading their pack. Meanwhile, Ivo – a man who had created a label in his own image, based on his intuitive love of music, and who had used music as a source of excitement, comfort and empathy – didn't even want to listen to music, let alone leave his house.

19 1995

FUCK YOU TIGER, WE'RE GOIN' SOUTH
(bad5001-tad5017)

In 1995, Will Oldham, under the alias Palace Music (and later Bonnie 'Prince' Billy), and Bill Callahan, as Smog, had released their first significant albums (*Viva Lost Blues* and *Wild Love* respectively). The likes of Wilco and The Jayhawks were also tapping the roots of American folk and country, albeit framed by a more fleshed-out Seventies rock sound. To document this progression, in January 1995 the US music trade title *Gavin Report* published a chart under the name, Americana: 'music that honors and is derived from the traditions of American roots music,' ran the editorial.

This musical and spiritual retreat was exactly where Ivo had found himself, expressed through the sound of Red House Painters, Heidi Berry and Lisa Germano, as Ivo looked inward, ignoring what was behind alt rock's passage into the pages of *Vogue* or who the major labels were splurging excessive budgets on. This was where Ivo had once found himself, a young record retail manager exploring Tim Buckley, Emmylou Harris and other folk and country rock pioneers when everyone around him was consuming rock of the heavy, progressive and glam variety. Trying to run a record company was causing Ivo irreparable harm, but running a record label was easy.

The gulf between the two ideals was again made blatant by the progress of The Wolfgang Press, as they edged ever-nearer to the mainstream. The trio's problem wasn't so much the music as the approach. Their new album *Funky Little Demons* had been ready for nine months, since spring 1994, but Warners' scheduling had interfered, and though it had kept the catalogue number signifying a 1994 release (wedged between Dead Can Dance and Lisa Germano albums), it had been put back to January 1995.

The new single 'Goin' South' appeared first, on 9 January. Promoted by several remixes and an expensive video set in Las Vegas that resuscitated the masked JFK and Jackie O figures from the 'Kansas' video, it charted in the UK at a depressing 117. In the States, it only reached 33 on the Alternative Modern Rock chart – 31 places lower than 'A Girl Like You' had despite a similarly slinky groove and a durable chorus. 'If I had 10 per cent of what 4AD spent on remixes and videos,' says Ivo, 'I'd be a wealthy man.'

Funky Little Demons followed two weeks later. 'The title was inspired by children and babies,' says Mick Allen. 'It was personal for me, and in a broader sense, also how the songs could be seen.' Yet the playful air belied the truth of its creation; Mark Cox had left the band after the album had been finished, even before the *All Virgos Are Mad* event. It was as if Allen had known what would happen. The term 'going south' is slang for 'a worse or inferior position … a decreased value'.

In the album track '11 Years', Allen sang, '*11 years of faking it/ Same clothes empty songs/ Believing it like most.*' 'That's very tongue in cheek, though, very hammy,' says Allen. 'Like, Why the fuck am I still doing this? Why I am here? But Elvis Presley has more right to sing that than me.'

Ivo: 'I hope "11 Years" wasn't about me!'

The album cover featured a typographical grid overlaid on the image of a tree. 'To signify past and present, like the music is a concoction of the latest technology with the roots of music,' says Allen. But this sign of strength masked the fact that the making of the album had severed the longest-serving alliance on 4AD, between Allen and Cox – and it had happened over a familiar bugbear: money.

The root of the problem was a hit single, but it wasn't even the band's own. Of all people to recognise The Wolfgang Press's way around a tune and to commission them to write a song for them, you would not have bet on Tom Jones, the trouper with the biggest lungs in showbiz, a singer and performer much admired by his peer Elvis Presley. It turned out that Jones had been scouting for songs and was sent a sampler of songs by Love and Rockets: '"A Girl Like You" was the next song on the tape,' says Allen. Jones had given the Wolfgang Press track a typically belting treatment for his album *The Lead And How to Swing It* and had asked the band to write a new song specifically for his new album. Inside 36 hours, says Allen, they had written 'Show Me (Some Devotion)'.

With this unexpected endorsement, the trio had begun to record an album, continuing their course towards a transparent commerciality with the now-customary field of guests (among them Dif Juz guitarist David Curtis and former Rema Rema/Mass comrade Gary Asquith). 'Derek The Confessor' pointed to a new, relaxed warmth, 'So Long Dead' was an angrier Wolfgang Press than they'd expressed for a while, and the electric piano triggering 'Christianity' was one of their most nagging riffs. But there was too much overworked, even bland, material, for example 'She's So Soft',which milked the rhythm of T. Rex's glam classic 'Get It On'. The record sounded jaded, and the band knew it.

'*Funky Little Demons* was a big mistake,' Mick Allen concludes. 'It went against what we were about, because we'd lost our way. Heads were turned. Mine was, anyway. Once you start thinking too much about what other people think of you, you lose the plot.'

'None of us were focused on what the sound should be,' adds Andrew Gray. 'We were all off at tangents.'

'*Queer* had taken ages to make, and I was surprised when they decided to go through it all again,' says Ivo. *Funky Little Demons* had been a nightmare to make too. 'The ideas didn't flow easily but musically, it mostly sounded joyous and lyrically Mick's observation of personal relationships was easier to follow than usual.'

The difference between *Queer*'s unqualified success and *Funky Little Demons*' failure was that the band had secured its own studio, partly through 'A Girl Like You' royalties. Freed up from the limitations of studio expense and bookings, they spent the best part of two years working on an album; to free up the creative block, producer Drostan Madden suggested each member demo three tracks at home. Gray says only he and Allen completed the task. 'Mark found it hard to work on his own, and he returned with some electronics that didn't go anywhere. And we were now under time and pressure to finish the album.'

Allen: 'Mark's confidence was shot too as he felt he wasn't given much support from us. We weren't the greatest at instilling confidence. But we were all big boys and we should have been able to come up with something.'

Strangely, the album's sole single writing credit was Cox's ambient instrumental 'New Glass', which sat awkwardly on a Wolfgang Press record. Allen says he should take part of the blame for the lack of direction. 'I was the driving force before but I'd started a family [with 4AD office manager Janice Chaplin], which had diverted my attention. Foolishly, I let Mark and Andrew steer things. It felt like we were carrying Mark, which actually had been going on for a while. It might sound ruthless but that's how it worked. The balance had shifted.'

'We'd always divided profits three ways, but some tracks were completely Mick or me,' Gray explains. 'In the end, we said that the publishing should be split according to the writing. Mark then said he'd leave.'

'*Queer* was the album we were always trying to make, which might explain why it all then fell apart,' Cox suggests. 'Tom Jones was the catalyst. People around us got excited, thinking we'd be millionaires, which turned into, "I wrote that song", after years of sharing everything. People have to treat me as an equal or I'm out of there. The Wolfgang Press was like an old married trio; we'd row over the milk, but we were solid on basic life morals, or so I thought. I'm aware of the others' complaints, but I believe strength comes from the ability to compromise.'

Cox even suggests that Ivo could have held the band together. 'Someone needed to get in the middle of us. But I'd watched Ivo, the youngest of eight, who didn't have children himself, except that he had a hundred children, all members of 4AD bands. Having since toured with Brendan [Perry] and Robin [Guthrie], seeing how the tour manager herded us around like spoilt children, I'm not surprised that Ivo burned out. He had to deal with all that fallout after this beautiful, harmonious growth.'

Ivo: 'The morning after the pivotal moment when I effectively had a breakdown, Mark had called to tell me he'd left; he was really upset, broken-hearted, confused and angry. We must have spoken for an hour, but he didn't realise that I was crying the whole time, because I was dealing with my own confusion.'

The Wolfgang Press had played *All Virgos Are Mad*, with David Curtis taking over Cox's keyboard parts. Cox did turn up in LA, to support Ivo and catch up with friends, but only after Allen and Gray had left town. The band continued to tour, but rumours swirled about them being dropped from 4AD. Andrew Gray had married an American and already elected to live in the States, and with Allen focused on his family in London, The Wolfgang Press officially went on sabbatical. A promo video was made for 'Christianity' but the track was only ever released as a promo. More money wasted, then. And would a song named after a mass religion, with provocative punk Mick Allen pulling crucifixion poses in the video, be supported anyway by an American corporation such as Warners?

Six months later, 4AD confirmed the band had been dropped following Warners' similar decision. 'We looked at the huge debt The Wolfgang Press had,' says Ivo. 'An American licensee was the only way it could now be financially viable, because it wasn't cheap to run offices in LA as well as London. It wasn't common for an English independent label to have such a set-up.'

The biggest flaw in the long-term contracts that 4AD were offering was the built-in option for the label to secure further albums, but only through paying increasingly bigger advances to the artist. 'It was becoming prohibitive, and one by one Warners wasn't interested in picking up those options,' Ivo recalls. 'It was almost like a domino effect.'

It seemed the odds were always stacked against The Wolfgang Press: never fashionable, never the new kids in town given their history with Rema-Rema and Mass, never supported by radio. When the band's publishing deal was also not renewed, the band was effectively cut adrift. Allen and Gray haven't recorded a note together since. Or spoken to Cox. 'I've held out a hand but they don't engage,' Cox says. 'We were so close for so long, like brothers. It felt like I'd been written out of the will.'

'I didn't like the fact Mark felt we'd been unreasonable,' says Allen. 'I might have been paranoid, but I also felt he used his friendship with Ivo to some effect, the fact that Mark was out in the cold, before we were dropped.'

'I'm not so sure,' Gray counters. 'I think Ivo saw us as a democracy, a family that had feuds, a family where you have to pull your weight, and if you don't, people will tell you so. It blew his vision of us. Remember, it was Mick and Mark right back at the start.'

What happened with The Wolfgang Press epitomised what had gone wrong at 4AD: commerce over commitment, money over art. Ivo's reaction reflected this, proving Allen was right to be paranoid, though not because of Cox.

'In many ways, what happened to The Wolfgang Press was the final straw,' says Ivo (and not for the first time – Tanya Donelly recalls Ivo saying much the same thing about Belly). 'These people I'd admired for so long for their principled approach as much as for their music were making the cardinal error of tearing apart the trust, respect and equality that made them so dear to me and unique to themselves. We let them go because it was no longer financially viable, but I was influenced by the way Mick and Andrew treated Mark.'

That left Dead Can Dance as the longest-serving 4AD personnel, followed by Throwing Muses. Both bands had negotiated potentially fatal family splits, and survived, all the stronger for it.

After the pain-free launch of Hersh's *Hips And Makers*, the Muses' first album as a trio, *University*, flexed its sinewy power-trio muscle over fourteen tracks and 48 minutes with a cohesion they hadn't achieved since 1987's *House Tornado*. But nothing in the Donelly era had had a

wah-wah guitar snaking through ('No Place In Hell'). There were delicate interludes, such as 'Calm Down, Come Down' and an acoustic
'Crabtown', introduced by Hersh's unabashed giggle. Hersh's two sons
Dylan and Ryder, alongside *Hips And Makers* producer Lenny Kaye,
sang on the title track, while 'Snakeface' had backing vocals by New
Orleans engineer Tina Shoemaker, who was to work with Hersh on
many of her following records. Another little family had begun to grow.

Hersh had good reason to celebrate as Sire had agreed to let her
contract expire after *University* if they could have the rights to *Hips
And Makers*, which hadn't been covered by the Muses' original deal.
Of course, Sire didn't make it easy. 'I'd made *Hips And Makers* for no
money, so I was immediately in the black,' Hersh recalls. 'But the day
that we left Warners, they put my album into debt and I've never
made another penny off it since. Warners know that I can't afford to
audit them.'

But Hersh and Throwing Muses were now finally free from the
yoke of Warners, and that was worth a lot. What Tanya Donelly would
have given at that moment for some intra-band harmony, and some
self-belief that the success she'd experienced around Belly's *Star* was
the right path to take.

'I had freaked out one night when I was in LA, and Ivo had come
to see me,' she confesses. 'We said to each other, what's happened?
Why can't we handle it? I hated talking about myself in interviews. I
didn't even know how to represent myself. I didn't understand why I
had to do so many interviews either. The British press with the Muses
had been so thoughtful, but schlepping from American radio station
to station got to me. It felt like I had no ownership of myself, my art
and my body.'

'I remember that night very well,' says Ivo. 'I don't often use the
term, but our conversation got very dark. That night it felt like, in
many ways, Tanya came to *my* rescue.'

Which made the recording of the new Belly album at Nassau's
plush and expensive Compass Point studios, with veteran British
producer Glyn Johns, seem like madness. The Bahamas was a glamorous jaunt for the rich, and Johns' former clients included The Beatles,

The Band, The Rolling Stones and The Eagles. Johns had also produced The Clash's *Combat Rock* album but he still seemed a bizarre choice for Belly – unless it was done with Sire's coercion, to initiate an inappropriate upgrade to make a proper rock star of Donelly, perhaps as the new Deborah Harry, Courtney Love or Stevie Nicks.

'Glyn's concept was to record us live, a simpler-is-better approach, which really appealed to us,' Donelly recalls. 'And we were Beatles devotees, so there was a historical appeal. We also got along extremely well and we liked his approach to the songs. Glyn needed to work outside the US for visa reasons, and we wanted someplace other than the UK. And Belly was a surfing beach bum band, after all! Recording in Nassau was much funkier and mellow than it sounds – we were not even aware of the island's glam side while we were there.'

After his hands-on steering of *Star*, Ivo's condition meant he wasn't involved this time, leaving Robin Hurley and Donelly's manager Gary Smith to negotiate the terrain. But the true problem lay internally.

'Band members were already not speaking,' Donelly confesses. 'That's what an eighteen-month tour can do. I still had a civil relationship with Chris and Gail, but they weren't talking to each other, and I wasn't speaking to Tom even though we were a great songwriting team. And being brothers, Tom and Chris fought like crazy. And I was a horrible bandleader. I didn't take the helm, and so the rudder was unmanned.

'In Nassau,' Donelly recalls, 'it was a question of who could be in the studio together. The answer was nobody. It was quite a juggling act.' But the real crime on *King* was Johns' anodyne production. Ivo first listened to the album, and says that when Tanya's voice came in, he couldn't believe it had been mixed so high. 'It was bonkers. After all, Glyn Johns had produced all those great early Steve Miller Band albums, including *Sailor*! It wasn't the album Tanya was hoping for. I didn't listen to it much after that.'

Donelly: 'For Ivo, not having a connection to the music he was imprinting was so antithetical to what 4AD was about. The connections we all felt had got colder and more clinical, because it was now about running a business.'

Of the six B-sides shared between the album's two singles 'Now They'll Sleep' (good) and 'Seal My Fate' (not so good), the four produced at Boston's trusted Apache Studio had the necessary fire that Johns had misplaced. The upgrade backfired as *King*'s sales also failed to match *Star*, though 350,000 in the US – and reaching number 6 in the UK national chart – showed that Belly had kept a dedicated fan base.

Removed from listening to music, making music and the business of music, Ivo had turned his attention to dogs after Brandi had suggested the couple own one. It turned out to be a great idea as it set Ivo off on a new journey that has since reshaped his life. It began with a Chinese Shar Pei, the only breed they could agree on, says Ivo. 'We got a boy and a girl from a breeder in Oregon. They were notorious for their lack of social skills regarding fellow canines but they proved to be a delightful handful. I might not have been going into the office every day but I was going to the dog park with the more sociable young dogs whilst walking the Shar Peis.'

At this point, Ivo decided to officially step down from running 4AD on a day-to-day basis. The board that had been nominally in charge was dissolved and Robin Hurley made president of 4AD worldwide. One of his first jobs was to tell Richard Hermitage he was no longer required. 'It was a shock, but the job had changed hugely,' Hermitage says. 'There wasn't room for two in that structure.'

Simon Harper recalls how Hermitage would arrive each morning carrying a briefcase, and that the receptionists would refer to him as Doctor Hermitage. It had been a frustrating experience for Hermitage to begin with, as he had accepted a job, and an office atmosphere, filled with uncertainty. 'The company had been running like a machine and we were financially very sound as the back catalogue was bringing in a fortune, but no significant signing was made while I was at 4AD,' he recalls. 'And we had a bloated staff count. It was easy to take people on when you're making money.'

'Richard was even-keeled and practical but in retrospect, employing him was a crazy decision,' says Simon Harper. 'It was like throwing someone into the extremely deep end of the swimming pool – are they drowning or waving? He had an impossible task to start with. Half the people at 4AD didn't know Richard, and were scratching their heads as to why we'd employed someone that hadn't any experience of working at a record company.'

Colin Wallace: 'Richard didn't have a clue. He began making cutbacks but he drove an expensive company car, like one rule for him and one for everyone else. But it must have been very strange for him. And my own judgement at the time was clouded by frustration and anger, because I was still taking drugs, even though I'd wanted to quit.'

In the two years that Wallace had been Ivo's A&R wingman, Ivo hadn't responded to one thing that he had sent him, and Wallace admits that he'd felt disillusioned by that, and with the general mood of the office. He was also experiencing a painful personal comedown. 'One time, my girlfriend said, "It's fucking boring doing drugs". Another time, Chris Bigg took me aside and said, "Your skin is grey and you're as thin as a rake, I'm really worried about you". Both really resonated with me, so I just stopped, went cold turkey. I couldn't go backstage for five years because of the association with cocaine.'

Even the v23 department had also pulled back from the druggy excesses, though Richard Hermitage had already been privileged, like Jim Beattie of Spirea X, to witness a Vaughan Oliver/glass roof episode, 'on a cold, wet, dark day, as if Vaughan had created himself as his own installation'. The design team was already under the cosh of a vastly increased workload of extra formats, marketing campaigns, and now had the demands of the new digital age to contend with. 'Neither Vaughan nor Chris could use a computer,' says Tim O'Donnell, a designer from New York who had written to v23 about a job and enclosed a handmade book of Samuel Beckett poems. It did the trick, and O'Donnell joined v23, but it would prove something of an education for the young American.

'Vaughan might disappear for days, and then turn up in the morning with a tray of gin and tonics from the pub across the road,' O'Donnell claims. 'He was still brilliant, and work would still carry on. We still had passionate, hilarious times, and awful times too, with people yelling … Vaughan was not your average employer. But it made the work better. He was constantly challenging everything but he would let us work, though we understood the work couldn't be middle of the road. If Vaughan hated it, he'd let you know immediately, which resulted in stronger work.'

Perhaps the new digital form was the underlying reason why many v23 sleeves of this era were beautifully decorative – a psychedelic array of textures, colours and shapes – but rarely mined the savage, permissive side of Oliver's creative brain. He was certainly having a rough time. First came the reduced size of the CD format, leaving him less of a canvas on which to create. Then he was forced to accept that his hands-on skills were being eroded as record companies began to refuse artwork unless it was in digitised form.

'The tools of my trade had been taken away from me – the parallel motion drawing board, the glue, the scalpel, the comma at the end of the scalpel, the sense of crafting,' Oliver recalls. 'I was used to sitting in front of black-and-white artwork imagining colours, and now printers would just run through twenty variations for the sake of it. It took me a while to stop resenting the change. I don't want to talk retro, but those were halcyon days, for music and for graphic design.'

For whatever reason, Oliver had underperformed for Red House Painters, with another solitary photo (of a windmill this time) in a sepia wash – an echo of the repeating textures of Cocteau Twins covers. Perhaps this was the point, to reflect the way the band's music had become so familiar, with Kozelek seemingly unable to move on either musically or lyrically.

He admits that their third album, *Ocean Beach*, 'had taken for ever to complete' – only Robin Hurley's intervention had encouraged Kozelek to put him out of his misery and accept it was finished. At 54 minutes (over an hour on double ten-inch vinyl, due to a bonus cover of 'Long Distance Runaround' by Kozelek's favourite prog rock behemoths Yes), the album was another lengthy consolidation, although admittedly it was still a fine record, especially the opening, meditative instrumental 'Cabazon', piano ballad 'Shadows' and the epic finale 'Drop'.

Yet even with Red House Painters, Ivo also felt something wasn't quite right. 'There were some things that, a year earlier, I'd have had the strength and ability to voice, to persuade Mark to alter. Like a crazy guitar solo [on 'Over My Head'] that just fizzled out. There's some gorgeous stuff there, and I'd probably feel more positive about it all now, but I was disappointed at the time.'

This sense of disappointment was to increase when lead guitarist Gorden Mack left the band. Kozelek's more restricted skills were now centre stage, at which point he expanded the guitar solos as part of a shift towards classic/progressive rock that indicated progress. Nothing Kozelek now did sat well with Ivo. Red House Painters was one of the very few bands he'd see live, 'but everything had become long and drawn out, and turned into comedy hour with Mark always talking,' he recalls. 'And his next lot of demos featured covers of Genesis and Wings songs that struck me as silly, with longer guitar solos. It all influenced my decision not to work with them again.'

Ivo's willingness to part ways with even Kozelek after the heights of their union showed his usual courage in putting a stop to something that he had lost touch with, but also that Ivo felt estranged from even his current favourite 4AD artists. Indeed, an 11-minute cover of Wings' 'Silly Love Songs' was not the band that he had first fallen for.

'Ivo had been my main contact and he was always there for me,' Kozelek recalls, 'but then I got word that Ivo wasn't happy. When he finally made contact, there was a hostility that wasn't like Ivo. It was the first time I was being told what to do, to lose the guitar solos and lose a few songs. It wasn't the 4AD I'd signed to and I suppose I wasn't the same artist anymore.'

Kozelek offered to buy himself out of the deal, which would cost £30,000. To his shock, Ivo agreed. 'I was in a state of disbelief, but I knew it was time to move on, and I felt confident that I could repay them,' Kozelek says. 'I didn't have the romantic connections associated with the label that other artists did. I felt confident I'd have a career with or without 4AD. I wanted to sing and play guitar and didn't care much about whose logo was on the record. I loved Black Sabbath, but who cared what label they were on?'

After Island had released Red House Painters' *Songs For A Blue Guitar* in 1996, Kozelek received a postcard from Ivo: 'It said, "beautiful record, Mark!"'*

Ivo: 'It was the right decision at the time to let them go, but in hindsight, it was probably the stupidest decision I made at 4AD – though hardly the worst decision 4AD ever took. I should have let them release *Songs For A Blue Guitar* on 4AD. But it was all falling apart for me.'

Ivo still had Heidi Berry and Lisa Germano to nurture, and he added eco-wood dweller Kendra Smith, another example of the folk rock stable that he was building, putting the music well before any idea of building careers, in the same manner as the Guernica venture. Even so, it was a bold move on Ivo's part: Smith was another artist that had been around for a while, rather than a new name that might spark any kind of breakthrough.

Smith didn't respond to email requests for this book, and perhaps she still lives without such mod cons as electricity. But by 1995, she had forsaken the 'off-the-grid community lifestyle' for a band and a mini-album under the name *The Guild Of Temporal Adventurers*. Enjoying its hazy, acid-folky style, Ivo had asked Hurley (who knew Smith from the Opal days at Rough Trade) if he could set up a meeting with Smith. It took place at a road lay-by.

Ivo: 'I got directions to drive from Eureka, way up at the top of northern California, to a particular road stop, opposite a wood cabin motel where I would be staying. Kendra arrived and drove me deep into the woods where she and her boyfriend had built a couple of small structures. We spent a few hours together talking more about life off the grid than music, but by the end of the night, she'd agreed to make an album.'

---

* The fact that Mark Kozelek has subsequently recorded entire albums of covers (by disparate sources such as AC/DC, John Denver and Modest Mouse), both under his own name and that of Sun Kil Moon – the band successor to Red House Painters – shows that he was not to be dissuaded from his new direction. At the same time, Kozelek has studiously taught himself to play more classical nylon-stringed guitar, supporting Ivo's view that American artists are always more self-improving than their British counterparts. Ivo maintains he has liked everything that Kozelek has recorded since they parted ways, saying, 'I still have an enormous soft spot for him.'

4AD's press release for *Five Ways Of Disappearing* quoted Smith as saying, 'I can deal directly with 4AD without the usual labyrinth of intermediaries and suits.' She described her way of life as: 'Primitive … it can be physically and "psychically" demanding. But it's satisfying to me. There are many opportunities to study nature and conduct scientific experiments. I know enough of humans already.'

Smith's interest in music had been rekindled by a love of playing the pump organ, the rich, droning hum of which was all over her album. 'I had intentionally stopped keeping up with new sounds on the "outside", and knew 4AD mainly by reputation, so I was pleased when I enjoyed the tapes that Ivo sent me,' the press release had continued. 'Meanwhile, I'm still listening to Syd [Barrett], Can, Faust, Eno and a good amount of Middle and Near Eastern music. Certain melodies and frequencies attract me, but I find them here and there and not entirely in commercially produced music. It's pretty obvious the artform has been vampirised, and its social and spiritual functions altered bizarrely by narcissism and greed.'

The title *Five Ways Of Disappearing* suited both Smith and Ivo's reticent nature, with drowsy lo-fi drones, a knit of violin, Turkish drums, Indian harmonium and fuzz guitar coloured by Smith's deep, sleepy voice and pump organ (which appeared on v23's cover artwork, alongside a cross section of a redwood tree). It was a little jauntier than both Opal and Temporal Adventurers records, as if life had been treating Smith better. 'In Your Head' was a sweet mid-tempo pop song and 'Maggots' more of a whimsical ditty. Ivo had wanted more of Smith's sadder disposition, and as with Red House Painters' *Ocean Beach*, felt let down.

'It was unusual for 4AD to work with someone that we'd admired from a distance,' he says. '"Aurelia" has always reminded me of Kevin Ayers and the cover of [Richard and Mimi Farina's] "Bold Marauder" was fantastic. But it didn't flow as well as the *Temporal Adventurers* record and I could have done without tracks like "Maggots". But I'm glad we managed to get Kendra back into the studio one more time, before she went back to the woods. She probably thought, Why did I bother to do that? Robin [Hurley] might have liked to carry on, but I didn't encourage it.'

There would be no 4AD release for almost two months, a worrying precedent for a label maintaining two offices and a demanding Warners licence deal. The drop in A&R activity after Ivo's breakdown had begun to show. A new project in the vein of This Mortal Coil that could have filled the gap, and given the media an angle, also failed to fire. 'I think Ivo realised it was too big for him,' says Lisa Germano.

Ivo had conceived of a series of ten-inch singles to unite a 4AD artist with a cover of his choosing. The first to be recorded was Slowdive's 'Dagger' with Brendan Perry producing Heidi Berry's cover, but Ivo didn't enjoy the result. Inexplicably, he also didn't like the luminous version of Neil Young's 'Round And Round' by Germano and her chosen backing band, Arizona's Giant Sand, whose lynchpin Howe Gelb conjured something of Young's sun-baked sound. Germano and Giant Sand believed in it, however, and they eventually released an album, *Slush*, under the mantle of OP8, on Thirsty Ear. 'They screwed us over as we never saw any money,' Germano recalls. 'At least Ivo had given us the money to start it, and people tell us they love the record.'

4AD staffer Chris Staley, who was co-ordinating the project for Ivo, says a video compilation also never came to fruition. Staley himself had left London for LA, for the same reason as Ivo, to try and resolve his depression. With Staley staying on the production side of the label, Ivo still single-handedly kept charge of A&R. But to his ears, nothing sounded good enough. Guernica had ended, Red House Painters wasn't coming back, and Ivo also felt that he hadn't been fulfilling his side of the deal with Paul Cox and Richard Roberts at Too Pure.

'I gave them access to 4AD's staff, warehouse space and distribution, but they got little guidance from me,' he says. 'Life was very busy and demanding and I later apologised to Paul and Richard, because I didn't give them what Martin [Mills] had given me, someone to take on aspects of daily business, which was the last thing I was good at or wanted to do. Martin eventually took on that role for Too Pure as well.'

If 4AD's trajectory was goin' south, the label's next release wasn't going to change that, with the same communication breakdown that had marred his relationships with Spirea X, Swallow and The Glee Club.

Liquorice was formed by Jenny Toomey, a respected musician and activist on the Washington, DC punk scene. She'd sung in the children's choir, absorbed her parents' love of jazz and showtunes, 'and the bad music you'd hear on the radio, like Foreigner', none of which hinted at the political resolve that would determine her future. 'I studied feminism and discovered it wasn't an accident that I thought I couldn't play music,' she says, 'and I immediately got into bands.'

To begin with, Toomey had joined forces with another former member of the children's choir, Amy Pickering, in Fire Party, a pioneering all-women hardcore punk band. In 1990, Toomey had launched the independent label Simple Machines, run from a shared house in Arlington, Virginia with Kristin Thompson, who was also her bandmate in Tsunami. Toomey had also formed Grenadine with moonlighting Unrest member Mark Robinson. The pair had also briefly dated, though Ivo – who was still enjoying music at that point – says it was the women of Tsunami (rather than yet another creative couple) that had captivated him, much like That Dog had: 'Jenny and Kristin's voices, straining at the top of their range, gave me the chills.'

Toomey and Ivo first met at an annual event that Robinson was staging for DC's indie fraternity. 'Mark organised it like a wedding,' Toomey recalls. 'Bands would sit at different tables, and he'd hand gold records out, and we'd all sing a cappella versions of songs. Ivo came to at least a couple of them. The fact he was running a big label but was totally jazzed by this little weirdo event seemed cool to me.'

With Grenadine over by 1994 and Tsunami committed to its own Simple Machines label, Toomey responded to Ivo's suggestion of an album with a suggestion of her own – an album of covers. Ivo wanted original songs, so Toomey suggested that she team up with Dan Littleton of New York trio Ida. Toomey recalls Robin Hurley – taking on Ivo's traditional role of mentor – buying her music that they thought she should listen to: 'I felt invested in, in a sweet and generous way. But Ivo was three steps removed for a lot of the time. He was like a mosquito that would come in real close, and then fade into the background.'

Warren Defever had produced Grenadine's second album, *Nopalitos*, so Toomey and Littleton employed him to produce theirs. With His Name Is Alive's regular drummer Trey Many joining up, Toomey christened the new trio Liquorice. She says they recorded twelve songs, 'but Warren did about 87 mixes, four full C90 cassette tapes of all the same songs but named differently. People think the record is broken because of scratches through some songs, but that was Warren experimenting with technology.'

Another sign of Ivo's altered perception was that in the past he'd often suggested releasing demos, yet Toomey says he told her the Liquorice album resembled demos, and that they should re-record the songs. 'It was a challenge with Ivo,' Toomey recalls. 'We wrote "Blew It" about how he was driving us nuts [*'You won the prize for step back and revise and redo it/ And you wouldn't sound so anaesthetised if you'd been through it/ But you blew it'*]. He didn't seem committed to us, or even interested, which was very frustrating. We had one hard conversation – he wasn't much for words – about stepping away from people like me, Warren and Unrest, and I remember writing to him, saying, we're the kind of people you should be betting on, because we'll always make great music.'

Liquorice's debut album *Listening Cap* was folkier and sparser than Tsunami's sound, and free of straining female harmonies. (Toomey left her political fervour at home too; did artists sense Ivo's avoidance of such leanings?) At least Ivo enjoyed the re-recorded version of the album: 'It was a surprisingly acoustic and soft record, with a lovely, delicate atmosphere.' But he didn't ask for more. 'It felt right as a one-off on 4AD. Years later, Jenny sent me a letter apologising for being very angry with me because we didn't carry on. I don't remember that anger.'

He suggests that Toomey's reaction derived from the fact she ran her own label. 'People think they'll get loads more exposure with a label like 4AD. It was no different to Geffen thinking that That Dog would be established with indie cred from being licensed to us. Those days seemed over.'*

Ivo didn't need to guide, reassure or even be present for Lisa Gerrard's first solo album. *The Mirror Pool* had been recorded at home in Gippsland, partly with the Melbourne-based Victorian Philharmonic Orchestra. Two tracks had been conceived during Dead Can Dance sessions: 'Sanvean: I Am Your Shadow' was one of the peak performances of Gerrard's career, sounding both serene and anguished, and the traditional 'Persian Love Song' first appeared on the duo's live album *Toward The Within*. The orchestrations were one facet of a more classical outlook: 'Largo' was the opening aria from Handel's opera *Serse*, and 'The Rite' came from a libretto Gerrard had written for a 1991 production of Sophocles' *Oedipus Rex*. The cinematic score of 'La Bas: Song Of The Drowned' and a more ceremonial 'Gloradin' were featured in director Michael Mann's crime thriller *Heat*, initiating an association with Hollywood that still thrives.

In the early days, Gerrard may have given the impression of being a fragile flower, but Dead Can Dance's continuing commitment and autonomy showed the same fearlessness that had led her into Melbourne's roughest pubs. Gerrard could see how Ivo was now the fragile one that needed support. 'Looking back, there were little clues,' she says. 'Ivo once sent me a few books on self-help that were not the kind of things I'd read, so why was he sending them? I didn't ask. Eventually, I saw he was burnt out. He had to be a sociopath all those years, the host for the 4AD party that never stopped. It came with the job, but it wasn't his nature.'

'Sanvean' was released as a single and rewarded with one of the few 4AD videos that would deserve a space on a compilation; it was directed by former 23 Envelope partner Nigel Grierson, and showed

---

* Simple Machines' annual guide to 'indie' was later transferred online as the Future of Music Coalition, embracing the new digital world that had opened up for artists. Jenny Toomey was awarded a grant for such work from the Ford Foundation, where she now works as a program officer for media rights and access in internet policy. She in turn gives grants to organisations that are 'fighting to ensure people have access to the internet as a right, and how to establish the rules of the internet, such as privacy and competition'.

again his Tarkovsky/*Stalker* influences, all refracted sunlight, shadow and water. He'd turned to directing music videos and adverts after a feeling of disconnect from record covers. 'It [designing artwork] wasn't as much fun as when Vaughan and I did it,' he says. 'We had played off each other so well, as a team.'*

By autumn of 1995, the mood around 4AD had turned dark, like its figurehead, a comedown after the peak success of 1993. But so had the mood across the music formerly known as 'alternative'. Kurt Cobain's suicide in 1994, alongside other cases of heroin addiction, felt like a curtain coming down on grunge; on the rise was the punishing industrial electro of Nine Inch Nails – whose 1989 debut *Pretty Hate Machine* had been partly produced by John Fryer – and the goth theatre of Reznor's protégé Marilyn Manson, a more extreme version of Peter Murphy and Bauhaus' patented 'dark glam'.

Looking back, Pixies was a total aberration for 4AD; Ivo wasn't remotely interested in the rock scene that followed in the band's wake, and none of 4AD's successes with Belly or The Breeders appeared to gve him any lasting pleasure. In Ivo's sunken and isolated state, he'd assembled a modest roster that happened to chime with the nascent Americana movement, and given the nature of preconception, core 4AD collectors were thrown by this, while equally committed fans of roots music thought of 4AD as a fountain of alternative rock. This wasn't to change even with 4AD's most striking additions in years.

The San Francisco-based quartet Tarnation was spearheaded by Paula Frazer, whose vocal style originated from the western side of country music, the sound of the lonesome prairie and Roy Orbison, and a perfect conduit for songs about crushed love. Raised in the

---

* Nigel Grierson concentrated on music videos (and TV commercials) in the Nineties, including The Beloved ('Sun Rising'), Robert Plant ('29 Palms'), David Sylvian ('Orpheus') and Rain Tree Crow ('Black Water'). Some drew on what Grierson calls his street photography, which he was developing at the same time as album sleeves at 4AD: 'I wanted videos to feel like turning the pages of a good photographic book – no continuity cuts, more stream of consciousness. It was partly a reaction against the narrative nonsense of videos in the first half of the Eighties. It was also pointless doing stuff that people would say looked like 4AD. Nevertheless, certain obsessions re-emerged in spite of myself' – water being the predominant reoccurring image.

hamlet of Sautee Nacoochee in Georgia's Smoky Mountains, Frazer had sung in her minister father's church choir. Her mother – who would say, 'What in tarnation?' rather than swear – taught Frazer piano and guitar, and introduced her to the best of America's music traditions – gospel, jazz, Fifties crooners and country, especially superstars Patsy Cline and George Jones.

Frazer was fourteen when the family moved to Eureka Springs, a Christian community nestled among the Ozarks mountains of Arkansas. But when Frazer struck out alone, to San Francisco, she tried her hand at punk rock, or what she called 'the moany, dirgier side of punk', in local bands such as Frightwig. This was goth by any other name. Frazer was rescued by joining Savina, a women's choir that specialised in Bulgarian choral music. Tarnation, born in late 1992, bottled a haunting blend of Appalachian and Balkan folk. 'I was always drawn to music of the imagination and landscape, such as [Italian composer Ennio] Morricone's spaghetti western soundtracks,' she says. 'So it fell into place for me to write that music myself.'

Le Mystère Des Voix Bulgares had led Frazer to 4AD, and on to This Mortal Coil, 'which,' she says, 'reminded me of choral music.' Mark Kozelek had alerted 4AD's LA office to Tarnation's debut album *I'll Give You Something To Cry About* released in 1993 by the tiny indie Nuf Sed. The label was run by the band's original lap steel guitarist Brandon Kearney, though the album had been recorded with guitarist Lincoln Allen, bassist Michelle Cernuto and drummer Matt Sullivan.

Ivo had immediately responded: 'Paula had an extraordinary, ancient-sounding, country voice, from a time before Emmylou, with a real edge to it. "Game Of Broken Hearts" was especially stunning.' Ivo's favourite track had been recorded by Frazer, alone at home, with an old microphone.

His preferred strategy for Tarnation's 4AD debut was to cherry-pick seven songs from the album and have the band record new material that fitted his choices – as expected, the band's maudlin side, for example 'Big O Motel', 'Do You Fancy Me' and 'The Well', abandoning the uptempo or overtly Nashville-influenced material. With its twisted roots and gothic aura, *Gentle Creatures* was 4AD's first release to blend

Ivo's love of Seventies country rock with classic Eighties 4AD, infused with the fumes of the Californian desert where he felt most at home.

In a role that Ivo might have adopted in the days when he felt engaged with his artists, Warren Defever remixed Tarnation's old tracks and oversaw the new recordings, giving Frazer's voice the necessary range of stark, haunting and blissful. 'Warren was great, like a mad professor,' she recalls. 'We had similar aesthetics, recording with interesting microphones and wire recorders from the Thirties, and using different rooms, like a garage.'

With *Listening Cap*, *The Mirror Pool* and *Gentle Creatures*, the quality and quantity of 4AD's schedule had gone north again. Next was Air Miami's debut album *Me Me Me*. The name was new but it was the same creative force as Unrest, namely Mark Robinson and Bridget Cross. Robinson had laid the Unrest name to bed six months after the release of *Perfect Teeth*: 'It was all the major label-type work we were doing,' he says. 'Constant interviews, travelling too much, no manager or a proper tour bus, performing at the distribution warehouse or in a boardroom … we got antsy.'

Drummer Phil Krauth had decided to record his own songs, and had been replaced by Gabriel Stout, which was enough for Robinson to strike up a new band name, honouring the Miami location where *Me Me Me* was recorded – the same studio where the Bee Gees had made *Saturday Night Fever* – 'all silly decisions made by me that Ivo went along with,' says Robinson. He and Cross ensured the album continued in Unrest's vein of superior guitar-pop, though Robinson rightly suggests that 'the songs were more succinct, shorter and pop-oriented'.

Two tracks, 'I Hate Milk' and a remixed 'Afternoon Train' formed half of a following EP that Ivo perversely insisted should be titled *Fuck You, Tiger*. Robinson willingly agreed, as it appealed to his sense of humour; *Me Me Me* was Air Miami's only album. 'I think Bridget and I both waited for the other to schedule a rehearsal, which never happened – I guess we lost interest,' says Robinson. 'The last Air Miami shows had Phil Krauth back on drums, so it was an Unrest reunion of sorts.'

Robinson persisted with the Teen-Beat label, as a labour of love, but was to concentrate on his new creative vocation of graphic design. Ivo couldn't be as flexible. 4AD was a much larger and unwieldy operation than Teen-Beat, with offices, staff, contracts ... Had he sold 4AD at this juncture, he would have been financially secure, but it would have taken a much bolder decision than Ivo was capable of making. The decision behind the label's next signing also lacked the necessary clarity. Scheer wasn't even Ivo's discovery, but Colin Wallace's, and Ivo's permission wasn't even linked to a true belief in the band's music.

From County Derry in Northern Ireland, Scheer had been formed by vocalist Audrey Gallagher, guitarist Neal Calderwood and bassist Peter Fleming who all met at university. After co-guitarist Paddy Leyden and drummer Joe Bates joined, the band released the single 'Wish You Were Dead' and EP *Psychobabble* on the local indie label SON. Calderwood loved Cocteau Twins, and Scheer had a delicate side, but Gallagher loved her hard rock and metal, acts like Thin Lizzy, AC/DC and Pantera, so, she says, 'I pushed for the heavier side of things.'

Wallace was smitten by Gallagher's voice and the band's musical clout. 'It was completely different from 4AD, but people in the office liked Scheer too. And bizarrely, Ivo kinda liked them, or Audrey's voice, or he thought it could do something. And they were great live.'

Ivo had hired Wallace to be an A&R filter rather than source, but admits, 'I knew Colin was disillusioned, so I needed to say yes to something. There was also again growing concern and despondency in the UK office that the focus was all on America. I did like Scheer's first records and Audrey's voice, but I mostly liked an acoustic demo. And I really enjoyed a semi-acoustic gig they did in New York.'

Perhaps it was more than the voice, but the look and the presence that had seduced Ivo. 'Audrey was a short, red-headed Northern Irish girl, completely at odds with her voice, which had that 4AD siren thing going on,' says Cliff Walton. 'She could make you weak at the knees.'

The next night, Ivo saw Scheer perform, in all their heavy, amplified glory, so he knew what he was taking on. It was like a repeat of

Swallow or Spirea X – a shift towards the 'here and now' of grunge. Once he had given the nod, Scheer began recording with Head, who'd done such a sterling job producing PJ Harvey's debut album *Dry*. But neither the band's *Schism* EP nor the promo version of 'Demon' were even worthy of the enticing description 'a turbo-charged Sundays', as one reviewer suggested. 'An Irish version of former Guernica signing Bettie Serveert' seemed more accurate.

Scheer wasn't an outright anomaly at 4AD – Pixies and The Breeders had rocked out just as hard; it was simply that Scheer's crunching power chords and grunge appeal had never been heard on a 4AD album. The collective view of the early adopters of internet fan forums was that the band represented a kind of betrayal. 'Despite the signing of bands like Tarnation and the loss of Red House Painters, [4AD] has never raised quite as many eyebrows as when they recently signed this not-so-shoegazing Irish rock band,' wrote Lee Graham Bridges at the online site WestNet. 'The event has been seen by many 4AD fans as, at best, quite a change in the way the label does business.'

Richard Hermitage, who was still at 4AD when Scheer were signed, admits not all of 4AD London supported Wallace. 'They were a mistake, with nothing to commend them,' he says. '4AD was in a very good situation since anything it signed would get immediate media attention, so confronting people by signing a band like Scheer wasn't helpful to the label.'

The band knew it wasn't popular with the 4AD cognoscenti. 'Ivo took a bit of a bashing in an interview, which he countered by saying he hadn't intentionally set out to create a brand, he was just signing music he liked,' says Neal Calderwood. 'It seemed people were fans of 4AD and not necessarily the bands. We plodded on anyway.'

It was thought Scheer might more easily fulfil the expectations of 4AD's licensing deal. On his first visit to Warners since 1993, Ivo joined Robin Hurley to sell Scheer to the licensees. 'Though Scheer was out of place on 4AD, Ivo sang the group's praises to Warners,' Hurley recalls. 'Since grunge was still ever-present, with a bit of luck with radio, a band like Scheer could connect.'

It had been a testing time for Warners, with internal problems that dwarfed anything 4AD was experiencing. 'We'd been ripped apart by the corporate heads,' recalls Tim Carr, and even Lenny Waronker and Mo Ostin had been ousted, leaving by the end of 1994 after a public conflict with Warner Music Group chairman Robert Morgado, who made Steven Baker the new president of the record company. Waronker ended up heading the A&R part of David Geffen's new label DreamWorks; he took Tim Carr with him. 'Ivo would have felt that I might be let go, but he'd always have Lenny and Mo,' says Carr. 'I'd worked at Capitol where the same guy that had signed The Beatles was still running it – you always felt you had stability. But all of that was ripped away from every single major label.'

4AD's biggest supporter at Warners had gone, as well as the head honcho who had sanctioned the deal, and though only Dead Can Dance had made a decent return on the major's investment, Steven Baker nevertheless picked up the option for a further two years, to take the deal through to the end of 1997.

'Ivo had a singular sensibility, like a colour,' Baker feels. 'Even Warners had a sensibility, which had become fractured since the days when it was a very LA-sounding folk rock label. But it was surviving because it had so many different parts, and 4AD was one of them. Warners was interested in individuals, like Tom Silverman at [rap label] Tommy Boy, who hadn't been hot for a while but Mo thought he was worth taking a shot on, and it turned out to be a great deal. Ivo fit into that category. Sometimes it's not the label, it's the individual, and 4AD as Ivo's brainchild was unique.'

Baker explains that few labels were so individually looked after as 4AD: 'Another was Daniel Miller at Mute, who would also moonlight as an artist, and he bought into a sound early on. By comparison, Tony Wilson at Factory was more mercenary about what he could sell. We renewed the deal with 4AD because Robin Hurley was smart and we still believed in Ivo as a signer of artists. Dead Can Dance was doing well, and knowing Belly, The Breeders and Lush, there was always potential for something wonderful to happen. We were lucky to be involved with Ivo and it made sense to consolidate the deal.'

The sensibility that Baker had defined was Ivo's ability to read the signs of the times. 4AD's mini-wave of Americana expanded to include a band that were almost tailor-made to give his love of west coast country rock a very English makeover, with an air of retreat and isolation.

Mojave 3 had risen from the ashes of Slowdive, paragons of shoegaze with a particularly billowing, symphonic style. They were also one of only two bands defined as shoegaze to have a male/female core (the other being the more overtly electronic duo Curve) in Neil Halstead and Rachel Goswell. Halstead was Slowdive's main songwriter and guitarist, but Goswell sang a lot of the lead vocals. The pair had been friends since primary school in Reading, and lovers from the age of eighteen until twenty-two. A self-confessed 'ex-goth', Goswell was a 4AD and Smiths fan while Halstead preferred the noisier end of things, such as My Bloody Valentine and The Jesus and Mary Chain. Both had been signed by Creation, so it made sense that Slowdive would be too.

As Heidi Berry had already discovered, Creation's support could evaporate quickly, especially once Britpop and Creation's flagship band Oasis had taken over. Goswell says the band's confidence had been dented by a press backlash; Richey Edwards of the politicically-charged Manic Street Preachers had labelled Slowdive 'worse than Hitler' – a great soundbite but the same blunt criticism that *Melody Maker*'s Everett True had levelled at Lush.

Ivo had adored the ethereal and progressive airs of Slowdive's early EPs: 'They were mournful and really pretty. They took the shimmering guitar approach that Robin Guthrie had possibly invented to a new level.' He'd been less fond of the band's albums, even the electro-ambient beauty *Pygmalion*. This was Neil Halstead's reaction to Creation's demand for a more commercial record, turning the other way instead towards his love of Talk Talk, electronics and Ecstasy. Creation subsequently dropped Slowdive, and, 'sick of music and the industry', Halstead went off travelling. On his return, he turned to acoustic music, he says, as a way back into enjoying music again. 'I also started to broaden my listening, into song-based country like Gram Parsons and Townes Van Zandt.'

Halstead's new songs were less Nashvillian country rock and more bucolic Britain in a Nick Drake vein. Halstead soon moved to the wild coast of Cornwall, at the south-west tip of the country, well out of reach of the music industry, where he took up surfing. A demo made with the help of Goswell and Slowdive drummer Ian McCutcheon reached Ivo via the band's manager Sheri Hood, who had also been representing Ultra Vivid Scene.

The demo tape had Slowdive's name on it, and Ivo recalls he had left it on the kitchen counter for a couple of weeks. 'I thought, if they'd been dropped and 4AD wasn't having a blazing success with anything, what could we do that Creation couldn't? But once I played the tape, I instantly adored it.'

'We were amazed that Ivo loved it, and that we'd jumped from one great label to another,' says Goswell. 'But we were tentative about how the 4AD office would take to us, because of our history. We imagined they'd think, What do we do with this lot? And I sensed their hesitancy when we met them. But Ivo had faith in us when no one else did.'

Ivo recalls Martin Mills later telling him about a huge resistance in the UK office towards this ex-Creation band: 'The staff needed something more vibrant. But the album was a consistently beautiful, sad record – some melodies even reminded me of Pearls Before Swine. Better than all that Britpop nonsense. No, not nonsense, but Britpop was for young people.'

'I remember being envious of all the excitement around Oasis taking off,' 4AD press officer Colleen Maloney recalls. 'The biggest music movement in the world was happening on our doorstep, but Ivo's signings reflected what was going on in his head.'

Warners president Steven Baker also had some reservations. 'Red House Painters and Mojave 3 were good examples of Ivo being ahead of his time; you hear so much stuff today that's reminiscent of those bands,' he says. 'But at the time, unfortunately I'd have been listening for a hit rather than the quality of the music, which is the worst way of listening. But radio is the most constrictive format possible; it only wants what's already a hit. Not even Blur and Oasis were revered in America.'

The management at 4AD were also aware that neither Ivo nor Colin Wallace, given his post-drug sobriety, were sufficiently driven to find an artist at grass roots level, by seeing them in their most formative stages, to network among other artists rather than await the demo alongside every other A&R person. There might not have been a business plan on the table but it had been decided to spend another salary for an injection of fresh ears.

Lewis Jamieson had replaced Colin Wallace as 4AD's warehouse manager, and followed his predecessor into A&R – it had even been Wallace's suggestion, which had secured Robin Hurley's support. From Lytham St Annes on the Lancashire coast, Jamieson had graduated in English and taken a Master's degree in media and communication studies, only to be distracted by music and clubbing. After moving to London to be closer to the action, he had sold advertising space to earn money. When his friend and DJ companion Tony Morley mentioned a vacancy in the warehouse when Wallace had been promoted to 'negative' A&R, Jamieson abandoned any pretence at a media career and joined 4AD.

'I didn't want to be lugging boxes, but it was a way in,' he recalls. 'And as an indie kid in the Eighties, I'll never forget walking in on my first day and seeing Bauhaus, Pixies and Cocteau Twins records. I was in heaven.

'It was an interesting time, because to me, 4AD was just on the downside of a peak,' says Jamieson. 'But I went to loads of gigs, and *Star* and *Last Splash* had meant 4AD's ambitions had increased, and there was a feeling we could push on if they had an A&R strategy. So it made sense to have someone younger and hooked in, like me. It didn't easily work out that way because labels are about the people out front, and 4AD's problem was that Ivo wasn't present. It was a very odd situation.'

It was going to be an interesting time, given that Ivo had only semi-approved of one artist that Colin Wallace had sent on, but Jamieson was willing to go to every show, travel to every country, seek out everything that could work. Yet he didn't discuss A&R with Ivo for another two years, and he was never briefed about any supposed A&R

strategy. For now, hopes for a new beginning rested on Tarnation and Slowdive – or Mojave 3 as the band renamed itself, in honour of their new sound. Both bands were committed to playing live, and had consummate songwriters. As singers, Halstead and Goswell weren't as distinctive or powerful as Tarnation's Paula Frazer, but they could carry the airy sentiments of the songs.

Mojave 3 were also willing to follow Red House Painters and have their demos form their first 4AD album, *Ask Me Tomorrow*, with only similarly minor tweaks to bring it up to scratch. Goswell sang the opening 'Love Songs On The Radio' with all the breathy languor of a sun-stoked desert afternoon, while 'Candle Song 3' had something of Leonard Cohen's nocturnal sound. The album only really woke up in the slowly escalating finale 'Mercy', driven by a guitar solo straight out of the progressive rock textbook. Notably, no single or video was attached to the album campaign. 4AD was turning into Guernica.

Halstead had been open to Ivo's suggestion of releasing demos, but pulled back at his request to add strings to 'Mercy'. 'I finally got to work with an orchestra!' Ivo recalls. 'I had suggested it because the song had reminded me of the album … *And Other Short Stories* by [UK progressive rock band) Barclay James Harvest, which featured magnificent orchestration, and in parts, a very similar guitar sound to "Mercy". Slowdive had reminded me of Barclay James, too. But Neil didn't like it, so the orchestrated version was never released.'

It was a rare excursion for Ivo into a pro-active A&R role, and didn't involve any kind of potentially damaging confrontation. Moreover, he was not about to step in on any level when Deal, 4AD's most lucrative asset on paper, decided to abandon The Breeders for a side project that had an element of fuck-you-tiger punk rock to it.

The trigger for this change of heart wasn't The Breeders' 1994 raw *Head To Toe* EP but twin sister Kelley. The Deal twins had made *Last Splash* on a varied diet of drugs, and after The Breeders had come off the Lollapalooza festival tour in September 1994, Kelley had been arrested for possession of heroin. She admits that she had been using for years – 'I was a drug addict and an alcoholic waiting to happen' – even when working in office jobs that required security checks.

The outcome of the court trial in January of 1995 was a spell in rehab, which she did in St Paul, Minnesota. Whatever was to follow for sister Kim, she knew it couldn't be The Breeders: 'I really didn't think they'd ever come back.' Josephine Wiggs says Deal announced that she wanted to pursue a solo project, 'something quick and dirty, under the radar,' says Wiggs. 'Something without the pressure of following up "Cannonball". It's always a good idea to do something in a different way. And why would you want to stop someone if that's what they want to do?'

Wiggs recalls that Kelley Deal had been concerned with this news. 'Kelley made moves to try and orchestrate us all playing on it, but I told Kim that if it was to be a Breeders record, I'd come out to Dayton, but it was clearly going to be a side project.'

But after Kim Deal had begun to record in her basement, she changed her mind and decided her new songs should be road-tested with a band. Tammy Ampersand and the Amps, later abbreviated to The Amps, was Kim, Breeders drummer Jim Macpherson and two other Dayton musicians, guitarist Nate Farley and bassist Luis Lerma. The songs duly road-tested, Deal then decided to use the band to record an album. It proved as difficult as the *Last Splash* sessions, a costly exercise, using five separate studios, one belonging to Robert Pollard of Guided By Voices ('I Am Decided' was a Deal–Pollard co-write). It wasn't Nassau, but it was still expensive, except that this time Deal was searching for a raw, unproduced sound closer to the Steve Albini model.

'Frankly, I was really struggling to deal with Kim's lo-fi,' says Ivo. 'I couldn't tell if it was truly a demo or if it was the sound she was trying to pursue. It was alike to Syd Barrett – she's got this unique language to making music, but I didn't understand the story and I couldn't give any input, except to be encouraging when she'd call. I felt bad about not having come up with an alternate approach that might've been less costly and more fruitful. But, ultimately, I thought it cool that she was releasing something far removed from what everyone would have expected as a follow-up to an enormously successful record.'

'Kim's idea was of being able to re-create songs live for a club audi-ence, without all that texture of *Last Splash*,' says Kelley. 'But really, she just wanted to break free.'

That's precisely what Elektra didn't want Kim to do. After the bankable success of *Last Splash*, Kim says the label had colluded with her manager to get her to sign an improved contract that would tie her to Elektra for much longer. 'It meant the advances were bigger, like a couple of hundred thousand dollars for the next album,' Deal recalls. 'I told them, "I might make a tuba record next, I'm from the Midwest, I'm just a normal person". I didn't want to present myself as a fraud, to take the money and then not make the record they wanted. I said that they'd got the wrong person. I've tried, but I don't have the killer spirit in me to generate chart sales for the sake of it.'

The Amps songs, such as the lead single 'Tipp City', a 128-second blast of bubblegum punk, showed exactly what she had meant. Nine out of twelve songs on the finished album, *Pacer*, came in under three minutes. Most were gristly scraps of lo-fi endeavour interspersed with weary melancholia, with none of *Last Splash*'s melodic summer. '*Pacer* was mostly a love song to Kelley,' Kim admits. 'I was feeling love, anger, worry, resentment, and grateful that nothing worse had happened.'

'I know a handful of people who think *Pacer* is one of Kim's best records,' says Ivo. 'I like it too, though it's coloured for me by how much money she spent on a record that sounds like it cost very little.'

'God damn, I was fucking nuts,' Kim recalls. 'I really did feel that I'd dropped the ball and the project lacked direction. I'd sent Ivo a demo of each song at a time, wrapped in a Polaroid, like a plug. It felt like an art project. I assumed he'd keep it like it was treasure, but he probably burned the cassettes in the backyard.'

Ivo says that Kim would sometimes stay in the flat above the 4AD office. 'Martin Mills told me she'd sometimes stroll over to the pub across the road in her pyjamas. After Chris Bigg had asked her for the lyrics to *Pacer*, Kim left the flat with the message that the lyrics were upstairs, and she'd written them all over the bedsheet!'

One of those demos, 'Empty Glasses', even made it to the B-side of 'Tipp City'. It's not hard to imagine Elektra's reaction to The Amps, though the label dutifully pressed up enough copies as if it was *Last Splash* part two instead of the anti-*Last Splash*. Unsurprisingly, *Pacer* sold poorly, leading to a surfeit of discounted copies in the shops that harmed further sales.

Deal wasn't unhappy at the commercial return on a project that was dear to her heart, only at the business arrangements that she felt restricted her. She had first been upset when Rough Trade America's licensing of *Pod* meant the album wasn't included as one of the three albums that Deal owed under the terms of her Pixies contract with Elektra. 'If I'd have stomped and screamed, Ivo would have let me go because he doesn't like working with anyone if they're not happy,' Deal contends. 'I had no reason to work with anyone else, but it didn't seem fair, it seemed skeevy. I understood it's a business, and a label puts in money and time, and then a band can break up. But no one was in the hole because of me.'

This time, she says, if she had refused to sign Elektra's improved offer, they said they'd stall on the money that was in the pipeline. 'Though Robin later told me they legally couldn't do that,' she adds. 'I signed, as it would have been irresponsible to the other Breeders not to. Like Jim had just become a father again. And where was Ivo in all this? What was going on?'

Ivo has since apologised to Kim for his unavoidable absence – at this time, except for Mark Cox, he had kept news of his breakdown even from his friends. Ivo was trying to discover what had exactly happened on his own through various self-help books. One promised, 'a three-step program to help us understand our place in the world and develop a sense of satisfaction with ourselves and others'. *Your Sacred Self* by Dr Wayne Dyer began with the words, 'You have been facing the wrong way.'

Ivo used the phrase *Facing The Wrong Way* for a promotional CD sampler given away in a UK retail campaign to anyone buying an album from 4AD's back catalogue. 'It just resonated for me,' Ivo recalls, 'like [fellow retail sampler] … *And Dogbones, Too*, which was

483

a phrase from [His Name Is Alive's] "The Dirt Eaters". Even if the title was, in one sense, throwaway, a marketing device associated with clinical depression was symptomatic of where Ivo and his record label had found themselves.

Ivo's trip to Warners to support Scheer was his first since that fateful Wolfgang Press meeting: 'I was happiest at home with Brandi,' he says. He was now giving their dogs the attention he might have given to music, and to his artists, though he'd also been trying to learn Photoshop as well as Cubase: 'I spent days and nights on the computer,' he admits.

Another new obsession that didn't require him to leave the house was photography. 'I'd lost the connection on a daily basis with music for some time, and I was trying to find other things to feel as strongly about as I'd felt about music in the previous decades of my life,' he says. Through 4AD's artwork, from Nigel Grierson to Simon Larbalestier, Ivo had a journeyman's appreciation of the medium, but now he had time to investigate the history of photography and start a small collection.

The image that had led the way was *Worker's Parade* from 1926, taken by Italian émigrée (and both political revolutionary and model) Tina Modotti: 'The most successful unknown photographer in the world,' Ivo reckons. 'It was taken from a bridge in Mexico, of protesting workers, a sea of sombreros. There was an inexplicable character to the image, a softness that wasn't sharp or out of focus. Something just happened to me.'

Ivo tracked down a rare copy of the print to a gallery in LA that was charging $40,000. He declined but saw, at the same gallery, an exhibition by Tom Baril, a photographer from New England who was living in New York. Baril had been celebrated photographer Robert Mapplethorpe's exclusive printer for fifteen years before embarking on his own striking monochromes of botany, cityscapes and seascapes, often with a handmade pinhole camera. His work had a textural detail, with a similar soft focus to Modotti's image. Baril was also responsible for printing the Mapplethorpe image of Cath Carroll on the cover of the Unrest album *Perfect Teeth*, so there was already a connection.

Ivo bought a Baril print of a Brooklyn skyline and warmed to the idea of publishing a book of Baril prints: 'To go back to the simplicity of saying, "I love your photos, can we do something? And, look, it can be of this quality".'

4AD had already published calendars and poster sets, but a fine art book was big leap. However, Ivo was adamant that it was the future, a new imprint that would have the quality of 4AD's packaging and the integrity that the label originally stood for. It was an upbeat end to 1995, a year that had begun shakily, with the fracturing of The Wolfgang Press, and Belly and The Breeders' enforced hiatus, but a year which also included the arrival of Tarnation and Mojave 3 to give 4AD a fresh identity and stronger roots for the foreseeable future.

The year concluded with another positive note: a festive EP from Kristin Hersh. *The Holy Single* included the message, 'Happy Holidays from all of us', with cover versions of Big Star's 'Jesus Christ', Christian hymn 'Amazing Grace', Dude's 'Sinkhole' (only previously recorded on the original Throwing Muses *Doghouse* cassette) and 'Can The Circle Be Unbroken', an adaptation of a Christian hymn that pleaded with the Lord for a place of heavenly rest for the narrator's deceased mother. Maybe the universe was listening and 4AD would get over its malaise, with a recovered Ivo back in the frame. Maybe Scheer would be 4AD's surprise rescue package. Maybe the circle would remain unbroken. Maybe.

20 1996

FEEL THE FEAR AND DO IT ANYWAY
(bad6001-bad6019)

Ivo recalls Martin Mills flying out to visit him. 'It was one of my darkest periods, when I was trying to understand the source of what was causing me so much sadness and confusion and my loss of connection to music, my career and my company. I turned to self-help books, meditation, yoga, everything. I told Martin about one self-help book after another and he said, "Have you thought of reading a novel?" In other words, get out of your head.'

Ivo was still unable to explain how depression had overtaken his life, despite dedicated bouts of research: 'I'd read several well-intentioned authors, on meditation, mindfulness and cognitive therapy.'

Wrapped up in dog-world and books, from self-help to photography, preferring the internet to people (besides Brandi), Ivo was increasingly distanced from 4AD. 'People didn't expect me at the office, or at gigs, and Robin stood in for me everywhere,' he says. 'But he didn't have the authority to sign bands. I just felt so awful for 4AD employees, being the boss who never turned up. And music would scare me by releasing too many emotions. It's embarrassing given how much I love [Duluth, Minnesota sadcore trio] Low now, but I remember Robin playing them to me and not being able to respond. Not connecting to music made me sadder. I'd spend a lot of time watching daytime TV, which is common among people with serious depression.'

Ivo did manage to find some respite with Brandi and with their Shar Pei dogs, Friday and Otis. His unconditional love of dogs turned into a mission when Brandi, while out walking Otis, found two abandoned adult dogs. Avoiding the dog shelter – 'it was full of terrified dogs and smelt like a death camp,' says Ivo – they adopted one (v23's Paul McMenamin took the other) and named him Rudy, after which Ivo and Brandi began to foster dogs from the shelter.

If Ivo was content communing with dogs, the staff and the artists in his care at 4AD might also have benefited from more nurturing. 'Like footballers and boxers, artists need a good manager, as security, in which they can express themselves and focus on what they do,' Nigel Grierson suggests. 'Ivo was that figure within 4AD, which gave a context for a lot of creative work, even when people had arguments, and few of those places exist.'

Lush, who had been concentrating on a third album throughout 1995 – they had only played seven shows all year – had felt the estrangement more than most, suffering from self-confidence issues after the chart downturn and mixed reviews of *Split*.

'We did feel let down, because Ivo just vanished,' says Miki Berenyi. 'If he'd just told us that he was having a breakdown, it would have been fine! There were rumours about what had happened, a lot of drugs, which didn't make me very sympathetic at a time when we really needed him. And when he told me about the therapy that he'd had, because of his chilled exterior, it seemed like he was toying with things rather than coming apart at the seams.'

Lush's isolation had been compounded by the departure of Tim Carr from Warners/Reprise and also that of manager Howard Gough. 'There's someone I never need speak to again,' says Berenyi. 'Even as far back as Lollapalooza, we'd pressed him on the accounts, and discovered he'd sometimes double-charged us. The music industry is geared towards ripping musicians off, full stop ... Howard said we should be grateful that he didn't take a cut of our tour money, which booking agents already did.'

Gough's departure was precipitated by a dinner that had been arranged to talk over Lush's forthcoming plans in the wake of *Split* – Robin Hurley had even flown over; given The Breeders' state of inactivity, Lush was now 4AD's best chance of hit records. 'Howard turned up, completely trashed, offering drugs, slagging off 4AD's bands but trying to be matey with 4AD because he used to work there,' Emma Anderson recalls. 'The next day, Simon Harper said that if we carried on working with Howard, it was over with 4AD. Suddenly Howard said he didn't want to manage us anymore. He decided to get in there first.'

In the search for Gough's replacement, 'Warners suggested an American and Emma rightly said we didn't want an American always pulling us over there,' says Berenyi. 'The focus on America was making Emma turn the other way, saying it wasn't why she'd formed Lush, that Europe was more our sensibility. Robin Guthrie said that [Cocteau manager] Ray Coffei was brilliant, that he'd sorted out their holiday and stuff, but we didn't need a babysitter.'

Lush eventually chose The Boo Radleys' manager Peter Felstead. 'He was a bit dull and pedestrian, but also a relief after Howard's craziness,' says Berenyi. 'And 4AD thought they could do business with Peter.'

Seven years on from Lush's Falcon show, the band didn't need knocking into shape, and Hurley agreed to let the band's live sound engineer Pete Bartlett produce the album: 'He knew us better than anyone,' says Anderson. Without the drama that had marred the recording of *Spooky* and *Split* – 'the mood was chipper,' says Berenyi – Bartlett got the desired results, with much less reliance on effects, to match the three-minute charge of the new tracks.

The first song that Berenyi had written for the album was 'Ladykillers'. 'I thought, right, if anyone thinks I'm incapable of writing a good song, I'll show you. I put everything in – handclaps, simpler harmonies, sudden stops ... even if my effort came out as dark and antagonistic.'

Berenyi had written pop songs before, for example 'Hypocrite', but nothing of the dynamic zip and intelligence of 'Ladykillers', with its sharp putdown of misplaced machismo that you'd have expected more from her former band The Baby Machines. Anderson's response was the ironic submission of 'Single Girl', a brilliantly bittersweet two minutes and 35 seconds with a marked Sixties lilt. 'It was us finally saying, we are quite good, we can do this, we don't have to cower and be embarrassed,' says Berenyi. 'We felt brasher, more upbeat.'

v23 joined in with a playful, enigma-stripping campaign, at odds with the Jim Friedman abstract Polaroids of Lush's early records or the singular objects (lemons, twigs, a bottle, a lampshade) used for the *Split* releases. Vaughan Oliver conceived of a series of spontaneously created street scenes of passers-by collared into holding up a large circular sign brandishing the band's name. 'Single Girl' became the lead single, and 4AD went to town on the formats, with two CDs and a seven-inch version necessitating seven new B-sides. A radio promo fronted by the exquisitely moody album cut 'Last Night' spanned six remixes. The machine had to be fed, no matter what the cost to physical and creative resources.

The upshot was 4AD's highest UK singles chart entry, at 21, and, at long last, an appearance on BBC TV'S *Top of the Pops*. Usually, that would have the knock-on effect of pushing a single up the chart, but this didn't happen. 'Ladykillers', which followed with indecent haste just six weeks later, even before an album was released, came in the same twin CD edition (and seven extra B-sides this time), charted at 22, but a second *Top of the Pops* appearance didn't send this further up the charts either. Lush's third album, *Lovelife*, followed a week later, reaching an encouraging number 8, but still finishing up one place lower than *Spooky*. Lush couldn't emulate those Britpop bands that were scoring top-three hits, but then Britpop was largely the domain of boisterous boy fans. Among the female-fronted bands defined as Britpop (Sleeper and Echobelly, among them), only Elastica sold more than a fraction of Blur, Pulp and Oasis's platinum units.

Did the UK press, still chipping away at Lush with relish, have anything to do with it? 'We were tapping the zeitgeist of Britpop, supposedly,' says Berenyi. Critics cited the presence of Pulp singer Jarvis Cocker, though he'd only been invited to duet on the playful

'Ciao!' after Chris Acland had reneged on a plan to make his vocal debut. But Lush had shared bills with Elastica and Blur, and Anderson admits there was an element of truth to the charge: 'It was like, everyone's having a bloody hit, let's have a go too.'

Not being a fan of anything that could be described as playful or jaunty, Ivo wasn't keen on 'Ciao!' or Jarvis Cocker. 'But I was no longer involved in making decisions. Everybody just got on with it. But finally, a group I was involved with was in a position to get on *Top of the Pops*, and would actually say yes! I've still not seen the footage.'

This shows how interested Ivo was in the fruits of success. His complete detachment from Scheer since selling them to Warners demonstrated how out of touch he had become with 4AD's daily motions, or even the urgent need to sell records. Maybe the Irish band stood a better chance than Lush. Hard rock and heavy metal culture made even less room for women, but Scheer had grunge appeal, with Audrey Gallagher the potential poster girl to follow Shirley Manson of the new rock *arrivistes* Garbage. In theory, all 4AD needed was Warners' muscle and the right record.

Scheer's debut album *Infliction* was trailed by two singles in quick suggestion: a battering 'Shéa' and 'Wish You Were Dead', which really did resemble a turbo-charged Cranberries song, with Gallagher's undulating Irish vocal, expressing much darker sentiments in tune with Shirley – and Marilyn – Manson. A further turbo-charged PJ Harvey might have made something like the bluesy 'Howling Boy', and a more measured 'In Your Head' showed co-guitarists Paddy Leyden and Neal Calderwood understood the art of dynamics. But Gallagher's melodies often played a secondary role to the guitars, except in the unexpectedly tender acoustic finale 'Goodbye'. A whole album of those would have thrilled 4AD, Ivo and all its dedicated fans.

After the band played St Louis, Missouri, WestNet writer Lee Graham Bridges judged Scheer, 'catchy, energetic, and a good listen … neither terribly boring nor incredibly interesting … a glittering, beautifully rough act in concert but standard rock stars on record.' A full commitment to tour-slogging across America might be the key. There were just a couple of hitches: both 4AD's London office and Warners had their doubts about the band.

'Scheer was a really good Irish rock band signed to the wrong label,' says 4AD PR Colleen Maloney. 'We had no experience of that kind of mainstream rock, unlike Beggars Banquet, where they should have been signed. The band needed a lot of guidance and we were grasping at the unknown.'

'4AD prioritised Scheer, and we took it seriously, but it also didn't seem like it was something we could succeed with,' says Warners president Steven Baker. 'It was 4AD's stab at working with a more conventional alternative rock band, and just because the band had a harder sound than other 4AD artists of the period, it didn't mean they would be more successful. Scheer had to stand out among other groups working with that sound, and in the end, they just didn't. One advantage of a big company like Warners is the ability of individuals to stand up for an artist that they think deserve to be prioritised in some way, and Scheer never received that vote of confidence from anyone.'

But the confusion over Scheer was nothing next to the jaw-dropping impact of 4AD's next album. Ivo had continued to enjoy watching San Diego's The Paladins, blues rock purveyors of good-time, hi-octane vibes. 'They were completely outside of anything to do with work, a total release,' says Ivo. Bringing them into the workplace was a risk but Ivo's keenness to release a Paladins album came from that place of pure emotional instinct, the tingle.

Ivo was also smitten with Paladins frontman Dave Gonzalez. 'He was the most hard-working, genuine musician I'd met, in love with everything to do with music. Dave was obsessed with the Fifties – the trucks in the yard, a Wurlitzer in the living room, the real deal. His uncle sold me my Dodge truck.'

The band had reached the stage where the trio's songs were stretching out to ten minutes with guitar solos. But while Red House Painters epics were exhausting, The Paladins' ten-minute tours de force such as 'Big Mary' and 'One Step' were driven by a constant blast of adrenalin. 'It was like watching a power trio with an upright bass,' Ivo recalls. 'I just wanted to capture this moment in time, just out of the pure love of doing it, and I thought it could help the band. Not because it was on 4AD, but that they didn't have any other outlet at the time. And it didn't cost much to do.'

Gonzalez is now based in Austin, but on the day we spoke, he was in Green Bay, Wisconsin where his current band Stone River Boys was headlining the local casino. He recalls that The Paladins had, incredibly, played more than three hundred shows a year, for twenty years. They'd started as a rockabilly outfit at the dawn of that genre's revival in the early Eighties, a brand of rebel music that had more in common with punk than the mainstream. The Paladins had even supported Bauhaus in 1982, and Gonzalez had heard of Pixies and Cocteau Twins.

By the early Nineties, The Paladins had added honky-tonk country, blues and rock, which they'd honed to perfection. Ivo's initial phone call, Gonzalez says, came out of the blue. 'He said how much he liked us, and he could name some of our songs! But he only wanted me to recommend some of my favourite blues guitarists. I told him [Fleetwood Mac's] Peter Green, who was awesome. There was also Jimmy Vaughan, and an older American guy called Hollywood Fats, who once sat in with The Paladins, and was a mentor to me. We just talked about music, for a year or so, before Ivo said he'd like to make a record with us. I wasn't expecting it, not from a guy who had pop hits on 4AD, who wanted to hear about other kinds of music to what was on his label. I couldn't believe he wanted to help us.'

Gonzalez initially said that he'd like to make a country music record, like early Willie Nelson. 'Ivo said, "No, you're a great blues guitarist, and I even know the seven songs I want on the album".' Gonzalez had many more he wanted to record, but they compromised on ten tracks, and picked the best versions from a dozen recorded shows.

Million Mile Club – named in honour of the distances the band's van had travelled over the years – was a scorcher. Gonzalez says the association with 4AD and Warners raised The Paladins' profile for years to come, enabling them to tour Europe and Australia. It did exactly what Ivo wanted, except entice Warners to lend its support.

'Warners didn't feel it like he did,' says Gonzalez. 'We weren't like anything that was on the radio. It frustrated Ivo that he couldn't get them to accept the records that he was giving them.'

So much for Steven Baker's claim that Warners was lucky to have Ivo. But 4AD was a victim of Ivo's delicate sensibilities and Warners simply had no channel to market The Paladins. At least Ivo could call the shots in the UK, and the band flew over to do promotion in Europe.

Nothing divided 4AD's newly expanded A&R team more than The Paladins. 'They were amongst the most pure and satisfying projects that I ever worked on,' says Ivo. 'The Paladins was a real head-in-hands moment for me,' recalls 4AD's newest A&R man Lewis Jamieson. 'Of course Ivo can put what he likes out on 4AD, but what could it add to the label, artistically or commercially?'

Jeff Keibel, whose comprehensive websites show an obsessive loyalty to 4AD, admits even he was initially tested by The Paladins. 'Many 4AD fans on the 4AD mailing list disowned or pretended *Million Mile Club* did not exist, but it was a learning experience for me. I wasn't ever a genuine blues fan yet I got what Ivo must have got when he heard this band play live, the sheer power and conviction.'

Robin Hurley also had trouble accepting The Paladins. 'They were an odd signing,' he concurs. 'I asked Ivo, what do we do with this? He got angry, and said, "Tell everyone to fucking work it, I've signed them". A lot of the London office thought that was it for Ivo. I had more history with him back from the beginning, when he'd say, "If I like something, I think others will as well". So that's how we treated it.'

The gulf between Ivo and 4AD's new A&R man was made abundantly clear early on in Lewis Jamieson's new role. In Ivo's mind, without the right aesthetic vision, 4AD didn't have a reason to exist. After Scheer, he was getting used to people questioning his choices. 'When we had signed Tarnation, there was enormous confusion – why had we signed a country band?' Ivo recalls. 'I didn't care if we weren't being obvious. If I'd followed those parameters, I would never have released a Birthday Party record.'

494

Jamieson was more of a commercially minded pragmatist. Seeing more cutbacks in the company, 'money that was spent on The Paladins should have gone towards people's wages,' he says.

The Paladins would have been trumped as 4AD's most unexpected part of the catalogue if Ivo had managed to license a compilation, *Bad Boy*, by a Fifties doo-wop troupe from New York. One of Brandi's favourites, The Jive Bombers were best known for their 1957 hit 'Bad Boy' that had been rediscovered via John Waters' hit film *Cry-Baby* – Brandi and Ivo would listen to the album (on the Australian reissues label Raven) on night-time drives around LA. Ivo particularly liked singer Clarence Palmer's strange and wonderful affectation, often scat-singing repeated syllables at the end of a word (*'I'm a bad boy-yoy-yoy-yoy-yoy'*). The album was even allocated a 4AD catalogue number, but the rights owner, Nippon Columbia – coincidentally 4AD's Japanese distributor – responded to Ivo's offer with the news that it would reissue the album instead (which never happened).

Another bone of contention between 4AD's boss and its youth spokesman was a band that, both artistically and commercially, could have given 4AD a noticeable boost, without pandering to Britpop or any other trend. The Scottish band Belle and Sebastian were a wonderful source of wistful and erudite folk-pop that quickly attracted a similarly fervent fan base as The Smiths, fusing the delicacy of Johnny Marr and Nick Drake. Jamieson had sent Ivo the band's debut album *Tigermilk*, which had been posted to Alma Road by the album's producer, former Associates member Alan Rankine.

'*Tigermilk* was brilliant,' recalls Jamieson. 'I'd usually play a customary 90 seconds of a track before dismissing it, but 37 minutes later, I was thinking I'd found our next signing. For a man who put out Air Miami records, Ivo didn't mind a bit of "twee". But he said, "It sounds like The Smiths, I still hate The Smiths, you can't sign them".'

Ivo: 'I can't remember talking to Lewis about Belle and Sebastian. The first time I ever heard them was reading reviews that compared them to Nick Drake. This was during a kind of overnight success for Drake after *Pink Moon* had been used in a VW commercial. I was intrigued but I listened sceptically, and I reacted negatively because I couldn't understand the lazy comparison to Nick Drake, someone whose music was dear to my heart. Belle and Sebastian didn't make me think of The Smiths either. But Lewis is right that I wouldn't have wanted to sign them to 4AD. Peculiarly out of context, I became a fan of some of Belle and Sebastian's earlier music after being seduced by their artwork once it was produced in fabulous Japanese replica sleeves.'

'Any indie label that was working properly would have signed that band,' Jamieson contends. 'Other people in the office got it, but it just got scuppered before I could do anything. Had Ivo gone for it, it would have been a cheap and easy deal as their album was already made, so we wouldn't have had to invest much money. It was such an odd situation to be in, as A&R for a label that belonged to a man I didn't meet until a year later.'

Jamieson says he should have flown to America to meet Ivo, but surely the onus was on 4AD's management to pair them up and unify a strategy that included fellow A&R man Colin Wallace. But Ivo led A&R, and he was in retreat: not even Robin Hurley decided to intervene.

'I felt a horrible conflict between the man that owned its vision and a music scene that had changed massively since he was last in it,' says Jamieson. 'The way 4AD had always sold records on the basis of its name had started to tail off as Britpop took hold, because the agenda for what constituted an indie band had changed, from interesting music that sold to a sub-culture of people, like Ultra Vivid Scene or His Name Is Alive, to how high you were in the charts and whether your record got on [BBC] Radio 1's B list. *NME* and radio liked 4AD but I felt they were interested in bigger things and that 4AD had been edged out: For example, Creation had Oasis, Teenage Fanclub and The Boo Radleys, who were all British. And 4AD needed to sell records here as it was a gateway to Europe. But we couldn't sign acts that appealed to a UK market that also made sense economically.'

The label combined three of its current young bands for an American tour. After the last of thirty-three British dates that had stretched across three months, Lush had just eight days' break before joining Mojave 3 and Scheer for twenty-eight dates in North America, starting in April. Ivo playfully named the tour Shaving The Pavement after a comment made by Mark Cox when he noticed a splodge of shaving foam at his feet; however, the bands quickly rechristened it Shagging The Pavement after Scheer's Audrey Gallagher and Neal Calderwood's newly minted relationship was reputedly one of several dalliances that took place during the six weeks on the road. 'The atmosphere was more hanging out, getting drunk and passing out, and less, you've got to break America,' says Emma Anderson.

But only two weeks after the Shaving/Shagging tour was over, Lush was back in the States for a series of radio-sponsored festivals prior to a Japanese tour. It wasn't at the punishing level of The Paladins, but then The Paladins didn't also have to zig-zag overseas with media duties at every stop as Lush did. One US show on the mini-tour was the KROQ Weenie Roast at LA's Irvine Meadows Amphitheatre, with Lush and new hip-hop superstars the Fugees on either side of a revolving stage. Another in blazing sunshine at a show in Hartford, Connecticut, where Miki Berenyi was repeatedly soaked by bottles of water chucked by an overheated crowd. 'She couldn't go near the microphone,' says Anderson. 'This massive boot came towards me and I ducked and put my guitar down and walked off. What was the point? It wasn't helping sell records. The radio station called us pussies ... That was the turning point for me. I hated the rest of the band and they hated me.'

Finally, one of 4AD's more enduring partnerships had begun to crack. 'Miki and Emma were like a rather strange, old bickering couple, though they were both beautiful and magnetic to watch,' recalls Simon Harper. Berenyi admits they'd had rivalries over songs, and it was clear that Anderson preferred the confines of the studio while Berenyi preferred the buzz of the stage. Manager Peter Felstead's machinations only widened the gulf. 'Peter started to behave like Howard Gough, dazzled by the prospect of making it in America,' says Berenyi. 'Emma couldn't stand him. I understood why, but we didn't have any choice, and so I went the other way, giving Peter the benefit of the doubt, which caused a big rift with Emma and we stopped talking.'

Anderson wanted to avoid returning to America: 'We were doing well in the UK, so why not tour here again?' she says. 'Even though our last UK tour had been very hard because 4AD hadn't given us enough tour support. Our support band, Coast, was staying at the Hilton hotel while we'd have a guest house with no heating and black dust coming out of the taps.'

Even tour veterans like Lush had problems with the lifestyle, but there were 4AD artists with much less confidence or experience of being out of their comfort zone, for example Lisa Germano. With Ivo in LA, it was left to Lewis Jamieson to be her artist liaison in the UK. 'Lisa was very challenging to work with,' he says. 'In Switzerland with Mojave 3, I was virtually cajoling her on to the stage because she was convinced nobody wanted her to play. In 4AD culture, the idea of the reluctant artist was acceptable. To my generation, that was anathema. You're in a band, that's your job, what do you mean you don't want to play? I said, we're the underdog and when we triumph, it will be even better! It wasn't about selling out – artistic validity was taken for granted. It was more, how can we get this to more people?'

Germano had already released her third album for 4AD. *Excerpts From A Love Circus* was another of her vulnerable gems, fitting in alongside the downbeat constituents of college-radio playlists such as Low, Codeine and Red House Painters. There were occasional signs of a less desperate frame of mind with the positively carefree 'I Love A Snot', the gypsy violin and breezy rhythm of the lead single 'Small Head', and sampled purrs from her cats Dorothy and Miamo-Tutti (whose names ended up in some of the song titles). But 'Lovesick' felt as disturbing as *Geek The Girl*'s '… A Psychopath', aimed at a figure who was, '*not my Yoko Ono*'.

But Ivo visited Germano at her home in Bloomington, showing he could engage when he still felt a bond to an artist. 'Ivo was there for me this time,' says Germano. 'He stayed with me, and we went for rides and hikes, and we talked about the songs.'

'People thought *Geek The Girl* was a bit difficult and bleak but, for me, *Excerpts* … was like an open wound,' says Ivo. Perhaps that explains why he didn't talk Germano out of including the sound of cat purrs. 'Tracks like "We Suck", "Baby On A Plane" and "Messages From Sophia" were all beautiful but Lisa was in an unhappy place. There's an on-the-edge-of-drunk feel to a lot of it. But this was the start of Lisa crafting her individuality in a sonic sense, which reminded me of Warren Defever's original approach. There was a lot of deconstruction possibly as a distraction from what she was singing about. I admire Lisa because she considered herself normal and average, and not one of the "cool" or smart people at 4AD, whoever they were. And yet she was making this cool, crazily imaginative music that came from her soul.'

Many years later, Ivo was furious to hear that Jamieson had, in his mind, bullied Germano on to the stage, and felt guilty that, in his absence, she was subject to a much more abrasive style of artist management. But then Ivo was not able to be around for several artists that had depended on him. Warren Defever was another. He no longer needed mentoring or remixing, but without this most sympathetic and empathic of label champions, he was exposed to the 'new' 4AD style, and having to work within the Warners system.

According to Defever, 'I signed a new long-term contract for five albums, starting with *Stars On ESP*, knowing that there was no one in charge anymore and that the LA and London offices didn't seem to communicate well. I felt I had a duty and a loyalty to commit to 4AD because of everything they had done for me, even though it was clear that things were going to be very different. Missed release dates, year-long delays, deleted catalogue titles, mixed-up catalogue numbers, poor promotion, dishonesty, accounting errors, late payments, broken promises … it was run in complete opposition to the way 4AD had been run in London.

'It got weird fast. Ivo assured me the LA office would put together a contract that solidified the terms that we currently worked under, with no new demands or additional pressures. This was not the case. I got a strictly scheduled recording plan with smaller advances than we were currently getting and none of the previous details of our working relationship were maintained. It sucked. I signed it. I regret it.'

At least musically everything was moving ahead without a single hitch. Defever had spent over three years recording a fourth album, with time allocated to production work for Tarnation and Liquorice and family affairs to attend to, such as the death of his mother. And Defever only needed his imagination, not big budgets, to record great albums.

The low maintenance joy that was His Name Is Alive's *Stars On ESP* kept 4AD's freak flag flying with Defever's usual gamut of strange currencies. Defever had a concept this time – a compilation of imagined singles on the experimental Sixties label ESP-Disk, best known for psych-folk mavericks like Pearls Before Swine, with his cut-up technique mirroring the turning of a radio dial between stations. He'd also found a way to get around samples that needed clearing: he would simply record his own version. For example, lead single 'Universal Frequencies' (the moustached man on the back cover was Vaughan Oliver, on his wedding day) was 'a sequel' to The Beach Boys' 'Good Vibrations'. Of the three different arrangements of 'This World Is Not My Home', 'I Can't Live In This World Anymore' was a clear Big Star homage, while Ivo had suggested Defever do a gospel arrangement, which became 'Last One'. It was another unique testament to Defever, 4AD's resident sonic boffin.

Ivo: 'Warren had developed into one of the most interesting producers and sound manipulators, with such an ear for accuracy. Listening to *Stars On ESP* now makes total sense in terms of his continued evolution away from his earliest work.'

Five co-writes showed Defever was increasingly open to collaborators, such as Mark Kozelek on the slow, sombre 'Across The Street'. Defever had also been recording with former Pale Saint Ian Masters. 'Ian sang high, choirboy style, without being overly precious or nice, and his lyrics were beautiful and crazy,' says Defever. After Masters had played bass for His Name Is Alive's *13 Year Itch* show, Ivo suggested the pair should record together. Masters duly flew to Michigan where an album was finished over the course of a month. 'Without Ivo's support or enthusiasm,' says Defever, '4AD just let it go.'

In return, Lewis Jamieson felt equally let down by Defever, who, like Lisa Germano, wasn't a stage natural. '*Stars On ESP* was marvellous, and it could have pushed His Name Is Alive beyond the cult world. But we needed him to tour.' Defever agreed, and HNIA flew over to play shows, but Jamieson recalls him turning up at Alma Road. 'Warren said he didn't feel he could do the rest of the tour. I was furious. Why spend money on a band that doesn't want to do this job? I was expecting support from the office but people said they could see Warren's point. If I'd been older and wiser, I'd have questioned if he'd really wanted to be bigger. I know 4AD, and especially me, were criticised for trying to make the label into something that it wasn't designed to be. With hindsight, I was trying to compete with Creation, and His Name Is Alive brought that into sharp relief.'

It was all so much easier when a band could be self-sufficient, not undone by paranoia, neglect or fear. So it was timely that Dead Can Dance should reappear now, a duo out of time and place, in their own universe, unbothered by the need for remixes, formats or management.

In this uncertain commercial climate, a stunning new Dead Can Dance album to emulate *Into The Labyrinth*'s half-million sales could mean salvation for 4AD. As ever, Brendan Perry was eager to incorporate new influences. With his brother Andrew, Perry had been hosting percussion workshops at his Quivvy Church studio in Ireland, and the new Dead Can Dance album *Spiritchaser* was a stab at transcendental Afro-Latin rhythm. Lisa Gerrard's vocal incantations were in support, but lengthy trance-inducing mantras such as 'Song Of The Stars' and 'Indus' were more National Geographic than KROQ. *Spiritchaser* topped Billboard's World Music charts, but it was the first Dead Can Dance album that lost some of the duo's ability to transcend their pool of influences.

The truth was, the periods of living and working apart had grown progressively longer; Gerrard was busy with motherhood and her own recordings, and the task of reuniting to restore the alchemical connection with Perry had been that much harder. '*Spiritchaser* was a bit stuffy and repetitive and I was constantly waiting for something to happen in the songs,' says Ivo. 'But when I saw them live in Santa Fe, it turned into a monster. They should have recorded the album after touring.'

Colleen Maloney admits that even though Pixies had brought in the most profit for 4AD, Dead Can Dance was promoted as the label's biggest act to shock people into paying attention. 'They'd sell out gigs in seconds. They wouldn't do much press so they retained a great sense of mystery, which made people even more eager when they were available. But with Brendan and Lisa not getting on anymore, it was hard to make it work.'

Perry admits that tensions were running high after the tour. Despite this, he and Gerrard did begin to record another album, which was eventually abandoned. 'We've always endeavoured to make every album sound unique in its own way,' he says. 'But the need to explore new territory brings its own stress. After *Spiritchaser*, we lost direction and out of frustration, turned on each other.'

The last of 4AD's old guard had finally crumbled and the pair finally surrendered and went their own way. 'We had a huge fight,' Gerrard recalls. 'We'd done that over the years, but this time we decided we just couldn't cope with each other anymore. The thing is, it's always to do with passion, and impatience, and a conflict. It's not that we didn't love or like each other or not want to work together. But it just became impossible.'

Heidi Berry was also about to record her last album for 4AD, showing how the turnaround of artists was that much faster, and more mercenary, than it had been in the Eighties when the likes of Dead Can Dance could be supported.

Berry had recorded her third consecutive 'bloody beautiful record', as Ivo put it – though the album had been finished for a year because he kept trying to improve it. 'I spent an unacceptably long time thinking about that album,' Ivo admits, 'but I really hoped that we could break Heidi in America, to have adequate success that would spread elsewhere. But it took me for ever to decide on anything, even what the single should be. I kept thinking something else needed to happen, like another track should be recorded, and this went on for months. But it was eventually released pretty much as is.'

Ivo feels that Berry's core band on *Miracle* (multi-instrumentalist brother Christopher Berry, bassist Laurence O'Keefe, drummer Jon Brookes and violinist Anna Wood) was 'the best playing ever on a 4AD record'. Woods' violin lent more pronounced Celtic flavours but there was the purer balladry of 'Only Human', 'the most naked of all my songs,' Berry says. She feels 'Northern Country' has her best vocal performance on record, and her take on Youngbloods' late-Sixties track 'Darkness, Darkness' captured its spirit of longing.

'Heidi was an incredible communicator and a very subtle one,' Ivo feels. 'Her music has great lasting value for me – the albums have stood the tests of time, and they've given me a degree of peace. But ironically, her albums turned out to be the ones that the fewest people have heard.'

In his song 'Fruit Tree', Nick Drake envisaged that fame might await people once they were no longer alive: certainly Berry's trio of 4AD albums would have benefited from some drama to hook in more people, but when *Miracle* was released, Colleen Maloney found there simply wasn't enough interest. For example, when she sent Berry's second album to the specialist monthly magazine *Folk Roots*, she recalls, 'They sent it back with a note saying, "this is not folk music". The British press was generally obsessed with what was trendy, and she wasn't – which was no failing on her part.'

Too folk for the hipsters, not trad enough for the folkies, Berry fell between two stools. In an effort to widen her appeal, 4AD used a dramatic close-up of her face on the cover of *Miracle*, in direct contrast to v23's usual delightful obfuscation. 'Robin Hurley wanted an image of me, so there was more of a presence and personality,' says Berry. 'Vaughan thought it was crappy, which was a shame. I should have stuck with the way that we'd worked before, but I didn't know if I was doing the right thing, or if I'd soon be starving to death.'

The marketing ploy made no difference, as *Miracle* sold the same as Berry's preceding two albums, around 25,000 copies. 'Warners wanted double that figure, and when that didn't happen, they pulled the plug,' says Berry. 'Robin told me in London that 4AD had to let me go as well. He felt so bad that I ended up comforting *him*! I started smoking cigarettes for the first time in ages, and we both got trashed on brandy. My hard feelings towards 4AD were only fleeting – I put them into a song and got it out of my system. But there was one time, when I saw Ivo, getting back into his BMW late at night after he was dropping me off, I thought, all right for some. But that feeling only lasted a day. If it hadn't been for Ivo, I wouldn't have had the most amazing experience of my life and got to know as much about myself as an artist and a person. I don't regret the relationship in any way.'*

Deborah Edgely says she could understand why artists like Berry might have felt similar twinges of envy or loss. 'Whatever toll it took on him, it took on others as well. Ivo made himself a future, but a lot of artists gave a huge amount of their lives to try and develop their future and careers and ended up with little or nothing.'

As Spirea X's Jim Beattie had noted, Ivo wasn't using any profits to fund a particular lifestyle beyond which a head of a thriving record label could expect. And Ivo was also known to fund things out of his own pocket. But in times of diminished sales, artists did suffer. Lush had seen tour support increasingly shaved, as did Lisa Germano when she'd planned to tour after *Excerpts From A Love Circus*. 'There wasn't a lot left,' she recalls. 'Dead Can Dance had broken up, Kim Deal didn't feel she had a hit record in her, and Pixies and Cocteau Twins were long gone. Everything making money for 4AD had, or was, breaking up and they needed to be very careful.'

This meant that investing in a nine-piece Icelandic multi-media electronic pop collective was risky. In hindsight, it was ludicrous. But it was also a sign that 4AD was still willing to be adventurous; the

---

* Berry subsequently recorded with Pieter Nooten and Michael Brook, 'but nothing happened,' she says. Nooten blames Brook's schedule and the cost of living in London: 'I moved back to Amsterdam and began work as an in-house producer in a dance/ambient-oriented studio. But I loved working with Heidi, and the material was gorgeous, ambient neo-classical material with her sulky voice on top.' A more complete and satisfying collaborator was former Kitchens of Distinction singer/bassist Patrick Fitzgerald, in a contemporary folk rock setting under the group alias Lost Girls. One track, 'Needle's Eye', was released in 1998 as a single and included on 4AD's 2001 Berry compilation *Pomegranate*. The remainder of the sessions sadly remain unreleased.

music had to be the reason to get involved. And if Lewis Jamieson and not Ivo was behind the band's signing, at least GusGus seemed much more suitable than Scheer, more individual and charismatic, more forward-looking rather than what had just been.

'An extravagant, unstable and, in the end, unsustainable project,' is how 4AD's own website summarises GusGus. The band was named after a line in German director Rainer Werner Fassbinder's 1974 film *Fear Eats the Soul*, where a woman cooks couscous for her lover but pronounces it '*gusgus*'. Its members had only assembled eighteen months earlier after aspiring filmmakers/designers Stefán Árni Þorgeirsson and Siggi Kjartansson had co-directed the short film *Pleasure*. The film's core cast of Daníel Ágúst, Magnús Jónsson and Hafdís Huld (who was only fifteen) were also singers who had decided to record an album together; Þorgeirsson and Kjartansson paired them with T-World, a.k.a. Birgir Þórarinsson (or Biggi Veira) and Magnús Guðmundsson (Herb Legowitz), a duo fashioning cool, chic electronic dance. The filmmakers joined in to add a visual aspect to the mix, while additional members such as Stephan Stephensen (a.k.a. President Bongo) and Emilíana Torrini Davíðsdóttir swelled the ranks, though Torrini had left by the time 1995's debut album *GusGus* was released in Iceland.

Lewis Jamieson had only been in the 4AD job for a week when his Icelandic friend played him the album. 'The job hadn't even become official, but I met their manager Baldur in a pub in Clapham Junction before Christmas,' Jamieson recalls. 'It was one of those moments of serendipity. It sounded contemporary but with a 4AD vibe, especially "Is Jesus Your Pal?" because to me, 4AD was much less about ethereal, warbling, gothic stuff and much more about skewed pop music, taking the genre and tilting it on its head and making it interesting again. I sent a copy to Ivo, saying we should sign them.'

'Ivo wouldn't have signed GusGus, or if he had, he would have made a different record,' says Robin Hurley. 'An electronic band was very rare for 4AD, but they did seem to fit.'

Ivo: 'I enjoyed the album but "Is Jesus Your Pal?" was the only track I truly loved. I said they had to release it as the single beforehand,

which everyone thought was stupid. I could understand their reason
– Emilíana sang it, and GusGus was working in the dance arena. [The
diaphanous ballad was also not a GusGus original, having been written by the Icelandic band Slowblow.] But it would have been a fantastic single. I think Lewis would have been happy to leave it off. I later
discovered he was a soul boy at heart. He wondered what had taken
me so long to figure that out.'

Talking from his home studio in the Icelandic capital of Reykjavík,
Biggi Veira says he was more of a fan of Mute, following the course of
electronic music, from Depeche Mode to club mixes. 'But I knew of
4AD, mostly Pixies. Everybody knew M/A/R/R/S too but we didn't
know it was on 4AD. Ivo was cool, but it felt like the old acts were
tired, and 4AD was unable to renew them. And in all our conversations with 4AD, I never got the feeling that he was involved.'

GusGus nevertheless knew 4AD, and Warners, were a reputable
gateway to a global audience. A svelte and springy 'Polyesterday' – a
remixed version from the Icelandic album – became the first release
under a new deal, making it 4AD's first original dance track (not
counting remixes) since 'Pump Up The Volume'. Anyone wanting
every version would have been stung, with one twelve-inch EP version,
three CD versions (one was an edit for radio) and, if fans could find
them, radio promos of a remixed 'Polydistortion' and of the forthcoming album track 'Chocolate'. But the single picked up enough
airplay – and the band enough media inches – to reach 55 in the UK
national charts, which still counted as a hit in 4AD terms.

Funding remixes was one thing; tour support for a multi-media
troupe was another. 'Being young and naïve, I just thought GusGus
was the greatest thing rather than a problem regarding finance and
investment,' says Jamieson. The bill for the band's London stage debut
wasn't crippling but it topped £10,000. 'They claimed they knew what
they were doing but they were making it up as they went,' Jamieson
reckons. 'They had two massive cinema projectors, and we spent the
day working out how to sync them with the music, before triggering
it with computers. Now it's all pre-programmed but everything was
done in real time back then.'

Jamieson readily admits that his tastes were different to Ivo's – in any other record company, they might be seen as complementing each other rather than clashing. Jamieson says his style of A&R was also not that of his boss: 'I was less nuts-and-bolts and more general vibing,' he says. Two of his preferred hangouts were the social heart of Britpop – The Good Mixer pub and the Blow Up club night at The Laurel Tree pub, both in Camden Town. Jamieson would play football with members of Blur; Ivo wouldn't even entertain a Blur record.

Wallace and Jamieson had still started their own record label, at Ivo's suggestion, to give them an outlet to sign bands without his rubber stamp of approval. Detox Artifacts was a separate entity, not an official offshoot of 4AD like Guernica, though the label could take advantage of 4AD's distribution and production facilities. But for the purposes of 4AD, the set-up was flawed.

'It was A&R by mad, dysfunctional committee,' says Simon Harper. 'For the right reasons, Lewis [Jamieson] was trying, in Ivo's absence, to embrace a more modern take on what 4AD could move towards, namely intelligent dance music. I don't think Ivo ever had time to sit down with Lewis. Maybe Lewis was too young, and diplomacy wasn't his natural forte, or even on his agenda. Ivo would sometimes come back with input and ideas, but a lot were confusing and frustrating. And it could get very feisty and competitive between Colin and Lewis, and a lot of my time was spent on various human resources issues. It was also impractical on a daily basis. Having three A&R people, for a company our size, was ridiculous.'

Jamieson admits his attitude did him few favours in the office environment. 'I became an arrogant little fucker. I was only about twenty-four; a lot of people I knew in Leeds had tried to do what I'd done, and more by luck than judgement, I was A&R-ing a band getting coverage in [style bible] *The Face* and on [BBC] Radio 1. I just wanted to swan around like my heroes, being a mouth like Alan McGee and telling everyone how great I was, at the point that GusGus looked like they were going to happen. 4AD didn't concentrate on one band but GusGus dominated the conversation from morning to night. It was a breath of fresh air for 4AD, a new dawn. And with Colin signing Scheer, the UK office was back in the frame.'

Kristin Hersh would have been happy not to be the topic of any conversation: 'From *Red Heaven* onward,' she admits, 'I wouldn't listen to any advice.' Chris Staley had taken over from Ivo the role of artist liaison with Throwing Muses, but Hersh, with husband/ manager Billy O'Connell, was a self-sufficient unit. Throwing Muses had a new US deal with independent label Rykodisc, and with the proceeds from recording and touring, the couple had put down a payment on a small house. Hersh's new blonde buzzcut served as a sign of renewal, with Sire and other traumas in the past.

The band's seventh album, *Limbo*, consolidated the steamrolling glee of *Red Heaven*, but the two singles – 'Shark' in the UK and 'Ruthie's Knocking' for America – showed Hersh still valued concise tunes. Two limited edition seven-inch versions of 'Shark' included alternative versions of album tracks, from the title track (the much looser 'Limbobo'), album highlight 'Serene' (the rockier 'Serene Swing') and a countrified version of 'Tar Moochers', but these were more fan collectables than marketing tools. Hersh wasn't going to be fooled again.

But operating outside of the Warners deal with 4AD, the band didn't have the kind of advances that could keep the band going by building up a debt to the label. Without sizeable sales, and with 4AD now unable to inject more tour support, Hersh admits they reached an impasse: 'We ran out of money,' she says. The band decided to go into hibernation, with Dave Narcizo setting up his own graphic design business called Lakuna.

But Hersh threw herself into a period of productivity, both as a solo artist and a pioneering businesswoman. She and O'Connell created the Throwing Music label and linked up with Donita Sparks of the all-women grunge band L7 to launch CASH Music. The Coalition of Artists and Stakeholders was a non-profit online organisation that pre-dated the Kickstarter model of private funding for creative projects by thirteen years: 'a way for audiences and creators to exchange creative perspectives and ideas,' the website claimed, or as Hersh put it, 'a way to circumvent the music industry'.

Since 1996, songs posted to Hersh's CASH Music have been released under a Creative Commons licence, to be downloaded and also remixed using 'stems' of each track's individual components. The cost ranges from free to one-off payments, at incremental levels with corresponding benefits, up to $5,000, which gives the subscriber an 'executive producer' credit on Hersh's next album. This single-minded response to the traditional relationship between artist and record label was an instinctive and brilliant vision of how outdated that relationship was, and how artists who valued independence and integrity needed to reinvent their means of survival.

Hersh had already felt her soul slip away by trying to house her music within the profiteering structure of major labels; some independent labels could be similarly exploitative, though 4AD was trying hard not to be turned into one of them. But it took a lot of courage and vision at that point to see how the music industry was stacked against the artist, with too much debt incurred by large advances and video/tour costs, and the constant pressure of trying to ascend to a higher level. That's where Lush were, in the summer of 1996, having played shows with the likes of Pulp, Sonic Youth, Garbage, Red Hot Chili Peppers, Nick Cave, Sepultura, Bush, Super Furry Animals, Beck and The Prodigy, like an endless Lollapalooza merry-go-round.

Following the last of their American dates, Lush returned to tour Europe and the UK in July as a third single was taken from *Lovelife*. A remixed version of '500' – now subtitled 'Shake Baby Shake' to boost its commercial sheen – reached 21 in the UK national charts – so tantalisingly close, yet again, to a confidence-boosting top 20 hit. But it was still the band's third top 22 hit in a row. Five more new B-sides were needed this time, meaning that Lush had had to write and record over an album's worth of bonus material. And then the band returned to the States, again, only eleven days after their final festival performance at Benicàssim in Spain.

Robin Hurley says that *Lovelife* sold a respectable 110,000 copies. 'But for Warners, it still wasn't enough to press the mythical button to turn 100,000 sales into 500,000.'

Tim Carr: 'Lush was the warhorse of all warhorses. But when they toured America, they could draw 2,000 people in New York or LA, but only about thirty people in Des Moines, Iowa, which would take the wind out of their sails. And in the days before the internet, they'd have to talk to every radio show and retail outlet. It was tough on them.'

Colleen Maloney: 'For young, impressionable indie kids, Lush were heroes. They had two sassy girls who looked great, without looking like they were trying too hard. They were living the life and having fun, even if the press would occasionally still give them a hammering. But I was aware more of frustration than unhappiness. Every band wants to sell records but I think that Lush was hungrier for recognition than sales and fame.'

For the first part of this third American tour of the year, Lush would be third on the bill in the unsuitable company of American rockers Goo Goo Dolls and the Gin Blossoms. 'I told the others, shall we say we won't do it?' says Emma Anderson. 'I waited for them to agree, but everyone looked down. Come on guys, help me here! I was dubbed the troublemaker, and anything I said was ignored. Our management started taunting me, saying, "For the next album, you won't play Britain, just America, you'll like that, won't you Emma?" Morale was rock bottom. I told Peter Felstead how unhappy we all were and he said, "Stop moaning, you're only there to keep them [Warners] interested or they'll move on to the next thing".'

Tim Carr: 'Warners realised Lush had hit a watershed and we weren't going to break through with them, as "Single Girl" hadn't taken them any higher. Lush wasn't The Sundays or The Cranberries, more a great low-level indie band.'

Miki Berenyi: 'It was madness, completely demoralising and it made the cracks spread rapidly.'

Anderson decided she needed outside help, and reached out to Ivo, without realising his present condition. They met for lunch in LA before Lush's flight to Hawaii. 'It was a very strange experience,' Anderson recalls. 'I wasn't talking to the same bloke that I used to know. Ivo wasn't listening to what I was saying, and what he was saying about therapy and new age stuff didn't have any relation to me.

He gave me some self-help books, such as [Susan Jeffers'] *Feel the Fear And Do It Anyway*. I felt so alone, like a bad dream. I decided I'd get through the tour and then I'd leave the band.'

Lush returned home from Tokyo on 18 September, eleven days after Chris Acland's thirtieth birthday was celebrated on stage at San Francisco's Fillmore. Anderson remembers that the last time she saw Acland the four Lush members were on the pavement after she'd called a meeting to announce her departure.

'Emma had hated all the criticism of us going Britpop and said she wasn't interested in that kind of music anymore,' says Berenyi. 'The most important thing for me was to keep the band together, as we only worked as a unit, so I agreed to get rid of Peter Felstead, and to do things her way. Emma was surprised, and then we agreed we'd do the European tour that had been booked and then redraw the whole template.'

Anderson says Acland admitted he felt unable to tour again. 'We suggested that we'd start with another drummer and maybe Chris could join us a week into the tour. He could go home to his parents, which would help.'

Ivo recalls his shock when he'd talked to Acland before the LA date of the Shaving The Pavement tour. 'Chris was one of the most relaxed, funny, gregarious individuals you could meet, who always made you feel comfortable. But here he was, confused and down. He told me, "Everybody's become friends on this tour, and I don't need any new friends, I have enough". It was such an odd thing to say.'

Berenyi: 'I know Chris was exhausted, but we all were. He had other stuff going on, like he'd turned thirty and he'd split with his girlfriend, and he was down about not having money or his own place to live. I'd known Chris since we were nineteen or so, and he'd always be having a great time. Sometimes he could be unapproachable, but he'd return home, recharge his batteries and things would be fine again.'

Exactly a month after Acland returned to his native Lake District, and ten days after 4AD released *Topolino*, an album of Lush B-sides for the Japanese market, his body was discovered in the garden of his parents' house; he'd hanged himself on a tree. 'No one had an inkling of what would happen,' says Ivo.

The shock was devastating for everyone who knew Acland, but especially Berenyi, who'd been closer to the drummer than anyone. 'We'd been students together, shared a house, I'd been his girlfriend and we'd been best mates for over a decade. He was one of the few reliably positive, consistently fun things about Lush. I still can't figure out why he killed himself. I understand people get depressed, and there was a history of depression in his family, but Chris wasn't bipolar.'

Acland had started taking the anti-depressant Prozac. 'Maybe he was diagnosed the wrong stuff,' Berenyi says. 'He told me he wasn't sleeping, and he'd been prescribed sleeping pills, but wasn't taking them as he associated it with taking drugs. I don't want to put it down to any drug, because that wasn't his weakness, though I thought Chris got into coke during that time, which pissed me off, because he could be slow one night and racing through the set the next night. I gave him a pep talk and said he should talk to someone as he hated talking to his mates. I phoned after the weekend, and his mum thought he'd gone out … he was dead by then. He'd made a very quick decision, and for such an unselfish person, it was the worst, most selfish thing he could have done. It was such an unspeakable, crushing waste.'

Acland's extreme reaction was proof that depression could take an unexplainable grip on the mind; Ivo knew that more than most. 'Ivo told me, "I could see me killing myself, or I could see you, but never in a million years could I imagine Chris would be the one",' says Tim Carr. 'The Chris I knew never had a dark thought in his head.'

Ivo: 'That last time I saw Chris he was about to turn thirty. I confessed I'd found it a really tricky birthday but things got better. We laughed a lot about growing old. But something had happened with him. I think his apparent first bout of serious depression was just too much. With no prior experience, he just needed to make it stop. It's also possible that the anti-depressants made things worse.'

The funeral in the Lake District united 4AD personnel past and present, including Ivo, Robin Guthrie and Howard Gough, in a gathering of profound sorrow where grievances could be set aside. When the dust had settled, it was Miki Berenyi and not Emma Anderson who decided she couldn't go on.

'For me, Chris was the glue that held things together, the core of the band more than me and Emma. Without Chris, Emma and I would have torn each other apart ages ago. We had respect for each other and we got on, but were at each other's throats too, and it was Chris and Phil that made it fun. I think even if Chris hadn't died, we'd eventually have had a blinding row and split up, but because of Chris, we had to be supportive of each other. And yet the problems were still there underneath.'*

As Marc Geiger had once pointed out, there did seem a pattern among Ivo's signings, of romantic relationships undermining the stability of bands. But there was another pattern – too many of the artists that Ivo signed, the shy and sensitive, the vulnerable and moody, simply buckled under the strain of success, or striving for it. Not even a seemingly brash Charles Thompson enjoyed the fruits of his labours. You'd have to go back to 4AD's earliest days, of Bauhaus and The Birthday Party, to find a predominance of artists that really thrived on attention.

Not even Belly could survive the unworkable marriage of its line-up during the making of second album *King*, but a much-needed spirit of rebirth came at the end of 4AD's most traumatic year – due to Chris Acland's death, the end of Dead Can Dance and Lush, the departure of Heidi Berry – with Tanya Donelly's new solo guise. She toured North America with a dream team of Throwing Muses drummer David Narcizo and bassist – and new husband – Dean Fisher, who joined her (alongside former Pixies drummer Dave Lovering) at

---

* Seventeen years after Lush's split, Miki Berenyi has yet to initiate any music of her own. 'I thought about it for a while,' she says. '[Her partner] Moose would love to do some music together, but I always did feel I was a bit of a chancer with music and that I'd never do as well as I did with Lush. And I didn't want to make a pale shadow. I got a job, I have kids … and music to me is hard work! It can't just be the odd evening, it's either full on or nothing.' She has sung on three projects, by invitation: The Rentals 1999 album *Seven More Minutes*, a remix of a Flat 7 track by Robin Guthrie, and the debut album by Seinking Ships, *Museum Quality Capture*.

Gary Smith's Fort Apache studio. The *Sliding & Diving* EP made *King* look like a bad dream. 'Bum' and 'Human' had more in common with and were as energetic as the current Throwing Muses, 'Restless' would have suited Gram Parsons, and 'Swoon' was well named. Donelly had come home.

Ivo was attempting to do the same. After the pursuit of one photographer, Tina Modotti, had inadvertently led to Tom Baril, so Baril had introduced Ivo to his picture framer Randolph Laub. Ivo took his small collection of photographs to Laub's home outside of Santa Fe in New Mexico to be framed: 'When I received them back,' says Ivo, 'each was mindblowing, in beautiful black matt, half-inch deep, just extraordinary. By giving Randolph complete freedom, I felt a correlation with the way that I'd worked with musicians and Vaughan.'

Ivo had wanted to visit Santa Fe ever since his brother Perry had shown him a photograph from his own trip. 'I immediately fell in love with the scenery,' he says, and an image, like a photograph in soft focus, grew in his mind of a place of rest and restoration, away from the big city and big business, to own land and build a house in the desert landscape.

In the early summer of 1996, Ivo had rented a house outside of Santa Fe for a month. When Dead Can Dance played in town, he had taken Gerrard and Perry to a plot of desert land he was thinking of buying. 'Ever since I'd been on holiday in Majorca with Vaughan, I'd been trying to re-create the peace and tranquillity of that trip. It was the most calm I'd ever felt in my life.'

Seeing Dead Can Dance's show that night only reinforced Ivo's feelings for the region. As he recalls, 'They played an outdoor auditorium in Santa Fe at the Native American Indian school. There was a blue moon that night, and you could see straight across to Colorado, and electrical storms in the distance … it was astonishing.'

The only thing was, the only way Ivo could pay for this dream was by selling his London flat, cutting off another tie with his home country, and to the past.

21 1997

AS CLOSE AS TWO COATS OF PAINT
ON A WINDSWEPT WALL
(tad7000-bad7012)

Dipping in and out of 4AD business, liaising with Ivo on occasion as two music fans and industry veterans, guitarist Michael Brook had the luxury of sizing up the label from a distance. 'Ivo just wasn't feeling the kind of enthusiasm and hunger that he had about music, which was part of why 4AD worked, and it wouldn't work if he didn't feel that way,' Brook recalls. 'In a way, 4AD was more like a band history than a label. It starts with a lot of excitement, and success builds, but it's usually finite.'

Since 1992's *Cobalt Blue* and its ... *Aquarium* companion album, Brook had had one track, 'Diffusing', included on the *All Virgos Are Mad* compilation and taken part in the live counterpart. He'd subsequently collaborated with the esteemed Pakistani *qawwali* singer Nusrat Fateh Ali Khan for the Real World label, and on a combined project with David Sylvian and King Crimson guitarist Robert Fripp while pursuing solo projects. Ivo agreed that 4AD should release his specially commissioned soundtrack to actor Kevin Spacey's directorial debut *Albino Alligator*. 'We all liked the film,' says Ivo, 'and 4AD seemed an appropriate outlet considering our connection with Michael.'

Brook's soundtrack was rich in *film noir* menace and edgy jazz, for a story of two petty criminals in New Orleans that take hostages,

515

culminating in a police siege. The film itself concluded with a humid arrangement of American composers Ted Koehler and Harold Arlen's 'Ill Wind', sung by Michael Stipe and venerated jazz veteran Jimmy Scott over the closing credits.

Like *Cobalt Blue*, the soundtrack album was a lovely boutique venture, but no money-spinner. With Ivo unable to muster enthusiasm for music that might sell enough records to keep the label afloat, as his choices in 4AD's early years had, then – unless Tanya Donelly could repeat Belly's success or Kim Deal could bring The Breeders back around – GusGus might be 4AD's only hope for recovery. The presence of the Icelandic band also felt like a doorway to a possible future rather than a reliance on the past. Warner Bros was on side this time: 'GusGus weren't just a typically alternative band, they had club potential, and the potential for having hits,' says Steven Baker. 'And it showed 4AD was branching out.'

Warners championed Tarnation too, to the point that responsibility for the band had been taken over by Reprise – 'the artist development portion of the company,' according to the band's singer Paula Frazer. Ivo believes that, on the surface, 4AD appeared to be functioning as it used to: 'We were trying to break artists like GusGus and Tanya Donelly; and Heidi Berry, Dead Can Dance and Lisa Germano had all had beautiful and intense campaigns.' He sees v23 as playing its part of giving the appearance of normality: 'From the visual reinvention of Lush, through Scheer and GusGus, the breadth of stylistic approach and the volume of work was staggering, especially when you see GusGus' campaign – seven- and twelve-inch singles, CDs, street and store posters ... If you knew nothing about 4AD, the artwork alone from this era was enough to convert you. This work, as much as the defining Cocteau Twins or Pixies sleeves, should have the same significance within the graphic design world.'

Even the least obvious contenders for formatting were getting the treatment, so Tarnation's new lead single 'You'll Understand' came in a CD and limited edition double seven-inch version with a limited edition seven-inch of 'There's Someone'. Both came from the band's forthcoming second album *Mirador*, recorded with a new line-up since the *Gentle Creatures* band had already splintered. 'Tarnation was my vision, but the other members wanted more of a partnership, and with four cooks the music was getting very diluted,' says Frazer.

Mutual friends had introduced her to the San Francisco trio Broken Horse. 'They were kinda Birthday Party stuff with a western swing and upright bass,' says Frazer, though *Mirador* was much more in tune with Nick Cave's brooding and measured Bad Seeds than the earlier band's chaotic drama. Broken Horse guitarist Alex Oropeza and drummer Yuma Joe Byrnes joined Tarnation; Frazer thought bassist Bill Cuevas's style was 'too busy' and so hired Jamie Meagan, formerly of Irish pop-punks Puppy Love Bomb, who Frazer was dating. 'The new Tarnation had a darker, edgier, alternative retro sound, which I loved,' she says.

Mirador was a bold step on from *Gentle Creatures*, a sultry gem that ranged from the tougher crust of 'Like A Ghost' and 'Christine' to shoring up the prairie ballads on 'Idly' and 'Destiny'. But if Frazer and Reprise saw progress, Ivo wasn't feeling it. 'Paula had her new band and went off into this swampy, sub-Kid Congo and Bad Seeds area that I felt was musically unoriginal and didn't suit her voice. Certain Virgo characteristics were peaking within me – nothing sounded good or essential, let alone perfect. I probably wouldn't have chosen to do a second album with Tarnation but our European licensees also really liked the band, and Simon [Harper] wanted a smooth flow of releases from bands we'd already worked with.'

It was a double disappointment for Ivo as he'd reached out to Frazer soon after the release of *Gentle Creatures* about a new collaborative venture. 'I gave Paula a couple of songs to think about how she might sing them, but I never got any feedback. It was such a shame because, like Elizabeth [Fraser], Lisa [Gerrard] and Kristin [Hersh], her voice might have helped redefine the label.'

That task was instead falling to GusGus. Ivo finally met the band when he was in London for one of his very rare visits to Alma Road. 'A handful of them were there, and I said hello to Hafdis, one of the singers,' Ivo recalls. 'She said, "Hello, what do you do?" It was indicative of my invisibility and how comfortable they must have felt there without me, which I took as a good sign.'

A bad sign was Ivo's reactions during an informal gathering that Ivo organised at the Alma pub. 'Ivo asked everyone to be very honest, and to say if we thought there were any bands that he shouldn't have signed,' says Colleen Maloney. 'Everyone was quiet, and Ivo said, "No, honestly, be blunt", and Lewis said something to the effect that he hadn't liked Lisa Germano's last album. At which point Ivo exploded, saying, "How dare you, Lisa's amazing ..." Lewis was faced with the impossible task of being expected to sign commercially minded acts but with the aesthetics of a man he never got to spend enough time with.'

Jamieson recalls a conversation with Ivo regarding their current favourites. 'Ivo said the new Low record, and I said Portishead and Massive Attack. We were clearly so unalike in our tastes.'

The pair had to be united for a meeting with Emma Anderson. Lush had split after the death of Chris Acland, but while Miki Berenyi had decided to lie low, Anderson had chosen to carry on, and 4AD had funded some new demos. 'Ivo and Lewis came to visit to break it to me gently,' she recalls. 'Lewis said they were really good songs, but Ivo said, "Not for us", so they dropped all of Lush. Our publishers dropped us too. We were on our own.'

GusGus still felt like a place where Jamieson and Ivo could conceivably overlap, and the band's visual side also chimed with 4AD's design identity. A variety of stills and original images gave v23 the necessary material to inspire some of the team's best artwork of the era, with a sumptuous twenty-page booklet for the GusGus debut 4AD album, *Polydistortion*.

Of course, the industry climate demanded more than great artwork, or even great music. The lead single 'Believe' came in three CD versions plus vinyl and radio promos and the album had exhausting single/double/limited edition permutations. The credited tracks (the unlisted 'Polybackwards' was an ambient epilogue) had been drawn from the band's original Icelandic album remixed for the 4AD version, to bring out the strengths of an hour-long odyssey of electronic dance, from sleek techno to lounge sophistication, Nordic funk to skewed pop.

GusGus began to build sizeable fan bases in the trend-setting cities of New York and LA, which The Wolfgang Press had never managed. But inexplicably, 'Believe' only reached 154 in the UK national charts, a significant failure after 'Polyesterday'. The album reached 130. Something was very wrong. 4AD staffer Cliff Walton thinks that the label's reputation had diminished: '4AD wasn't mainstream enough anymore, so we couldn't cross over a band like GusGus, despite the big buzz about them. But they were arty and eccentric, and didn't play by the rules, which made them more fun to work on.'

This scenario was even more inexplicable as the band's press profile had been sky-high after a very expensive media trip to Iceland. 'It was insane,' recalls Tim Hall, who 4AD had employed in 1996 to run the new website and mail order department. 'We took about forty press, radio and TV people to a hydro-electric plant where we had a huge meal and a nice hotel for two nights, all for one concert.'

Lewis Jamieson: 'It really disappointed and frustrated me that we couldn't convert all these cool points into sales. On "Believe", we just couldn't get singles away. This was still the height of Britpop and 4AD was culturally out of step. The indie label identity that [BBC] Radio 1 preferred was personified by Creation, the feeling of being part of a wave that was sweeping the UK. Everyone was metaphorically out having fun in the [affects Liam Gallagher's Mancunian accent] *sunshiiine* and 4AD didn't really do fun. GusGus got loads of style and music press but radio didn't respond. I think we relied on the label to get us going and 4AD didn't have that networking power anymore.'

'Despite the fact we utilised great pluggers, club promotion people and had great national and regional press, Radio 1 had the perception that 4AD was an albums label,' says Simon Harper. 'We were also dealing with a non-UK resident act. It's fine to have shitloads of press around the release and tour cycle, but the media window tends to close quickly for developing bands when they leave the country. Being available at short notice for radio or TV and just by being present in the public's field of vision can be a real asset.'

Since Colourbox in 1982, the number of British-based artists that Ivo had signed long-term was four: Lush, Pale Saints, Heidi Berry and Mojave 3.

Given the heights Belly had reached, there was hope invested in Tanya Donelly's debut solo album. David Narcizo played on the four tracks produced by Muses/Pixies buddy – and Donelly's new manager – Gary Smith, and the drummer was to join the live band that toured the album across America alongside husband Dean Fisher on bass.

Donelly's new album emulated Belly's debut and, in large parts, bettered it. Lead single 'Pretty Deep' and the follow-up 'Bright Light' were crunchy and effervescent, 'Acrobat' was tender and haunting and 'Mysteries Of The Unexplained' is a contender for the best ballad that Donelly has ever written. But MTV Buzz Bin wasn't interested anymore and the wave that had carried Belly along had beached a long time ago. The video to 'Pretty Deep' was aired on the new MTV2 channel, set up to siphon off whatever popular music was deemed alternative, and also on MTV's new 'adult contemporary' strand VH1. Both had much lower viewer figures than the main MTV channel, which was busy making itself over as a youth TV mouthpiece that preferred celebrity and reality TV programming. Donelly was an underdog all over again.

The only chart placing *Lovesongs For Underdogs* won was Billboard's Northeast Heatseekers chart, where it reached number 20. 'I've given up trying to figure out what the music industry is about,' Donelly told me at the time. 'It's so changeable; I can't predict it. There were high hopes around 4AD and Sire, which I'm trying to stay away from! People need to have high hopes to get through the process, but in my own heart, I have to keep an even keel. I don't want to make records to try and maintain a momentum; whichever way the wind blows this time, I'll be OK.'

'I very much liked Tanya's album and I thought it would be enormously successful,' says Ivo. 'But it didn't happen.' Neither had the track listing that he chose for Donelly, which began with 'Acrobat'. 'Gary Smith's response was that we didn't want to scare people away from the listening posts in record shops,' Ivo says. 'A few years earlier,

I'd have felt strong enough to express my emotional investment in a record and in Tanya, but Gary spoke louder to Sire about editing "Pretty Deep", so they cut the reference to a "dead body" [*'Remember when we all went out to Fire Island/ You thought you saw a body on the beach'*]. These were lovely and creative people doing the best to have successful records. With me at the helm or not, 4AD was never meant to be that. Let's not forget why independent labels were created in the first place – as an alternative way of having an outlet, a career in the music industry, without following the sell-your-soul route to success.'

In Ivo's mind, and as Michael Brook had seen it, 4AD was predicated on Ivo's purist way of working, or it couldn't work … the present compromise in both the UK and LA offices certainly wasn't sustainable. Lewis Jamieson saw a potential fatal flaw in Ivo's continued absence. 'The roster wasn't renewed properly, so its once great strength, a unified vision of music, wasn't present anymore. There was GusGus, Ivo's bands, Scheer, and none of them fit together. The base of people buying nearly every release because it was on 4AD started to fall, and we didn't have the marketing expertise to replace that reliance on label loyalty.'

'4AD whore' Craig Roseberry was one of those mad collectors of old who was about to call a halt to his obsessive need to own everything 4AD released, and filed in order of catalogue numbers. 'After years of frenzied devotion to all things 4AD,' Roseberry says, 'things began to turn around 1995. Even if I hadn't been in love with a release, I still felt it was interesting, collectable and a crucial part of the ethos of 4AD's image and identity. But I could no longer see cohesion or unified vision. There were awkward transitional records by bands trying to figure out their next steps, and I found the rash of newer signings like Heidi Berry, Scheer, Tarnation, Air Miami, Mojave 3 and Lisa Germano lacklustre and uninspiring. But GusGus was a great signing – they were unique, interesting and "other".

But then everything changes. I had changed too. I was no longer that sullen and idealistic post-punk-goth-indie kid wanting to kick against the pricks and to cling to everything I felt embodied the same ideals. I was working as an artist manager and record exec in the dance and electronic worlds – I was more into acid jazz and trip hop, soul and deep house. And 4AD was *not* that. Many of the label's later releases represented a significant page or chapter from my earlier life that was slipping away.'

To counteract the loss of such core collectors, 4AD had to pursue marketing campaigns, even to the point of changing the emphasis of those record covers. Ivo attributes much of 4AD's appearance of success to v23's continuing sterling efforts. There could be dips in quality, arguably down to the office resources being unfairly stretched by the need for multiple formats. Artists were now more likely to be seen on record covers, such as on *Lovesongs For Underdogs*, which featured a functional, rather than imaginative, image of an outstretched Tanya Donelly, dominated by typography. The demand by GusGus singer Daníel Ágúst to have his image – underwater in skimpy swimming trunks and cap – on the front of *Polydistortion* scuppered v23's own idea but Vaughan Oliver still had a lavish twenty-page booklet in the CD artwork in which to juxtapose stills from the band's film and photo archive with v23's own contributions.

The tree husks of *Mirador* – photographed on London's Hampstead Heath as there wasn't the budget to shoot them in Oliver's preferred Mojave desert location – were also memorable, but the Scheer sleeves and the silver oven mittens (the outline of Warren Defever's home state of Michigan is mitten-shaped) of *Stars On ESP* and an accompanying image combining forks and whales were inspired. 'We were still turning something banal into something exciting,' says Oliver. 'Warren allowed me to do the most random, surreal things, anything but just another record sleeve.'

Defever recalls his periodic visits to v23 with great fondness. 'Their dungeon office was always so much fun and filled with loud music, dancing and occasional screaming. I remember staying in the flat two floors above the office and hearing Vaughan howling like a wolf or a demon one night. I was too terrified to investigate. The next day, everything seemed fine and nobody mentioned anything. When I hear 4AD artists whining about their experience working with him, I always think, you fucking idiot, you have no idea how lucky you are, let me know when you find a better designer to work with.'

Vaughan Oliver wasn't the only one working hard. Despite what might have struck the 4AD staff as rehearsals for Ivo's retirement, he had again been hatching plans for a follow-up to This Mortal Coil. 'I found I was missing not having a project to obsess about, which to me was a good sign, because before then, I just wanted to get things *off* my mind. I remember telling Lisa Germano that if I didn't start something, I'd forget about ever doing another record. She said why didn't I just start it? So I did.'

It couldn't be This Mortal Coil, and it wasn't to be *Blood* either. But Ivo still felt a covers project had legs, though it needed to stand apart from the past, which precluded John Fryer's participation, and that of Jon Turner. Unable to commit to co-ordinating and engaging in prolonged sessions, a large and revolving collective felt too difficult and grand. What began to gel in Ivo's head centred on the sublime bass playing of Laurence O'Keefe from Heidi Berry's house band (and Brendan Perry's *13 Year Itch* performance). 'For the sake of simplicity,' Ivo says, 'I thought of a record that would just be bass guitar and strings.'

O'Keefe instantly wanted to take part, so on his spring trip to London, Ivo organised a session with engineer Alex Russell at Protocol studios, now that the trusted Blackwing had closed down, with a view to releasing an album in 1998. Eight backing tracks were laid down, with the subtlest addition of some sampled effects that Ivo had brought with him, such as ocean waves and his bedroom's air conditioning unit (the tape of which helped him sleep when travelling). 'Eight tracks was all I wanted to do,' he says. 'And more than ever, I felt like [film director] Robert Altman, who said, "Once you have your script and cast, 98 per cent of the work is done".'

Ivo hadn't intended to have just one singer after he'd heard what former This Mortal Coil contributor Louise Rutkowski had recorded for the demos. 'It was to help me pick a direction, but I just fell in love with what she did, so we kept them,' says Ivo. 'Most were done in one or two takes.'

Rutkowski had been working for the British Arts Council when she got Ivo's call. Like other artists that Ivo favoured, she had struggled to survive making music after This Mortal Coil had given her the desire to put integrity before anything. She admits that she had virtually abandoned singing. 'It's much easier being independent nowadays, but back then, it was much harder because you had to rely on so many people – labels, managers and more. Being involved with Ivo, there wasn't that level of falseness; it was about the music. He was like a film director in that he could capture some essence of oneself in a very true way, as I had nothing on the tracks to bounce off, which meant I had to work harder. Nothing that I've been involved in before or after working with Ivo has brought me anything like the same happiness.'

Rather than use TMC foil Martin McCarrick, Ivo added string arrangements by cellist Audrey Riley, who had worked on *Static & Silence*, Ivo's favourite album by The Sundays. With the odd vocal retouch and Richie Thomas's modest contribution – drums on 'Hanky Panky Nohow', saxophone on 'Sweet Unknown' – an album was completed. 'There were very few people involved and very little preparation,' Ivo recalls. 'I just played games of musical consequences, passing ideas around. I was less concerned with my tangible role and just delighted to be the enabler of the project. It was all so beautifully relaxed and easy.'

Ivo hadn't talked to John Fryer since the *Blood* sessions in 1994, but changed his mind about using his former ally for the album's mixing in New York. 'Why make life harder by not using John? I gave him much more freedom than with This Mortal Coil. Back in London, I'd also let Laurence stay on in the studio for a couple of nights to play whatever he wanted. But in the end, everyone who played on the album expressed surprise by how stripped down it became.'

Ivo also retired the songs he'd tried out with Joanne Loughman/ *Blood*, choosing songs either because they spoke loudly to him, or just because they had beautiful melodies and memories, such as Brian Eno's 'Spider & I' and former Velvet Underground member John Cale's 'Hanky Panky Nohow'. The sessions' third song by a British art rock icon, 'Let The Happiness In' by David Sylvian, did have a profound resonance – it had been the soundtrack in Ivo's mind during his father's funeral in 1987.

Three tracks had concrete connections to 4AD. Slowblow's 'Is Jesus Your Pal?' was chosen purely for its melody, but the message in Heidi Berry's 'Only Human' seemed all too clear: *'If anyone should offer your heart/ Could you give the same way?/ You're too afraid/ You're too far gone/ But you know you'll find a way to be.'* The meaning inferred in Neil Halstead's 'Dagger' was open to interpretation, however: *'The sunshine girl is sleeping/ She falls and dreams alone/ And me I am her dagger/ Too numb to feel her pain.'*

'I'd rather not be too literal,' says Ivo. 'Songs just resonate, don't they? "Only Human", well, we are, aren't we? I chose "Dagger" for the atmosphere. I'm not sure I know what it's about.'

That left two tracks. 'Sweet Unknown', written by British shoegazers Cranes, echoed 'Song To The Siren' in describing the inevitability of lost love: *'I loved it when you would hold me tight/ And for a while our world seemed bright…/ And I hope one day you find the things you really need …'* But it was only 'The Outer Skin' whose lyric was included in the artwork. The song had been written by Chris Knox of the inventive New Zealand art-pop duo Tall Dwarfs. The lines locate the narrator in the grip of isolation, with a black-eyed dog barring the door: *'We're as close as two coats of paint on a windswept wall/ But we'll never know what sits at the other's core'*, as well as, *'Self-obsessed on a crumbling couch for hours/ Quite alone as is usual for the things we are quite unable to go beyond what's ours/ And it feels like nothing on earth has ever got in.'*

The name of this new project was The Hope Blister, a phrase that had popped into Ivo's head while he sat in a traffic jam. 'I wanted two words that worked together that normally don't. It means different things to me, but the meaning is pretty much contained within the name, simultaneously positive and negative. Like waiting for the agony to stop and letting the happiness in. Virtually everything in life is like that.'

But the aftermath of Ivo's visit to the London office was much more about agony than happiness. The ongoing round of financial trimming that had affected artist tour support and design projects finally had staff numbers in its sights. 'Memos had been going around,' recalls Cliff Walton, 'that we'd not had the success we'd hoped for, and a reference to the label being supported by Ivo's own money.' (Not true, he says.)

In June, Robin Hurley flew to London to announce who was to be let go; those staying were to double up on duties, for example Tim Hall would take over record plugging. 'I was told how to do the job in two hours one afternoon,' he says. Colleen Maloney was to run international PR as well as the UK side – and single-handed too, as Tony Morley had already left to concentrate full-time on his record label Leaf.*

A&R also had to be cut down. Ivo naturally wanted to retain Colin Wallace, his old friend who had been employed longer than Lewis Jamieson, who Ivo didn't get on with anyway. But he was persuaded otherwise. 'Lewis' character jarred with what 4AD was used to, like he'd get shitfaced with the bands like a Creation Records A&R man would do,' says Hurley, 'but Lewis came with GusGus.'

Wallace, of course, came with Scheer. It was no contest. And he had signed precisely one band at 4AD during three and a half years in the job, while his and Jamieson's Detox Artifacts imprint had only lasted a year, to no noticeable effect.† 'Ultimately, we did make a choice to go with Lewis, based primarily on the overall artistic direction 4AD

---

* Tony Morley and fellow PR Julian Carerra had started Leaf in late 1994, concentrating on instrumental/electronic music. After being hospitalised for three months after a car crash in September 1995, Morley decided to concentrate on Leaf full-time: 'It was an opportunity to do something different.' Today, Morley runs Leaf from his West Yorkshire home. 'I've been influenced by what Ivo did,' he says, 'a label driven by one person, not making decisions based on market share. But Leaf has never had something sell enough to fund other things, as other labels have, which snowballed for them to the point of becoming money machines. And what labels did in the Eighties isn't possible anymore, to get that level of success without kowtowing to get to that point.'

† Of the six acts Detox Artifacts released, the Aeroplane single 'Signs Of Life' featuring Heidi Berry was the best. Toüçan, Stellar, Thrush Puppies, Ajax Disco Spanner and Suckle were the other five bands of no fixed reputation, and none went past recording a single or EP for the label. 'Ivo didn't like any of it!' says Colin Wallace.

seemed to be heading towards, coupled with the fact Colin didn't seem very happy with that direction,' says Simon Harper.

Sixteen years earlier, Wallace had chauffeured Cocteau Twins from Grangemouth to London and beyond, seen his pals Robin Guthrie and Liz Fraser help mould the template for 4AD's success, and witnessed, close hand, the success of M/A/R/R/S and Pixies before finding himself helping Ivo steer a way forward. The Cocteaus had first slipped away and now Wallace was himself removed.

'4AD was my second family, where I absolutely loved working,' he says. 'It must have been unbelievably painful for Ivo and Robin to cut everyone loose. Martin Mills told me that 4AD resembled a Rolls-Royce being run on the budget of a Citroën 2CV, which was unsustainable. I thought it would go on for ever, and get bigger and better, but in the end, I was seeing my friends and colleagues leaving one after the other, some in tears, and it was just very, very sad. I was taken care of financially, and the next day after I left, I went to Jamaica, smoked lots of *sensimilla*, and had a fantastic holiday.'

Cliff Walton, and Simon Harper's assistant in the International department, were also let go, while v23's Paul McMenamin had already moved to LA. Vaughan Oliver admits that morale was down in every department of the label, and despite the workload, he realised he could no longer depend on a privileged safety. 'At one point, years earlier, Ivo had told me that things would end at a certain point, after he'd made his mark. I was shocked that he'd have an end game in sight. I felt secure enough, but it still felt devastating, to have this amazing galleon that was charting new waters and getting lost – and then the captain might want to stand down? Other people can take the helm, but they weren't big enough, and they still had Ivo over their shoulder, thinking, what would he like?'

Ivo: 'Vaughan was angry that I had never discussed moving to America, and he was now working for a company that was populated by what he regarded as fools. I wasn't thinking clearly or honestly when I allowed them to let Colin go, because he was my friend, but I was doing something in order to save the company, to follow the vision to sell records at any cost. Shame on me for agreeing.'

But Ivo had come up with no other alternative. He hadn't signed the right artists, so what were the remaining staff members to do in that absence? On top of Ivo's new studio project, he had been busy on two others, both of which had no tangible commercial portfolio, but then that was never his consideration. Ivo had expressed to Robin Hurley his interest in working on a film as music supervisor: 'Seventy-two hours later, Robin called, saying, "You won't believe it, I've just been asked if you'd be interested in working on a film called *Joyride*". The director was a big 4AD fan.'

The crime thriller starring Tobey Maguire (with Benicio del Toro in a supporting role) was screenwriter Quinton Peeples' first stab at directing. Assisted by 4AD LA office co-ordinator Chris Staley, Ivo assembled a soundtrack of fourteen 4AD tracks, taking the opportunity to use personal favourites such as Tarnation's 'Game Of Broken Hearts', This Mortal Coil's 'Ivy And Neet', Lush's 'Desire Lines' and Dif Juz's 'No Motion'. He also added three slices of suspenseful ambient darkness from German artists Baked Beans and Oliver Lieb. 'It was an interesting, if frustrating experience,' Ivo recalls. 'I used far too much music that served no purpose and ultimately was barely audible in the film. I do like the opening credits using "Spirea Rising", though.'*

The *Joyride* soundtrack was only released in America. The second project wasn't even on sale in record stores, only in bookshops.

The self-titled Tom Baril book had finally come together after a series of meetings. The photographer, born a year before Ivo, did have more in common with Ivo than simply the work; Baril had grown up making a racket in the family basement with his brother, aping James Brown, The Rolling Stones and The Yardbirds, before progressing to jazz. He hadn't heard of 4AD when Ivo got in touch; Ivo, for his part, must have kept very quiet about 4AD's music, as Baril says he still doesn't know who This Mortal Coil are. But he did get acquainted

---

* Ivo was also credited as music supervisor for the soundtrack that Brendan Perry's brother Robert composed for Gary Tieche's 1997 film *Nevada*, though, he says, 'I did little more than introduce Gary to Rob and commission a version each of "Danny Boy" by Michael Brook and Paula Frazer. I also gave Rob some money to start a solo record that never materialised.'

with 4AD's commitment to production: 'It was clear Ivo was detail-orientated, and I knew he'd do a special book, and do it right, with the best paper and printing. It was hand-bound, and it got very expensive.' Baril says that the book almost didn't happen: 'Ivo knew how he wanted the book to be designed, these very small prints, only two or three inches high … he was into precious little images. But most of my work was large-scale. We compromised in the end.'

Ivo sequenced the order as he would an album. 'I found a starting point, removed just three photos, and 40 minutes later I had something that flowed beautifully, almost mirroring the journey through an album that I'd always found so important. I sent it to Tom, he moved one image, and that was it. I'm so proud of that book, the way it came about, the quality of work, materials and reproduction, the simplicity of design and the purity of intention behind the whole project.'

For the printing, Ivo tracked down a couple in Connecticut after seeing the quality of Alfred Stieglitz's book of Georgia O'Keeffe portraits. The couple's trademark was to painstakingly print in black and white as they did the traditional four-colour process – one ink at a time.

Tom Baril was a stunning 176-page monograph that included a wide range of subjects, a prized piece of art that displayed Ivo's love of the medium. He wanted to press 5,000 copies but the distributor, DAP, was wary of 4AD's ability as a new publisher and convinced Ivo to go for half that amount. There was also a limited edition of fifty copies with a gelatine silver print (yours now for $2,500). 'Everything sold out immediately, proving the experts wrong,' says Ivo. 'We did a second run of fifty limited editions with a different print. But we still lost quite a bit of money.'

There was a chance that Robin Hurley would see Ivo's interest in photography as a distraction from the main task of heading a record label, but he fully supported Ivo's plan for a book-publishing division. 'I'd seen how photography had taken the place of Ivo's enthusiasm for music and it felt very positive for the label, to get Ivo re-connected,' says Hurley. 'The experience of the Baril book was a rare, unique success. We'd hit on an artist rising up in the photographic world and we'd made a precious and beautiful book that had immediately sold out.'

Baril: 'Everyone loved the book. It was a big deal when it came out, and people started to make books that looked like that.'

Two more books were lined up, one by San Diego photographer Robert Maxwell, who specialised in dramatic portraiture, the other from Han Nguyen, a Vietnamese photographer who had settled in San Diego, and whose singular vision and gorgeous compositions chimed with Vaughan Oliver's love of texture. Maxwell had already done a Lisa Germano shoot, and the relationship was moving along, when he told Ivo that his agent – who also represented Tom Baril – had persuaded him to go with a more established publisher, despite the job that 4AD had done.

'The agent felt it would be better for Robert's career in the long run,' says Ivo. 'I felt betrayed by a man whose client we had already given a major career boost. The only reason I'd got into publishing was to return to the purity of reasoning that I'd cherished in 4AD's early years and I was very disappointed to discover identical mercenary individuals in photography. Rather than offering any apology, the agent simply asked why I'd imagined the photography business would be any different. Combined with losing money on Tom's book and Robert's withdrawal, I then had my own very difficult conversation with Han to explain I wasn't going to carry on with the book imprint.'

To compound another premature end to a project with so much promise, Warners president Steven Baker had come to the same decision regarding the 4AD licensing deal. Despite the promise of GusGus and the suggestion that 4AD was branching out, he hadn't seen enough progress since he'd extended the agreement in 1995 – which he says he still doesn't regret. 'I now look back at the people as opposed to the charts, and I cherish all the bands that I dealt with at 4AD. A lot of that music makes a lot of sense to me now, which happens with a lot of cool music.'

'For me, Warners not renewing the option was the turning point,' says Hurley. In theory, 4AD was finally free to find a label that might prioritise 4AD, but the Warners money was funding 4AD's LA office. Hurley was faced with finding smaller premises and to reduce the staff count, which left just himself and Rich Holtzman.

Holtzman had been a witness to the way 4AD had risen and fallen in the space of just four years. In 1993, he was working in college promotions at IRS Records when his friend, Muses manager Billy O'Connell, mentioned a vacant job at 4AD, 'the coolest label on the planet,' says Holtzman. 'After his job interview with Hurley, Holtzman had met Ivo at a Red House Painters show. 'To a young kid like me from the New York suburbs, Ivo was very mysterious, the wizard behind the scenes. But he was this regular person when we met.' But perhaps not a regular record label chief: Ivo didn't stay for long at the show, nor did Hurley; finally Holtzman was left standing on his own. 'It was the era of Red House Painters' interminably long shows, and everyone was exhausted,' he recalls. 'But getting Ivo to any show was hard. Because he was Ivo, he got away with it. Bands never expected him so no one got upset when he didn't turn up. It was the same with meetings.'

Holtzman had arrived in time for 4AD's second golden era, spearheaded by The Breeders' 'Cannonball' and Dead Can Dance's 'The Ubiquitous Mr Lovegrove': 'They were awesome songs that people wanted to play, and not just on college radio, where we were the kings. Every record we released went to number 1 on the college radio charts: Red House Painters, Unrest, Air Miami. Even Insides did really well. We even got The Glee Club to number 1. Even the Paladins got a look-in! People were like, where did *this* come from?'

Holtzman had worked in marketing, label management and production, and when Robin Hurley started to run 4AD, some artist liaison. 'We ran things our way, and hoped Warners would come along for the ride. It often didn't seem like they did. We gave them very cool artists, but by the time it ended, alternative radio had become hard rock and rap rock, all things we clearly didn't fit in with, other than Scheer, which might have been the last record through Warners.'

A series of limited edition releases served the hardcore fan base: the Scheer EP *Demon*, a US-only GusGus remix EP, *Standard Stuff For*

Drama (which was given a Warners catalogue number), and the mail order-only His Name Is Alive EP *Nice Day*, which Warren Defever had recorded in 1996 only for 4AD to delay the release by a year.* The hardcore fan would probably also need to buy into 4AD's more mercenary programme of starting to recycle its venerated back catalogue to provide a necessary revenue stream.

Singles and rarities had previously been gathered and turned into compilations on vinyl and subsequently CD. But *Death To The Pixies* was 4AD's first 'Best Of …' compilation. 'When Pixies split up, I was asked if 4AD would release a "Best Of" album,' says Ivo. 'I said if they saw one, it was because either the band or the label was desperate for money.'

'Using the back catalogue felt like we were conning the fan base,' says Lewis Jamieson. 'At least the track listing for *Death To The Pixies* wasn't a typical reissue. And they didn't do a Best Of Cocteau Twins for years. A Throwing Muses compilation would have sold too. But Ivo's approach was totally ethical. He had this label that was still operating in a world where purity was no longer valued. But times had changed and it was now less about 4AD and more about the artists – or less about the artists and more about single tracks.'

Chris Bigg recalls that Simon Larbalestier and Vaughan Oliver had fallen out (the photographer won't say why; the designer says he can't remember), so the rock covered with Pixies images on the cover *Death To The Pixies* was v23's own idea: 'The planet of *Bossanova* exploded into fragments,' Oliver explains. 'We shot the old artwork and stuck them on to rock and reshot the image. It made sense at the time.'

What didn't make sense at the time was how *Surfer Rosa* only donated two tracks while three were taken off *Bossanova*. What made sense, though it was a cynical exercise, was to take 'Debaser' from *Doolittle* as a single to promote the compilation. Ivo was equally dismayed when he pulled out the CD booklet 'and the paper just

---

* While His Name Is Alive's *Nice Day* EP was originally a mail order-only release of a thousand copies, the EP was re-pressed and sold in stores as well as added to the 1998 reissue of *Stars On ESP*.

flopped, it was so thin'. He adds that 'Sales across the board weren't great and it was clear that, financially, we were struggling badly. But I'd rather have fired everyone than cut back on the quality of production.'

Ironically, *Death To The Pixies* led the way for the record industry's deluxe 'heritage' reissues that now feed the collectors market (with the Japanese paper sleeve the top of that particular market).* It had two special limited edition CDs, one with a bonus live album and the other a 'Golden Ticket' version adding two early Charles Thompson demos. There was a ten-inch vinyl box set too. The humble cassette even got a look in. 'Debaser' came in live, studio and demo versions, proving that a job worth doing well is clearly worth overkilling.

'Debaser' reached 23 in the UK chart, the highest Pixies ever got, but plummeting sales figures for singles meant this wasn't a real achievement. The album's shock chart placing of 20 could be blamed on having two CD formats that didn't count towards one set of sales. 'The chart rules were changing every week,' says Cliff Walton. 'But even so, we thought a Pixies compilation would be a bigger event given the love for the individual albums, the references from Nirvana, and an appreciation for Pixies that had continued to rise.'

Was it that 4AD no longer had the power to sell its most popular band, or just that it was too soon for a retrospective? The rock on the album cover suggested an archaeological find but Pixies had only split up five years earlier. 'The head of music at [BBC] Radio 1 said Pixies was an oldies band, and I was better off talking to Radio 2,' says Tim

---

* 4AD's reissues for the American market were less impressive and reinforced Ivo's dismay over production quality. Jeff Keibel, who runs the comprehensive online site Fedge, wrote, 'Things first started going wrong in the 4AD catalogue number system in July 1998 when the label was faced with reissuing key titles after the end of their US Warner Bros distribution deal. The reissues included M/A/R/R/S, all three This Mortal Coil albums, Bauhaus' *In The Flat Field*, Dead Can Dance's *A Passage In Time*, His Name Is Alive's *Stars On ESP/ Nice Day*, The Birthday Party *Hits* and *Lonely Is An Eyesore*. All these reissues were hastily thrown together, using cheap paper and strange-smelling ink. Certain graphics were omitted from the designs as well. For example, *It'll End In Tears* is missing its front cover logo. To cut costs, 4AD even reduced the beautiful *Lonely Is An Eyesore* booklet to a single sheet with the reverse side blank, but did make up for it by offering to send fans a full booklet in the mail.'

Hall. Not that Radio 2's older demographic would appreciate Charles Thompson's scream and Joe Santiago's sympatico guitar, meaning exposure on radio was relegated to those specialist indie-rock stations such as XFM.

It wasn't only in the UK the album struggled. *Death To The Pixies* limped to 180 in the US. Yet it was still 4AD's most popular album in four years. The fan base had become selective. As Lewis Jamieson had noted, it was now more about the artists than the label.

Behind the façade of normality, says Jamieson, 'it was the maddest, most eclectic release schedule, with two rosters running in parallel with nothing in common, a contemporary side for a younger audience and a left-field side targeted at a more mature audience'. And in the thick of it, he adds, 'was a battle for the soul of the label'.

22 1998

SMILE'S OK, A LAST GASP
(tad8001-4adm1)

Any struggle over the soul of 4AD was put on hold for the unified display, and sound, of the first release of 1998. *Anakin* was a compilation engineered to raise the label's profile after the end of the Warners deal; it neatly confirmed 4AD's rich and varied roster while stressing the downbeat and serene folk/country focus at the heart of its owner.

After the recycled nature of the *All Virgos Are Mad* compilation, Ivo was back in charge of *Anakin* and the eleven tracks were new and exclusive, and programmed to give goosebumps. 'I wasn't interested in a compilation to start with, but then I began to pick tracks to present the softer side of 4AD,' he says. 'For me, it felt like a last gasp, a left turn when everyone was expecting a right. The soft, acoustic nature of most of *Anakin* was not yet where everyone else was going.'

The album title wasn't Ivo's but the collective choice of 4AD's LA office, to honour Rich Holtzman's Siberian husky that had been named after Anakin Skywalker from *Star Wars*. Robin Hurley had found the dog wandering near the office: 'We couldn't find an owner and Anakin quickly owned me,' Holtzman recalls. Anakin joined him in the office every day and even attended in-store shows until she suddenly died of a massive heart attack. Vaughan Oliver was sent a commemorative photo of Anakin for the cover, which he re-shot, in a negative print, stuck to the back of his own head. 'I was appalled at the sentimentality,' he says. A psychotherapist might have seen it as a subconscious act of wrestling back control on behalf of the London office.

Even artists that didn't distil those particular roots provided acoustic ballads, starting with His Name Is Alive's 'Ain't No Lie' – a fabrication since the track was both written and played by Ida duo Dan Littleton and Elizabeth Mitchell. Scheer's second album trailer, 'Say What You Came To Say', showed what kind of exquisite ballads were being shouldered out of the way for the electric guitars. Album previews came from Kristin Hersh, Lisa Germano, Lisa Gerrard – with new collaborator Pieter Bourke – and The Hope Blister. Mojave 3 and GusGus provided demos: '"To Whom Should I Write" was Neil Halstead doing his Nick Drake,' says Ivo, while the Icelanders' 'Blue Mug' was a sequel of sorts to 'Is Jesus Your Pal?' written by the band's filmmaker Siggi Kjartansson and sung by Hafdís Huld. The different arrangements took *Anakin* away from a depiction of roots music and into the realm of an expertly flowing chillout mix.

But a new chapter was about to break. The most revealing aspect of *Anakin* was the unveiling of three new signings to 4AD. These potential harbingers of survival – two of which were based in London – had come from three different sources: Thievery Corporation via Rich Holtzman, Cuba via Lewis Jamieson, and starry smooth hound (lower case intentional), Ivo's first signing to 4AD since Tarnation.

Vinny Miller's alluring alias 'starry smooth hound' had been conjured up in a tearoom meeting with Robin Hurley and Colin Wallace. Growing up in south-west England, Miller's voice was an early gift; he'd been a young chorister at Salisbury cathedral but European ecclesiastical music had made way for Boney M's disco popsicle 'Ma Baker'. 'It was like an arrow through my head,' he says. His teenage years reverberated to The Police, The Beatles, Adam Ant and U2, but he had rejected rock and pop by his early twenties: 'It seemed empty to me. I wanted to hear things that would last beyond their moment of promotional saturation.'

Miller turned to the intense troubadours of folk-blues: Van Morrison, Roy Harper, Tim Buckley, Nick Drake, Fred Neil, Tim Rose, Ritchie Havens – an Ivo covers project in the making. By the time he'd recorded a demo, Miller had been shaped further: 'Drones and bird-song … and how [Talk Talk's] Mark Hollis sounded like a reed wind instrument, where word formation melts into pure tone, so you're unsure what you're listening to.'

Of all his influences, Miller's voice was closest to Tim Buckley's, though his raw, nervous energy put him close to Tim's son Jeff Buckley, especially the demos Jeff had been recording in preparation for his follow-up to his ecstatically received album debut *Grace*. Ivo, with his habitual preconceptions, had found it hard to accept Jeff because of his love for father Tim, but now Ivo had his own version, albeit at a much earlier stage of development.

Miller's lack of interest in contemporary music meant he hadn't heard of 4AD when a friend advised him to contact the label. 'If it hadn't been for 4AD, I'd have ducked out at that point,' Miller claims, in a premature admission of unsuitability for the business of music. 'It was typically tedious of me to record something and hate it the next day, and it happened too many times to mention.'

Miller first met Ivo when the latter was in London for The Hope Blister session. 'Ivo gave me a tape with Scott Walker's *Climate Of Hunter* and *Tilt* album tracks, and with songs by [Screaming Trees frontman] Mark Lanegan and Tim Buckley. He wanted to know which one of The Corrs I'd most like to shag – I said all of them at once. He said, "You know all these [artist/label] relationships have to end at some point?" After that, we kept in contact by phone, usually every couple of weeks.'

Ivo: 'Had I still lived in London, I think we would've made a good pairing. I enjoyed Vinny's playful intelligence and it was clear we shared some demons. I can't remember having The Corrs conversation but it is a valid question.'

Over distance, it remained an unusual relationship. 'When we did my contract, Ivo predicted we'd hate each other within eighteen months,' Miller recalls. 'That never happened, probably because we were rarely in the same place. But the bit of Ivo that I saw appeared at peace with himself. He was living quite a Zen existence away from the circus, surrounded by animals and continuing to explore art.'

Miller's *Anakin* cut, 'Dreamt U In A Dream', had been recorded at Protocol with producer Guy Fixsen, who had engineered records by Ultra Vivid Scene, The Breeders and The Wolfgang Press. Fixsen had also formed Too Pure signing Laika with Margaret Fiedler of Too Pure signing Moonshake. Only one other track ('Coco Crush', still unreleased) was recorded. 'I wish he'd carried on working with Guy, but Vinny was headed in a different direction,' says Ivo. 'He'd already started to be influenced by glitchy laptop stuff. His songs went through quite a few different versions or possibilities, much like Ultra Vivid Scene before him.'

Miller: 'Ivo ended up being really hands off. Occasionally, he'd get stuff from me but often half-formed and binned by the time it reached him. He wanted "prettiness" in music; not exclusively, but something that would meet that aesthetic. The easiest way for someone like me to achieve that would be through melody, not a squelchy sound off a sampler. Ivo cautioned me a couple of times about prospects for artists, like Tim Buckley ended up as a cab driver. But I never got any "give me the hits" nonsense.'

As Ivo's newest signing battled with demons before he'd even got started, 4AD's other new arrivals were employing samplers in a much more organised fashion. Thievery Corporation had come together after Rob Garza walked into Eighteenth Street Lounge, a bar in Washington, DC co-owned by Eric Hilton. On the phone from his home in San Francisco, the half-Mexican Garza recalls growing up listening to mariachi and soul, 'but also new wave and hardcore punk,' he adds. He'd known of 4AD through Pixies: 'I loved the fact Pixies had songs in Spanish but I also saw them live. They blew my mind and captured my imagination.'

An electronic music course at high school had sent Garza in another direction, as had the moment he walked into Eighteenth Street Lounge and heard 'March' by Brazilian bossa nova legend Antônio Carlos Jobim. 'Brazilian music wasn't commonly heard outside of South America,' says Garza. 'Eric and I started talking, and soon we'd started recording. We wanted to combine music from around the world with something futuristic and electronic.'

Dub, bossa nova, jazz and easy listening fed into three singles the duo released in 1996 on their own Eighteenth Street Lounge (ESL) Music label. 'The Foundation', 'Shaolin Satellite' and '2001 A Spliff Odyssey' also slotted into the debut album *Sounds From The Thievery Hi-Fi* that a friend in Washington had sent to Rich Holtzman, who commissioned the duo to remix GusGus' 'Polyesterday'.

Lewis Jamieson liked what he heard. 'They reminded me of how Massive Attack had projected itself on to the world, with a record label, club and lifestyle vibe. Their album took elements of dub and easy listening, a unique combination, and treated them in very delicate ways.' Jamieson's suggestion that 4AD license Thievery Corporation's album outside of North America got the green light. 'Eric and Rob didn't want to deal with majors, so why not talk to us?' says Jamieson. 'Rich was key in this as we had the same agenda. His job was to convince Ivo to go for it.'

'We saw 4AD going in a different direction with GusGus and we thought it was a great label,' says Garza. 'Bauhaus, Dead Can Dance, Cocteau Twins, Pixies of course, even M/A/R/R/S – it was a real artist's label. Nobody used the word "boutique" then but it was that kind of label, which was what mostly attracted us.'

Ivo didn't return the same level of appreciation but he took a pragmatic view. 'It just wasn't the kind of music I was interested in, but it was nice to give Rich the confidence that he could bring something to the label, and he got on well with them. But if my true feelings had been known, 4AD would only have been releasing three records a year. To say no to people, you need a degree of confidence in your own decision-making process and to make alternative suggestions, which I didn't have.'

After a deal was struck, Garza and Hilton flew to Europe and met the 4AD London office. 'You'd hear Ivo's name a lot, but we only met him the once,' says Garza. 'For someone that you associate with bringing this whole scene together, he was the opposite of what I expected, very clean-cut. I wasn't focused on the structure and politics behind that but I loved the label, its music and the legacy, and I think they did a great job for us. We were darlings of the UK press, and had great relationships with 4AD's label partners in Europe. People held 4AD in very high esteem.'

Lewis Jamieson's signing, Cuba, had an altogether more strained relationship with 4AD. For starters, Ivo says the Anglo-American duo of Christopher Andrews and Ashley Bates was his 'least favourite act on 4AD'. But Robin Hurley – who says that he had personally enjoyed Cuba – took the pragmatic view: 'It had a chance of being successful in the current British climate. And we were keen to have some success.'

Born in Toronto, Canada, Andrews now lives in Chicago where he works as an account director for advertising agency Leo Burnett, having been based in Amsterdam. He was born in Toronto but left Canada for London in 1994: 'I wanted to live somewhere different and to play music for a living. I wasn't a particular Anglophile but I'd grown up with British music.'

Andrews had met Bates, the former drummer of Home Counties shoegazers Chapterhouse, at a party. 'I knew the band, so we'd started chatting,' says Andrews. 'We didn't set out to form a band, but Ashley is technically fantastic and a great engineer, so armed with a sampler, some loops and guitars, we had the shell of a track after one day.'

Jamieson had been pursuing his A&R job at an alarming pace: 'I was in Iceland one minute and then the Miami dance conference, the South By Southwest festival in Austin, the College Music Journal festival in New York, Warners in Burbank, going to gigs all the time, flying the 4AD flag, and burning out quite heavily.' But the route to Cuba was easy; Andrews had recently married Rachel Goswell of Mojave 3 (they met at a Slowdive show in Toronto). Jamieson visited the couple, who lived around the corner from him, and heard the Cuba demo 'Fiery Cross'. 'He said he loved it and wanted to release it,' says Andrews.

Jamieson: 'Cuba was the biggest break from the 4AD tradition, because they were the most obviously English, and had attracted the traditional British kind of vibe through the music papers. But to me, it was marrying guitars and technology, like the best ideas of My Bloody Valentine and Primal Scream.'

Ashley Bates' experience at the RCA faux-indie offshoot Dedicated, which had mercilessly pushed Chapterhouse into writing more clear-cut singles and accepting a 'name' producer before being dropped for not delivering the requisite goods, had moved on to secure employment as a drum tutor and studio engineer. Cuba, and 4AD, provided the means for a new creative outlet, but he was still wary. 'I wasn't sure how serious to take the offer. I wondered what 4AD was after because I knew we were a strange signing for them. But 4AD had the best back catalogue around. I was an old goth, and my brother was a graphic designer, so we had more faith in and respect for 4AD than any other label.'

Andrews had no such qualms. 'From the outside, 4AD always seemed like a sanctuary, an island of art, very of itself, a very cool club. I knew if 4AD signed someone, it wouldn't be an obvious signing.'

It helped that Cuba was a self-reliant duo, as opposed to GusGus' expensively maintained collective, but Cuba (named after the birthplace of Andrews' mother) was about as obvious a signing as Scheer. At least Thievery Corporation shared some DNA with The Wolfgang Press and Colourbox, but 'Fiery Cross' occupied the same landscape as Chemical Brothers' thumping sampledelia that was known as Big Beat. Jamieson knew it, so he decided on a touch of subterfuge.

'I was amazed that 4AD was letting me do Thievery Corporation as they were so not a 4AD band,' Jamieson says. 'By Cuba, I'd long gone past caring. So I used some of the promotional budget and cut 500 [vinyl] white labels of "Hot Shit" that I sent to a few people without anyone else knowing, and [Radio 1 DJ] Steve Lamacq went for it. Before, we couldn't get a record away on radio to save our lives, so this was serious. I had to put my hands up – I'd done something bad, but this was the result. It was a confrontational approach but I'd lost Belle and Sebastian. I would have repaid the money if 4AD had asked, but we had such a desire to get something properly away that Robin and Simon said to carry on.'

Ivo had heard a demo, 'Havana': 'I felt it could be a good twelve-inch single, for the clubs,' he says, so there was some support. The track was included on *Anakin* but as a hidden last track, completely at odds with what came before it. Andrews recalls that Ivo's name had only cropped up at the end of contract negotiations. 'We knew he had to sign off on our deal, and we got the sense some arm-twisting went on. But Robin was president and this was a whole new world.'

As a trial by fire, Jamieson persuaded Cuba to make their live debut at the University of London Union on a 4AD showcase with Thievery Corporation and headliners GusGus. This one-nighter demonstrated the shift that had taken place since *All Virgos Are Mad*, but it retained a boutique feel across three diverse and creative exponents of electronic dance music.

In between the reissued GusGus single 'Polyesterday' and forthcoming Thievery Corporation and Cuba debuts, 4AD's old guard was still rallying, having found a way to work without unnecessary compromise. Kristin Hersh's decision to put Throwing Muses into hibernation had been tough – the sleeve dedication on her new album *Strange Angels* was to her husband, three sons and 'TM (1984–97)'. But having a solo outlet made it bearable. 'It was a relief,' she admits. 'People wanted pencil sketches instead of the bright colours I was used to painting with, but I no longer had to work with dollar-to-decibel or dollar-to-production-values. And Ivo treated the songs with even more deference than Muses records.'

Ivo's bond with Hersh had re-opened the channel to lending A&R support and friendship. 'We would allude to each other's struggles but we saw our time together as a respite from struggle,' says Hersh. 'We'd talk about the desert and music because that was all we cared about at the time. I'd run away to the desert even before he did, into forty acres of moonscape.'

After giving birth to her third son, Wyatt, Hersh and family had felt their now habitual wanderlust, renting out their east coast house and moving to a friend's plot in Pioneertown, California, a small town originally built in the 1940s as a Wild West film set near Joshua Tree

Monument Park. The location provided some refuge, just not enough. 'We learnt the vocabulary of the moon and coyotes and owls and cacti, but I'd tried to run away and it hadn't worked. My son that I'd lost custody of couldn't come with us and I found that umbilical cords only stretched so far.'

Hersh's problems only got worse as the lithium that she was taking for her bipolar disorder had deadened her creative senses. 'I felt I couldn't write anymore, so *Strange Angels* was a bunch of leftover songs. And I hadn't been able to listen to music for years. I was sleep-walking and I later toured the album in a half-arsed manner. Ivo was bemused but there was nothing he could do, or say.'

Ivo was also bemused by his credit on *Strange Angels*. Now Hersh was the one providing support and succour. 'Kristin was looking for my input when they were mixing the album in LA, to help make a track into a single. I made some suggestions, not heartfelt ones, and they peculiarly made me executive producer. It was so sweet that they were reaching out to me, to draw me back in, but I didn't need it, and I didn't do anything anyway. It was an odd combination of genuine friendship and a clinical misreading.'

Strange Angels lacked the undulating range and luminosity of *Hips And Makers*, and its fifteen songs were a lot if its songwriter didn't truly believe in them. But even Hersh's leftovers wove a persuasive spell, with her particularly urgent brand of gentleness, or gentle brand of urgency. 'Gazebo Tree' and 'Like You' – released as a limited edition single in time for her tour – were career highlights, and 'Home' was a fine album intro. And Hersh's creative energy and her love of music were both to return, on that supposed half-arsed tour, while out buying coffee.

Hersh: 'I could see music again, coming out of the speakers in 3D, and I remembered how I'd thrown my life away. Tears were streaming down my face. This old Indian guy, Leonard Crow Dog, was burning herbs over a guitar, and Billy told him, "My wife is crying about music, did you do this?" He said he was doing a musical blessing, and he must have hit me in the back! He had me play the guitar, and hoped the blessing would rub off on me.'

Lisa Gerrard had also been adjusting to a new way of life, without the safety net and collaborative spirit of Dead Can Dance and Brendan Perry, her foil for eighteen years. But she'd found another in Australian composer, multi-instrumentalist and engineer Pieter Bourke, who had played on Gerrard's solo album *The Mirror Pool* and in Dead Can Dance's *Spiritchaser* tour band. She invited Bourke to engineer and play percussion on a track that she had begun recording at home in Gippsland, which blossomed into a co-writing venture and the album *Duality*.

The album had the same blend of ethnic and medieval moods, but tracks such as 'Forest Veil' and 'Pilgrimage Of Lost Children' were sparser than previous Gerrard recordings, though it didn't deviate from her default shivery settings. 'Sacrifice', heavy on the choral and Balkan influences, and a more percussive 'Tempest' would be included in Gerrard and Bourke's 1999 soundtrack to *The Insider*, Michael Mann's follow-up to *Heat*; soundtracks would singularly occupy Gerrard's time for the next six years, giving her the chance to stay in Australia and yet embrace the wider world.

Brendan Perry, however, says he didn't feel neglected. 'I made a conscious decision not to work in film,' he says. 'To leave edits up to the production, to manipulate your ideas … It feels like a job as opposed to being true to my art.' Hearing this, Gerrard calmly responds: 'I'm brought in as an artist, to do what I make, not to do generic film scores.'

In Ireland, Perry had been working for years on a solo album, going through different permutations of arrangements that his perfectionist nature wouldn't let him finish.

The Hope Blister album *smile's ok* completed a trio of releases by 4AD's entrenched survivors, giving the core fan base a reason to stick around. The album title was another metaphor, as the surface image of coping with depression is often far from reality.

Each track on the *Anakin* compilation had an attached commentary on the sleeve: a lyric, information or a comment. Under the Hope Blister track 'Dagger' were the words: 'Is this the idiot bastard son of This Mortal Coil?' Well, yes and no. The album's cover versions drew on a well of loneliness similar to the Mortal Coil trinity. Louise Rutkowski was a clear link to the past. But there was no Pallas Citroen on the cover, just a blurry image that Ivo had photographed with an old, leaky Polaroid of a vase in his London flat. The starkness matched the reduced numbers under Ivo's direction and the monastic sound, stripped of extraneous detail.

'It [smile's ok] went against the grain of much modern music, and gladly so,' Ivo told me at the time. 'This record takes me on a journey to somewhere I want to go. I find very little music does that these days. I like the feeling of comfort and being at home within music. You know, like you're in safe hands. It's music for people who don't like to go out.'

Even if the core fan base swooned, The Hope Blister could never emulate the success of This Mortal Coil; the past was a foreign country, as Tanya Donelly and Kristin Hersh's solo albums were proof of. The UK's latest breakthrough band, for example, was The Verve; Radiohead had headlined Glastonbury in the wake of its masterpiece *OK Computer*. Epic rock, Britpop, Big Beat ... this was music to go out to. Multi-cultural trip-hop pioneers Massive Attack – whose 1997 single 'Teardrop' had been sung by guest vocalist Liz Fraser after Cocteau Twins had finally split up – was the kind of music that people wanted to stay in to. The first Labour government in nearly two decades brought a sense of optimism after the Conservative years. But just as with *Blood*, going against the grain was all the more reason for The Hope Blister.

'We wanted to do our best for Ivo,' says Colleen Maloney, 'but it was a very difficult record and we were very careful who we targeted in the press because it was risky to cast the net wide. It wasn't a trendy form of music.'

'A melancholic, yet oddly soothing record ... what fascinates is the uniformity of themes and treatments, creating the illusion that all the songs were written by the same person,' said *MOJO* magazine. But *NME*'s review read like an uninformed sneer: 'It's not a particularly good start, is it? That name. Lifted from the humourless depths of gothsville and no doubt intended to symbolise some kind of Yin and

Yang of joy and ultimate pain.' It continued in the same vein, raising the comparison of 'the deadly earnest neo-folk wibblings of Enya or Clannad'.

Ivo flew to London to do promotion. He talked to *The Independent* newspaper about being one of the few survivors from the independent label boom of the Eighties: 'It's only us, Beggars Banquet and Mute left now, I think. Someone did ask yesterday if it would be possible to start a label with £2,000 and yes, absolutely, that can still be done, but to start a label like this one, which would have some sort of consistent thread or identity, would cost a huge amount of money.'

Ivo added that he hoped to do more Hope Blister albums: 'Given that he owns the label they appear on, it seems a safe bet,' wrote journalist Andrew Mueller. But – understandably – nothing was mentioned by Ivo about depression, or the true state of 4AD. 'It was such a surreal experience,' Ivo recalls. 'I felt like a musician visiting a record company that didn't really know who I was or why I'd been signed.

'I started to get an idea of some of the concerns that certain artists had raised with me,' he says, 'to deal with an uninterested record company ... and I still owned half of it! To be fair, I know that The Hope Blister would not have been something Lewis, or anyone besides Chris Bigg, who always had such a genuine and heartfelt response to music, would've responded to had it been pulled out of the demo basket. Tim Hall had arranged an interview with a local London radio station and as I was being miced up, they were playing a great song that I'd not heard before. When it finished, and I was on air, I said, "That sounds just like the Pixies". It was Blur's "Song 2". That really showed how out of touch I was.'

Ivo was spot on about Lewis Jamieson, who admits that he would have let go those 4AD artists that 'commercially speaking, were ridiculous, like His Name Is Alive, or even The Hope Blister'. About This Mortal Coil he says, '[It] had been a moment in time, built around a label with a strong identity, which encapsulated the label vision, not just the guy who runs it but the artists on it. Now 4AD was just schizophrenic and it didn't fit. Ivo was this vague, shadowy figure, completely impenetrable, so it was like this weird, autonomous republic that couldn't shift itself from its anarchic ruler. But we had some great records and some great moments when we were doing something right.'

Ivo and Jamieson would at least have agreed on the brilliant, emerging Icelandic quartet Sigur Rós, whose mission to take the shoe-gazing's beautiful noise in a more classical direction – with a made-up language to match Elizabeth's Fraser – was still to be discovered outside of its own country. Jamieson was advantageously placed to approach them, but he says the idea of dealing with two Icelandic bands 'would have been unreasonable for my mental health'.

Jamieson thinks the likes of Sigur Rós, who quickly achieved global success, would have attracted bands of a similar magnitude. 'I'm sure a band such as [now hugely popular northern English band] Elbow, who had elements of Pink Floyd and Talk Talk, which might appeal to Ivo [he does indeed like Elbow], would have wanted to be on 4AD, because we'd embody a certain spirit that made up for the fact we were offering less money. But the major labels had marched into our stomping ground. I saw a queue of A&Rs at Elbow's show and no way could 4AD compete anymore. [Beggars Banquet dance offshoot] XL, for example, was higher up the list in a manager's mind than 4AD. No young British band would be attracted to 4AD because of The Paladins and Tarnation. In the late 1980s, Lush and Pale Saints were feeling validated by Pixies' label phoning them! But the cycle had turned.'

Things could maybe improve if Ivo could receive a Native American's blessing in a coffee shop, as Kristin Hersh had experienced, and so rediscover his passion for music. Or if he had an A&R accomplice who could help broaden and strengthen his vision, not oppose it – an empathic ear like Ed Horrox, the A&R contact for Beggars Banquet's newest subsidiary label. Mantra had primarily been created in 1995 by Beggars Banquet press officer John Empson to plug the gap between the other in-house labels; less rock than Beggars Banquet, less dance than XL, less artful than 4AD. When Ivo was in the London office, Simon Harper had suggested he talk to

Horrox, who gave him a copy of *Secret Name* by Low, the much-loved trio famed for its heartache brand of sadcore that Robin Hurley had tried to interest Ivo in two years earlier, with no luck. Geoff Travis had already licensed the album to his Rough Trade subsidiary Tugboat.

Ivo played the tape on the drive to Oundle to visit his mother. 'I've never fallen in love with an album so immediately,' he recalls. 'When I arrived, I immediately called Robin and we had to release it in America if the band didn't already have an outlet. I didn't know Low was signed to [US indie] Kranky and that Tugboat was part of Rough Trade. I was disappointed but extremely happy to discover that the connection to gorgeous music was still alive and kicking inside me. I had begun to wonder.'

Ivo was still a His Name Is Alive fan. Similarly, though he was disgruntled with 4AD's business practices, Warren Defever had enjoyed more creative freedom and support than he'd ever have experienced elsewhere. If he was as much out on a limb as The Hope Blister, Defever's presently enhanced blend of soul, funk, psychedelia and hard rock was, in theory, a sound for the times, a rich mutant brew of past and present that could slip in alongside 4AD's new dance faction. Stressing electronica, Motown and rockabilly influences, Defever and company arrived at *Ft. Lake*, as extraordinary in its own way as *Livonia* though the two locations couldn't be further apart.

Once His Name Is Alive could be compared to This Mortal Coil; now it was more a rocking Wolfgang Press. There were frequent echoes of Sly & The Family Stone's liquefied groove and 'Wish I Had A Wishing Ring' even raised the ghost of Jimi Hendrix (Defever had employed Steve King, who had produced legends of the calibre of Aretha Franklin and George Clinton, to add authentic finishing touches). Karin Oliver was still involved but Defever had promoted Lovetta Pippen from the vibrant gospel choir used on *Stars On ESP*. 'Can't Always Be Loved' was an eminently radio-friendly single with a pronounced Motown gait and a fast-cut promo video that captured HNIA's creative zip as the Brothers Quay had captured their former weirdness.

Of course, Defever could never lose his maverick touch, reflected in the tape edits and hairpin-bend changes that ensured *Ft. Lake* transcended retro but also put it out of reach of US radio. 'So few people got Warren at all,' says Ivo. 'He's the only musician I've worked with that brings Zappa to mind in his diversity, playfulness and originality.'

Colleen Maloney saw how His Name Is Alive was symptomatic of 4AD's conundrum. 'They were very much Ivo's love, and we were all extremely fond of His Name Is Alive in the office, but there was the realisation that the amount of money spent on records that didn't sell, and the artwork, just wasn't adding up.'

The clubby swish of *Sounds From The Thievery Hi-Fi* was much more likely to find a wider appreciation. 'Thievery Corporation was part of a diverse roster of bands that made the best of their particular type of music, with a strong visual sense,' says Colleen Maloney. '4AD was the world leader at signing bands like that, from Cocteau Twins to Throwing Muses and Pixies.'

The lead single '.38.45 (A Thievery Number)' was a foray into the modern jittery world of dubstep beats, and the second single 'Lebanese Blonde' had an inviting mix of trip-hop sitar, even if the promo video was as bland as any 4AD had been involved in. The ugly sentiment of the line, '*We come annihilate the bloodclot nation*' – using derogatory Jamaican patois for menstruation – was also new for 4AD. It felt especially disrespectful of all the women that had found freedom at 4AD, but this was a more callous age. 'They were a very good signing in terms of profile and sales and it ticked the boxes as an A&R is supposed to do – to attract other people to the label and give PRs things to talk about,' says Jamieson. 'In any case, the deals we struck were tiny. I never spent any money of note at 4AD.'

There was no doubt Garza and Hilton looked the part, and several guest singers (including Brazilian bossa nova singer Bebel Gilberto) helped spice up a mix that advertising agencies would doubtless appreciate. However 4AD's long-standing reputation had not been built on ticking boxes, but providing something that felt either groundbreaking or emotionally resonant. Maybe Garza and Hilton weren't trying – ultimately Thievery Corporation reflected, but could never transcend, the duo's influences. Portishead, for example, would have been a much more ideal accomplice for 4AD's transition into modernity.

Cuba was also guilty of lacking transcendence. But in callous commercial terms, the duo could snare both indie kids and rock fans – a wider net than the more select followers of Thievery Corporation's sophisticated groove. And the duo was based in London, not Iceland. It was another weighty irony that Ivo's least favourite 4AD act stood the best chance of salvaging a future, at least in the short term.

After releasing a second white label twelve-inch 'Fiery Cross', Cuba had recorded an album, on the cheap with a home studio and with Ashley Bates engineering and producing. 'Chris took the driving role,' says Bates. 'He was what I'd call "the vibesman". He got people excited. And he was a great guitarist.'

Andrews was also a confident motormouth in the established tradition of Oasis frontman Liam Gallagher, something that further isolated Cuba in 4AD-world. 'I think we are being reasonable in expecting to be the most critically successful band on 4AD since the Pixies,' he told *Music Week*'s online site Dotmusic. 'We want to be its most commercially successful. I think that's possible and I think 4AD believe that.'

Andrews was less of a natural singer, but luckily for him, the trend in British dance music, from Massive Attack to Chemical Brothers, was to deploy guest singers. At Lewis Jamieson's suggestion, Cuba had approached Shara Nelson, who had sung Massive Attack's iconic hits 'Safe From Harm' and 'Unfinished Sympathy'. She agreed to sing for Cuba too, as did the equally soulful Angie Brown and British rapper Michael Gifts, known as Mau, who had sung for Massive Attack's Bristol trip-hop peers Earthling.

Mau fronted 'Cross The Line', the first of three official twelve-inch Cuba singles released across the space of a few months. After the instrumental 'Urban Light', Mau returned for 'Havana'. 'The radio edit sucked all the power out,' says Andrews. 'I understood the decision, but we weren't a radio band.' But radio, and not clubs, was helping bands sell records and cross over, as GusGus knew. The only real complaint that could be upheld against 4AD was the bizarre timing of 'Havana', released in the mad rush up to Christmas rather than at the start of the new year.

Not that it seemed to matter. 'I felt "Havana" was my last throw of the dice,' says Jamieson. 'It got a lot of attention, but there was no finance or energy left at 4AD. Death In Vegas came along shortly after and became the coolest thing for a year, with shoegazy guitars and slight gothy overtones with a trip-hop feel. Sometimes it's not about who does it first.'

The pendulum swung back to the folkier side with a new Mojave 3 album, *Out Of Tune*. It's a shame that R.E.M. had beaten them to it, but *Out Of Time* would have been a much more suitable title, in its literal interpretation. Perhaps *Out Of Tune* was more honest in a self-deprecating don't-count-on-us manner.

The three were now five, after adding keyboardist Alan Forrester and ex-Chapterhouse guitarist Simon Rowe. Forrester's Hammond organ underlined Halstead's fondness for Sixties Bob Dylan/Band chord progressions on lead single 'Some Kind Of Angels' and 'Keep It All Hid', with Nick Drake's gently aching feel more audible on second lead single 'Who Do You Love' and the pedal steel winding through 'Baby's Coming Home'.

Both singles were among a handful of tracks engineered by Belle and Sebastian's trusted studio ally Tony Doogan, at Jamieson's suggestion, knowing that not only was Halstead a Belle and Sebastian fan but his demos needed sprucing up to give Mojave 3 more heft on record. But Halstead's commercial instinct only went so far; it had, after all, been three years since Mojave 3's first album, and while Belle and Sebastian frontman Stuart Murdoch had a jauntier pop side and a humorous outlook (no wonder Ivo didn't initially enjoy them), Mojave 3's own frontman was shy and retiring. The photo of surfers shot in Cornwall for the album cover showed where his priorities might lie.

'The songs tickle by, softly floating timelessly, tirelessly, and the vocals are like a pillow for your head as you listen, enraptured,' raved

Allmusic; Pitchfork's subsequent review suggested *Out Of Tune*, 'could very well be the first 4AD album to be fully embraced by both AAA [Adult Adult Alternative] radio stations and your mom'. Given the parlous state of play, this could only be a good thing.

Halstead's own, sarcastic view of *Out Of Tune* was how Mojave 3 had changed 'from slow country to mid-slow tempo country-rock'. A more palpable shift was Rachel Goswell's diminished vocal presence. On a press trip in 1996, her eardrum had burst midflight between LA and New York, which necessitated an emergency stop in Denver and a week's recovery before she could fly home. Goswell's subsequent panic attacks were diagnosed as post-traumatic stress disorder, and on the Shaving The Pavement tour, future husband Christopher Andrews had come along as carer and supporter. Goswell says Ivo had given her self-help manuals that addressed crisis and depression, and slowly she had returned to a point of normality, playing bass but only contributing harmonies to *Out Of Tune*.

Two weeks further into October, 4AD released Lisa Germano's new album *Slide*, which persisted in sombre ballads as fragile as the butterfly shown on the cover. The enigmatic sign-off in the album credits – 'thank you Dash, I think we're done now' – felt ominous. Warners had paid for the recording, and Germano admits the major had even allowed her to add two more songs despite already spending her budget. That had delayed *Slide*'s release, and by the time it was on sale, the licensing deal was over, and Robin Hurley had prepared Germano with the news that 4AD would let her go too if the album didn't outsell its predecessors.

Since *Slide* sounded like it was purpose-built alongside *smile's ok* for candlelit baths at 4am, it wasn't to be, and yet another artist that should have been a protected species at 4AD left the label. 'I was just glad to make a beautiful record,' Germano declares. 'I don't regret anything because it was a great relationship with 4AD. I just couldn't sell enough records to pay for them.'

4AD's meagre collective sales meant that Robin Hurley was forced to announce more cutbacks at 4AD's London office. 'That was a dark day,' says v23 designer Tim O'Donnell. 'Even though Robin was

English, it was this weird feeling of the boss flying in from this other office, and no one knowing if Ivo was involved anymore. Robin read out some numbers, like we'd all been in this bubble and hadn't considered the business side. He said something like, "We haven't had a successful record in the last eighteen months, they're each selling about 1,500 copies worldwide, but we're printing the sleeves in eight colours". It was a sudden wake-up call.'

Proof that the old order had irrevocably collapsed was Hurley telling v23 that 4AD could no longer afford their retainer and they'd have to go freelance. 'I thought, hold on a minute,' says Vaughan Oliver. 'Think back to 1994, when I was in the middle of the *This Rimy River* exhibition. 4AD had the new office in LA and I'd just been hired by a company there to do motion graphics and to direct adverts, the first being Microsoft that paid me £30,000 for six weeks' work. I thought my fucking boat has come in. And now I'm being told 4AD doesn't want me anymore, despite the enormous workload and daily deadlines.'

Oliver had also taken the twin blows of Ivo using v23's former assistant Paul McMenamin to design The Hope Blister's … *smile's ok* and the Tom Baril book. McMenamin was conveniently close to hand in LA, but Oliver knew there was another reason: 'Ivo told me, this way, he could get exactly what he wanted.'

Opting out of giving Oliver free rein, as all 4AD artists had been encouraged to do, was hypocritical on Ivo's side, but these were different times; as with This Mortal Coil and The Hope Blister, Ivo needed a safe and considerate collaboration. 'Vaughan and I were hurting each other by then,' he recalls. 'Can you imagine how I felt when I'd return to the UK office, by which time the speed of artwork was dictating when records would actually get released, to see the walls covered with Vaughan's freelance work? And I knew the [Baril] book wouldn't look the way it did with Vaughan. I had a pretty clear idea of how I wanted it to look, and Paul [McMenamin] was fantastic, alongside Robin Hurley, at monitoring every stage of the origination and printing process. Tom's book is one of the proudest achievements of my life.'

Oliver negotiated his severance from 4AD, and v23 moved into an office in Battersea, a mile away from Wandsworth. Sentimentality was not an Oliver trait, and Colleen Maloney recalls him assembling a bonfire of artwork in Alma Road's backyard. 'He was burning stuff, beautiful mock-ups of the artwork assembled in layers on boards that would have been precious to many,' she says. 'I tried to rescue some stuff but I had to give up, things were too far-gone. You might have thought it was cathartic for Vaughan, to get rid of the old before they moved, but there was a lot of anger there.'

An interview with Oliver in *Computer Arts* magazine talked of new artistic directions – adverts, book jackets, digital media, and new roles, including being Creative Director on a series of Sony Playstation adverts and directing the promo video for Pixies' 'Debaser'. On a presumably tight budget, Oliver cut between fuzzy live footage of the band, flashing typography and more interesting images, such as a woman in fetish gear with an e-collar. 'MTV liked it but I don't think [ITV's] *The Chart Show* liked all the noise and dirt,' Oliver said.

Oliver also claimed the three-man v23 team would remain intact, but O'Donnell decided not to continue working with Oliver and Chris Bigg. 'There might be a month when we'd only do two covers, and two *NME* ads,' he recalls. 'I love Vaughan, and he's brilliant, but he wasn't the world's best businessman. It had become less stable, and less fun. Paul in LA had got some high-profile accounts, and Vaughan thought Paul was trading on his name and reputation, and then suddenly there was more distrust of the third person, namely me, and I didn't feel respected. He'd had dozens of people saying that they'd work for Vaughan for free, so he was shocked when I went.'

One of v23's first commissions in its new office was a CD of 4AD tracks, which was to be cover-mounted on the November 1998 issue of the UK music monthly magazine *Uncut*. There were tracks by GusGus, Thievery Corporation and Cuba, yet it embodied the cold fact that as a popular cause, 4AD was dependent on the past with Pixies, Lush, This Mortal Coil, Dead Can Dance, Cocteau Twins, Colourbox and The Birthday Party all present. 4AD itself went back to the archives for new releases. *Pixies At The BBC* was a self-explanatory compilation of radio sessions that gave fans access to something rare rather than recycled; even rarer was Throwing Muses' double CD *In A Doghouse*, combining the band's debut album, *Chains Changed* EP, the pre-4AD demo tape *The Doghouse Cassette* and five songs written in 1983 but recorded in 1996 by the Muses trio.

Kristin Hersh fans were also treated to another solo album in one year, to launch 4AD's new mail order-only service. *Murder, Misery And Then Goodnight* was a collection of doomy Appalachian ballads that Hersh's father had played to her as a child before bedtime (something that arguably goes some way towards explaining her own fearless approach to songwriting). At no point did Hersh's commitment to her art waver. She couldn't do it any other way. And neither could Ivo.

Yet Hersh, Donelly and Defever, familiar faces all, couldn't collectively provide a secure future. Mojave 3 couldn't take the weight of any expectations. And what of The Amps? More to the point, what of The Breeders? In either incarnation, Kim Deal was the one 4AD artist missing from *Anakin* except in the liner notes: 'also recording: The Breeders'.

Deal had not released anything since The Amps' *Pacer* in 1995. The *Uncut* CD included The Breeders' 'Saints', already six years old. The band had even got back together, after a fashion. In 1996, Deal had decided The Amps' live set needed bolstering with Breeders songs, and so that audiences didn't get confused, she decided to resuscitate the band's name. 'It was ... fine,' demurs Josephine Wiggs. 'I've thought a lot about this, and I've concluded that The Breeders is whatever Kim is doing.'

Kelley Deal, meanwhile, had followed the path of rehab by staying on in St Paul, Minnesota: 'I didn't know anyone in Dayton who wasn't always shit-faced,' she says. With a less demanding schedule, she'd formed a new band, The Kelley Deal 6000, and recorded two albums, 1996's *Go To The Sugar Altar* and 1997's *Boom! Boom! Boom!*, both similar in feel to Kim's *modus operandi*. In 1997, Breeders bassist Josephine Wiggs says Kim had called to ask if she wanted in on a new Breeders album, but knowing that drugs might still be in the equation, Wiggs politely declined.

Kim had rehired *Last Splash* co-producer Mark Freegard to record a new album with the former Amps, plus Kelley when the timing was right. Kim not only had an advance for the new record, but a considerable amount of royalties from the sampling of *Last Splash* cut 'S.O.S.' by The Prodigy for the British electronic band's global smash single 'Firestarter'. 'Even after seven weeks, and a studio cost of two thousand dollars a day, we had nothing to hear,' says Freegard. 'Kim got totally lost. She was taking substances and not wanting to go to bed, but she wouldn't let the other musicians play. I had to give up on her.'

Drummer Jim Macpherson also bailed. 'Kim had changed,' he agrees. 'The band had a totally different feel, and I was drinking and smoking with Nate and Luis. And I felt I wasn't wanted. I also had two small children.'

On the subject of drugs, Kim simply says, 'Pot, opiates and beer, I still love them all. I just don't do them anymore.' At the time, it turned her search for a sound that was only in her head into a purist obsession. 'Digital production had burned through recording studios like crack,' she recalls. 'Everyone was densely layering everything, making keyboards sound like guitars, and I'm so reactive. I could have put a hundred melodies on top but for me it's more about drums and clean guitar. I worked really hard to keep it that hard and basic and people said it sounded unfinished! I was obviously doing the wrong thing.'

By 1998, she decided to jack it in and go AWOL in New York. 'It was a lost year, and a lot of fun,' she says, unrepentant. 'I'd been touring consistently since 1987. So what was the worst that could happen? I finally met some guys in LA and moved out there, and I learnt to play drums, so it wasn't wasted time.'

Everyone was deploying their best coping mechanism to deal with the changes that had swept through the industry. Ivo would have empathised with Neil Halstead finding peace in reclusion and a new obsession, though Ivo was not at the beach, among the waves, but still dreaming of a desert. He had looked, unsuccessfully, for the right plot of land on which to build a house, but he needed finance for when it would happen.

In the summer, he and Martin Mills had discussed a way forward. 'It was the what-ifs,' Ivo says. 'The options were carrying on, which meant the likelihood of more layoffs and cutbacks, or shutting the whole thing down to a one-office operation back in the UK as effectively a catalogue label, or Martin buying me out. I knew that Martin wasn't in a position to at that time but we both agreed that, should that become my preference, he'd try and find a way. We agreed to carry on thinking.'

In the meantime, 4AD was left drifting, much like the helpless narrator of 'Song To The Siren', lying lovelorn on the rocks.

23 1999

EVERYTHING MUST GO
(bad9001-4adm2)

Chris Bigg recalls an email from Ivo in mid-1999 that included a confession: 'We're trying to play a game we're not equipped to play.'

None of Ivo, Robin Hurley and Simon Harper can remember the exact date in 1999 that the trio convened in Twentynine Palms in California, just outside the Joshua Tree National Park. 'Ivo said that we needed to talk about the future of the label, and his future in it, and what Robin and I both wanted, with or without him,' recalls Simon Harper. 'It was only on the second night that he said he wanted out. It wasn't a shock. I didn't fall off the sun lounger. The writing was on the wall.'

'I only fully decided that I wanted to leave the company on that night in Joshua Tree,' Ivo recalls. 'Simon saying he wanted to move to New York, for family reasons, and that he'd no longer be part of 4AD London helped me express what I'd been scared to admit, even to myself, for years. The next morning, I told Robin and Simon that I wanted out.'

'It was clear for a long time that Ivo was desperate to get out, that he was totally disconnected from it all,' says Martin Mills. 'He was pretty clear he wanted the money to live on for the rest of his life, and

559

fair enough, who wouldn't? But he valued the company at a level that we couldn't afford.'

Beggars Banquet was in a particularly prosperous state following its dance-label offspring XL's signing of The Prodigy. The band's 1996 album *The Fat Of The Land* had entered the American and UK charts at number 1 on the back of the 'Firestarter' single and had eventually topped charts in twenty-six countries. But Mills was not in the habit of funding one label off the back of another (despite being forced to borrow funds from 4AD to defeat the court case against Nick Austin in 1989/1990). So an agreement had been shelved, and Ivo had carried on.

There was still hope that GusGus could make good on their investment, after the expensive videos, the top-drawer DJ remixes (including Carl Craig, Amon Tobin and DJ Vadim) and another media trip to Iceland for the band's second album *This Is Normal*. 'A huge amount of money was being spent on GusGus because we believed they would break,' says Colleen Maloney.

But there was a marked difference between the extravagant booklet that accompanied *Polydistortion* and the standard bland CD jewel case that housed *This Is Normal*. The bulk of GusGus' new tracks, largely written between Daníel Ágúst and Siggi Kjartansson, stood every chance of succeeding. The album had nothing as definable as Big Beat, trip hop or factory-produced pop – just the troupe's usual progressive and inventive brand of Nordic soul, equal parts melody, beats and bleeps. Yet factions within GusGus blamed 4AD for bullying them into a less adventurous and atmospheric record.

'We first sent a demo of "Teenage Sensation" and 4AD said, "What are you trying to do, music for space scientists?"' recalls Biggi Veira. 'It was too weird and electronic for them, so we changed it to what you hear on the album. *This Is Normal* wasn't interesting enough and a lot of older fans would have hated it. We hadn't progressed from *Polydistortion*, which combined different people and backgrounds without any ambition besides having fun. After signing to 4AD and touring, the opinions and desires of other members didn't sync with mine, which were more electronic than pop. We knew GusGus would split after *This Is Normal*.'

If *This Is Normal* was in some way unadventurous, it was still a sublime collection of tracks. Sung breathily by Hafdís Huld, 'Teenage Sensation' was about as definable as GusGus got, with a loping trip-hop feel. 'Bambi' had the strings-lined dreaminess of classic 4AD, 'Ladyshave' was 4AD's best dance hit-in-waiting since The Wolfgang Press's 'A Girl Like You', complete with gospel-tinged backing vocals. 'I was convinced "Ladyshave" would be an enormous hit,' says Ivo (Colleen Maloney claims the track paved the way for American disco campers Scissor Sisters). Being ahead of your time is only rewarding in posterity: at the time, the UK chart placing of 64 – much higher than 'Believe' but still lower than 'Polyesterday' – was a grave disappointment for the label.

A second single was released before the album followed six weeks later. The smoother techno pulse of 'Starlovers' reached 62. *This Is Normal* only scraped the UK top 100 at 94. Wasn't 4AD an albums label? It seemed GusGus' fan base was more of a discerning club crowd that didn't care much about albums on top of singles. 'VIP', the third single drawn from the album, reached 86 to conclude another dismaying sales campaign. 'GusGus had to get on Radio 1 to break in the UK,' says Maloney, 'and we weren't like a major label that goes in every week plugging bands that can make the playlist.'

Biggi Veira thinks 4AD should share the responsibility for the failure. 'Our manager Baldur said "Ladyshave" had sold out in its first week of release, and 4AD didn't press enough copies to get it into the top 40. I also think 4AD was putting too much faith in too few active acts. The older artists, for example Kim Deal, had nothing going on at the time. 4AD should have had lots of cool artists with low recording costs, not loads but enough releases to have things going on. The crowd keeps buying everything from the label, and there is also the chance that some albums will sell more. And maybe 4AD should have been more careful on what they spent on GusGus!'

4AD returned once again to its back catalogue. Compiled for the American market, *Always Stay Sweet* drew from those His Name Is Alive records that had gone out of print. *Soundpool* made Dif Juz music finally available on CD, combining *Huremics* and *Vibrating Air* tracks with *Lonely Is An Eyesore*'s 'No Motion'. The Birthday Party's *Live 1981–82* was more mercenary since it contained the whole 1981 Venue show (bar, this time, the cover of The Stooges' 'Loose') that the band had previously reckoned wasn't good enough to release in full.

Ivo was at least involved in one half of Red House Painters' *Retrospective* double CD compilation of the band's 4AD years. His exacting attitude was illustrated by his decision to exclude 'Take Me Out', his all-time favourite 4AD track. 'I couldn't get it to fit the running order. Leaving it off spoke to something bigger and more important about the record, and I'm proud of that.'

Mark Kozelek sequenced the second CD, subtitled *Demos, Outtakes, Live (1989–1995)*. He recalls that he and Ivo had reconnected in a mastering suite where *Retrospective* was being cut, followed by dinner. 'He seemed happier than I'd ever seen him,' Kozelek recalls.

This might have been because Martin Mills and Ivo had finally agreed a sale price for 4AD: 'a seven-figure sum,' says Mills. 'We didn't negotiate,' says Ivo. 'I didn't hire a lawyer. We just did it. Martin had once again just been there for me.'

Ivo had first approached Marc Geiger about buying out his 50 per cent share of 4AD. Geiger had recently left American Recordings in 1996 to launch ARTISTdirect, one of the first companies to recognise the internet as the future of the music industry: alongside a booking agency and start-up record label (in partnership with major label RCA-BMG), ARTISTdirect had an e-commerce division, which was establishing individual 'stores' to create a business and information link between artist and fan – the Kristin Hersh model writ (very) large. But Ivo's offer came in just as ARTISTdirect was about to become a public company, and the stock market crashed.

'I desperately wanted to do it,' says Geiger. 'But I ended up losing all my stock and couldn't make it happen, or afford it. I was *very* bummed.'

The architect of the successful arrangement turned out to be former 4AD staffer Rich Holtzman. Mindful of 4AD's problems and what limited career opportunities lay ahead, Holtzman had jumped before he could be pushed and joined Atomic Pop as label and marketing manager. The LA-based company was at the forefront of the new digital era, building up a portfolio of rights to a wealth of music from numerous independent labels: in PR speak, 'a compelling platform to promote, market, and distribute their music digitally directly to consumers'.

The offer to license music from Beggars Banquet and its associated labels was enough to fund buying Ivo's share of 4AD. 'It was a short licensing deal but a big wad of cash,' says Holtzman. 'Digital rights weren't going to mean that much for a few years to come, and by then Martin would get the rights back. But it was the right deal to strike.'*

Determined to arrest 4AD's financial drain, Mills wanted to quickly announce the sale and to initiate another round of staff redundancies. The decision was taken for Robin Hurley to fly over to Alma Road and break the news, face to face.

In the meantime, Kristin Hersh's new single 'Echo' was released in June. The sultry electric piano underpinning each verse gave way to the gritty Muses-lite rock for the chorus and signified a change of approach: its parent album, *Sky Motel*, was Hersh's first part-electric solo album. There were drums on six tracks (ex-Muse David Narcizo played on two). Hersh had not just relocated her mojo but the family had relocated to New England, though the new album had again been recorded in New Orleans with her trusted friend and engineer Trina Shoemaker. The face on the back cover wore an unconditionally happy smile, as if the burdens of the past had again been lifted. But when the photograph was taken, Hersh hadn't known that Ivo, her friend and long-term supporter, would have to leave her behind.

Sky Motel was released on the Monday following the annual Glastonbury festival weekend, where GusGus had been playing. The 4AD London office had attended en masse. 'Martin said, "Let's not do

---

* The dotcom boom and crash of the late Nineties and early Noughties meant that Atomic Pop's IPO (Initial Public Offering) to issue shares never took place, and the day that the Atomic Pop label's first artist (Slum Village) made the Billboard Top 100, its staff were let go. 'Martin, as everyone knows, is a pretty tough negotiator and he got Atomic Pop to agree to a clause that allowed the rights to revert to 4AD should their company go bust,' says Ivo. 'That's exactly what happened! Luck of the devil, that man.'

it now, let's do it after the staff have had their fun",' says Robin Hurley, 'and GusGus was one band that the office all believed in. But it fucked me up, having to return to Alma Road but not being able to tell them [about the sale and redundancies] until after Glastonbury. I remember trudging up that hill on the Monday, and a calmness coming over me, because it was inevitable, and the right thing to do for the company.'

'The way it all ended was perverse in the extreme,' says A&R man Lewis Jamieson. 'GusGus were second headliners on the dance stage, and they played a great set to eight thousand people, and it felt like it was finally going to happen, with the clubs going mad for "VIP". We came back into the office after the weekend, where Robin was sitting, saying he needed to talk to us all. Colleen disappeared for an early lunch and the rest of us were told that we were being let go, immediately, because the label was out of money. It felt very savage and I felt betrayed. But that's the music industry. I've seen it happen to plenty of people since, at big and small labels.'

Maloney had disappeared early as she was to be the only staff member retained by 4AD's new outright owner, Martin Mills. 'There were no guarantees to start with,' she says. 'So I went clothes shopping and bought an interview outfit, just in case. It was a very tough, emotional time. I was offered a job by Rough Trade but Martin asked me to stay and become head of press for the whole of Beggars Banquet, and I thought at least the bands would know someone if I stayed. It wasn't the easiest place to work as people so identified with Ivo, and he wasn't there. We just had to get on with it.'

There was a one-month lull before Cuba's album *Leap Of Faith* was released, a spectacularly ironic title given that, as Jamieson says, '4AD was in no state to promote it by then'.

4AD was in no state to design it either. *Leap Of Faith* was the first sleeve since Vaughan Oliver's arrival not to be even laid out by v23, and the simplistic band logo, jazzed up with spotlight effects, showed what one-dimensional blandness could look like without a unique overview by a visionary designer. Cuba's next single 'Black Island' limped out, with the artwork in complete contrast to the euphoric sound.

Fortunately, Ivo had managed to ensure that there was still time to leave his imprint by agreeing to release a record by David Narcizo. With his wife Misi, the former Throwing Muses drummer was running his graphic design company, Lakuna, Inc, but had also been recording kaleidoscopic instrumentals, from ambient to loops-based rhythm created from samples of Fifties and Sixties records. 'I was attracted to the idea of making a sound that has bits of past and present stuck to it in a truly random fashion,' Narcizo told Jeff Keibel.

Under the name Lakuna (the Sri Lankan word for 'symbol'), Narcizo released the single 'So Happy', followed by the album *Castle Of Crime*. With former Belly drummer Tom Gorman, Kristin Hersh and Bernard Georges among the guests, the record resembled a final reunion of some of Ivo's most cherished 4AD contacts, given Throwing Muses had been his all-important entry into the country he had since made his home, and hopefully for good. But Ivo wasn't home and dry yet. 'Everyone was keen to support David because he's such a lovely bloke,' he recalls. 'He was reaching out to me, looking for input, but I had nothing to give. I couldn't feel it … or anything, still. That was what was so ultimately depressing.'

Another solo project that had finally come to fruition, with very bad timing, was Brendan Perry's album. *Eye Of The Hunter* had been in the works for six years, since his *13 Year Itch* debut solo show, until he had finally considered it finished and handed it over, with a release date of October. That meant it was to fall in the period between Ivo's departure and the arrival of a potential replacement.

Perry's album eschewed the songs that he'd unveiled on Dead Can Dance's live album *Toward The Within*,* though he did include another Tim Buckley cover, 'I Must Have Been Blind'. Although Scott Walker's measured gravity was still part of Perry's DNA, the album's eight ballads included a newfound falsetto inspired by his Tim Buckley covers. 'When I moved to Ireland, I found a big folk scene, and I started using Buckley's songs as a template to develop my own

---

* 'Sloth' had been performed on stage with Dead Can Dance, and a 1993 radio session from 1993 was released on the box set *Dead Can Dance (1981–1998)*.

acoustic guitar technique and the range of my voice, from high to low, which helped bring it out,' says Perry. 'It was a real transition for me.'

The constant re-working of tracks, occasionally daubed in pedal steel guitar or strings, was Ivo's given reason for why he felt slightly disappointed in *Eye Of The Hunter*. 'I didn't hear enough of the human, organic feel that Brendan's songs have in concert. But his singing was absolutely stunning. I'm still confused as to why singers with half his talent are twice as successful.'

It would have been fitting had Perry provided the end of a tumultuous year, decade and even a lifetime of Ivo's steering of 4AD. Perry had been a 4AD artist for fifteen years, making decisions based on intuition not on any concept of market share, just as Kristin Hersh had, and as Ivo preferred. Perry's former foil, Lisa Gerrard, would have been an equally perfect way for Ivo to bow out, except that her and Pieter Bourke's soundtrack for *The Insider* was released in 1999 on Sony Records, not 4AD. 'It was still a big deal, the first soundtrack to a big movie done by a 4AD artist,' says Ivo.

As it was, with one last resounding note of irony, a Cuba single closed up shop. 'Starshine' was to fare no better than 'Black Island' and Christopher Andrews' boast to Dotmusic that Cuba had the potential to emulate Pixies as 4AD's biggest band felt horribly premature. 'We had swagger, and we really thought we had something,' Andrews recalls. 'I still think we could have been a really big band, but the stars have to align.'

In that same Dotmusic feature, Lewis Jamieson had been quoted as saying, 'The ethos at 4AD is that if you sign a band or a musical project and you value it, it should have the legs and the ideas to develop over time.' The ethos was already out of date, and 4AD cut Cuba loose after contract negotiations for a second album stalled. Rather than claim they were misled by the non-declaration of 4AD's porous finances, Ashley Bates and Andrews both shoulder responsibility. The contract negotiations, Bates says, had been fundamentally flawed: '4AD were cutting their losses, but it didn't help that our management were asking for more money than we'd originally signed for.'

'I was shell-shocked when Lewis said 4AD was pulling out, but I have to take some blame myself,' Andrews continues. 'We were negotiating too hard for an advance that included a reasonable share of licensing deals, and tour support. It was a real shame because I genuinely think we'd have hit our stride on the next album. Other labels were calling us too, but when we didn't re-sign with 4AD, our publishing deal wasn't renewed either, and the interest dried up. Labels easily move on to the next thing, and we lost momentum. Things stagnated and I decided to go off travelling. But I still think of 4AD as music lovers running a business that was more than a record business.'*

Both Tarnation and Scheer had already been informed that 4AD was not going to continue the relationship. Tarnation had only signed a two-album deal, and without supporters at the label, it didn't make sense to continue. Singer Paula Frazer immediately saw what would happen without 4AD's protection. 'Reprise offered to put out an album if I went with a country Nashville sound and a producer of their choosing. But I said no. I'd heard enough horror stories about that kind of set-up.'

Scheer had recorded a second album, but they'd also lost key support with Colin Wallace's departure, and it was clear that 4AD didn't know what to do with them. 'The writing was on the wall,' says singer Audrey Gallagher. 'No one fought on either side.' In any case, Gallagher and guitarist-boyfriend Neal Calderwood wanted a change, and veered off into the realm of dance music, bearing no grudge. 'Compared to our experiences since, 4AD was a caring label that wasn't just out to make money,' says Calderwood. 'They did have genuine belief in the music and the bands. We just joined at the wrong time.'

It would have been the most poignant sign-off of all had Ivo been the instigator of the final release under his stewardship. But *Underarms*, a Hope Blister album of instrumental out-takes, had been

---

* The experience was enough for even a 'vibesman' such as Christopher Andrews to get disillusioned, and he became yet another signing to abandon music after his relationship with 4AD disintegrated, switching his swagger to the advertising industry.

released in April, the second in 4AD's mail order operation, and the last. 'There was a lack of belief, or leadership, particularly out of the UK office,' says Robin Hurley.

As was Ivo's perverse way, in a fuck-you-tiger manner, the inspiration for the album title was a voicemail message left by the wife of the album's Swedish studio engineer. A dominatrix (according to Ivo) calling herself Sheena Bizarre had called the studio and left details complaining about her journey into work. 'She had been standing there next to people with stinking underarms,' Ivo recalls. It was both a very strange title and association for the seven dark, dreamy neo-classical instrumentals, part strings and part ambient drone, but it was a fitting conclusion to Ivo's recorded output, a textural sound-scape of restless, withdrawn beauty, just for its own sake.*

Mission accomplished, money in the bank, Ivo returned to his beloved dogs that he and Brandi were still regularly fostering from the animal shelter. Walks, house training and finding new homes for them took priority over trying to find musicians and singers a safe space in which to be themselves.

News of 4AD's new structure under Martin Mills was only publically announced in November, five months after the staff had been told. '4AD HQ returns to London,' ran the headline in *Music Week*.

'4AD has a profile, reputation and image which I hope will be enhanced,' said Mills. 'I hope 4AD in the future will be more so and better. The spirit of 4AD will live on.'

While a large part of the world was wondering if the end of the millennium would end in Armageddon, or at least a technology melt-down that would redefine life, Ivo saw it as a chance to begin again for the better. 'I felt relaxed and off the hook, and no longer guilty about

---

* Ivo had a huge boost when working on *Underarms*. 'The track "White On White" was recorded and mixed the very last day at Battery in New York,' he explains. 'Originally it was called "Dali Herzog" but I sent it off to Bauhaus, who were just about to commence their first reunion tour, with a suggestion that they use it as their intro music on the assumption they would be kicking off live shows with "Double Dare". They were and, much to my delight and surprise, they used it throughout the tour. I also gave the track to my then neighbour Harold Budd, who said that he was jealous and wished he had written it. Can you *imagine* how I felt?'

not being available to people whose future depended on me,' he says today. Ivo had finally found the right plot of land outside Santa Fe on which to build a sanctuary, to clean up, to calm his tempestuous mind, to heal. He had no clue as to the future; neither did the record label he was leaving behind.

In 1998, when he was still living in LA, Ivo had been contemplating a move to the desert while considering the tracks to be covered for The Hope Blister project. He decided against 'At Last I Am Free' by American R&B legends Chic, which Robert Wyatt had made his own with a cover in 1982. A second discarded idea was 'Place Of My Own' by Pink Floyd's progressive rock contemporaries Caravan. Ivo thinks the lyric could have been written for him today.

'Yesterday's face is not the one I choose to see/ Nor is the face of someone who gets much too close to me/ I've got this place of my own where I can go when I feel I'm coming down.'

The year 2000: Forward!

24

FULL OF DUST AND GUITARS

I'm full of dust and guitars. The only work I've done the last two years
is interviews. I'm very good at it.

(Syd Barrett, 1971)

'We're at the foot of the future and it's kicking us up the past'
('Don't Even Know Which Day It Is' – Edgar Broughton Band)

If the spirit of 4AD was to live on, as Martin Mills had suggested, it
would have to do so not just without Ivo but without trusted lieuten-
ants Simon Harper and Robin Hurley. The latter had been offered the
chance to run 4AD from Beggars' New York base, but he didn't want
to move back to the east coast, and he didn't feel it was a viable option.
'I realised that I would really miss Ivo and I had no confidence that
4AD would thrive without him.'

Like Ivo, Hurley believes that 4AD should have changed
tack, to survive and even thrive – as a back catalogue operation.
He suggests Ivo could have made that a condition of the sale:
'The purchase price from Martin wouldn't have been noticeably
lower.'

Mills knew that particular course of action would have been financially prudent. 'We needed to generate an income from 4AD, and the easiest way over a period of time would have been to run it as a museum piece, knowing 4AD was Ivo, and it could never be the same again. But that would have been a waste. There was something great there that we couldn't just give up on. I wanted to reinvent 4AD in Ivo's image, a label that he would continue to be proud of. I don't know if we succeeded, but we tried.'

With Simon Harper making his move to the USA, Mills needed to find someone to head the label.* Just as 4AD's A&R team after Ivo's move to America had been plucked from the warehouse, Mills looked within the company rather than bringing in an outsider. Chris Sharp had joined Beggars Banquet's press department in 1995, progressing to head both Beggars and XL press operations after successful high-profile campaigns including The Prodigy. 'It was an incredible opportunity,' says Sharp. Given his incisive business brain, communication skills and good taste, he was a capable choice. Responsibilities were to be shared with new head of A&R Ed Horrox, now that Beggars Banquet's subsidiary label Mantra had been shut down.

Sharp's first task was to examine 4AD's existing contracts and accounts, and to visit the relevant artists to discuss the future. He made contact with Kim Deal, Warren Defever, Tanya Donelly, Kristin Hersh, Brendan Perry, Lisa Gerrard, Mojave 3, GusGus, The Thievery Corporation and Vinny Miller – not a bad roster to inherit.

Sharp was confronted with mixed reactions to Ivo's departure. 'Ivo didn't tell me he was leaving, I heard it from Brendan,' says Lisa Gerrard. 'I was devastated. I had tried calling Ivo a few times in the

---

* Simon Harper originally took a role as a consultant for Beggars Banquet in New York, but in 2001 he left the company to follow his ex-wife and son to North Carolina, where he worked as a consultant for the Haw River-based independent label Yep Roc. Harper now lives in Hillsborough, and works as general manager at Bud Matthews Inc, a residential building and service company in Chapel Hill. 'As a result, I now enjoy music a lot more,' he says. Robin Hurley joined Atomic Pop/Artists Direct, but the dotcom boom-and-bust of the early Noughties saw him out of a job after nine months, 'so,' he says, 'maybe I should have taken the 4AD job!' After working for Warners-owned reissue specialists Rhino for a decade, Hurley now runs his own consultancy business in Los Angeles.

Nineties, but Brandi began to ask why I was calling – she felt I was putting him under pressure, and so I'd stopped.'

Sharp says Hersh and Donelly appreciated the fact that someone was now offering a sense of direction. Warren Defever was more suspicious, adding: 'His view was that His Name Is Alive had been releasing records with diminishing returns, so could I still pursue my vision to make R&B records? And did anyone at 4AD truly care?' Thievery Corporation's Eric Hilton was the toughest negotiator: 'He wanted 4AD to drop them so he could make lots of money if they could re-sell the overseas rights to a second album,' says Sharp. 'But we wanted to keep them.'

There was just one person Sharp couldn't reach: 'Kim Deal was off the radar. She was in the thick of her drink and drugs period, but she popped up a year later.'

Vinny Miller's case was even more complicated. As starry smooth hound, he'd received an advance for an album that remained unfinished, three years on. In Sharp's mind, 'Ivo had given Vinny the spiel, that he was a genius, and that he was a rough diamond that Ivo could polish. But he never did, which left Vinny in limbo. Ivo's hands-off approach had left a few people potentially unprotected.'

Sharp was as obsessed with music as Ed Horrox, and the connection that Horrox had made with Ivo regarding Low showed the potential for a continuity of Ivo's original spirit. 'I was aware of this label that had been as great as any other, and incredibly attractive,' says Horrox. 'It was a case of just trying to sign the things that you love, or that you see as important. I loved how key records on 4AD went their own way.'

As a teenager during, he says, 'one blissful summer', Horrox had been entrusted the family house on his own for the first time – the soundtrack to this time was dominated by This Mortal Coil, Cocteau Twins and Le Voix Bulgares. Horrox's own path shows how the times had changed, as he dived deep into club music, from house to Madchester. He'd tried, and failed, to forge a career as a jobbing musician but at least this provided common ground with the artists that he was trying to sign as an A&R man.

In 1993, Horrox joined Island as an A&R scout, moving to London Records and then Mantra, where his more imaginative and eclectic tastes could prosper. There, he signed The Delgados (pensive, orchestrated rock), Six By Seven (expansive rock) and Gorky's Zygotic Mynci (wistful, folky psychedelia; Ivo had once been keen on the Welshmen). He couldn't sign Low, but he had turned Ivo on to their album *Secret Name*. 'Ivo called to say the album had brought him to tears, and why weren't people sending him this kind of stuff?' Horrox recalls. 'It was a nice little encounter, but we didn't speak again until I was at 4AD.'

Martin Mills was again to take a hands-off approach. He says he hadn't understood Colin Wallace and Lewis Jamieson's promotions to A&R, or Scheer's signing, but then he admits he didn't get Pixies' *Come On Pilgrim* either. 'But I know Robin and Simon managed things to the best of their ability. And it wasn't my role to second-guess their A&R.'

So could Sharp and Horrox rebuild 4AD by bringing in new artists to match 4AD's original ethos, and also inspire those remaining artists that had initially helped create it? To begin with, nothing appeared to have changed on the surface. 4AD in the twenty-first century began with Kristin Hersh's single 'A Cleaner Light' taken from *Sky Motel*. The reserved optimism sounded perfect for Ivo: *'I was trying to skip out on this high … but in a cleaner light, it's OK.'* Three live versions of Throwing Muses classics added continuity with the past.

A new album, *GusGus vs. T-World*, did much the same. It was a devious title as the tracks featured songs from remaining members Biggi Veira and Herb Legowitz recorded in their former T-World days. This explained the album's series of techno instrumentals, with just seven tracks, the closing 'Esja' at 11 minutes long. And that was GusGus out of the picture.

Mojave 3 were content to stay, and released its third album *Excuses For Travellers*: song titles such as 'Bringin' Me Home' and 'Got My Sunshine' expressed the simple sentiments and melodies, but Vaughan Oliver would most probably have refused to use the primitive and child-like drawing that ended up on the cover. The absence of v23's visual flair was the most obvious difference between the old and new 4AD, without even a surface beauty to keep the doubters at bay.

After a second Thievery Corporation album, *The Mirror Conspiracy*, Rob Garza and Eric Hilton were to follow GusGus. On 4AD's side, the album suggested a new artful and budget-conscious outlook. The lead single, titled 'Sound File 001', was released only on ten-inch vinyl, fronted by a remix of the album track 'Focus On Sight'. The following ten-inch single 'Sound File 002' was led by the album track 'Shadows Of Ourselves'. Both releases had inexpensive videos, and there were no other remixes. With far fewer staff members and less overheads, there was less anxiety over bringing in money.

4AD's first new signing since starry smooth hound was a sign of how things might be restructured; something esoteric, modern, select, with a touch of continuity with the past. It wasn't folk, America, dance, singer-songwriter balladry or a sound built to compete with Creation, but one that paralleled the leading British independent Warp, at the experimental end of electronica.

If the movie *Blade Runner* had been made in the year 2000 and not 1982, it might have had a soundtrack by Magnétophone rather than Vangelis. Dark, dystopian and restless in mood, jagged and soothing in equal measure, Birmingham duo Matt Huish Saunders and John Hanson's debut album *I Guess Sometimes I Need To Be Reminded Of How Much You Love Me* wasn't the same ear-buzzing challenge as that offered by Warp's prominent artists Aphex Twin and Autechre, but they nevertheless tapped into 'glitch', the sound of machine malfunction, hum and hiss.

Musically, Ivo would never have gone there: 'A glitch was something I'd spent hours in the studio, or when mastering, asking engineers to get rid of,' he comments. 'To have it as the fabric of a piece, a style even of music, just didn't suit my brain, and still doesn't, but in many ways that's good and proper. Each generation should be offending the previous one with its originality and disregard for what is acceptable. Unfortunately, most offend for the opposite reason – a complete lack of originality.'

'Uppermost in our minds,' says Sharp, 'was that 4AD had squandered its credibility having hit records, with endless Cuba twelve-inch remixes, in a desperate attempt to be on the radio and have hits. All previous successes on 4AD had happened organically. Ed and I were into labels such as Warp, so we looked for artists with integrity and staying power to re-establish 4AD as a home for uncompromised creativity. Perhaps we were naïve in signing bands that lacked commercial ambition, but that had been the problem before. At the same time, we were under much more direct financial scrutiny than Ivo ever was. He never needed to seek Martin's approval. We had to make tiny deals, never over £5,000 an album.'

The artwork for *I Guess Sometimes I Need To Be Reminded Of How Much You Love Me* was pure v23, with the photos and credits printed on the *inside* of an inner slipcase, and the track listing on a strip of card at the rear. Yet cost-saving was involved. The designer was Martin Andersen, a v23 assistant working under Vaughan Oliver's art direction, which was a cheaper option than using the head honcho.

4AD continued to repackage its enviable back catalogue, with compilations from Heidi Berry (*Pomegranate: An Anthology*) and, finally, a Cocteau Twins collection (*Stars And Topsoil: A Collection*)* before the year was out.†

More discerning collectors were engaged by the compilation *Fwd>Motion* given away free at a 4AD-sponsored event at an abandoned foam factory in London, featuring Magnétophone, future 4AD signing Minotaur Shock, and a live recording by electro-ambient duo Paul Schütze and Simon Hopkins. More decisive esoterica came from

---

* 4AD once considered reissuing Cocteau Twins' two subsequent albums on Fontana, *Four-Calendar Café* and *Milk & Kisses*, though the only 4AD release containing Fontana material is the 2006 singles collection *Lullabies To Violaine*.

† The floodgates were to open over the next years, with compilations from Modern English (*The Best Of ... Life In The Gladhouse: 1980–1984*), Lush (*Ciao! Best Of ...*), Pixies (*Complete 'B' Sides*), The Wolfgang Press (*Everything Is Beautiful: [A Retrospective 1983–1995]*), Colourbox (*Best Of 82/87*), Dead Can Dance (*1981–1998*) and Belly (*Sweet Ride: The Best Of ...*). An especially beautiful four-CD Cocteau Twins compilation, *Lullabies To Violaine*, followed in 2006.

Piano Magic's 4AD debut, the ambient soundtrack to Spanish director Bigas Luna's art-house film *Son de Mar* – not even Dead Can Dance's early film soundtracks were so indulged. The Sharp/Horrox version of 4AD appeared to be moving closer to Ivo's post-Bauhaus years, of Gilbert/Lewis and David J/René Halkett, and disregarding any sense of clear-cut trends.

Son de Mar was already Piano Magic's fifth album, and 4AD was the London trio's fourth label, but the soundtrack was more of an introduction to the main event. Released in 2001, *Writers Without Homes* was a contemporary reading of a familiar blueprint: Sharp says core member Glen Johnson 'was obsessed with This Mortal Coil, and the album was to keep in with the old 4AD spirit of collaboration'.

Johnson had a more eclectic reach than This Mortal Coil, drawing on shoegaze and post-rock, but guest performers included long-lost folk singer Vashti Bunyan, former Cocteau Twin and TMC contributor Simon Raymonde, and the stunning, dolorous baritone of John Grant.* v23's sublime artwork – with Vaughan Oliver at the helm – maintained the image and feel of old. There was one weak spot: the concept. Sharp felt that Johnson hadn't fully delivered on his collaborative promise. More ominously, there were echoes of the 4AD–Warners relationship of old.

'4AD's press and marketing people struggled with the album and I never sensed much enthusiasm for Piano Magic around Alma Road,' says Sharp. Johnson's plan to write a rockier album for the live incarnation of Piano Magic didn't alleviate Sharp's concerns. 'I was put off by the prospect of getting the project through the Beggars system, so we didn't pick up the option.'

In its eclectic reach and quirkier feel, *Writers Without Homes* was more His Name Is Alive than This Mortal Coil, and now it was the

---

* Now an acclaimed solo artist, in 2003 John Grant was still fronting The Czars, whose uniquely broody, dark roots had a touch of *Tarnation*'s western/prairie character. In fact, Paula Frazer added backing vocals to several Czars songs, found on the band's first two Bella Union albums, *Before … But Longer* (2000) and *The Ugly People Vs. The Beautiful People* (2002).

turn of the real thing. With 2001's *Someday My Blues Will Cover The Earth*, Warren Defever persisted with his progressive R&B evolution, though without Karin Oliver for the first time. But Defever couldn't settle, and sought a working environment that was unencumbered by contracts and strangers at 4AD's office. After one last album for the label, 2002's *Last Night*, 'I begged to be released from our contract one record early,' he says.*

Kristin Hersh had already established career independence with her consumer-funded organisation CASH Music, but had agreed to persist with 4AD as the budgets, though smaller than they once were at the label, gave her a profile. Some of the old demons, though, returned during the making of her fifth solo album, 2002's *Sunny Border Blue*. 'It was some of my best work, but I sang about things I shouldn't have and played things I shouldn't have – it was like a mania. Things could be insular and a mindfuck, and lonely without Ivo, and I'd already lost Dave [Narcizo], the only two people who spoke my musical language. So I compensated with my first real work of obsession since I was a teenager. I'd get drunk in the studio and call people, and they'd say, "Tell the truth, it will be fine, just record it". And it wasn't my 4AD any longer. And I'd been there longer than the other employees! Piece by piece, we'd lost the family, but it was inevitable. The entire music industry was collapsing. But it was fine too. It was about the music again instead of the family, and I still had some good people on my side.'

In 2000, there had been a very brief Throwing Muses reunion, with Tanya Donelly also on board, for two fan gatherings (in Massachusetts and at a Rhode Island music festival) christened 'Gut Pageant'. Hersh then got busy. Her fourth son Brodie was born in November 2002, followed by her sixth solo album *The Grotto*. It was

---

* Defever subsequently released a varying spread of music through his Time Stereo label before co-founding the Silver Mountain Media label and getting major label Sony-BMG on side to distribute 2006's *Detrola* and 2007's *Xmmer* albums, both of which restored His Name Is Alive's original idiosyncratic mystery. *Detrola* became Defever's most commercial and critical success in ten years; *Pitchfork* described it as, 'Fantastic art, full of depth and warmth and creativity. It's probably the best thing Defever's ever done.'

the most nakedly acoustic album she'd yet made, but this was partly down to siphoning off the electricity for a new Throwing Muses album. Husband Billy had noticed Hersh was writing Muses-style songs, and suggested she use part of her advance for the solo album on a band record, so Hersh, Narcizo and Georges reconvened after seven years apart.

Hersh named the album *Throwing Muses*, like the 1986 debut, in the spirit of starting over. Recorded over two weekends, the album had an intensely knotty mood – 'quick and dirty, playing by the seat of our pants,' says Hersh. Both the solo and band album were released on the same day in March 2003: 'They were two sides of the same coin,' says Hersh. 'I didn't want either to suffer because of the other, and they came from the same time and place. They're related.'

Throwing Muses even featured a guest backing vocalist – Tanya Donelly. It was an extraordinary moment for them both. 'I just asked her,' Hersh recalls. 'I thought she'd be too busy, as she had had a baby. She wrote all these crazy melodies around mine, and by the end, I couldn't tell whose voice was whose. We were both in tears, because it felt like we were singing together.'

Hersh wanted Throwing Muses to tour; with Narcizo committed to his design company, he helped find a replacement drummer, Rob Ahlers. Since Hersh saw Narcizo as an irreplaceable Muse, she named the new trio 50 Foot Wave. It took on a life of its own, recording 2004's self-titled mini-album and 2005's full-length *Golden Ocean*, in which Ahler's more aggressive style pushed Hersh to blistering heights.

'Since *Hips And Makers*, I'd been releasing a record a year, and touring until I wore out my welcome,' she recalls. 'I saw 50 Foot Wave as an opportunity to not think about solo material and to travel in a different sphere. Different sound, clubs, engineers. And then to come back with fresh ears and impulses.'

Like Hersh, Donelly too had found a way to combine motherhood with music. Her 2002 second solo album *Beautysleep* again featured husband/bassist Dean Fisher and Narcizo, before the entrancing acoustic *Whiskey Tango Ghosts* finished her 4AD contract on a high, in a country/folk reverie that spoke of her present state ten years on from Belly.*

However, the most anticipated return was Kim Deal – with Kelley again by her side. The sisters had been recording piecemeal since 1998, but the only track they'd managed was a cover of The James Gang's 'Collage' (the B-side of the first single they'd bought together) for the 1999 soundtrack of *The Mod Squad*. Five other tracks from this period ended up on the new Breeders album, but it wasn't until 2001 that Kim and Kelley toured again under that name, with three Breeders debutantes: guitarist Richard Presley and bassist Mando Lopez from the LA punk band Fear, and drummer Jose Medeles. The same year, Steve Albini was recalled to record the rest of the album, which Kim called *Title TK*. 'That was the title I wanted to call *Last Splash*, but it didn't make so much sense for that record,' she says. 'But here, it worked. *Title TK* sounds like I know nothing, even after fighting for so many rounds, not even a title for the fucking record! I thought it was funny.'

Although there were five Breeders on the credits, the album's sombre, skeletal feel resembled the solo album that Kim had once intended to make. She was even playing some of the drums. 4AD bravely released 'Off You' as the lead single, a haunting ballad that laid bare the suffering and doubt that the sisters had endured. It couldn't have been a greater contrast to 'Cannonball', and all the energies of Elektra to keep her on side failed.

Deal had also to contend with the fact 4AD had changed. 'I was very suspicious when I first met Ed Horrox, because he wasn't Ivo. I also talked to Ivo, and to Vaughan, and it was all confusing. I didn't know what anyone was doing. I don't know if anyone suggested producers, but I'd wanted to shoo away everyone since everything had gone digital. But my 4AD contract ended with *Title TK*.'

In 2002, 4AD had also released the debut album *Nonument* by Sybarite, a neo-classical-ambient-electronic assemblage by Brooklyn-

---

* Tanya Donelly's band name lives on in one sense, as her own experience of the traumatic birth of her daughter Gracie led to her working as a qualified doula, assisting in pregnancies and childbirth. She says she has finally done more recordings, and is about to release them in a series.

based multi-instrumentalist Xian Hawkins. But it wasn't all edgy electronica, as other signings The Mountain Goats and Cass McCombs represented a new vanguard of Americana.

The Mountain Goats was a loose collective arranged around the poetic, narrative strengths of Californian singer-songwriter John Darnielle, who had released numerous lo-fi tracks across cassette, vinyl and CD before 2002's *Tallahassee*. It was the first of six albums that 4AD was to release over the next seven years, as success in America – though very little outside – made it worthwhile continuing.

McCombs, another Californian, was even more of a curio, living as a restless hobo, sleeping in cars, on couches and at campsites across the country. Asked what he'd like on his tombstone, he said, 'HOME AT LAST'. His 2002 EP debut *Not The Way* shared Alex Chilton's resigned, mournful stamp, and McCombs could have been the new 4AD's Mark Kozelek. But after two albums, *A* (2003) and *PREfection* (2005), McCombs moved on, to the London-based Domino label, just as he'd moved on to other cars, couches and campsites.

Another character who would have slotted in alongside McCombs's tormented nature was Vinny Miller. He had dropped the starry smooth hound alias, and finally completed an album. 4AD released *On The Block* in 2004, six years after his *Anakin* demo. Fittingly, the album is one of the label's most buried treasures, as Miller was in no reasonable state to promote it bar a few shows in America. He didn't even have the will to continue making music.

Miller recalls how hopeless he'd felt during those intervening years. 'I blew opportunities most musicians would give their teeth for. I dived headfirst into music tech with hardware samplers and hard disk recorders, when I should have spent the time being creative. The momentum gets lost and the length of time becomes a burden in itself. If you've worked 12-hour days for two and a half years but haven't completed even one piece, something's gone badly wrong. At the least, you're not cut out for a career in music. They [Ed and Chris] wanted to help, but however supportive or tuned in somebody is, they can't finish your record for you. And finishing it was a matter of recognising my own mediocrity.'

Chris Sharp recalls an upsetting conversation where Miller expressed 'a paranoid hallucinatory belief that Vaughan [Oliver] was this male force, trying to control, or damage, his career'. Miller's finished album careered over twelve wildly undulating tracks, his fevered voice couched in hushed and violent outbursts. 'It's not super-dark,' he reflects today. 'If it's mad, it's benevolently so. A lot of it came from boredom. I'd do something beautiful, melodic and atmospheric and then be so sick of that sound that I'd do something different for a bit. Then I'd get something shouty to a finishing point and be exhausted by it.'

Ivo heard *On The Block* at a point, he says, where it was best he didn't listen to 4AD releases: 'But, of course, I did. It's not the overall album that I'd imagined when I contacted Vinny years earlier. In some ways, it's better. It's almost like he jumped straight to his second album. He'd got very glitch and "laptop" and I'm happy Ed and Chris didn't necessarily respond positively to that approach. For me, it was Vinny's voice. It was before the era when post-Jeff Buckley wannabes became a dime a dozen, without the voices to deliver the emotion. Vinny seemed to have returned to a place where he wanted to allow his voice to be heard, to shine. I find the recording unnecessarily lo-fi for my taste, but the arrangements, and his voice, were fabulous.'

Yet Miller was still intent on a sense of disruption. For starters (literally), 'The Yes/No Game' has to be the most bizarre opening track in 4AD's canon – two minutes of conversation between Miller and an east London pirate radio DJ. 'He popped up while I was flicking through for radio samples,' Miller recalls. 'I wasn't prank-calling … I originally wanted a taped shout-out, then wanted to win his game. It's supposed to disorientate.'

The album cover portrayed Miller tarred and feathered, eyes heavily lidded, as if drugged or hypnotised. 'It is to date, the worst album sleeve concept ever released on 4AD,' he states. 'I'm chuffin' proud of that. It was by accident but I remembered Sebastião Salgado's photo of the Gulf War oil well-capping guys. It was for purposes of liberation too. With every new track being completed, it felt like unzipping a skin from the top of my head right the way down to my feet. It was a fucking great feeling.'

Yet *On The Block* had no lasting cathartic effect. When Miller's concert in the tiny backroom of London pub The Water Rats was shut down by a fire between the soundcheck and the show, it seemed to be an omen. Miller says that 4AD's decision to terminate the relationship 'was pretty merciful, as things panned out'. He now works as a nurse with people suffering from 'severe and enduring mental illness'.

How perfect that Ivo's last signing at 4AD was someone whose mental fragility couldn't make enough sense of the business of music. 'I like obscurity. It's underrated,' concludes Miller, adding, 'There are too many records out there. Some of them are great. Bands have creative differences and split, solo artists isolate and go nuts. I don't regret leaving.'

The same year saw Lisa Gerrard's departure after twenty-two years on the label. In 2002, 4AD had released her soundtrack to the film *Whale Rider*, a widely successful (and independently released) magic-realist saga based around Maori culture, and *Immortal Memory* followed in 2004. It was her first original album in six years, recorded with a new collaborator, Irish classical composer Patrick Cassidy. '4AD after Ivo was like someone had lifted up the house and put a new one on top, and you don't know where anything is. I decided to see out my agreement, and that was it.'

So where was Ivo during these developments? Having twice failed to buy land in the Santa Fe region on a neighbouring ridge to where he'd first searched, he had purchased a plot of ten acres in 2000, initiated building in August 2001 and taken possession of his new house in June 2002. The stress of 4AD had gone, but not the clinical depression. Despite a couple of moments of clarity where he'd considered making music again, to the point of sending out tapes of cover versions to a couple of people, 'I couldn't go through with it,' he recalls. 'In any case, I haven't had an original idea for years. Just like so much modern music.'

Considerate towards 4AD's legacy and aware its founder's aura still hovered over Alma Road, Ed Horrox kept in touch with Ivo, posting him compilations. 'It was mostly unsigned, emerging little bands, and he [Ivo] would write most of them off. He'd say, "Twelve of those thirteen tracks were shit, but I really like that Shins song".'

In 2001, when Horrox flew to Texas to see XL signings The White Stripes at the South By Southwest festival, he paid Ivo a visit: 'It felt like I was visiting the guru. I was looking at a fire that was nearly out, but nurturing the embers … and I wanted to say hello, music fan to music fan. We mostly talked about old music, like Spirit, Steve Miller, Judy Henske, or about dogs, but never about how or why things had tailed off for him. He even gave the impression he wasn't listening to music.'

Horrox didn't even get a positive reaction to Blonde Redhead's brilliant 2004 album *Misery Is A Butterfly*, despite the New York-based trio's inventive twist on the dream-pop dynamic. Japanese singer Kazu Makino and Italian twin brothers Amedeo and Simone Pace had had roots in a noisier dissonance – early albums were released on Sonic Youth drummer Steve Shelley's label Smells Like. But by the time they signed to 4AD, they were mining a more concentrated, swooning sound, part vintage shoegaze in the style of Lush (especially 'Equus') and part baroque Gallic pop in the style of Serge Gainsbourg's Sixties classic *Histoire De Melody Nelson*. Makino was a Lush, Cocteau Twins and This Mortal Coil fan. 'Those people made the kind of records you had to make a choice to listen to,' she explains. 'I'd never imagined I had what it took to make a record like that, with that kind of conviction.'

'*Misery Is A Butterfly* was the first time we felt we were making a step forward,' says Chris Sharp. 'It opened 4AD up to America again, which led directly to TV On The Radio, which was another step up – the hottest band on the planet – and we could be taken seriously again. Things began to accelerate.'

Brooklyn-based multi-racial quintet TV On The Radio had released its debut EP *Young Liars* in 2003 on the US indie Touch & Go. The record had infused art rock with a funk/soul perspective, and had original ideas: the EP's hidden track, for example, was an a cappella version of Pixies' 'Mr Greaves'. 'It was the first thing I sent Ivo that he freaked out about,' says Horrox. 'I thought, fucking hell, wow, something's going on here.'

'I felt like it was almost a Rema-Rema moment for Chris and Ed, something that really didn't sound like anything else, a starting point of something real,' says Ivo.

The band's guitarist and producer Dave Sitek was a 4AD obsessive to the point that he'd call studios where 4AD records had been recorded, asking for insider tips. 'You could hear Cocteau Twins in Dave's guitars, Gerard [Smith, the band's bassist/keyboardist who died of lung cancer in 2011] was a massive fan of His Name Is Alive, and they knew 4AD's catalogue inside out,' says Sharp.

Sitek even called Ivo at home, 'trying to be a fan, and trying to be kind,' Ivo recalls. But Ivo still wasn't ready to reconnect with 4AD, even after six years away from the front line. 'I was still listening to much less music, and it took me a long time to be able to go back and listen to anything on 4AD for pleasure,' he says. 'In 2002, I'd moved into this house where the environment was appropriate to re-create that feeling of that Majorca trip, where Vaughan and I mostly just listened to Eno. When I moved into this house, I banished voices and drums and that's when my true love of Stars of the Lid and their offshoots blossomed. I found there was a finite amount of time one can listen to ambient music from the Eno camp on a loop.'

Stars of the Lid was the Austin, Texas duo Adam Wiltzie and Brian McBride, specialists in drone-based, orchestral ambience that created a spellbinding sense of awe. Ivo started buying their albums, and with his name cropping up on sales reports, Wiltzie had emailed Ivo about concerns over the duo's European distribution. 'Adam didn't know I had left 4AD,' Ivo recalls. 'I said Ed and Chris were the ones to contact, and I emailed Ed, whose response was, "Love them, love to hear something". But he later told Adam that 4AD needed to be signing things that sold. That was an alarm bell in all sorts of directions. That's the best example of how the post-Ivo model of 4AD differed, because I'd have done anything to have worked with Stars of the Lid.'

Ivo also saw 4AD's attempt to keep him in the loop as a cynical exercise. 'They were trying to suggest I was still involved by never announcing I was not involved. People like Warren and Kim kept telling me that it had never really been made clear that I had been gone since 1999.'

Ivo did re-engage with 4AD on one occasion when the label reissued The Hope Blister's previous mail order-only *Underarms* in 2005, packaged with *Sideways*, a bonus CD of *Underarm* remixes by the Bavarian ambient composer Markus Guentner. 'It was an excuse to get my dearly and recently departed [Shar Pei] Otis on the cover,' Ivo admits. 'The carrot to get Ed and Chris involved was Marcus, to create something new out of the record.'

There might have been a Dead Can Dance album too, but after Gerrard and Perry had reformed for a tour in 2005, they again butted heads and egos and decided against persisting. Perry then decided he would leave 4AD too. 'I'd become a bit of a nature boy, and a father, and it was the only time I ever needed a kick up the arse, to get back to making music,' he says. 'But no one [from 4AD] got in touch to ask how things were going. I also thought the label had lost kudos with its new signings. And all the old faces had gone. I had one album left on the band-cum-solo deal but I left by mutual agreement. There was a healthy debt that *Eye Of The Hunter* hadn't put a dent in, and I later discovered that if I'd done a second solo album, 4AD would have cross-collateralised the debt from Dead Can Dance and so there would have been no income. That's the old antiquated contracts for you.'

In contrast, Mojave 3 had stuck around. Neil Halstead says the band hadn't missed Ivo as other artists had since they'd only had a direct relationship with him before their debut album in 1995. Horrox and Sharp treated them reverently, allowing Halstead and Rachel Goswell to record respective solo albums *Sleeping On Roads* (2002) and *Waves Are Universal* (2004) that were released either side of the band's fourth album *Spoon And Rafter*.

'There was a lot of good will towards them at 4AD, including Martin [Mills],' says Sharp. 'I always felt that Neil was an underrated songwriter. His solo album was a relative surprise; it picked up good reviews and did pretty well in America, which worked as a good springboard between *Excuses For Travellers* and *Spoon And Rafter*, which became their best-selling record. So it felt like they were always on an upward trajectory, albeit a gradual one.'

A fifth band album, *Puzzles Like You* (2006), fulfilled Mojave 3's five-album contract with a more upbeat take on country/folk roots, though it remains the band's last album to date. 'It didn't really take them any further audience-wise, so there wasn't a huge sense of urgency on either side to do another deal,' says Sharp. 'And the band was increasingly precarious as an entity thanks to the long gaps between records, people's different side projects and the increasing need all of them had to cope with real life.'*

Nor was there urgency to persist with the standard v23 had set for artwork, going by Mojave 3's twee folk-art imagery. The graphic design studio was only occasionally re-employed, to bring something special to the table, such as for Magnétophone's second album *The Man Who Ate The Man*: enigmatic image, exquisite typeface and a little insert for eight small cards, with lyrical phrases on one side ('walk beneath bad light'; 'who are you here for?') and a graphic image on the back that could be assembled into one complete picture, in a homage to the cardboard joy inside packets of bubblegum.

The Man Who Ate The Man wasn't just about the packaging. It was a more approachable listening experience than its predecessor, weaving in folk influences with guest folk singers King Creosote and James Yorkston. But the surprise was to be found on the buzzing instrumental 'Kel's Vintage Thought' – with Kim Deal on drums and sister Kelley on violin and guitar. 'Getting Kim and Kelley involved was a tactic for widening their musical horizons,' says Sharp. 'Ed had some Magnétophone demos with him when he was visiting them in Dayton, and they knocked up some bass and guitar in Kim's home studio.'

Perhaps the Deals swayed it, but 'Kel's Vintage Thought' was a wayward choice for a lead single and hardly the vehicle to promote the

* Neil Halstead has recorded two solo albums, 2008's *Oh! Mighty Engine* and 2012's *Palindrome Hunches*. Goswell is raising a daughter and Ian McCutcheon is a member of the band The Loose Salute. Though Mojave 3 reformed for live shows in 2011, Halstead maintains the band is still on hiatus though his commitment to surfing never wavers.

album, which ranks as another neglected 4AD jewel. 'I'd be surprised if it sold a thousand copies worldwide,' says Sharp. 'More attention should have been paid to the realpolitik of fighting for people's commitment at Beggars. Plus it was an abrasive and abstract record in places, so there weren't many obvious ways in. [Magnétophone's] Matt and John were knocked back by the experience as they'd seen 4AD as a significant step up.'

The spin-offs designed to promote the album had been an inspired choice, from a limited twelve-inch of Sonic Boom's 20-minute remix of 'Benny Insobriety' to John-Mark Lapham's impressionistic mix of the entire album. Lapham would play an unheralded part in 4AD's next phase. Of the nine new acts unveiled between 2005 and 2007, The Late Cord was the best – Ivo agrees – and most frustratingly, the briefest.

The Late Cord was Lapham's collaboration with singer Micah P. Hinson, a fellow Texan out of the Cass McCombs mould of troubled souls who was trying to overcome a history of addiction and homelessness. Lapham had been the studio mastermind behind the Anglo-American quartet The Earlies, whose two albums patented an adventurous blend of folk and electronica. His motivation for working with Hinson, he says, 'was to create my own "early 4AD sound". I wasn't trying to replicate it, but it was a massive influence.'

Without knowing of Lapham's reverence for the label, Ed Horrox had asked The Earlies if they wanted to remix a Rachel Goswell song. 'I jumped at the chance to do something for 4AD,' Lapham says. After hearing the Lapham/Hinson demos, Horrox offered to release a record, which became the mini-album *Lights From The Wheelhouse*, a filmic serving of sad, restless mystery with long stretches of ambient darkness, etched by titles such as 'My Most Meaningful Relationships Are With Dead People' and 'Hung On The Cemetery Gates'. A full album was meant to follow, but Hinson fell off the radar and Lapham was forced to concede defeat. Having connected with Ivo, the pair talked about a This Mortal Coil-style project with Lapham handling the music, but it never got further than a conversation.

At least Ivo was rediscovering a love of music. Hearing Danish quintet Mew's *And The Glass Handed Kites* – a progressive rock record out of its time, from an unexpected source – was the trigger for a fuller investigation of the gatefold sleeves of the progressive genre, which led to the artwork of many British prog rock labels, 'especially those that didn't work,' he says, 'like Deram Nova, I don't know why.'

An online search led Ivo to the Japanese paper-sleeve box set of King Crimson's *In The Court Of The Crimson King*, which kickstarted a love for the paper-sleeve format. 'Since I was buying these records, I thought I might as well listen to them, with the feeling of a boy in a record shop, or working in a record shop,' he says. 'I was delighted to find genuinely exciting, original musicianship that really impressed me at a point in time when I was always running an inventory in my head of what contemporary music reminded me of, so it was a relief to be challenged. It was an emotional response to something that existed in the arts, like photography, rather than getting frustrated with what was meant to be in fashion.'

Ivo did find time for current records too – the country melancholy of South San Gabriel, or Richmond Fontaine. It wasn't remotely original but it clearly hit the right spot – worn and sad, authentic and true. There was one more 4AD album that Ivo fully endorsed – Jóhann Jóhannsson's second 4AD album, 2008's *Fordlandia*, another cinematic – but wholly instrumental – composition. The ambient minimalist from Iceland was as likely to incorporate orchestras as electronics in his work, and used concepts to shape his music. Released in 2006, *IBM 1401, A User's Manual* was based on a Seventies recording of an IBM mainframe computer by Jóhann's father (Jóhann Gunnarsson); *Fordlandia* was the name of American motor industrialist Henry Ford's fantasy-style settlement in the Amazonian jungle, set up to source the rubber needed for car tyres.

So far, Sharp and Horrox had slowly amassed an impressive body of work, mostly with an esoteric appeal, but a sense of adventure. Yet besides TV On The Radio, there was little significant sign of advancing the label. And this wasn't going to happen with Celebration. The

Brooklyn trio's self-titled debut album, produced by Dave Sitek, shared much of TV On The Radio's restless energy, but not their charisma or groove. Nor with the electronic instrumentalist Minotaur Shock, a.k.a. British-born David Edwards, who released two albums, *Maritime* (2005) and *Amateur Dramatics* (2008). Nor was there much chance with Portland, Oregon singer-songwriter-guitarist M. Ward, whose two albums, 2006's *Post-War* (a rare political treatise for 4AD, concerning the United States' reaction to the war in Iraq through its creative resources) and 2009's *Hold Time*, were licensed from US indie Merge.

With Australian quartet Wolf & Cub, the Sharp–Horrox A&R model even started to resemble the confused roster of late-Nineties 4AD, a rare excursion into rock that combined Sixties and shoegaze versions of psychedelia, with two drummers. But *Vessels* became the band's only 4AD album. 'They were originally more angular and sprightly but changed their minds and wrote long, lumpy, proggy songs that sank without trace,' says Sharp. The solo album *Watch The Fireworks* from Emma Pollock, the singer of Scots band The Delgados that Ed Horrox had signed to Mantra, was similarly underwhelming and wasn't followed by another.

Pollock and Wolf & Cub were the newest kids on the bill of *1980: Forward*, 4AD's 25th-anniversary showcase in the tradition of *The 13 Year Itch* and *All Virgos Are Mad*. Shows at venues across London included Kristin Hersh playing Throwing Muses and solo songs; The Breeders, with Kim and Kelley Deal sober and sorted, according to special guest Josephine Wiggs; even Mark Kozelek, performing Red House Painters songs. It served to draw a line under most of what 4AD had so far achieved. TV On The Radio had been important, but the label lacked the kind of signing that would create a story, to make other artists – and journalists – wonder what was going on at 4AD. This would happen in 2006 with the surprise signing of Scott Walker, whose presence alone could command the right level of respect for the label.

As one third of the Sixties idols The Walker Brothers, the man born Scott Engel specialised in grand, lugubrious melodramas in the style of Phil Spector's kitchen sink productions. His rich, sonorous voice had iced several astonishing solo albums through the late Sixties, the cavernous arrangements and funereal tempos framing lyrics set in a definitively non-swinging part of London. Having retreated from fame and survived a series of MOR and country covers, and then The Walker Brothers' patchily successful reunion in the Seventies, Engel only re-emerged for 1984's sleek and audacious album *Climate Of Hunter* and, after an even lengthier retreat, 1995's alarming, electronic-fused *Tilt* for major label imprint Fontana.

Walker had always recorded for the majors. 'But his manager has played the major label game for too long,' says Sharp, 'and he understood the integrity of a label like 4AD. I only talked to him after the deal had been done, but he said that it felt like a great place to be.'

Walker had declined to make his 4AD debut in 1986 on This Mortal Coil's *Filigree & Shadow*, but he would have already known of Ivo's achievements. As it was, he arrived at the label with 2006's *The Drift*, another avant-rock, neo-classical mass with a quaking industrial core, as challenging as it was rewarding. By increments, 4AD began to build on Walker's residency, a signing that was never going to bring in the profits but proved 4AD was a viable option, an artist's label.

Zachary Francis Condon was next on board. Condon, who performed under the name of Beirut, was 'incredibly important' to the revival of 4AD, says Horrox. There were two – admittedly tenuous – links to Ivo: Condon hailed from Santa Fe, where, like Ivo, he developed a taste for the joyous Mexican folk sound of mariachi, to add to his love of Balkan folk, making his debut album *Gulag Orkestar* (licensed from the American label Ba Da Bing!) the first 4AD record rooted in ethnic folk since Dead Can Dance.

Condon was only twenty when *Gulag Orkestar* was released, and widely acclaimed. When he toured with a nine-piece version of Beirut, 'in the middle of having a nervous breakdown,' says Horrox, there was cause for concern. But he bounced back, and a second album, *The Flying Club Cup*, was released, blending new influences from French *chanson* including Serge Gainsbourg and Yves Montand. TV On The Radio's second 4AD album *Return To Cookie Mountain*

(2006) – with Vaughan Oliver sleeve and Chris Bigg assistance – consolidated 4AD's upward curve, with David Bowie and Blonde Redhead's Kazu Makino among the guest singers. But the relationship ended when TV On The Radio's US label Touch & Go was bought by Universal, which then assumed responsibility for the indie label's overseas licensing.

Even though she was now out of contract with 4AD, Kim Deal returned in 2008, after a gap of six years – her tardiness this time could be blamed on the Pixies' reunion in 2004 for a series of tours that continue, sporadically, to this day. The fourth Breeders album *Mountain Battles* retained Mando Lopez, Jose Medeles and engineer Steve Albini, bridging the raw nature of *Title TK* with more of the detail of *Last Splash*.

The loss of TV On The Radio was compensated by the licensing of a new singer-songwriter who was to prove even more influential. Bon Iver – after *bon hiver*, French for 'good winter' – was the pen name of American singer-songwriter Justin Vernon, who handled the break-up of a relationship and his band DeYarmond Edison by leaving his native North Carolina for an extended winter sojourn in his father's log cabin deep in the Medford, Wisconsin woods. While debilitated by glandular fever, Vernon recorded a set of demos – just voice, guitar and the occasional drum, which seeped an air of restorative isolation.

These demos were merely intended to secure a record deal until Vernon realised the value of his intense, stark sketches and released 500 copies of an album, titled *For Emma, Forever Ago*. The blogsphere – which had expanded at an exponential rate, to create a whole new marketplace for artists – reacted with unanimous fervour and Vernon was chased by every independent label who could muster an offer.

Ed Horrox had witnessed Bon Iver's breakthrough show in 2007, at the annual College Music Journal convention in New York. Chris Sharp was able to catch footage online. 'We offered a worldwide deal with 4AD, but Justin and [US indie label] Jagjaguwar had a Midwest connection, so we got to license the album instead,' says Sharp. 'I left 4AD the week before it was released.'

If Sharp had been successful in licensing Arcade Fire's own break-through album *Funeral* (Rough Trade won out) in 2005, it could have been a very different story for him. But Martin Mills was a pragmatic – as well as ruthless – businessman, judging by Sharp's memory of a meeting that took place only weeks after he'd returned from compassionate leave.*

Sharp: 'Martin said something like, "I get the impression you're losing your enthusiasm, is there anything you'd like to say?" I said I was still excited working at 4AD, and we agreed to revisit the conversation. Ed and I went to Nottingham to see The Breeders play. It was fantastic, Kim was clean and having a great time, and it was one of those evenings where you think, This is why I do this, to hang out with great people, it's a privilege to work with these artists. The next day, Martin asked me to leave. He never did give me a clear explanation.'

The reason turned out to be Simon Halliday, the new general manager for Beggars Banquet's associated labels. In his formative teenage years, Halliday had been a committed fan of Echo & The Bunnymen, New Order and Cocteau Twins, and says the first This Mortal Coil album 'is near perfection for me'. Halliday, like Horrox, was also smitten by club music – from R&B and soul to hip-hop and house: 'It balanced out the ethereal,' he says. 'Though I always thought Cocteau Twins weren't a guitar band, but more dance, because of their beats.'

Halliday had promoted clubs nights in Manchester before joining the London-based promotions company Streets Ahead and then

---

* Paul Cox at Too Pure had also found Martin Mills tougher to deal with than Ivo. In 1998, the label finally stopped signing bands and became a Singles Club, releasing one single a month, on a subscription basis. 'Control had slipped out of my hands by then,' Cox recalls. '[Partner] Richard [Roberts] emigrated to Australia in 1998, and I couldn't afford to buy his shareholding, so Martin bought it. With Richard's replacement, Nick West, we had started a little Too Pure in LA, out of American Recording, and then Martin brought Nick back to help run things in the UK and asked me to give him some of my share to motivate him. Eventually we became another Beggars Banquet label, working in their office, run by Jason White. I was A&R consultant. Around 2000, he let me go. I never felt I could prevent losing my job. It may have been a different story if Ivo had remained. We loved the 4AD office vibe much more than Beggars.'

RTM, the distribution and marketing company that had risen from the ashes of Rough Trade Distribution. After working with labels such as 4AD and Tommy Boy, he'd joined Warp full-time, handling A&R and marketing before moving to New York to head the label's US wing. In 2008, Halliday had departed over internal disagreements, but soon received Martin Mills' offer of a job.

More plugged-in to the new generation of young beats-infused pop and electronica being fussed over by the fresh legions of blog writers, Halliday was hired to provide a jolt in the arm for the revitalised 4AD. His first idea was to unite most of Beggars' labels. XL, Rough Trade (Mills had just purchased half of Rough Trade from its owner Geoff Travis) and Matador (an American label founded in New York by Gerard Cosnoy that Beggars had also bought into) were strong enough to stand alone, but Mills agreed that both Beggars Banquet and Too Pure labels should be mothballed, those bands deemed surplus to requirements let go, and those worth retaining to be affiliated under one roof. 'Simpler is easier,' says Halliday. 'And the strongest element was 4AD.'

That was enough of a vision for Mills to finally interfere with the running of 4AD and make Halliday the new label head. 'It was just the next phase,' Mills explains. 'The A&R needed to become more dynamic and energetic, and Simon was very ambitious.'

Chris Sharp and Ed Horrox had tried to restore, even expand, Ivo's original aesthetic, not in his image but with respect for it. But releases such as *Plague Songs*, a concept album about the ten plagues of Egypt commissioned by the British arts organisation Artangel for its project *The Margate Exodus*, and even perhaps Scott Walker, were too left field to be financially viable. As Sharp says of Minotaur Shock's *Maritime*, 'This delicate, complex, melodic, tricky electronic record, in time-honoured, beautiful packaging … but it just didn't happen. We already knew from Magnétophone how hard it was in the current market.'

'The Ed and Chris model proved not to be particularly successful in a commercial sense,' says Ivo. 'But I'd really admired how, clearly, they were releasing music that they loved. I like both of them immensely as people and had appreciated how both, for a while anyway, would send me music that they were enjoying, regardless of whether they were thinking about releasing it. But the last time Ed came to visit, I chastised him for not having signed one band or individual that hadn't already released a record with someone else. In his response, I realised that, once again, the pressure and need to sign something that would sell had raised its ugly head. But that decision was taken away from Ed and Chris by Martin.'

Under Simon Halliday's charge, Brooklyn's majestically brooding The National, the eclectic, art-rocking St. Vincent (Oklahoma singer-songwriter Annie Clark) and the indefatigable, gravel-voiced Mark Lanegan moved from Beggars Banquet to 4AD. Krautrock/lounge fusioneers Stereolab, after enjoying a long association with Too Pure, also moved over.

Sharp says that Beirut left 4AD as a result of his dismissal, but otherwise little changed. 'Martin's been hugely successful because he's always made moves to preserve the business,' Sharp says, magnanimously. 'And it was a great opportunity for them to weed out the roster. But it was unfair to say I wasn't interested anymore. It didn't help my state of mind that Bon Iver's album quickly sold 50,000 copies.'

Another disgruntled individual was Ivo, who was incandescent about the folding of labels into 4AD: 'At the time, I was very hurt he didn't let me know what he intended to do. I still don't understand the decision, effectively just to start calling Beggars 4AD, but I can't deny it's proved to be a sound business move.'

'After Jac Holzman sold Elektra, lock-stock-and-barrel to Warner Brothers in the early Seventies, he was probably not pleased that [hard rockers] Staind ended up on his old label,' says Robin Hurley. 'But Jac put his label behind him. Ivo hasn't.'

In 2011, Martin Mills and Ivo met face to face for the first time in twelve years when Mills visited Ivo's home in Lamy after concluding some business Stateside. 'It was very moving to see Ivo,' recalls Mills. 'He's always been an odd fish, which I'm sure he'd take as a compliment! He's incredibly pure and principled – ascetic, if you like.'

Ivo: 'It was really good to see Martin and be reminded of the man himself and not the man of business. He's put up with so much from me over the years, eager to play devil's advocate or just to let me vent. He's supported me in more ways than anyone will ever know.'

Mills: 'I know that it's more than just about business with Ivo. And he's been very good in saying he's forfeited the opportunity to voice an opinion, and he's never told me what to do. He left, and we had no choice but to carry on, and I think 4AD is stronger for having those extra bands. It's not like they wouldn't fit within a broader definition of 4AD. [Beggars dance act] Basement Jaxx clearly wouldn't have fitted. Even M/A/R/R/S shows how catholic 4AD could be. And [current 4AD acts] tUnE-yArDs, Grimes and St. Vincent are not just female singers but are totally compatible with Ivo's purist ethos. But 4AD couldn't have survived without changing. The growth and broadening of 4AD is consistent with its history. And Grimes is clearly a Cocteaus fan.'

The artists that Mills mentions as fitting Ivo's purist ethos are a wide-ranging collection, and in the case of tUnE-yArDs and Grimes, their penchant for glitchy rhythm and jarring textures makes this highly unlikely.*

Yet Grimes – the adopted name of Vancouver-born Claire Boucher – is at 4AD mostly because of Ivo. In 2012, 4AD licensed her third album *Visions* from the Montreal label Arbutus. Leading online music site Pitchfork made the lead single 'Oblivions' its number one track of 2012, for its 'steely, hyper-minimal beat, layered vocals, and hypnotic, circular melody', and the lyric 'beautifully fragmented and open to interpretation'.

---

* Regarding his feelings towards contemporary music, on 4AD or otherwise, Ivo says, 'It takes a lot for something to really stand out for me. I just long for real singers that hit the mark as Gene Clark or Roy Harper did.' After loving 2011's King Creosote/ Jon Hopkins' *Diamond Mine*, he finally found something in 2013's *Perils From The Sea*, a similarly folk/ electronic collaboration between Jimmy Lavalle of The Album Leaf and – bringing it on back home – Mark Kozelek. 'When I made that comment about *Diamond Mine* for Domino's press release, I had the first three Red House Painters albums in mind,' says Ivo. 'How fitting the album I've enjoyed the most since is *Perils From The Sea*. Two tracks – "Ceiling Gazing" and "Somehow The Wonder Of Life Prevails" – are quite possibly the most beautiful songs I've heard in my entire life.'

Boucher's tough, flighty, imaginative 'cyborg-pop' has seen her compared to Abba and Aphex Twin, Björk and Enya, though at high school, Boucher was more besotted with Pixies and Cocteau Twins. 'I was really into female vocalists, and I'd started listening to Yeah Yeah Yeahs, but someone said Cocteau Twins were better,' she recalls. 'Pixies were big for me too. I didn't know Birthday Party was on 4AD, but I'd listen to them too. Their aesthetic was just so intense and scary, and it was music that my parents wouldn't like! I started finding out about Bauhaus, New Order, Dead Can Dance … but Cocteau Twins are one of my biggest influences. If Liz wasn't singing lyrics, I didn't need to either. I like to improvise, but it's not free jazz or jamming; it's beautiful, raw vocal expression. With Pixies, it was more "I'm sixteen and getting wasted!"'

Boucher says that most other record labels wanted her to change her material in some way, but that 4AD's reputation was the real deal-maker. 'I'd always felt that, if the music industry was The Simpsons, then 4AD is Lisa Simpson. She's not the most popular person in the family but the cool, intelligent, subversive one. 4AD don't sign buzz bands, they're super-tasteful, and distinctively feminine a lot of the time.'

Interestingly, the number of female artists signed in the Halliday–Horrox era matches that of Ivo's, whose support helped women become so visible in contemporary music. But in other respects, '4AD Present' is a very different label to '4AD Past'. For example, the feminine was emphatically absent in June 2012 when 4AD released its first rap act, SpaceGhostPurrp, the self-styled leader of underground rap group Raider Klan Mafia. Judging by his album *Mysterious Phonk: The Chronicles Of SpaceGhostPurrp*, Miami rapper/producer Markese Roller is a master of hypnotic, slurred rhythm, but he's still a contentious presence among the label's traditional followers, which have baulked at lines such as, *'Grind on me/ I got your bitch on my dick, bitch.'*

'I'm sure SpaceGhostPurrp is appropriate for some label out there,' reckons 4AD keeper of the flame Jeff Keibel. 'But it simply doesn't belong in the 4AD universe. It forever taints the legacy of the label.'

'Most great hip-hop has lyrics that can offend people, and some lyrics aren't to my personal taste, but I tend to be liberal when I like a beat,' Halliday responds. 'But I think he's insulting other competing rappers and producers, not women. There's a lot of love for women on that album.'*

Halliday says his approach with SpaceGhostPurrp is no different to every 4AD artist: 'We try to get the purist form of that person's artistry or expression. We trust our big acts like Bradford and Ariel, so we don't get involved. They have the vision. The more involved we are, the more scared I am that it's not going right.'

Alongside Grimes, the big acts that Halliday trusts in are more typical of 4AD's original valued currency, less in the margins alongside Scott Walker (whose second 4AD album, 2012's *Bish Bosch*, was no less experimental) and firmly in the flourishing concourse of modern popular culture. As the frontmen of Atlanta quartet Deerhunter and Ariel Pink's Haunted Graffiti respectively, Bradford Cox and Ariel Marcus Rosenberg are mercurial, dictatorial auteurs with their own particularly skewed outlook. Deerhunter's three 4AD albums, *Microcastle*, *Halcyon Digest* and *Monomania*, reveal a uniquely eerie, heavy-lidded and cryptic vision of psychedelia, loose like Cox's beloved Breeders and tight like his beloved Echo & The Bunnymen. Ariel Pink is more of the loopier Syd Barrett brand, though his two 4AD albums to date, *Before Today* and *Mature Themes*, are increasingly soulful and accessible.

Both declared champions of 4AD, Cox and Pink helped compile tracks for a Japanese-only 4AD sampler to coincide with a Far East tour of Deerhunter, Ariel Pink and Blonde Redhead. Showing a more slapdash approach to visuals, the compilation had no title, with only Cox's lyric on the cover: '*What did you want to see/ What did you want to be/ When you grew up?*' which craftily showed 4AD's ability to shape impressionable brains. Displaying his teen goth roots, Pink chose

---

* The comment that accompanies the official download of SpaceGhostPurrp's recent – and self-released – mixtape *B.M.W.* EP will only inflame the doubters: 'Instructions before listening to this EP: 1. Get yo weed 2. Get yo drank 3. Get yo pillz 4. Get yo coke 5. Get yo bitch 6. Get Phucked up 7. Then blast this shit.'

tracks by Clan Of Xymox, Xmal Deutschland and Cocteau Twins as his answers. Ever the Kim Deal aficionado, Cox picked The Breeders, The Amps and Pixies. Blonde Redhead (whose subsequent *23* and *Penny Sparkle* albums refined their dream-pop exotica) chose Lush, Stereolab and TV On The Radio.

'New' 4AD signing The National chose tracks by Cocteau Twins and St. Vincent, while The Big Pink (London electronic rock duo Robbie Furze and Milo Cordell, behind two albums of booming electronic rock, 2009's promising *A Brief History Of Love* and 2012's less promising *Future This*) chose Unrest and M/A/R/R/S.

The compilation was an acknowledgement of Ivo's years by the new Halliday era, but more recent signings have a similar hallmark to Grimes' 4AD Present. Two are even male-female couples. Montreal duo Corin Roddick and Megan James make beats-driven dream-pop as Purity Ring (unlike Grimes, they were unaware of 4AD in their youth), while the tempestuous rock trio Daughter is the sound of London-based couple Elena Tonra and Igor Haefeli. Indians, a.k.a. Denmark's singular and gentler enigma Søren Løkke Juul, would have fitted into Ivo's 4AD.

'I'm very glad there was a period between Ivo and myself,' Halliday concludes. 'Chris and Ed had an almost impossible task in taking over the reins from Ivo. 4AD's personality was so big that it would have been hard not to be too reverential, to prop up the legacy, and to make Ivo happy. I don't want to be dismissive of Ivo, who I've never met, but now 4AD just does what 4AD does. We don't want to destroy the past, and we don't want to not allude to it. Now I know that we're good and we're relevant, I'm more open to the past and how glorious it was. We have a weighty inheritance, but we still care more about today than yesterday.'

The number of artists on the current roster far outweighs what Ivo would have assembled, and so it is inevitably more fractured than cohesive, but then what did connect Colourbox to Dead Can Dance or Pixies to Mojave 3, other than being the best at what they did? The same can be said for LA's digi-soul brothers inc., Oxford folk-pop band Stornoway, UK dubstep/grime artist Joker, the similarly beats-based Zomby, Scots indie-pop band Camera Obscura, American synth-pop revivalist Twin Shadow, Denmark's orchestral Efterklang, Manhattan's progressive Gang Gang Dance, the sombre Americana of Iron and Wine (whose 4AD debut *Kiss Each Other Clean* was the first co-operative Warners/4AD venture since 1997) …

'Being spontaneous about decisions seemed the best thing to do,' Halliday concludes. 'We didn't plan Purity Ring being a throwback, for example. I've tried to make sure that there is a core running through, but with some deviations from the core, as there were in Ivo's era. But I'm not Ivo, and so 4AD is a different label, but hopefully our legacy in years to come will match his. And I do believe that 4AD has blossomed again.'

Halliday is not the only one. 'The difference between the bands signed now and the first phase after Ivo is that someone now has the spirit of the original Ivo,' reckons Tim Carr. 'I'm amazed that every time I like any record, it's on 4AD.'

Marc Geiger agrees: 'The current roster is as good as 4AD's heyday. It's like someone is channelling from Santa Fe. I don't know how you get this many right, record for record, artist for artist.'

'The 4AD that exists now is the label I was trying to shape at the time,' Lewis Jamieson claims. 'It's regained its artistic vision after the dead years after Ivo, which saw the second wave of Britpop with The Libertines and The Strokes. 4AD is again very cool with twenty-year-old journalists.'

'It's heresy to say it, but I think the 4AD roster is stronger than it's ever been,' Ed Horrox contends. 'It's just been a journey to get there. At times, we weren't in a position to do what we've done in more recent years. It's like a fire – it grew and burned brightly under Ivo, and then it nearly went out. For years, we had to convince people we were still active. Something that had such a strong identity, to become of your time as well, is a process of reinvention, and convincing the artistic community, like Blonde Redhead, who Dave Sitek almost stalked, and to get the trust of people like Kim Deal to release *Title TK* and *Mountain Battles*.'

But Deal won't be returning again. In 2009, she pressed and distributed The Breeders' EP *Fate To Fatal* herself and has so far released two limited edition solo singles through her website. 'I don't even know if music sells anymore, or that bands exist as they used to,' she says. 'Ivo and I have talked about the death of the music industry, and there is so much more of it to die. People no longer look at a band, their life, their reality, the sub-culture they've created, as 40 minutes' worth of their time. I don't even know the value of music anymore. I downloaded Miles Davis' *Kind Of Blue* for 99 cents and I know that's not the value of it.'

Kristin Hersh feels the same way. 50 Foot Wave's 2005 EP *Free Music* had even pioneered the name-your-own-price model three years before Radiohead's much-publicised *In Rainbows*. The old record label model, of giving artists the platform to release music that appealed to enough people to purchase it, was changing, and Hersh was going to ride the wave rather than get crushed by it. Yet for a while, she stayed with 4AD, and in 2007 released her first solo album in four years, *Learn To Sing Like A Star*. It was never less than vital, engaging and uncompromising, but it was to be her last original 4AD album, after twenty-one years in the family.

In 2011, 4AD released *Anthology*, a double CD of band-chosen highlights and rarities timed with another Throwing Muses reunion tour, but the limited budget and pressing allocated left Hersh feeling short-changed, and her 2010 solo album was not even released by a record company but a book publisher, HarperCollins. *Crooked* took the form of a handsome book of photographs, lyrics, essays and a download link to what her website called 'a treasure trove' of online content, including: 'The full *Crooked* album, full recording stems for every track allowing fan remixes, track-by-track audio commentary by Kristin, the opening chapters of her forthcoming memoir, exclusive video content, outtakes, and a forum enabling fans to interact with Kristin, ask questions, and participate in live web chats.'

This close interaction with fans is what Hersh had been working towards since co-founding CASH Music. There may be fewer fans now than at Throwing Muses' peak, but every one is rewarded for their support. Every new solo and Throwing Muses demo is now posted online, to be downloaded for free, or for a suggested donation of $3. All Hersh's recordings, and the new Throwing Muses album due out in autumn 2013, are CASH Music-funded.

Nevertheless, contrary to Hersh's unconventional model, and Kim Deal's suspicions, the old record label model still lives on. Artists still make records and play shows, which is how 4AD still manages to prosper. Across its three A&R sources – Horrox at Alma Road, Halliday's desk in Beggars' Manhattan office, and an additional A&R scout in LA – 4AD is once again a very desirable destination for artists. Martin Mills must imagine that the spirit of Ivo lives on.

Yet, for fans of music, it's no longer a question of trusting a record label enough to collect everything on it. Not only can consumers try first online, but MP3 downloads are invisible: there will never again be the same joyful feeling of imagining what lies inside the enigma of a 4AD album cover. It's also doubtful that there will ever again be a record label like the original 4AD, one with the attention to design and packaging, within current economic constraints. It's hard to imagine The Wolfgang Press would now get the support they once did. Perhaps all record labels are record companies now.*

Yet Ed Horrox remains hopeful. 'The challenge,' he concludes, 'is to consistently keep finding artists from the underground or the left of centre, the music makers, which is what Ivo did with Deb and Vaughan and Nigel and the others, to create something lasting, that speaks to a new generation. That is hooked on the same dream, living through spellbinding music.'

---

* One tangible difference between 4AD Past and Present was encapsulated by a website posting by Rob Sanders titled *Modern-era 4AD, Revized* on a website for US graphic design company, The Mystery Parade (it has now been archived at the company's Facebook page): Wrote Sanders, 'This post is admittedly a reaction to the 4AD record label's de-emphasizing of their cover art that was once one of their trademarks. The brief is to basically utilize existing cover art and attempt to create new art and capture at least some of the essence of the older, beautifully designed covers.' For example, Sanders redesigned Bon Iver's *For Emma* ... album with artwork by Shinro Ohtake. 'It's such a shame that 4AD has decided not to put the care, time, and effort those old packagings by v23/23 Envelope used to have,' wrote one respondent. 'I recently read an Ivo interview and in it he talks about the passion they had for creating something beautiful.'

25

FACING THE OTHER WAY

August 2012. Elizabeth Fraser has reached the last song of her second show at London's Royal Festival Hall. She's appearing as a special favour to Antony Hegarty of Antony and the Johnsons, this year's curator at the RFH's annual arts festival Meltdown. These are her first solo concerts in the fifteen years since Cocteau Twins split in 1997, during which time Fraser had recorded enough songs for an album but only released one of them – and that was as a tribute to a friend who died tragically in a motorbike accident, released in 2009. The atmosphere throughout the night has been pregnant with expectation, and she's back on stage for her second, and presumably final, encore. What will she choose to complete this most auspicious occasion?

Fraser hasn't yet sung 'Teardrop', the track she fronted for Massive Attack in 1998, and the most popular song, in terms of sales, that she has ever sung. Nor has she performed one of her two contributions to Peter Jackson's *The Lord of the Rings* films. Maybe it will be another of her new songs, ripe for a live interpretation. Maybe it will be another Cocteau Twins song; she's already sung nine, including 'Pearly-Dewdrops' Drops' (Robin Guthrie needn't have worried about the way Fraser's backing band would play his music; their fluid, ambient-tinged treatments are lovely but can't hold a candle to his beautiful noise).

The encore begins with a slow draw of cellos and guitar drone. It's hard to pick out what the song is until Fraser begins to sing: *'Long afloat on shipless oceans I did all my best to smile ...'* It's 'Song To The Siren'.

'We probably did get a bee in our bonnet about [Song To The Siren] not being Cocteau Twins,' Fraser told *Volume* magazine in 1992. 'That was *Head Over Heels* time and it felt more right to have success because of Cocteau Twins music. Having said that, though, I heard it played in a shop ... and I liked it. I realised why I got in such a pickle and it wasn't because it was a bad recording of an amazing song. It is a beautiful song.'

Contrary to Guthrie's memory that Ivo wouldn't let the track be featured in a film, Ivo did allow the This Mortal Coil version of 'Song To The Siren' to be used – twice, in fact. Ivo hadn't been the only one heartbroken by the greed of Tim Buckley's estate in 1985. In an interview, David Lynch admitted that not getting the song for *Blue Velvet* 'broke my heart'. The director subsequently gave some of his own lyrics to the composer Angelo Badalamenti and asked for 'something cosmic, angelic, very beautiful', which led to 'Mysteries Of Love', sung by Julee Cruise. By the time of his 1997 cryptic *film noir Lost Highway*, Lynch had another scene that required the same mood, and he could now afford the asking price. Instead of the surreal prom scene planned for *Blue Velvet*, Fraser and Guthrie's cosmic, angelic and very beautiful sound accompanied Patricia Arquette and Balthazar Getty's characters Alice and Pete making love bathed in the white glow of their car headlamps.

But Guthrie had been partially right: Ivo wouldn't allow Lynch to put 'Song To The Siren' on the soundtrack, in order to limit what he saw as commercial exploitation. 'I didn't want people coming to it unsuitably squished between two other tracks, but rather on its own, or to take them to hear it on a This Mortal Coil album,' Ivo explains.

Yet he agreed to have 'Song To The Siren' included on the prospective soundtrack to Peter Jackson's 2009 film *The Lovely Bones*, 'because [Brian] Eno was involved,' says Ivo. But no soundtrack was ever released: Guthrie loses again. At least the version is in the film, accompanying an afterlife sequence where the lead character is watching over her family. 'It's good music for a funeral,' claims one YouTube contributor.* But not as good for a superhero movie, perhaps. Ivo rejected the request from Marc Webb, the director of 2012's *The Amazing Spider-Man*. 'He wrote me a pleading letter, saying he'd listened to This Mortal Coil throughout his youth. But I just couldn't say yes.'†

October 2012. Dead Can Dance is near the end of its first London show in sixteen years following the release of *Anastasis*. It's time for the encore, and Brendan Perry and the present DCD live band return without Lisa Gerrard to sing a particularly emotional version of … 'Song To The Siren'. 'We're doing it precisely for the *wow* factor,' Perry tells me afterwards.

It's not the first time Perry has sung Tim Buckley's deathless classic. In 2011, Perry did a rare solo tour across America, with a solo Robin Guthrie in support, scotching any leftover rumours of animosity between Cocteau Twins and Dead Can Dance.‡ On the first night, Guthrie says he was backstage following his opening set when he

---

* Another layer of mystique to the aquatic setting and tragic demeanour of 'Song To The Siren' is the fate of Jeff Buckley. After hearing Elizabeth Fraser's interpretation of his father Tim's song, Jeff had contacted Fraser and the pair embarked on a brief affair in the mid-Nineties, even recording the (unreleased) duet 'All Flowers In Time Bend Towards The Sun'. In 1997, Buckley drowned in Memphis as he prepared to record his second album. He was thirty, just two years older than Tim was when he died. 'I always felt there was a prophecy of death in that song,' says Sinead O'Connor. Fraser subsequently met Damon Reece, Massive Attack's drummer. The pair live in Bristol and have one daughter, Lily.

† For any filmgoers starved of 'Song To The Siren', Tim Buckley's original appeared in Neil Armfield's 2006 film *Candy*, a story of doomed junkie lovers starring the late Heath Ledger. The same year, it was sung by Ivri Lider in Israeli director Eytan Fox's film *HaBuah* (*The Bubble*).

‡ Before the Perry–Guthrie tour, Perry had planned a similar touring venture with former Bauhaus singer Pete Murphy, which fell apart before it got started. 'Whoever suggested that, I mean, have they ever met either of them?' says Ivo. 'Through my entire life, I've attracted mad people.' Perry reports that Murphy's demands were impossible; the singer certainly showed his madder side in March 2013 when he was involved in an accident while driving in LA, and subsequently charged with misdemeanour DUI, hit-and-run driving and methamphetamine possession. He had pleaded not guilty and at the time of writing is due back in court, though he remains on course to tour through North America and Europe, 'celebrating 35 years of Bauhaus' and performing only Bauhaus material.

heard Perry start to sing … '*Long afloat on shipless oceans I did all my best to smile …*'

'I didn't know Brendan was going to do "Song To The Siren" in his set,' Guthrie recalls. 'I heard this sound and thought, What the fuck's that? Oh, fuck! The next night, he asked me to play it with him and I thought, Why not? So I noodled along and did my thing. But most nights, I just watched the audience, and saw the rapture on their faces, which made me happy. That's what entertainment's about, isn't it?'

Ivo was sent a YouTube clip of Perry singing 'Song To The Siren' on a radio session. Robin Guthrie has made his peace with the song that had given him so much turmoil, but Ivo was unable to watch the clip – the weight of memory still too heavy. But he did watch Liz Fraser's live version on YouTube, unable to resist, curious to hear how she now sounded. Ivo hasn't talked with Fraser for many years, though he is in sporadic email contact with Guthrie following a long gap after an initial reconciliation in the late Nineties.

'I can't remember how we got back in touch,' says Ivo. 'But I later visited Robin and Simon at their September Sound studio, and as I left, we hugged, and Robin said, "I'm so glad you're back in my life". Possibly with Robin and Simon now running their own [Bella Union] label, they'd experienced life on the other side. Simon said how difficult it must have been to have Raymond Coffer in the picture, as he knew, for good or bad, how managers get in the way of a direct relationship.'

In the mid-Nineties, Robin Guthrie had entered rehab, and has never taken drugs again. 'Robin really benefited from doing the twelve-step programme,' Ivo believes. 'He was able to express warmth towards me, and vice versa. He said that the worst thing that ever happened to the band was leaving 4AD, which implies, as I let them go, that the biggest mistake they made was in not addressing the problems that existed between us. I certainly am not afraid or ashamed to admit that was my own biggest regret. We just didn't talk.

'I last spoke to Robin in April 2012 when he called me, incredibly upset, having just found out that Liz was to perform at the Meltdown festival and was going to be singing Cocteau Twins songs. During our conversation, I confessed that our "split" remained a huge disappointment in my life. He laughed and said that by letting them go, my problems with Cocteau Twins were over whereas for him, the problems were only just beginning.'

'Signing to [major label] Fontana in 1992, after we fell out with 4AD, was the biggest mistake we ever made,' says Guthrie. 'Fontana was a faceless, corporate-wank entity, who pressured us into album-tour-album-tour work. We had to keep recording extra formats for singles so we were constantly thrust together in the studio. I cringe when I hear our *Twinlights* and *Otherness* EPs [both 1995]. *Twinlights* was acoustic and has violins and shite like that, and *Otherness* was some pointless remixes of our songs. Neither was what Cocteau Twins was all about, but I wasn't in control then. I'd come out of rehab and I thought I should make the band a democracy. But our musical legacy was joyous. Even our dark and melancholic stuff sounds exuberant. When I hear the odd Cocteaus track, I'm so happy I wasn't in Kajagoogoo.'*

Robin Guthrie and Vaughan Oliver had re-connected. Despite all the wrangling over artwork in the 4AD era, Guthrie asked Oliver to work on his first post-Cocteaus project, Violet Indiana (a collaboration with singer Siobhan de Maré). 'All the things that Robin and Vaughan used to argue over were still there!' says Chris Bigg. 'There was still that element of control, a real battle.'

Bigg had experienced his own battles with Oliver. The pair had entered into an equal business partnership in 1998, which was severed in 2009. 'Vaughan wanted to take us to the next level, beyond music design, but he was very embittered about everything, after all the pioneering work that he'd done – he'd get angry and aggressive, and

---

* Ivo: 'Robin once told me, what was the point of making music, post-Cocteaus? He said it would either be Cocteaus music without a vocalist or Cocteaus music with a vocalist and without Elizabeth. Well, he's now done both. I called him recently, excited after listening to *Heaven Or Las Vegas* again, to encourage him to rethink a band. There are, surely, many vocalists out there that partially fill Liz's shoes and, frankly, outshine the modern Liz. But he couldn't hear me on the phone, so I rang off. And I didn't call back.'

it wasn't really him,' Bigg concludes. 'We get on fine now as there isn't the burden of work.'

Despite the talk of plans in 1998, v23 had not expanded into new ventures and mediums. Oliver admits that self-promotion was neither his nor Bigg's strength, and that not enough new work found them. 'It took me about three years to come to terms with having no retainer anymore,' he says. 'We ran up too much debt because we had to have assistants, due to the technological revolution – we still couldn't work the computers.'

Oliver was also to discover that, before v23 had moved out of the 4AD office into its own, Bigg had been offered Oliver's job – which Bigg had turned down out of loyalty. 'That's business for you,' says Oliver. But there was a positive outcome. Like Bigg, Oliver now lectures in graphic design: he holds an honorary Master's degree (for achievement in industry) at Epsom's University of the Creative Arts, and the title of Visiting Professor at University of Greenwich. 'Given my work's maverick nature, to be recognised by the academic establishment is OK,' he says. 'But more importantly, it recognises the cultural significance of the simple old record sleeve, or a simple piece of printed ephemera.'

Since his 23 Envelope partnership with Oliver disintegrated, Nigel Grierson also found the terrain difficult to manage. Through the Nineties, he'd worked for the London-based production house Limelight. 'Like with 4AD,' he says, 'the consistency of working at one place creates a strong public following, but once you're freelance, it's only industry people who know what's going on and who's doing what. Vaughan seemed to hang on to 4AD like a life raft, but I understand more now, knowing what else is out there. It's rare to have such an experience, on a family level, and you end up talking about the era as a golden age.'*

---

* Nigel Grierson has been working for years on a book of nature-based photographs (working title: *Passing Through*), but it will be preceded with a volume of his 4AD work, *Photographs*, scheduled for publication in March 2014. 'It's closer to what people know of me,' he explains. 'It seems important to build on any kind of foundation, however depleted it's become, that I already have – most people from that era think I died years ago.'

Another former clash of head and heart found a way back, from Dead Can Dance to Charles Thompson and Kim Deal. While fronting his own band Frank Black and the Catholics, Thompson had regularly dismissed the possibility of a Pixies reunion, but after he'd begun to play Pixies songs on stage, got divorced and had therapy, a Pixies reunion tour was brokered by Marc Geiger, who had left ARTISTdirect and was now heading the booking agency William Morris. In April 2004, Pixies played a show for the first time in twelve years.

But there was one relationship that not even an arbitrator such as Geiger could fix. Cocteau Twins had split up in 1997 while recording a new album: 'Things just reached the point when I knew we couldn't do it anymore, but Liz was first to say so,' says Robin Guthrie. 'It was the formative music of my life, so in effect to be stopped by someone else was hurtful. Now I can see it couldn't have ended any other way.'

Eight years later, Guthrie received a call from Geiger, asking if Cocteau Twins would play the annual Coachella festival in California. 'I had to be coaxed into it as I wanted to protect myself from getting fucked up by walking back into the same situation,' Guthrie says. 'But it was explained to me, as with Pixies, we were all older and wiser, and human beings in our own right. I thought, OK, I can deal with that. We had a long meeting and got along very well and decided to try it. Shortly after, we were advertised to play, but at some point Liz got cold feet. Maybe we just fell back into our own dynamic. I did, however, think it was inexcusable, really, to commit to something for the fans and then pull out.'

Steven Cantor, who co-directed the 2004 Pixies tour documentary loudQuietloud, told Billboard that he felt the Pixies reunion was, '75 per cent … for money, but the other 25 per cent was because of the fact that they're legends'. The mended relationship extended as far as Charles Thompson's magnanimous gesture to record Kim Deal's song 'Bam Thwok' as the only new Pixies song as yet released since the reformation. It seemed Deal held more power than in the past; when talk of a new album spread in 2006, Thompson told NME, 'We're rehearsing in January, if we can persuade Kim to come out of her house. We offered to go to her but we figured if we book the rehearsals she'll show up.' The proposed album has still not happened, though Pixies finally went back in the studio with producer Gil Norton in late 2012, and in June 2013 released (via a free download) the band's first new track in nine years, 'Bagboy', which followed two weeks after the announcement that Kim Deal had left the band. She didn't comment publically on her decision; however, according to Ivo, 'she never felt that they were back together as a band, and faced with recording and more touring, thought it best if she stopped.'

I had met with the band in a London hotel in 2009, before they were to play the launch party for an exhibition of photographs taken from the latest memorable collaboration with Vaughan Oliver, and found them to be outwardly cheery and relaxed. Then, and through-out Pixies' reformation, Deal had not shown any resistance to the arrangement.

Pixies had agreed that a box set of the band's 4AD albums was worth supporting if their favourite designer was involved. And there is no one else in record sleeve design who would have proposed such a radical artwork interpretation as Oliver did for *Minotaur*.

Jeff Anderson, the owner of the American label A+R (short for Artist in Residence) that specialises in collector's sets, told Oliver he wanted to assemble a Pixies box set, covering all the studio albums. The rights had reverted back to Thompson, and with his support, Oliver saw his chance to do something extraordinary. *Minotaur* ended up a mammoth entity, surely the largest ever product masquerading as a music project at almost two foot high, to house vinyl and CD copies, DVDs and posters, with gold-plated CDs and new artwork throughout. This included a ninety-six-page booklet, the images for which Oliver called on his students at Epsom's University of the Creative Arts to help originate; he also contacted Simon Larbalestier for more of his illuminating photographs. 'You don't make the pack-age monumental for it to become pompous or pretentious, which is all the things that Pixies isn't,' Oliver explains. 'But it needed to be dramatic and substantial.'

Oliver even came up with the title *Minotaur*, after the figure from Greek mythology – continuing the animalistic theme of Pixies artwork – and a surrealist magazine from the Thirties. 'Charles loved the name *Minotaur* when I suggested it,' Oliver recalls. 'I was thinking more of the magazine but it's a beast of a package, so the half-bull, half-man is appropriate.'

Minotaur costs a considerable $449.99, but for cheapskates there is a 'deluxe' model (just $169.99). Anyone claiming that *Minotaur* is a rip-off because it contains no new Pixies music was missing the point, says Oliver. 'This is about the packaging, which of course comes out of the music, as it always does with me when I'm designing, but I wanted to challenge the convention of what the record sleeve does.'

To Oliver, *Minotaur* is less a box set than, 'a visual exploration'. Charles Thompson plumps for 'art project'. Either way, it is the complete antithesis of MP3 culture, where artwork and packaging has disappeared into the ether. 'It's the responsibility of our generation to remind people otherwise,' says Oliver. 'I gave this talk and some kids came up afterwards and said, "We know the music you're describing but we haven't seen the sleeve" – which is something that can enhance the whole experience of the music. It's tragic!'

Ivo guardedly views *Minotaur* as 'what you get when Vaughan is let loose'. His own version of restoration was embodied by the limited edition box set of This Mortal Coil's entire recordings that 4AD released in 2011, in his favourite Japanese paper-sleeve CD format on to which original vinyl artwork was shrunk down. On a much smaller scale than *Minotaur*, Ivo had Oliver expand the original artwork with out-takes from Nigel Grierson's Pallas Citroen shoots and new gatefold sleeves, with everything manufactured to the highest spec by the Tokyo-based printers Ichikudo. A fourth CD of rarities was named *Dust & Guitars* after Syd Barrett's quote from 1971.

'Barrett's words just made sense to me when I first read them,' says Ivo. 'It was fairly fresh in my mind when Ed [Horrox] or Chris [Sharp] asked me if I'd agree to include [the This Mortal Coil track] "Sixteen Days/Gathering Dust" on an iTunes exclusive download [in 2006], and would I come up with a title? It was wasted on the silly, disparate sampler that they put together, so I reclaimed it, in part, for the box set. Believe it or not, I only made the "Gathering Dust" connection after all of that had happened!'*

The rarities' CD also included a cover of Neil Young's 'We Never Danced' left over from the *Blood* sessions, which was destined to be released through Rough Trade's singles club until Ivo changed his mind. 'I just didn't think it was good enough. Though I now love its over-the-top drama.'†

Compare This Mortal Coil's box set manufacture to that of the comprehensive Colourbox box set that 4AD released in 2012. Ivo deems the latter to be a travesty of perfunctory packaging, and printing, with no additional images or information. 'It's not particularly 4AD,' says Martin Mills, 'but today's market economies won't allow us to do what should be done.' In other words, the spirit of Ivo does not live on. Profit overrules art.

Today, the spirit of '4AD Past' exists most strongly as music – and as memories. In an appearance in January 2013 on the BBC Radio 4 staple *Desert Island Discs* (in which public figures choose eight all-time favourite pieces of music to be stranded with, and then pick which of the eight they favour over all the others) British comedian Dawn French chose This Mortal Coil's 'Song To The Siren' as her

---

* The *This Mortal Coil* box set gave Ivo the chance to put some personal words on the spine of each original album sleeve. On *It'll End In Tears*, it reads: 'Every day takes figuring out, all over again how to live', as said by the character Calamity Jane in the TV series *Deadwood*. The first part of *Filigree & Shadow*'s quote, 'You know that I don't like riddles', comes from Ivo's mother Gina, and the second part, 'You know that thinking makes me ill', from Charles Dickens. *Blood*'s message, 'but life is not a succession of urgent "nows", it's a listless trickle of "why should I?"'s' was spoken by Johnny Depp's character, the Earl of Rochester, in the film *The Libertine*.

† The cover version of 'We Never Danced' was inspired as much by Alan Rudolph's 1987 film *Made in Heaven*, 'an odd, beautiful little film,' Ivo recalls. The angel, played by Kelly McGillis, says those very words to Timothy Hutton's recently deceased character, and back on earth, the couple indeed do get to dance, to Young's song (the film's theme tune) sung on the soundtrack by Martha Davis of The Motels. On *Filigree & Shadow*, Ivo re-created some of *Made in Heaven*'s incidental sound: 'an intake of breath, a sigh, running water and tinkling bells', underneath the voice of cellist Emily Proctor, who says, 'You know what we never did? We never danced.' It can be heard right before 'Nature's Way'. 'I can't even dance in front of the mirror without getting embarrassed,' Ivo confesses. 'Chris Bigg says he likes nothing more than dancing. I should dance one time before I die.'

penultimate choice. Following many years of marriage that resulted in separation, French had met a new beau who had introduced her to the track. 'I knew when I heard this song that it was an offer,' she told interviewer Kirsty Young. 'You would fall in love, wouldn't you, with somebody who gave you that song?'

'I have done some good after all, haven't I?' says Ivo, when he hears the news.

Five years earlier, in 2008, Ivo read *Shoot the Damn Dog: A Memoir of Depression*, and felt his fog of bewilderment lift. Sally Brampton, the founding editor of the women's magazine *Elle*, had named her book after Winston Churchill's 'black dog'.

Ivo: 'Sally Brompton had gone from great success to literally not being able to function, for years. My collapse was minor in comparison, but it was still the same blueprint, of depression taking hold and you're never the same again.'

Ivo was never facing the wrong way; he was just facing the other way. Just as 4AD was, throughout the time that he ran it. And his spirit continues to live on in the more uniquely slanted of 4AD Present's signings.

And take the wide-ranging influence Ivo's 4AD has had on contemporary music, on a wildly diverse set of current genres: dream-pop, industrial, shoegaze, nu-gaze, ambient, nu-goth, synth-pop and its R&B counterpart chillwave.

Or 2012's cult film *The Perks of Being a Wallflower*, the twenty-first-century equivalent of the Eighties coming-of-age saga *The Breakfast Club*. Directed by the author of the book by the same name, Stephen Chbosky, the setting is an American high school in the early Nineties, where the introspective lead character Charlie finds acceptance among a bunch of other misfit adolescents who use music and mixtapes as a shared language. Michael Brook wrote the film's incidental soundtrack, but the pivotal tracks are David Bowie's 'Heroes', The Smiths, Nick Drake and Cocteau Twins: Charlie's friend Sam admits she had a personal epiphany the first time she heard 'Pearly-Dewdrops' Drops', and finally knew her true self.

Take the 20th-anniversary reunion tour of The Breeders' *Last Splash*. The four that recorded the album have reunited to play it, and some of the band's non-hits. Kim Deal says she will enjoy it much more this time around, minus all the expectations and stress. 'I think she still really enjoys doing music that's just unadulterated,' says bassist Josephine Wiggs. 'For me, it's a chance to replace the memory of how The Breeders ended so oddly. It's a much happier ending this time.'

Everyone has downed tools to take part; Kim from her Pixies and solo projects, Jim Macpherson from his work as a carpenter, Wiggs from her soundtrack recordings, Kelley from her musical sideline R Ring, part-time job in a funeral home and her bespoke knitting, the hobby that replaced her heroin addiction for a different set of needles.

Take south Londoner Daniel Woolhouse, who calls himself Deptford Goth, though ironically, as his music wouldn't go down well in The Batcave Club; it's more haunting electronic soul, but his 2012 debut album *Life After Defo* has as beautiful and sad an aura as a certain Tim Buckley cover. "Song To The Siren" still sounds really new, and it would not just be popular and trendy now, but a new sound,' Woodhouse maintains. '[This Mortal Coil's] "Kangaroo" is another, the big, echoey bass sound ... every time it repeats, it reels you in a bit more. Those tracks are doing two things – pulling you in and seducing you, and you're identifying with the sadness but they also build, up and up. It's like a sad euphoria. It's the best kind of music.'

Take the example of Waves On Canvas, the alias of Sardinian composer Stefano Guzzetti, whose 2012 album *Into The Northsea* features 4AD Past luminaries Louise Rutkowski, Ian Masters and Pieter Nooten in combined settings of electronica, ambient and soundtrack that is quintessential This Mortal Coil; Vaughan Oliver even did the artwork. That so few people know of Waves On Canvas shows how much has changed since *It'll End In Tears*. But 4AD began as a cult; when Ivo departed, it was still a cult, and that's what its descendants are too – something to be treasured whether a hit or not. Something worth hearing because it was made. The artefact.

Take the fact that Tim Buckley's 'Song To The Siren' has now become a modern standard, covered twenty-four times since This Mortal Coil's version, by singers such as Robert Plant, Sinead O'Connor, George Michael, Bryan Ferry and Sheila Chandra, not forgetting dance versions (Lost Witness's remix reached the UK top 30), punk parodists Half Man Half Biscuit and Elvis impersonator Jimmy 'The King' Brown.*

'I was always afraid to record it, because I knew that it would bring up more grief,' says O'Connor. 'I'd sing a line and then cry for twenty minutes. It was when my eldest child Jake had left home; you'd think someone had died from my reaction. So it became important for me to sing it out, and move on. That's what's so powerful about music; if you could describe music, you wouldn't need music. It does all the shit there aren't words for. And Liz Fraser's version – you can apply any kind of pain or grief or longing or hunger, she just has all these things in her voice that just speak to your soul and stop you in your tracks.'

All this is 4AD's lasting legacy. 'Revisiting every release for this book has done me a lot of good,' Ivo concludes. 'For once I am able to look at it all, which I fail so badly to do in my daily life, with a cup of well-over-half-full perspective. I remember those crazy, beautiful days, full of idealism, if temporarily, but the young people we all were, and the product of our passion and inventiveness is there to be seen and admired … in homes dotted around the world, or in museums rather than record shops, sadly.

'But 4AD was a fantastic opportunity. And for a while, we all participated in something quite pure and unique. Those records are a reflection of an idea that became a dream that became a reality that will continue to vibrate long after I have ceased to do so myself. Whether people connect to them or not is down to personal taste, but I've yet to hear music, before they were made or since, that sounds anything like them. That can't be bad.'

---

* 'Song To The Siren' had cast other shadows. In the extra-terrestrial TV series *The X Files*, 'Scully's Theme' written by Mark Snow was 'Song To The Siren' in all but name, while series creator Chris Carter titled one episode *This Mortal Coil*.

In Altmusic's online list of the top 20 independent labels of all time, Mute is number 13, Factory is number 7, Creation is number 4 and 4AD is ... number 1. 'Perhaps the greatest of all record labels ...' the review starts.

'4AD was a significant supernova that gave birth to a legion of landmark artists that continue to influence generations of discerning music lovers,' claims 4AD whore Craig Roseberry. 'They set the bar and mould which many labels, major and indie, tried to emulate.'

'Ivo's legacy was the music that he introduced everyone to,' says Simon Raymonde. 'Prince and Madonna loved Cocteau Twins, Robert Plant and Perry Farrell were massive 4AD fans. And Vaughan's designs have been copied by advertising, graphics and films. 4AD's ripples continue to move through the water.'

Kristin Hersh added her own, coursing through the years, inspiring anyone to face the fear and do it anyway. Listening to her commentary on her 2010 album *Crooked* about her creative process, it's clear that it's only music that truly matters. This was her struggle, right from the start, to serve the song, and to be true to herself as she handed the song over to the listener.

Hersh's fight with her impulses, her songs and her need to get them out formed the crux of her 2011 memoir *Paradoxical Undressing/Rat Girl*. The book concentrates on events between early 1985 and early 1986, concluding with a new relationship formed with an enigmatic English gentleman called Ivo, and the alien experience of recording an album. Without Ivo, Hersh acknowledges, she would never have experienced the freedom of expression and the foundations of a career that thrives to this day. 'Ivo is my hero,' Hersh concludes, 'the person who allowed me to be my own version of Ivo, musically and in the music business, shy and more like a dog than a person. He made it look good and facilitated the work that reflected that perspective.'

The last time she and Ivo met, in Santa Fe, 'We spent the day together and he then drove me over to the show,' says Hersh. 'As we were driving, we looked at the desert stars, and how quiet it was, and Ivo said, "You know what we should do, we should just keep driving".

That's what we always wanted anyway. There had always been too much turning up, too much talking, too much failure. Really, we just wanted to be the music.'

LIST OF ILLUSTRATIONS

All care has been taken to accredit illustrations to their photographers; however, due to the age of the images and the nature of the archives some images are not fully attributed.

Bauhaus and Peter Kent, O'Hare airport, Chicago, 1980
Peter Murphy of Bauhaus, 1980 (*Kevin Cummins, Getty Images*)
Rema-Rema, Royal Albert Hall, London, 1980 (*Paul Stahl*)
Modern English, South Bank, London, 1981 (*4AD promotional photo*)
The Birthday Party's creative core, London, 1982 (*Bleddyn Butcher*)
Cyrus Bruton of Dance Chapter, The Africa Centre, London 1980 (*Helen Bruton*)
Dif Juz, 1985 (*4AD promotional photo*)
Matt Johnson, aka The The, 1981 (*Peter Ashworth*)
Colourbox, 1983 (*4AD promotional photo*)
Xmal Deutschland, London, 1983 (*Chris Garnham, 4AD promotional photo*)
Cocteau Twins mark I, 1980 (*4AD promotional photo*)
Cocteau Twins mark II, 1985 (*4AD promotional photo*)
Vaughan Oliver, 4AD office, 1983

On holiday in Corfu, 1984

23 Envelope, 1990

23 Envelope, 1990

Ivo on the cover of *The Offense Newsletter*, December 1986

Ivo and Deborah, 1984

Cocteau Twins/Wolfgang Press European tour, 1985 (*supplied by the artist*)

Dead Can Dance, 1984 (*4AD promotional photo*)

Xymox, 1985 (*4AD promotional photo*)

Poster for The Carnival Of Light tour, 1986 (*supplied by the artist*)

The Wolfgang Press, 1988 (*Stephen Gray, 4AD promotional photo*)

Throwing Muses, 1986 (*Kristen Sweder, 4AD promotional photo*)

Pixies, 1989 (*Millicent Harvey, 4AD promotional photo*)

A.R. Kane, Alex Ayuli, 1987 (*4AD promotional photo*)

A.R. Kane, Rudy Tambala, 1987 (*4AD promotional photo*)

M/A/R/R/S (without A.R. Kane) (*Juergen Teller, 4AD promotional photo*)

Kurt Ralske, aka Ultra Vivid Scene (*Renaud Montfourney, 4AD promotional photo*)

Pale Saints, 1990 (*Bleddyn Butcher, 4AD promotional photo*)

His Name Is Alive, 1993 (*4AD promotional photo*)

This Mortal Coil muse Pallas Citroen: outtake from 1990 session (*Nigel Grierson*)

Heidi Berry, 1992 (*Justin De Deny, 4AD promotional photo*)

Mark Kozelek of Red House Painters (*Joe Dilworth, 4AD promotional photo*)

Belly mark II (*Danny Clinch, 4AD promotional photo*)

Unrest (*Joe Dilworth, 4AD promotional photo*)

The Breeders mark II, 1992 (*Michael Lavine, 4AD promotional photo*)

The Breeders mark III, 1994 (*Tim Mosenfelder, Corbis*)

Ivo's 'bitches', 1993

The Amps, 1995 (*4AD promotional photo*)

The Breeders mark IV, 2001 (*Michael Lavine, 4AD promotional photo*)

Lush and Pale Saints on tour, France, March 1990 (*supplied by the artist*)

Tanya Donnelly and Chris Acland, Los Angeles, September 1990 (*supplied by the artist*)

Lush mark II, on the Lollapalooza tour, San Francisco, 1992 (*supplied by the artist*)

Backstage at The Ubu, Rennes, 1994 (*supplied by the artist*)

Kristin Hersh and Miki Berenyi at the Reading Festival, 1995 (*supplied by the artist*)

Lisa Germano (*Greg Allen, 4AD promotional photo*)

Mojave 3, 1995 (*Phil Nicholls, 4AD promotional photo*)

Scheer, 1996 (*Steve Gullick, 4AD promotional photo*)

Paula Frazer of Tarnation, 1996 (*Lyn Gaza, 4AD promotional photo*)

GusGus, Iceland, 1998 (*4AD promotional photo*)

Publicity shot for The Hope Blister, 1998 (*Martyn Welch, 4AD promotional photo*)

Vinny Miller, aka starry smooth hound, 2004 (*The Green Project, 4AD promotional photo*)

Ivo with Moke, Lamy, New Mexico, April 2012

Ivo with the author, Lamy, New Mexico, April 2012

Vaughan Oliver at the Surfer Rosa shoot, 1989

Vaughan Oliver sketch for Modern English's debut album, working title Five Sided Figure, 1981

Vaughan Oliver sketches for 4AD logos

INDEX

Facing the Other Way
THE STORY OF 4AD

MARTIN ASTON

ALSO BY MARTIN ASTON

Björkgraphy
Pulp